NEVADA

CRIMINAL PROCEDURE

2018 EDITION

NEVADA REVISED STATUTES

TITLE 14 - PROCEDURE IN CRIMINAL CASES

TABLE OF CONTENTS

CHAPTER 169 - PRELIMINARY PROVISIONS

NRS 169.015 Short title. This title may be known and cited as the Nevada Criminal Procedure Law.
(Added to NRS by 1967, 1398)

NRS 169.025 Scope.
1. This title governs the procedure in the courts of the State of Nevada and before magistrates in all criminal proceedings.
2. Except as otherwise provided in NRS 62C.330, this title does not apply to proceedings against children conducted pursuant to title 5 of NRS.
(Added to NRS by 1967, 1398; A 1981, 1195; 2003, 1118)

NRS 169.035 Purpose; construction. This title is intended to provide for the just determination of every criminal proceeding. Its provisions shall be construed to secure simplicity in procedure, fairness in administration and the elimination of unjustifiable expense and delay.
(Added to NRS by 1967, 1398)

NRS 169.045 Definitions. As used in this title, unless the context otherwise requires, the words and terms defined in NRS 169.049 to 169.205, inclusive, have the meanings ascribed to them in those sections.
(Added to NRS by 1967, 1398; A 1977, 1571; 1997, 2364)

NRS 169.049 "Case in chief of the defendant" defined. "Case in chief of the defendant" means the first opportunity of the defendant to present evidence after the close of the case in chief of the State.
(Added to NRS by 1997, 2364)

NRS 169.055 "Criminal action" defined. "Criminal action" means the proceedings by which a party charged with a public offense is accused and brought to trial and punishment. A criminal action is prosecuted in the name of the State of Nevada, as plaintiff.
(Added to NRS by 1967, 1398)

NRS 169.065 "Defendant" defined. "Defendant" means the party prosecuted in a criminal action.
(Added to NRS by 1967, 1398)

NRS 169.075 "District attorney" defined. "District attorney" includes any deputy district attorney.
(Added to NRS by 1967, 1398)

NRS 169.085 "Law" defined. "Law" includes statutes and judicial decisions.
(Added to NRS by 1967, 1398)

NRS 169.095 "Magistrate" defined. "Magistrate" means an officer having power to issue a warrant for the arrest of a person charged with a public offense and includes:
1. Justices of the Supreme Court;
2. Judges of the Court of Appeals;
3. Judges of the district courts;
4. Justices of the peace;
5. Municipal judges; and
6. Others upon whom are conferred by law the powers of a justice of the peace in criminal cases.
(Added to NRS by 1967, 1398; A 1983, 901; 2013, 1752)

NRS 169.097 "Master" defined. "Master" means a person appointed by the district court to inform defendants of their rights, assign counsel for indigent defendants and perform other similar administrative duties assigned by the court.
(Added to NRS by 1977, 1570)

NRS 169.105 "Month" defined. "Month" means a calendar month unless otherwise expressed.
(Added to NRS by 1967, 1398)

NRS 169.115 "Oath" defined. "Oath" includes an affirmation.
(Added to NRS by 1967, 1398)

NRS 169.125 "Peace officer" defined. "Peace officer" includes any person upon whom some or all of the powers of a peace officer are conferred pursuant to NRS 289.150 to 289.360, inclusive.
(Added to NRS by 1967, 1398; A 1969, 55, 1130, 1423; 1971, 255, 2077; 1973, 89, 922, 1583; 1975, 112, 989, 1344; 1977, 858, 1120, 1441; 1979, 127, 280, 902; 1981, 330, 1104, 2008; 1983, 854, 1242; 1985, 246; 1989, 889, 968; 1993, 2527)

NRS 169.145 "Personal property" defined. "Personal property" includes money, goods, chattels, things in action and evidences of debt.
(Added to NRS by 1967, 1399)

NRS 169.155 "Property" defined. "Property" includes both real and personal property.
(Added to NRS by 1967, 1399)

NRS 169.164 "Public officer" defined. "Public officer" means a person elected or appointed to a position which:
1. Is established by the constitution or a statute of this State, or by a charter or ordinance of a political subdivision of this State; and
2. Involves the continuous exercise, as part of the regular and permanent administration of the government, of a public power, trust or duty.
(Added to NRS by 1967, 1399)

NRS 169.175 "Real property" defined. "Real property" is coextensive with lands, tenements and hereditaments.
(Added to NRS by 1967, 1399)

NRS 169.185 "State" defined. "State," when applied to the different parts of the United States, includes the District of Columbia and the territories.
(Added to NRS by 1967, 1399)

NRS 169.195 "Trial" defined.
1. "Trial" means that portion of a criminal action which:
(a) If a jury is used, begins with the impaneling of the jury and ends with the return of the verdict, both inclusive.
(b) If no jury is used, begins with the opening statement, or if there is no opening statement, when the first witness is sworn, and ends with the closing argument or upon submission of the cause to the court without argument, both inclusive.
2. "Trial" does not include any proceeding had upon a plea of guilty or guilty but mentally ill to determine the degree of guilt or to fix the punishment.
(Added to NRS by 1967, 1399; A 1995, 2448; 2003, 1456; 2007, 1404)

NRS 169.205 "United States" defined. "United States" may include the District of Columbia, Puerto Rico, territories or insular possessions.
(Added to NRS by 1967, 1399)

NRS 169.215 Interpretation.
1. Writing includes printing and typewriting.

2. Every mode of oral statement, under oath or affirmation, is embraced by the term "testify," and every written one in the term "depose."

(Added to NRS by 1967, 1399; A 1977, 186)

NRS 169.225 Signature by mark. When a signature of a person is required by this title, the mark of a person, if the person cannot write, shall be deemed sufficient, the name of the person making the mark being written near it, and the mark being witnessed by a person who writes his or her own name as a witness.

(Added to NRS by 1967, 1399)

NRS 169.235 Superseding of criminal law no bar to punishment unless specifically expressed. The superseding of any law creating a criminal offense shall not be held to constitute a bar to the prosecution and punishment of a crime already committed, or to bar the trial and punishment of a crime where a prosecution has been already begun, for a violation of the law so superseded, unless the intention to bar such prosecution and punishment, or trial and punishment where a prosecution has been already begun is expressly declared in the superseding act.

(Added to NRS by 1967, 1399)

NRS 169.245 Bonds and undertakings in criminal actions or proceedings: Approval by clerk.

1. In all criminal actions or proceedings where a bond or other undertaking is required by the provisions of this title or by the Nevada Rules of Civil Procedure or the Nevada Rules of Appellate Procedure, the bond or undertaking shall be presented to the clerk, of the court in which the action or proceeding is pending, for the clerk's approval before being filed or deposited.

2. The clerk of the court may refuse approval of a surety for any bond or other undertaking if a power of attorney-in-fact, which covers the agent whose signature appears on the bond or other undertaking, is not on file with the clerk of the court.

(Added to NRS by 1975, 1196)

CHAPTER 170 - PREVENTION OF PUBLIC OFFENSES

NRS 170.040 Intervention of officers of justice by requiring surety to keep peace. Public offenses may be prevented by the intervention of the officers of justice by requiring surety to keep the peace.

[1911 Cr. Prac. § 12; RL § 6862; NCL § 10661] — (NRS A 1967, 1400)

NRS 170.060 Complaint for threatening offense against person or property; may be filed in municipal court.

1. A complaint may be filed and warrant issued, as in other criminal cases, for the arrest of any person who has threatened to commit an offense against the person or property of another.

2. Such a complaint may also be filed in a municipal court. The city attorney shall act as prosecutor, and the proceedings shall conform to the requirements of NRS 170.070 to 170.170, inclusive.

[1911 Cr. Prac. § 14; A 1925, 9; NCL § 10663] — (NRS A 1967, 1400)

NRS 170.070 Trial to proceed as in criminal cases. When the person complained of is brought before the justice of the peace or magistrate, the trial on the charge shall proceed as in other criminal cases.

[1911 Cr. Prac. § 17; A 1925, 9; NCL § 10664]

NRS 170.080 Person complained of: When to be discharged. If it appears that there is no just reason to fear the commission of the offense alleged to have been threatened, the person complained of must be discharged.

[1911 Cr. Prac. § 18; RL § 6868; NCL § 10665]

NRS 170.090 Security to keep peace.

1. If, however, there is a just reason to fear the commission of the offense, the person complained of may be required to enter into a bond, in such sum, not exceeding $5,000, as the magistrate may direct, with one or more sufficient sureties, to keep the peace toward the people of this State, and particularly toward the complainant.

2. The bond shall be valid and binding for 6 months, and may, upon the renewal of the complaint, be extended for a longer period or a new bond may be required.

[1911 Cr. Prac. § 19; RL § 6869; NCL § 10666]

NRS 170.100 Effect of giving or refusing to give security.

1. If the bond required by NRS 170.090 is given, the person complained of shall be discharged.

2. If the person complained of does not give it, the magistrate must commit the person to prison until the person gives such bond, specifying in the warrant the requirement to give security, the amount thereof, and the omission to pay the same; but in no event shall the person complained of be confined in prison for a period of longer than 6 months for a failure or omission to give such bond.

[1911 Cr. Prac. § 20; A 1915, 16; 1919 RL § 6870; NCL § 10667]

NRS 170.110 Person committed may give security later. If the person complained of is committed for not giving the bond required, the person complained of may be discharged by any magistrate upon giving the same.

[1911 Cr. Prac. § 21; RL § 6871; NCL § 10668]

NRS 170.120 Bond to be filed. A bond given, as provided in NRS 170.090, must be filed by the magistrate in the office of the clerk of the county.

[1911 Cr. Prac. § 22; RL § 6872; NCL § 10669]

NRS 170.130 Breach of peace before magistrate; when security required. Any person who, in the presence of a court or magistrate, assaults or threatens to assault another or to commit any offense against a person or property, or who shall contend with another with angry words, may be ordered by the court or magistrate to give security, as provided in NRS 170.090, or if the person refuses to do so, the person may be committed as provided in NRS 170.100.

[1911 Cr. Prac. § 23; RL § 6873; NCL § 10670]

NRS 170.140 Bond to keep peace: When broken. A bond to keep the peace must be deemed broken when the person complained against is convicted of a breach of the peace.

[1911 Cr. Prac. § 24; RL § 6874; NCL § 10671]

NRS 170.150 Bond to keep peace: When and how prosecuted. Upon the district attorney's producing evidence of such conviction to the district court of the county, the court must order the bond to be prosecuted, and the district attorney must thereupon commence an action on the same, in the name of the State.

[1911 Cr. Prac. § 25; RL § 6875; NCL § 10672]

NRS 170.160 Allegation and evidence of breach. In the action, the offense stated in the record of conviction must be alleged as the breach of the bond, and such record is conclusive evidence of the breach.

[1911 Cr. Prac. § 26; RL § 6876; NCL § 10673]

NRS 170.170 Security for peace or good behavior not required except in accordance with this chapter. No security to keep the peace, or to be of good behavior, is required except as prescribed in this chapter.

[1911 Cr. Prac. § 27; RL § 6877; NCL § 10674]

CHAPTER 171 - PROCEEDINGS TO COMMITMENT

LOCAL JURISDICTION OF PUBLIC OFFENSES

NRS 171.010 Jurisdiction of offense committed in State.
NRS 171.015 Jurisdiction of offense commenced without, but consummated within, this State; consummation through agent.
NRS 171.020 Act within this State culminating in crime in this or another state.
NRS 171.025 Death by dueling.
NRS 171.030 Offense committed partly in one county and partly in another.
NRS 171.035 Offense committed on or near boundary.
NRS 171.040 Offense committed on vessel in state waters, common carrier or private motor vehicle or aircraft.
NRS 171.045 Offenses concerning animals ranging in two or more counties.
NRS 171.055 Bigamy and incest.
NRS 171.060 Burglary, robbery, larceny or embezzlement: Venue when property is taken in one county and brought into another.
NRS 171.065 Accessory: Venue in either county where offense of accessory was committed or where principal offense committed.
NRS 171.070 Conviction or acquittal in another state or territory is bar where jurisdiction is concurrent.
NRS 171.075 Conviction or acquittal in another county is bar where venue is concurrent.

CALIFORNIA-NEVADA COMPACT FOR JURISDICTION ON INTERSTATE WATERS

NRS 171.076 Enactment.
NRS 171.077 Text of Compact.

INTERSTATE COMPACT FOR JURISDICTION ON THE COLORADO RIVER

NRS 171.078 Enactment.
NRS 171.079 Text of Compact.

TIME OF COMMENCING CRIMINAL ACTIONS

NRS 171.080 No statute of limitation for murder or terrorism.
NRS 171.083 No limitation for sexual assault or sex trafficking if written report filed with law enforcement officer during period of limitation; effect of disability on period of limitation.
NRS 171.084 Limitation for kidnapping or attempted murder extended if written report filed with law enforcement officer during period of limitation.
NRS 171.085 Limitations for felonies.
NRS 171.090 Limitations for gross and simple misdemeanors.
NRS 171.095 Limitations for offenses committed in secret manner, offenses constituting sexual abuse or sex trafficking of child and offenses regarding personal identifying information.
NRS 171.100 Indictment found when it is presented and filed.

WARRANT OR SUMMONS UPON COMPLAINT

NRS 171.102 Complaint defined; oath or declaration required.
NRS 171.103 Court clerk may accept complaint filed electronically; procedure; service.
NRS 171.104 Arrest defined; by whom made.
NRS 171.106 Issuance of warrant or summons upon complaint or citation.
NRS 171.108 Contents of warrant of arrest.
NRS 171.112 Contents of summons.
NRS 171.114 Execution of warrant and service of summons: By whom.
NRS 171.116 When magistrate may depute person to act as constable.
NRS 171.118 Execution of warrant and service of summons: Territorial limits.
NRS 171.122 Manner in which execution of warrant and service of summons are made; issuance of citation in lieu of execution of warrant of arrest.

INVESTIGATION OF SUSPECTED CRIMINAL ACTIVITY; DETENTION AND IDENTIFICATION OF SUSPECTS

ARREST: BY WHOM AND HOW MADE

INTERSTATE FRESH PURSUIT (UNIFORM ACT)

INTRASTATE FRESH PURSUIT (UNIFORM ACT)

CITATION FOR MISDEMEANOR

PROCEEDINGS BEFORE MAGISTRATE

LOCAL JURISDICTION OF PUBLIC OFFENSES

NRS 171.010 Jurisdiction of offense committed in State. Every person, whether an inhabitant of this state, or any other state, or of a territory or district of the United States, is liable to punishment by the laws of this state for a public offense committed therein, except where it is by law cognizable exclusively in the courts of the United States.

[1911 Cr. Prac. § 58; RL § 6908; NCL § 10705]

NRS 171.015 Jurisdiction of offense commenced without, but consummated within, this State; consummation through agent. When the commission of a public offense, commenced without the State, is consummated within its boundaries, the defendant is liable to punishment therefor in this State, though the defendant was out of the State at the time of the commission of the offense charged. If the defendant consummated it in this State, through the intervention of an innocent or guilty agent, or any other means proceeding directly from the defendant, in such case the jurisdiction is in the county in which the offense is consummated.

[1911 Cr. Prac. § 59; RL § 6909; NCL § 10706]

NRS 171.020 Act within this State culminating in crime in this or another state. Whenever a person, with intent to commit a crime, does any act within this State in execution or part execution of such intent, which culminates in the commission of a crime, either within or without this State, such person is punishable for such crime in this State in the same manner as if the same had been committed entirely within this State.

[1911 Cr. Prac. § 59a; added 1927, 87; NCL § 10707]

NRS 171.025 Death by dueling. When an inhabitant or resident of this state, by previous appointment or engagement, fights a duel or is concerned as second therein, out of the jurisdiction of this state, and in the duel a wound is inflicted upon a person, whereof the person dies in this state, the jurisdiction of the offense is in the county where the death happens.

[1911 Cr. Prac. § 60; RL § 6910; NCL § 10708]

NRS 171.030 Offense committed partly in one county and partly in another. When a public offense is committed in part in one county and in part in another or the acts or effects thereof constituting or requisite to the consummation of the offense occur in two or more counties, the venue is in either county.
[1911 Cr. Prac. § 61; RL § 6911; NCL § 10709] — (NRS A 1963, 47)

NRS 171.035 Offense committed on or near boundary. When an offense is committed on the boundary of two or more counties, or within 500 yards thereof, the venue is in either county.
[1911 Cr. Prac. § 62; RL § 6912; NCL § 10710] — (NRS A 1963, 47)

NRS 171.040 Offense committed on vessel in state waters, common carrier or private motor vehicle or aircraft. When an offense is committed in this state:
1. On board a vessel navigating a river, slough, lake or canal, or lying therein, in the prosecution of a voyage, the venue is in any county through which the vessel is navigated in the course of the voyage, or in the county where the voyage terminates;
2. On a railroad train, car, stage or other public conveyance, or on a private motor vehicle, prosecuting its trip, the venue is in any county through which the train, car, stage or other public conveyance, or private motor vehicle, passes in the course of its trip, or in the county where the trip terminates; or
3. On an aircraft prosecuting its trip, the venue is in any county over which the aircraft passes in the course of its trip, or in the county where the trip terminates. However, venue under this subsection shall be only in a county over or into which the aircraft passes prior to the first landing of such aircraft after the crime is discovered by or reported to the person in charge of such aircraft.
[1911 Cr. Prac. § 63; RL § 6913; NCL § 10711] — (NRS A 1959, 215; 1963, 47)

NRS 171.045 Offenses concerning animals ranging in two or more counties. When a public offense concerns any neat cattle, horse, mule or other animal running at large upon any range which extends into more than one county of this state, such offense may be prosecuted in either of the counties, and, upon the trial of any such offense, proof that such animal is the property of the owner, or person occupying the range, and was at the time the offense was committed running at large upon the range, shall be prima facie evidence that the offense was committed within the jurisdiction of the court.
[1911 Cr. Prac. § 64; RL § 6914; NCL § 10712]

NRS 171.055 Bigamy and incest. When the offense, either of bigamy or incest, is committed in one county and the defendant is apprehended in another, the venue is in either county.
[1911 Cr. Prac. § 66; RL § 6916; NCL § 10714] — (NRS A 1963, 47)

NRS 171.060 Burglary, robbery, larceny or embezzlement: Venue when property is taken in one county and brought into another. When property taken in one county by burglary, robbery, larceny or embezzlement has been brought into another, the venue of the offense is in either county, but if, at any time before the conviction of the defendant in the latter, the defendant is indicted in the former county, the sheriff of the latter county must, upon demand, deliver the defendant to the sheriff of the former.
[1911 Cr. Prac. § 67; RL § 6917; NCL § 10715] — (NRS A 1963, 47)

NRS 171.065 Accessory: Venue in either county where offense of accessory was committed or where principal offense committed. In the case of an accessory in the commission of a public offense, the venue is in either the county where the offense of the accessory was committed, or where the principal offense was committed.
[1911 Cr. Prac. § 68; RL § 6918; NCL § 10716] — (NRS A 1963, 48)

NRS 171.070 Conviction or acquittal in another state or territory is bar where jurisdiction is concurrent. When an act charged as a public offense is within the jurisdiction of another state or territory, as well as of this state, a conviction or acquittal thereof in the former is a bar to the prosecution or indictment therefor in this state.
[1911 Cr. Prac. § 69; RL § 6919; NCL § 10717] — (NRS A 2009, 2734)

NRS 171.075 Conviction or acquittal in another county is bar where venue is concurrent. When an offense is within the venue of two or more counties, a conviction or acquittal thereof in one county is a bar to the prosecution or indictment therefor in another.
[1911 Cr. Prac. § 70; RL § 6920; NCL § 10718] — (NRS A 1963, 48)

CALIFORNIA-NEVADA COMPACT FOR JURISDICTION ON INTERSTATE WATERS

NRS 171.076 Enactment. The California-Nevada Compact for Jurisdiction on Interstate Waters, set forth in full in NRS 171.077, is hereby enacted into law.
(Added to NRS by 1987, 309)

NRS 171.077 Text of Compact. The California-Nevada Compact for Jurisdiction on Interstate Waters is as follows:

ARTICLE I — Purpose and Policy

1. The Legislature finds that law enforcement has been impaired in sections of Lake Tahoe and Topaz Lake forming an interstate boundary between California and Nevada because of difficulty in determining precisely where a criminal act was committed.

2. The Legislature intends that a person committing an act which is illegal in both states not be freed merely because neither state could establish that a crime was committed within its boundaries.

3. The California-Nevada Compact for Jurisdiction on Interstate Waters is enacted to provide for enforcement of the laws of this state with regard to certain acts committed on Lake Tahoe or Topaz Lake, on either side of the boundary line between California and Nevada.

ARTICLE II — Definitions

As used in this compact, unless the context otherwise requires, "party state" means a state which has enacted this compact.

ARTICLE III — Concurrent Jurisdiction

1. If conduct is prohibited by the party states, courts and law enforcement officers in either state who have jurisdiction over criminal offenses committed in a county where Lake Tahoe or Topaz Lake forms a common interstate boundary have concurrent jurisdiction to arrest, prosecute and try offenders for the prohibited conduct committed anywhere on the body of water forming a boundary between the two states.

2. This compact does not authorize:

(a) Prosecution of any person for conduct which is lawful in the state where it was committed.

(b) Any conduct prohibited by a party state.

ARTICLE IV — Ratification

This compact is ratified by enactment of the language of this compact, or substantially similar language expressing the same purpose, by the State of California and the State of Nevada.

(Added to NRS by 1987, 309)

INTERSTATE COMPACT FOR JURISDICTION ON THE COLORADO RIVER

NRS 171.078 Enactment. The Interstate Compact for Jurisdiction on the Colorado River, set forth in full in NRS 171.079, is hereby enacted into law.

(Added to NRS by 1987, 378)

NRS 171.079 Text of Compact. The Interstate Compact for Jurisdiction on the Colorado River is as follows:

ARTICLE I — Purpose and Policy

1. The Legislature finds that law enforcement has been impaired in sections of the Colorado River forming an interstate boundary because of difficulty in determining precisely where a criminal act was committed.

2. The Legislature intends that a person committing an act which is illegal in both states not be freed merely because neither state could establish that a crime was committed within its boundaries.

3. The Interstate Compact for Jurisdiction on the Colorado River is enacted to provide for enforcement of the laws of this State with regard to certain acts committed on the Colorado River, or any lake formed by or a part of the Colorado River, on either side of the boundary line with an adjoining state.

ARTICLE II — Definitions

As used in this Compact, unless the context otherwise requires, "party state" means a state which has enacted this Compact.

ARTICLE III — Concurrent Jurisdiction

1. If conduct is prohibited by two adjoining party states, courts and law enforcement officers in either state who have jurisdiction over criminal offenses committed in a county where the Colorado River, or any lake formed by or a part of the Colorado River, forms a common interstate boundary have concurrent jurisdiction to arrest, prosecute and try offenders for the prohibited conduct committed anywhere on the body of water forming a boundary between the two states and concurrent jurisdiction to arrest offenders for the prohibited conduct committed on any land mass within 5 air miles of the Colorado River or any lake formed by or a part of the Colorado River.

2. This Compact does not authorize:

(a) Prosecution of any person for conduct which is lawful in the state where it was committed.

(b) Any conduct prohibited by a party state.

3. If any claim, including a counterclaim or cross-claim, is brought in a civil action which is filed in a party state and which is:

(a) Brought against a present or former officer or employee of another party state or an agency or political subdivision of that other party state; and

(b) Based on any alleged act or omission that is related to his or her official duties or employment and conducted under the authority of this Compact,

□ the claim is subject to the conditions and limitations on civil actions, including, without limitation, the provisions regarding sovereign immunity, established by the party state in which that officer or employee is or was an officer or employee.

ARTICLE IV — Ratification

This Compact is ratified by enactment of the language of this Compact, or substantially similar language expressing the same purpose, by at least two states of which the Colorado River forms a common boundary.

(Added to NRS by 1987, 378; A 2005, 303)

TIME OF COMMENCING CRIMINAL ACTIONS

NRS 171.080 No statute of limitation for murder or terrorism. There is no limitation of the time within which a prosecution for:

1. Murder must be commenced. It may be commenced at any time after the death of the person killed.
2. A violation of NRS 202.445 must be commenced. It may be commenced at any time after the violation is committed.

[1911 Cr. Prac. § 71; RL § 6921; NCL § 10719] — (NRS A 2003, 2952)

NRS 171.083 No limitation for sexual assault or sex trafficking if written report filed with law enforcement officer during period of limitation; effect of disability on period of limitation.

1. If, at any time during the period of limitation prescribed in NRS 171.085 and 171.095, a victim of a sexual assault, a person authorized to act on behalf of a victim of a sexual assault, or a victim of sex trafficking or a person authorized to act on behalf of a victim of sex trafficking, files with a law enforcement officer a written report concerning the sexual assault or sex trafficking, the period of limitation prescribed in NRS 171.085 and 171.095 is removed and there is no limitation of the time within which a prosecution for the sexual assault or sex trafficking must be commenced.
2. If a written report is filed with a law enforcement officer pursuant to subsection 1, the law enforcement officer shall provide a copy of the written report to the victim or the person authorized to act on behalf of the victim.
3. If a victim of a sexual assault or sex trafficking is under a disability during any part of the period of limitation prescribed in NRS 171.085 and 171.095 and a written report concerning the sexual assault or sex trafficking is not otherwise filed pursuant to subsection 1, the period during which the victim is under the disability must be excluded from any calculation of the period of limitation prescribed in NRS 171.085 and 171.095.
4. For the purposes of this section, a victim of a sexual assault or sex trafficking is under a disability if the victim is insane, intellectually disabled, mentally incompetent or in a medically comatose or vegetative state.
5. As used in this section, "law enforcement officer" means:

(a) A prosecuting attorney;
(b) A sheriff of a county or the sheriff's deputy;
(c) An officer of a metropolitan police department or a police department of an incorporated city; or
(d) Any other person upon whom some or all of the powers of a peace officer are conferred pursuant to NRS 289.150 to 289.360, inclusive.

(Added to NRS by 1997, 890; A 2013, 683, 2418)

NRS 171.084 Limitation for kidnapping or attempted murder extended if written report filed with law enforcement officer during period of limitation.

1. If, at any time during the period of limitation prescribed in NRS 171.085 and 171.095, a victim of kidnapping or attempted murder, or a person authorized to act on behalf of such a victim, files with a law enforcement officer a written report concerning the offense, the period of limitation prescribed in NRS 171.085 and 171.095 is extended for 5 years.
2. If a written report is filed with a law enforcement officer pursuant to subsection 1, the law enforcement officer shall provide a copy of the written report to the victim or the person authorized to act on behalf of the victim.
3. As used in this section, "law enforcement officer" has the meaning ascribed to it in NRS 171.083.

(Added to NRS by 2001, 3031)

NRS 171.085 Limitations for felonies. Except as otherwise provided in NRS 171.080, 171.083, 171.084 and 171.095, an indictment for:

1. Theft, robbery, burglary, forgery, arson, sex trafficking, a violation of NRS 90.570, a violation punishable pursuant to paragraph (c) of subsection 3 of NRS 598.0999 or a violation of NRS 205.377 must be found, or an information or complaint filed, within 4 years after the commission of the offense.
2. Sexual assault must be found, or an information or complaint filed, within 20 years after the commission of the offense.
3. Any felony other than the felonies listed in subsections 1 and 2 must be found, or an information or complaint filed, within 3 years after the commission of the offense.

[1911 Cr. Prac. § 72; RL § 6922; NCL § 10720] — (NRS A 1963, 371; 1977, 1630; 1985, 2167; 1997, 890; 2001, 3031; 2003, 20th Special Session, 273; 2005, 1426; 2009, 146; 2013, 2418;2015, 583)

NRS 171.090 Limitations for gross and simple misdemeanors. Except as otherwise provided in NRS 171.095, 202.885 and 624.800, an indictment for:

1. A gross misdemeanor must be found, or an information or complaint filed, within 2 years after the commission of the offense.
2. Any other misdemeanor must be found, or an information or complaint filed, within 1 year after the commission of the offense.

[1911 Cr. Prac. § 73; RL § 6923; NCL § 10721] — (NRS A 1981, 771; 1985, 2167; 1999, 3525; 2005, 1209)

NRS 171.095 Limitations for offenses committed in secret manner, offenses constituting sexual abuse or sex trafficking of child and offenses regarding personal identifying information.

1. Except as otherwise provided in subsection 2 and NRS 171.083 and 171.084:

(a) If a felony, gross misdemeanor or misdemeanor is committed in a secret manner, an indictment for the offense must be found, or an information or complaint filed, within the periods of limitation prescribed in NRS 171.085, 171.090 and 624.800 after the discovery of the offense, unless a longer period is allowed by paragraph (b) or (c) or the provisions of NRS 202.885.

(b) An indictment must be found, or an information or complaint filed, for any offense constituting sexual abuse of a child as defined in NRS 432B.100 or sex trafficking of a child as defined in NRS 201.300, before the victim is:

(1) Thirty-six years old if the victim discovers or reasonably should have discovered that he or she was a victim of the sexual abuse or sex trafficking by the date on which the victim reaches that age; or

(2) Forty-three years old if the victim does not discover and reasonably should not have discovered that he or she was a victim of the sexual abuse or sex trafficking by the date on which the victim reaches 36 years of age.

(c) If a felony is committed pursuant to NRS 205.461 to 205.4657, inclusive, against a victim who is less than 18 years of age at the time of the commission of the offense, an indictment for the offense must be found, or an information or complaint filed, within 4 years after the victim discovers or reasonably should have discovered the offense.

2. If any indictment found, or an information or complaint filed, within the time prescribed in subsection 1 is defective so that no judgment can be given thereon, another prosecution may be instituted for the same offense within 6 months after the first is abandoned.

[1911 Cr. Prac. § 74; RL § 6924; NCL § 10722] — (NRS A 1981, 771; 1985, 2167; 1989, 1443; 1993, 305; 1997, 891; 1999, 3525; 2001, 3031; 2005, 1209; 2011, 131; 2013, 247, 2419)

NRS 171.100 Indictment found when it is presented and filed. An indictment is found, within the meaning of this chapter, when it is presented by the grand jury in open court, and there received and filed.

[1911 Cr. Prac. § 75; RL § 6925; NCL § 10723]

WARRANT OR SUMMONS UPON COMPLAINT

NRS 171.102 Complaint defined; oath or declaration required. The complaint is a written statement of the essential facts constituting the public offense charged. It must be made upon:

1. Oath before a magistrate or a notary public; or
2. Declaration which is made subject to the penalty for perjury.

(Added to NRS by 1967, 1400; A 1969, 387; 1983, 446)

NRS 171.103 Court clerk may accept complaint filed electronically; procedure; service.

1. A court clerk may accept a complaint filed pursuant to this chapter that is filed electronically. A complaint that is filed electronically must contain an image of the signature of the prosecuting attorney.

2. If a court clerk accepts a complaint that is filed electronically pursuant to subsection 1, the court clerk shall acknowledge receipt of the complaint by an electronic time stamp and shall electronically return the complaint with the electronic time stamp to the prosecuting attorney. A complaint that is filed and time-stamped electronically pursuant to this section may be converted into a printed document and served upon a defendant in the same manner as a complaint that is not filed electronically.

(Added to NRS by 1997, 892)

NRS 171.104 Arrest defined; by whom made. An arrest is the taking of a person into custody, in a case and in the manner authorized by law. An arrest may be made by a peace officer or by a private person.

(Added to NRS by 1967, 1400)

NRS 171.106 Issuance of warrant or summons upon complaint or citation. If it appears from the complaint or a citation issued pursuant to NRS 484A.730, 488.920 or 501.386, or from an affidavit or affidavits filed with the complaint or citation that there is probable cause to believe that an offense, triable within the county, has been committed and that the defendant has committed it, a warrant for the arrest of the defendant shall be issued by the magistrate to any peace officer. Upon the request of the district attorney a summons instead of a warrant shall issue. More than one warrant or summons may issue on the same complaint or citation. If a defendant fails to appear in response to the summons, a warrant shall issue.

(Added to NRS by 1967, 1400; A 1971, 830)

NRS 171.108 Contents of warrant of arrest. The warrant of arrest is an order in writing in the name of the State of Nevada which shall:

1. Be signed by the magistrate with the magistrate's name of office;
2. Contain the name of the defendant or, if the defendant's name is unknown, any name or description by which the defendant can be identified with reasonable certainty;
3. State the date of its issuance, and the county, city or town where it was issued;
4. Describe the offense charged in the complaint; and
5. Command that the defendant be arrested and brought before the nearest available magistrate.

(Added to NRS by 1967, 1400)

NRS 171.112 Contents of summons. The summons shall be in the same form as the warrant except that it shall summon the defendant to appear before a magistrate at a stated time and place. Upon a complaint against a corporation, the magistrate must issue a summons, signed by the magistrate, with the magistrate's name of office, requiring the corporation to appear before the magistrate at a specified time and place to answer the charge, the time to be not less than 10 days after the issuing of the summons.

(Added to NRS by 1967, 1400)

NRS 171.114 Execution of warrant and service of summons: By whom. The warrant shall be directed to and executed by a peace officer. The summons may be served by any person authorized to serve a summons in a civil action.

(Added to NRS by 1967, 1401)

NRS 171.116 When magistrate may depute person to act as constable. A magistrate may depute in writing any suitable and discreet person to act as constable when no constable is at hand and the nature of the business requires immediate action.

(Added to NRS by 1967, 1401)

NRS 171.118 Execution of warrant and service of summons: Territorial limits. The warrant may be executed or the summons may be served at any place within the jurisdiction of the State of Nevada.

(Added to NRS by 1967, 1401)

NRS 171.122 Manner in which execution of warrant and service of summons are made; issuance of citation in lieu of execution of warrant of arrest.

1. Except as otherwise provided in subsection 2, the warrant must be executed by the arrest of the defendant. The officer need not have the warrant in the officer's possession at the time of the arrest, but upon request the officer must show the warrant to the defendant as soon as possible. If the officer does not have a warrant in the officer's possession at the time of the arrest, the officer shall then inform the defendant of the officer's intention to arrest the defendant, of the offense charged, the authority to make it and of the fact that a warrant has or has not been issued. The defendant must not be subjected to any more restraint than is necessary for the defendant's arrest and detention. If the defendant either flees or forcibly resists, the officer may, except as otherwise provided in NRS 171.1455, use all necessary means to effect the arrest.

2. In lieu of executing the warrant by arresting the defendant, a peace officer may issue a citation as provided in NRS 171.1773 if:

(a) The warrant is issued upon an offense punishable as a misdemeanor;

(b) The officer has no indication that the defendant has previously failed to appear on the charge reflected in the warrant;

(c) The defendant provides satisfactory evidence of his or her identity to the peace officer;

(d) The defendant signs a written promise to appear in court for the misdemeanor offense; and

(e) The officer has reasonable grounds to believe that the defendant will keep a written promise to appear in court.

3. The summons must be served upon a defendant by delivering a copy to the defendant personally, or by leaving it at the defendant's dwelling house or usual place of abode with some person then residing in the house or abode who is at least 16 years of age and is of suitable discretion, or by mailing it to the defendant's last known address. In the case of a corporation, the summons must be served at least 5 days before the day of appearance fixed in the summons, by delivering a copy to an officer or to a managing or general agent or to any other agent authorized by appointment or by law to receive service of process and, if the agent is one authorized by statute to receive service and the statute so requires, by also mailing a copy to the corporation's last known address within the State of Nevada or at its principal place of business elsewhere in the United States.

(Added to NRS by 1967, 1401; A 1985, 618; 1993, 143, 931, 932)

INVESTIGATION OF SUSPECTED CRIMINAL ACTIVITY; DETENTION AND IDENTIFICATION OF SUSPECTS

NRS 171.1223 Peace officer with limited jurisdiction must notify primary law enforcement agency of commission of certain felonies; transfer of investigation to primary law enforcement agency.

1. Except as otherwise provided in subsection 3, in a county whose population is 100,000 or more, a peace officer with limited jurisdiction who witnesses a category A felony being committed or attempted in the officer's presence, or has reasonable cause for believing a person has committed or attempted to commit a category A felony in an area that is within the officer's jurisdiction, shall immediately notify the primary law enforcement agency in the city or county, as appropriate, where the offense or attempted offense was committed.

2. Upon arrival of an officer from the primary law enforcement agency notified pursuant to subsection 1, a peace officer with limited jurisdiction shall immediately transfer the investigation of the offense or attempted offense to the primary law enforcement agency.

3. The provisions of subsection 1 do not:

(a) Apply to an offense or attempted offense that is a misdemeanor, gross misdemeanor or felony other than a category A felony;

(b) Apply to an officer of the Nevada Highway Patrol, a member of the police department of the Nevada System of Higher Education, an agent of the Investigation Division of the Department of Public Safety or a ranger of the Division of State Parks of the State Department of Conservation and Natural Resources;

(c) Apply to a peace officer with limited jurisdiction if an interlocal agreement between the officer's employer and the primary law enforcement agency in the city or county in which a category A felony was committed or attempted authorizes the peace officer with limited jurisdiction to respond to and investigate the felony without immediately notifying the primary law enforcement agency; or

(d) Prohibit a peace officer with limited jurisdiction from:

(1) Contacting a primary law enforcement agency for assistance with an offense that is a misdemeanor, gross misdemeanor or felony that is not a category A felony; or

(2) Responding to a category A felony until the appropriate primary law enforcement agency arrives at the location where the felony was allegedly committed or attempted, including, without limitation, taking any appropriate action to provide assistance to a victim of the felony, to apprehend the person suspected of committing or attempting to commit the felony, to secure the location where the felony was allegedly committed or attempted and to protect the life and safety of the peace officer and any other person present at that location.

4. As used in this section:

(a) "Peace officer with limited jurisdiction" means:

(1) A school police officer who is appointed or employed pursuant to subsection 2 of NRS 391.281;

(2) An airport guard or police officer who is appointed pursuant to NRS 496.130;

(3) A person employed to provide police services for an airport authority created by a special act of the Legislature; and

(4) A marshal or park ranger who is part of a unit of specialized law enforcement established pursuant to NRS 280.125.

(b) "Primary law enforcement agency" means:

(1) A police department of an incorporated city;

(2) The sheriff's office of a county; or

(3) If the county is within the jurisdiction of a metropolitan police department, the metropolitan police department.

(Added to NRS by 2001, 1868; A 2003, 102; 2015, 3834)

NRS 171.1225 Peace officer to provide information to suspected victims of domestic violence.

1. When investigating an act of domestic violence, a peace officer shall:

(a) Make a good faith effort to explain the provisions of NRS 171.137 pertaining to domestic violence and advise victims of all reasonable means to prevent further abuse, including advising each person of the availability of a shelter or other services in the community.

(b) Provide a person suspected of being the victim of an act of domestic violence with a written copy of the following statements:

(1) My name is officer .... (naming the investigating officer). Nevada law requires me to inform you of the following information.

(2) If I have probable cause to believe that a battery has been committed against you, your minor child or the minor child of the person believed to have committed the battery in the last 24 hours by your spouse, your former spouse, any other person to whom you are related by blood or marriage, a person with whom you are or were actually residing, a person with whom you have had or are having a dating relationship or a person with whom you have a child in common, I am required, unless mitigating circumstances exist, to arrest the person suspected of committing the battery.

(3) If I am unable to arrest the person suspected of committing the battery, you have the right to request that the prosecutor file a criminal complaint against the person. I can provide you with information on this procedure. If convicted, the person who committed the battery may be placed on probation, ordered to see a counselor, put in jail or fined.

(4) The law provides that you may seek a court order for the protection of you, your minor children or any animal that is owned or kept by you, by the person who committed or threatened the act of domestic violence or by the minor child of either such person against further threats or acts of domestic violence. You do not need to hire a lawyer to obtain such an order for protection.

(5) An order for protection may require the person who committed or threatened the act of domestic violence against you to:

(I) Stop threatening, harassing or injuring you or your children;

(II) Move out of your residence;

(III) Stay away from your place of employment;

(IV) Stay away from the school attended by your children;

(V) Stay away from any place you or your children regularly go;

(VI) Avoid or limit all communication with you or your children;

(VII) Stop physically injuring, threatening to injure or taking possession of any animal that is owned or kept by you or your children, either directly or through an agent; and

(VIII) Stop physically injuring or threatening to injure any animal that is owned or kept by the person who committed or threatened the act or his or her children, either directly or through an agent.

(6) A court may make future orders for protection which award you custody of your children and require the person who committed or threatened the act of domestic violence against you to:

(I) Pay the rent or mortgage due on the place in which you live;

(II) Pay the amount of money necessary for the support of your children;

(III) Pay part or all of the costs incurred by you in obtaining the order for protection; and

(IV) Comply with the arrangements specified for the possession and care of any animal owned or kept by you or your children or by the person who committed or threatened the act or his or her children.

(7) To get an order for protection, go to room number .... (state the room number of the office at the court) at the court, which is located at .... (state the address of the court). Ask the clerk of the court to provide you with the forms for an order of protection.

(8) If the person who committed or threatened the act of domestic violence against you violates the terms of an order for protection, the person may be arrested and, if:

(I) The arresting officer determines that such a violation is accompanied by a direct or indirect threat of harm;

(II) The person has previously violated a temporary or extended order for protection; or

(III) At the time of the violation or within 2 hours after the violation, the person has a concentration of alcohol of 0.08 or more in the person's blood or breath or an amount of a prohibited substance in the person's blood or urine that is equal to or greater than the amount set forth in subsection 3 of NRS 484C.110,

□ the person will not be admitted to bail sooner than 12 hours after arrest.

(9) You may obtain emergency assistance or shelter by contacting your local program against domestic violence at .... (state name, address and telephone number of local program) or you may call, without charge to you, the Statewide Program Against Domestic Violence at .... (state toll-free telephone number of Statewide Program).

2. The failure of a peace officer to carry out the requirements set forth in subsection 1 is not a defense in a criminal prosecution for the commission of an act of domestic violence, nor may such an omission be considered as negligence or as causation in any civil action against the peace officer or the officer's employer.

3. As used in this section:

(a) "Act of domestic violence" means any of the following acts committed by a person against his or her spouse, former spouse, any other person to whom he or she is related by blood or marriage, a person with whom he or she is or was actually residing, a person with whom he or she has had or is having a dating relationship, a person with whom he or she has a child in common, the minor child of any of those persons or his or her minor child:

(1) A battery.

(2) An assault.

(3) Compelling the other by force or threat of force to perform an act from which he or she has the right to refrain or to refrain from an act which he or she has the right to perform.

(4) A sexual assault.

(5) A knowing, purposeful or reckless course of conduct intended to harass the other. Such conduct may include, but is not limited to:

(I) Stalking.

(II) Arson.

(III) Trespassing.

(IV) Larceny.

(V) Destruction of private property.

(VI) Carrying a concealed weapon without a permit.

(VII) Injuring or killing an animal.

(6) False imprisonment.

(7) Unlawful entry of the other's residence, or forcible entry against the other's will if there is a reasonably foreseeable risk of harm to the other from the entry.

(b) "Dating relationship" means frequent, intimate associations primarily characterized by the expectation of affectional or sexual involvement. The term does not include a casual relationship or an ordinary association between persons in a business or social context.

(Added to NRS by 1989, 64; A 1993, 2771; 1995, 899; 1997, 1800; 2001, 1221; 2007, 1015; 2013, 40)

NRS 171.1227 Peace officer to submit written report concerning suspected acts of domestic violence; information from reports to be aggregated and forwarded to Central Repository; content of report.

1. If a peace officer investigates an act that constitutes domestic violence pursuant to NRS 33.018, the peace officer shall prepare and submit a written report of the investigation to the peace officer's supervisor or to another person designated by the peace officer's supervisor, regardless of whether the peace officer makes an arrest.

2. If the peace officer investigates a mutual battery that constitutes domestic violence pursuant to NRS 33.018 and finds that one of the persons involved was the primary physical aggressor, the peace officer shall include in the report:

(a) The name of the person who was the primary physical aggressor; and

(b) A description of the evidence which supports the peace officer's finding.

3. If the peace officer does not make an arrest, the peace officer shall include in the report the reason the peace officer did not do so.

4. The information contained in a report made pursuant to subsections 1 and 2 must be:

(a) Aggregated each month; and

(b) Forwarded by each jurisdiction to the Central Repository for Nevada Records of Criminal History not later than the 15th day of the following month.

5. The Director of the Department of Public Safety shall prescribe the form on which the information described in subsection 4 must be reported to the Central Repository. In addition to the information required pursuant to subsections 1 and 2, the form must also require the inclusion of the following information from each report:

(a) The gender, age and race of the persons involved;

(b) The relationship of the persons involved;

(c) The date and time of day of the offense;

(d) The number of children present, if any, at the time of the offense;

(e) Whether or not an order for protection against domestic violence was in effect at the time of the offense;

(f) Whether or not any weapons were used during the commission of the offense;

(g) Whether or not any person required medical attention;

(h) Whether or not any person was given a domestic violence card that contains information about appropriate counseling or other supportive services available in the community in which that person resides;

(i) Whether or not the primary physical aggressor, if identified, was arrested and, if not, any mitigating circumstances explaining why an arrest was not made; and

(j) Whether or not any other person was arrested.

(Added to NRS by 1997, 1533; A 2007, 2482)

NRS 171.1228 Investigation of alleged sexual offense: Alleged victim not required to submit to polygraphic examination or other similar examination.

1. A law enforcement officer, prosecutor or other employee of a governmental entity shall not, as a condition of investigating an alleged sexual offense, request or require a victim of the alleged sexual offense to take or submit to a polygraphic examination or other similar examination that is used, or the results of which are used, for the purpose of rendering a diagnostic opinion regarding the honesty or dishonesty of a person.

2. As used in this section, "sexual offense" has the meaning ascribed to it in NRS 179D.097.

(Added to NRS by 2007, 95)

NRS 171.1229 Fingerprinting of persons detained and cited for committing suspected acts of domestic violence; fingerprints to be forwarded to Central Repository. If a peace officer:

1. Detains a person for violating a county, city or town ordinance or state law that:

(a) Is punishable as a misdemeanor; and

(b) Constitutes domestic violence pursuant to NRS 33.018; and

2. Issues the person a citation in lieu of taking the person before a magistrate,

□ the peace officer shall obtain not less than one fingerprint of the person and shall forward any fingerprint taken and the report that the peace officer is required to prepare pursuant to NRS 171.1227 to the Central Repository for Nevada Records of Criminal History.

(Added to NRS by 1997, 1533)

NRS 171.123 Temporary detention by peace officer of person suspected of criminal behavior or of violating conditions of parole or probation: Limitations.

1. Any peace officer may detain any person whom the officer encounters under circumstances which reasonably indicate that the person has committed, is committing or is about to commit a crime.

2. Any peace officer may detain any person the officer encounters under circumstances which reasonably indicate that the person has violated or is violating the conditions of the person's parole or probation.

3. The officer may detain the person pursuant to this section only to ascertain the person's identity and the suspicious circumstances surrounding the person's presence abroad. Any person so detained shall identify himself or herself, but may not be compelled to answer any other inquiry of any peace officer.

4. A person must not be detained longer than is reasonably necessary to effect the purposes of this section, and in no event longer than 60 minutes. The detention must not extend beyond the place or the immediate vicinity of the place where the detention was first effected, unless the person is arrested.

(Added to NRS by 1969, 535; A 1973, 597; 1975, 1200; 1987, 1172; 1995, 2068)

NRS 171.1231 Arrest if probable cause appears. At any time after the onset of the detention pursuant to NRS 171.123, the person so detained shall be arrested if probable cause for an arrest appears. If, after inquiry into the circumstances which prompted the detention, no probable cause for arrest appears, such person shall be released.

(Added to NRS by 1969, 535)

NRS 171.1232 Search to ascertain presence of dangerous weapon; seizure of weapon or evidence.

1. If any peace officer reasonably believes that any person whom the peace officer has detained or is about to detain pursuant to NRS 171.123 is armed with a dangerous weapon and is a threat to the safety of the peace officer or another, the peace officer may search such person to the extent reasonably necessary to ascertain the presence of such weapon. If the search discloses a weapon or any evidence of a crime, such weapon or evidence may be seized.

2. Nothing seized by a peace officer in any such search is admissible in any proceeding unless the search which disclosed the existence of such evidence is authorized by and conducted in compliance with this section.

(Added to NRS by 1969, 535)

NRS 171.1235 Gaming licensee may detain person suspected of having committed felony in gaming establishment.

1. As used in this section:

(a) "Establishment" means any premises whereon any gaming is done or any premises owned or controlled by a licensee for the purpose of parking motor vehicles owned or operated by patrons of such licensee.

(b) "Licensee" has the meaning ascribed to it in NRS 463.0171.

2. Any licensee or the licensee's officers, employees or agents may take into custody and detain any person when such licensee or the licensee's officers, employees or agents have reasonable cause to believe the person detained has committed a felony, whether or not in the presence of such licensee or the licensee's officers, employees or agents.

3. Detention pursuant to this section shall be in the establishment, in a reasonable manner, for a reasonable length of time and solely for the purpose of notifying a peace officer. Such taking into custody and detention shall not render the licensee or the licensee's officers, employees or agents criminally or civilly liable for false arrest, false imprisonment, slander or unlawful detention unless such taking into custody and detention are unreasonable under all the circumstances.

4. No licensee or the licensee's officers, employees or agents are entitled to the immunity from liability provided for in this section unless there is displayed in a conspicuous place in the establishment a notice in boldface type clearly legible and in substantially this form:

> Any gaming licensee or the licensee's officers, employees or agents who have reasonable cause to believe that any person has committed a felony may detain such person in the establishment for the purpose of notifying a peace officer.

(Added to NRS by 1973, 1700; A 2003, 20th Special Session, 15)

NRS 171.1237 Identification of suspect by live lineup, photo lineup or show-up: Law enforcement agencies to adopt policies and procedures governing use.

1. Each law enforcement agency shall adopt policies and procedures governing the use of live lineups, photo lineups and show-ups.

2. As used in this section:

(a) "Live lineup" means an identification procedure in which a group of persons, including the suspect, is displayed to an eyewitness to determine whether the eyewitness identifies the suspect as the perpetrator of a crime.

(b) "Photo lineup" means an identification procedure in which an array of photographs, including a photograph of the suspect, is displayed to an eyewitness in hard copy or by digital image to determine whether the eyewitness identifies the suspect as the perpetrator of a crime.

(c) "Show-up" means an identification procedure in which the suspect appears individually for possible identification by the eyewitness as the perpetrator of a crime.

(Added to NRS by 2011, 325)

ARREST: BY WHOM AND HOW MADE

NRS 171.124 Arrest by peace officer or officer of Drug Enforcement Administration.

1. Except as otherwise provided in subsection 3 and NRS 33.070 and 33.320, a peace officer or an officer of the Drug Enforcement Administration designated by the Attorney General of the United States for that purpose may make an arrest in obedience to a warrant delivered to him or her, or may, without a warrant, arrest a person:

(a) For a public offense committed or attempted in the officer's presence.

(b) When a person arrested has committed a felony or gross misdemeanor, although not in the officer's presence.

(c) When a felony or gross misdemeanor has in fact been committed, and the officer has reasonable cause for believing the person arrested to have committed it.

(d) On a charge made, upon a reasonable cause, of the commission of a felony or gross misdemeanor by the person arrested.

(e) When a warrant has in fact been issued in this State for the arrest of a named or described person for a public offense, and the officer has reasonable cause to believe that the person arrested is the person so named or described.

2. A peace officer or an officer of the Drug Enforcement Administration designated by the Attorney General of the United States for that purpose may also, at night, without a warrant, arrest any person whom the officer has reasonable cause for believing to have committed a felony or gross misdemeanor, and is justified in making the arrest, though it afterward appears that a felony or gross misdemeanor has not been committed.

3. An officer of the Drug Enforcement Administration may only make an arrest pursuant to subsections 1 and 2 for a violation of chapter 453 of NRS.

(Added to NRS by 1967, 1401; A 1975, 755; 1979, 834; 1983, 1651; 1985, 1171, 2022, 2170; 2001, 2850; 2003, 888; 2013, 2946; 2015, 2521)

NRS 171.1245 Arrest by agent of Federal Bureau of Investigation or Secret Service. An agent of the Federal Bureau of Investigation or Secret Service may, without a warrant, arrest a person:

1. For a public offense committed or attempted in the agent's presence.

2. When a person arrested has committed a felony or gross misdemeanor, although not in the agent's presence.

3. When a felony or gross misdemeanor has in fact been committed, and the agent has reasonable cause for believing the person arrested to have committed it.

4. On a charge made, upon a reasonable cause, of the commission of a felony or gross misdemeanor by the person arrested.

5. When a warrant has in fact been issued in this State for the arrest of a named or described person for a public offense, and the agent has reasonable cause to believe that the person arrested is the person so named or described.

(Added to NRS by 1985, 451)

NRS 171.1255 Arrest by officer or agent of Bureau of Indian Affairs or police officer employed by Indian tribe.

1. Except as otherwise provided in subsection 2, an officer or agent of the Bureau of Indian Affairs or a person employed as a police officer by an Indian tribe may make an arrest in obedience to a warrant delivered to him or her, or may, without a warrant, arrest a person:

(a) For a public offense committed or attempted in the officer or agent's presence.

(b) When a person arrested has committed a felony or gross misdemeanor, although not in the officer or agent's presence.

(c) When a felony or gross misdemeanor has in fact been committed, and the officer or agent has reasonable cause for believing the person arrested to have committed it.

(d) On a charge made, upon a reasonable cause, of the commission of a felony or gross misdemeanor by the person arrested.

(e) When a warrant has in fact been issued in this State for the arrest of a named or described person for a public offense, and the officer or agent has reasonable cause to believe that the person arrested is the person so named or described.

(f) When the peace officer has probable cause to believe that the person to be arrested has committed a battery upon that person's spouse and the peace officer finds evidence of bodily harm to the spouse.

2. Such an officer or agent may make an arrest pursuant to subsection 1 only:

(a) Within the boundaries of an Indian reservation or Indian colony for an offense committed on that reservation or colony; or

(b) Outside the boundaries of an Indian reservation or Indian colony if the officer or agent is in fresh pursuit of a person who is reasonably believed by the officer or agent to have committed a felony within the boundaries of the reservation or colony or has committed, or attempted to commit, any criminal offense within those boundaries in the presence of the officer or agent.

 For the purposes of this subsection, "fresh pursuit" has the meaning ascribed to it in NRS 171.156.

(Added to NRS by 1985, 452)

NRS 171.1257 Arrest by postal inspector of United States Postal Inspection Service.

1. A postal inspector of the United States Postal Inspection Service may make an arrest in obedience to a warrant delivered to him or her, or may, without a warrant, arrest a person:

(a) For a public offense related to postal matters committed or attempted in the postal inspector's presence.

(b) When the person arrested has committed a felony or gross misdemeanor related to postal matters, although not in the postal inspector's presence.

(c) When a felony or gross misdemeanor related to postal matters has in fact been committed, and the postal inspector has reasonable cause for believing the person arrested to have committed it.

(d) On a charge made, upon a reasonable cause, of the commission of a felony or gross misdemeanor related to postal matters by the person arrested.

(e) When a warrant has in fact been issued in this State for the arrest of a named or described person for a public offense related to postal matters, and the postal inspector has reasonable cause to believe that the person arrested is the person so named or described.

2. As used in this section, "postal matters" means any act related to mail service, including, without limitation, delivering and collecting mail, mail theft and mail fraud.

(Added to NRS by 2007, 2173)

NRS 171.126 Arrest by private person. A private person may arrest another:

1. For a public offense committed or attempted in the person's presence.

2. When the person arrested has committed a felony, although not in the person's presence.

3. When a felony has been in fact committed, and the private person has reasonable cause for believing the person arrested to have committed it.

(Added to NRS by 1967, 1402)

NRS 171.128 Magistrate may order arrest for committing or attempting to commit offense in magistrate's presence. A magistrate may orally order a peace officer or private person to arrest anyone committing or attempting to commit a public offense in the presence of the magistrate, and may thereupon proceed as if the offender had been brought before the magistrate on a warrant of arrest.

(Added to NRS by 1967, 1402)

NRS 171.132 Person making arrest may summon assistance. Any person making an arrest may orally summon as many persons as the person making the arrest deems necessary to aid him or her therein.

(Added to NRS by 1967, 1402)

NRS 171.134 Escape or rescue of arrested person: Pursuit and retaking at any time and place in State. If a person arrested escapes or is rescued, the person from whose custody he or she escaped or was rescued may immediately pursue and retake the person at any time and in any place within the State.

(Added to NRS by 1967, 1402)

NRS 171.136 When arrest may be made.

1. If the offense charged is a felony or gross misdemeanor, the arrest may be made on any day, and at any time of day or night.

2. If it is a misdemeanor, the arrest cannot be made between the hours of 7 p.m. and 7 a.m., except:

(a) Upon the direction of a magistrate, endorsed upon the warrant;

(b) When the offense is committed in the presence of the arresting officer;

(c) When the person is found and the arrest is made in a public place or a place that is open to the public and:

(1) There is a warrant of arrest against the person; and

(2) The misdemeanor is discovered because there was probable cause for the arresting officer to stop, detain or arrest the person for another alleged violation or offense;

(d) When the offense is committed in the presence of a private person and the person makes an arrest immediately after the offense is committed;

(e) When the offense charged is battery that constitutes domestic violence pursuant to NRS 33.018 and the arrest is made in the manner provided in NRS 171.137;

(f) When the offense charged is a violation of a temporary or extended order for protection against domestic violence issued pursuant to NRS 33.017 to 33.100, inclusive;

(g) When the person is already in custody as a result of another lawful arrest; or

(h) When the person voluntarily surrenders himself or herself in response to an outstanding warrant of arrest.

(Added to NRS by 1967, 1402; A 1977, 874; 1985, 6, 2023; 1991, 331; 1993, 119; 2001, 1431)

NRS 171.137 Arrest required for suspected battery constituting domestic violence; exceptions.

1. Except as otherwise provided in subsection 2, whether or not a warrant has been issued, a peace officer shall, unless mitigating circumstances exist, arrest a person when the peace officer has probable cause to believe that the person to be arrested has, within the preceding 24 hours, committed a battery upon his or her spouse, former spouse, any other person to whom he or she is related by blood or marriage, a person with whom he or she is or was actually residing, a person with whom he or she has had or is having a dating relationship, a person with whom he or she has a child in common, the minor child of any of those persons or his or her minor child.

2. If the peace officer has probable cause to believe that a battery described in subsection 1 was a mutual battery, the peace officer shall attempt to determine which person was the primary physical aggressor. If the peace officer determines that one of the persons who allegedly committed a battery was the primary physical aggressor involved in the incident, the peace officer is not required to arrest any other person believed to have committed a battery during the incident. In determining whether a person is a primary physical aggressor for the purposes of this subsection, the peace officer shall consider:

(a) Prior domestic violence involving either person;

(b) The relative severity of the injuries inflicted upon the persons involved;

(c) The potential for future injury;

(d) Whether one of the alleged batteries was committed in self-defense; and

(e) Any other factor that may help the peace officer decide which person was the primary physical aggressor.

3. A peace officer shall not base a decision regarding whether to arrest a person pursuant to this section on the peace officer's perception of the willingness of a victim or a witness to the incident to testify or otherwise participate in related judicial proceedings.

4. As used in this section, "dating relationship" means frequent, intimate associations primarily characterized by the expectation of affectional or sexual involvement. The term does not include a casual relationship or an ordinary association between persons in a business or social context.

(Added to NRS by 1985, 2170; A 1989, 23; 1995, 901; 1997, 1533, 1802; 1999, 486)

NRS 171.138 Breaking open door or window: Making arrest. To make an arrest, a private person, if the offense is a felony, and in all cases a peace officer, may break open a door or window of the house, structure or other place of concealment in which the person to be arrested is, or in which there is reasonable grounds for believing the person to be, after having demanded admittance and explained the purpose for which admittance is desired.

(Added to NRS by 1967, 1402; A 1983, 244)

NRS 171.142 Breaking open door or window: Upon detention after making arrest. Any person who has entered a house, structure or other place of concealment to make an arrest may break open a door or window if that is necessary to liberate himself or herself. An officer may do the same to liberate a person who, acting in the officer's aid, entered to make an arrest and is detained inside.

(Added to NRS by 1967, 1402; A 1983, 244)

NRS 171.144 Breaking open door or window: Retaking person arrested. To retake a person arrested who has escaped or been rescued, the person pursuing may break open an outer or inner door or window of a dwelling house, structure or other place of concealment, if, after notice of his or her intention, the person pursuing is refused admittance.

(Added to NRS by 1967, 1402)

NRS 171.1455 Use of deadly force to effect arrest: Limitations. If necessary to prevent escape, an officer may, after giving a warning, if feasible, use deadly force to effect the arrest of a person only if there is probable cause to believe that the person:

1. Has committed a felony which involves the infliction or threat of serious bodily harm or the use of deadly force; or

2. Poses a threat of serious bodily harm to the officer or to others.

(Added to NRS by 1993, 931)

NRS 171.146 Weapon may be taken from person arrested. Any person making an arrest may take from the person arrested all dangerous and offensive weapons which the person arrested may have about his or her person.

(Added to NRS by 1967, 1402)

NRS 171.147 Duties of arresting officer where person arrested appears to be intoxicated or not in control of the person's physical functions.

1. Every peace officer shall, when arresting any person who appears to be intoxicated or not in control of the person's physical functions, investigate in a reasonable manner to determine whether or not that person is wearing a bracelet, necklace, other visible device or other identification identifying a medical condition which might account for the actions of the person.

2. Any arresting officer who discovers identification of a medical condition during an investigation conducted pursuant to subsection 1 shall take reasonable steps to aid the afflicted person in receiving medication or other treatment for the medical condition.

(Added to NRS by 1981, 781)

NRS 171.148 Warrant of arrest by telegram authorized.

1. A warrant of arrest may be transmitted by telegram. A copy of a warrant transmitted by telegram may be sent to one or more peace officers, and the copy is as effectual in the hands of any officer, and the officer must proceed in the same manner under it, as though the officer held an original warrant issued by the magistrate before whom the original complaint in the case was laid.

2. Every officer causing a warrant to be transmitted by telegram pursuant to subsection 1 must certify as correct a copy of the warrant and endorsement thereon, and must return the original with a statement of the officer's action thereunder.

3. As used in this section, "telegram" includes every method of electric or electronic communication by which a written as distinct from an oral message is transmitted.

(Added to NRS by 1967, 1402; A 1973, 598; 2003, 984)

NRS 171.152 Return of warrant after execution by arrest or issuance of citation; return of summons after service; cancellation by district attorney before execution or service; reissuance.

1. The peace officer executing a warrant by arrest shall make return thereof to the magistrate before whom the defendant is brought pursuant to NRS 171.178 and 171.184. At the request of the district attorney any unexecuted warrant must be returned to the magistrate by whom it was issued and must be cancelled.

2. The peace officer executing a warrant by issuance of a citation pursuant to subsection 2 of NRS 171.122 shall:

(a) Record on the warrant the number assigned to the citation issued thereon;

(b) Attach the warrant to the citation issued thereon; and

(c) Return the warrant and citation to the magistrate before whom the defendant is scheduled to appear.

3. On or before the return day the person to whom a summons was delivered for service shall make return thereof to the magistrate before whom the summons is returnable.

4. At the request of the district attorney made at any time while the complaint is pending, a warrant returned unexecuted and not cancelled or a summons returned unserved or a duplicate thereof may be delivered by the magistrate to a peace officer for execution or service.

(Added to NRS by 1967, 1403; A 1993, 144)

NRS 171.153 Right of person arrested to make telephone calls.

1. Any person arrested has the right to make a reasonable number of completed telephone calls from the police station or other place at which the person is booked immediately after the person is booked and, except where physically impossible, no later than 3 hours after the arrest. Such telephone calls may be limited to local calls, except that long distance calls may be made by the arrested person at his or her own expense.

2. A reasonable number of calls must include one completed call to a friend or bail agent and one completed call to an attorney.

(Added to NRS by 1973, 724; A 1997, 3393)

NRS 171.1536 Arrest of person with communications disability: Interpreter to be made available. Upon the arrest of a person with a communications disability as defined in NRS 50.050, and before any interrogation or the taking of a statement, the peace officer in actual charge of the station, headquarters or other facility to which the person with a communications disability has been brought shall make an interpreter available at public expense to that person in accordance with the provisions of NRS 50.050 to 50.053, inclusive.

(Added to NRS by 1975, 309; A 1979, 657; 2001, 1776; 2007, 170)

NRS 171.1537 Arrest of person with disability: Right to communicate by mail or telephone. When a person with a disability is detained in custody, the detaining authority shall make available a reasonable means of communication, at least pencil and paper, and at least two envelopes and first-class postage stamps. If the person with a disability so requests, the proper officer of the detaining authority shall make on the person's behalf the same number and kind of telephone calls which a person arrested is authorized by law or custom to make and shall mail any letters written by that person.

(Added to NRS by 1975, 309; A 2001, 1776)

NRS 171.1538 Arrest of person with communications disability: Waiver of right to interpretation or communication.

1. The rights to interpretation and communication provided in NRS 171.1536 and 171.1537 may not be waived except knowingly and voluntarily by the person with a communications disability by a written statement indicating a desire not to be so assisted. At any time after arrest but before the termination of any custody, the person may retract a waiver by indicating a desire to be so assisted.

2. Unless there is a waiver under this section, there must be no interrogation or taking of the statement of a person with a communications disability without the assistance of an interpreter in accordance with the provisions of NRS 50.050 to 50.053, inclusive.

(Added to NRS by 1975, 309; A 2001, 1776; 2007, 170)

INTERSTATE FRESH PURSUIT (UNIFORM ACT)

NRS 171.154 Short title. NRS 171.154 to 171.164, inclusive, may be cited as the Uniform Act on Interstate Fresh Pursuit.

(Added to NRS by 1967, 1403)

NRS 171.156 Definitions. As used in NRS 171.154 to 171.164, inclusive, unless the context or subject matter otherwise requires:

1. "Fresh pursuit" includes fresh pursuit as defined by the common law and also the pursuit of a person who has committed a felony or who is reasonably suspected of having committed a felony. It shall also include the pursuit of a person suspected of having committed a supposed felony, though no felony has actually been committed, if there is reasonable ground for believing that a felony has been committed. Fresh pursuit as used in NRS 171.154 to 171.164, inclusive, shall not necessarily imply instant pursuit, but pursuit without unreasonable delay.

2. "State" includes the District of Columbia for the purpose of NRS 171.154 to 171.164, inclusive.

(Added to NRS by 1967, 1403)

NRS 171.158 Arrests within this State by foreign officers; hearing before magistrate.

1. Any member of a duly organized state, county or municipal peace unit of another state of the United States who enters this State in fresh pursuit, and continues within this State in fresh pursuit, of a person in order to arrest the person on the ground that the person is believed to have committed a felony in the other state, shall have the same authority to arrest and hold such person in custody, as has any member of any duly organized state, county or municipal peace unit of this State, to arrest and hold in custody a person on the ground that the person is believed to have committed a felony in this State.

2. The officer of another state making an arrest within this State shall take the person arrested before a magistrate of the county in which the arrest was made, without unnecessary delay. The magistrate shall conduct a hearing for the purpose of determining the lawfulness of the arrest. If the magistrate determines that the arrest was lawful, the magistrate shall commit the person arrested to await for a reasonable time the issuance of an extradition warrant by the Governor of this State or admit the person to bail for such purpose. If the magistrate determines the arrest was unlawful the magistrate shall discharge the person arrested.

3. This section shall not be construed so as to make unlawful any arrest in this State which would otherwise be lawful.

(Added to NRS by 1967, 1403)

NRS 171.162 Duty of Secretary of State. On March 4, 1955, the Secretary of State shall certify a copy of NRS 171.154 to 171.164, inclusive, to the executive department of each of the states of the United States.

(Added to NRS by 1967, 1404)

NRS 171.164 Severability. If any part of NRS 171.154 to 171.164, inclusive, is for any reason declared void, it is declared to be the intent of NRS 171.154 to 171.164, inclusive, that such invalidity shall not affect the validity of the remaining portions of those sections.

(Added to NRS by 1967, 1404)

INTRASTATE FRESH PURSUIT (UNIFORM ACT)

NRS 171.166 Short title. NRS 171.166 to 171.176, inclusive, may be cited as the Uniform Act on Intrastate Fresh Pursuit.

(Added to NRS by 1967, 1404)

NRS 171.168 Definitions. "Fresh pursuit" as used in NRS 171.166 to 171.176, inclusive, shall include fresh pursuit as defined by the common law and also the pursuit of a person who has committed a felony or is reasonably suspected of having committed a felony in this state, or who has committed or attempted to commit any criminal offense in this state in the presence of the arresting officer referred to in NRS 171.172 or for whom such officer holds a warrant of arrest for a criminal offense. It shall also include the pursuit of a person suspected of having committed a supposed felony in this state, though no felony has actually been committed, if there is reasonable ground for so believing. Fresh pursuit as used in NRS 171.166 to 171.176, inclusive, shall not necessarily imply instant pursuit, but pursuit without unreasonable delay.

(Added to NRS by 1967, 1404)

NRS 171.172 When officer may arrest. Any peace officer of this state in fresh pursuit of a person who is reasonably believed by the peace officer to have committed a felony in this state or has committed, or attempted to commit, any criminal offense in this state in the presence of such officer, or for whom such officer holds a warrant of arrest, may hold in custody such person anywhere in this state.

(Added to NRS by 1967, 1404)

NRS 171.174 Procedure after arrest. If such an arrest is made in obedience to a warrant, the disposition of the prisoner shall be as in other cases of arrest under a warrant. If the arrest is without a warrant, the prisoner shall without unnecessary delay be taken before a municipal court or a justice of the peace or other magistrate of the county wherein such an arrest was made, and such court shall admit such person to bail, if the offense is bailable, by taking security by way of recognizance for the appearance of such prisoner before the court having jurisdiction of such criminal offense.

(Added to NRS by 1967, 1404)

NRS 171.176 Limitation. NRS 171.172 shall not make unlawful an arrest which would otherwise be lawful.

(Added to NRS by 1967, 1404)

CITATION FOR MISDEMEANOR

NRS 171.177 When person detained must be taken before magistrate. Except as otherwise provided in NRS 171.122 and 171.178, whenever any person is detained by a peace officer for any violation of a county, city or town ordinance or a state law which is punishable as a misdemeanor, the person must be taken without unnecessary delay before the proper magistrate, as specified in NRS 171.178 and 171.184, in the following cases:

1. When the person demands an immediate appearance before a magistrate;
2. When the person is detained pursuant to a warrant for the person's arrest;
3. When the person is arrested by a peace officer; or
4. In any other event when the person is issued a misdemeanor citation by an authorized person and refuses to give a written promise to appear in court as provided in NRS 171.1773.

(Added to NRS by 1973, 156; A 1975, 1200; 1993, 144)

NRS 171.1771 Issuance of citation when person detained by peace officer. Whenever any person is detained by a peace officer for any violation of a county, city or town ordinance or a state law which is punishable as a misdemeanor and the person is not required to be taken before a magistrate, the person shall, in the discretion of the peace officer, either be given a misdemeanor citation, or be taken without unnecessary delay before the proper magistrate. Any such person shall be taken before the magistrate when the person does not furnish satisfactory evidence of identity or when the peace officer has reasonable and probable grounds to believe the person will disregard a written promise to appear in court.

(Added to NRS by 1973, 156)

NRS 171.1772 Issuance of citation after arrest by private person. Whenever any person is arrested by a private person, as provided in NRS 171.126, for any violation of a county, city or town ordinance or state law which is punishable as a misdemeanor, such person arrested may be issued a misdemeanor citation by a peace officer in lieu of being immediately taken before a magistrate by the peace officer if:

1. The person arrested furnishes satisfactory evidence of identity; and
2. The peace officer has reasonable grounds to believe that the person arrested will keep a written promise to appear in court.

(Added to NRS by 1973, 1157; A 1975, 1201; 2001, 2023)

NRS 171.1773 Form and contents of citation: When person detained by peace officer.

1. Whenever a person is detained by a peace officer for any violation of a county, city or town ordinance or a state law which is punishable as a misdemeanor and the person is not taken before a magistrate as required or permitted by NRS 171.177, 171.1771 or 171.1772, the peace officer may prepare a misdemeanor citation manually or electronically in the form of a complaint issuing in the name of "The State of Nevada" or in the name of the respective county, city or town, containing a notice to appear in court, the name and address of the person, the state registration number of the person's vehicle, if any, the offense charged, including a brief description of the offense and the NRS or ordinance citation, the time when and place where the person is required to appear in court, and such other pertinent information as may be necessary. The citation must be signed by the peace officer. If the citation is prepared electronically, the officer shall sign the copy of the citation that is delivered to the person charged with the violation.
2. The time specified in the notice to appear must be at least 5 days after the alleged violation unless the person charged with the violation demands an earlier hearing.
3. The place specified in the notice must be before a magistrate, as designated in NRS 171.178 and 171.184.
4. The person charged with the violation may give a written promise to appear in court by signing at least one copy of the misdemeanor citation prepared by the peace officer, in which event the peace officer shall deliver a copy of the citation to the person, and thereupon the peace officer shall not take the person into physical custody for the violation. If the citation is prepared electronically, the officer shall deliver the signed copy of the citation to the person and shall indicate on the electronic record of the citation whether the person charged gave a written promise to appear. A copy of the citation that is signed by the person charged or the electronic record of the citation which indicates that the person charged gave a written promise to appear suffices as proof of service.

(Added to NRS by 1973, 156; A 1991, 16; 1999, 1141)

NRS 171.1774 Form and contents of citation: When issued after arrest by private person.

1. In those instances described in NRS 171.1772, the peace officer summoned after the arrest shall prepare a misdemeanor citation manually or electronically in the form of a complaint issuing in the name of "The State of Nevada" or in the name of the respective county, city or town, and containing:
   (a) A notice to appear in court;
   (b) The name and address of the person;
   (c) The state registration number of the person's vehicle, if any;
   (d) The offense charged, including a brief description of the offense and the NRS or ordinance citation;
   (e) The time when and place where the person is required to appear in court;
   (f) Such other pertinent information as may be necessary; and
   (g) The signatures of the private person making the arrest and the peace officer preparing the citation.
2. The time specified in the notice to appear must be at least 5 days after the alleged violation unless the person charged with the violation demands an earlier hearing.
3. The place specified in the notice must be before a magistrate, as designated in NRS 171.178 and 171.184.
4. The person charged with the violation may give a written promise to appear in court by signing at least one copy of the misdemeanor citation prepared by the peace officer, in which event the peace officer shall deliver a copy of the citation to the person, and thereupon the peace officer shall not take the person into physical custody for the violation. If the citation is prepared electronically, the officer shall deliver the signed copy of the citation to the person and shall indicate on the electronic record of the citation whether the person charged gave a written promise to appear. A copy of the citation that is signed by the person charged or the electronic record of the citation which indicates that the person charged gave a written promise to appear suffices as proof of service.

(Added to NRS by 1973, 1157; A 1991, 16; 1999, 1142)

NRS 171.1775 Preparation of citations: Use of citation book or electronic device; maintenance of records relating to citation book or electronic device.

1. Every county, city or town law enforcement agency in this state shall provide in appropriate form misdemeanor citations containing notices to appear which must meet the requirements of NRS 171.177 to 171.1779, inclusive, and be:
   (a) Issued in books; or
   (b) Available through an electronic device used to prepare the citations.

2. The chief administrative officer of each law enforcement agency is responsible for the issuance of such books and electronic devices and shall maintain a record of each book, each electronic device and each citation contained therein issued to individual members of the law enforcement agency. The chief administrative officer shall require and retain a receipt for every book and electronic device that is issued.

(Added to NRS by 1973, 157, 1158; A 1991, 17; 1999, 1143)

NRS 171.17751 Designation of certain state, county and city officers to prepare, sign and serve citations.

1. Any board of county commissioners or governing body of a city may designate the chief officer of the organized fire department or any employees designated by the chief officer, and certain of its inspectors of solid waste management, building, housing and licensing inspectors, zoning enforcement officers, parking enforcement officers, animal control officers, traffic engineers, marshals and park rangers of units of specialized law enforcement established pursuant to NRS 280.125, and other persons charged with the enforcement of county or city ordinances, to prepare, sign and serve written citations on persons accused of violating a county or city ordinance.

2. The Chief Medical Officer and the health officer of each county, district and city may designate certain employees to prepare, sign and serve written citations on persons accused of violating any law, ordinance or regulation of a board of health that relates to public health.

3. The Chief of the Manufactured Housing Division of the Department of Business and Industry may designate certain employees to prepare, sign and serve written citations on persons accused of violating any law or regulation of the Division relating to the provisions of chapters 118B, 461, 461A and 489 of NRS.

4. The State Contractors' Board may designate certain of its employees to prepare, sign and serve written citations on persons pursuant to subsection 2 of NRS 624.115.

5. An employee designated pursuant to this section:

(a) May exercise the authority to prepare, sign and serve citations only within the field of enforcement in which the employee works;

(b) May, if employed by a city or county, prepare, sign and serve a citation only to enforce an ordinance of the city or county by which the employee is employed; and

(c) Shall comply with the provisions of NRS 171.1773.

(Added to NRS by 1979, 871; A 1981, 564, 858; 1987, 377; 1989, 279; 1993, 81, 1330, 1511, 2515; 1995, 583; 1999, 2966; 2005, 1382)

NRS 171.1776 Issued citations: Filing with court; disposition of charges by court; unlawful acts; maintenance of records.

1. Every peace officer upon issuing a misdemeanor citation, pursuant to NRS 171.177 to 171.1779, inclusive, to an alleged violator of any provision of a county, city or town ordinance or of a state law which is punishable as a misdemeanor shall file manually or, if the provisions of subsection 2 are satisfied, file electronically the original or a copy of such misdemeanor citation with a court having jurisdiction over the alleged offense.

2. A copy of a misdemeanor citation that is prepared electronically may be filed electronically with a court having jurisdiction over the alleged offense if the court:

(a) Authorizes such electronic filing;

(b) Has the ability to receive and store the citation electronically; and

(c) Has the ability to physically reproduce the citation upon request.

3. Upon the filing of the original or a copy of such misdemeanor citation with a court having jurisdiction over the alleged offense, such original or copy of such misdemeanor citation may be disposed of only by trial in such court or other official action by a judge of such court.

4. It is unlawful and official misconduct for any peace officer or other officer or public employee to dispose of a misdemeanor citation or copies thereof or of the record of the issuance of a misdemeanor citation in a manner other than as required in this section.

5. The chief administrative officer of every county, city or town law enforcement agency shall require the return of a physical copy or electronic record of every misdemeanor citation issued by an officer under the chief administrative officer's supervision to an alleged misdemeanant and of all physical copies or electronic records of every misdemeanor citation which has been spoiled or upon which any entry has been made and not issued to an alleged misdemeanant.

6. Such chief administrative officer shall also maintain or cause to be maintained in connection with every misdemeanor citation issued by an officer under the chief administrative officer's supervision a record of the disposition of the charge by the court in which the original or copy of the misdemeanor citation was filed.

(Added to NRS by 1973, 157, 1158; A 1999, 1143)

NRS 171.1777 Issued citations: Audit of records. Every record of misdemeanor citations required by NRS 171.177 to 171.1779, inclusive, shall be audited at least semiannually by the appropriate fiscal officer of the governmental agency to which the law enforcement agency is responsible.

(Added to NRS by 1973, 158, 1159)

NRS 171.1778 Citation filed with court deemed complaint for purpose of prosecution. If the form of citation:

1. Includes information whose truthfulness is attested as required for a complaint charging commission of the offense alleged in the citation to have been committed; or

2. Is prepared electronically,

□ then the citation when filed with a court of competent jurisdiction shall be deemed to be a lawful complaint for the purpose of prosecution.

(Added to NRS by 1973, 158, 1159; A 1983, 446; 1999, 1144)

NRS 171.17785 Effect of violation of written promise to appear; appearance by counsel in lieu of personal appearance authorized.

1. It is unlawful for a person to violate a written promise to appear given to a peace officer upon the issuance of a misdemeanor citation prepared manually or electronically, regardless of the disposition of the charge for which the citation was originally issued.

2. A person may comply with a written promise to appear in court by an appearance by counsel.
3. A warrant may issue upon a violation of a written promise to appear.
(Added to NRS by 1999, 1141)

NRS 171.1779 NRS 171.177 to 171.1779, inclusive, not applicable to violations of traffic laws. The provisions of NRS 171.177 to 171.1779, inclusive, do not apply to those situations in which a person is detained by a peace officer for any violation of chapters 484A to 484E, inclusive, of NRS.
(Added to NRS by 1973, 158, 1159)

PROCEEDINGS BEFORE MAGISTRATE

NRS 171.178 Appearance before magistrate; release from custody by arresting officer.
1. Except as otherwise provided in subsections 5 and 6, a peace officer making an arrest under a warrant issued upon a complaint or without a warrant shall take the arrested person without unnecessary delay before the magistrate who issued the warrant or the nearest available magistrate empowered to commit persons charged with offenses against the laws of the State of Nevada.
2. A private person making an arrest without a warrant shall deliver the arrested person without unnecessary delay to a peace officer. Except as otherwise provided in subsections 5 and 6 and NRS 171.1772, the peace officer shall take the arrested person without unnecessary delay before the nearest available magistrate empowered to commit persons charged with offenses against the laws of the State of Nevada.
3. If an arrested person is not brought before a magistrate within 72 hours after arrest, excluding nonjudicial days, the magistrate:
(a) Shall give the prosecuting attorney an opportunity to explain the circumstances leading to the delay; and
(b) May release the arrested person if the magistrate determines that the person was not brought before a magistrate without unnecessary delay.
4. When a person arrested without a warrant is brought before a magistrate, a complaint must be filed forthwith.
5. Except as otherwise provided in NRS 178.484 and 178.487, where the defendant can be admitted to bail without appearing personally before a magistrate, the defendant must be so admitted with the least possible delay, and required to appear before a magistrate at the earliest convenient time thereafter.
6. A peace officer may immediately release from custody without any further proceedings any person the peace officer arrests without a warrant if the peace officer is satisfied that there are insufficient grounds for issuing a criminal complaint against the person arrested. Any record of the arrest of a person released pursuant to this subsection must also include a record of the release. A person so released shall be deemed not to have been arrested but only detained.
(Added to NRS by 1967, 1404; A 1971, 574; 1975, 1201; 1979, 323, 1190; 1997, 3356; 2001, 2023)

NRS 171.182 Proceedings before another magistrate. If the defendant is brought before a magistrate in the same county, other than the one who issued the warrant, the affidavits and depositions on which the warrant was granted, if the defendant insists upon an examination, must be sent to that magistrate, or, if they cannot be procured, the prosecutor and the prosecutor's witnesses must be summoned to give their testimony anew.
(Added to NRS by 1967, 1405)

NRS 171.184 Proceedings upon complaint for offenses triable in another county.
1. When a complaint is laid before a magistrate of the commission of a public offense triable in another county of the State, but showing that the defendant is in the county where the complaint is laid, the same proceedings must be had as prescribed in this chapter except that the warrant must require the defendant to be taken before the nearest or most accessible magistrate of the county in which the offense is triable, and the depositions of the complainant or prosecutor, and of the witnesses who may have been produced, must be delivered by the magistrate to the officer to whom the warrant is delivered.
2. The officer who executed the warrant must take the defendant before the nearest or most accessible magistrate of the county in which the offense is triable, and must deliver the depositions and the warrant, with the officer's return endorsed thereon, and the magistrate must then proceed in the same manner as upon a warrant issued by the magistrate.
3. If the offense charged in the warrant issued pursuant to subsection 1 is a misdemeanor, the officer must, upon being required by the defendant, take the defendant before a magistrate of the county in which the warrant was issued, who must admit the defendant to bail, and immediately transmit the warrant, depositions and undertaking to the justice of the peace or clerk of the court in which the defendant is required to appear.
(Added to NRS by 1967, 1405)

NRS 171.1845 Proceedings upon discovery of another arrest warrant outstanding in another county.
1. If a person is brought before a magistrate under the provisions of NRS 171.178 or 171.184, and it is discovered that there is a warrant for the person's arrest outstanding in another county of this State, the magistrate may release the person in accordance with the provisions of NRS 178.484 or 178.4851 if:
(a) The warrant arises out of a public offense which constitutes a misdemeanor; and
(b) The person provides a suitable address where the magistrate who issued the warrant in the other county can notify the person of a time and place to appear.
2. If a person is released under the provisions of this section, the magistrate who releases the person shall transmit the cash, bond, notes or agreement submitted under the provisions of NRS 178.502 or 178.4851, together with the person's address, to the magistrate who issued the warrant. Upon receipt of the cash, bonds, notes or agreement and address, the magistrate who issued the warrant shall notify the person of a time and place to appear.

3. Any bail set under the provisions of this section must be in addition to and apart from any bail set for any public offense with which a person is charged in the county in which a magistrate is setting bail. In setting bail under the provisions of this section, a magistrate shall set the bail in an amount which is sufficient to induce a reasonable person to travel to the county in which the warrant for the arrest is outstanding.

4. A person who fails to appear in the other county as ordered is guilty of failing to appear and shall be punished as provided in NRS 199.335. A sentence of imprisonment imposed for failing to appear in violation of this section must be imposed consecutively to a sentence of imprisonment for the offense out of which the warrant arises.

(Added to NRS by 1973, 612; A 1981, 1583; 1999, 1844)

NRS 171.186 Rights of defendant before preliminary examination. The magistrate or master shall inform the defendant of the complaint and of any affidavit filed therewith, of the right to retain counsel, of the right to request the assignment of counsel if the defendant is unable to obtain counsel, and of the right to have a preliminary examination. The magistrate or master shall also inform the defendant that the defendant is not required to make a statement and that any statement made may be used against him or her. The magistrate shall allow the defendant reasonable time and opportunity to consult counsel, and shall admit the defendant to bail as provided in this title.

(Added to NRS by 1967, 1405; A 1977, 1571)

NRS 171.188 Procedure for appointment of attorney for indigent defendant.

1. Any defendant charged with a public offense who is an indigent may, by oral statement to the district judge, justice of the peace, municipal judge or master, request the appointment of an attorney to represent the defendant.

2. The request must be accompanied by the defendant's affidavit, which must state:

(a) That the defendant is without means of employing an attorney; and

(b) Facts with some particularity, definiteness and certainty concerning the defendant's financial disability.

3. The district judge, justice of the peace, municipal judge or master shall forthwith consider the application and shall make such further inquiry as he or she considers necessary. If the district judge, justice of the peace, municipal judge or master:

(a) Finds that the defendant is without means of employing an attorney; and

(b) Otherwise determines that representation is required,

□ the judge, justice or master shall designate the public defender of the county or the State Public Defender, as appropriate, to represent the defendant. If the appropriate public defender is unable to represent the defendant, or other good cause appears, another attorney must be appointed.

4. The county or State Public Defender must be reimbursed by the city for costs incurred in appearing in municipal court. The county shall reimburse the State Public Defender for costs incurred in appearing in Justice Court. If a private attorney is appointed as provided in this section, the private attorney must be reimbursed by the county for appearance in Justice Court or the city for appearance in municipal court in an amount not to exceed $75 per case.

(Added to NRS by 1967, 1405; A 1969, 478; 1971, 1412; 1973, 357; 1977, 1571; 1983, 901)

NRS 171.192 Certification of bail; discharge of defendant. On admitting the defendant to bail, the magistrate shall certify on the warrant the fact of having done so, and deliver the warrant and recognizance to the officer having charge of the defendant. The officer shall forthwith discharge the defendant from arrest, and shall, without delay, deliver the warrant and recognizance to the justice of the peace, magistrate or clerk of the court at which the defendant is required to appear.

(Added to NRS by 1967, 1406)

NRS 171.194 Procedure when arrest for capital offense. The defendant, when arrested under a warrant for a capital offense, must be held in custody by the sheriff of the county in which the complaint is filed, unless admitted to bail after an examination or upon a writ of habeas corpus.

(Added to NRS by 1967, 1406)

NRS 171.196 Preliminary examination: Waiver; time for conducting; postponement; introduction of evidence and cross-examination of witnesses by defendant; admissibility of hearsay evidence.

1. If an offense is not triable in the Justice Court, the defendant must not be called upon to plead. If the defendant waives preliminary examination, the magistrate shall immediately hold the defendant to answer in the district court.

2. If the defendant does not waive examination, the magistrate shall hear the evidence within 15 days, unless for good cause shown the magistrate extends such time. Unless the defendant waives counsel, reasonable time must be allowed for counsel to appear.

3. Except as otherwise provided in this subsection, if the magistrate postpones the examination at the request of a party, the magistrate may order that party to pay all or part of the costs and fees expended to have a witness attend the examination. The magistrate shall not require a party who requested the postponement of the examination to pay for the costs and fees of a witness if:

(a) It was not reasonably necessary for the witness to attend the examination; or

(b) The magistrate ordered the extension pursuant to subsection 4.

4. If application is made for the appointment of counsel for an indigent defendant, the magistrate shall postpone the examination until:

(a) The application has been granted or denied; and

(b) If the application is granted, the attorney appointed or the public defender has had reasonable time to appear.

5. The defendant may cross-examine witnesses against him or her and may introduce evidence in his or her own behalf.

6. Hearsay evidence consisting of a statement made by the alleged victim of the offense is admissible at a preliminary examination conducted pursuant to this section only if the defendant is charged with one or more of the following offenses:

(a) A sexual offense committed against a child who is under the age of 16 years if the offense is punishable as a felony. As used in this paragraph, "sexual offense" has the meaning ascribed to it in NRS 179D.097.
(b) Abuse of a child pursuant to NRS 200.508 if the offense is committed against a child who is under the age of 16 years and the offense is punishable as a felony.
(c) An act which constitutes domestic violence pursuant to NRS 33.018, which is punishable as a felony and which resulted in substantial bodily harm to the alleged victim.
(Added to NRS by 1967, 1406; A 1971, 159; 1997, 116; 2015, 576)

NRS 171.1965 Discovery by defendant before preliminary examination; material subject to discovery; effect of failure to permit discovery.
1. At the time a person is brought before a magistrate pursuant to NRS 171.178, or as soon as practicable thereafter, but not less than 5 judicial days before a preliminary examination, the prosecuting attorney shall provide a defendant charged with a felony or a gross misdemeanor with copies of any:
(a) Written or recorded statements or confessions made by the defendant, or any written or recorded statements made by a witness or witnesses, or any reports of statements or confessions, or copies thereof, within the possession or custody of the prosecuting attorney;
(b) Results or reports of physical or mental examinations, scientific tests or scientific experiments made in connection with the particular case, or copies thereof, within the possession or custody of the prosecuting attorney; and
(c) Books, papers, documents or tangible objects that the prosecuting attorney intends to introduce in evidence during the case in chief of the State, or copies thereof, within the possession or custody of the prosecuting attorney.
2. The defendant is not entitled, pursuant to the provisions of this section, to the discovery or inspection of:
(a) An internal report, document or memorandum that is prepared by or on behalf of the prosecuting attorney in connection with the investigation or prosecution of the case.
(b) A statement, report, book, paper, document, tangible object or any other type of item or information that is privileged or protected from disclosure or inspection pursuant to the Constitution or laws of this State or the Constitution of the United States.
3. The provisions of this section are not intended to affect any obligation placed upon the prosecuting attorney by the Constitution of this State or the Constitution of the United States to disclose exculpatory evidence to the defendant.
4. The magistrate shall not postpone a preliminary examination at the request of a party based solely on the failure of the prosecuting attorney to permit the defendant to inspect, copy or photograph material as required in this section, unless the court finds that the defendant has been prejudiced by such failure.
(Added to NRS by 1997, 2364; A 2009, 486)

NRS 171.197 Use of affidavit at preliminary examination: When permitted; notice by district attorney; circumstances under which district attorney must produce person who signed affidavit; continuances.
1. If a witness resides outside this State or more than 100 miles from the place of a preliminary examination, the witness's affidavit may be used at the preliminary examination if it is necessary for the district attorney to establish as an element of any offense that:
(a) The witness was the owner, possessor or occupant of real or personal property; and
(b) The defendant did not have the permission of the witness to enter, occupy, possess or control the real or personal property of the witness.
2. If a financial institution does not maintain any principal or branch office within this State or if a financial institution that maintains a principal or branch office within this State does not maintain any such office within 100 miles of the place of a preliminary examination, the affidavit of a custodian of the records of the financial institution or the affidavit of any other qualified person of the financial institution may be used at the preliminary examination if it is necessary for the district attorney to establish as an element of any offense that:
(a) When a check or draft naming the financial institution as drawee was drawn or passed, the account or purported account upon which the check or draft was drawn did not exist, was closed or held insufficient money, property or credit to pay the check or draft in full upon its presentation; or
(b) When a check or draft naming the financial institution as drawee was presented for payment to the financial institution, the account or purported account upon which the check or draft was drawn did not exist, was closed or held insufficient money, property or credit to pay the check or draft in full.
3. The district attorney shall provide either written or oral notice to the defendant, not less than 10 days before the scheduled preliminary examination, that the district attorney intends to use an affidavit described in this section at the preliminary examination.
4. If, at or before the time of the preliminary examination, the defendant establishes that:
(a) There is a substantial and bona fide dispute as to the facts in an affidavit described in this section; and
(b) It is in the best interests of justice that the person who signed the affidavit be cross-examined,
□ the magistrate may order the district attorney to produce the person who signed the affidavit and may continue the examination for any time it deems reasonably necessary in order to receive such testimony.
(Added to NRS by 1993, 548; A 1999, 163)

NRS 171.1975 Use of audiovisual technology to present live testimony at preliminary examination: Requirements.
1. If a witness resides more than 100 miles from the place of a preliminary examination or is unable to attend the preliminary examination because of a medical condition, or if good cause otherwise exists, the magistrate must allow the witness to testify at the preliminary examination through the use of audiovisual technology.
2. If a witness testifies at the preliminary examination through the use of audiovisual technology:
(a) The testimony of the witness must be transcribed by a certified court reporter; and

(b) Before giving testimony, the witness must be sworn and must sign a written declaration, on a form provided by the magistrate, which acknowledges that the witness understands that he or she is subject to the jurisdiction of the courts of this state and may be subject to criminal prosecution for the commission of any crime in connection with his or her testimony, including, without limitation, perjury, and that the witness consents to such jurisdiction.

3. Audiovisual technology used pursuant to this section must ensure that the witness may be:

(a) Clearly heard and seen; and

(b) Examined and cross-examined.

4. As used in this section, "audiovisual technology" includes, without limitation, closed-circuit video and videoconferencing.

(Added to NRS by 2001, 543; A 2015, 577)

NRS 171.198 Reporting testimony of witnesses.

1. Except as otherwise provided in subsection 2, a magistrate shall employ a certified court reporter to take down all the testimony and the proceedings on the hearing or examination and, within such time as the court may designate, have such testimony and proceedings transcribed into typewritten transcript.

2. A magistrate who presides over a preliminary hearing in a justice court, in any case other than in a case in which the death penalty is sought, may employ a certified court reporter to take down all the testimony and the proceedings on the hearing or appoint a person to use sound recording equipment to record all the testimony and the proceedings on the hearing. If the magistrate appoints a person to use sound recording equipment to record the testimony and proceedings on the hearing, the testimony and proceedings must be recorded and transcribed in the same manner as set forth in NRS 4.390 to 4.420, inclusive. Any transcript of the testimony and proceedings produced from a recording conducted pursuant to this subsection is subject to the provisions of this section in the same manner as a transcript produced by a certified court reporter.

3. When the testimony of each witness is all taken and transcribed by the reporter, the reporter shall certify to the transcript in the same manner as for a transcript of testimony in the district court, which certificate authenticates the transcript for all purposes of this title.

4. Before the date set for trial, either party may move the court before which the case is pending to add to, delete from or otherwise correct the transcript to conform with the testimony as given and to settle the transcript so altered.

5. The compensation for the services of a reporter employed as provided in this section are the same as provided in NRS 3.370, to be paid out of the county treasury as other claims against the county are allowed and paid.

6. Testimony reduced to writing and authenticated according to the provisions of this section must be filed by the examining magistrate with the clerk of the district court of the magistrate's county, and if the prisoner is subsequently examined upon a writ of habeas corpus, such testimony must be considered as given before such judge or court. A copy of the transcript must be furnished to the defendant and to the district attorney.

7. The testimony so taken may be used:

(a) By the defendant; or

(b) By the State if the defendant was represented by counsel or affirmatively waived his or her right to counsel,

□ upon the trial of the cause, and in all proceedings therein, when the witness is sick, out of the State, dead, or persistent in refusing to testify despite an order of the judge to do so, or when the witness's personal attendance cannot be had in court.

(Added to NRS by 1967, 1406; A 1973, 1322; 1987, 911; 1989, 1272; 1993, 75, 1411, 2024; 1995, 570; 2009, 633)

NRS 171.202 District attorney to prosecute at preliminary examination where felony or gross misdemeanor charged. The district attorney of the proper county shall be present at and conduct the prosecution in all preliminary examinations where a felony or gross misdemeanor is charged.

(Added to NRS by 1967, 1407)

NRS 171.204 Exclusion of persons; exceptions.

1. Except as otherwise provided in subsection 2, the magistrate may, if good cause is shown and upon the request of any party or on the magistrate's own motion, exclude from the examination every person except:

(a) The magistrate's clerk;

(b) The Attorney General;

(c) The prosecuting attorney;

(d) An investigating officer, after the investigating officer has testified as a prosecuting witness and the investigating officer's cross-examination has been completed;

(e) Any counsel for the victim;

(f) The victim, after the victim has testified as a prosecuting witness and the victim's cross-examination has been completed;

(g) The defendant and the defendant's counsel;

(h) The witness who is testifying;

(i) The officer having the defendant or a witness in the officer's custody;

(j) An attendant to a witness designated pursuant to NRS 178.571; and

(k) Any other person whose presence is found by the magistrate to be necessary for the proper conduct of the examination.

2. A person who is called as a witness primarily for the purpose of identifying the victim may not be excluded from the examination except in the discretion of the magistrate.

3. As used in this section, "victim" includes any person described in NRS 178.569.

(Added to NRS by 1967, 1407; A 1969, 628; 1983, 891; 1995, 72, 996; 1997, 72, 513)

NRS 171.206 Procedure following preliminary examination. If from the evidence it appears to the magistrate that there is probable cause to believe that an offense has been committed and that the defendant has committed it, the magistrate shall forthwith hold the defendant to answer in the district court; otherwise the magistrate shall discharge the defendant. The magistrate shall admit the defendant to bail as provided in this title. After concluding the proceeding the magistrate shall transmit forthwith to the clerk of the district court all papers in the proceeding and any bail.

(Added to NRS by 1967, 1407)

NRS 171.208 Remand for preliminary examination. If a preliminary examination has not been had and the defendant has not unconditionally waived the examination, the district court may for good cause shown at any time before a plea has been entered or an indictment found remand the defendant for preliminary examination to the appropriate justice of the peace or other magistrate, and the justice or other magistrate shall then proceed with the preliminary examination as provided in this chapter.

(Added to NRS by 1967, 1407; A 1987, 1188)

CHAPTER 172 - PROCEEDINGS AFTER COMMITMENT AND BEFORE INDICTMENT

GENERAL PROVISIONS

FORMATION OF GRAND JURY

POWERS AND DUTIES OF GRAND JURY

MISCELLANEOUS PROVISIONS

GENERAL PROVISIONS

NRS 172.005 Definitions. As used in this chapter, unless the context otherwise requires:

1. An indictment is an accusation in writing, presented by a grand jury to a competent court, charging a person with a public offense.
2. A presentment is an informal statement in writing, by the grand jury, representing to the court that a public offense has been committed, which is triable within the district, and that there is reasonable ground for believing that a particular person, named or described, has committed it.

(Added to NRS by 1967, 1409)

NRS 172.015 Prosecution of public offenses. Every public offense must be prosecuted by indictment or information, except:

1. Where proceedings are had for the removal of a civil officer.
2. Offenses arising in the militia when in actual service in time of war, or which this State may keep, with the consent of Congress, in time of peace.
3. Offenses tried in municipal or Justice Courts, which shall be prosecuted by complaint.

(Added to NRS by 1967, 1407; A 1969, 20)

NRS 172.025 Prosecution by accusation. When proceedings are had for the removal of district, county, municipal or township officers, they may be commenced by accusation, in writing, as provided in chapter 283 of NRS.

(Added to NRS by 1967, 1407)

NRS 172.035 Accusations, indictments and informations to be found or filed in district court. All accusations, informations and indictments against district, county, municipal and township officers must be found or filed in the district court.

(Added to NRS by 1967, 1408)

FORMATION OF GRAND JURY

NRS 172.045 Impaneling grand juries. Grand juries shall be impaneled as provided in chapter 6 of NRS.

(Added to NRS by 1967, 1408)

NRS 172.047 Grand jury impaneled for specific limited purpose. A district judge may impanel a grand jury to inquire into a specific limited matter among those set forth in NRS 172.175. In that case, the judge shall charge the grand jury as to its limited duties and give it such information as the judge deems necessary. A grand jury that is impaneled for a specific limited purpose shall not inquire into matters not related to that purpose. A grand jury impaneled for a specific limited purpose may be discharged after the grand jury completes its investigation and submits its report. If the grand jury has not completed its investigation and submitted its report within 1 year after it was impaneled, it shall, in a closed hearing, show cause to the judge why it should not be discharged. If the judge determines that it is in the public interest for the grand jury to continue its investigation, the grand jury may continue for a period which does not exceed 1 year.

(Added to NRS by 1985, 556)

NRS 172.055 Challenges to grand jury and to grand jurors: How made and tried. The district attorney or a defendant who has been held to answer in the district court may challenge the array of jurors on the ground that the grand jury was not selected, drawn or summoned in accordance with law, and may challenge an individual juror on the ground that the juror is not legally qualified. Challenges may be oral or in writing and shall be tried by the court.

(Added to NRS by 1967, 1408)

NRS 172.065 Motion to dismiss presentment or indictment based on objections to grand jurors. A motion to dismiss the presentment or indictment may be based on objections to the array or on the lack of legal qualification of an individual juror, if not previously determined upon challenge. A presentment or indictment shall not be dismissed on the ground that one or more members of the grand jury were not legally qualified if it appears from the record kept pursuant to NRS 172.075 that 12 or more jurors, after deducting the number not legally qualified, concurred in finding the presentment or indictment.

(Added to NRS by 1967, 1408)

NRS 172.075 Officers of grand jury. The jury shall elect one of its members to be foreman, another to be deputy foreman and a third to be secretary. The foreman shall have power to administer oaths and affirmations and shall sign all presentments and indictments. The secretary shall keep a record of the number of jurors concurring in the finding of every presentment or indictment and shall file the record with the clerk of the court, but the record shall not be made public except on order of the court. During the absence of the foreman, the deputy foreman shall act as foreman, and if both are absent, the jury shall elect a temporary foreman.

(Added to NRS by 1967, 1408)

NRS 172.085 Oath of grand jurors. The following oath must be administered to the grand jury:

> You, as grand jurors, will diligently inquire into, and true presentment make, of all offenses against the State of Nevada committed or triable within this county, (or city, in the case of Carson City) of which you shall have or can obtain legal evidence. You will keep your own counsel, and that of your fellows and the Government, and will not, except when required in the due course of judicial proceedings, disclose the testimony of any witness examined before you, nor anything which you or any other grand juror may have said, nor the manner in which you or any other grand juror may have voted on any matter before you. You will present no person through malice, hatred, or ill will, nor leave any unpresented through fear, favor, or affection, or for any reward, or the promise or hope thereof; but in all your presentments you will present the truth, the whole truth, and nothing but the truth, according to the best of your skill and understanding, so help you God.

(Added to NRS by 1967, 1408; A 1969, 316)

NRS 172.095 Charges to be given to grand jury by court; district attorney to inform grand jury of specific elements of public offense considered as basis of indictment.

1. The grand jury being impaneled and sworn, must be charged by the court. In doing so, the court shall:

(a) Give the grand jurors such information as is required by law and any other information it deems proper regarding their duties and any charges for public offenses returned to the court or likely to come before the grand jury.

(b) Inform the grand jurors of the provisions of NRS 172.245 and the penalties for its violation.

(c) Give each regular and alternate grand juror a copy of the charges.

(d) Inform the grand jurors that the failure of a person to exercise the right to testify as provided in NRS 172.241 must not be considered in their decision of whether or not to return an indictment.

2. Before seeking an indictment, or a series of similar indictments, the district attorney shall inform the grand jurors of the specific elements of any public offense which they may consider as the basis of the indictment or indictments.

(Added to NRS by 1967, 1408; A 1985, 554, 1028)

NRS 172.097 Supervision of grand jury by impaneling judge; limitations on and review of expenditures; monthly statement by county treasurer.

1. The district judge impaneling a grand jury shall supervise its proceedings.

2. The grand jury shall submit an itemized list of its expenditures no less often than every 3 months or a fraction thereof to the judge who impaneled it.

3. The grand jury shall not spend money or incur a debt exceeding the amount of money budgeted for its use unless it first obtains the approval of the judge who impaneled it. The judge shall inform the board of county commissioners of any expenditure or indebtedness the judge so approves.

4. The county treasurer shall provide to the grand jury a monthly statement of its expenditures for the preceding month and the balance remaining of the money appropriated for its use.

(Added to NRS by 1985, 556)

POWERS AND DUTIES OF GRAND JURY

NRS 172.105 Powers. The grand jury may inquire into all public offenses triable in the district court or in a Justice Court, committed within the territorial jurisdiction of the district court for which it is impaneled.

(Added to NRS by 1967, 1408)

NRS 172.107 Limitations on use of grand jury. A district attorney shall not use a grand jury to discover tangible, documentary or testimonial evidence to assist in the prosecution of a defendant who has already been charged with the public offense by indictment or information.

(Added to NRS by 1985, 1028)

NRS 172.135 Evidence receivable before grand jury.

1. In the investigation of a charge, for the purpose of either presentment or indictment, the grand jury can receive no other evidence than such as is given by witnesses produced and sworn before them or furnished by legal documentary evidence or by the deposition of witnesses taken as provided in this title, except that the grand jury may receive any of the following:

(a) An affidavit or declaration from an expert witness or other person described in NRS 50.315 in lieu of personal testimony or a deposition.

(b) An affidavit of an owner, possessor or occupant of real or personal property or other person described in NRS 172.137 in lieu of personal testimony or a deposition.

2. Except as otherwise provided in this subsection, the grand jury can receive none but legal evidence, and the best evidence in degree, to the exclusion of hearsay or secondary evidence. The grand jury can receive hearsay evidence consisting of a statement made by the alleged victim of an offense if the defendant is alleged to have committed one or more of the following offenses:

(a) A sexual offense committed against a child who is under the age of 16 years if the offense is punishable as a felony. As used in this paragraph, "sexual offense" has the meaning ascribed to it in NRS 179D.097.

(b) Abuse of a child pursuant to NRS 200.508 if the offense is committed against a child who is under the age of 16 years and the offense is punishable as a felony.

(c) An act which constitutes domestic violence pursuant to NRS 33.018, which is punishable as a felony and which resulted in substantial bodily harm to the alleged victim.

3. A statement made by a witness at any time that is inconsistent with the testimony of the witness before the grand jury may be presented to the grand jury as evidence.

(Added to NRS by 1967, 1409; A 1975, 649; 1983, 1917; 1993, 86, 549; 1999, 164; 2015, 578)

NRS 172.137 Use of affidavit before grand jury: When permitted; notice by district attorney; circumstances under which district attorney must produce person who signed affidavit; continuances.

1. If a witness resides outside this State or more than 100 miles from the place of a grand jury proceeding, the witness's affidavit may be used at the proceeding if it is necessary for the district attorney to establish as an element of any offense that:

(a) The witness was the owner, possessor or occupant of real or personal property; and

(b) The defendant did not have the permission of the witness to enter, occupy, possess or control the real or personal property of the witness.

2. If a financial institution does not maintain any principal or branch office within this State or if a financial institution that maintains a principal or branch office within this State does not maintain any such office within 100 miles of the place of a grand jury proceeding, the affidavit of a custodian of the records of the financial institution or the affidavit of any other qualified person of the financial institution may be used at the proceeding if it is necessary for the district attorney to establish as an element of any offense that:

(a) When a check or draft naming the financial institution as drawee was drawn or passed, the account or purported account upon which the check or draft was drawn did not exist, was closed or held insufficient money, property or credit to pay the check or draft in full upon its presentation; or

(b) When a check or draft naming the financial institution as drawee was presented for payment to the financial institution, the account or purported account upon which the check or draft was drawn did not exist, was closed or held insufficient money, property or credit to pay the check or draft in full.

3. If the defendant has been subpoenaed to appear before the grand jury or if the defendant has requested to testify pursuant to NRS 172.241, the district attorney shall provide either written or oral notice to the defendant, within a reasonable time before the scheduled proceeding of the grand jury, that an affidavit described in this section will be used at the proceeding.

4. If, at or before the time of the proceeding, the defendant establishes that:

(a) There is a substantial and bona fide dispute as to the facts in an affidavit described in this section; and

(b) It is in the best interests of justice that the person who signed the affidavit be examined or cross-examined,

□ the grand jury may request that the district attorney produce the person who signed the affidavit and may continue the proceeding for any time it deems reasonably necessary in order to receive such testimony.

(Added to NRS by 1993, 548; A 1999, 164)

NRS 172.138 Use of audiovisual technology to present live testimony before grand jury: Requirements.

1. If a witness resides more than 100 miles from the place of a grand jury proceeding or is unable to attend the grand jury proceeding because of a medical condition, or if good cause otherwise exists, the district judge supervising the proceedings of the grand jury must allow a witness to testify before the grand jury through the use of audiovisual technology.

2. If a witness testifies at the grand jury proceeding through the use of audiovisual technology:

(a) The testimony of the witness must be transcribed by a certified court reporter appointed pursuant to NRS 172.215 in accordance with the provisions of NRS 172.225; and

(b) Before giving testimony, the witness must be sworn and must sign a written declaration, on a form provided by the district judge, which acknowledges that the witness understands that he or she is subject to the jurisdiction of the courts of this state and may be subject to criminal prosecution for the commission of any crime in connection with his or her testimony, including, without limitation, perjury, and that the witness consents to such jurisdiction.

3. Audiovisual technology used pursuant to this section must ensure that the witness may be:

(a) Clearly heard and seen; and

(b) Examined.

4. As used in this section, "audiovisual technology" includes, without limitation, closed-circuit video and videoconferencing.

(Added to NRS by 2001, 545; A 2015, 579)

NRS 172.139 District attorney and grand jury prohibited from questioning attorney regarding matters learned for client or issuing subpoena for work done by attorney for client. During a grand jury proceeding, the district attorney and the grand jurors shall not:

1. Question an attorney or an attorney's employee regarding matters which were learned during a legitimate investigation for a client.

2. Issue a subpoena for the production of the private notes or other matters representing work done by the attorney or the attorney's employee regarding the legal services which the attorney provided for a client.

(Added to NRS by 1985, 1028)

NRS 172.145 Defendant entitled to submit statement regarding preliminary hearing which grand jury must receive; grand jury required to hear and district attorney required to submit known evidence which will explain away charge; invitations and issuance of process for witnesses.

1. The grand jury is not bound to hear evidence for the defendant, except that the defendant is entitled to submit a statement which the grand jury must receive providing whether a preliminary hearing was held concerning the matter and, if so, that the evidence presented at the preliminary hearing was considered insufficient to warrant holding the defendant for trial. It is their duty, however, to weigh all evidence submitted to them, and when they have reason to believe that other evidence within their reach will explain away the charge, they shall order that evidence to be produced, and for that purpose may require the district attorney to issue process for the witnesses.

2. If the district attorney is aware of any evidence which will explain away the charge, the district attorney shall submit it to the grand jury.

3. The grand jury may invite any person, without process, to appear before the grand jury to testify.

(Added to NRS by 1967, 1409; A 1985, 555; 2011, 287)

NRS 172.155 Degree of evidence to warrant indictment; objection.

1. The grand jury ought to find an indictment when all the evidence before them, taken together, establishes probable cause to believe that an offense has been committed and that the defendant has committed it.

2. The defendant may object to the sufficiency of the evidence to sustain the indictment only by application for a writ of habeas corpus.

(Added to NRS by 1967, 1409; A 1979, 331)

NRS 172.165 Grand juror must declare knowledge as to commission of public offense; investigation. If a member of the grand jury knows or has reason to believe that a public offense has been committed, which is triable within the jurisdiction of the district court which has impaneled such grand jury, the member must declare such knowledge or belief to the member's fellow jurors, who shall thereupon investigate the alleged offense.

(Added to NRS by 1967, 1409; A 1969, 6)

NRS 172.175 Matters into which grand jury shall and may inquire.

1. Each grand jury that is not impaneled for a specific limited purpose shall inquire into:

(a) The case of every person imprisoned in the jail of the county, on a criminal charge, against whom an indictment has not been found or an information or complaint filed.

(b) The condition and management of any public prison located within the county.

(c) The misconduct in office of public officers of every description within the county which may constitute a violation of a provision of chapter 197 of NRS.

2. A grand jury that is not impaneled for another specific limited purpose may inquire into any and all matters affecting the morals, health and general welfare of the inhabitants of the county, or of any administrative division thereof, or of any township, incorporated city, irrigation district or town therein.

(Added to NRS by 1967, 1409; A 1973, 1274; 1985, 556, 701)

NRS 172.185 Grand jury entitled to enter jails and examine records. The grand jury shall be entitled to free access, at all reasonable times, to all public prisons and to the examination without charge of all public records within its district.

(Added to NRS by 1967, 1409)

NRS 172.195 Issuance of subpoenas by grand jury; subpoenaed witnesses must be informed of general nature of inquiry.

1. Except as otherwise provided in NRS 172.139, the grand jury may issue subpoenas, subscribed by the foreman or by the deputy or temporary foreman when acting for the foreman, for witnesses within the State and for the production of books, papers or documents.

2. The grand jury shall orally inform any witness so subpoenaed of the general nature of the grand jury's inquiry before the witness testifies. Such a statement must be included in the transcript of the proceedings.

(Added to NRS by 1967, 1409; A 1985, 573, 1029)

NRS 172.197 Procedure when person subpoenaed to appear before grand jury intends to assert constitutional privilege against self-incrimination.

1. If a person who has been subpoenaed to appear before a grand jury informs the district attorney that the person intends to refuse to testify and to assert the person's constitutional privilege against self-incrimination, the district attorney shall:

(a) Move for an order of immunity pursuant to NRS 178.572;

(b) Challenge the existence of a valid privilege by filing in any court of record a motion to compel the testimony of the person; or

(c) Withdraw the subpoena.

2. All proceedings which are held on a motion filed pursuant to subsection 1 must be closed.

3. If the existence of the privilege is challenged, the court shall hear the evidence of both parties and determine whether or not a valid privilege exists and to which matters, if any, it extends.

4. The district attorney shall not call a person to testify before a grand jury regarding matters which have been so determined to be within the person's constitutional privilege against self-incrimination.

(Added to NRS by 1985, 554)

NRS 172.205 Power to engage services of skilled persons. The grand jury shall have the power, with the consent of the board of county commissioners, to engage the services of an attorney other than and in addition to the district attorney, certified or registered public accountants, and such other skilled persons as may be necessary in the performance of its inquisitorial powers.

(Added to NRS by 1967, 1410)

NRS 172.215 Certified court reporter: Appointment; compensation; material required for and prohibited from inclusion in notes.

1. Whenever criminal causes are being investigated by the grand jury, it shall appoint a certified court reporter. If the certified court reporter is not an official reporter of the district court, the certified court reporter shall, before entering upon his or her duties, take and subscribe the constitutional oath of office. The certified court reporter is entitled to receive the same compensation for services as an official reporter of the district court.

2. Except as otherwise provided in subsection 3, the certified court reporter shall include in the notes taken of a grand jury proceeding all criminal matters which come before the grand jury including:

(a) The charge by the impaneling judge;

(b) Any subsequent instructions or statements made by the judge;

(c) Each statement made by the district attorney;

(d) Each question asked of and response given by the witnesses who appear before the grand jury; and

(e) Any statements made by the grand jurors during the proceeding.

3. The certified court reporter shall not include in his or her notes:

(a) Any confidential communication between a witness and the witness's legal counsel, if the legal counsel is allowed to accompany the witness before the grand jury; or

(b) The deliberations and voting of the grand jury.

(Added to NRS by 1967, 1410; A 1973, 1323; 1985, 1029; 1993, 1411)

NRS 172.225 Transcripts: Preparation; public record.

1. If an indictment has been found or accusation presented against a defendant, the stenographic reporter shall certify and file with the county clerk an original transcription of his or her notes and a copy thereof and as many additional copies as there are defendants.

2. The reporter shall complete the certification and filing within 10 days after the indictment has been found or the accusation presented unless the court for good cause makes an order extending the time.

3. The county clerk shall:

(a) Deliver a copy of the transcript so filed with the county clerk to the district attorney immediately upon receipt thereof;

(b) Retain one copy for use only by judges in proceedings relating to the indictment or accusation; and

(c) Deliver a copy of the transcript to each defendant who is in custody or has given bail or to the defendant's attorney.

4. Any defendant to whom a copy has not been delivered is entitled upon motion to a continuance of the defendant's arraignment until a date 10 days after the defendant actually receives a copy.

5. If several criminal charges against a defendant are investigated on one investigation and thereafter separate indictments are returned or accusations presented upon the several charges, the delivery to the defendant or his or her attorney of one copy of the transcript of the investigation is a compliance with this section as to all of the indictments or accusations.

6. Upon the filing of such a transcript with the county clerk, the transcript and any related physical evidence exhibited to the grand jury become a matter of public record unless the court:

(a) Orders that the presentment or indictment remain secret until the defendant is in custody or has been given bail; or

(b) Upon motion, orders the transcript and evidence to remain secret until further order of the court.

(Added to NRS by 1967, 1410; A 1975, 910; 1983, 359)

NRS 172.235 Who may be present when grand jury is in session.

1. Except as otherwise provided in subsection 2, the following persons may be present while the grand jury is in session:

(a) The district attorney;

(b) A witness who is testifying;

(c) An attorney who is accompanying a witness pursuant to NRS 172.239;

(d) Any interpreter who is needed;

(e) The certified court reporter who is taking stenographic notes of the proceeding;

(f) Any person who is engaged by the grand jury pursuant to NRS 172.205; and

(g) Any other person requested by the grand jury to be present.

2. No person other than the jurors may be present while the grand jury is deliberating or voting.

(Added to NRS by 1967, 1410; A 1985, 555; 1993, 1412)

NRS 172.239 Legal counsel for certain persons who appear before grand jury.

1. A person whose indictment the district attorney intends to seek or the grand jury on its own motion intends to return may be accompanied by legal counsel during any appearance before the grand jury.

2. The legal counsel who accompanies a person pursuant to subsection 1 may advise his or her client but shall not:

(a) Address directly the members of the grand jury;

(b) Speak in such a manner as to be heard by the members of the grand jury; or

(c) In any other way participate in the proceedings of the grand jury.

3. The court or the foreman of the grand jury may have the legal counsel removed if the legal counsel violates any of the provisions of subsection 2 or in any other way disrupts the proceedings of the grand jury.

4. The district attorney or the foreman of the grand jury shall give a person entitled to legal counsel notice of the provisions of this section at the time the person is served with a subpoena to appear before the grand jury. If such a person is invited without process to appear, the grand jury shall include with the invitation notice of the provisions of this section.

(Added to NRS by 1985, 554)

NRS 172.241 Right of certain persons to appear before grand jury; notice of consideration of indictment; withholding of notice; effect of inadequate notice.

1. A person whose indictment the district attorney intends to seek or the grand jury on its own motion intends to return, but who has not been subpoenaed to appear before the grand jury, may testify before the grand jury if the person requests to do so and executes a valid waiver in writing of the person's constitutional privilege against self-incrimination.

2. A district attorney or a peace officer shall serve reasonable notice upon a person whose indictment is being considered by a grand jury unless the court determines that adequate cause exists to withhold notice. The notice is adequate if it:

(a) Is given to the person, the person's attorney of record or an attorney who claims to represent the person and gives the person not less than 5 judicial days to submit a request to testify to the district attorney; and

(b) Advises the person that the person may testify before the grand jury only if the person submits a written request to the district attorney and includes an address where the district attorney may send a notice of the date, time and place of the scheduled proceeding of the grand jury.

3. The district attorney may apply to the court for a determination that adequate cause exists to withhold notice if the district attorney:

(a) Determines that the notice may result in the flight of the person whose indictment is being considered, on the basis of:

(1) A previous failure of the person to appear in matters arising out of the subject matter of the proposed indictment;

(2) The fact that the person is a fugitive from justice arising from charges in another jurisdiction;

(3) Outstanding local warrants pending against the person; or

(4) Any other objective factor;

(b) Determines that the notice may endanger the life or property of other persons; or

(c) Is unable, after reasonable diligence, to notify the person.

4. If a district attorney applies to the court for a determination that adequate cause exists to withhold notice, the court shall hold a closed hearing on the matter. Upon a finding of adequate cause, the court may order that no notice be given.

5. If notice required to be served upon a person pursuant to subsection 2 is not adequate, the person must be given the opportunity to testify before the grand jury. If the person testifies pursuant to this subsection, the grand jury must be instructed to deliberate again on all the charges contained in the indictment following such testimony.

(Added to NRS by 1985, 554; A 1991, 1063; 1997, 188; 2015, 580)

NRS 172.245 Secrecy of proceedings of grand jury; permitted disclosures; penalty.

1. The disclosure of:

(a) Evidence presented to the grand jury;

(b) Information obtained by the grand jury;

(c) The results of an investigation made by the grand jury; and

(d) An event occurring or a statement made in the presence of the grand jury other than its deliberations and the vote of a juror,

□ may be made to the district attorney for use in the performance of the district attorney's duties.

2. Except as otherwise provided in subsection 3, the Attorney General or a member of the Attorney General's staff, a grand juror, district attorney or member of the district attorney's staff, peace officer, clerk, stenographer, interpreter, witness or other person invited or allowed to attend the proceedings of a grand jury shall not disclose:

(a) Evidence presented to the grand jury;

(b) An event occurring or a statement made in the presence of the grand jury;

(c) Information obtained by the grand jury; or

(d) The results of an investigation made by the grand jury.

3. A person may disclose his or her knowledge concerning the proceedings of a grand jury:

(a) When so directed by the court preliminary to or in connection with a judicial proceeding;

(b) When permitted by the court at the request of the defendant upon a showing that grounds may exist for a motion to dismiss the presentment or indictment because of matters occurring before the grand jury;

(c) If the person was a witness before the grand jury and is disclosing his or her knowledge of the proceedings to the person's own attorney; or

(d) As provided in NRS 172.225.

4. No obligation of secrecy may be imposed upon any person except in accordance with this section. The court may direct that a presentment or indictment be kept secret until the defendant is in custody or has been given bail, and the clerk shall seal the presentment or indictment. It is unlawful for any person to disclose the finding of the secret presentment or indictment except when necessary for the issuance and execution of a warrant or summons.

5. A person who violates any of the provisions of this section is guilty of a gross misdemeanor and contempt of court.

6. The Attorney General or district attorney shall investigate and prosecute a violation of this section.

7. The grand jury shall inform each person who appears before the grand jury of the provisions of this section and the penalties for its violation.

(Added to NRS by 1967, 1410; A 1985, 552)

NRS 172.255 Finding and return of presentment or indictment; effect of failure to indict.

1. A presentment or indictment may be found only upon the concurrence of 12 or more jurors.

2. The jurors shall vote separately on each person and each count included in a presentment or indictment.

3. The presentment or indictment must be returned by the grand jury to a judge in open court or, in the absence of the judge, to the clerk of the court in open court, who shall determine that 12 or more jurors concurred in finding a presentment or indictment. If the defendant

has been held to answer and 12 jurors do not concur in finding a presentment or indictment, the foreman shall so report to the court in writing forthwith.

4. The failure to indict does not prevent the same charge from being again submitted to a grand jury if resubmission is approved by the court.

(Added to NRS by 1967, 1411; A 1971, 208; 1985, 1030)

NRS 172.259 Publication of fact that no indictment was issued by grand jury. After a grand jury investigation is concluded:

1. A person who was the subject of the investigation but against whom an indictment was not returned; or
2. A district attorney, with the permission of that person,

□ may make public the fact that no indictment was issued as a result of the grand jury's investigation.

(Added to NRS by 1985, 1028)

NRS 172.265 Names of witnesses inserted or endorsed at foot of indictment. When an indictment is found, the names of the witnesses examined before the grand jury shall be inserted at the foot of the indictment, or endorsed thereon before it is presented to the court.

(Added to NRS by 1967, 1411)

NRS 172.267 Report of grand jury: Scope; purpose; limitations.

1. A grand jury may issue a report concerning a matter into which it may lawfully inquire.
2. The report must be issued for the sole purpose of reporting on the matter. The report must not:

(a) Contain material the sole effect of which is to ridicule or abuse a person or otherwise subject the person to public disgrace or embarrassment;

(b) Contain material which is personal in nature and does not relate to any lawful inquiry; or

(c) Accuse a named or unnamed person directly or by innuendo, imputation or otherwise of an act that, if true, constitutes an indictable offense unless the report is accompanied by a presentment or an indictment of the person for the offense mentioned in the report.

3. The judge impaneling a grand jury shall include the provisions of this section in the judge's charge to the grand jury.

(Added to NRS by 1985, 700)

NRS 172.269 Report of grand jury: Inclusion of recommendations to public officers or agencies; criticism must be constructive; positive statement of no indictable activity required, if applicable. A grand jury may include in its report recommendations to a public officer or agency for actions which will reduce costs, increase efficiency or result in better service to the public. Any criticism made therein must be constructive and made in support of the recommendations. If such recommendations and criticism are included in a report and the report is not accompanied by a related indictment or presentment, the report must include a positive statement that no indictable criminal activity was found.

(Added to NRS by 1985, 701)

NRS 172.271 Report of grand jury: Preliminary review by court; notification of identified persons; procedure to expunge improper material; filing and distribution.

1. The grand jury shall submit a draft of the report that it wishes to make to the court which impaneled it.
2. The court shall review its contents and, if it contains any material which violates paragraph (a) of subsection 2 of NRS 172.267, require the grand jury to expunge that material from the draft.
3. The court shall send to any person identified in the draft in violation of paragraph (b) of subsection 2 of NRS 172.267 the pertinent part of the draft and notify the person that the person has been identified in the draft of the report of the grand jury in connection with possible criminal conduct. The person may, within 5 days after receiving the notice and the portion of the draft, submit a written request to the court for a hearing in chambers to consider a motion to expunge that portion of the draft from the final report.
4. The court shall rule on any such motion to expunge material within 20 days after the completion of the hearing on the motion.
5. If the court determines that the draft:

(a) Violates in its entirety a provision of NRS 172.267; or

(b) After the removal of a portion pursuant to NRS 172.267, is so incomplete that it is meaningless,

□ it shall not file the report with the clerk of the district court but shall file instead a written statement describing, generally, its action and the basis for it.

6. The court shall file either the draft, the draft as corrected or the statement with the clerk of the district court within 60 days after receiving the draft from the grand jury. Upon filing, the draft becomes the final report of the grand jury.
7. Within 5 days after the report is filed, the clerk shall mail a copy of the pertinent portion of the report to each person or governmental entity mentioned in the report.

(Added to NRS by 1985, 701)

MISCELLANEOUS PROVISIONS

NRS 172.275 Discharge of grand jury; discharge or excuse of juror.

1. A grand jury shall serve until discharged by the court and may be so discharged at any time after the expiration of 1 year. At any time for cause shown the court may excuse a juror either temporarily or permanently, and in the latter event the court may impanel an alternate grand juror in place of the juror excused.

2. Where the court is composed of more than one judge, any judge may discharge or excuse a juror; but if any other judge notifies the judge so acting, in writing within 24 hours after the action is taken, that the judge objects, the action stands rescinded and is not effective unless the concurrence of a majority of the judges composing the court is obtained.

(Added to NRS by 1967, 1411; A 1985, 557)

NRS 172.285 Warrant on presentment.

1. If the court deems that the facts stated in a presentment constitute a public offense triable:

(a) In the district court of the county, it shall direct the clerk to issue a warrant for the arrest of the defendant.

(b) In another court of the county, it shall forward the presentment to such court.

2. The clerk, or justice of the peace in a case forwarded to the justice of the peace, may accordingly at any time thereafter issue a warrant under the signature and seal of the court, if it has a seal.

3. The magistrate before whom the defendant is brought shall proceed to examine the charge contained in the presentment and hold the defendant to answer such charge, or discharge the defendant, in the same manner as upon a warrant of arrest on complaint.

(Added to NRS by 1967, 1411)

NRS 172.295 Review by person of person's prior testimony before testifying before grand jury again. A person who:

1. Is called to testify before a grand jury; and

2. Has testified regarding the same matter at another time before the same or another grand jury,

 may, upon request, review the transcript or recording of the person's prior testimony before testifying again.

(Added to NRS by 1985, 1028)

NRS 172.305 Failure to disclose subject of grand jury's inquiry to defendant not cause for dismissal of subsequent presentment or indictment. A presentment or indictment may not be dismissed on the ground that the specific subject of the inquiry was not disclosed to the defendant pursuant to NRS 172.195 or subsection 5 of NRS 174.315.

(Added to NRS by 1985, 572; A 1993, 118; 2013, 1202)

CHAPTER 173 - INDICTMENT AND INFORMATION

GENERAL PROCEDURE

NRS 173.015 First pleading by State. The first pleading on the part of the State is the indictment or information.
(Added to NRS by 1967, 1411)

NRS 173.025 Courts may act upon information for all offenses. The several courts of this state shall have and may exercise the same power and jurisdiction to try and determine prosecutions upon information for crimes, misdemeanors and offenses, to issue writs and process and do all other acts therein as in cases of like prosecution under indictment.
(Added to NRS by 1967, 1412)

NRS 173.035 Information may be filed following preliminary examination when accused is bound over or when preliminary examination is waived; when information is filed on affidavit; limitation of time; amended information may include additional charges if plea agreement is rejected or withdrawn.

1. An information may be filed against any person for any offense when the person:

(a) Has had a preliminary examination as provided by law before a justice of the peace, or other examining officer or magistrate, and has been bound over to appear at the court having jurisdiction; or

(b) Has waived the right to a preliminary examination.

2. If, however, upon the preliminary examination the accused has been discharged, or the affidavit or complaint upon which the examination has been held has not been delivered to the clerk of the proper court, the Attorney General when acting pursuant to a specific statute or the district attorney may, upon affidavit of any person who has knowledge of the commission of an offense, and who is a competent witness to testify in the case, setting forth the offense and the name of the person or persons charged with the commission thereof, upon being furnished with the names of the witnesses for the prosecution, by leave of the court first had, file an information, and process must forthwith be issued thereon. The affidavit need not be filed in cases where the defendant has waived a preliminary examination, or upon a preliminary examination has been bound over to appear at the court having jurisdiction.

3. The information must be filed within 15 days after the holding or waiver of the preliminary examination. Each information must set forth the crime committed according to the facts.

4. If, with the consent of the prosecuting attorney, a defendant waives the right to a preliminary examination in accordance with an agreement by the defendant to plead guilty, guilty but mentally ill or nolo contendere to a lesser charge or to at least one, but not all, of the initial charges, the information filed against the defendant pursuant to this section may contain only the offense or offenses to which the defendant has agreed to enter a plea of guilty, guilty but mentally ill or nolo contendere. If, for any reason, the agreement is rejected by the district court or withdrawn by the defendant, the prosecuting attorney may file an amended information charging all of the offenses which were in the criminal complaint upon which the preliminary examination was waived. The defendant must then be arraigned in accordance with the amended information.

(Added to NRS by 1967, 1412; A 1975, 654; 1979, 1093; 1989, 163; 1993, 82; 1995, 2448; 2003, 1456; 2007, 1404)

NRS 173.045 District attorney or Attorney General to be informant; endorsement of names of witnesses; affidavits.

1. All informations must be filed in the court having jurisdiction of the offenses specified therein, by the Attorney General when acting pursuant to a specific statute or by the district attorney of the proper county as informant, and his or her name must be subscribed thereto by him or her or by his or her deputy.

2. The district attorney or the Attorney General shall endorse thereon the names of such witnesses as are known at the time of filing the information. The district attorney or Attorney General shall not endorse the name of any witness whom he or she does not reasonably expect to call.

3. In all cases in which the defendant has not had or waived a preliminary examination there must be filed with the information the affidavit of some credible person verifying the information upon the personal knowledge of affiant that the offense was committed.

(Added to NRS by 1967, 1412; A 1975, 655; 1989, 163; 1997, 2365)

NRS 173.049 Court clerk may accept information filed electronically; procedure; service.

1. A court clerk may accept an information filed pursuant to this chapter that is filed electronically. An information that is filed electronically must contain an image of the signature of the prosecuting attorney.

2. If a court clerk accepts an information that is filed electronically pursuant to subsection 1, the court clerk shall acknowledge receipt of the information by an electronic time stamp and shall electronically return the information with the electronic time stamp to the prosecuting attorney. An information that is filed and time-stamped electronically pursuant to this section may be converted into a printed document and served upon a defendant in the same manner as an information that is not filed electronically.

(Added to NRS by 1997, 892)

NRS 173.055 Duties of district attorney or Attorney General; written statement containing reasons why information not filed.

1. The Attorney General when acting pursuant to a specific statute or the district attorney of the proper county shall inquire into all cases of preliminary examinations as provided by law, concerning the commission of any offense, whether the offenders are committed to jail, recognized or held to bail.

2. If the district attorney or the Attorney General determines in any such case that an information ought not to be filed, the district attorney or Attorney General shall file with the clerk of the court having jurisdiction of the supposed offense a written statement containing the reasons, in fact and in law, for not filing any information in the case. The statement must be filed within 15 days after the holding of the preliminary examination.

(Added to NRS by 1967, 1412; A 1975, 655; 1979, 1093; 1989, 164)

NRS 173.065 Judge may require Attorney General to prosecute if district attorney refuses. The judge of the court having jurisdiction may in extreme cases, upon affidavit filed with the judge of the commission of a crime, require all available evidence to be delivered to the Attorney General for prosecution, if the district attorney refuses to prosecute any person for such crime.

(Added to NRS by 1967, 1413)

FORM AND AMENDMENT

NRS 173.075 Nature and contents generally.

1. The indictment or the information must be a plain, concise and definite written statement of the essential facts constituting the offense charged. It must be signed by the Attorney General acting pursuant to a specific statute or the district attorney. It need not contain a formal commencement, a formal conclusion or any other matter not necessary to the statement.

2. Allegations made in one count may be incorporated by reference in another count. It may be alleged in a single count that the means by which the defendant committed the offense are unknown or that the defendant committed it by one or more specified means.

3. The indictment or information must state for each count the official or customary citation of the statute, rule, regulation or other provision of law which the defendant is alleged therein to have violated. Error in the citation or its omission is not a ground for dismissal of the indictment or information or for reversal of a conviction if the error or omission did not mislead the defendant to the defendant's prejudice.

(Added to NRS by 1967, 1413; A 1975, 655; 1989, 164)

NRS 173.085 Surplusage. The court on motion of the defendant may strike surplusage from the indictment or information.
(Added to NRS by 1967, 1413)

NRS 173.095 Amendment; notice of habitual criminality, habitually fraudulent felon or habitual felon.

1. The court may permit an indictment or information to be amended at any time before verdict or finding if no additional or different offense is charged and if substantial rights of the defendant are not prejudiced.

2. If an indictment is found charging a primary offense upon which a charge of habitual criminality may be based, the prosecuting attorney may file a notice of habitual criminality with the court. If an indictment is found charging a primary offense upon which a charge of:

(a) Habitually fraudulent felon may be based, the prosecuting attorney shall file a notice of habitually fraudulent felon with the court.

(b) Habitual felon may be based, the prosecuting attorney shall file a notice of habitual felon with the court.

3. The court shall permit an information to be amended pursuant to subsection 4 of NRS 173.035.

(Added to NRS by 1967, 1413; A 1985, 1026; 1993, 82; 1995, 857, 1245)

NRS 173.105 Charging defendant by fictitious or erroneous name: Insertion of true name. When a defendant is charged by a fictitious or erroneous name, and in any stage of the proceedings the defendant's true name is discovered, it must be inserted in the subsequent proceedings referring to the fact of the defendant's being charged by the name mentioned in the indictment or information.
(Added to NRS by 1967, 1413)

JOINDER OF OFFENSES AND OF DEFENDANTS

NRS 173.115 Joinder of offenses. Two or more offenses may be charged in the same indictment or information in a separate count for each offense if the offenses charged, whether felonies or misdemeanors or both, are:

1. Based on the same act or transaction; or

2. Based on two or more acts or transactions connected together or constituting parts of a common scheme or plan.

(Added to NRS by 1967, 1413)

NRS 173.125 Prosecution not required to elect between different offenses or counts; plea of guilty or guilty but mentally ill to one offense does not preclude prosecution for other offenses. The prosecution is not required to elect between the different offenses or counts set forth in the indictment or information, and a plea of guilty or guilty but mentally ill to one or more offenses charged in the indictment or information does not preclude prosecution for the other offenses.
(Added to NRS by 1967, 1413; A 1995, 2449; 2003, 1457; 2007, 1404)

NRS 173.135 Joinder of defendants. Two or more defendants may be charged in the same indictment or information if they are alleged to have participated in the same act or transaction or in the same series of acts or transactions constituting an offense or offenses. Such defendants may be charged in one or more counts together or separately and all of the defendants need not be charged in each count.
(Added to NRS by 1967, 1413)

WARRANTS AND SUMMONSES

NRS 173.145 Issuance of warrant or summons.

1. Upon the request of the Attorney General acting pursuant to a specific statute or the district attorney, the court shall issue a warrant for each defendant named in the indictment or information.

2. The clerk shall issue a summons instead of a warrant upon the request of the district attorney, the Attorney General or by direction of the court.

3. Upon like request or direction the clerk shall issue more than one warrant or summons for the same defendant.

4. The clerk shall deliver the warrant or summons to the peace officer or other person authorized by law to execute or serve it.

5. If a defendant fails to appear in response to the summons, a warrant must be issued.

(Added to NRS by 1967, 1413; A 1975, 656; 1989, 164)

NRS 173.155 Form of warrant; fixing and endorsement of amount of bail. The form of the warrant shall be as provided in NRS 171.108 except that it shall be signed by the clerk, it shall describe the offense charged in the indictment or information and it shall command that the defendant be arrested and brought before the court. The amount of bail may be fixed by the court and endorsed on the warrant.
(Added to NRS by 1967, 1414)

NRS 173.165 Manner of proceeding on giving bail in another county. If the offense charged in the warrant is bailable, and the defendant is arrested in another county, the officer must, upon being required by the defendant, take the defendant before the most convenient magistrate in that or any adjoining county, who must admit the defendant to bail in the amount fixed in the warrant and take bail from the defendant accordingly, naming therein a time, not more than 10 days after the time of taking such bail, for the defendant to appear before the court in which the warrant was issued; or, in case the court is not in session at the time so fixed for the defendant to appear, for the defendant to appear before the court in which the warrant was issued at the first time it is in session thereafter.
(Added to NRS by 1967, 1414)

NRS 173.175 Ordering defendant charged with felony into custody unless increased bail is given. When the indictment or information is for a felony and the defendant before the filing thereof has given bail for the defendant's appearance to answer the charge, the court in which the indictment or information is presented, or in which it is pending, may order the defendant to be committed to actual custody unless the defendant gives bail in an increased amount, to be specified in the order.

(Added to NRS by 1967, 1414)

NRS 173.185 Form of summons. The summons shall be in the same form as the warrant except that it shall summon the defendant to appear before the court at a stated time and place.

(Added to NRS by 1967, 1414)

NRS 173.195 Execution of warrant and service of summons. The warrant shall be executed or the summons served as provided in NRS 171.114, 171.118 and 171.122. A summons to a corporation shall be served as provided in NRS 171.122. The officer executing the warrant shall bring the arrested person promptly before the court or, for the purpose of admission to bail, before a magistrate.

(Added to NRS by 1967, 1414)

NRS 173.205 Return of warrant and summons; reissuance.

1. The peace officer executing a warrant shall make return thereof to the court. At the request of the Attorney General acting pursuant to a specific statute or the district attorney any unexecuted warrant must be returned and cancelled.
2. On or before the return day the person to whom a summons was delivered for service shall make return thereof.
3. At the request of the Attorney General acting pursuant to a specific statute or the district attorney, made at any time while the indictment or information is pending, a warrant returned unexecuted and not cancelled or a summons returned unserved or a duplicate thereof may be delivered by the clerk to a peace officer or other authorized person for execution or service.

(Added to NRS by 1967, 1414; A 1975, 656; 1989, 165)

CHAPTER 174 - ARRAIGNMENT AND PREPARATION FOR TRIAL

ARRAIGNMENT

PLEAS

PLEADINGS AND MOTIONS BEFORE TRIAL; DEFENSES AND OBJECTIONS

JOINDER AND RELIEF THEREFROM

DEPOSITIONS

VIDEOTAPED DEPOSITIONS AND TESTIMONY

DISCOVERY AND INSPECTION

SUBPOENA

ATTENDANCE OF WITNESSES OUTSIDE STATE (UNIFORM ACT)

REMOVAL OF ACTION BEFORE TRIAL

TIME OF TRIAL

ARRAIGNMENT

NRS 174.015 Conduct of arraignment.

1. Arraignment shall be conducted in open court and shall consist of reading the indictment or information to the defendant or stating the substance of the charge and calling on the defendant to plead thereto. The defendant shall be given a copy of the indictment or information before the defendant is called upon to plead.

2. In Justice Court, before the trial commences, the complaint must be distinctly read to the defendant before the defendant is called upon to plead.

(Added to NRS by 1967, 1414)

NRS 174.025 Proceedings respecting name of defendant; entry of true name in minutes; subsequent proceedings in true name. When the defendant is arraigned, the defendant must be informed that if the name by which the defendant is prosecuted is not his or her true name the defendant must then declare his or her true name, or be proceeded against by the name in the indictment, information or complaint. If the defendant gives no other name, the court may proceed accordingly; but, if the defendant alleges that another name is his or her true name, the court must direct an entry thereof in the minutes of the arraignment, and the subsequent proceedings on the information, indictment or complaint may be had against the defendant by that name, referring also to the name by which the defendant was first charged therein.

(Added to NRS by 1967, 1415)

PLEAS

NRS 174.035 Types of pleas; procedure for entering plea.

1. A defendant may plead not guilty, guilty, guilty but mentally ill or, with the consent of the court, nolo contendere. The court may refuse to accept a plea of guilty or guilty but mentally ill.

2. If a plea of guilty or guilty but mentally ill is made in a written plea agreement, the agreement must be in substantially the form prescribed in NRS 174.063. If a plea of guilty or guilty but mentally ill is made orally, the court shall not accept such a plea or a plea of nolo contendere without first addressing the defendant personally and determining that the plea is made voluntarily with understanding of the nature of the charge and consequences of the plea.

3. With the consent of the court and the district attorney, a defendant may enter a conditional plea of guilty, guilty but mentally ill or nolo contendere, reserving in writing the right, on appeal from the judgment, to a review of the adverse determination of any specified pretrial motion. A defendant who prevails on appeal must be allowed to withdraw the plea.

4. A plea of guilty but mentally ill must be entered not less than 21 days before the date set for trial. A defendant who has entered a plea of guilty but mentally ill has the burden of establishing the defendant's mental illness by a preponderance of the evidence. Except as otherwise provided by specific statute, a defendant who enters such a plea is subject to the same criminal, civil and administrative penalties and procedures as a defendant who pleads guilty.

5. The defendant may, in the alternative or in addition to any one of the pleas permitted by subsection 1, plead not guilty by reason of insanity. A plea of not guilty by reason of insanity must be entered not less than 21 days before the date set for trial. A defendant who has not so pleaded may offer the defense of insanity during trial upon good cause shown. Under such a plea or defense, the burden of proof is upon the defendant to establish by a preponderance of the evidence that:

(a) Due to a disease or defect of the mind, the defendant was in a delusional state at the time of the alleged offense; and

(b) Due to the delusional state, the defendant either did not:

(1) Know or understand the nature and capacity of his or her act; or

(2) Appreciate that his or her conduct was wrong, meaning not authorized by law.

6. If a defendant refuses to plead or if the court refuses to accept a plea of guilty or guilty but mentally ill or if a defendant corporation fails to appear, the court shall enter a plea of not guilty.

7. A defendant may not enter a plea of guilty or guilty but mentally ill pursuant to a plea bargain for an offense punishable as a felony for which:

(a) Probation is not allowed; or

(b) The maximum prison sentence is more than 10 years,

□ unless the plea bargain is set forth in writing and signed by the defendant, the defendant's attorney, if the defendant is represented by counsel, and the prosecuting attorney.

8. If the court accepts a plea of guilty but mentally ill pursuant to this section, the court shall cause, within 5 business days after acceptance of the plea, on a form prescribed by the Department of Public Safety, a record of that plea to be transmitted to the Central Repository for Nevada Records of Criminal History along with a statement indicating that the record is being transmitted for inclusion in each appropriate database of the National Instant Criminal Background Check System.

9. As used in this section:

(a) "Disease or defect of the mind" does not include a disease or defect which is caused solely by voluntary intoxication.

(b) "National Instant Criminal Background Check System" has the meaning ascribed to it in NRS 179A.062.

(Added to NRS by 1967, 1415; A 1991, 301, 1062; 1995, 1534, 2450; 1997, 641; 2003, 1457; 2007, 1405; 2009, 2484; 2015, 1795)

NRS 174.055 Proceedings on plea of guilty or guilty but mentally ill in justice court. In a justice court, if the defendant pleads guilty or guilty but mentally ill, the court may, before entering such a plea or pronouncing judgment, examine witnesses to ascertain the gravity of the offense committed. If it appears to the court that a higher offense has been committed than the offense charged in the complaint, the court may order the defendant to be committed or admitted to bail or to answer any indictment that may be found against the defendant or any information which may be filed by the district attorney.

(Added to NRS by 1967, 1415; A 1995, 2450; 2003, 1458; 2007, 1406)

NRS 174.061 Plea bargaining: General requirements; prohibited agreements.

1. If a prosecuting attorney enters into an agreement with a defendant in which the defendant agrees to testify against another defendant in exchange for a plea of guilty, guilty but mentally ill or nolo contendere to a lesser charge or for a recommendation of a reduced sentence, the agreement:

(a) Is void if the defendant's testimony is false.

(b) Must be in writing and include a statement that the agreement is void if the defendant's testimony is false.

2. A prosecuting attorney shall not enter into an agreement with a defendant which:

(a) Limits the testimony of the defendant to a predetermined formula.

(b) Is contingent on the testimony of the defendant contributing to a specified conclusion.

(Added to NRS by 1991, 291; A 1995, 2450; 2003, 1458; 2007, 1406)

NRS 174.063 Written plea agreement for plea of guilty or guilty but mentally ill: Form; contents.

1. If a plea of guilty or guilty but mentally ill is made in a written plea agreement, the agreement must be substantially in the following form:

Case No. ....
Dept. No. ....

IN THE .... JUDICIAL DISTRICT COURT OF THE
STATE OF NEVADA IN AND FOR THE COUNTY OF............,

The State of Nevada,
PLAINTIFF,

v.

(Name of defendant),
DEFENDANT.

GUILTY OR GUILTY BUT MENTALLY ILL PLEA AGREEMENT

I hereby agree to plead guilty or guilty but mentally ill to: (List charges to which defendant is pleading guilty or guilty but mentally ill), as more fully alleged in the charging document attached hereto as Exhibit 1.

My decision to plead guilty or guilty but mentally ill is based upon the plea agreement in this case which is as follows:

(State the terms of the agreement.)

CONSEQUENCES OF THE PLEA

I understand that by pleading guilty or guilty but mentally ill I admit the facts which support all the elements of the offenses to which I now plead as set forth in Exhibit 1.

I understand that as a consequence of my plea of guilty or guilty but mentally ill I may be imprisoned for a period of not more than (maximum term of imprisonment) and that I (may or will) be fined up to (maximum amount of fine). I understand that the law requires me to pay an administrative assessment fee.

I understand that, if appropriate, I will be ordered to make restitution to the victim of the offenses to which I am pleading guilty or guilty but mentally ill and to the victim of any related offense which is being dismissed or not prosecuted pursuant to this agreement. I will also be ordered to reimburse the State of Nevada for expenses relating to my extradition, if any.

I understand that I (am or am not) eligible for probation for the offense to which I am pleading guilty or guilty but mentally ill. (I understand that, except as otherwise provided by statute, the question of whether I receive probation is in the discretion of the sentencing judge, or I understand that I must serve a mandatory minimum term of (term of imprisonment) or pay a minimum mandatory fine of (amount of fine) or serve a mandatory minimum term (term of imprisonment) and pay a minimum mandatory fine of (amount of fine).)

I understand that if more than one sentence of imprisonment is imposed and I am eligible to serve the sentences concurrently, the sentencing judge has the discretion to order the sentences served concurrently or consecutively.

I understand that information regarding charges not filed, dismissed charges or charges to be dismissed pursuant to this agreement may be considered by the judge at sentencing.

I have not been promised or guaranteed any particular sentence by anyone. I know that my sentence is to be determined by the court within the limits prescribed by statute. I understand that if my attorney or the State of Nevada or both recommend any specific punishment to the court, the court is not obligated to accept the recommendation.

I understand that the Division of Parole and Probation of the Department of Public Safety may or will prepare a report for the sentencing judge before sentencing. This report will include matters relevant to the issue of sentencing, including my criminal history. I understand that this report may contain hearsay information regarding my background and criminal history. My attorney (if represented by counsel) and I will each have the opportunity to comment on the information contained in the report at the time of sentencing.

WAIVER OF RIGHTS

By entering my plea of guilty or guilty but mentally ill, I understand that I have waived the following rights and privileges:

1. The constitutional privilege against self-incrimination, including the right to refuse to testify at trial, in which event the prosecution would not be allowed to comment to the jury about my refusal to testify.

2. The constitutional right to a speedy and public trial by an impartial jury, free of excessive pretrial publicity prejudicial to the defense, at which trial I would be entitled to the assistance of an attorney, either appointed or retained. At trial, the State would bear the burden of proving beyond a reasonable doubt each element of the offense charged.

3. The constitutional right to confront and cross-examine any witnesses who would testify against me.

4. The constitutional right to subpoena witnesses to testify on my behalf.

5. The constitutional right to testify in my own defense.

6. The right to appeal the conviction, with the assistance of an attorney, either appointed or retained, unless the appeal is based upon reasonable constitutional, jurisdictional or other grounds that challenge the legality of the proceedings and except as otherwise provided in subsection 3 of NRS 174.035.

VOLUNTARINESS OF PLEA

I have discussed the elements of all the original charges against me with my attorney (if represented by counsel) and I understand the nature of these charges against me.

I understand that the State would have to prove each element of the charge against me at trial.

I have discussed with my attorney (if represented by counsel) any possible defenses and circumstances which might be in my favor.

All of the foregoing elements, consequences, rights and waiver of rights have been thoroughly explained to me by my attorney (if represented by counsel).

I believe that pleading guilty or guilty but mentally ill and accepting this plea bargain is in my best interest and that a trial would be contrary to my best interest.

I am signing this agreement voluntarily, after consultation with my attorney (if represented by counsel) and I am not acting under duress or coercion or by virtue of any promises of leniency, except for those set forth in this agreement.

I am not now under the influence of intoxicating liquor, a controlled substance or other drug which would in any manner impair my ability to comprehend or understand this agreement or the proceedings surrounding my entry of this plea.

My attorney (if represented by counsel) has answered all my questions regarding this guilty or guilty but mentally ill plea agreement and its consequences to my satisfaction and I am satisfied with the services provided by my attorney.

Dated: This .... day of the month of .... of the year ....

....
Defendant.

Agreed to on this .... day of the month of .... of the year ....

....
Deputy District Attorney.

2. If the defendant is represented by counsel, the written plea agreement must also include a certificate of counsel that is substantially in the following form:

CERTIFICATE OF COUNSEL

I, the undersigned, as the attorney for the defendant named herein and as an officer of the court hereby certify that:

1. I have fully explained to the defendant the allegations contained in the charges to which guilty or guilty but mentally ill pleas are being entered.

2. I have advised the defendant of the penalties for each charge and the restitution that the defendant may be ordered to pay.

3. All pleas of guilty or guilty but mentally ill offered by the defendant pursuant to this agreement are consistent with all the facts known to me and are made with my advice to the defendant and are in the best interest of the defendant.

4. To the best of my knowledge and belief, the defendant:

(a) Is competent and understands the charges and the consequences of pleading guilty or guilty but mentally ill as provided in this agreement.

(b) Executed this agreement and will enter all guilty or guilty but mentally ill pleas pursuant hereto voluntarily.

(c) Was not under the influence of intoxicating liquor, a controlled substance or other drug at the time of the execution of this agreement.

Dated: This .... day of the month of .... of the year ....

....
Attorney for defendant.

(Added to NRS by 1995, 1531; A 2001, 36, 2565; 2007, 1406)

NRS 174.065 When plea may specify degree of crime or punishment. Except as otherwise provided in NRS 174.061:

1. On a plea of guilty or guilty but mentally ill to an information or indictment accusing a defendant of a crime divided into degrees, when consented to by the prosecuting attorney in open court and approved by the court, the plea may specify the degree, and in such event the defendant shall not be punished for a higher degree than that specified in the plea.

2. On a plea of guilty or guilty but mentally ill to an indictment or information for murder of the first degree, when consented to by the prosecuting attorney in open court and approved by the court, the plea may specify a punishment less than death. The specified punishment, or any lesser punishment, may be imposed by a single judge.

(Added to NRS by 1967, 1416; A 1973, 1801; 1977, 1543; 1991, 291, 651; 1993, 828; 1995, 2451; 2003, 1458; 2007, 1409)

PLEADINGS AND MOTIONS BEFORE TRIAL; DEFENSES AND OBJECTIONS

NRS 174.075 Pleadings and motions.

1. Pleadings in criminal proceedings are the indictment, the information and, in justice court, the complaint, and the pleas of guilty, guilty but mentally ill, not guilty, not guilty by reason of insanity and nolo contendere.

2. All other pleas, demurrers and motions to quash are abolished, and defenses and objections raised before trial which could have been raised by one or more of them may be raised only by motion to dismiss or to grant appropriate relief, as provided in this title.

(Added to NRS by 1967, 1416; A 1995, 2451; 2003, 1459; 2007, 1409)

NRS 174.085 Proceedings not constituting acquittal; effect of acquittal on merits; proceedings constituting bar to another prosecution; retrial after discharge of jury; effect of voluntary dismissal.

1. If a defendant was formerly acquitted on the ground of a variance between the indictment, information or complaint and proof, or the indictment, information, or complaint was dismissed upon an objection to its form or substance, or in order to hold a defendant for a higher offense without a judgment of acquittal, it is not an acquittal of the same offense.

2. If a defendant is acquitted on the merits, the defendant is acquitted of the same offense, notwithstanding a defect in the form or substance in the indictment, information, or complaint on which the trial was had.

3. When a defendant is convicted or acquitted, or has been once placed in jeopardy upon an indictment, information or complaint, except as otherwise provided in subsections 5 and 6, the conviction, acquittal or jeopardy is a bar to another indictment, information or complaint for the offense charged in the former, or for an attempt to commit the same, or for an offense necessarily included therein, of which the defendant might have been convicted under that indictment, information or complaint.

4. In all cases where a jury is discharged or prevented from giving a verdict by reason of an accident or other cause, except where the defendant is discharged during the progress of the trial or after the cause is submitted to them, the cause may be again tried.

5. The prosecuting attorney, in a case that the prosecuting attorney has initiated, may voluntarily dismiss a complaint:

(a) Before a preliminary hearing if the crime with which the defendant is charged is a felony or gross misdemeanor; or

(b) Before trial if the crime with which the defendant is charged is a misdemeanor,

□ without prejudice to the right to file another complaint, unless the State of Nevada has previously filed a complaint against the defendant which was dismissed at the request of the prosecuting attorney. After the dismissal, the court shall order the defendant released from custody or, if the defendant is released on bail, exonerate the obligors and release any bail.

6. If a prosecuting attorney files a subsequent complaint after a complaint concerning the same matter has been filed and dismissed against the defendant:

(a) The case must be assigned to the same judge to whom the initial complaint was assigned; and

(b) A court shall not issue a warrant for the arrest of a defendant who was released from custody pursuant to subsection 5 or require a defendant whose bail has been exonerated pursuant to subsection 5 to give bail unless the defendant does not appear in court in response to a properly issued summons in connection with the complaint.

7. The prosecuting attorney, in a case that the prosecuting attorney has initiated, may voluntarily dismiss an indictment or information before the actual arrest or incarceration of the defendant without prejudice to the right to bring another indictment or information. After the arrest or incarceration of the defendant, the prosecuting attorney may voluntarily dismiss an indictment or information without prejudice to the right to bring another indictment or information only upon good cause shown to the court and upon written findings and a court order to that effect.

(Added to NRS by 1967, 1416; A 1971, 596; 1997, 2391)

NRS 174.095 Defenses and objections which may be raised by motion. Any defense or objection which is capable of determination without the trial of the general issue may be raised before trial by motion.

(Added to NRS by 1967, 1416)

NRS 174.098 Motion to declare that defendant is intellectually disabled: When authorized; procedure.

1. A defendant who is charged with murder of the first degree in a case in which the death penalty is sought may, not less than 10 days before the date set for trial, file a motion to declare that the defendant is intellectually disabled.

2. If a defendant files a motion pursuant to this section, the court must:

(a) Stay the proceedings pending a decision on the issue of intellectual disability; and

(b) Hold a hearing within a reasonable time before the trial to determine whether the defendant is intellectually disabled.

3. The court shall order the defendant to:

(a) Provide evidence which demonstrates that the defendant is intellectually disabled not less than 30 days before the date set for a hearing conducted pursuant to subsection 2; and

(b) Undergo an examination by an expert selected by the prosecution on the issue of whether the defendant is intellectually disabled at least 15 days before the date set for a hearing pursuant to subsection 2.

4. For the purpose of the hearing conducted pursuant to subsection 2, there is no privilege for any information or evidence provided to the prosecution or obtained by the prosecution pursuant to subsection 3.

5. At a hearing conducted pursuant to subsection 2:

(a) The court must allow the defendant and the prosecution to present evidence and conduct a cross-examination of any witness concerning whether the defendant is intellectually disabled; and

(b) The defendant has the burden of proving by a preponderance of the evidence that the defendant is intellectually disabled.

6. If the court determines based on the evidence presented at a hearing conducted pursuant to subsection 2 that the defendant is intellectually disabled, the court must make such a finding in the record and strike the notice of intent to seek the death penalty. Such a finding may be appealed pursuant to NRS 177.015.

7. For the purposes of this section, "intellectually disabled" means significant subaverage general intellectual functioning which exists concurrently with deficits in adaptive behavior and manifested during the developmental period.

(Added to NRS by 2003, 766; A 2013, 684, 1752)

NRS 174.105 Defenses and objections which must be raised by motion.

1. Defenses and objections based on defects in the institution of the prosecution, other than insufficiency of the evidence to warrant an indictment, or in the indictment, information or complaint, other than that it fails to show jurisdiction in the court or to charge an offense, may be raised only by motion before trial. The motion shall include all such defenses and objections then available to the defendant.

2. Failure to present any such defense or objection as herein provided constitutes a waiver thereof, but the court for cause shown may grant relief from the waiver.

3. Lack of jurisdiction or the failure of the indictment, information or complaint to charge an offense shall be noticed by the court at any time during the pendency of the proceeding.

(Added to NRS by 1967, 1416)

NRS 174.115 Time of making motion. The motion shall be made before the plea is entered, but the court may permit it to be made within a reasonable time thereafter.

(Added to NRS by 1967, 1417)

NRS 174.125 Certain motions required to be made before trial.

1. All motions in a criminal prosecution to suppress evidence, for a transcript of former proceedings, for a preliminary hearing, for severance of joint defendants, for withdrawal of counsel, and all other motions which by their nature, if granted, delay or postpone the time of trial must be made before trial, unless an opportunity to make such a motion before trial did not exist or the moving party was not aware of the grounds for the motion before trial.

2. In any judicial district in which a single judge is provided:

(a) All motions subject to the provisions of subsection 1 must be made in writing, with not less than 10 days' notice to the opposite party unless good cause is shown to the court at the time of trial why the motion could not have been made in writing upon the required notice.

(b) The court may, by written order, shorten the notice required to be given to the opposite party.

3. In any judicial district in which two or more judges are provided:

(a) All motions subject to the provisions of subsection 1 must be made in writing not less than 15 days before the date set for trial, except that if less than 15 days intervene between entry of a plea and the date set for trial, such a motion may be made within 5 days after entry of the plea.

(b) The court may, if a defendant waives hearing on the motion or for other good cause shown, permit the motion to be made at a later date.

4. Grounds for making such a motion after the time provided or at the trial must be shown by affidavit.

(Added to NRS by 1967, 1417; A 1981, 1955)

NRS 174.135 Hearing on motion.

1. A motion before trial raising defenses or objections shall be determined before trial unless the court orders that it be deferred for determination at the trial of the general issue.

2. An issue of fact shall be tried by a jury if a jury trial is required under the Constitution of the United States or of the State of Nevada or by statute.

3. All other issues of fact shall be determined by the court with or without a jury or on affidavits or in such other manner as the court may direct.

(Added to NRS by 1967, 1417)

NRS 174.145 Effect of determination.

1. If a motion is determined adversely to the defendant, the defendant shall be permitted to plead if the defendant had not previously pleaded. A plea previously entered shall stand.

2. If the court grants a motion based on a defect in the institution of the prosecution or in the indictment, information or complaint, it may also order that the defendant be held in custody or that the defendant's bail be continued for a specified time pending the filing of a new indictment, information or complaint.

3. Nothing in this section shall affect the provisions of any statute relating to periods of limitations.

(Added to NRS by 1967, 1417)

JOINDER AND RELIEF THEREFROM

NRS 174.155 Trial together of indictments or informations. The court may order two or more indictments or informations or both to be tried together if the offenses, and the defendants if there is more than one, could have been joined in a single indictment or information. The procedure shall be the same as if the prosecution were under such single indictment or information.

(Added to NRS by 1967, 1418)

NRS 174.165 Relief from prejudicial joinder.

1. If it appears that a defendant or the State of Nevada is prejudiced by a joinder of offenses or of defendants in an indictment or information, or by such joinder for trial together, the court may order an election or separate trials of counts, grant a severance of defendants or provide whatever other relief justice requires.

2. In ruling on a motion by a defendant for severance the court may order the district attorney to deliver to the court for inspection in chambers any statements or confessions made by the defendants which the State intends to introduce in evidence at the trial.

(Added to NRS by 1967, 1418)

DEPOSITIONS

NRS 174.171 Applicability. The provisions of NRS 174.171 to 174.225, inclusive, do not apply to a deposition taken pursuant to NRS 174.227 or used pursuant to NRS 174.228, or both.

(Added to NRS by 1985, 1423; A 1993, 252)

NRS 174.175 When taken.

1. If it appears that a prospective witness is an older person or a vulnerable person or may be unable to attend or prevented from attending a trial or hearing, that the witness's testimony is material and that it is necessary to take the witness's deposition in order to prevent a failure of justice, the court at any time after the filing of an indictment, information or complaint may, upon motion of a defendant or of the State and notice to the parties, order that the witness's testimony be taken by deposition and that any designated books, papers, documents or tangible objects, not privileged, be produced at the same time and place. If the motion is for the deposition of an older person or a vulnerable person, the court may enter an order to take the deposition only upon good cause shown to the court. If the deposition is taken upon motion of the State, the court shall order that it be taken under such conditions as will afford to each defendant the opportunity to confront the witnesses against him or her.

2. If a witness is committed for failure to give bail to appear to testify at a trial or hearing, the court, on written motion of the witness and upon notice to the parties, may direct that the witness's deposition be taken. After the deposition has been subscribed, the court may discharge the witness.

3. This section does not apply to the prosecutor, or to an accomplice in the commission of the offense charged.

4. As used in this section:

(a) "Older person" means a person who is 70 years of age or older.

(b) "Vulnerable person" has the meaning ascribed to it in NRS 200.5092.

(Added to NRS by 1967, 1418; A 2009, 2552; 2015, 825)

NRS 174.185 Notice of taking. The party at whose instance a deposition is to be taken shall give to every other party reasonable written notice of the time and place for taking the deposition. The notice shall state the name and address of each person to be examined. On motion of a party upon whom the notice is served, the court for cause shown may extend or shorten the time.

(Added to NRS by 1967, 1418)

NRS 174.195 Defendant's counsel and payment of expenses. If a defendant is without counsel the court shall advise the defendant of his or her right and assign counsel to represent the defendant unless the defendant elects to proceed without counsel or is able to obtain counsel. If it appears that a defendant at whose instance a deposition is to be taken cannot bear the expense thereof, the court may direct that the expenses of the court reporter and of travel and subsistence of the defendant's attorney for attendance at the examination must be paid as provided in NRS 7.135.

(Added to NRS by 1967, 1418; A 1987, 1301)

NRS 174.205 How taken. A deposition shall be taken in the manner provided in civil actions. The court at the request of a defendant may direct that a deposition be taken on written interrogatories in the manner provided in civil actions.

(Added to NRS by 1967, 1418)

NRS 174.215 Use of deposition.

1. At the trial or upon any hearing, a part or all of a deposition, so far as otherwise admissible under the rules of evidence, may be used if it appears:

(a) That the witness is dead;

(b) That the witness is out of the State of Nevada, unless it appears that the absence of the witness was procured by the party offering the deposition;

(c) That the witness cannot attend or testify because of sickness or infirmity;

(d) That the witness has become of unsound mind; or

(e) That the party offering the deposition could not procure the attendance of the witness by subpoena.

2. Any deposition may also be used by any party to contradict or impeach the testimony of the deponent as a witness.

3. If only a part of a deposition is offered in evidence by a party, an adverse party may require the party to offer all of it which is relevant to the part offered and any party may offer other parts.

(Added to NRS by 1967, 1418; A 1989, 588)

NRS 174.225 Objections to admissibility. Objections to receiving in evidence a deposition or part thereof may be made as provided in civil actions.

(Added to NRS by 1967, 1419)

VIDEOTAPED DEPOSITIONS AND TESTIMONY

NRS 174.227 Videotaped depositions: Order of court; notice to parties; cross-examination; use.

1. A court on its own motion or on the motion of the district attorney may, for good cause shown, order the taking of a videotaped deposition of:

(a) A victim of sexual abuse as that term is defined in NRS 432B.100;

(b) A prospective witness in any criminal prosecution if the witness is less than 14 years of age; or

(c) A victim of sex trafficking as that term is defined in subsection 2 of NRS 201.300. There is a rebuttable presumption that good cause exists where the district attorney seeks to take the deposition of a person alleged to be the victim of sex trafficking.

□ The court may specify the time and place for taking the deposition and the persons who may be present when it is taken.

2. The district attorney shall give every other party reasonable written notice of the time and place for taking the deposition. The notice must include the name of the person to be examined. On the motion of a party upon whom the notice is served, the court:

(a) For good cause shown may release the address of the person to be examined; and

(b) For cause shown may extend or shorten the time.

3. If at the time such a deposition is taken, the district attorney anticipates using the deposition at trial, the court shall so state in the order for the deposition and the accused must be given the opportunity to cross-examine the deponent in the same manner as permitted at trial.

4. Except as limited by NRS 174.228, the court may allow the videotaped deposition to be used at any proceeding in addition to or in lieu of the direct testimony of the deponent. It may also be used by any party to contradict or impeach the testimony of the deponent as a witness. If only a part of the deposition is offered in evidence by a party, an adverse party may require the party to offer all of it which is relevant to the part offered and any party may offer other parts.

(Added to NRS by 1985, 1423; A 1993, 252; 2013, 2419)

NRS 174.228 Videotaped depositions: Use. A court may allow a videotaped deposition to be used instead of the deponent's testimony at trial only if:

1. In the case of a victim of sexual abuse, as that term is defined in NRS 432B.100:

(a) Before the deposition is taken, a hearing is held by a justice of the peace or district judge who finds that:

(1) The use of the videotaped deposition in lieu of testimony at trial is necessary to protect the welfare of the victim; and

(2) The presence of the accused at trial would inflict trauma, more than minimal in degree, upon the victim; and

(b) At the time a party seeks to use the deposition, the court determines that the conditions set forth in subparagraphs (1) and (2) of paragraph (a) continue to exist. The court may hold a hearing before the use of the deposition to make its determination.

2. In the case of a victim of sex trafficking as that term is defined in subsection 2 of NRS 201.300:

(a) Before the deposition is taken, a hearing is held by a justice of the peace or district judge and the justice or judge finds that cause exists pursuant to paragraph (c) of subsection 1 of NRS 174.227; and

(b) Before allowing the videotaped deposition to be used at trial, the court finds that the victim is unavailable as a witness.

3. In all cases:

(a) A justice of the peace or district judge presides over the taking of the deposition;

(b) The accused is able to hear and see the proceedings;

(c) The accused is represented by counsel who, if physically separated from the accused, is able to communicate orally with the accused by electronic means;

(d) The accused is given an adequate opportunity to cross-examine the deponent subject to the protection of the deponent deemed necessary by the court; and

(e) The deponent testifies under oath.

(Added to NRS by 1993, 251; A 2013, 2420)

NRS 174.229 Videotaped testimony. If a prospective witness who is scheduled to testify before a grand jury or at a preliminary hearing is less than 14 years of age, the court shall, upon the motion of the district attorney, and may, upon its own motion, order the child's testimony to be videotaped at the time it is given.

(Added to NRS by 1985, 1424)

NRS 174.231 Effect of NRS 174.227, 174.228 and 174.229. The provisions of NRS 174.227, 174.228 and 174.229 do not preclude:

1. The submission of videotaped depositions or testimony which are otherwise admissible as evidence in court.

2. A victim or prospective witness from testifying at a proceeding without the use of his or her videotaped deposition or testimony.

(Added to NRS by 1985, 1424; A 1993, 252)

DISCOVERY AND INSPECTION

NRS 174.233 Disclosure by defendant of intent to claim alibi; defendant to disclose list of alibi witnesses; prosecuting attorney to disclose list of rebuttal witnesses; continuing duty to disclose; sanctions.

1. In addition to the written notice required by NRS 174.234, a defendant in a criminal case who intends to offer evidence of an alibi in his or her defense shall, not less than 10 days before trial or at such other time as the court may direct, file and serve upon the prosecuting attorney a written notice of the defendant's intention to claim the alibi. The notice must contain specific information as to the place at which

the defendant claims to have been at the time of the alleged offense and, as particularly as are known to defendant or the defendant's attorney, the names and last known addresses of the witnesses by whom the defendant proposes to establish the alibi.

2. Not less than 10 days after receipt of the defendant's list of witnesses, or at such other time as the court may direct, the prosecuting attorney shall file and serve upon the defendant the names and last known addresses, as particularly as are known to the prosecuting attorney, of the witnesses the State proposes to offer in rebuttal to discredit the defendant's alibi at the trial of the cause.

3. Both the defendant and the prosecuting attorney have a continuing duty to disclose promptly the names and last known addresses of additional witnesses which come to the attention of either party after filing their respective lists.

4. If a defendant fails to file and serve a copy of the notice required by this section, the court may exclude evidence offered by the defendant to prove an alibi, except the testimony of the defendant. If the notice is given by a defendant, the court may exclude the testimony of any witness offered by the defendant to prove an alibi if the name and last known address of the witness, as particularly as are known to the defendant or the defendant's attorney, are not stated in the notice.

5. If the prosecuting attorney fails to file and serve a copy on the defendant of a list of witnesses as required by this section, the court may exclude evidence offered by the State in rebuttal to the defendant's evidence of alibi. If the list is filed and served by the prosecuting attorney, the court may exclude the testimony of any witness offered by the prosecuting attorney for the purpose of rebutting the evidence of alibi if the name and last known address of the witness, as particularly as are known to the prosecuting attorney, are not stated in the notice. For good cause shown the court may waive the requirements of this section.

(Added to NRS by 1969, 350; A 1971, 283; 1991, 301; 1995, 263; 1997, 2365)

NRS 174.234 Reciprocal disclosure of lists of witnesses and information relating to expert testimony; continuing duty to disclose; protective orders; sanctions.

1. Except as otherwise provided in this section, not less than 5 judicial days before trial or at such other time as the court directs:

(a) If the defendant will be tried for one or more offenses that are punishable as a gross misdemeanor or felony:

(1) The defendant shall file and serve upon the prosecuting attorney a written notice containing the names and last known addresses of all witnesses the defendant intends to call during the case in chief of the defendant; and

(2) The prosecuting attorney shall file and serve upon the defendant a written notice containing the names and last known addresses of all witnesses the prosecuting attorney intends to call during the case in chief of the State.

(b) If the defendant will not be tried for any offenses that are punishable as a gross misdemeanor or felony:

(1) The defendant shall file and serve upon the prosecuting attorney a written notice containing the name and last known address of any witness the defendant intends to call during the case in chief of the defendant whose name and last known address have not otherwise been provided to the prosecuting attorney pursuant to NRS 174.245; and

(2) The prosecuting attorney shall file and serve upon the defendant a written notice containing the name and last known address or place of employment of any witness the prosecuting attorney intends to call during the case in chief of the State whose name and last known address or place of employment have not otherwise been provided to the defendant pursuant to NRS 171.1965 or 174.235.

2. If the defendant will be tried for one or more offenses that are punishable as a gross misdemeanor or felony and a witness that a party intends to call during the case in chief of the State or during the case in chief of the defendant is expected to offer testimony as an expert witness, the party who intends to call that witness shall file and serve upon the opposing party, not less than 21 days before trial or at such other time as the court directs, a written notice containing:

(a) A brief statement regarding the subject matter on which the expert witness is expected to testify and the substance of the testimony;

(b) A copy of the curriculum vitae of the expert witness; and

(c) A copy of all reports made by or at the direction of the expert witness.

3. After complying with the provisions of subsections 1 and 2, each party has a continuing duty to file and serve upon the opposing party:

(a) Written notice of the names and last known addresses of any additional witnesses that the party intends to call during the case in chief of the State or during the case in chief of the defendant. A party shall file and serve written notice pursuant to this paragraph as soon as practicable after the party determines that the party intends to call an additional witness during the case in chief of the State or during the case in chief of the defendant. The court shall prohibit an additional witness from testifying if the court determines that the party acted in bad faith by not including the witness on the written notice required pursuant to subsection 1.

(b) Any information relating to an expert witness that is required to be disclosed pursuant to subsection 2. A party shall provide information pursuant to this paragraph as soon as practicable after the party obtains that information. The court shall prohibit the party from introducing that information in evidence or shall prohibit the expert witness from testifying if the court determines that the party acted in bad faith by not timely disclosing that information pursuant to subsection 2.

4. Each party has a continuing duty to file and serve upon the opposing party any change in the last known address, or, if applicable, last known place of employment, of any witness that the party intends to call during the case in chief of the State or during the case in chief of the defendant as soon as practicable after the party obtains that information.

5. Upon a motion by either party or the witness, the court shall prohibit disclosure to the other party of the address of the witness if the court determines that disclosure of the address would create a substantial threat to the witness of bodily harm, intimidation, coercion or harassment. If the court prohibits disclosure of an address pursuant to this subsection, the court shall, upon the request of a party, provide the party or the party's attorney or agent with an opportunity to interview the witness in an environment that provides for protection of the witness.

6. In addition to the sanctions and protective orders otherwise provided in subsections 3 and 5, the court may upon the request of a party:

(a) Order that disclosure pursuant to this section be denied, restricted or deferred pursuant to the provisions of NRS 174.275; or

(b) Impose sanctions pursuant to subsection 2 of NRS 174.295 for the failure to comply with the provisions of this section.

7. A party is not entitled, pursuant to the provisions of this section, to the disclosure of the name or address of a witness or any other type of item or information that is privileged or protected from disclosure or inspection pursuant to the Constitution or laws of this state or the Constitution of the United States.

(Added to NRS by 1995, 263; A 1997, 2366; 1999, 152)

NRS 174.235 Disclosure by prosecuting attorney of evidence relating to prosecution; limitations.

1. Except as otherwise provided in NRS 174.233 to 174.295, inclusive, at the request of a defendant, the prosecuting attorney shall permit the defendant to inspect and to copy or photograph any:

(a) Written or recorded statements or confessions made by the defendant, or any written or recorded statements made by a witness the prosecuting attorney intends to call during the case in chief of the State, or copies thereof, within the possession, custody or control of the State, the existence of which is known, or by the exercise of due diligence may become known, to the prosecuting attorney;

(b) Results or reports of physical or mental examinations, scientific tests or scientific experiments made in connection with the particular case, or copies thereof, within the possession, custody or control of the State, the existence of which is known, or by the exercise of due diligence may become known, to the prosecuting attorney; and

(c) Books, papers, documents, tangible objects, or copies thereof, which the prosecuting attorney intends to introduce during the case in chief of the State and which are within the possession, custody or control of the State, the existence of which is known, or by the exercise of due diligence may become known, to the prosecuting attorney.

2. The defendant is not entitled, pursuant to the provisions of this section, to the discovery or inspection of:

(a) An internal report, document or memorandum that is prepared by or on behalf of the prosecuting attorney in connection with the investigation or prosecution of the case.

(b) A statement, report, book, paper, document, tangible object or any other type of item or information that is privileged or protected from disclosure or inspection pursuant to the Constitution or laws of this state or the Constitution of the United States.

3. The provisions of this section are not intended to affect any obligation placed upon the prosecuting attorney by the Constitution of this state or the Constitution of the United States to disclose exculpatory evidence to the defendant.

(Added to NRS by 1967, 1419; A 1995, 264; 1997, 2367)

NRS 174.245 Disclosure by defendant of evidence relating to defense; limitations.

1. Except as otherwise provided in NRS 174.233 to 174.295, inclusive, at the request of the prosecuting attorney, the defendant shall permit the prosecuting attorney to inspect and to copy or photograph any:

(a) Written or recorded statements made by a witness the defendant intends to call during the case in chief of the defendant, or copies thereof, within the possession, custody or control of the defendant, the existence of which is known, or by the exercise of due diligence may become known, to the defendant;

(b) Results or reports of physical or mental examinations, scientific tests or scientific experiments that the defendant intends to introduce in evidence during the case in chief of the defendant, or copies thereof, within the possession, custody or control of the defendant, the existence of which is known, or by the exercise of due diligence may become known, to the defendant; and

(c) Books, papers, documents or tangible objects that the defendant intends to introduce in evidence during the case in chief of the defendant, or copies thereof, within the possession, custody or control of the defendant, the existence of which is known, or by the exercise of due diligence may become known, to the defendant.

2. The prosecuting attorney is not entitled, pursuant to the provisions of this section, to the discovery or inspection of:

(a) An internal report, document or memorandum that is prepared by or on behalf of the defendant or the defendant's attorney in connection with the investigation or defense of the case.

(b) A statement, report, book, paper, document, tangible object or any other type of item or information that is privileged or protected from disclosure or inspection pursuant to the Constitution or laws of this state or the Constitution of the United States.

(Added to NRS by 1967, 1419; A 1969, 350; 1995, 265; 1997, 2368)

NRS 174.275 Protective orders. Upon a sufficient showing, the court may at any time order that discovery or inspection pursuant to NRS 174.234 to 174.295, inclusive, be denied, restricted or deferred, or make such other order as is appropriate. Upon motion by the defendant or prosecuting attorney, the court may permit the defendant or prosecuting attorney to make such showing, in whole or in part, in the form of a written statement to be inspected by the court in chambers. If the court enters an order granting relief following a showing in chambers, the entire text of the written statement must be sealed and preserved in the records of the court to be made available to the appellate court in the event of an appeal.

(Added to NRS by 1967, 1420; A 1995, 265; 1997, 2369)

NRS 174.285 Time limits.

1. A request made pursuant to NRS 174.235 or 174.245 may be made only within 30 days after arraignment or at such reasonable later time as the court may permit. A subsequent request may be made only upon a showing of cause why the request would be in the interest of justice.

2. A party shall comply with a request made pursuant to NRS 174.235 or 174.245 not less than 30 days before trial or at such reasonable later time as the court may permit.

(Added to NRS by 1967, 1420; A 1995, 265; 1997, 2369)

NRS 174.295 Continuing duty to disclose; failure to comply; sanctions.

1. If, after complying with the provisions of NRS 174.235 to 174.295, inclusive, and before or during trial, a party discovers additional material previously requested which is subject to discovery or inspection under those sections, the party shall promptly notify the other party or the other party's attorney or the court of the existence of the additional material.

2. If at any time during the course of the proceedings it is brought to the attention of the court that a party has failed to comply with the provisions of NRS 174.234 to 174.295, inclusive, the court may order the party to permit the discovery or inspection of materials not previously disclosed, grant a continuance, or prohibit the party from introducing in evidence the material not disclosed, or it may enter such other order as it deems just under the circumstances.

(Added to NRS by 1967, 1420; A 1995, 265; 1997, 2370)

SUBPOENA

NRS 174.305 Subpoena for attendance of witnesses; form; issuance. Except as provided in NRS 172.195 and 174.315:

1. A subpoena must be issued by the clerk under the seal of the court. It must state the name of the court and the title, if any, of the proceeding, and must command each person to whom it is directed to attend and give testimony at the time and place specified therein. The clerk shall issue a subpoena, signed and sealed but otherwise in blank, to a party requesting it, who shall fill in the blanks before it is served.

2. A subpoena must be issued by a justice of the peace in a proceeding before the justice of the peace under the seal of the court.

(Added to NRS by 1967, 1420; A 1967, 1367; 1987, 124)

NRS 174.315 Issuance of subpoena by prosecuting attorney or attorney for defendant; promise to appear; informing witness of general nature of grand jury's inquiry; calendaring of certain subpoenas.

1. A prosecuting attorney may issue subpoenas subscribed by the prosecuting attorney for witnesses within the State, in support of the prosecution or whom a grand jury may direct to appear before it, upon any investigation pending before the grand jury.

2. A prosecuting attorney or an attorney for a defendant may issue subpoenas subscribed by the issuer for:

(a) Witnesses within the State to appear before the court at which a preliminary hearing is to be held or an indictment, information or criminal complaint is to be tried.

(b) Witnesses already subpoenaed who are required to reappear in any Justice Court at any time the court is to reconvene in the same case within 60 days, and the time may be extended beyond 60 days upon good cause being shown for its extension.

3. Witnesses, whether within or outside of the State, may accept delivery of a subpoena in lieu of service, by a written or oral promise to appear given by the witness. Any person who accepts an oral promise to appear shall:

(a) Identify himself or herself to the witness by name and occupation;

(b) Make a written notation of the date when the oral promise to appear was given and the information given by the person making the oral promise to appear identifying the person as the witness subpoenaed; and

(c) Execute a certificate of service containing the information set forth in paragraphs (a) and (b).

4. A peace officer may accept delivery of a subpoena in lieu of service, via electronic means, by providing a written promise to appear that is transmitted electronically by any appropriate means, including, without limitation, by electronic mail transmitted through the official electronic mail system of the law enforcement agency which employs the peace officer.

5. A prosecuting attorney shall orally inform any witness subpoenaed as provided in subsection 1 of the general nature of the grand jury's inquiry before the witness testifies. Such a statement must be included in the transcript of the proceedings.

6. Any subpoena issued by an attorney for a defendant for a witness to appear before the court at which a preliminary hearing is to be held must be calendared by filing a motion that includes a notice of hearing setting the matter for hearing not less than 2 full judicial days after the date on which the motion is filed. A prosecuting attorney may oppose the motion orally in open court. A subpoena that is properly calendared pursuant to this subsection may be served on the witness unless the court quashes the subpoena.

(Added to NRS by 1967, 1368; A 1979, 130; 1985, 573; 1989, 685; 1991, 302; 1993, 118; 2013, 1202)

NRS 174.325 Production of prisoner as witness.

1. When it is necessary to have a person imprisoned in the state prison brought before any district court, or a person imprisoned in the county jail brought before a district court sitting in another county, an order for that purpose may be made by the district court or district judge, at chambers, and executed by the sheriff of the county when it is made. The order can only be made upon motion of a party upon affidavit showing the nature of the action or proceeding, the testimony expected from the witness, and its materiality.

2. When a person required as a witness before a district court is imprisoned, the judge thereof may order the sheriff to bring the prisoner before the court at the expense of the State or, in the judge's discretion, at the expense of the defendant.

(Added to NRS by 1967, 1420)

NRS 174.335 Subpoena for production of documentary evidence and of objects.

1. Except as otherwise provided in NRS 172.139, a subpoena may also command the person to whom it is directed to produce the books, papers, documents or other objects designated therein.

2. The court on motion made promptly may quash or modify the subpoena if compliance would be unreasonable or oppressive.

3. The court may direct that books, papers, documents or objects designated in the subpoena be produced before the court at a time before the trial or before the time when they are to be offered in evidence and may, upon their production, permit the books, papers, documents or objects or portions thereof to be inspected by the parties and their attorneys.

(Added to NRS by 1967, 1421; A 1985, 1030)

NRS 174.345 Service of subpoena.

1. Except as otherwise provided in NRS 174.315 and subsection 2, a subpoena may be served by a peace officer or by any other person who is not a party and who is not less than 18 years of age. Except as otherwise provided in NRS 289.027, service of a subpoena must be made by delivering a copy thereof to the person named.

2. Except as otherwise provided in NRS 174.315, a subpoena to attend a misdemeanor trial may be served by mailing the subpoena to the person to be served by registered or certified mail, return receipt requested from that person, in a sealed postpaid envelope, addressed to the person's last known address, not less than 10 days before the trial which the subpoena commands the person to attend.

3. If a subpoena is served by mail, a certificate of the mailing must be filed with the court within 2 days after the subpoena is mailed.

(Added to NRS by 1967, 1421; A 1977, 638; 1989, 685; 2007, 2816)

NRS 174.365 Place of service. A subpoena requiring the attendance of a witness at a hearing or trial may be served at any place within the State of Nevada.

(Added to NRS by 1967, 1421)

NRS 174.375 Subpoena for taking depositions; place of examination.

1. An order to take a deposition authorizes the issuance by the clerk of the court for the county in which the deposition is to be taken of subpoenas for the persons named or described therein.

2. A resident of this state may be required to attend an examination only in the county wherein the resident resides or is employed or transacts business in person. A nonresident of this state may be required to attend only in the county where the nonresident is served with a subpoena or within 40 miles from the place of service or at such other place as is fixed by the court.

(Added to NRS by 1967, 1421)

NRS 174.385 Contempt. Failure by any person without an adequate excuse to obey a subpoena of a court, a prosecuting attorney or an attorney for a defendant served upon the person or, in the case of a subpoena issued by a prosecuting attorney or an attorney for a defendant, delivered to the person and accepted, shall be deemed a contempt of the court from which the subpoena issued or, in the case of a subpoena issued by a prosecuting attorney or an attorney for a defendant, of the court in which a preliminary hearing is to be held, an investigation is pending or an indictment, information or complaint is to be tried.

(Added to NRS by 1967, 1421; A 1979, 130; 1995, 1082; 2013, 1203)

ATTENDANCE OF WITNESSES OUTSIDE STATE (UNIFORM ACT)

NRS 174.395 Short title. NRS 174.395 to 174.445, inclusive, may be cited as the Uniform Act To Secure the Attendance of Witnesses From Without a State in Criminal Proceedings.

(Added to NRS by 1967, 1421)

NRS 174.405 Definitions. As used in NRS 174.395 to 174.445, inclusive:

1. "State" shall include any territory of the United States and the District of Columbia.
2. "Summons" shall include a subpoena, order or other notice requiring the appearance of a witness.
3. "Witness" shall include a person whose testimony is desired in any proceeding or investigation by a grand jury or in a criminal action, prosecution or proceeding.

(Added to NRS by 1967, 1421)

NRS 174.415 Summoning witness in this State to testify in another state.

1. If a judge of a court of record in any state which by its laws has made provision for commanding persons within that state to attend and testify in this State certifies under the seal of such court that there is a criminal prosecution pending in such court, or that a grand jury investigation has commenced or is about to commence, that a person being within this State is a material witness in such prosecution, or grand jury investigation, and that the person's presence will be required for a specified number of days, upon presentation of such certificate to any judge of a court of record in the county in which such person is, such judge shall fix a time and place for a hearing, and shall make an order directing the witness to appear at a time and place certain for the hearing.

2. If at a hearing the judge determines that the witness is material and necessary, that it will not cause undue hardship to the witness to be compelled to attend and testify in the prosecution or a grand jury investigation in the other state, and that the laws of the state in which the prosecution is pending, or grand jury investigation has commenced or is about to commence (and of any other state through which the witness may be required to pass by ordinary course of travel), will give the witness protection from arrest and the service of civil and criminal process, the judge shall issue a summons, with a copy of the certificate attached, directing the witness to attend and testify in the court where the prosecution is pending, or where a grand jury investigation has commenced or is about to commence at a time and place specified in the summons. In any such hearing the certificate shall be prima facie evidence of all the facts stated therein.

3. If the certificate recommends that the witness be taken into immediate custody and delivered to an officer of the requesting state to assure the witness's attendance in the requesting state, such judge may, in lieu of notification of the hearing, direct that such witness be forthwith brought before the judge for hearings; and the judge at the hearing being satisfied of the desirability of such custody and delivery, for which determination the certificate shall be prima facie proof of such desirability, may, in lieu of issuing subpoena or summons, order that the witness be forthwith taken into custody and delivered to an officer of the requesting state.

4. If the witness, who is summoned as above provided, after being paid or tendered by some properly authorized person the amount required by NRS 50.225 for subsistence and travel expenses, fails without good cause to attend and testify as directed in the summons, the witness shall be punished in the manner provided for the punishment of any witness who disobeys a summons issued from a court of record in this State.

(Added to NRS by 1967, 1421; A 1987, 550)

NRS 174.425 Witness from another state summoned to testify in this State.

1. If a person in any state, which by its laws has made provision for commanding persons within its borders to attend and testify in criminal prosecutions, or grand jury investigations commenced or about to commence, in this State, is a material witness in a prosecution pending in a court of record in this State, or in a grand jury investigation which has commenced or is about to commence, a judge of such a court may issue a certificate under the seal of the court stating these facts and specifying the number of days the witness will be required. The certificate may include a recommendation that the witness be taken into immediate custody and delivered to an officer of this State to ensure the witness's attendance in this State. This certificate must be presented to a judge of a court of record in the county in which the witness is found.

2. If the witness is summoned to attend and testify in this State the witness is entitled to receive the amount required by NRS 50.225 for subsistence and travel expenses. A witness who has appeared in accordance with the provisions of the summons shall not be required to remain within this State a longer period of time than the period mentioned in the certificate unless otherwise ordered by the court. If such witness, after coming into this State, fails without good cause to attend and testify as directed in the summons, the witness shall be punished in the manner provided for the punishment of any witness who disobeys a summons issued from a court of record in this State.

(Added to NRS by 1967, 1422; A 1987, 551)

NRS 174.435 Exemption from arrest and service of process.

1. If a person comes into this state in obedience to a summons directing the person to attend and testify in this state the person shall not while in this state pursuant to such summons be subject to arrest or the service of process, civil or criminal, in connection with matters which arose before the person's entrance into this state under the summons.

2. If a person passes through this state while going to another state in obedience to a summons to attend and testify in that state or while returning therefrom, the person shall not while so passing through this state be subject to arrest or the service of process, civil or criminal, in connection with matters which arose before the person's entrance into this state under the summons.

(Added to NRS by 1967, 1423)

NRS 174.445 Uniformity of interpretation. NRS 174.395 to 174.445, inclusive, shall be so interpreted and construed as to effectuate their general purpose to make uniform the law of the states which enact them.

(Added to NRS by 1967, 1423)

REMOVAL OF ACTION BEFORE TRIAL

NRS 174.455 Ground for removal; application not to be granted until after voir dire examination; appeal of order changing or refusing to change place of trial.

1. A criminal action prosecuted by indictment, information or complaint may be removed from the court in which it is pending, on application of the defendant or state, on the ground that a fair and impartial trial cannot be had in the county where the indictment, information or complaint is pending.

2. An application for removal of a criminal action shall not be granted by the court until after the voir dire examination has been conducted and it is apparent to the court that the selection of a fair and impartial jury cannot be had in the county where the indictment, information or complaint is pending.

3. An order in a criminal action changing or refusing to change the place of trial is appealable only on appeal from the final judgment.

(Added to NRS by 1967, 1423; A 1969, 378; 1981, 1707)

NRS 174.464 Application for removal: Making and service; hearing and determination in absence of defendant.

1. The application for removal must be made in open court, and in writing, verified by the affidavit of the defendant or district attorney, and a copy of the affidavit must be served on the adverse party, at least 1 day prior to the hearing of the application.

2. The application may be supported or opposed by other affidavits or other evidence, or other witnesses may be examined in open court.

3. Whenever the affidavit of the defendant shows that the defendant cannot safely appear in person to make such application, because popular prejudice is so great as to endanger the defendant's personal safety, and such statement is sustained by other testimony, such application may be made by the defendant's attorney and must be heard and determined in the absence of the defendant, notwithstanding the charge then pending against the defendant be a felony, and the defendant has not, at the time of such application, been arrested or given bail, or been arraigned, or pleaded to the indictment or information.

(Added to NRS by 1967, 1423)

NRS 174.475 Order transferring action: When to be made. If the court is satisfied that the representations of the applicant are true, an order must be made transferring the action to the district court of some convenient county free from a like objection.

(Added to NRS by 1967, 1423)

NRS 174.485 Entry of order of removal; transmittal of papers. The order of removal must be entered on the minutes, and the clerk must immediately make out and transmit to the court to which the action is removed a certified copy of the order of removal, record, pleadings, and proceedings in the action, including the undertakings for the appearance of the defendant and of the witnesses.

(Added to NRS by 1967, 1423)

NRS 174.495 Proceedings on removal when defendant is in custody. If the defendant is in custody, the order must direct the defendant's removal and the defendant must be forthwith removed by the sheriff of the county where the defendant is imprisoned, to the custody of the sheriff of the county to which the action is removed.

(Added to NRS by 1967, 1423)

NRS 174.505 Authority of court to which action is removed; transmission of original papers. The court to which the action is removed must proceed to trial and judgment therein as if the action had been commenced in such court. If it is necessary to have any of the original pleadings or other papers before such court, the court from which the action is removed must, at any time, on the application of the district attorney or the defendant, order such papers or pleadings to be transmitted by the clerk, a certified copy thereof being retained.

(Added to NRS by 1967, 1424)

TIME OF TRIAL

NRS 174.511 Right of State to trial within 60 days after arraignment; exceptions. The State, upon demand, has the right to a trial of the defendant within 60 days after arraignment. The court may postpone the trial if:

1. It finds that more time is needed by the defendant to prepare a defense; or
2. The number of other cases pending in the court prohibits the acceptance of the case for trial within that time.

(Added to NRS by 1983, 1670)

NRS 174.515 Postponement: When and how ordered; court may require depositions of and undertakings by witnesses; court may consider adverse effect upon child who is victim or witness.

1. When an action is called for trial, or at any time previous thereto, the court may, upon sufficient cause shown by either party by affidavit, direct the trial to be postponed to another day. In all cases where a continuance is granted upon the application of either party the court may require, as a condition of granting such continuance, that the party applying therefor consent to taking, forthwith, or at any time to be fixed by the court, of the deposition of any witness summoned by the opposite party whose deposition has not previously been taken.
2. The court also may require all witnesses to enter into undertakings in such sum as the court may order, with or without sureties, to appear and testify on the day to which the case may be continued, but any witness who is unable to procure sureties for the witness's attendance may be discharged on the witness's own recognizance, upon giving a deposition in the manner prescribed in NRS 174.175 and 174.205.
3. If the trial involves acts committed against a child less than 16 years of age or involving acts witnessed by a child less than 16 years of age, the court may consider any adverse effect a continuance or other postponement might have upon the mental or emotional health or well-being of the child. The court may deny a continuance or other postponement if the delay will adversely affect the mental or emotional health or well-being of the child.

(Added to NRS by 1967, 1424; A 1989, 588; 1995, 400)

NRS 174.519 Request for preference in setting date for trial where child is victim or witness; court may consider effect on child of delay in commencement of trial. If the trial involves acts committed against a child less than 16 years of age or involving acts witnessed by a child less than 16 years of age, the prosecuting attorney shall request the court, in its discretion, to give preference in setting a date for the trial of the defendant. In making a ruling, the court may consider the effect a delay in the commencement of the trial might have on the mental or emotional health or well-being of the child.

(Added to NRS by 1995, 400; A 1997, 511)

CHAPTER 175 - TRIAL

TRIAL BY JURY OR COURT

CONDUCT OF TRIAL

CONDUCT OF JURY

VERDICT

ACQUITTAL

HEARING TO DETERMINE WHETHER SEXUALLY MOTIVATED OFFENSE

PENALTY HEARING FOR FIRST DEGREE MURDER

TRIAL BY JURY OR COURT

NRS 175.011 Trial by jury.

1. In a district court, cases required to be tried by jury must be so tried unless the defendant waives a jury trial in writing with the approval of the court and the consent of the State. A defendant who pleads not guilty to the charge of a capital offense must be tried by jury.

2. In a Justice Court, a case must be tried by jury only if the defendant so demands in writing not less than 30 days before trial. Except as otherwise provided in NRS 4.390 and 4.400, if a case is tried by jury, a reporter must be present who is a certified court reporter and shall report the trial.

(Added to NRS by 1967, 1424; A 1983, 749; 1987, 614; 1993, 1412)

NRS 175.021 Formation of jury; number of jurors.

1. Trial juries for criminal actions are formed in the same manner as trial juries in civil actions.

2. Except as provided in subsection 3, juries must consist of 12 jurors, but at any time before verdict, the parties may stipulate in writing with the approval of the court that the jury consist of any number less than 12 but not less than six.

3. Juries must consist of six jurors for the trial of a criminal action in a Justice Court.

(Added to NRS by 1967, 1424; A 1983, 749)

NRS 175.031 Examination of trial jurors. The court shall conduct the initial examination of prospective jurors, and defendant or the defendant's attorney and the district attorney are entitled to supplement the examination by such further inquiry as the court deems proper. Any supplemental examination must not be unreasonably restricted.

(Added to NRS by 1967, 1424; A 1971, 246; 1979, 213)

NRS 175.036 Challenges for cause for individual jurors: Grounds; trial of challenge.

1. Either side may challenge an individual juror for disqualification or for any cause or favor which would prevent the juror from adjudicating the facts fairly.

2. Challenges for cause shall be tried by the court. The juror challenged and any other person may be examined as a witness on the trial of the challenge.

(Added to NRS by 1968, 45)

NRS 175.041 Limitation of defendants' right to sever in challenges. When several defendants are tried together, they cannot sever their peremptory challenges, but must join therein.

(Added to NRS by 1967, 1425)

NRS 175.051 Number of peremptory challenges.

1. If the offense charged is punishable by death or by imprisonment for life, each side is entitled to eight peremptory challenges.

2. If the offense charged is punishable by imprisonment for any other term or by fine or by both fine and imprisonment, each side is entitled to four peremptory challenges.

3. The State and the defendant shall exercise their challenges alternately, in that order. Any challenge not exercised in its proper order is waived.

(Added to NRS by 1967, 1425)

NRS 175.061 Alternate jurors.

1. The court may direct that not more than six jurors in addition to the regular jury be called and impaneled to sit as alternate jurors.

2. Alternate jurors, in the order in which they were called, shall replace jurors who become unable or disqualified to perform their duties.

3. Alternate jurors shall:

(a) Be drawn in the same manner;
(b) Have the same qualifications;
(c) Be subject to the same examination and challenges;

(d) Take the same oath; and
(e) Have the same functions, powers, facilities and privileges, as the regular jurors.
4. If an alternate juror is required to replace a regular juror after the jury has retired to consider its verdict, the judge shall recall the jury, seat the alternate and resubmit the case to the jury.
5. Each side is entitled to one peremptory challenge in addition to those otherwise allowed by law if one or two alternate jurors are to be impaneled, two peremptory challenges if three or four alternate jurors are to be impaneled, and three peremptory challenges if five or six alternate jurors are to be impaneled. The additional peremptory challenges may be used against an alternate juror only, and the other peremptory challenges allowed by statute may not be used against an alternate juror.
(Added to NRS by 1967, 1425; A 2005, 306)

NRS 175.071 Discharge of juror where juror dies or unable to perform duty. If, before the conclusion of the trial, and there being no alternate juror called or available, a juror dies, or becomes disqualified or unable to perform the juror's duty, the court may duly order the juror to be discharged and a new juror may be sworn and the trial begun anew, or the jury may be discharged and a new jury then or afterward impaneled.
(Added to NRS by 1967, 1425)

NRS 175.081 Discharge of jury after retirement upon accident or cause. If, after the retirement of the jury, any accident or cause occurs to prevent their being kept for deliberation, the jury may be discharged.
(Added to NRS by 1967, 1425)

NRS 175.091 Disability of judge during trial. If by reason of death, sickness or other disability the judge before whom a jury trial has commenced is unable to proceed with the trial, any other judge regularly sitting in or assigned to the court, upon certifying that the judge has familiarized himself or herself with the record of the trial, may proceed with and finish the trial.
(Added to NRS by 1967, 1425)

NRS 175.101 Disability of judge after verdict or finding of guilty or guilty but mentally ill. If by reason of absence from the judicial district, death, sickness or other disability the judge before whom the defendant has been tried is unable to perform the duties to be performed by the court after a verdict or finding of guilty or guilty but mentally ill, any other judge regularly sitting in or assigned to the court may perform those duties, but if such other judge is satisfied that he or she cannot perform those duties because he or she did not preside at the trial or for any other reason, the judge may in his or her discretion grant a new trial.
(Added to NRS by 1967, 1425; A 2007, 1410)

CONDUCT OF TRIAL

NRS 175.111 Oath of jurors. When the jury has been impaneled, the court shall administer the following oath:

> Do you and each of you solemnly swear that you will well and truly try this case, now pending before this court, and a true verdict render according to the evidence given, so help you God.

(Added to NRS by 1967, 1426)

NRS 175.121 Personal knowledge of jurors.
1. The judge shall then admonish the jury that:
(a) No juror may declare to any fellow jurors any fact relating to the case as of the juror's own knowledge; and
(b) If any juror discovers during the trial or after the jury has retired that he or she or any other juror has personal knowledge of any fact in controversy in the case, the juror shall disclose such situation to the judge out of the presence of the other jurors.
2. When any such disclosure is made, the judge shall examine the juror who admits or is alleged to have personal knowledge, under oath, in the presence of counsel for the parties, and may allow such counsel to examine the juror.
3. If the juror has disclosed the juror's own knowledge to the judge and it appears that the juror has not declared any fact relating to the case to any fellow jurors as of the juror's own knowledge, the judge shall after the examination decide whether the juror shall remain or shall be replaced by an alternate juror.
4. If it appears that the juror has declared any fact relating to the case to any fellow jurors as of the juror's own knowledge, or that the juror's vote was influenced by such knowledge undisclosed, the judge shall declare a mistrial.
(Added to NRS by 1967, 1426)

NRS 175.131 Judge to inform jury of right to take notes. Before any evidence has been introduced the judge may inform the jury they may individually take notes during the trial, but the judge shall further caution them not to rely upon their respective notes in case of conflict among them, because the reporter's notes contain the complete and authentic record of the trial.
(Added to NRS by 1967, 1426)

NRS 175.141 Order of trial. The jury having been impaneled and sworn, the trial shall proceed in the following order:
1. If the indictment or information be for a felony, the clerk must read it and state the plea of the defendant to the jury. In all other cases this formality may be dispensed with.

2. The district attorney, or other counsel for the State, must open the cause. The defendant or the defendant's counsel may then either make the defendant's opening statement or reserve it to be made immediately prior to the presentation of evidence in the defendant's behalf.

3. The State must then offer its evidence in support of the charge, and the defendant may then offer evidence in his or her defense.

4. The parties may then respectively offer rebutting testimony only, unless the court, for good reasons, in furtherance of justice, permit them to offer evidence upon their original cause.

5. When the evidence is concluded, unless the case is submitted to the jury on either side, or on both sides, without argument, the district attorney, or other counsel for the State, must open and must conclude the argument.

(Added to NRS by 1967, 1426)

NRS 175.151 Number of counsel who may argue case. If the indictment or information be for an offense punishable with death, two counsel on each side may argue the case to the jury, but in such case, as well as in all others, the counsel for the State must open and conclude the argument. If it be for any other offense, the court may, in its discretion, restrict the argument to one counsel on each side.

(Added to NRS by 1967, 1426)

NRS 175.161 Instructions.

1. Upon the close of the argument, the judge shall charge the jury. The judge may state the testimony and declare the law, but may not charge the jury in respect to matters of fact. The charge must be reduced to writing before it is given; and no charge or instructions may be given to the jury otherwise than in writing, unless by the mutual consent of the parties. If either party requests it, the court must settle and give the instructions to the jury before the argument begins, but this does not prevent the giving of further instructions which may become necessary by reason of the argument.

2. In charging the jury, the judge shall state to them all such matters of law the judge thinks necessary for their information in giving their verdict.

3. Either party may present to the court any written charge, and request that it be given. If the court thinks it correct and pertinent, it must be given; if not, it must be refused.

4. An original and one copy of each instruction requested by any party must be tendered to the court. The copies must be numbered and indicate who tendered them. Copies of instructions given on the court's own motion or modified by the court must be so identified. When requested instructions are refused, the judge shall write on the margin of the original the word "refused" and initial or sign the notation. The instructions given to the jury must be firmly bound together and the judge shall write the word "given" at the conclusion thereof and sign the last of the instructions to signify that all have been given. After the instructions are given, the judge may not clarify, modify or in any manner explain them to the jury except in writing unless the parties agree to oral instructions.

5. After the jury has reached a verdict and been discharged, the originals of all instructions, whether given, modified or refused, must be preserved by the clerk as part of the proceedings.

6. Conferences with counsel to settle instructions must be held out of the presence of the jury and may be held in chambers at the option of the court.

7. When the offense charged carries a possible penalty of life without possibility of parole a charge to the jury that such penalty does not exclude executive clemency is a correct and pertinent charge, and must be given upon the request of either party.

(Added to NRS by 1967, 1427; A 1969, 401; 1981, 410)

NRS 175.171 No special instructions to be given relating exclusively to defendant's testimony. In the trial of all indictments, complaints and other proceedings against persons charged with the commission of crimes or offenses, the person so charged shall, at the person's own request, but not otherwise, be deemed a competent witness, the credit to be given the person's testimony being left solely to the jury, under the instructions of the court, but no special instruction shall be given relating exclusively to the testimony of the defendant.

(Added to NRS by 1967, 1427)

NRS 175.181 Instruction not to be given relative to failure of defendant to testify.

1. No instruction shall be given relative to the failure of the person charged with the commission of crime or offense to testify, except, upon the request of the person so charged, the court shall instruct the jury that, in accordance with a right guaranteed by the Constitution, no person can be compelled, in a criminal action, to be a witness against himself or herself.

2. Nothing herein contained shall be construed as compelling any such person to testify.

(Added to NRS by 1967, 1427)

NRS 175.186 Instructions in prosecution for sexual assault or statutory sexual seduction: Use of certain terms and instructions prohibited.

1. In any prosecution for sexual assault or statutory sexual seduction or for an attempt to commit or conspiracy to commit either crime, the term "unchaste character" may not be used with reference to the alleged victim of the crime in any instruction to the jury.

2. In a prosecution for sexual assault or statutory sexual seduction, the court may not give any instructions to the jury to the effect that it is difficult to prove or establish the crime beyond a reasonable doubt.

(Added to NRS by 1975, 1132; A 1977, 1630; 1991, 126)

NRS 175.191 Presumption of innocence: Acquittal in case of reasonable doubt. A defendant in a criminal action is presumed to be innocent until the contrary is proved; and in case of a reasonable doubt whether the defendant's guilt is satisfactorily shown, the defendant is entitled to be acquitted.

(Added to NRS by 1967, 1427)

NRS 175.201 Presumption of innocence: Conviction of lowest degree of offense. Every person charged with the commission of a crime shall be presumed innocent until the contrary is proved by competent evidence beyond a reasonable doubt; and when an offense has been proved against the person, and there exists a reasonable doubt as to which of two or more degrees the person is guilty, the person shall be convicted only of the lowest.

(Added to NRS by 1967, 1427)

NRS 175.211 Definition of reasonable doubt; no other definition to be given to juries.

1. A reasonable doubt is one based on reason. It is not mere possible doubt, but is such a doubt as would govern or control a person in the more weighty affairs of life. If the minds of the jurors, after the entire comparison and consideration of all the evidence, are in such a condition that they can say they feel an abiding conviction of the truth of the charge, there is not a reasonable doubt. Doubt to be reasonable must be actual, not mere possibility or speculation.

2. No other definition of reasonable doubt may be given by the court to juries in criminal actions in this State.

(Added to NRS by 1967, 1427; A 1991, 257)

NRS 175.221 Evidence.

1. In all trials the testimony of witnesses shall be taken orally in open court, unless otherwise provided by statute.

2. The admissibility of evidence and the competency and privileges of witnesses shall be governed by:

(a) The general provisions of title 4 of NRS;

(b) The specific provisions of any other applicable statute; and

(c) Where no statute applies, the principles of the common law as they may be interpreted by the courts of the State of Nevada in the light of reason and experience.

(Added to NRS by 1967, 1428; A 1971, 803)

NRS 175.241 Proof of corporate existence generally. If, upon a trial or proceeding in a criminal case, the existence, constitution or powers of any corporation shall become material, or be in any way drawn in question, it is not necessary to produce a certified copy of the articles or acts of incorporation, but the same may be proved by general reputation, or by the printed statutes of the state, or government, or country by which such corporation was created.

(Added to NRS by 1967, 1428)

NRS 175.251 Conspiracy: Allegation and proof of overt act; evidence of overt acts not alleged. Upon a trial for conspiracy, in a case where an overt act shall be necessary to constitute the offense, the defendant shall not be convicted unless one or more overt acts shall be expressly alleged in the indictment or information, nor unless one of the acts alleged shall have been proved; but other overt acts not alleged may be given in evidence.

(Added to NRS by 1967, 1428)

NRS 175.261 False pretenses: What evidence necessary. Upon a trial for having, with an intent to cheat or defraud another designedly, by any false pretense, obtained the signature of any person, to a written instrument, or having obtained from any person any money, personal property, or valuable thing, the defendant shall not be convicted if the false pretense shall have been expressed in language, unaccompanied by a false token or writing, unless the pretense or some note or memorandum thereof be in writing, subscribed by or in the handwriting of the defendant, or unless the pretense be proved by the testimony of two witnesses, or that of one witness and corroborating circumstances; but this section shall not apply to a prosecution for falsely representing or personating another, and, in such assumed character, marrying, or receiving any money or property.

(Added to NRS by 1967, 1428)

NRS 175.271 Expert witnesses.

1. The court may order the defendant or the State or both to show cause why expert witnesses should not be appointed, and may request the parties to submit nominations.

2. The court may appoint any expert witnesses agreed upon by the parties, and may appoint witnesses of its own selection. An expert witness shall not be appointed by the court unless the witness consents to act.

3. A witness so appointed shall be informed of the witness's duties by the court in writing, a copy of which shall be filed with the clerk, or at a conference in which the parties shall have the opportunity to participate.

4. A witness so appointed shall advise the parties of the witness's findings, if any, and may thereafter be called to testify by the court or by any party. The witness shall be subject to cross-examination by each party.

5. The court may determine the reasonable compensation of such a witness and direct its payment out of such funds as may be provided by law.

6. The parties also may call expert witnesses of their own selection.

7. An expert witness, whether appointed by the court or called by a party, may in the discretion of the judge be excluded from the courtroom during the testimony of other witnesses.

(Added to NRS by 1967, 1428)

NRS 175.282 Plea bargain: Inspection by jury; instruction of jury; cross-examination of defendant. If a prosecuting attorney enters into an agreement with a defendant in which the defendant agrees to testify against another defendant in exchange for a plea of guilty, guilty but mentally ill or nolo contendere to a lesser charge or for a recommendation of a reduced sentence, the court shall:

1. After excising any portion it deems irrelevant or prejudicial, permit the jury to inspect the agreement;

2. If the defendant who is testifying has not entered a plea or been sentenced pursuant to the agreement, instruct the jury regarding the possible related pressures on the defendant by providing the jury with an appropriate cautionary instruction; and

3. Allow the defense counsel to cross-examine fully the defendant who is testifying concerning the agreement.

(Added to NRS by 1991, 291; A 1995, 2451; 2003, 1460; 2007, 1410)

NRS 175.291 Testimony of accomplice must be corroborated; sufficiency of corroboration; accomplice defined.

1. A conviction shall not be had on the testimony of an accomplice unless the accomplice is corroborated by other evidence which in itself, and without the aid of the testimony of the accomplice, tends to connect the defendant with the commission of the offense; and the corroboration shall not be sufficient if it merely shows the commission of the offense or the circumstances thereof.

2. An accomplice is hereby defined as one who is liable to prosecution, for the identical offense charged against the defendant on trial in the cause in which the testimony of the accomplice is given.

(Added to NRS by 1967, 1429)

NRS 175.301 Testimony of person upon or with whom abortion was allegedly committed. Upon a trial for procuring or attempting to procure an abortion, or aiding or assisting therein, the defendant must not be convicted upon the testimony of the person upon or with whom the offense has allegedly been committed, unless:

1. The testimony of that person is corroborated by other evidence; or

2. The person giving the testimony is, and was at the time the crime is alleged to have taken place, a police officer or deputy sheriff who was performing his or her duties as such.

(Added to NRS by 1967, 1429; A 1979, 302; 1981, 1029; 2005, 308)

NRS 175.311 Procedure when higher offense is shown by evidence. If it appears by the testimony that the facts proved constitute an offense of a higher nature than that charged in the indictment or information, the court may direct the jury to be discharged, and all proceedings on the indictment or information to be suspended, and may order the defendant to be committed, or continued on, or admitted to bail, to answer any new indictment or information which may be found or filed against the defendant for the higher offense.

(Added to NRS by 1967, 1429)

NRS 175.321 Procedure if higher offense ignored. If an indictment for the higher offense be dismissed by the grand jury, or be not found at its next session, or if an information be not filed before the next session of the grand jury, the court shall again proceed to try the defendant on the original indictment or information.

(Added to NRS by 1967, 1429)

NRS 175.331 When defendant on bail appears for trial defendant may be committed and held. When a defendant who has given bail appears for trial, the court may, in its discretion, at any time after the defendant's appearance for trial, order the defendant to be committed to the custody of the proper officer, to abide the judgment or further order of the court, and the defendant must be committed and held in custody accordingly.

(Added to NRS by 1967, 1429)

NRS 175.341 Mistake in charging proper offense: Defendant not discharged; commitment or bail. When it appears, at any time before verdict or judgment, that a mistake has been made in charging the proper offense, the defendant must not be discharged, if there appears good cause to detain the defendant in custody; but the court must commit the defendant, or require the defendant to give bail for his or her appearance to answer to the offense; and may also require the witnesses to give bail for their appearance.

(Added to NRS by 1967, 1429)

NRS 175.351 Discharge of defendant when jury discharged for want of jurisdiction. If the jury is discharged because the court has not jurisdiction of the offense charged, and it appears that it was committed out of the jurisdiction of this state, the defendant must be discharged, unless the court orders that the defendant be detained for a reasonable time, to be specified in the order, to enable the district attorney to communicate with the chief executive officer of the country, state, territory or district where the offense was committed.

(Added to NRS by 1967, 1429)

NRS 175.361 Offense committed in other county: Commitment to await warrant; admission to bail; transmittal of papers to district attorney of proper county; expense of transmission. If the offense was committed within the jurisdiction of another county of this state, the court may direct the defendant to be committed for such time as it deems reasonable, to await a warrant from the proper county for the defendant's arrest, or it may admit the defendant to bail in an undertaking, with sufficient sureties that the defendant will, within such time as the court may appoint, render himself or herself amenable to a warrant for arrest from the proper county; and, if not sooner arrested thereon, will attend at the office of the sheriff of the county where the trial was had, at a certain time particularly specified in the undertaking, to surrender himself or herself upon the warrant, if issued, or that the defendant's bail will forfeit such sum as the court may fix, to be mentioned in the undertaking; and the clerk must forthwith transmit a certified copy of the indictment or information, and of all the papers filed in the action, to the district attorney of the proper county, the expenses of which transmission are chargeable to that county.

(Added to NRS by 1967, 1430)

NRS 175.371 Discharge where defendant not arrested on warrant from other county; proceedings in case of arrest.

1. If the defendant is not arrested on a warrant from the proper county, as provided in NRS 175.361, the defendant must be discharged from custody, or the defendant's bail in the action is exonerated, or money deposited instead of bail must be refunded, as the case may be, and the sureties in the undertaking, as mentioned in that section, must be discharged.

2. If the defendant is arrested, the same proceedings must be had thereon as upon the arrest of a defendant in another county on a warrant issued by a magistrate.

(Added to NRS by 1967, 1430)

NRS 175.381 Court may advise jury to acquit defendant when evidence on either side closed; motion for judgment of acquittal after verdict of guilty or guilty but mentally ill; subsequent motion for new trial.

1. If, at any time after the evidence on either side is closed, the court deems the evidence insufficient to warrant a conviction, it may advise the jury to acquit the defendant, but the jury is not bound by such advice.

2. The court may, on a motion of a defendant or on its own motion, which is made after the jury returns a verdict of guilty or guilty but mentally ill, set aside the verdict and enter a judgment of acquittal if the evidence is insufficient to sustain a conviction. The motion for a judgment of acquittal must be made within 7 days after the jury is discharged or within such further time as the court may fix during that period.

3. If a motion for a judgment of acquittal after a verdict of guilty or guilty but mentally ill pursuant to this section is granted, the court shall also determine whether any motion for a new trial should be granted if the judgment of acquittal is thereafter vacated or reversed. The court shall specify the grounds for that determination. If the motion for a new trial is granted conditionally, the order thereon does not affect the finality of the judgment. If the motion for a new trial is granted conditionally and the judgment is reversed on appeal, the new trial must proceed unless the appellate court has otherwise ordered. If the motion is denied conditionally, the defendant on appeal may assert error in that denial, and if the judgment is reversed on appeal, subsequent proceedings must be in accordance with the order of the appellate court.

(Added to NRS by 1967, 1430; A 1991, 651; 2007, 1410)

NRS 175.383 Withdrawal, discharge or change of defense counsel; limitations. If a counsel seeks to withdraw from the case or is discharged by the defendant for the purpose of delaying the trial, the court shall not allow the counsel to be changed. The counsel for a defendant may not be changed after a trial has commenced except upon good cause shown to the court.

(Added to NRS by 1971, 596)

NRS 175.387 Misconduct of defendant; sanctions.

1. Whenever a defendant interferes with the orderly course of a trial by disruptive, disorderly or disrespectful conduct, the court may:

(a) Order the defendant bound and gagged.

(b) Cite the defendant for contempt.

(c) Order the defendant removed from the courtroom and proceed with the trial.

2. No such order or citation shall issue except after the defendant has been fully and fairly informed that the defendant's conduct is wrong and intolerable and has been warned of the consequences of continued misconduct.

3. A defendant who has been removed from the courtroom may be returned upon the defendant's promise to discontinue such misconduct. If the defendant's misconduct continues after the defendant's return the court may proceed as provided in subsection 1.

(Added to NRS by 1971, 847)

CONDUCT OF JURY

NRS 175.391 Separation or custody of jury before submission. The jurors sworn to try a criminal action may, at any time before the submission of the case to the jury, in the discretion of the court, be permitted to separate, depart for home overnight or be kept in charge of a proper officer. Upon commencing deliberation, the jurors shall be kept in charge of a proper officer, unless at the discretion of the court they are permitted to depart for home overnight. When the jurors are kept together, the officer in charge shall keep the jurors in some private and convenient place and separate from other persons. The officer shall not permit any communication to be made to them, or make any personally, unless by order of the court, except to ask them if they have agreed upon their verdict. The officer shall not, before the verdict is rendered, communicate to any person the state of their deliberations or the verdict agreed upon. The officer shall return them into court when they have reached their verdict or when ordered by the court.

(Added to NRS by 1967, 1430; A 1977, 882)

NRS 175.401 Jury to be admonished at each adjournment. At each adjournment of the court, whether the jurors are permitted to separate or depart for home overnight, or are kept in charge of officers, they must be admonished by the judge or another officer of the court that it is their duty not to:

1. Converse among themselves or with anyone else on any subject connected with the trial;

2. Read, watch or listen to any report of or commentary on the trial or any person connected with the trial by any medium of information, including without limitation newspapers, television and radio; or

3. If they have not been charged, form or express any opinion on any subject connected with the trial until the cause is finally submitted to them.

(Added to NRS by 1967, 1430; A 1977, 883; 1981, 318)

NRS 175.421 Accommodations for jury upon retirement; power of court to furnish. A room shall be provided by the sheriff of each county for the use of the jury upon their retirement for deliberation, with suitable furniture, fuel, lights and stationery, unless such necessaries have been already furnished by the county. The court may order the sheriff to do so, and the expenses incurred by the sheriff in carrying the order into effect, when certified by the court, shall be a county charge.

(Added to NRS by 1967, 1431)

NRS 175.431 Jury provided food and lodging when kept together. While the jury are kept together, either during the progress of the trial or after their retirement for deliberation, they shall be provided, at the expense of the county, with suitable and sufficient food and lodging.

(Added to NRS by 1967, 1431)

NRS 175.441 Jury may take written instructions, materials received in evidence, certain papers and own notes of trial on retiring for deliberation. Upon retiring for deliberation, the jury may take with them:

1. All papers and all other items and materials which have been received as evidence in the case, except depositions or copies of such public records or private documents given in evidence as ought not, in the opinion of the court, to be taken from the person having them in possession.
2. The written instructions given, and notes of the testimony or other proceedings on the trial, taken by themselves or any of them, but none taken by any other person.

(Added to NRS by 1967, 1431)

NRS 175.451 Return of jury for information. After the jury have retired for deliberation, if there is any disagreement between them as to any part of the testimony, or if they desire to be informed on any point of law arising in the cause, they must require the officer to conduct them into court. Upon their being brought into court, the information required shall be given in the presence of, or after notice to, the district attorney and the defendant or the defendant's counsel.

(Added to NRS by 1967, 1431)

NRS 175.461 Jury not to be discharged after cause submitted; exceptions. Except as provided in NRS 175.081, the jury shall not be discharged after the cause is submitted to them, until they have agreed upon their verdict and rendered it in open court, unless by the consent of both parties, entered upon the minutes, or unless, at the expiration of such time as the court may deem proper, it satisfactorily appears that there is no reasonable probability that the jury can agree.

(Added to NRS by 1967, 1431)

NRS 175.471 Adjournment of court during absence of jury. While the jury are absent, the court may adjourn from time to time, as to other business, but it shall nevertheless be deemed to be open for every purpose connected with the cause submitted to the jury, until a verdict be rendered or the jury discharged.

(Added to NRS by 1967, 1431)

VERDICT

NRS 175.481 Return. The verdict shall be unanimous. It shall be returned by the jury to the judge in open court.

(Added to NRS by 1967, 1431)

NRS 175.491 Verdict where there are several defendants. If there are two or more defendants, the jury at any time during its deliberations may return a verdict or verdicts with respect to a defendant or defendants as to whom it has agreed; if the jury cannot agree with respect to all, the defendant or defendants as to whom it does not agree may be tried again.

(Added to NRS by 1967, 1431)

NRS 175.501 Jury may convict of lesser included offense or attempt. The defendant may be found guilty or guilty but mentally ill of an offense necessarily included in the offense charged or of an attempt to commit either the offense charged or an offense necessarily included therein if the attempt is an offense.

(Added to NRS by 1967, 1431; A 2007, 1411)

NRS 175.511 When offenses to be stated separately. When the defendant may be convicted of more than one offense charged, each offense of which the defendant is convicted must be stated in the verdict or the finding of the court.

(Added to NRS by 1967, 1431)

NRS 175.531 Polling jury; further deliberation or discharge. When a verdict is returned and before it is recorded the jury shall be polled at the request of any party or upon the court's own motion. If upon the poll there is not unanimous concurrence, the jury may be directed to retire for further deliberation or may be discharged.

(Added to NRS by 1967, 1432)

NRS 175.533 Finding of guilty but mentally ill upon plea of not guilty by reason of insanity; required findings; effect of finding.

1. During a trial, upon a plea of not guilty by reason of insanity, the trier of fact may find the defendant guilty but mentally ill if the trier of fact finds all of the following:

(a) The defendant is guilty beyond a reasonable doubt of an offense;

(b) The defendant has established by a preponderance of the evidence that due to a disease or defect of the mind, the defendant was mentally ill at the time of the commission of the offense; and

(c) The defendant has not established by a preponderance of the evidence that the defendant is not guilty by reason of insanity pursuant to subsection 5 of NRS 174.035.

2. Except as otherwise provided by specific statute, a defendant who is found guilty but mentally ill is subject to the same criminal, civil and administrative penalties and procedures as a defendant who is found guilty.

3. If the trier of fact finds a defendant guilty but mentally ill pursuant to subsection 1, the court shall cause, within 5 business days after the finding, on a form prescribed by the Department of Public Safety, a record of the finding to be transmitted to the Central Repository for Nevada Records of Criminal History, along with a statement indicating that the record is being transmitted for inclusion in each appropriate database of the National Instant Criminal Background Check System.

4. As used in this section:

(a) "Disease or defect of the mind" does not include a disease or defect which is caused solely by voluntary intoxication.

(b) "National Instant Criminal Background Check System" has the meaning ascribed to it in NRS 179A.062.

(Added to NRS by 2007, 1410; A 2009, 2485; 2015, 1796)

ACQUITTAL

NRS 175.539 Acquittal by reason of insanity: Defendant to be examined; hearing to be held to determine whether defendant is mentally ill; procedure for committing defendant to custody of Division of Public and Behavioral Health.

1. Where on a trial a defense of insanity is interposed by the defendant and the defendant is acquitted by reason of that defense, the finding of the jury pending the judicial determination pursuant to subsection 2 has the same effect as if the defendant were regularly adjudged insane, and the judge must:

(a) Order a peace officer to take the person into protective custody and transport the person to a forensic facility for detention pending a hearing to determine the person's mental health;

(b) Order the examination of the person by two psychiatrists, two psychologists, or one psychiatrist and one psychologist who are employed by a division facility; and

(c) At a hearing in open court, receive the report of the examining advisers and allow counsel for the State and for the person to examine the advisers, introduce other evidence and cross-examine witnesses.

2. If the court finds, after the hearing:

(a) That there is not clear and convincing evidence that the person is a person with mental illness, the court must order the person's discharge; or

(b) That there is clear and convincing evidence that the person is a person with mental illness, the court must order that the person be committed to the custody of the Administrator of the Division of Public and Behavioral Health of the Department of Health and Human Services until the person is discharged or conditionally released therefrom in accordance with NRS 178.467 to 178.471, inclusive.

□ The court shall issue its finding within 90 days after the defendant is acquitted.

3. The Administrator shall make the reports and the court shall proceed in the manner provided in NRS 178.467 to 178.471, inclusive.

4. If the court accepts a verdict acquitting a defendant by reason of insanity pursuant to this section, the court shall cause, within 5 business days after accepting the verdict, on a form prescribed by the Department of Public Safety, a record of that verdict to be transmitted to the Central Repository for Nevada Records of Criminal History, along with a statement indicating that the record is being transmitted for inclusion in each appropriate database of the National Instant Criminal Background Check System.

5. As used in this section, unless the context otherwise requires:

(a) "Division facility" has the meaning ascribed to it in NRS 433.094.

(b) "Forensic facility" means a secure facility of the Division of Public and Behavioral Health of the Department of Health and Human Services for offenders and defendants with mental disorders. The term includes, without limitation, Lakes Crossing Center.

(c) "National Instant Criminal Background Check System" has the meaning ascribed to it in NRS 179A.062.

(d) "Person with mental illness" has the meaning ascribed to it in NRS 178.3986.

(Added to NRS by 2003, 1459; A 2007, 1411; 2009, 2486; 2015, 1797)

NRS 175.541 Discharge of defendant after acquittal. If judgment of acquittal be given on a verdict, and the defendant be not detained for any other legal cause, the defendant must be discharged as soon as the verdict is given.

(Added to NRS by 1967, 1432)

NRS 175.543 Notice to defendant of provisions concerning sealing of records of proceedings leading to acquittal. Upon the entry of a judgment of acquittal, the court shall provide the defendant with a written notice of the provisions of NRS 179.255 which concern the sealing of records of the proceedings leading to the acquittal.

(Added to NRS by 2001, 1690)

HEARING TO DETERMINE WHETHER SEXUALLY MOTIVATED OFFENSE

NRS 175.547 Notice of intent to request hearing; time of hearing; evidence; court to enter finding; "sexually motivated" defined.

1. In any case in which a defendant pleads or is found guilty or guilty but mentally ill of murder in the first or second degree, kidnapping in the first or second degree, false imprisonment, burglary or invasion of the home, the court shall, at the request of the prosecuting attorney, conduct a separate hearing to determine whether the offense was sexually motivated. A request for such a hearing may not be submitted to

the court unless the prosecuting attorney, before the commencement of the trial, files and serves upon the defendant a written notice of the prosecuting attorney's intention to request such a hearing.

2. A hearing requested pursuant to subsection 1 must be conducted before:

(a) The court imposes its sentence; or

(b) A separate penalty hearing is conducted.

3. At the hearing, only evidence concerning the question of whether the offense was sexually motivated may be presented. The prosecuting attorney must prove beyond a reasonable doubt that the offense was sexually motivated.

4. The court shall enter its finding in the record.

5. For the purposes of this section, an offense is "sexually motivated" if one of the purposes for which the person committed the offense was the person's sexual gratification.

(Added to NRS by 1995, 413; A 1997, 1666; 2007, 1412)

PENALTY HEARING FOR FIRST DEGREE MURDER

NRS 175.552 When required; procedure; evidence.

1. Except as otherwise provided in subsection 2, in every case in which there is a finding that a defendant is guilty or guilty but mentally ill of murder of the first degree, whether or not the death penalty is sought, the court shall conduct a separate penalty hearing. The separate penalty hearing must be conducted as follows:

(a) If the finding is made by a jury, the separate penalty hearing must be conducted in the trial court before the trial jury, as soon as practicable.

(b) If the finding is made upon a plea of guilty or guilty but mentally ill or a trial without a jury and the death penalty is sought, the separate penalty hearing must be conducted before a jury impaneled for that purpose, as soon as practicable.

(c) If the finding is made upon a plea of guilty or guilty but mentally ill or a trial without a jury and the death penalty is not sought, the separate penalty hearing must be conducted as soon as practicable before the judge who conducted the trial or who accepted the plea.

2. In a case in which the death penalty is not sought or in which a court has made a finding that the defendant is intellectually disabled and has stricken the notice of intent to seek the death penalty pursuant to NRS 174.098, the parties may by stipulation waive the separate penalty hearing required in subsection 1. When stipulating to such a waiver, the parties may also include an agreement to have the sentence, if any, imposed by the trial judge. Any stipulation pursuant to this subsection must be in writing and signed by the defendant, the defendant's attorney, if any, and the prosecuting attorney.

3. During the hearing, evidence may be presented concerning aggravating and mitigating circumstances relative to the offense, defendant or victim and on any other matter which the court deems relevant to the sentence, whether or not the evidence is ordinarily admissible. Evidence may be offered to refute hearsay matters. No evidence which was secured in violation of the Constitution of the United States or the Constitution of the State of Nevada may be introduced. The State may introduce evidence of additional aggravating circumstances as set forth in NRS 200.033, other than the aggravated nature of the offense itself, only if it has been disclosed to the defendant before the commencement of the penalty hearing.

4. In a case in which the death penalty is not sought or in which a court has found the defendant to be intellectually disabled and has stricken the notice of intent to seek the death penalty pursuant to NRS 174.098, the jury or the trial judge shall determine whether the defendant should be sentenced to life with the possibility of parole or life without the possibility of parole.

(Added to NRS by 1977, 1543; A 1993, 322; 1995, 258, 2451; 2003, 767, 1460, 2082; 2007, 1412; 2013, 684)

NRS 175.554 Death penalty cases: Instructions to jury; determinations; findings and verdict; hearing to set aside sentence of defendant alleged to be intellectually disabled. In cases in which the death penalty is sought:

1. The court shall instruct the jury at the end of the penalty hearing, and shall include in its instructions the aggravating circumstances alleged by the prosecution upon which evidence has been presented during the trial or at the hearing. The court shall also instruct the jury as to the mitigating circumstances alleged by the defense upon which evidence has been presented during the trial or at the hearing.

2. The jury shall determine:

(a) Whether an aggravating circumstance or circumstances are found to exist;

(b) Whether a mitigating circumstance or circumstances are found to exist; and

(c) Based upon these findings, whether the defendant should be sentenced to imprisonment for a definite term of 50 years, life imprisonment with the possibility of parole, life imprisonment without the possibility of parole or death.

3. The jury may impose a sentence of death only if it finds at least one aggravating circumstance and further finds that there are no mitigating circumstances sufficient to outweigh the aggravating circumstance or circumstances found.

4. If a jury imposes a sentence of death, the jury shall render a written verdict signed by the foreman. The verdict must designate the aggravating circumstance or circumstances which were found beyond a reasonable doubt, and must state that there are no mitigating circumstances sufficient to outweigh the aggravating circumstance or circumstances found.

5. If a sentence of death is imposed and a prior determination regarding intellectual disability has not been made pursuant to NRS 174.098, the defendant may file a motion to set aside the penalty on the grounds that the defendant is intellectually disabled. If such a motion is filed, the court shall conduct a hearing on that issue in the manner set forth in NRS 174.098. If the court determines pursuant to such a hearing that the defendant is intellectually disabled, it shall set aside the sentence of death and order a new penalty hearing to be conducted. Either party may appeal such a determination pursuant to NRS 177.015.

(Added to NRS by 1977, 1543; A 1993, 322; 1995, 258; 2003, 768, 2083; 2013, 685, 1752)

NRS 175.556 Procedure when jury unable to reach unanimous verdict.

1. In a case in which the death penalty is sought, if a jury is unable to reach a unanimous verdict upon the sentence to be imposed, the district judge who conducted the trial or accepted the plea of guilty shall sentence the defendant to life imprisonment without the possibility of parole or impanel a new jury to determine the sentence.

2. In a case in which the death penalty is not sought, if a jury is unable to reach a unanimous verdict upon the sentence to be imposed, the trial judge shall impose the sentence.

(Added to NRS by 1977, 1543; A 1995, 259; 2003, 2083)

CHAPTER 176 - JUDGMENT AND EXECUTION

NRS 176.075 Rate of imprisonment in default of administrative assessment, fine or forfeiture.
NRS 176.085 Reduction of excessive fine or administrative assessment; payment in installments.
NRS 176.087 Imposition of community service as punishment or condition of probation.

Preservation of Biological Evidence and Genetic Marker Analysis

NRS 176.0911 Definitions.
NRS 176.09111 "Agency of criminal justice" defined.
NRS 176.09112 "Biological specimen" defined.
NRS 176.09113 "CODIS" defined.
NRS 176.09114 "DNA" defined.
NRS 176.09115 "DNA profile" defined.
NRS 176.09116 "DNA record" defined.
NRS 176.09117 "Forensic laboratory" defined.
NRS 176.09118 "Genetic marker analysis" defined.
NRS 176.09119 "State DNA Database" defined.
NRS 176.0912 Biological evidence secured in connection with investigation or prosecution; required preservation.
NRS 176.09121 State DNA Database: Establishment; duties.
NRS 176.09123 Collection of biological specimen from persons arrested for felony; submission to forensic laboratory; identifying information submitted to Central Repository; genetic marker analysis; creation of DNA profile; information included in criminal history record.
NRS 176.09125 Destruction of biological specimen and purging of DNA record: Grounds; written request; duties of Central Repository, forensic laboratory and State DNA Database.
NRS 176.09127 Payment of costs for obtaining biological specimen, destroying biological specimen and purging DNA record.
NRS 176.09129 Storage and maintenance of biological specimen, DNA profile, DNA record and information; release of information; confidentiality; penalty for unauthorized disclosure of information.
NRS 176.0913 Biological specimen to be obtained from certain defendants; identifying information submitted to Central Repository; genetic marker analysis; release of information; costs.
NRS 176.0915 Fee for obtaining biological specimen and for analysis; inclusion in sentence; creation of county fund; use of money in fund.
NRS 176.0916 Biological specimen to be obtained from certain probationers and parolees; release of information; penalty; fee for obtaining and analyzing specimen; identifying information submitted to Central Repository; creation of Fund for Genetic Marker Analysis; use of money in Fund.
NRS 176.09165 Establishment of standard form concerning use and destruction of biological specimen and purging of DNA record; law enforcement to provide form to person in certain circumstances.
NRS 176.0917 County to designate forensic laboratory to conduct or oversee analysis; criteria.
NRS 176.09173 Powers and duties of forensic laboratory; prohibited use of biological specimen, DNA profile and DNA record.
NRS 176.09177 Limitation on civil and criminal liability for acts relating to collection of biological specimen.
NRS 176.0918 Petition requesting genetic marker analysis by person convicted of felony; procedure; notice to victim.
NRS 176.09183 Grounds for granting or dismissing petition; appeal.
NRS 176.09187 Genetic marker analysis: Motion for new trial authorized when results favorable to petitioner; petitioner deemed to consent to submission, release and use of certain information; costs; remedy not exclusive.
NRS 176.0919 Execution stayed pending results of genetic marker analysis.

Sex Offenders and Offenders Convicted of a Crime Against a Child

NRS 176.0921 Definitions.
NRS 176.0922 "Central Repository" defined.
NRS 176.0923 "Crime against a child" defined.
NRS 176.0924 "Record of registration" defined.
NRS 176.0925 "Sexual offense" defined.
NRS 176.0926 Crime against child: Notice of conviction to Central Repository; defendant to be informed of duty to register; effect of failure to inform.
NRS 176.0927 Sexual offense: Notice of conviction to Central Repository; defendant to be informed of duty to register; effect of failure to inform.

Lifetime Supervision

NRS 176.0931 Special sentence for sex offenders; petition for release from lifetime supervision.

Miscellaneous Provisions

NRS 176.095 State Board of Parole Commissioners may direct release of state prisoner on parole.
NRS 176.105 Judgment in criminal action generally.
NRS 176.115 Judgment against complainant for malicious prosecution when defendant not found guilty; costs; enforcement of judgment.
NRS 176.125 Entry of judgment of conviction; what papers constitute record of action.

INVESTIGATION BY DIVISION OF PAROLE AND PROBATION

NRS 176.133 Definitions.
NRS 176.135 Presentence investigation and report: When required; time for completing.
NRS 176.139 Presentence investigation and report: Psychosexual evaluation of certain sex offenders required; standards and methods for conducting evaluation; access to records; rights of confidentiality and privileges deemed waived; costs.
NRS 176.145 Presentence investigation and report: Contents of report.
NRS 176.151 General investigation and report on defendant convicted of category E felony: When required; time for completing; contents of report.
NRS 176.153 Disclosure of report of presentence investigation.
NRS 176.156 Disclosure of report of presentence or general investigation; persons entitled to use report; confidentiality of report.
NRS 176.159 Delivery of report of presentence or general investigation to Director of Department of Corrections.
NRS 176.161 Portion of certain presentence or general investigations and reports to be paid by county in which indictment found or information filed.

WITHDRAWAL OF PLEA

NRS 176.165 When plea of guilty, guilty but mentally ill or nolo contendere may be withdrawn.

EXECUTION

NRS 176.265 Fines to be paid into State Treasury.
NRS 176.275 Judgment for fine, administrative assessment, payment of restitution or repayment of expenses is lien; additional provisions concerning judgment for payment of restitution.
NRS 176.278 Payment of restitution from civil judgment or settlement in favor of defendant and against State, political subdivision, officer, employee or contractor.
NRS 176.285 Fines in Justice Court to be paid to county treasurer; due date.
NRS 176.295 Costs when criminal action removed before trial; clerk to certify costs to auditor.
NRS 176.305 Judgment for imprisonment or fine and imprisonment until satisfied: Commitment and detention.
NRS 176.315 Judgment of imprisonment in county jail: How executed.
NRS 176.325 Judgment of imprisonment in state prison: How executed.
NRS 176.335 Duty of sheriff on receiving copies of judgment of imprisonment; Director of Department of Corrections to receive prisoner from sheriff; when term of imprisonment begins.
NRS 176.337 Court to notify defendant convicted of domestic violence concerning possession, shipment, transportation or receipt of firearm or ammunition.
NRS 176.345 Proceedings when conviction carries death penalty.
NRS 176.355 Execution of death penalty: Method; time and place; witnesses.
NRS 176.357 Request for notification of execution of death penalty; request to attend.
NRS 176.365 Director of Department of Corrections to make return on death warrant.

SUSPENSION OF EXECUTION OF DEATH PENALTY

General Provisions

NRS 176.415 When execution of death penalty may be stayed.

Insanity or Pregnancy

NRS 176.425 Sanity investigation: Filing of petition; stay of execution.
NRS 176.435 Sanity investigation: Conduct of hearing.
NRS 176.445 Execution of judgment when defendant found sane.
NRS 176.455 Suspension of execution when defendant found insane; proceedings on recovery of sanity.
NRS 176.465 Investigation of pregnancy: Procedure; hearing.
NRS 176.475 Proceedings after investigation: Execution of judgment; suspension of execution; issuance of warrant on termination of pregnancy.
NRS 176.485 Costs of investigations borne by State; manner of payment.

Petition for Postconviction Relief

NRS 176.486 Authority to enter stay of execution.
NRS 176.487 Determination of whether to enter stay of execution.
NRS 176.488 Entry of stay of execution and necessary orders.
NRS 176.489 Vacation of stay of execution.
NRS 176.491 Stay of execution following denial of appeal.
NRS 176.492 Dissolution of stay of execution which was improperly entered.

NEW ORDER TO EXECUTE JUDGMENT OF DEATH

NEW TRIAL OR MOTION TO VACATE JUDGMENT

ARREST OF JUDGMENT

MISCELLANEOUS PROVISIONS

GENERAL PROVISIONS

NRS 176.002 "Division" defined. As used in this chapter, unless the context otherwise requires, "Division" means the Division of Parole and Probation of the Department of Public Safety.

(Added to NRS by 1993, 1512; A 2001, 2568)

ADVISORY COMMISSION ON THE ADMINISTRATION OF JUSTICE

NRS 176.0121 "Commission" defined. As used in NRS 176.0121 to 176.0129, inclusive, "Commission" means the Advisory Commission on the Administration of Justice.

(Added to NRS by 1995, 1353; A 2007, 2818; 2009, 1351, 2569; 2013, 1064, 2989, 3699)

NRS 176.0123 Creation; members and appointing authorities; Chair; terms; vacancies; salaries and per diem; staff.

1. The Advisory Commission on the Administration of Justice is hereby created. The Commission consists of:

(a) One member who is a municipal judge or justice of the peace, appointed by the governing body of the Nevada Judges of Limited Jurisdiction;

(b) One member who is a district judge, appointed by the governing body of the Nevada District Judges Association;

(c) One member who is a justice of the Supreme Court of Nevada or a retired justice of the Supreme Court of Nevada, appointed by the Chief Justice of the Supreme Court of Nevada;

(d) One member who is a district attorney, appointed by the governing body of the Nevada District Attorneys Association;

(e) One member who is an attorney in private practice, experienced in defending criminal actions, appointed by the governing body of the State Bar of Nevada;

(f) One member who is a public defender, appointed by the governing body of the State Bar of Nevada;

(g) One member who is a representative of a law enforcement agency, appointed by the Governor;

(h) One member who is a representative of the Division of Parole and Probation of the Department of Public Safety, appointed by the Governor;

(i) One member who has been a victim of a crime or is a representative of an organization supporting the rights of victims of crime, appointed by the Governor;

(j) One member who is a representative of an organization that advocates on behalf of inmates, appointed by the Governor;

(k) One member who is a representative of the Nevada Sheriffs' and Chiefs' Association, appointed by the Nevada Sheriffs' and Chiefs' Association;

(l) One member who is a member of the State Board of Parole Commissioners, appointed by the State Board of Parole Commissioners;

(m) The Director of the Department of Corrections;

(n) Two members who are Senators, one of whom is appointed by the Majority Leader of the Senate and one of whom is appointed by the Minority Leader of the Senate; and

(o) Two members who are members of the Assembly, one of whom is appointed by the Speaker of the Assembly and one of whom is appointed by the Minority Leader of the Assembly.

□ If any association listed in this subsection ceases to exist, the appointment required by this subsection must be made by the association's successor in interest or, if there is no successor in interest, by the Governor.

2. The Attorney General is an ex officio voting member of the Commission.

3. Each appointed member serves a term of 2 years. Members may be reappointed for additional terms of 2 years in the same manner as the original appointments. Any vacancy occurring in the membership of the Commission must be filled in the same manner as the original appointment not later than 30 days after the vacancy occurs.

4. The Legislators who are members of the Commission are entitled to receive the salary provided for a majority of the members of the Legislature during the first 60 days of the preceding session for each day's attendance at a meeting of the Commission.

5. At the first regular meeting of each odd-numbered year, the members of the Commission shall elect a Chair by majority vote who shall serve until the next Chair is elected.

6. The Commission shall meet at least once every 3 months and may meet at such further times as deemed necessary by the Chair.

7. A majority of the members of the Commission constitutes a quorum for the transaction of business, and a majority of those members present at any meeting is sufficient for any official action taken by the Commission.

8. While engaged in the business of the Commission, to the extent of legislative appropriation, each member of the Commission is entitled to receive the per diem allowance and travel expenses provided for state officers and employees generally.

9. To the extent of legislative appropriation, the Director of the Legislative Counsel Bureau shall provide the Commission with such staff as is necessary to carry out the duties of the Commission.

(Added to NRS by 1995, 1353; A 2001, 2568; 2005, 581; 2007, 2818; 2009, 2569; 2015, 236)

NRS 176.0124 Subcommittee on Juvenile Justice: Creation; Chair; members; duties; salaries and per diem.

1. There is hereby created the Subcommittee on Juvenile Justice of the Commission.

2. The Chair of the Commission shall appoint the members of the Subcommittee and designate one of the members of the Subcommittee as Chair of the Subcommittee. The Chair of the Subcommittee must be a member of the Commission.

3. The Subcommittee shall meet at the times and places specified by a call of the Chair. A majority of the members of the Subcommittee constitutes a quorum, and a quorum may exercise any power or authority conferred on the Subcommittee.

4. The Subcommittee shall consider issues related to juvenile justice and shall evaluate, review and submit a report to the Commission with recommendations concerning such issues.

5. Any Legislators who are members of the Subcommittee are entitled to receive the salary provided for a majority of the members of the Legislature during the first 60 days of the preceding session for each day's attendance at a meeting of the Subcommittee.

6. While engaged in the business of the Subcommittee, to the extent of legislative appropriation, each member of the Subcommittee is entitled to receive the per diem allowance and travel expenses provided for state officers and employees generally.

(Added to NRS by 2009, 2568)

NRS 176.01245 Subcommittee on Victims of Crime: Creation; Chair; members; duties; salaries and per diem.

1. There is hereby created the Subcommittee on Victims of Crime of the Commission.

2. The Chair of the Commission shall appoint the members of the Subcommittee and designate one of the members of the Subcommittee as Chair of the Subcommittee. The Chair of the Subcommittee must be a member of the Commission.

3. The Subcommittee shall meet at the times and places specified by a call of the Chair. A majority of the members of the Subcommittee constitutes a quorum, and a quorum may exercise any power or authority conferred on the Subcommittee.

4. The Subcommittee shall consider issues related to victims of crime and shall evaluate, review and submit a report to the Commission with recommendations concerning such issues.

5. Any Legislators who are members of the Subcommittee are entitled to receive the salary provided for a majority of the members of the Legislature during the first 60 days of the preceding session for each day's attendance at a meeting of the Subcommittee.

6. While engaged in the business of the Subcommittee, to the extent of legislative appropriation, each member of the Subcommittee is entitled to receive the per diem allowance and travel expenses provided for state officers and employees generally.

(Added to NRS by 2009, 2569)

NRS 176.01246 Subcommittee to Review Arrestee DNA: Creation; Chair; members; duties; salaries and per diem.

1. There is hereby created the Subcommittee to Review Arrestee DNA of the Commission.

2. The Chair of the Commission shall appoint the members of the Subcommittee which must include, without limitation:

(a) A member experienced in defending criminal actions.

(b) A member of a minority community organization whose mission includes the protection of civil rights for minorities.

3. The Chair of the Commission shall designate one of the members of the Subcommittee as Chair of the Subcommittee.

4. The Subcommittee shall meet at the times and places specified by a call of the Chair. A majority of the members of the Subcommittee constitutes a quorum, and a quorum may exercise any power or authority conferred on the Subcommittee.

5. The Subcommittee shall consider issues relating to DNA of arrested persons and shall evaluate, review and submit a report to the Commission with recommendations concerning such issues. The issues considered by the Subcommittee and the report submitted by the Subcommittee must include, without limitation:

(a) The costs and procedures relating to the methods, implementation and utilization of the provisions for the destruction of biological specimens and purging of DNA profiles and DNA records of arrested persons; and

(b) The collection and review of information concerning the number of requests for the destruction of biological specimens and purging of DNA profiles and DNA records of arrested persons and the number and percentage of such requests that are denied.

6. Any Legislators who are members of the Subcommittee are entitled to receive the salary provided for a majority of the members of the Legislature during the first 60 days of the preceding session for each day's attendance at a meeting of the Subcommittee.

7. While engaged in the business of the Subcommittee, to the extent of legislative appropriation, each member of the Subcommittee is entitled to receive the per diem allowance and travel expenses as provided for state officers and employees generally.

8. As used in this section:

(a) "Biological specimen" has the meaning ascribed to it in NRS 176.09112.

(b) "DNA" has the meaning ascribed to it in NRS 176.09114.

(c) "DNA profile" has the meaning ascribed to it in NRS 176.09115.

(d) "DNA record" has the meaning ascribed to it in NRS 176.09116.

(Added to NRS by 2013, 1063)

NRS 176.01247 Subcommittee on Medical Use of Marijuana: Creation; Chair; members; duties; salaries and per diem.

1. There is hereby created the Subcommittee on the Medical Use of Marijuana of the Commission.

2. The Chair of the Commission shall appoint the members of the Subcommittee. The Subcommittee must consist of legislative and nonlegislative members, including, without limitation:

(a) At least four Legislators, who may or may not be members of the Commission.

(b) A representative of the Division of Public and Behavioral Health of the Department of Health and Human Services.

(c) A patient who holds a valid registry identification card to engage in the medical use of marijuana pursuant to chapter 453A of NRS.

(d) An owner or operator of a cultivation facility that is certified to operate pursuant to chapter 453A of NRS.

(e) An owner or operator of a facility for the production of edible marijuana products or marijuana-infused products that is certified to operate pursuant to chapter 453A of NRS.

(f) An owner or operator of a medical marijuana dispensary that is certified to operate pursuant to chapter 453A of NRS.

(g) A representative of the Attorney General.

(h) A representative of a civil liberties organization.

(i) A representative of an organization which advocates for persons who use marijuana for medicinal purposes.

(j) A representative of a law enforcement agency located within the jurisdiction of Clark County.

(k) A representative of a law enforcement agency located within the jurisdiction of Washoe County.

(l) A representative of local government.

3. The Chair of the Commission shall designate one of the legislative members of the Commission as Chair of the Subcommittee.

4. The Subcommittee shall meet at the times and places specified by a call of the Chair. A majority of the members of the Subcommittee constitutes a quorum, and a quorum may exercise any power or authority conferred on the Subcommittee.

5. The Subcommittee shall:

(a) Consider issues concerning the medical use of marijuana, the dispensation of marijuana for medical use and the implementation of provisions of law providing for the dispensation of marijuana for medical use; and

(b) Evaluate, review and submit a report to the Commission with recommendations concerning such issues.

6. Any Legislators who are members of the Subcommittee are entitled to receive the salary provided for a majority of the members of the Legislature during the first 60 days of the preceding session for each day's attendance at a meeting of the Subcommittee.

7. While engaged in the business of the Subcommittee, to the extent of legislative appropriation, each member of the Subcommittee is entitled to receive the per diem allowance and travel expenses provided for state officers and employees generally.

(Added to NRS by 2013, 3698)

NRS 176.0125 Duties of Commission. The Commission shall:

1. Identify and study the elements of this State's system of criminal justice which affect the sentences imposed for felonies and gross misdemeanors.

2. Evaluate the effectiveness and fiscal impact of various policies and practices regarding sentencing which are employed in this State and other states, including, but not limited to, the use of plea bargaining, probation, programs of intensive supervision, programs of regimental discipline, imprisonment, sentencing recommendations, mandatory and minimum sentencing, mandatory sentencing for crimes involving the possession, manufacture and distribution of controlled substances, structured or tiered sentencing, enhanced penalties for habitual criminals, parole, credits against sentences, residential confinement and alternatives to incarceration.

3. Recommend changes in the structure of sentencing in this State which, to the extent practicable and with consideration for their fiscal impact, incorporate general objectives and goals for sentencing, including, but not limited to, the following:

(a) Offenders must receive sentences that increase in direct proportion to the severity of their crimes and their histories of criminality.

(b) Offenders who have extensive histories of criminality or who have exhibited a propensity to commit crimes of a predatory or violent nature must receive sentences which reflect the need to ensure the safety and protection of the public and which allow for the imprisonment for life of such offenders.

(c) Offenders who have committed offenses that do not include acts of violence and who have limited histories of criminality must receive sentences which reflect the need to conserve scarce economic resources through the use of various alternatives to traditional forms of incarceration.

(d) Offenders with similar histories of criminality who are convicted of similar crimes must receive sentences that are generally similar.

(e) Offenders sentenced to imprisonment must receive sentences which do not confuse or mislead the public as to the actual time those offenders must serve while incarcerated or before being released from confinement or supervision.

(f) Offenders must not receive disparate sentences based upon factors such as race, gender or economic status.

(g) Offenders must receive sentences which are based upon the specific circumstances and facts of their offenses, including the nature of the offense and any aggravating factors, the savagery of the offense, as evidenced by the extent of any injury to the victim, and the degree of criminal sophistication demonstrated by the offender's acts before, during and after commission of the offense.

4. Evaluate the effectiveness and efficiency of the Department of Corrections and the State Board of Parole Commissioners with consideration as to whether it is feasible and advisable to establish an oversight or advisory board to perform various functions and make recommendations concerning:

(a) Policies relating to parole;
(b) Regulatory procedures and policies of the State Board of Parole Commissioners;
(c) Policies for the operation of the Department of Corrections;
(d) Budgetary issues; and
(e) Other related matters.

5. Evaluate the effectiveness of specialty court programs in this State with consideration as to whether such programs have the effect of limiting or precluding reentry of offenders and parolees into the community.

6. Evaluate the policies and practices concerning presentence investigations and reports made by the Division of Parole and Probation of the Department of Public Safety, including, without limitation, the resources relied on in preparing such investigations and reports and the extent to which judges in this State rely on and follow the recommendations contained in such presentence investigations and reports.

7. Evaluate, review and comment upon issues relating to juvenile justice in this State, including, but not limited to:
(a) The need for the establishment and implementation of evidence-based programs and a continuum of sanctions for children who are subject to the jurisdiction of the juvenile court; and
(b) The impact on the criminal justice system of the policies and programs of the juvenile justice system.

8. Compile and develop statistical information concerning sentencing in this State.

9. Identify and study issues relating to the application of chapter 241 of NRS to meetings held by the:
(a) State Board of Pardons Commissioners to consider an application for clemency; and
(b) State Board of Parole Commissioners to consider an offender for parole.

10. Identify and study issues relating to the operation of the Department of Corrections, including, without limitation, the system for allowing credits against the sentences of offenders, the accounting of such credits and any other policies and procedures of the Department which pertain to the operation of the Department.

11. Evaluate the policies and practices relating to the involuntary civil commitment of sexually dangerous persons.

12. Identify and study the impacts and effects of collateral consequences of convictions in this State. Such identification and study:
(a) Must cause to be identified any provision in the Nevada Constitution, the Nevada Revised Statutes and the Nevada Administrative Code which imposes a collateral sanction or authorizes the imposition of a disqualification, and any provision of law that may afford relief from a collateral consequence;
(b) May rely on the study of this State's collateral sanctions, disqualifications and relief provisions prepared by the National Institute of Justice described in section 510 of the Court Security Improvement Act of 2007, Public Law 110-177; and
(c) Must include the posting of a hyperlink on the Commission's website to any study of this State's collateral sanctions, disqualifications and relief provisions prepared by the National Institute of Justice described in section 510 of the Court Security Improvement Act of 2007, Public Law 110-177.

13. For each regular session of the Legislature, prepare a comprehensive report including the Commission's recommended changes pertaining to the administration of justice in this State, the Commission's findings and any recommendations of the Commission for proposed legislation. The report must be submitted to the Director of the Legislative Counsel Bureau for distribution to the Legislature not later than September 1 of each even-numbered year.

(Added to NRS by 1995, 1354; A 2007, 2819, 3194; 2011, 231; 2013, 2777)

NRS 176.01255 Grants, bequests, devises, donations and gifts; Special Account for the Support of the Advisory Commission on the Administration of Justice.

1. The Chair of the Commission may apply for and accept any available grants and may accept any bequests, devises, donations or gifts from any public or private source to carry out the provisions of NRS 176.0121 to 176.0129, inclusive.

2. Any money received pursuant to this section must be deposited in the Special Account for the Support of the Advisory Commission on the Administration of Justice, which is hereby created in the State General Fund. Interest and income earned on money in the Account must be credited to the Account. Money in the Account may only be used for the support of the Commission and its activities pursuant to NRS 176.0121 to 176.0129, inclusive.

(Added to NRS by 2013, 2989)

NRS 176.0126 Subpoenas: Power to issue; compelling performance.

1. To carry out its powers and duties pursuant to NRS 176.0121 to 176.0129, inclusive, the Commission, or any member thereof acting on behalf of the Commission with a concurrence of a majority of the members of the Commission, may issue subpoenas to compel the attendance of witnesses and the production of books, records, documents or other papers and testimony.

2. If any person fails to comply with a subpoena issued by the Commission or any member thereof pursuant to this section within 20 days after the date of service of the subpoena, the Commission may petition the district court for an order of the court compelling compliance with the subpoena.

3. Upon such a petition, the court shall enter an order directing the person subpoenaed to appear before the court at a time and place to be fixed by the court in its order, the time to be not more than 20 days after the date of service of the order, and show cause why the person has not complied with the subpoena. A certified copy of the order must be served upon the person subpoenaed.

4. If it appears to the court that the subpoena was regularly issued by the Commission or a member thereof pursuant to this section, the court shall enter an order compelling compliance with the subpoena, and upon failure to obey the order the person shall be dealt with as for contempt of court.

(Added to NRS by 2007, 2817)

NRS 176.0127 Department of Corrections and Division of Parole and Probation to provide information to and assist Commission.

1. The Department of Corrections shall:

(a) Provide the Commission with any available statistical information or research requested by the Commission and assist the Commission in the compilation and development of information requested by the Commission, including, but not limited to, information or research concerning the facilities and institutions of the Department of Corrections, the offenders who are or were within those facilities or institutions, rates of recidivism, the effectiveness of educational and vocational programs and the sentences which are being served or were served by those offenders;

(b) If requested by the Commission, make available to the Commission the use of the computers and programs which are owned by the Department of Corrections; and

(c) Provide the independent contractor retained by the Department of Administration pursuant to NRS 176.0129 with any available statistical information requested by the independent contractor for the purpose of performing the projections required by NRS 176.0129.

2. The Division shall:

(a) Provide the Commission with any available statistical information or research requested by the Commission and assist the Commission in the compilation and development of information concerning sentencing, probation, parole and any offenders who are or were subject to supervision by the Division;

(b) If requested by the Commission, make available to the Commission the use of the computers and programs which are owned by the Division; and

(c) Provide the independent contractor retained by the Department of Administration pursuant to NRS 176.0129 with any available statistical information requested by the independent contractor for the purpose of performing the projections required by NRS 176.0129.

(Added to NRS by 1995, 1355; A 2001 Special Session, 214; 2009, 1352)

NRS 176.0128 Central Repository for Nevada Records of Criminal History to facilitate data collection and provide data and information to Commission. The Central Repository for Nevada Records of Criminal History shall:

1. Facilitate the collection of statistical data in the manner approved by the Director of the Department of Public Safety and coordinate the exchange of such data with agencies of criminal justice within this State, including:

(a) State and local law enforcement agencies;

(b) The Office of the Attorney General;

(c) The Court Administrator;

(d) The Department of Corrections; and

(e) The Division.

2. Provide the Commission with available statistical data and information requested by the Commission.

(Added to NRS by 2009, 1351)

NRS 176.0129 Annual projections of persons imprisoned, on probation, on parole and in residential confinement. The Department of Administration shall, on an annual basis, contract for the services of an independent contractor, in accordance with the provisions of NRS 333.700, to:

1. Review sentences imposed in this State and the practices of the State Board of Parole Commissioners and project annually the number of persons who will be:

(a) In a facility or institution of the Department of Corrections;

(b) On probation;

(c) On parole; and

(d) Serving a term of residential confinement,

 during the 10 years immediately following the date of the projection; and

2. Review preliminary proposals and information provided by the Commission and project annually the number of persons who will be:

(a) In a facility or institution of the Department of Corrections;

(b) On probation;

(c) On parole; and

(d) Serving a term of residential confinement,

 during the 10 years immediately following the date of the projection, assuming the preliminary proposals were recommended by the Commission and enacted by the Legislature.

(Added to NRS by 1995, 1355; A 2001 Special Session, 215; 2009, 2231)

SENTENCE AND JUDGMENT; GENETIC MARKER ANALYSIS

Hearing

NRS 176.015 Prompt hearing; court may commit defendant or continue or alter bail before hearing; statement by defendant; presentation of mitigating evidence; rights of victim; notice of hearing.

1. Sentence must be imposed without unreasonable delay. Pending sentence, the court may commit the defendant or continue or alter the bail.

2. Before imposing sentence, the court shall:

(a) Afford counsel an opportunity to speak on behalf of the defendant; and

(b) Address the defendant personally and ask the defendant if:

(1) The defendant wishes to make a statement in his or her own behalf and to present any information in mitigation of punishment; and

(2) The defendant is a veteran or a member of the military. If the defendant is a veteran or a member of the military and meets the qualifications of paragraphs (b) and (c) of subsection 2 of NRS 176A.285, the court may, if appropriate, assign the defendant to:

(I) A program of treatment established pursuant to NRS 176A.280; or

(II) If a program of treatment established pursuant to NRS 176A.280 is not available for the defendant, a program of treatment established pursuant to NRS 176A.250 or 453.580.

3. After hearing any statements presented pursuant to subsection 2 and before imposing sentence, the court shall afford the victim an opportunity to:

(a) Appear personally, by counsel or by personal representative; and

(b) Reasonably express any views concerning the crime, the person responsible, the impact of the crime on the victim and the need for restitution.

4. The prosecutor shall give reasonable notice of the hearing to impose sentence to:

(a) The person against whom the crime was committed;

(b) A person who was injured as a direct result of the commission of the crime;

(c) The surviving spouse, parents or children of a person who was killed as a direct result of the commission of the crime; and

(d) Any other relative or victim who requests in writing to be notified of the hearing.

□ Any defect in notice or failure of such persons to appear are not grounds for an appeal or the granting of a writ of habeas corpus. All personal information, including, but not limited to, a current or former address, which pertains to a victim or relative and which is received by the prosecutor pursuant to this subsection is confidential.

5. For the purposes of this section:

(a) "Member of the military" has the meaning ascribed to it in NRS 176A.043.

(b) "Relative" of a person includes:

(1) A spouse, parent, grandparent or stepparent;

(2) A natural born child, stepchild or adopted child;

(3) A grandchild, brother, sister, half brother or half sister; or

(4) A parent of a spouse.

(c) "Veteran" has the meaning ascribed to it in NRS 176A.090.

(d) "Victim" includes:

(1) A person, including a governmental entity, against whom a crime has been committed;

(2) A person who has been injured or killed as a direct result of the commission of a crime; and

(3) A relative of a person described in subparagraph (1) or (2).

6. This section does not restrict the authority of the court to consider any reliable and relevant evidence at the time of sentencing.

(Added to NRS by 1967, 1432; A 1989, 1425; 1991, 90; 1995, 371; 1997, 3236; 2001, 889; 2009, 100)

NRS 176.017 Imposition of sentence on person convicted as adult for offense committed when person was under age of 18 years: Additional considerations. If a person is convicted as an adult for an offense that the person committed when he or she was less than 18 years of age, in addition to any other factor that the court is required to consider before imposing a sentence upon such a person, the court shall consider the differences between juvenile and adult offenders, including, without limitation, the diminished culpability of juveniles as compared to that of adults and the typical characteristics of youth.

(Added to NRS by 2015, 618)

Sentence of Death; Terms of Imprisonment; Restitution

NRS 176.025 Sentence of death or life imprisonment without possibility of parole not to be imposed on person under age of 18 years. A sentence of death or life imprisonment without the possibility of parole must not be imposed or inflicted upon any person convicted of a crime now punishable by death or life imprisonment without the possibility of parole who at the time of the commission of the crime was less than 18 years of age. As to such a person, the maximum punishment that may be imposed is life imprisonment with the possibility of parole.

(Added to NRS by 1967, 1432; A 2005, 63; 2011, 19; 2015, 618)

NRS 176.033 Sentence of imprisonment required or permitted by statute: Definite period for misdemeanor or gross misdemeanor; minimum and maximum term for felony unless definite term required by statute; restitution; modification of sentence.

1. If a sentence of imprisonment is required or permitted by statute, the court shall:

(a) If sentencing a person who has been found guilty of a misdemeanor or a gross misdemeanor, sentence the person to imprisonment for a definite period of time within the maximum limit or the minimum and maximum limits prescribed by the applicable statute, taking due account of the gravity of the particular offense and of the character of the individual defendant.

(b) If sentencing a person who has been found guilty of a felony, sentence the person to a minimum term and a maximum term of imprisonment, unless a definite term of imprisonment is required by statute.

(c) If restitution is appropriate, set an amount of restitution for each victim of the offense and for expenses related to extradition in accordance with NRS 179.225.

2. At any time after a prisoner has been released on parole and has served one-half of the period of parole, or 10 consecutive years on parole in the case of a prisoner sentenced to life imprisonment, the State Board of Parole Commissioners, upon the recommendation of the Division, may petition the court of original jurisdiction requesting a modification of sentence. The Board shall give notice of the petition and hearing thereon to the Attorney General or district attorney who had jurisdiction in the original proceedings. Upon hearing the recommendation of the State Board of Parole Commissioners and good cause appearing, the court may modify the original sentence by

reducing the maximum term of imprisonment but shall not make the term less than the minimum term prescribed by the applicable penal statute.

(Added to NRS by 1967, 527; A 1973, 844; 1975, 652; 1977, 414; 1987, 395; 1989, 678; 1993, 934, 1512; 1995, 551, 1248)

NRS 176.035 Conviction of two or more offenses; concurrent and consecutive sentences; aggregating consecutive sentences.

1. Except as otherwise provided in subsection 3, whenever a person is convicted of two or more offenses, and sentence has been pronounced for one offense, the court in imposing any subsequent sentence may provide that the sentences subsequently pronounced run either concurrently or consecutively with the sentence first imposed. Except as otherwise provided in subsections 3 and 4, if the court makes no order with reference thereto, all such subsequent sentences run concurrently. For offenses committed on or after July 1, 2014, if the court imposes the sentences to run consecutively, the court must pronounce the minimum and maximum aggregate terms of imprisonment pursuant to subsection 2, unless the defendant is sentenced to life imprisonment without the possibility of parole or death.

2. When aggregating terms of imprisonment pursuant to subsection 1:

(a) If at least one sentence imposes a maximum term of imprisonment for life with the possibility of parole, the court must aggregate the minimum terms of imprisonment to determine the minimum aggregate term of imprisonment, and the maximum aggregate term of imprisonment shall be deemed to be imprisonment in the state prison for life with the possibility of parole.

(b) If all the sentences impose a minimum and maximum term of imprisonment, the court must aggregate the minimum terms of imprisonment to determine the minimum aggregate term of imprisonment and must aggregate the maximum terms of imprisonment to determine the maximum aggregate term of imprisonment.

3. Except as otherwise provided in this subsection, whenever a person under sentence of imprisonment for committing a felony commits another crime constituting a felony and is sentenced to another term of imprisonment for that felony, the latter term must not begin until the expiration of all prior terms, including the expiration of any prior aggregated terms. If the person is a probationer at the time the subsequent felony is committed, the court may provide that the latter term of imprisonment run concurrently with any prior terms or portions thereof. If the person is sentenced to a term of imprisonment for life without the possibility of parole, the sentence must be executed without reference to the unexpired term of imprisonment and without reference to eligibility for parole.

4. Whenever a person under sentence of imprisonment commits another crime constituting a misdemeanor or gross misdemeanor, the court shall provide expressly whether the sentence subsequently pronounced runs concurrently or consecutively with the one first imposed.

5. Whenever a person under sentence of imprisonment commits another crime for which the punishment is death, the sentence must be executed without reference to the unexpired term of imprisonment.

6. This section does not prevent the State Board of Parole Commissioners from paroling a person under consecutive sentences of imprisonment from a current term of imprisonment to a subsequent term of imprisonment.

(Added to NRS by 1967, 1432; A 1973, 181, 674; 1987, 591; 1997, 1187; 2001, 1936; 2013, 221)

NRS 176.045 Imposition of concurrent or consecutive sentence on person under sentence in another jurisdiction.

1. Whenever a person convicted of a public offense in this State is under sentence of imprisonment pronounced by another jurisdiction, federal or state, whether or not the prior sentence is for the same offense, the court in imposing any sentence for the offense committed in this State may, in its discretion, provide that such sentence shall run either concurrently or consecutively with the prior sentence.

2. If the court provides that the sentence shall run concurrently, and the defendant is released by the other jurisdiction prior to the expiration of the sentence imposed in this State, the defendant shall be returned to the State of Nevada to serve out the balance of such sentence, unless the defendant is eligible for parole under the provisions of chapter 213 of NRS, and the Board of Parole Commissioners directs that the defendant be released on parole as provided in that chapter.

3. If the court makes an order pursuant to this section, the clerk of the court shall provide the Director of the Department of Corrections with a certified copy of judgment and notification of the place of out-of-state confinement.

4. If the court makes no order pursuant to this section, the sentence imposed in this State shall not begin until the expiration of all prior sentences imposed by other jurisdictions.

(Added to NRS by 1967, 1432; A 1973, 180; 1977, 859; 2001 Special Session, 215)

NRS 176.055 Credit against sentence of imprisonment.

1. Except as otherwise provided in subsection 2, whenever a sentence of imprisonment in the county jail or state prison is imposed, the court may order that credit be allowed against the duration of the sentence, including any minimum term or minimum aggregate term, as applicable, thereof prescribed by law, for the amount of time which the defendant has actually spent in confinement before conviction, unless the defendant's confinement was pursuant to a judgment of conviction for another offense. Credit allowed pursuant to this subsection does not alter the date from which the term of imprisonment is computed.

2. A defendant who is convicted of a subsequent offense which was committed while the defendant was:

(a) In custody on a prior charge is not eligible for any credit on the sentence for the subsequent offense for time the defendant has spent in confinement on the prior charge, unless the charge was dismissed or the defendant was acquitted.

(b) Imprisoned in a county jail or state prison or on probation or parole from a Nevada conviction is not eligible for any credit on the sentence for the subsequent offense for the time the defendant has spent in confinement which is within the period of the prior sentence, regardless of whether any probation or parole has been formally revoked.

(Added to NRS by 1967, 1433; A 1971, 243; 1973, 161; 1981, 479; 2013, 222)

NRS 176.057 Effect of finding of guilty but mentally ill or acceptance of such plea.

1. If a defendant is found guilty but mentally ill pursuant to NRS 175.533 or the court accepts the defendant's plea of guilty but mentally ill entered pursuant to NRS 174.035, and the court finds by a preponderance of the evidence that:

(a) The defendant is not mentally ill at the time of sentencing, the court shall impose any sentence that the court is authorized to impose upon a defendant who pleads or is found guilty of the same offense; or

(b) The defendant is mentally ill at the time of sentencing, the court shall:

(1) Impose any sentence that the court is authorized to impose upon a defendant who pleads or is found guilty of the same offense; and

(2) Include in that sentence an order that the defendant, during the period of confinement or probation, be given or obtain such treatment as is medically indicated for the defendant's mental illness.

2. If the sentence of a defendant includes a period of confinement at a state correctional facility, the Department of Corrections shall separate such a person from the general population of the prison and shall not return the person to that population until a licensed psychiatrist or psychologist employed by the Department finds that the person no longer requires acute mental health care. If the person is returned to the general population, the person must continue to be given or obtain such treatment as is medically indicated for the person's mental illness.

(Added to NRS by 2007, 1413)

Administrative Assessments, Fines, Fees, Forfeitures and Community Service

NRS 176.059 Administrative assessment for misdemeanor: Collection; distribution; limitations on use.

1. Except as otherwise provided in subsection 2, when a defendant pleads guilty or guilty but mentally ill or is found guilty or guilty but mentally ill of a misdemeanor, including the violation of any municipal ordinance, the justice or judge shall include in the sentence the sum prescribed by the following schedule as an administrative assessment and render a judgment against the defendant for the assessment:

Fine	Assessment
$5 to $49	$30
50 to 59	45
60 to 69	50
70 to 79	55
80 to 89	60
90 to 99	65
100 to 199	75
200 to 299	85
300 to 399	95
400 to 499	105
500 to 1,000	120

If the justice or judge sentences the defendant to perform community service in lieu of a fine, the justice or judge shall include in the sentence the amount of the administrative assessment that corresponds with the fine for which the defendant would have been responsible as prescribed by the schedule in this subsection.

2. The provisions of subsection 1 do not apply to:

(a) An ordinance regulating metered parking; or

(b) An ordinance which is specifically designated as imposing a civil penalty or liability pursuant to NRS 244.3575 or 268.019.

3. The money collected for an administrative assessment must not be deducted from the fine imposed by the justice or judge but must be taxed against the defendant in addition to the fine. The money collected for an administrative assessment must be stated separately on the court's docket and must be included in the amount posted for bail. If bail is forfeited, the administrative assessment included in the amount posted for bail pursuant to this subsection must be disbursed in the manner set forth in subsection 5 or 6. If the defendant is found not guilty or the charges are dismissed, the money deposited with the court must be returned to the defendant. If the justice or judge cancels a fine because the fine has been determined to be uncollectible, any balance of the fine and the administrative assessment remaining unpaid shall be deemed to be uncollectible and the defendant is not required to pay it. If a fine is determined to be uncollectible, the defendant is not entitled to a refund of the fine or administrative assessment the defendant has paid and the justice or judge shall not recalculate the administrative assessment.

4. If the justice or judge permits the fine and administrative assessment to be paid in installments, the payments must be first applied to the unpaid balance of the administrative assessment. The city treasurer shall distribute partially collected administrative assessments in accordance with the requirements of subsection 5. The county treasurer shall distribute partially collected administrative assessments in accordance with the requirements of subsection 6.

5. The money collected for administrative assessments in municipal court must be paid by the clerk of the court to the city treasurer on or before the fifth day of each month for the preceding month. The city treasurer shall distribute, on or before the 15th day of that month, the money received in the following amounts for each assessment received:

(a) Two dollars to the county treasurer for credit to a special account in the county general fund for the use of the county's juvenile court or for services to juvenile offenders. Any money remaining in the special account after 2 fiscal years must be deposited in the county general fund if it has not been committed for expenditure. The county treasurer shall provide, upon request by a juvenile court, monthly reports of the revenue credited to and expenditures made from the special account.

(b) Seven dollars for credit to a special revenue fund for the use of the municipal courts. Any money remaining in the special revenue fund after 2 fiscal years must be deposited in the municipal general fund if it has not been committed for expenditure. The city treasurer shall provide, upon request by a municipal court, monthly reports of the revenue credited to and expenditures made from the special revenue fund.

(c) Five dollars to the State Controller for credit to the State General Fund.

(d) The remainder of each assessment to the State Controller for credit to a special account in the State General Fund for distribution as provided in subsection 8.

6. The money collected for administrative assessments in justice courts must be paid by the clerk of the court to the county treasurer on or before the fifth day of each month for the preceding month. The county treasurer shall distribute, on or before the 15th day of that month, the money received in the following amounts for each assessment received:

(a) Two dollars for credit to a special account in the county general fund for the use of the county's juvenile court or for services to juvenile offenders. Any money remaining in the special account after 2 fiscal years must be deposited in the county general fund if it has not been committed for expenditure. The county treasurer shall provide, upon request by a juvenile court, monthly reports of the revenue credited to and expenditures made from the special account.

(b) Seven dollars for credit to a special revenue fund for the use of the justice courts. Any money remaining in the special revenue fund after 2 fiscal years must be deposited in the county general fund if it has not been committed for expenditure. The county treasurer shall provide, upon request by a justice court, monthly reports of the revenue credited to and expenditures made from the special revenue fund.

(c) Five dollars to the State Controller for credit to the State General Fund.

(d) The remainder of each assessment to the State Controller for credit to a special account in the State General Fund for distribution as provided in subsection 8.

7. The money apportioned to a juvenile court, a justice court or a municipal court pursuant to this section must be used, in addition to providing services to juvenile offenders in the juvenile court, to improve the operations of the court, or to acquire appropriate advanced technology or the use of such technology, or both. Money used to improve the operations of the court may include expenditures for:

(a) Training and education of personnel;

(b) Acquisition of capital goods;

(c) Management and operational studies; or

(d) Audits.

8. Of the total amount deposited in the State General Fund pursuant to paragraph (d) of subsection 5 and paragraph (d) of subsection 6, the State Controller shall distribute the money received to the following public agencies in the following manner:

(a) Not less than 51 percent to the Office of Court Administrator for allocation as follows:

(1) Thirty-six and one-half percent of the amount distributed to the Office of Court Administrator for:

(I) The administration of the courts;

(II) The development of a uniform system for judicial records; and

(III) Continuing judicial education.

(2) Forty-eight percent of the amount distributed to the Office of Court Administrator for the Supreme Court.

(3) Three and one-half percent of the amount distributed to the Office of Court Administrator for the payment for the services of retired justices, retired judges of the Court of Appeals and retired district judges.

(4) Twelve percent of the amount distributed to the Office of Court Administrator for the provision of specialty court programs.

(b) Not more than 49 percent must be used to the extent of legislative authorization for the support of:

(1) The Central Repository for Nevada Records of Criminal History;

(2) The Peace Officers' Standards and Training Commission;

(3) The operation by the Department of Public Safety of a computerized interoperative system for information related to law enforcement;

(4) The Fund for the Compensation of Victims of Crime;

(5) The Advisory Council for Prosecuting Attorneys; and

(6) Programs within the Office of the Attorney General related to victims of domestic violence.

9. Any money deposited in the State General Fund pursuant to paragraph (d) of subsection 5 and paragraph (d) of subsection 6 that is not distributed or used pursuant to paragraph (b) of subsection 8 must be transferred to the uncommitted balance of the State General Fund.

10. As used in this section:

(a) "Juvenile court" has the meaning ascribed to it in NRS 62A.180.

(b) "Office of Court Administrator" means the Office of Court Administrator created pursuant to NRS 1.320.

(Added to NRS by 1983, 907; A 1985, 907; 1987, 1417; 1989, 1058, 1980; 1991, 1554, 2181; 1993, 604, 867; 1995, 2453; 1997, 1508; 1999, 2426; 2001, 375, 2353, 2919; 2003, 1118, 1461, 2098; 2007, 40, 1413, 1741; 2009, 979; 2010, 26th Special Session, 81; 2013, 1753)

NRS 176.0611 Additional administrative assessment for misdemeanor: Authorization; collection; distribution; limitations on use. [Effective through June 30, 2017.]

1. A county or a city, upon recommendation of the appropriate court, may, by ordinance, authorize the justices or judges of the justice or municipal courts within its jurisdiction to impose for not longer than 50 years, in addition to the administrative assessments imposed pursuant to NRS 176.059, 176.0613 and 176.0623, an administrative assessment for the provision of court facilities.

2. Except as otherwise provided in subsection 3, in any jurisdiction in which an administrative assessment for the provision of court facilities has been authorized, when a defendant pleads guilty or guilty but mentally ill or is found guilty or guilty but mentally ill of a misdemeanor, including the violation of any municipal ordinance, the justice or judge shall include in the sentence the sum of $10 as an administrative assessment for the provision of court facilities and render a judgment against the defendant for the assessment. If the justice or judge sentences the defendant to perform community service in lieu of a fine, the justice or judge shall include in the sentence the administrative assessment required pursuant to this subsection.

3. The provisions of subsection 2 do not apply to:

(a) An ordinance regulating metered parking; or

(b) An ordinance that is specifically designated as imposing a civil penalty or liability pursuant to NRS 244.3575 or 268.019.

4. The money collected for an administrative assessment for the provision of court facilities must not be deducted from the fine imposed by the justice or judge but must be taxed against the defendant in addition to the fine. The money collected for such an administrative assessment must be stated separately on the court's docket and must be included in the amount posted for bail. If bail is forfeited, the administrative assessment included in the amount posted for bail pursuant to this subsection must be disbursed in the manner set forth in subsection 6 or 7. If the defendant is found not guilty or the charges are dismissed, the money deposited with the court must be returned to the defendant. If the justice or judge cancels a fine because the fine has been determined to be uncollectible, any balance of the fine and the administrative assessment remaining unpaid shall be deemed to be uncollectible and the defendant is not required to pay it. If a fine is determined to be uncollectible, the defendant is not entitled to a refund of the fine or administrative assessment the defendant has paid and the justice or judge shall not recalculate the administrative assessment.

5. If the justice or judge permits the fine and administrative assessment for the provision of court facilities to be paid in installments, the payments must be applied in the following order:

(a) To pay the unpaid balance of an administrative assessment imposed pursuant to NRS 176.059;

(b) To pay the unpaid balance of an administrative assessment for the provision of court facilities pursuant to this section;

(c) To pay the unpaid balance of an administrative assessment for the provision of specialty court programs pursuant to NRS 176.0613;

(d) To pay the unpaid balance of an administrative assessment for obtaining a biological specimen and conducting a genetic marker analysis pursuant to NRS 176.0623;

(e) To pay the unpaid balance of the specialty courts fee pursuant to NRS 484C.515; and

(f) To pay the fine.

6. The money collected for administrative assessments for the provision of court facilities in municipal courts must be paid by the clerk of the court to the city treasurer on or before the fifth day of each month for the preceding month. The city treasurer shall deposit the money received in a special revenue fund. The city may use the money in the special revenue fund only to:

(a) Acquire land on which to construct additional facilities for the municipal courts or a regional justice center that includes the municipal courts.

(b) Construct or acquire additional facilities for the municipal courts or a regional justice center that includes the municipal courts.

(c) Renovate or remodel existing facilities for the municipal courts.

(d) Acquire furniture, fixtures and equipment necessitated by the construction or acquisition of additional facilities or the renovation of an existing facility for the municipal courts or a regional justice center that includes the municipal courts. This paragraph does not authorize the expenditure of money from the fund for furniture, fixtures or equipment for judicial chambers.

(e) Acquire advanced technology for use in the additional or renovated facilities.

(f) Pay debt service on any bonds issued pursuant to subsection 3 of NRS 350.020 for the acquisition of land or facilities or the construction or renovation of facilities for the municipal courts or a regional justice center that includes the municipal courts.

□ Any money remaining in the special revenue fund after 5 fiscal years must be deposited in the municipal general fund for the continued maintenance of court facilities if it has not been committed for expenditure pursuant to a plan for the construction or acquisition of court facilities or improvements to court facilities. The city treasurer shall provide, upon request by a municipal court, monthly reports of the revenue credited to and expenditures made from the special revenue fund.

7. The money collected for administrative assessments for the provision of court facilities in justice courts must be paid by the clerk of the court to the county treasurer on or before the fifth day of each month for the preceding month. The county treasurer shall deposit the money received to a special revenue fund. The county may use the money in the special revenue fund only to:

(a) Acquire land on which to construct additional facilities for the justice courts or a regional justice center that includes the justice courts.

(b) Construct or acquire additional facilities for the justice courts or a regional justice center that includes the justice courts.

(c) Renovate or remodel existing facilities for the justice courts.

(d) Acquire furniture, fixtures and equipment necessitated by the construction or acquisition of additional facilities or the renovation of an existing facility for the justice courts or a regional justice center that includes the justice courts. This paragraph does not authorize the expenditure of money from the fund for furniture, fixtures or equipment for judicial chambers.

(e) Acquire advanced technology for use in the additional or renovated facilities.

(f) Pay debt service on any bonds issued pursuant to subsection 3 of NRS 350.020 for the acquisition of land or facilities or the construction or renovation of facilities for the justice courts or a regional justice center that includes the justice courts.

□ Any money remaining in the special revenue fund after 5 fiscal years must be deposited in the county general fund for the continued maintenance of court facilities if it has not been committed for expenditure pursuant to a plan for the construction or acquisition of court facilities or improvements to court facilities. The county treasurer shall provide, upon request by a justice court, monthly reports of the revenue credited to and expenditures made from the special revenue fund.

8. If money collected pursuant to this section is to be used to acquire land on which to construct a regional justice center, to construct a regional justice center or to pay debt service on bonds issued for these purposes, the county and the participating cities shall, by interlocal agreement, determine such issues as the size of the regional justice center, the manner in which the center will be used and the apportionment of fiscal responsibility for the center.

(Added to NRS by 1995, 1024; A 1995, 2482; 1997, 140; 2003, 526, 1463, 2100; 2007, 1416; 2013, 1064, 1988, 3683; 2015, 2955)

NRS 176.0611 Additional administrative assessment for misdemeanor: Authorization; collection; distribution; limitations on use. [Effective July 1, 2017.]

1. A county or a city, upon recommendation of the appropriate court, may, by ordinance, authorize the justices or judges of the justice or municipal courts within its jurisdiction to impose for not longer than 50 years, in addition to the administrative assessments imposed pursuant to NRS 176.059, 176.0613 and 176.0623, an administrative assessment for the provision of court facilities.

2. Except as otherwise provided in subsection 3, in any jurisdiction in which an administrative assessment for the provision of court facilities has been authorized, when a defendant pleads guilty or guilty but mentally ill or is found guilty or guilty but mentally ill of a misdemeanor, including the violation of any municipal ordinance, the justice or judge shall include in the sentence the sum of $10 as an administrative assessment for the provision of court facilities and render a judgment against the defendant for the assessment. If the justice or judge sentences the defendant to perform community service in lieu of a fine, the justice or judge shall include in the sentence the administrative assessment required pursuant to this subsection.

3. The provisions of subsection 2 do not apply to:

(a) An ordinance regulating metered parking; or

(b) An ordinance that is specifically designated as imposing a civil penalty or liability pursuant to NRS 244.3575 or 268.019.

4. The money collected for an administrative assessment for the provision of court facilities must not be deducted from the fine imposed by the justice or judge but must be taxed against the defendant in addition to the fine. The money collected for such an administrative assessment must be stated separately on the court's docket and must be included in the amount posted for bail. If bail is forfeited, the administrative assessment included in the amount posted for bail pursuant to this subsection must be disbursed in the manner set forth in subsection 6 or 7. If the defendant is found not guilty or the charges are dismissed, the money deposited with the court must be returned to the defendant. If the justice or judge cancels a fine because the fine has been determined to be uncollectible, any balance of the fine and the administrative assessment remaining unpaid shall be deemed to be uncollectible and the defendant is not required to pay it. If a fine is determined to be uncollectible, the defendant is not entitled to a refund of the fine or administrative assessment the defendant has paid and the justice or judge shall not recalculate the administrative assessment.

5. If the justice or judge permits the fine and administrative assessment for the provision of court facilities to be paid in installments, the payments must be applied in the following order:

(a) To pay the unpaid balance of an administrative assessment imposed pursuant to NRS 176.059;

(b) To pay the unpaid balance of an administrative assessment for the provision of court facilities pursuant to this section;

(c) To pay the unpaid balance of an administrative assessment for the provision of specialty court programs pursuant to NRS 176.0613;

(d) To pay the unpaid balance of an administrative assessment for obtaining a biological specimen and conducting a genetic marker analysis pursuant to NRS 176.0623; and

(e) To pay the fine.

6. The money collected for administrative assessments for the provision of court facilities in municipal courts must be paid by the clerk of the court to the city treasurer on or before the fifth day of each month for the preceding month. The city treasurer shall deposit the money received in a special revenue fund. The city may use the money in the special revenue fund only to:

(a) Acquire land on which to construct additional facilities for the municipal courts or a regional justice center that includes the municipal courts.

(b) Construct or acquire additional facilities for the municipal courts or a regional justice center that includes the municipal courts.

(c) Renovate or remodel existing facilities for the municipal courts.

(d) Acquire furniture, fixtures and equipment necessitated by the construction or acquisition of additional facilities or the renovation of an existing facility for the municipal courts or a regional justice center that includes the municipal courts. This paragraph does not authorize the expenditure of money from the fund for furniture, fixtures or equipment for judicial chambers.

(e) Acquire advanced technology for use in the additional or renovated facilities.

(f) Pay debt service on any bonds issued pursuant to subsection 3 of NRS 350.020 for the acquisition of land or facilities or the construction or renovation of facilities for the municipal courts or a regional justice center that includes the municipal courts.

□ Any money remaining in the special revenue fund after 5 fiscal years must be deposited in the municipal general fund for the continued maintenance of court facilities if it has not been committed for expenditure pursuant to a plan for the construction or acquisition of court facilities or improvements to court facilities. The city treasurer shall provide, upon request by a municipal court, monthly reports of the revenue credited to and expenditures made from the special revenue fund.

7. The money collected for administrative assessments for the provision of court facilities in justice courts must be paid by the clerk of the court to the county treasurer on or before the fifth day of each month for the preceding month. The county treasurer shall deposit the money received to a special revenue fund. The county may use the money in the special revenue fund only to:

(a) Acquire land on which to construct additional facilities for the justice courts or a regional justice center that includes the justice courts.

(b) Construct or acquire additional facilities for the justice courts or a regional justice center that includes the justice courts.

(c) Renovate or remodel existing facilities for the justice courts.

(d) Acquire furniture, fixtures and equipment necessitated by the construction or acquisition of additional facilities or the renovation of an existing facility for the justice courts or a regional justice center that includes the justice courts. This paragraph does not authorize the expenditure of money from the fund for furniture, fixtures or equipment for judicial chambers.

(e) Acquire advanced technology for use in the additional or renovated facilities.

(f) Pay debt service on any bonds issued pursuant to subsection 3 of NRS 350.020 for the acquisition of land or facilities or the construction or renovation of facilities for the justice courts or a regional justice center that includes the justice courts.

□ Any money remaining in the special revenue fund after 5 fiscal years must be deposited in the county general fund for the continued maintenance of court facilities if it has not been committed for expenditure pursuant to a plan for the construction or acquisition of court facilities or improvements to court facilities. The county treasurer shall provide, upon request by a justice court, monthly reports of the revenue credited to and expenditures made from the special revenue fund.

8. If money collected pursuant to this section is to be used to acquire land on which to construct a regional justice center, to construct a regional justice center or to pay debt service on bonds issued for these purposes, the county and the participating cities shall, by interlocal agreement, determine such issues as the size of the regional justice center, the manner in which the center will be used and the apportionment of fiscal responsibility for the center.

(Added to NRS by 1995, 1024; A 1995, 2482; 1997, 140; 2003, 526, 1463, 2100; 2007, 1416; 2013, 1064, 1988, 3683; 2015, 2955, effective July 1, 2017)

NRS 176.0613 Additional administrative assessment for misdemeanor: Authorization; collection; distribution; limitations on use. [Effective through June 30, 2017.]

1. The justices or judges of the justice or municipal courts shall impose, in addition to an administrative assessment imposed pursuant to NRS 176.059, 176.0611 and 176.0623, an administrative assessment for the provision of specialty court programs.

2. Except as otherwise provided in subsection 3, when a defendant pleads guilty or guilty but mentally ill or is found guilty or guilty but mentally ill of a misdemeanor, including the violation of any municipal ordinance, the justice or judge shall include in the sentence the sum of $7 as an administrative assessment for the provision of specialty court programs and render a judgment against the defendant for the assessment. If a defendant is sentenced to perform community service in lieu of a fine, the sentence must include the administrative assessment required pursuant to this subsection.

3. The provisions of subsection 2 do not apply to:

(a) An ordinance regulating metered parking; or

(b) An ordinance which is specifically designated as imposing a civil penalty or liability pursuant to NRS 244.3575 or 268.019.

4. The money collected for an administrative assessment for the provision of specialty court programs must not be deducted from the fine imposed by the justice or judge but must be taxed against the defendant in addition to the fine. The money collected for such an administrative assessment must be stated separately on the court's docket and must be included in the amount posted for bail. If bail is forfeited, the administrative assessment included in the bail pursuant to this subsection must be disbursed pursuant to subsection 6 or 7. If the defendant is found not guilty or the charges are dismissed, the money deposited with the court must be returned to the defendant. If the justice or judge cancels a fine because the fine has been determined to be uncollectible, any balance of the fine and the administrative assessment remaining unpaid shall be deemed to be uncollectible and the defendant is not required to pay it. If a fine is determined to be uncollectible, the defendant is not entitled to a refund of the fine or administrative assessment the defendant has paid and the justice or judge shall not recalculate the administrative assessment.

5. If the justice or judge permits the fine and administrative assessment for the provision of specialty court programs to be paid in installments, the payments must be applied in the following order:

(a) To pay the unpaid balance of an administrative assessment imposed pursuant to NRS 176.059;

(b) To pay the unpaid balance of an administrative assessment for the provision of court facilities pursuant to NRS 176.0611;

(c) To pay the unpaid balance of an administrative assessment for the provision of specialty court programs;

(d) To pay the unpaid balance of an administrative assessment for obtaining a biological specimen and conducting a genetic marker analysis pursuant to NRS 176.0623;

(e) To pay the unpaid balance of the specialty courts fee pursuant to NRS 484C.515; and

(f) To pay the fine.

6. The money collected for an administrative assessment for the provision of specialty court programs in municipal court must be paid by the clerk of the court to the city treasurer on or before the fifth day of each month for the preceding month. On or before the 15th day of that month, the city treasurer shall deposit the money received for each administrative assessment with the State Controller for credit to a special account in the State General Fund administered by the Office of Court Administrator.

7. The money collected for an administrative assessment for the provision of specialty court programs in justice courts must be paid by the clerk of the court to the county treasurer on or before the fifth day of each month for the preceding month. On or before the 15th day of that month, the county treasurer shall deposit the money received for each administrative assessment with the State Controller for credit to a special account in the State General Fund administered by the Office of Court Administrator.

8. The Office of Court Administrator shall allocate the money credited to the State General Fund pursuant to subsections 6 and 7 to courts to assist with the funding or establishment of specialty court programs.

9. Money that is apportioned to a court from administrative assessments for the provision of specialty court programs must be used by the court to:

(a) Pay for the treatment and testing of persons who participate in the program; and

(b) Improve the operations of the specialty court program by any combination of:

(1) Acquiring necessary capital goods;

(2) Providing for personnel to staff and oversee the specialty court program;

(3) Providing training and education to personnel;

(4) Studying the management and operation of the program;

(5) Conducting audits of the program;

(6) Supplementing the funds used to pay for judges to oversee a specialty court program; or

(7) Acquiring or using appropriate technology.

10. As used in this section:

(a) "Office of Court Administrator" means the Office of Court Administrator created pursuant to NRS 1.320; and

(b) "Specialty court program" means a program established by a court to facilitate testing, treatment and oversight of certain persons over whom the court has jurisdiction and who the court has determined suffer from a mental illness or abuses alcohol or drugs. Such a program includes, without limitation, a program established pursuant to NRS 176A.250, 176A.280 or 453.580.

(Added to NRS by 2003, 2096; A 2007, 1418; 2009, 101; 2013, 1990, 3686; 2015, 2955)

NRS 176.0613 Additional administrative assessment for misdemeanor: Authorization; collection; distribution; limitations on use. [Effective July 1, 2017.]

1. The justices or judges of the justice or municipal courts shall impose, in addition to an administrative assessment imposed pursuant to NRS 176.059, 176.0611 and 176.0623, an administrative assessment for the provision of specialty court programs.

2. Except as otherwise provided in subsection 3, when a defendant pleads guilty or guilty but mentally ill or is found guilty or guilty but mentally ill of a misdemeanor, including the violation of any municipal ordinance, the justice or judge shall include in the sentence the sum of $7 as an administrative assessment for the provision of specialty court programs and render a judgment against the defendant for the assessment. If a defendant is sentenced to perform community service in lieu of a fine, the sentence must include the administrative assessment required pursuant to this subsection.

3. The provisions of subsection 2 do not apply to:

(a) An ordinance regulating metered parking; or

(b) An ordinance which is specifically designated as imposing a civil penalty or liability pursuant to NRS 244.3575 or 268.019.

4. The money collected for an administrative assessment for the provision of specialty court programs must not be deducted from the fine imposed by the justice or judge but must be taxed against the defendant in addition to the fine. The money collected for such an administrative assessment must be stated separately on the court's docket and must be included in the amount posted for bail. If bail is forfeited, the administrative assessment included in the bail pursuant to this subsection must be disbursed pursuant to subsection 6 or 7. If the defendant is found not guilty or the charges are dismissed, the money deposited with the court must be returned to the defendant. If the justice or judge cancels a fine because the fine has been determined to be uncollectible, any balance of the fine and the administrative assessment remaining unpaid shall be deemed to be uncollectible and the defendant is not required to pay it. If a fine is determined to be uncollectible, the defendant is not entitled to a refund of the fine or administrative assessment the defendant has paid and the justice or judge shall not recalculate the administrative assessment.

5. If the justice or judge permits the fine and administrative assessment for the provision of specialty court programs to be paid in installments, the payments must be applied in the following order:

(a) To pay the unpaid balance of an administrative assessment imposed pursuant to NRS 176.059;

(b) To pay the unpaid balance of an administrative assessment for the provision of court facilities pursuant to NRS 176.0611;

(c) To pay the unpaid balance of an administrative assessment for the provision of specialty court programs;

(d) To pay the unpaid balance of an administrative assessment for obtaining a biological specimen and conducting a genetic marker analysis pursuant to NRS 176.0623; and

(e) To pay the fine.

6. The money collected for an administrative assessment for the provision of specialty court programs in municipal court must be paid by the clerk of the court to the city treasurer on or before the fifth day of each month for the preceding month. On or before the 15th day of that month, the city treasurer shall deposit the money received for each administrative assessment with the State Controller for credit to a special account in the State General Fund administered by the Office of Court Administrator.

7. The money collected for an administrative assessment for the provision of specialty court programs in justice courts must be paid by the clerk of the court to the county treasurer on or before the fifth day of each month for the preceding month. On or before the 15th day of that month, the county treasurer shall deposit the money received for each administrative assessment with the State Controller for credit to a special account in the State General Fund administered by the Office of Court Administrator.

8. The Office of Court Administrator shall allocate the money credited to the State General Fund pursuant to subsections 6 and 7 to courts to assist with the funding or establishment of specialty court programs.

9. Money that is apportioned to a court from administrative assessments for the provision of specialty court programs must be used by the court to:

(a) Pay for the treatment and testing of persons who participate in the program; and

(b) Improve the operations of the specialty court program by any combination of:

(1) Acquiring necessary capital goods;

(2) Providing for personnel to staff and oversee the specialty court program;

(3) Providing training and education to personnel;

(4) Studying the management and operation of the program;

(5) Conducting audits of the program;

(6) Supplementing the funds used to pay for judges to oversee a specialty court program; or

(7) Acquiring or using appropriate technology.

10. As used in this section:

(a) "Office of Court Administrator" means the Office of Court Administrator created pursuant to NRS 1.320; and

(b) "Specialty court program" means a program established by a court to facilitate testing, treatment and oversight of certain persons over whom the court has jurisdiction and who the court has determined suffer from a mental illness or abuses alcohol or drugs. Such a program includes, without limitation, a program established pursuant to NRS 176A.250, 176A.280 or 453.580.

(Added to NRS by 2003, 2096; A 2007, 1418; 2009, 101; 2013, 1066, 1990, 3686; 2015, 2955, effective July 1, 2017)

NRS 176.062 Administrative assessment for felony or gross misdemeanor: Collection; distribution; limitations on use.

1. When a defendant pleads guilty or guilty but mentally ill or is found guilty or guilty but mentally ill of a felony or gross misdemeanor, the judge shall include in the sentence the sum of $25 as an administrative assessment and render a judgment against the defendant for the assessment.

2. The money collected for an administrative assessment:

(a) Must not be deducted from any fine imposed by the judge;

(b) Must be taxed against the defendant in addition to the fine; and

(c) Must be stated separately on the court's docket.

3. The money collected for administrative assessments in district courts must be paid by the clerk of the court to the county treasurer on or before the fifth day of each month for the preceding month. The county treasurer shall distribute, on or before the 15th day of that month, the money received in the following amounts for each assessment received:

(a) Five dollars for credit to a special account in the county general fund for the use of the district court.

(b) The remainder of each assessment to the State Controller.

4. The State Controller shall credit the money received pursuant to subsection 3 to a special account for the assistance of criminal justice in the State General Fund, and distribute the money from the account to the Attorney General as authorized by the Legislature. Any amount received in excess of the amount authorized by the Legislature for distribution must remain in the account.

(Added to NRS by 1987, 846; A 1991, 1153; 1995, 2455; 2001, 2921; 2003, 1465; 2007, 1420)

NRS 176.0623 Additional administrative assessment for felony, gross misdemeanor or misdemeanor: Authorization; collection; distribution; limitations on use.

1. In addition to any other administrative assessment imposed, when a defendant pleads guilty, is found guilty or enters a plea of nolo contendere to a misdemeanor, gross misdemeanor or felony, including the violation of any municipal ordinance, on or after July 1, 2013, the justice or judge of the justice, municipal or district court, as applicable, shall include in the sentence the sum of $3 as an administrative assessment for obtaining a biological specimen and conducting a genetic marker analysis and shall render a judgment against the defendant for the assessment. If a defendant is sentenced to perform community service in lieu of a fine, the sentence must include the administrative assessment required pursuant to this subsection.

2. The money collected for an administrative assessment for obtaining a biological specimen and conducting a genetic marker analysis must not be deducted from the fine imposed by the justice or judge but must be taxed against the defendant in addition to the fine. The money collected for such an administrative assessment must be stated separately on the court's docket and must be included in the amount posted for bail. If bail is forfeited, the administrative assessment included in the bail pursuant to this subsection must be disbursed pursuant to subsection 4. If the defendant is found not guilty or the charges are dismissed, the money deposited with the court must be returned to the defendant. If the justice or judge cancels a fine because the fine has been determined to be uncollectible, any balance of the fine and the administrative assessment remaining unpaid shall be deemed to be uncollectible, and the defendant is not required to pay it. If a fine is determined to be uncollectible, the defendant is not entitled to a refund of the fine or administrative assessment he or she has paid, and the justice or judge shall not recalculate the administrative assessment.

3. If the justice or judge permits the fine and administrative assessment for the provision of genetic marker analysis to be paid in installments, the payments must be applied in the following order:

(a) To pay the unpaid balance of an administrative assessment imposed pursuant to NRS 176.059;

(b) To pay the unpaid balance of an administrative assessment for the provision of court facilities pursuant to NRS 176.0611;

(c) To pay the unpaid balance of an administrative assessment for the provision of specialty court programs pursuant to NRS 176.0613;

(d) To pay the unpaid balance of an administrative assessment for obtaining a biological specimen and conducting a genetic marker analysis pursuant to this section; and

(e) To pay the fine.

4. The money collected for an administrative assessment for the provision of genetic marker analysis must be paid by the clerk of the court to the county treasurer on or before the fifth day of each month for the preceding month for credit to the fund for genetic marker analysis pursuant to NRS 176.0915.

(Added to NRS by 2013, 1062)

NRS 176.0625 Administrative assessment, fine or fee for felony or gross misdemeanor: Collection by certain entities.

1. If a fine, administrative assessment or fee is imposed pursuant to this chapter upon a defendant who pleads guilty or guilty but mentally ill or is found guilty or guilty but mentally ill of a felony or gross misdemeanor, the district court entering the judgment of conviction shall forward to the county treasurer or other office assigned by the county to make collections the information necessary to collect the fine, administrative assessment or fee. The county treasurer or other office assigned by the county to make collections is responsible for such collection efforts and has the authority to collect the fine, administrative assessment or fee.

2. If the county treasurer or other office assigned by the county to make collections is unable to collect the fine, administrative assessment or fee after 60 days, the county treasurer may assign to the Office of the State Controller the responsibility for collection of the fine, administrative assessment or fee through a cooperative agreement pursuant to NRS 353.650, so long as the Office of the State Controller is willing and able to make such collection efforts.

3. If the county treasurer and the Office of the State Controller enter into a cooperative agreement pursuant to NRS 353.650, the county treasurer or other county office assigned by the county to make collections shall forward to the Office of the State Controller the necessary information. For the purposes of this section, the information necessary to collect the fine, administrative assessment or fee shall be considered and limited to:

(a) The name of the defendant;

(b) The date of birth of the defendant;

(c) The social security number of the defendant;

(d) The last known address of the defendant; and

(e) The nature and the amount of money owed by the defendant.

4. If the Office of the State Controller is successful in collecting the fine, administrative assessment or fee, the money collected must be returned to the originating county, minus the costs and fees actually incurred in collecting the fine, administrative assessment or fee pursuant to NRS 176.0635.

5. Any money collected pursuant to subsection 4 must be deposited in the State Treasury, pursuant to NRS 176.265.

6. Any record created pursuant to subsection 3 that contains personal identifying information shall not be considered a public record pursuant to NRS 239.010 and must be treated pursuant to NRS 239.0105.

7. Unless otherwise prohibited by law, the entity responsible for collecting the fine, administrative assessment or fee pursuant to this section has the authority to compromise the amount to be collected for the purpose of satisfying the judgment.

(Added to NRS by 2011, 909)

NRS 176.063 Administrative assessment, fine or fee for felony or gross misdemeanor: Court must advise defendant regarding lien. If a district court imposes a fine, administrative assessment or fee upon a defendant who pleads guilty or guilty but mentally ill or is found guilty or guilty but mentally ill of a felony or gross misdemeanor, the district court judge shall advise the defendant at the time of sentencing that:

1. The judgment constitutes a lien, pursuant to NRS 176.275; and

2. If the defendant does not satisfy the lien, collection efforts may be undertaken against the defendant pursuant to the laws of this State.

(Added to NRS by 2011, 910)

NRS 176.0635 Administrative assessment, fine or fee for felony or gross misdemeanor: Additional costs and fees for collection.

1. A defendant who pleads guilty or guilty but mentally ill or is found guilty or guilty but mentally ill who owes a fine, administrative assessment or fee, pursuant to NRS 176.0625, must be assessed by and pay to the county treasurer or other office assigned by the county to make collections the following costs and fees if the county treasurer or other office assigned by the county to make collections is successful in collecting the fine, administrative assessment or fee:

(a) The costs and fees actually incurred in collecting the fine, administrative assessment or fee; and

(b) A fee payable to the county treasurer in the amount of 2 percent of the amount of the fine, administrative assessment or fee assigned to the county treasurer or other office assigned by the county to make collections.

2. The total amount of the costs and fees required to be collected pursuant to subsection 1 must not exceed 35 percent of the amount of the fine, administrative assessment or fee or $50,000, whichever is less.

(Added to NRS by 2011, 910)

NRS 176.064 Collection fee for unpaid administrative assessment, fine, fee or restitution; use of collection agency; report to credit agencies; civil judgment; attachment or garnishment; suspension of driver's license; imprisonment.

1. If a fine, administrative assessment, fee or restitution is imposed upon a defendant pursuant to this chapter, whether or not the fine, administrative assessment, fee or restitution is in addition to any other punishment, and the fine, administrative assessment, fee or restitution or any part of it remains unpaid after the time established by the court for its payment, the defendant is liable for a collection fee, to be imposed by the court at the time it finds that the fine, administrative assessment, fee or restitution is delinquent, of:

(a) Not more than $100, if the amount of the delinquency is less than $2,000.

(b) Not more than $500, if the amount of the delinquency is $2,000 or greater, but is less than $5,000.

(c) Ten percent of the amount of the delinquency, if the amount of the delinquency is $5,000 or greater.

2. A state or local entity that is responsible for collecting a delinquent fine, administrative assessment, fee or restitution may, in addition to attempting to collect the fine, administrative assessment, fee or restitution through any other lawful means, take any or all of the following actions:

(a) Report the delinquency to reporting agencies that assemble or evaluate information concerning credit.

(b) Request that the court take appropriate action pursuant to subsection 3.

(c) Contract with a collection agency licensed pursuant to NRS 649.075 to collect the delinquent amount and the collection fee. The collection agency must be paid as compensation for its services an amount not greater than the amount of the collection fee imposed pursuant to subsection 1, in accordance with the provisions of the contract.

3. The court may, on its own motion or at the request of a state or local entity that is responsible for collecting the delinquent fine, administrative assessment, fee or restitution, take any or all of the following actions, in the following order of priority if practicable:

(a) Enter a civil judgment for the amount due in favor of the state or local entity that is responsible for collecting the delinquent fine, administrative assessment, fee or restitution. A civil judgment entered pursuant to this paragraph may be enforced and renewed in the manner provided by law for the enforcement and renewal of a judgment for money rendered in a civil action. If the court has entered a civil judgment pursuant to this paragraph and the person against whom the judgment is entered is not indigent and has not satisfied the judgment within the time established by the court, the person may be dealt with as for contempt of court.

(b) Request that a prosecuting attorney undertake collection of the delinquency, including, without limitation, the original amount of the civil judgment entered pursuant to paragraph (a) and the collection fee, by attachment or garnishment of the defendant's property, wages or other money receivable.

(c) Order the suspension of the driver's license of the defendant. If the defendant does not possess a driver's license, the court may prohibit the defendant from applying for a driver's license for a specified period. If the defendant is already the subject of a court order suspending or delaying the issuance of the defendant's driver's license, the court may order the additional suspension or delay, as appropriate, to apply consecutively with the previous order. At the time the court issues an order suspending the driver's license of a defendant pursuant to this paragraph, the court shall require the defendant to surrender to the court all driver's licenses then held by the defendant. The court shall, within 5 days after issuing the order, forward to the Department of Motor Vehicles the licenses, together with a copy of the order. At the time the court issues an order pursuant to this paragraph delaying the ability of a defendant to apply for a driver's license, the court shall, within 5 days after issuing the order, forward to the Department of Motor Vehicles a copy of the order. The Department of Motor Vehicles shall report a suspension pursuant to this paragraph to an insurance company or its agent inquiring about the defendant's driving record, but such a suspension must not be considered for the purpose of rating or underwriting.

(d) For a delinquent fine or administrative assessment, order the confinement of the person in the appropriate prison, jail or detention facility, as provided in NRS 176.065 and 176.075.

4. Money collected from a collection fee imposed pursuant to subsection 1 must be distributed in the following manner:

(a) Except as otherwise provided in paragraph (d), if the money is collected by or on behalf of a municipal court, the money must be deposited in a special fund in the appropriate city treasury. The city may use the money in the fund only to develop and implement a program for the collection of fines, administrative assessments, fees and restitution and to hire additional personnel necessary for the success of such a program.

(b) Except as otherwise provided in paragraph (d), if the money is collected by or on behalf of a justice court or district court, the money must be deposited in a special fund in the appropriate county treasury. The county may use the money in the special fund only to:

(1) Develop and implement a program for the collection of fines, administrative assessments, fees and restitution and to hire additional personnel necessary for the success of such a program; or

(2) Improve the operations of a court by providing funding for:

(I) A civil law self-help center; or

(II) Court security personnel and equipment for a regional justice center that includes the justice courts of that county.

(c) Except as otherwise provided in paragraph (d), if the money is collected by a state entity, the money must be deposited in an account, which is hereby created in the State Treasury. The Court Administrator may use the money in the account only to develop and implement a program for the collection of fines, administrative assessments, fees and restitution in this State and to hire additional personnel necessary for the success of such a program.

(d) If the money is collected by a collection agency, after the collection agency has been paid its fee pursuant to the terms of the contract, any remaining money must be deposited in the state, city or county treasury, whichever is appropriate, to be used only for the purposes set forth in paragraph (a), (b) or (c) of this subsection.

(Added to NRS by 1997, 899; A 1999, 425; 2001, 2569; 2013, 530)

NRS 176.065 Rate of additional imprisonment in default of administrative assessment, fine or forfeiture.

1. Except as otherwise provided in subsection 2, when a person is sentenced to both fine and imprisonment, or to pay a forfeiture in addition to imprisonment, the court may, pursuant to NRS 62B.420 or 176.064, order that the person be confined in the state prison, the city or county jail or a detention facility, whichever is designated in the person's sentence of imprisonment, for an additional period of 1 day for each $75 of the amount until the administrative assessment and the fine or forfeiture are satisfied or the maximum term of imprisonment prescribed by law for the offense committed has elapsed, whichever is earlier, but the person's eligibility for parole is governed only by the person's sentence of imprisonment.

2. The provisions of this section do not apply to indigent persons.

(Added to NRS by 1967, 1433; A 1973, 32; 1983, 434, 908; 1989, 1178; 1997, 901; 2013, 532)

NRS 176.075 Rate of imprisonment in default of administrative assessment, fine or forfeiture.

1. Except as otherwise provided in subsection 2, when a person is sentenced to pay a fine or forfeiture without an accompanying sentence of imprisonment, the court may, pursuant to NRS 62B.420 or 176.064, order that the person be confined in the city or county jail or detention facility for a period of not more than 1 day for each $75 of the amount until the administrative assessment and the fine or forfeiture are satisfied.

2. The provisions of this section do not apply to indigent persons.

(Added to NRS by 1967, 1433; A 1983, 434, 908; 1989, 1178; 1997, 901; 2013, 532)

NRS 176.085 Reduction of excessive fine or administrative assessment; payment in installments. Whenever, after a fine and administrative assessment have been imposed but before they have been discharged by payment or confinement, it is made to appear to the judge or justice imposing the fine or administrative assessment or his or her successor:

1. That the fine or administrative assessment is excessive in relation to the financial resources of the defendant, the judge or justice or his or her successor may reduce the fine accordingly.

2. That the discharge of the fine or administrative assessment is not within the defendant's present financial ability to pay, the judge or justice or his or her successor may direct that the fine be paid in installments.

(Added to NRS by 1967, 1433; A 1973, 388; 1983, 908)

NRS 176.087 Imposition of community service as punishment or condition of probation.

1. Except where the imposition of a specific criminal penalty is mandatory, a court may order a convicted person to perform supervised community service:

(a) In lieu of all or a part of any fine or imprisonment that may be imposed for the commission of a misdemeanor; or

(b) As a condition of probation granted for another offense.

2. The community service must be performed for and under the supervising authority of a county, city, town or other political subdivision or agency of the State of Nevada or a charitable organization that renders service to the community or its residents.

3. The court may require the convicted person to deposit with the court a reasonable sum of money to pay for the cost of policies of insurance against liability for personal injury and damage to property or for industrial insurance, or both, during those periods in which the person performs the community service, unless, in the case of industrial insurance, it is provided by the authority for which the person performs the community service.

4. The following conditions apply to any such community service imposed by the court:

(a) The court must fix the period of community service that is imposed as punishment or a condition of probation and distribute the period over weekends or over other appropriate times that will allow the convicted person to continue employment and to care for the person's family. The period of community service fixed by the court must not exceed, for a:

(1) Misdemeanor, 200 hours;

(2) Gross misdemeanor, 600 hours; or

(3) Felony, 1,000 hours.

(b) A supervising authority listed in subsection 2 must agree to accept the convicted person for community service before the court may require the convicted person to perform community service for that supervising authority. The supervising authority must be located in or be the town or city of the convicted person's residence or, if that placement is not possible, one located within the jurisdiction of the court or, if that placement is not possible, the authority may be located outside the jurisdiction of the court.

(c) Community service that a court requires pursuant to this section must be supervised by an official of the supervising authority or by a person designated by the authority.

(d) The court may require the supervising authority to report periodically to the court or to a probation officer the convicted person's performance in carrying out the punishment or condition of probation.

(Added to NRS by 1981, 486; A 1991, 1930; 1997, 33; 2001 Special Session, 133)

Preservation of Biological Evidence and Genetic Marker Analysis

NRS 176.0911 Definitions. As used in NRS 176.0911 to 176.0919, inclusive, unless the context otherwise requires, the words and terms defined in NRS 176.09111 to 176.09119, inclusive, have the meanings ascribed to them in those sections.

(Added to NRS by 1997, 1668; A 2001, 3032; 2009, 1846; 2013, 1068)

NRS 176.09111 "Agency of criminal justice" defined. "Agency of criminal justice" has the meaning ascribed to it in NRS 179A.030.

(Added to NRS by 2013, 1056)

NRS 176.09112 "Biological specimen" defined. "Biological specimen" means a biological sample, tissue, fluid or other bodily sample suitable for genetic marker analysis, obtained from a person or from physical evidence.

(Added to NRS by 2013, 1056)

NRS 176.09113 "CODIS" defined. "CODIS" means the Federal Bureau of Investigation's Combined DNA Index System that allows for the storage and exchange of DNA records submitted by federal, state and local forensic DNA laboratories. The term includes the National DNA Index System administered and operated by the Federal Bureau of Investigation.

(Added to NRS by 2013, 1056)

NRS 176.09114 "DNA" defined. "DNA" means deoxyribonucleic acid which is located in the cells of a person and which provides the genetic blueprint of a person.

(Added to NRS by 2013, 1057)

NRS 176.09115 "DNA profile" defined. "DNA profile" means the genetic constitution of a person at defined locations in the DNA of the person.

(Added to NRS by 2013, 1057)

NRS 176.09116 "DNA record" defined. "DNA record" means a database record, stored in the State DNA Database or CODIS, that includes the DNA profile of a person and data required to manage the record, including, without limitation, the identity of the agency submitting the database record, the identification number of the biological specimen and the names of personnel who conducted the genetic marker analysis.

(Added to NRS by 2013, 1057)

NRS 176.09117 "Forensic laboratory" defined. "Forensic laboratory" means any laboratory designated pursuant to NRS 176.0917.

(Added to NRS by 2013, 1057)

NRS 176.09118 "Genetic marker analysis" defined. "Genetic marker analysis" means the analytical testing process of a biological specimen that results in a DNA profile.

(Added to NRS by 2013, 1057)

NRS 176.09119 "State DNA Database" defined. "State DNA Database" means the database established pursuant to NRS 176.09121.

(Added to NRS by 2013, 1057)

NRS 176.0912 Biological evidence secured in connection with investigation or prosecution; required preservation.

1. Except as otherwise provided in this section, upon the conviction of a defendant for a category A or B felony, an agency of criminal justice that has in its possession or custody any biological evidence secured in connection with the investigation or prosecution of the defendant shall preserve such evidence until the expiration of any sentence imposed on the defendant.

2. Biological evidence subject to the requirements of this section may be consumed for testing upon notice to the defendant.

3. An agency of criminal justice may establish procedures for:

(a) Retaining probative samples of biological evidence subject to the requirements of this section; and

(b) Disposing of bulk evidence that does not affect the suitability of such probative samples for testing.

4. The provisions of this section must not be construed to restrict or limit an agency of criminal justice from establishing procedures for the retention, preservation and disposal of biological evidence secured in connection with other criminal cases.

5. As used in this section, "biological evidence" means any semen, blood, saliva, hair, skin tissue or other identified biological material removed from physical evidence.

(Added to NRS by 2009, 1845; A 2013, 1068)

NRS 176.09121 State DNA Database: Establishment; duties.

1. The State DNA Database is hereby established to serve as this State's repository for DNA records and to provide DNA records to the Federal Bureau of Investigation.

2. The Forensic Science Division of the Washoe County Sheriff's Office shall oversee, manage and administer the State DNA Database and shall:

(a) Implement policies for the management and administration of the State DNA Database, including, without limitation, any system for the identification of DNA profiles and DNA records that is necessary to support agencies of criminal justice.

(b) Adopt policies and protocols and enter into any necessary agreements to implement the provisions of NRS 176.0911 to 176.0919, inclusive.

(c) Ensure that all searches of the State DNA Database are performed in accordance with state and federal law.

(d) Act as a liaison between the Federal Bureau of Investigation and other state agencies of criminal justice relating to this State's participation in CODIS.

(Added to NRS by 2013, 1057)

NRS 176.09123 Collection of biological specimen from persons arrested for felony; submission to forensic laboratory; identifying information submitted to Central Repository; genetic marker analysis; creation of DNA profile; information included in criminal history record.

1. If a person is arrested for a felony pursuant to a warrant, the law enforcement agency making the arrest shall:

(a) Submit the name, date of birth, fingerprints and any other information identifying the person to the Central Repository for Nevada Records of Criminal History;

(b) Upon booking the person into a city or county jail or detention facility, and before the person is released from custody, obtain a biological specimen from the person, through a cheek swab, pursuant to the provisions of this section; and

(c) Submit the biological specimen to the appropriate forensic laboratory for genetic marker analysis in accordance with the provisions of this section.

2. If a person is arrested for a felony without a warrant, the law enforcement agency making the arrest shall:

(a) Submit the name, date of birth, fingerprints and any other information identifying the person to the Central Repository for Nevada Records of Criminal History;

(b) Upon booking the person into a city or county jail or detention facility, and before the person is released from custody, obtain a biological specimen from the person, through a cheek swab, pursuant to the provisions of this section;

(c) Submit the biological specimen to the appropriate forensic laboratory for genetic marker analysis in accordance with the provisions of this section after receiving notice that a court or magistrate has determined that probable cause existed for the person's arrest; and

(d) If a court or magistrate determines that probable cause did not exist for the person's arrest, destroy the biological specimen within 5 business days after receiving notice of the determination by the court or magistrate.

3. A law enforcement agency shall not knowingly obtain a biological specimen from a person who has previously submitted such a specimen for an arrest or conviction of a prior offense unless the law enforcement agency or a court or magistrate determines that an additional specimen is necessary.

4. If a law enforcement agency has not already obtained a biological specimen from a person arrested for an offense for which a biological specimen must be obtained pursuant to this section at the time a court or magistrate sets bail or considers releasing a person on his or her own recognizance, the court or magistrate shall:

(a) Require the person to provide a biological specimen as a condition of being admitted to bail or released on his or her own recognizance; and

(b) Require the biological specimen to be provided to the appropriate forensic laboratory.

5. The Attorney General or a district attorney may petition a district court for an order requiring a person arrested for an offense for which a biological specimen must be obtained pursuant to this section to provide a biological specimen:

(a) Through a cheek swab; or

(b) By alternative means, if the person will not cooperate.

□ Nothing in this subsection shall be construed to prevent the collection of a biological specimen by order of a court of competent jurisdiction or the collection of a biological specimen from a person who is required to provide such a specimen pursuant to this section.

6. Upon receipt of a biological specimen, the forensic laboratory shall proceed with a genetic marker analysis. If the forensic laboratory determines that the biological specimen is inadequate or otherwise unusable, the law enforcement agency may obtain an additional biological specimen from the person arrested unless the person arrested is eligible to request destruction of the biological specimen and purging of his or her DNA profile or DNA record pursuant to this section.

7. Upon completion of a genetic marker analysis of a person pursuant to this section, the forensic laboratory shall inform the Central Repository for Nevada Records of Criminal History that the forensic laboratory has created a DNA profile of the person and will be submitting the DNA profile of the person for inclusion in the State DNA Database and CODIS. The Central Repository for Nevada Records of Criminal

History shall include an indication on the criminal history record of the person regarding the collection of a biological specimen and the creation of a DNA profile, but may not include, in its records, any other information relating to the biological specimen, DNA profile or DNA record of the person.

(Added to NRS by 2013, 1058)

NRS 176.09125 Destruction of biological specimen and purging of DNA record: Grounds; written request; duties of Central Repository, forensic laboratory and State DNA Database.

1. A person whose record of criminal history indicates the collection of a biological specimen and whose DNA profile and DNA record have been included in the State DNA Database and CODIS pursuant to NRS 176.09123 may make a written request to the Central Repository for Nevada Records of Criminal History, using the form created pursuant to NRS 176.09165, that the biological specimen be destroyed and the DNA profile and DNA record be purged from the forensic laboratory, the State DNA Database and CODIS on the grounds that:

(a) The conviction on which the authority for keeping the biological specimen or the DNA profile or DNA record has been reversed and the case dismissed; or

(b) The arrest which led to the inclusion of the biological specimen or the DNA profile or DNA record:

(1) Has resulted in a felony charge that has been resolved by a dismissal, the successful completion of a preprosecution diversion program, a conditional discharge, an acquittal or an agreement entered into by a prosecuting attorney and a defendant in which the defendant, in exchange for a plea of guilty, guilty but mentally ill or nolo contendere, receives a charge other than a felony; or

(2) Has not resulted in any additional criminal charge for a felony within 3 years after the date of the arrest.

2. Within 6 weeks after receiving a written request pursuant to subsection 1, the Central Repository for Nevada Records of Criminal History shall forward the request and all supporting documentation to the forensic laboratory holding the biological specimen. Except as otherwise provided in subsection 3, upon receipt of the written request, the forensic laboratory shall destroy any biological specimen from the person and purge the DNA profile of the person if the written request is accompanied by:

(a) A certified copy of the court order reversing and dismissing the conviction; or

(b) For any biological specimen obtained pursuant to an arrest for which a biological specimen must be provided pursuant to NRS 176.09123:

(1) A certified copy of the dismissal, the successful completion of a preprosecution diversion program, a conditional discharge, an acquittal or the agreement entered into by the prosecuting attorney and the defendant in which the defendant, in exchange for a plea of guilty, guilty but mentally ill or nolo contendere, received a charge other than a felony; or

(2) A sworn affidavit from the law enforcement agency which submitted the biological specimen that no felony charges arising from the arrest have been filed within 3 years after the date of the arrest.

3. The forensic laboratory shall not destroy a biological specimen or purge the DNA profile of a person if the forensic laboratory is notified by a law enforcement agency that the person has a prior felony, a new felony arrest or a pending felony charge for which collection of a biological specimen is authorized pursuant to NRS 176.09123.

4. If a forensic laboratory:

(a) Determines that the requirements to destroy a biological specimen or purge a DNA profile or DNA record of a person have not been met, the forensic laboratory shall notify the Central Repository of Nevada Records of Criminal History of that fact. The Central Repository shall, as soon as reasonably practicable, notify the person that his or her request has been denied.

(b) Destroys a biological specimen and purges a DNA profile pursuant to this section, the forensic laboratory shall take the following actions:

(1) Notify the State DNA Database that the DNA profile and DNA record of the person must be purged from the State DNA Database and from CODIS. Upon receipt of such notification, the DNA profile and DNA record of the person must be purged from the State DNA Database and CODIS.

(2) Notify the Central Repository for Nevada Records of Criminal History that the forensic laboratory has destroyed the biological specimen and purged the DNA profile of the person and has notified the State DNA Database that the DNA profile and DNA record of the person must be purged from the State DNA Database and CODIS. Upon receipt of such notification, the Central Repository shall, as soon as reasonably practicable, notify the person that his or her request has been granted, his or her biological specimen has been destroyed by the forensic laboratory and his or her DNA profile and DNA record have been purged from the forensic laboratory, the State DNA Database and CODIS.

(Added to NRS by 2013, 1058)

NRS 176.09127 Payment of costs for obtaining biological specimen, destroying biological specimen and purging DNA record. Any cost that is incurred to obtain a biological specimen from a person pursuant to NRS 176.09123 or to destroy a biological specimen or to purge a DNA profile or DNA record from a forensic laboratory, the State DNA Database or CODIS pursuant to NRS 176.09125:

1. Is a charge against the county in which the person was arrested; and
2. Must be paid as provided in NRS 176.0915.

(Added to NRS by 2013, 1058)

NRS 176.09129 Storage and maintenance of biological specimen, DNA profile, DNA record and information; release of information; confidentiality; penalty for unauthorized disclosure of information.

1. The biological specimen, DNA profile, DNA record and any other information identifying or matching a biological specimen with a person must, at all times, be stored and maintained in the forensic laboratory, State DNA Database or CODIS, as applicable, and may only be made available in accordance with the provisions of this section. The biological specimen, DNA profile, DNA record, other information identifying or matching a biological specimen with a person and all computer software used by the forensic laboratory and the State DNA Database for the State DNA Database and for CODIS are confidential and are not public books or records within the meaning of NRS 239.010.

2. If any information related to a biological specimen, DNA profile or DNA record contained in CODIS is requested, the forensic laboratory shall comply with all applicable provisions of federal law and all applicable statutes and regulations governing the release of such information. All requests for any such information must be directed through the casework CODIS administrator of the forensic laboratory. To minimize duplication in the collection of a biological specimen and the conducting of a genetic marker analysis, a forensic laboratory may make information available to any agency of criminal justice to verify whether a biological specimen has been collected from a person and a genetic marker analysis has been conducted.

3. Except as otherwise authorized by this section or NRS 176.09123, 176.09125 or 176.09127, by federal law or by another specific statute, a biological specimen obtained pursuant to NRS 176.09123, a DNA profile, a DNA record and any other information identifying or matching a biological specimen with a person must not be shared with or disclosed to any person other than the authorized personnel who have possession and control of the biological specimen, DNA profile, DNA record or other information identifying or matching a biological specimen with a person, except pursuant to:

(a) A court order; or

(b) A request from a law enforcement agency during the course of an investigation.

□ A person who violates any provision of this subsection is guilty of a category C felony and shall be punished as provided in NRS 193.130.

(Added to NRS by 2013, 1058)

NRS 176.0913 Biological specimen to be obtained from certain defendants; identifying information submitted to Central Repository; genetic marker analysis; release of information; costs.

1. If a defendant is convicted of an offense listed in subsection 4:

(a) The name, social security number, date of birth, fingerprints and any other information identifying the defendant must be submitted to the Central Repository for Nevada Records of Criminal History; and

(b) Unless a biological specimen was previously obtained upon arrest pursuant to NRS 176.09123, a biological specimen must be obtained from the defendant pursuant to the provisions of this section and the specimen must be used for a genetic marker analysis. If a biological specimen was previously obtained upon arrest pursuant to NRS 176.09123, the court shall notify the Central Repository for Nevada Records of Criminal History, who in turn shall notify the appropriate forensic laboratory.

2. If the defendant is committed to the custody of the Department of Corrections, the Department of Corrections shall arrange for the biological specimen to be obtained from the defendant. The Department of Corrections shall provide the specimen to the forensic laboratory that has been designated by the county in which the defendant was convicted to conduct or oversee genetic marker analysis for the county pursuant to NRS 176.0917.

3. If the defendant is not committed to the custody of the Department of Corrections, the Division shall arrange for the biological specimen to be obtained from the defendant. The Division shall provide the specimen to the forensic laboratory that has been designated by the county in which the defendant was convicted to conduct or oversee genetic marker analysis for the county pursuant to NRS 176.0917. Any cost that is incurred to obtain a biological specimen from a defendant pursuant to this subsection is a charge against the county in which the defendant was convicted and must be paid as provided in NRS 176.0915.

4. Except as otherwise provided in subsection 5, the provisions of subsection 1 apply to a defendant who is convicted of:

(a) A felony;

(b) A crime against a child as defined in NRS 179D.0357;

(c) A sexual offense as defined in NRS 179D.097;

(d) Abuse or neglect of an older person or a vulnerable person pursuant to NRS 200.5099;

(e) A second or subsequent offense for stalking pursuant to NRS 200.575;

(f) An attempt or conspiracy to commit an offense listed in paragraphs (a) to (e), inclusive;

(g) Failing to register with a local law enforcement agency as a convicted person as required pursuant to NRS 179C.100, if the defendant previously was:

(1) Convicted in this State of committing an offense listed in paragraph (a), (d), (e) or (f); or

(2) Convicted in another jurisdiction of committing an offense that would constitute an offense listed in paragraph (a), (d), (e) or (f) if committed in this State;

(h) Failing to register with a local law enforcement agency after being convicted of a crime against a child as required pursuant to NRS 179D.450; or

(i) Failing to register with a local law enforcement agency after being convicted of a sexual offense as required pursuant to NRS 179D.450.

5. If it is determined that a defendant's biological specimen has previously been submitted for conviction of a prior offense, an additional sample is not required.

6. Except as otherwise authorized by federal law or by specific statute, a biological specimen obtained pursuant to this section, the DNA profile, the DNA record and any other information identifying or matching a biological specimen with a person must not be shared with or disclosed to any person other than the authorized personnel who have possession and control of the biological specimen, the DNA profile, the DNA record or other information identifying or matching a biological specimen with a person, except pursuant to:

(a) A court order; or

(b) A request from a law enforcement agency during the course of an investigation.

7. A person who violates any provision of subsection 6 is guilty of a category C felony and shall be punished as provided in NRS 193.130.

(Added to NRS by 1989, 376; A 1995, 414; 1997, 1669; 2001, 1852, 3032, 3037; 2001 Special Session, 215; 2003, 289, 2684; 2005, 1115; 2007, 749, 2745; 2009, 80; 2013, 1068)

NRS 176.0915 Fee for obtaining biological specimen and for analysis; inclusion in sentence; creation of county fund; use of money in fund.

1. If a biological specimen is obtained from a person pursuant to NRS 176.09123 or 176.0913, and the person is convicted of the offense for which the biological specimen was obtained, the court, in addition to any other penalty, shall order the person, to the extent of the person's financial ability, to pay the sum of $150 as a fee for obtaining the specimen and for conducting the genetic marker analysis. The fee:

(a) Must be stated separately in the judgment of the court or on the docket of the court;

(b) Must be collected from the person before or at the same time that any fine imposed by the court is collected from the person; and

(c) Must not be deducted from any fine imposed by the court.

2. All money that is collected pursuant to subsection 1 must be paid by the clerk of the court to the county treasurer on or before the fifth day of each month for the preceding month.

3. The board of county commissioners of each county shall by ordinance create in the county treasury a fund to be designated as the fund for genetic marker analysis. The county treasurer shall deposit money that is collected pursuant to subsection 2 in the fund for genetic marker analysis. The money must be accounted for separately within the fund.

4. Each month, the county treasurer shall use the money deposited in the fund for genetic marker analysis to pay for the actual amount charged to the county for obtaining a biological specimen from a person pursuant to NRS 176.09123 or 176.0913.

5. The board of county commissioners of each county may apply for and accept grants, gifts, donations, bequests or devises which the board of county commissioners shall deposit with the county treasurer for credit to the fund for genetic marker analysis.

6. If money remains in the fund after the county treasurer makes the payments required by subsection 4, the county treasurer shall pay the remaining money each month to the forensic laboratory that is designated by the county pursuant to NRS 176.0917 to conduct or oversee genetic marker analysis for the county. A forensic laboratory that receives money pursuant to this subsection shall use the money to cover any expense related to genetic marker analysis.

(Added to NRS by 1997, 1668; A 2001, 3033; 2009, 82; 2013, 1070)

NRS 176.0916 Biological specimen to be obtained from certain probationers and parolees; release of information; penalty; fee for obtaining and analyzing specimen; identifying information submitted to Central Repository; creation of Fund for Genetic Marker Analysis; use of money in Fund.

1. If the Division is supervising a probationer or parolee pursuant to an interstate compact and the probationer or parolee is or has been convicted in another jurisdiction of violating a law that prohibits the same or similar conduct as an offense listed in subsection 4 of NRS 176.0913, unless a biological specimen was previously obtained upon arrest pursuant to NRS 176.09123, the Division shall arrange for a biological specimen to be obtained from the probationer or parolee.

2. After a biological specimen is obtained from a probationer or parolee pursuant to this section, the Division shall:

(a) Provide the biological specimen to the forensic laboratory that has been designated by the county in which the probationer or parolee is residing to conduct or oversee genetic marker analysis for the county pursuant to NRS 176.0917; and

(b) Submit the name, social security number, date of birth, fingerprints and any other information identifying the probationer or parolee to the Central Repository.

3. Except as otherwise authorized by federal law or by specific statute, a biological specimen obtained pursuant to this section, the DNA profile, the DNA record and any other information identifying or matching a biological specimen with a person must not be shared with or disclosed to any person other than the authorized personnel who have possession and control of the biological specimen, the DNA profile, the DNA record or other information identifying or matching a biological specimen with a person, except pursuant to:

(a) A court order; or

(b) A request from a law enforcement agency during the course of an investigation.

4. A person who violates any provision of subsection 3 is guilty of a category C felony and shall be punished as provided in NRS 193.130.

5. A probationer or parolee, to the extent of his or her financial ability, shall pay the sum of $150 to the Division as a fee for obtaining the biological specimen and for conducting the genetic marker analysis. Except as otherwise provided in subsection 6, the fee required pursuant to this subsection must be collected from a probationer or parolee at the time the biological specimen is obtained from the probationer or parolee.

6. A probationer or parolee may arrange to make monthly payments of the fee required pursuant to subsection 5. If such arrangements are made, the Division shall provide a probationer or parolee with a monthly statement that specifies the date on which the next payment is due.

7. Any unpaid balance for a fee required pursuant to subsection 5 is a charge against the Division.

8. The Division shall deposit money that is collected pursuant to this section in the Fund for Genetic Marker Analysis, which is hereby created in the State General Fund. The money deposited in the Fund for Genetic Marker Analysis must be used to pay for the actual amount charged to the Division for obtaining biological specimens from probationers and parolees, and for conducting genetic marker analysis of the biological specimens.

(Added to NRS by 2001, 3032; A 2007, 750; 2013, 1070)

NRS 176.09165 Establishment of standard form concerning use and destruction of biological specimen and purging of DNA record; law enforcement to provide form to person in certain circumstances.

1. The Department of Public Safety shall establish a standard form for use by every law enforcement agency in this State that:

(a) Sets forth the authorized use of a biological specimen pursuant to NRS 176.0911 to 176.0919, inclusive.

(b) Identifies the circumstances and process under which a person may have his or her biological specimen destroyed and his or her DNA profile or DNA record purged from the forensic laboratory, the State DNA Database and CODIS.

(c) May be completed and submitted to the Central Repository for Nevada Records of Criminal History by a person to request that his or her biological specimen be destroyed and his or her DNA profile or DNA record be purged from the forensic laboratory, the State DNA Database and CODIS.

2. A law enforcement agency shall provide the form to a person:

(a) Before obtaining a biological specimen;

(b) Upon release from custody if the person has submitted a biological specimen; or

(c) At the request of the person, if the person believes that he or she is eligible to have his or her biological specimen destroyed and his or her DNA profile or DNA record purged from the forensic laboratory, the State DNA Database and CODIS.

(Added to NRS by 2013, 1061)

NRS 176.0917 County to designate forensic laboratory to conduct or oversee analysis; criteria.

1. The board of county commissioners of each county shall designate a forensic laboratory to conduct or oversee for the county any genetic marker analysis that is required pursuant to NRS 176.09123, 176.0913 or 176.0916.

2. The forensic laboratory designated by the board of county commissioners pursuant to subsection 1:

(a) Must be operated by this State or one of its political subdivisions; and

(b) Must satisfy or exceed the standards for quality assurance that are established by the Federal Bureau of Investigation for participation in CODIS.

(Added to NRS by 1997, 1668; A 2001, 3034; 2013, 1071)

NRS 176.09173 Powers and duties of forensic laboratory; prohibited use of biological specimen, DNA profile and DNA record.

1. A forensic laboratory shall:

(a) Prescribe protocols and procedures for the collection, submission, identification, genetic marker analysis, storage, maintenance, uploading and disposition of biological specimens, DNA profiles and DNA records.

(b) Securely upload DNA records to the State DNA Database.

(c) Acquire and maintain computer hardware and software necessary to store, maintain and upload DNA profiles and DNA records relating to:

(1) Crime scene evidence and forensic casework;

(2) Persons arrested for a felony and persons convicted of an offense listed in subsection 4 of NRS 176.0913 who are required to provide a biological specimen;

(3) Persons required to register as sex offenders pursuant to NRS 179D.445, 179D.460 or 179D.480;

(4) Unidentified persons or body parts;

(5) Missing persons;

(6) Relatives of missing persons;

(7) Anonymous DNA profiles used for forensic validation, forensic protocol development, quality control purposes or establishment of a population statistics database for use by criminal justice agencies; and

(8) Voluntarily submitted DNA profiles.

2. A forensic laboratory may:

(a) Use all or part of the remainder of any biological specimen stored in the forensic laboratory for:

(1) Retesting to confirm or update the original genetic marker analysis; or

(2) Quality control testing of new forensic methods for genetic marker analysis, provided that no personal identifying information is included.

(b) Contract with providers of services to perform a genetic marker analysis or to carry out functions on behalf of the forensic laboratory. Any provider of services who contracts with a forensic laboratory to perform a genetic marker analysis or to carry out functions on behalf of the forensic laboratory is subject to the same restrictions and requirements as the forensic laboratory.

3. A forensic laboratory shall not use any biological specimen, DNA profile or DNA record for the purpose of identification of any medical or genetic disorder.

(Added to NRS by 2013, 1057)

NRS 176.09177 Limitation on civil and criminal liability for acts relating to collection of biological specimen. Any person authorized to collect a biological specimen pursuant to NRS 176.0911 to 176.0919, inclusive, may not be held civilly or criminally liable for any act relating to the collection of a biological specimen if the person performed that act in good faith and in a reasonable manner.

(Added to NRS by 2013, 1063)

NRS 176.0918 Petition requesting genetic marker analysis by person convicted of felony; procedure; notice to victim.

1. A person convicted of a felony who otherwise meets the requirements of this section may file a postconviction petition requesting a genetic marker analysis of evidence within the possession or custody of the State which may contain genetic marker information relating to the investigation or prosecution that resulted in the judgment of conviction. If the case involves a sentence of death, the petition must include, without limitation, the date scheduled for the execution, if it has been scheduled.

2. Such a petition must be filed with the clerk of the district court for the county in which the petitioner was convicted on a form prescribed by the Department of Corrections. A copy of the petition must be served by registered mail upon:

(a) The Attorney General; and

(b) The district attorney in the county in which the petitioner was convicted.

3. A petition filed pursuant to this section must be accompanied by a declaration under penalty of perjury attesting that the information contained in the petition does not contain any material misrepresentation of fact and that the petitioner has a good faith basis relying on particular facts for the request. The petition must include, without limitation:

(a) Information identifying specific evidence either known or believed to be in the possession or custody of the State that can be subject to genetic marker analysis;

(b) The rationale for why a reasonable possibility exists that the petitioner would not have been prosecuted or convicted if exculpatory results had been obtained through a genetic marker analysis of the evidence identified in paragraph (a);

(c) An identification of the type of genetic marker analysis the petitioner is requesting to be conducted on the evidence identified in paragraph (a);

(d) If applicable, the results of all prior genetic marker analysis performed on evidence in the trial which resulted in the petitioner's conviction; and

(e) A statement that the type of genetic marker analysis the petitioner is requesting was not available at the time of trial or, if it was available, that the failure to request genetic marker analysis before the petitioner was convicted was not a result of a strategic or tactical decision as part of the representation of the petitioner at the trial.

4. If a petition is filed pursuant to this section, the court may:

(a) Enter an order dismissing the petition without a hearing if the court determines, based on the information contained in the petition, that the petitioner does not meet the requirements set forth in this section;

(b) After determining whether the petitioner is indigent pursuant to NRS 171.188 and whether counsel was appointed in the case which resulted in the conviction, appoint counsel for the limited purpose of reviewing, supplementing and presenting the petition to the court; or

(c) Schedule a hearing on the petition. If the court schedules a hearing on the petition, the court shall determine which person or agency has possession or custody of the evidence and shall immediately issue an order requiring, during the pendency of the proceeding, each person or agency in possession or custody of the evidence to:

(1) Preserve all evidence within the possession or custody of the person or agency that may be subjected to genetic marker analysis pursuant to this section;

(2) Within 90 days, prepare an inventory of all evidence relevant to the claims in the petition within the possession or custody of the person or agency that may be subjected to genetic marker analysis pursuant to this section; and

(3) Within 90 days, submit a copy of the inventory to the petitioner, the prosecuting attorney and the court.

5. Within 90 days after the inventory of all evidence is prepared pursuant to subsection 4, the prosecuting attorney may file a written response to the petition with the court.

6. If the court holds a hearing on a petition filed pursuant to this section, the hearing must be presided over by the judge who conducted the trial that resulted in the conviction of the petitioner, unless that judge is unavailable. Any evidence presented at the hearing by affidavit must be served on the opposing party at least 15 days before the hearing.

7. If a petitioner files a petition pursuant to this section, the court schedules a hearing on the petition and a victim of the crime for which the petitioner was convicted has requested notice pursuant to NRS 178.5698, the district attorney in the county in which the petitioner was convicted shall provide to the victim notice of:

(a) The fact that the petitioner filed a petition pursuant to this section;

(b) The time and place of the hearing scheduled by the court as a result of the petition; and

(c) The outcome of any hearing on the petition.

(Added to NRS by 2003, 1892; A 2009, 1197; 2013, 1409) — (Part substituted in revision by NRS 176.09183 and 176.09187)

NRS 176.09183 Grounds for granting or dismissing petition; appeal.

1. The court shall order a genetic marker analysis, after considering the information contained in the petition pursuant to subsection 3 of NRS 176.0918 and any other evidence, if the court finds that:

(a) A reasonable possibility exists that the petitioner would not have been prosecuted or convicted if exculpatory results had been obtained through a genetic marker analysis of the evidence identified in the petition;

(b) The evidence to be analyzed exists; and

(c) Except as otherwise provided in subsection 2, the evidence was not previously subjected to a genetic marker analysis.

2. If the evidence was previously subjected to a genetic marker analysis, the court shall order a genetic marker analysis pursuant to subsection 1 if the court finds that:

(a) The result of the previous analysis was inconclusive;

(b) The evidence was not subjected to the type of analysis that is now requested and the requested analysis may resolve an issue not resolved by the previous analysis; or

(c) The requested analysis would provide results that are significantly more accurate and probative of the identity of the perpetrator than the previous analysis.

3. If the court orders a genetic marker analysis pursuant to subsection 1 or 2, the court shall:

(a) Order the analysis to be conducted promptly under reasonable conditions designed to protect the interest of the State and the petitioner in the integrity of the evidence and the analysis process.

(b) Select a forensic laboratory to conduct or oversee the analysis. The forensic laboratory selected by the court must:

(1) Be operated by this state or one of its political subdivisions, when possible; and

(2) Satisfy the standards for quality assurance that are established for forensic laboratories by the Federal Bureau of Investigation.

(c) Order the forensic laboratory selected pursuant to paragraph (b) to perform a genetic marker analysis of evidence. The analysis to be performed and evidence to be analyzed must:

(1) Be specified in the order; and

(2) Include such analysis, testing and comparison of genetic marker information contained in the evidence and the genetic marker information of the petitioner as the court determines appropriate under the circumstances.

(d) Order the production of any reports that are prepared by a forensic laboratory in connection with the analysis and any data and notes upon which the report is based.

(e) Order the preservation of evidence used in a genetic marker analysis performed pursuant to this section and NRS 176.0918 and 176.09187 for purposes of a subsequent proceeding or analysis, if any.

(f) Order the results of the genetic marker analysis performed pursuant to this section and NRS 176.0918 and 176.09187 to be sent to the State Board of Parole Commissioners if the results of the genetic marker analysis are not favorable to the petitioner.

4. If the court orders a genetic marker analysis pursuant to subsection 1 or 2, the State may appeal to the appellate court of competent jurisdiction pursuant to the rules fixed by the Supreme Court pursuant to Section 4 of Article 6 of the Nevada Constitution within 30 days after the notice of the entry of the order by filing a notice of appeal with the clerk of the district court.

5. The court shall enter an order dismissing a petition filed pursuant to NRS 176.0918 if:

(a) The requirements for ordering a genetic marker analysis pursuant to this section and NRS 176.0918 and 176.09187 are not satisfied; or

(b) The results of a genetic marker analysis performed pursuant to this section and NRS 176.0918 and 176.09187 are not favorable to the petitioner.

6. If the court enters an order dismissing a petition filed pursuant to NRS 176.0918, the person aggrieved by the order may appeal to the appellate court of competent jurisdiction pursuant to the rules fixed by the Supreme Court pursuant to Section 4 of Article 6 of the Nevada Constitution within 30 days after the notice of the entry of the order by filing a notice of appeal with the clerk of the district court.

(Added to NRS by 2003, 1892; A 2009, 1197; 2013, 1409) — (Substituted in revision for part of NRS 176.0918)

NRS 176.09187 Genetic marker analysis: Motion for new trial authorized when results favorable to petitioner; petitioner deemed to consent to submission, release and use of certain information; costs; remedy not exclusive.

1. If the results of a genetic marker analysis performed pursuant to this section and NRS 176.0918 and 176.09183 are favorable to the petitioner:

(a) The petitioner may bring a motion for a new trial based on the ground of newly discovered evidence pursuant to NRS 176.515; and

(b) The restriction on the time for filing the motion set forth in subsection 3 of NRS 176.515 is not applicable.

2. For the purposes of a genetic marker analysis pursuant to this section and NRS 176.0918 and 176.09183, a person who files a petition pursuant to NRS 176.0918 shall be deemed to consent to the:

(a) Submission of a biological specimen by the petitioner to determine genetic marker information; and

(b) Release and use of genetic marker information concerning the petitioner.

3. The petitioner shall pay the cost of a genetic marker analysis performed pursuant to this section and NRS 176.0918 and 176.09183, unless the petitioner is incarcerated at the time the petitioner files the petition, found to be indigent pursuant to NRS 171.188 and the results of the genetic marker analysis are favorable to the petitioner. If the petitioner is not required to pay the cost of the analysis pursuant to this subsection, the expense of an analysis ordered pursuant to this section and NRS 176.0918 and 176.09183 is a charge against the Department of Corrections and must be paid upon approval by the Board of State Prison Commissioners as other claims against the State are paid.

4. The remedy provided by this section and NRS 176.0918 and 176.09183 is in addition to, is not a substitute for and is not exclusive of any other remedy, right of action or proceeding available to a person convicted of a crime.

(Added to NRS by 2003, 1892; A 2009, 1197; 2013, 1409) — (Substituted in revision for part of NRS 176.0918)

NRS 176.0919 Execution stayed pending results of genetic marker analysis.

1. After a judge grants a petition requesting a genetic marker analysis pursuant to NRS 176.0918, 176.09183 and 176.09187, if the case involves a sentence of death and a judge determines that the genetic marker analysis cannot be completed before the date of the execution of the petitioner, the judge shall stay the execution of the judgment of death pending the results of the analysis.

2. If the case involves a sentence of death and the results of an analysis ordered and conducted pursuant to NRS 176.0918, 176.09183 and 176.09187 are not favorable to the petitioner:

(a) Except as otherwise provided in paragraph (b), the Director of the Department of Corrections shall, in due course, execute the judgment of death.

(b) If the judgment of death has been stayed pursuant to subsection 1, the judge shall cause a certified copy of the order staying the execution of the judgment and a certified copy of the report of genetic marker analysis that indicates results which are not favorable to the petitioner to be immediately forwarded by the clerk of the court to the district attorney. Upon receipt, the district attorney shall pursue the issuance of a new warrant of execution of the judgment of death in the manner provided in NRS 176.495.

(Added to NRS by 2003, 1894; A 2009, 1200)

Sex Offenders and Offenders Convicted of a Crime Against a Child

NRS 176.0921 Definitions. As used in NRS 176.0921 to 176.0927, inclusive, unless the context otherwise requires, the words and terms defined in NRS 176.0922 to 176.0925, inclusive, have the meanings ascribed to them in those sections.

(Added to NRS by 1997, 1666)

NRS 176.0922 "Central Repository" defined. "Central Repository" means the Central Repository for Nevada Records of Criminal History.

(Added to NRS by 1997, 1666)

NRS 176.0923 "Crime against a child" defined. "Crime against a child" has the meaning ascribed to it in NRS 179D.0357.
(Added to NRS by 1997, 1666; A 2007, 2746)

NRS 176.0924 "Record of registration" defined. "Record of registration" has the meaning ascribed to it in NRS 179D.070.
(Added to NRS by 1997, 1666)

NRS 176.0925 "Sexual offense" defined. "Sexual offense" has the meaning ascribed to it in NRS 179D.097.
(Added to NRS by 1997, 1666; A 2007, 2746)

NRS 176.0926 Crime against child: Notice of conviction to Central Repository; defendant to be informed of duty to register; effect of failure to inform.

1. If a defendant is convicted of a crime against a child, the court shall, following the imposition of a sentence:

(a) Notify the Central Repository of the conviction of the defendant, so the Central Repository may carry out the provisions for registration of the defendant pursuant to NRS 179D.450.

(b) Inform the defendant of the requirements for registration, including, but not limited to:

(1) The duty to register initially pursuant to NRS 179D.445;

(2) The duty to register in this State during any period in which the defendant is a resident of this State or a nonresident who is a student or worker within this State and the time within which the defendant is required to register pursuant to NRS 179D.450;

(3) The duty to register in any other jurisdiction, including, without limitation, any jurisdiction outside the United States, during any period in which the defendant is a resident of the other jurisdiction or a nonresident who is a student or worker within the other jurisdiction;

(4) If the defendant moves from this State to another jurisdiction, including, without limitation, any jurisdiction outside the United States, the duty to register with the appropriate law enforcement agency in the other jurisdiction;

(5) The duty to notify the local law enforcement agency in whose jurisdiction the defendant formerly resided, in person or in writing, if the defendant changes the address at which the defendant resides, including if the defendant moves from this State to another jurisdiction, including, without limitation, any jurisdiction outside the United States, or changes the primary address at which the defendant is a student or worker; and

(6) The duty to notify immediately the appropriate local law enforcement agency if the defendant is, expects to be or becomes enrolled as a student at an institution of higher education or changes the date of commencement or termination of enrollment at an institution of higher education or if the defendant is, expects to be or becomes a worker at an institution of higher education or changes the date of commencement or termination of the defendant's work at an institution of higher education.

(c) Require the defendant to read and sign a form stating that the requirements for registration have been explained and that the defendant understands the requirements for registration.

2. The failure to provide the defendant with the information or confirmation form required by paragraphs (b) and (c) of subsection 1 does not affect the duty of the defendant to register and to comply with all other provisions for registration pursuant to NRS 179D.010 to 179D.550, inclusive.

(Added to NRS by 1997, 1666; A 1999, 1284; 2001, 2050; 2003, 564; 2005, 2860; 2007, 2746, 3245)

NRS 176.0927 Sexual offense: Notice of conviction to Central Repository; defendant to be informed of duty to register; effect of failure to inform.

1. If a defendant is convicted of a sexual offense, the court shall, following the imposition of a sentence:

(a) Notify the Central Repository of the conviction of the defendant, so the Central Repository may carry out the provisions for registration of the defendant pursuant to NRS 179D.450.

(b) Inform the defendant of the requirements for registration, including, without limitation:

(1) The duty to register initially pursuant to NRS 179D.445;

(2) The duty to register in this State during any period in which the defendant is a resident of this State or a nonresident who is a student or worker within this State and the time within which the defendant is required to register pursuant to NRS 179D.460;

(3) The duty to register in any other jurisdiction during any period in which the defendant is a resident of the other jurisdiction or a nonresident who is a student or worker within the other jurisdiction;

(4) If the defendant moves from this State to another jurisdiction, the duty to register with the appropriate law enforcement agency in the other jurisdiction;

(5) The duty to notify the local law enforcement agency in whose jurisdiction the defendant formerly resided, in person or in writing, if the defendant changes the address at which the defendant resides, including if the defendant moves from this State to another jurisdiction, or changes the primary address at which the defendant is a student or worker; and

(6) The duty to notify immediately the appropriate local law enforcement agency if the defendant is, expects to be or becomes enrolled as a student at an institution of higher education or changes the date of commencement or termination of enrollment at an institution of higher education or if the defendant is, expects to be or becomes a worker at an institution of higher education or changes the date of commencement or termination of the defendant's work at an institution of higher education.

(c) Require the defendant to read and sign a form stating that the requirements for registration have been explained and that the defendant understands the requirements for registration.

2. The failure to provide the defendant with the information or confirmation form required by paragraphs (b) and (c) of subsection 1 does not affect the duty of the defendant to register and to comply with all other provisions for registration pursuant to NRS 179D.010 to 179D.550, inclusive.

(Added to NRS by 1997, 1667; A 1999, 1285; 2001, 2051; 2003, 565; 2005, 2861; 2007, 2747)

Lifetime Supervision

NRS 176.0931 Special sentence for sex offenders; petition for release from lifetime supervision.

1. If a defendant is convicted of a sexual offense, the court shall include in sentencing, in addition to any other penalties provided by law, a special sentence of lifetime supervision.

2. The special sentence of lifetime supervision commences after any period of probation or any term of imprisonment and any period of release on parole.

3. A person sentenced to lifetime supervision may petition the sentencing court or the State Board of Parole Commissioners for release from lifetime supervision. The sentencing court or the Board shall grant a petition for release from a special sentence of lifetime supervision if:

(a) The person has complied with the requirements of the provisions of NRS 179D.010 to 179D.550, inclusive;

(b) The person has not been convicted of an offense that poses a threat to the safety or well-being of others for an interval of at least 10 consecutive years after the person's last conviction or release from incarceration, whichever occurs later; and

(c) The person is not likely to pose a threat to the safety of others, as determined by a person professionally qualified to conduct psychosexual evaluations, if released from lifetime supervision.

4. A person who is released from lifetime supervision pursuant to the provisions of subsection 3 remains subject to the provisions for registration as a sex offender and to the provisions for community notification, unless the person is otherwise relieved from the operation of those provisions pursuant to the provisions of NRS 179D.010 to 179D.550, inclusive.

5. As used in this section:

(a) "Offense that poses a threat to the safety or well-being of others" includes, without limitation:

(1) An offense that involves:

(I) A victim less than 18 years of age;

(II) A crime against a child as defined in NRS 179D.0357;

(III) A sexual offense as defined in NRS 179D.097;

(IV) A deadly weapon, explosives or a firearm;

(V) The use or threatened use of force or violence;

(VI) Physical or mental abuse;

(VII) Death or bodily injury;

(VIII) An act of domestic violence;

(IX) Harassment, stalking, threats of any kind or other similar acts;

(X) The forcible or unlawful entry of a home, building, structure, vehicle or other real or personal property; or

(XI) The infliction or threatened infliction of damage or injury, in whole or in part, to real or personal property.

(2) Any offense listed in subparagraph (1) that is committed in this State or another jurisdiction, including, without limitation, an offense prosecuted in:

(I) A tribal court.

(II) A court of the United States or the Armed Forces of the United States.

(b) "Person professionally qualified to conduct psychosexual evaluations" has the meaning ascribed to it in NRS 176.133.

(c) "Sexual offense" means:

(1) A violation of NRS 200.366, subsection 4 of NRS 200.400, NRS 200.710, 200.720, subsection 2 of NRS 200.730, NRS 201.180, 201.230, 201.450, 201.540 or 201.550 or paragraph (a) or (b) of subsection 4 or paragraph (a) or (b) of subsection 5 of NRS 201.560;

(2) An attempt to commit an offense listed in subparagraph (1); or

(3) An act of murder in the first or second degree, kidnapping in the first or second degree, false imprisonment, burglary or invasion of the home if the act is determined to be sexually motivated at a hearing conducted pursuant to NRS 175.547.

(Added to NRS by 1995, 414; A 1997, 1671; 2001, 2789; 2003, 1381; 2005, 2862; 2007, 2748; 2013, 1160; 2015, 1436)

Miscellaneous Provisions

NRS 176.095 State Board of Parole Commissioners may direct release of state prisoner on parole. The State Board of Parole Commissioners may direct that any prisoner confined in the state prison, or confined in another jurisdiction as provided in NRS 176.045, shall be released on parole as provided in chapter 213 of NRS, if eligible for parole under the provisions of such chapter.

(Added to NRS by 1967, 1433; A 1973, 180)

NRS 176.105 Judgment in criminal action generally.

1. If a defendant is found guilty and is sentenced as provided by law, the judgment of conviction must set forth:

(a) The plea;

(b) The verdict or finding;

(c) The adjudication and sentence, including the date of the sentence, any term of imprisonment, the amount and terms of any fine, restitution or administrative assessment, a reference to the statute under which the defendant is sentenced and, if necessary to determine eligibility for parole, the applicable provision of the statute; and

(d) The exact amount of credit granted for time spent in confinement before conviction, if any.

2. If the defendant is found not guilty, or for any other reason is entitled to be discharged, judgment must be entered accordingly.

3. The judgment must be signed by the judge and entered by the clerk.

(Added to NRS by 1967, 1433; A 1973, 161; 1979, 1124; 1989, 938; 1993, 78; 1997, 905)

NRS 176.115 Judgment against complainant for malicious prosecution when defendant not found guilty; costs; enforcement of judgment.

1. In all cases of criminal prosecution where the defendant is not found guilty, the court may require the complainant, if it appears that the prosecution was malicious or without probable cause, to pay the costs of the action, or to give security to pay the same within 30 days.

2. If the complainant does not comply with the order of the court, judgment may be entered against the complainant for the amount thereof.

3. Such judgments may be enforced and appealed from in the same manner as those rendered in civil actions.

(Added to NRS by 1967, 1433)

NRS 176.125 Entry of judgment of conviction; what papers constitute record of action. When judgment upon a conviction is rendered, the clerk shall, within 5 days, annex together and file the following papers, which shall constitute the record of the action:

1. A copy of the minutes of any challenge which may have been interposed by the defendant to the panel of the grand jury, or to any individual grand juror, and the proceedings thereon.
2. The indictment or information and a copy of the minutes of the plea.
3. A copy of the minutes of any challenge which may have been interposed to any juror, and the proceedings thereon.
4. A copy of the minutes of the trial.
5. A copy of the judgment.
6. The decision of the court upon matters of law deemed excepted to, if such decision is in writing, and a copy of the minutes showing any decision deemed excepted to.
7. Any written charges given or refused by the court, with the endorsements thereon.
8. The affidavits and counter-affidavits, if any, used on the hearing of a motion for a new trial.

(Added to NRS by 1967, 1433)

INVESTIGATION BY DIVISION OF PAROLE AND PROBATION

NRS 176.133 Definitions. As used in NRS 176.133 to 176.161, inclusive, unless the context otherwise requires:

1. "Person professionally qualified to conduct psychosexual evaluations" means a person who has received training in conducting psychosexual evaluations and is:

(a) A psychiatrist licensed to practice medicine in this State and certified by the American Board of Psychiatry and Neurology, Inc.;
(b) A psychologist licensed to practice in this State;
(c) A social worker holding a master's degree in social work and licensed in this State as a clinical social worker;
(d) A registered nurse holding a master's degree in the field of psychiatric nursing and licensed to practice professional nursing in this State;
(e) A marriage and family therapist licensed in this State pursuant to chapter 641A of NRS; or
(f) A clinical professional counselor licensed in this State pursuant to chapter 641A of NRS.

2. "Psychosexual evaluation" means an evaluation conducted pursuant to NRS 176.139.

3. "Sexual offense" means:

(a) Sexual assault pursuant to NRS 200.366;
(b) Statutory sexual seduction pursuant to NRS 200.368, if punished as a felony;
(c) Battery with intent to commit sexual assault pursuant to NRS 200.400;
(d) Abuse of a child pursuant to NRS 200.508, if the abuse involved sexual abuse or sexual exploitation and is punished as a felony;
(e) An offense involving pornography and a minor pursuant to NRS 200.710 to 200.730, inclusive;
(f) Incest pursuant to NRS 201.180;
(g) Open or gross lewdness pursuant to NRS 201.210, if punished as a felony;
(h) Indecent or obscene exposure pursuant to NRS 201.220, if punished as a felony;
(i) Lewdness with a child pursuant to NRS 201.230;
(j) Sexual penetration of a dead human body pursuant to NRS 201.450;
(k) Sexual conduct between certain employees of a school or volunteers at a school and a pupil pursuant to NRS 201.540;
(l) Sexual conduct between certain employees of a college or university and a student pursuant to NRS 201.550;
(m) Luring a child or a person with mental illness pursuant to NRS 201.560, if punished as a felony;
(n) An attempt to commit an offense listed in paragraphs (a) to (m), inclusive, if punished as a felony; or
(o) An offense that is determined to be sexually motivated pursuant to NRS 175.547 or 207.193.

(Added to NRS by 1997, 1637; A 1999, 1188; 2001, 2790; 2003, 1381; 2007, 3078; 2011, 2473; 2013, 1161, 2705; 2015, 1438)

NRS 176.135 Presentence investigation and report: When required; time for completing.

1. Except as otherwise provided in this section and NRS 176.151, the Division shall make a presentence investigation and report to the court on each defendant who pleads guilty, guilty but mentally ill or nolo contendere to, or is found guilty or guilty but mentally ill of, a felony.

2. If a defendant is convicted of a felony that is a sexual offense, the presentence investigation and report:

(a) Must be made before the imposition of sentence or the granting of probation; and
(b) If the sexual offense is an offense for which the suspension of sentence or the granting of probation is permitted, must include a psychosexual evaluation of the defendant.

3. If a defendant is convicted of a felony other than a sexual offense, the presentence investigation and report must be made before the imposition of sentence or the granting of probation unless:

(a) A sentence is fixed by a jury; or

(b) Such an investigation and report on the defendant has been made by the Division within the 5 years immediately preceding the date initially set for sentencing on the most recent offense.

4. Upon request of the court, the Division shall make presentence investigations and reports on defendants who plead guilty, guilty but mentally ill or nolo contendere to, or are found guilty or guilty but mentally ill of, gross misdemeanors.

(Added to NRS by 1967, 1434; A 1969, 406; 1981, 369, 464; 1985, 148; 1987, 592; 1993, 1512; 1995, 2456; 1997, 642, 1639; 1999, 1189, 1285; 2001, 77; 2003, 1466; 2007, 1420)

NRS 176.139 Presentence investigation and report: Psychosexual evaluation of certain sex offenders required; standards and methods for conducting evaluation; access to records; rights of confidentiality and privileges deemed waived; costs.

1. If a defendant is convicted of a sexual offense for which the suspension of sentence or the granting of probation is permitted, the Division shall arrange for a psychosexual evaluation of the defendant as part of the Division's presentence investigation and report to the court.

2. The psychosexual evaluation of the defendant must be conducted by a person professionally qualified to conduct psychosexual evaluations.

3. The person who conducts the psychosexual evaluation of the defendant must use diagnostic tools that are generally accepted as being within the standard of care for the evaluation of sex offenders, and the psychosexual evaluation of the defendant must include:

(a) A comprehensive clinical interview with the defendant; and

(b) A review of all investigative reports relating to the defendant's sexual offense and all statements made by victims of that offense.

4. The psychosexual evaluation of the defendant may include:

(a) A review of records relating to previous criminal offenses committed by the defendant;

(b) A review of records relating to previous evaluations and treatment of the defendant;

(c) A review of the defendant's records from school;

(d) Interviews with the defendant's parents, the defendant's spouse or other persons who may be significantly involved with the defendant or who may have relevant information relating to the defendant's background; and

(e) The use of psychological testing, polygraphic examinations and arousal assessment.

5. The person who conducts the psychosexual evaluation of the defendant must be given access to all records of the defendant that are necessary to conduct the evaluation, and the defendant shall be deemed to have waived all rights of confidentiality and all privileges relating to those records for the limited purpose of the evaluation.

6. The person who conducts the psychosexual evaluation of the defendant shall:

(a) Prepare a comprehensive written report of the results of the evaluation;

(b) Include in the report all information that is necessary to carry out the provisions of NRS 176A.110; and

(c) Provide a copy of the report to the Division.

7. If a psychosexual evaluation is conducted pursuant to this section, the court shall:

(a) Order the defendant, to the extent of the defendant's financial ability, to pay for the cost of the psychosexual evaluation; or

(b) If the defendant was less than 18 years of age when the sexual offense was committed and the defendant was certified and convicted as an adult, order the parents or guardians of the defendant, to the extent of their financial ability, to pay for the cost of the psychosexual evaluation. For the purposes of this paragraph, the court has jurisdiction over the parents or guardians of the defendant to the extent that is necessary to carry out the provisions of this paragraph.

(Added to NRS by 1997, 1638; A 1999, 1286; 2001, 1636)

NRS 176.145 Presentence investigation and report: Contents of report.

1. The report of any presentence investigation must contain:

(a) Any prior criminal record of the defendant;

(b) Information concerning the characteristics of the defendant, the defendant's financial condition, the circumstances affecting the defendant's behavior and the circumstances of the defendant's offense that may be helpful in imposing sentence, in granting probation or in the correctional treatment of the defendant;

(c) Information concerning the effect that the offense committed by the defendant has had upon the victim, including, without limitation, any physical or psychological harm or financial loss suffered by the victim, to the extent that such information is available from the victim or other sources, but the provisions of this paragraph do not require any particular examination or testing of the victim, and the extent of any investigation or examination is solely at the discretion of the court or the Division and the extent of the information to be included in the report is solely at the discretion of the Division;

(d) Information concerning whether the defendant has an obligation for the support of a child, and if so, whether the defendant is in arrears in payment on that obligation;

(e) Data or information concerning reports and investigations thereof made pursuant to chapter 432B of NRS that relate to the defendant and are made available pursuant to NRS 432B.290;

(f) The results of the evaluation of the defendant conducted pursuant to NRS 484C.300, if such an evaluation is required pursuant to that section;

(g) A recommendation of a minimum term and a maximum term of imprisonment or other term of imprisonment authorized by statute, or a fine, or both;

(h) A recommendation, if the Division deems it appropriate, that the defendant undergo a program of regimental discipline pursuant to NRS 176A.780;

(i) If a psychosexual evaluation of the defendant is required pursuant to NRS 176.139, a written report of the results of the psychosexual evaluation of the defendant and all information that is necessary to carry out the provisions of NRS 176A.110; and

(j) Such other information as may be required by the court.

2. The Division may include in the report any additional information that it believes may be helpful in imposing a sentence, in granting probation or in correctional treatment.

(Added to NRS by 1967, 1434; A 1973, 178; 1981, 21, 1208; 1985, 148; 1989, 1853; 1993, 8, 1513, 2016; 1995, 667, 1248; 1997, 837, 1639; 1999, 1190, 1287; 2001, 77, 1637)

NRS 176.151 General investigation and report on defendant convicted of category E felony: When required; time for completing; contents of report.

1. If a defendant pleads guilty, guilty but mentally ill or nolo contendere to, or is found guilty or guilty but mentally ill of, one or more category E felonies, but no other felonies, the Division shall not make a presentence investigation and report on the defendant pursuant to NRS 176.135, unless the Division has not made a presentence investigation and report on the defendant pursuant to NRS 176.135 within the 5 years immediately preceding the date initially set for sentencing on the category E felony or felonies and:

(a) The court requests a presentence investigation and report; or

(b) The prosecuting attorney possesses evidence that would support a decision by the court to deny probation to the defendant pursuant to paragraph (b) of subsection 1 of NRS 176A.100.

2. If the Division does not make a presentence investigation and report on a defendant pursuant to subsection 1, the Division shall, not later than 45 days after the date on which the defendant is sentenced, make a general investigation and report on the defendant that contains:

(a) Any prior criminal record of the defendant;

(b) Information concerning the characteristics of the defendant, the circumstances affecting the defendant's behavior and the circumstances of the defendant's offense that may be helpful to persons responsible for the supervision or correctional treatment of the defendant;

(c) Information concerning the effect that the offense committed by the defendant has had upon the victim, including, without limitation, any physical or psychological harm or financial loss suffered by the victim, to the extent that such information is available from the victim or other sources, but the provisions of this paragraph do not require any particular examination or testing of the victim, and the extent of any investigation or examination and the extent of the information included in the report is solely at the discretion of the Division;

(d) Data or information concerning reports and investigations thereof made pursuant to chapter 432B of NRS that relate to the defendant and are made available pursuant to NRS 432B.290; and

(e) Any other information that the Division believes may be helpful to persons responsible for the supervision or correctional treatment of the defendant.

(Added to NRS by 1999, 1188; A 2003, 1466; 2007, 1421)

NRS 176.153 Disclosure of report of presentence investigation. Except as otherwise provided in this section, the Division shall disclose to the prosecuting attorney, the counsel for the defendant, the defendant and the court, not later than 14 calendar days before the defendant will be sentenced, the factual content of the report of any presentence investigation made pursuant to NRS 176.135 and the recommendations of the Division. The defendant may waive the minimum period required by this section.

(Added to NRS by 2013, 2704; A 2013, 2706; 2015, 540)

NRS 176.156 Disclosure of report of presentence or general investigation; persons entitled to use report; confidentiality of report.

1. The Division shall disclose to the prosecuting attorney, the counsel for the defendant and the defendant the factual content of the report of:

(a) Any presentence investigation made pursuant to NRS 176.135 and the recommendations of the Division, in the period provided in NRS 176.153.

(b) Any general investigation made pursuant to NRS 176.151.

The Division shall afford an opportunity to each party to object to factual errors in any such report and to comment on any recommendations.

2. Unless otherwise ordered by a court, upon request, the Division shall disclose the content of a report of a presentence investigation or general investigation to a law enforcement agency of this State or a political subdivision thereof and to a law enforcement agency of the Federal Government for the limited purpose of performing their duties, including, without limitation, conducting hearings that are public in nature.

3. Unless otherwise ordered by a court, upon request, the Division shall disclose the content of a report of a presentence investigation or general investigation to the Division of Public and Behavioral Health of the Department of Health and Human Services for the limited purpose of performing its duties, including, without limitation, evaluating and providing any report or information to the Division concerning the mental health of:

(a) A sex offender as defined in NRS 213.107; or

(b) An offender who has been determined to be mentally ill.

4. Unless otherwise ordered by a court, upon request, the Division shall disclose the content of a report of a presentence investigation or general investigation to the Nevada Gaming Control Board for the limited purpose of performing its duties in the administration of the provisions of chapters 462 to 467, inclusive, of NRS.

5. Except for the disclosures required by subsections 1 to 4, inclusive, a report of a presentence investigation or general investigation and the sources of information for such a report are confidential and must not be made a part of any public record.

(Added to NRS by 1967, 1434; A 1969, 405; 1975, 576; 1981, 1209; 1985, 149; 1993, 1513; 1995, 1057; 1997, 54; 1999, 103, 1190; 2013, 2705)

NRS 176.159 Delivery of report of presentence or general investigation to Director of Department of Corrections.

1. Except as otherwise provided in subsection 2, when a court imposes a sentence of imprisonment in the state prison or revokes a program of probation and orders a sentence of imprisonment to the state prison to be executed, the court shall cause a copy of the report of the presentence investigation to be delivered to the Director of the Department of Corrections, if such a report was made. The report must be delivered not later than when the judgment of imprisonment is delivered pursuant to NRS 176.335. Delivery of the report may, at the court's discretion, also be accomplished by electronic transmission or by affording the Department of Corrections the required electronic access necessary to retrieve the report.

2. If a presentence investigation and report were not required pursuant to paragraph (b) of subsection 3 of NRS 176.135 or pursuant to subsection 1 of NRS 176.151, the court shall cause a copy of the previous report of the presentence investigation or a copy of the report of the general investigation, as appropriate, to be delivered to the Director of the Department of Corrections in the manner provided pursuant to subsection 1.

(Added to NRS by 1969, 871; A 1973, 67; 1977, 859; 1997, 130; 1999, 1191; 2001, 217; 2013, 1369)

NRS 176.161 Portion of certain presentence or general investigations and reports to be paid by county in which indictment found or information filed.

1. Seventy percent of the expense of any presentence or general investigation and report made by the Division pursuant to NRS 176.135 or 176.151, other than the expense of a psychosexual evaluation conducted pursuant to NRS 176.139, must be paid by the county in which the indictment was found or the information filed.

2. Each county shall pay to the Division all expenses required pursuant to subsection 1 according to a schedule established by the Division, which must require payment on at least a quarterly basis.

(Added to NRS by 2011, 2473)

WITHDRAWAL OF PLEA

NRS 176.165 When plea of guilty, guilty but mentally ill or nolo contendere may be withdrawn. Except as otherwise provided in this section, a motion to withdraw a plea of guilty, guilty but mentally ill or nolo contendere may be made only before sentence is imposed or imposition of sentence is suspended. To correct manifest injustice, the court after sentence may set aside the judgment of conviction and permit the defendant to withdraw the plea.

(Added to NRS by 1967, 1434; A 1989, 1983; 1995, 2456; 2003, 1467; 2007, 1421)

EXECUTION

NRS 176.265 Fines to be paid into State Treasury. The full amount of all fines imposed and collected under and for violation of any penal law of this State shall be paid into the State Treasury.

(Added to NRS by 1967, 1437)

NRS 176.275 Judgment for fine, administrative assessment, payment of restitution or repayment of expenses is lien; additional provisions concerning judgment for payment of restitution.

1. A judgment which imposes a fine or administrative assessment or requires a defendant to pay restitution or repay the expenses of a defense constitutes a lien in like manner as a judgment for money rendered in a civil action.

2. A judgment which requires a defendant to pay restitution:

(a) May be recorded, docketed and enforced as any other judgment for money rendered in a civil action.

(b) Does not expire until the judgment is satisfied.

3. An independent action to enforce a judgment which requires a defendant to pay restitution may be commenced at any time.

(Added to NRS by 1967, 1437; A 1975, 217; 1977, 337; 1983, 909; 1993, 149; 2015, 2573)

NRS 176.278 Payment of restitution from civil judgment or settlement in favor of defendant and against State, political subdivision, officer, employee or contractor.

1. Except as otherwise provided in subsection 4, if a person who is or was imprisoned in the state prison or a county or city jail or detention facility is awarded a judgment against:

(a) The State of Nevada, a county or a city;

(b) A department, commission, board or other agency of the State of Nevada, a county or a city; or

(c) A current or former officer, employee or contractor of the State of Nevada, a county or a city,

arising from a civil action that accrued while the person was imprisoned in the state prison or county or city jail or detention facility, the person or governmental entity that pays the judgment shall deposit the money for the judgment with the court. The court shall deduct from the money received from the judgment any amount of money owed by the person for restitution and send the money to the appropriate person, governmental agency or political subdivision of a governmental agency to whom restitution is owed.

2. Except as otherwise provided in subsection 4, if a person enters into a settlement for money in an action described in subsection 1, the person or governmental entity that pays the settlement shall deposit the money for the settlement with the court in which the action was filed or the district court of the county in which the person resides if no action was filed. The court shall deduct from the money deposited with the court any amount of money owed by the person for restitution and send the money to the appropriate person, governmental agency or political subdivision of a governmental agency to whom restitution is owed.

3. If any money remains after the court makes the deduction pursuant to subsection 1 or 2, the court shall forward the remaining money to the person who initiated the action.

4. The provisions of this section do not apply to a judgment or settlement in a case that involves the death of a person who was imprisoned.

(Added to NRS by 1999, 67)

NRS 176.285 Fines in Justice Court to be paid to county treasurer; due date. In Justice Court, when a fine is paid or bail is forfeited, the justice must pay the same to the county treasurer on or before the fifth day of the month immediately following the month in which the fine is paid or bail is forfeited.

(Added to NRS by 1967, 1437; A 2015, 2566)

NRS 176.295 Costs when criminal action removed before trial; clerk to certify costs to auditor.

1. In every case where a criminal action may have been or shall be removed before trial, the costs accruing upon such removal and trial shall be a charge against the county in which the cause of the indictment or information occurred.

2. The clerk of the county to which such action is or may be removed shall certify the amount of the costs to the auditor of the county in which the indictment was found, or the information filed, which shall be examined, allowed and paid as other county charges.

(Added to NRS by 1967, 1437)

NRS 176.305 Judgment for imprisonment or fine and imprisonment until satisfied: Commitment and detention. If the judgment be imprisonment, or a fine and imprisonment until it is satisfied, the defendant must forthwith be committed to the custody of the proper officer, and detained until the judgment is complied with.

(Added to NRS by 1967, 1437)

NRS 176.315 Judgment of imprisonment in county jail: How executed. A judgment of imprisonment to be served in a county jail must be executed by delivering the defendant into the custody of the sheriff or other officer in charge of the county jail. A copy of the judgment of conviction, duly certified by the judge or justice, is a sufficient warrant for the doing of every act necessary or proper in the due execution thereof. The officer shall, upon discharging the defendant, return such copy to the justice, with an account of the officer's doings endorsed thereon, and must at the same time pay over to the justice all money which the officer may have received from the defendant in payment of the fine.

(Added to NRS by 1967, 1437; A 1999, 1047)

NRS 176.325 Judgment of imprisonment in state prison: How executed. When a judgment of imprisonment to be served in the state prison has been pronounced, triplicate certified paper or electronic copies of the judgment of conviction, attested by the clerk under the seal of the court, must forthwith be furnished to the officers whose duty it is to execute the judgment, as provided by NRS 176.335, and no other warrant or authority is necessary to justify or require the execution thereof, except when a judgment of death is rendered.

(Added to NRS by 1967, 1438; A 1973, 30; 1989, 938; 1993, 79; 1995, 1252; 1999, 1047; 2013, 1369)

NRS 176.335 Duty of sheriff on receiving copies of judgment of imprisonment; Director of Department of Corrections to receive prisoner from sheriff; when term of imprisonment begins.

1. If a judgment is for imprisonment in the state prison, the sheriff of the county shall, on receipt of the triplicate certified paper or electronic copies of the judgment of conviction, immediately notify the Director of the Department of Corrections and the Director shall, without delay, send some authorized person to the county where the prisoner is held for commitment to receive the prisoner.

2. When such an authorized person presents to the sheriff holding the prisoner an order for the delivery of the prisoner, the sheriff shall deliver to the authorized person two of the certified copies of the judgment of conviction and take from the person a receipt for the prisoner, and the sheriff shall make return upon the certified copy of the judgment of conviction, showing the sheriff's proceedings thereunder, and both that copy with the return affixed thereto and the receipt from the authorized person must be filed with the county clerk.

3. The term of imprisonment designated in the judgment of conviction must begin on the date of sentence of the prisoner by the court.

(Added to NRS by 1967, 1438; A 1973, 30; 1977, 859; 1997, 130; 1999, 1047, 1191; 2001, 77; 2001 Special Session, 217; 2003, 668; 2013, 1369)

NRS 176.337 Court to notify defendant convicted of domestic violence concerning possession, shipment, transportation or receipt of firearm or ammunition. If a defendant is convicted of a misdemeanor or felony that constitutes domestic violence pursuant to NRS 33.018, the court shall notify the defendant that possession, shipment, transportation or receipt of a firearm or ammunition by the defendant may constitute a felony pursuant to NRS 202.360 or federal law.

(Added to NRS by 2007, 95)

NRS 176.345 Proceedings when conviction carries death penalty.

1. When a judgment of death has been pronounced, a certified copy of the judgment of conviction must be forthwith executed and attested in triplicate by the clerk under the seal of the court. There must be attached to the triplicate copies a warrant signed by the judge, attested by the clerk, under the seal of the court, which:

(a) Recites the fact of the conviction and judgment;

(b) Appoints a week, the first day being Monday and the last day being Sunday, within which the judgment is to be executed, which must not be less than 60 days nor more than 90 days from the time of judgment; and

(c) Directs the sheriff to deliver the prisoner to such authorized person as the Director of the Department of Corrections designates to receive the prisoner, for execution. The prison must be designated in the warrant.

2. The original of the triplicate copies of the judgment of conviction and warrant must be filed in the office of the county clerk, and two of the triplicate copies must be immediately delivered by the clerk to the sheriff of the county. One of the triplicate copies must be delivered by the sheriff, with the prisoner, to such authorized person as the Director of the Department of Corrections designates, and is the warrant and authority of the Director for the imprisonment and execution of the prisoner, as therein provided and commanded. The Director shall return the certified copy of the judgment of conviction to the county clerk of the county in which it was issued. The other triplicate copy is the warrant and authority of the sheriff to deliver the prisoner to the authorized person designated by the Director. The final triplicate copy must be returned to the county clerk by the sheriff with the sheriff's proceedings endorsed thereon.

(Added to NRS by 1967, 1438; A 1977, 860; 1989, 390; 1999, 1048; 2001 Special Session, 218)

NRS 176.355 Execution of death penalty: Method; time and place; witnesses.

1. The judgment of death must be inflicted by an injection of a lethal drug.

2. The Director of the Department of Corrections shall:

(a) Execute a sentence of death within the week, the first day being Monday and the last day being Sunday, that the judgment is to be executed, as designated by the district court. The Director may execute the judgment at any time during that week if a stay of execution is not entered by a court of appropriate jurisdiction.

(b) Select the drug or combination of drugs to be used for the execution after consulting with the Chief Medical Officer.

(c) Be present at the execution.

(d) Notify those members of the immediate family of the victim who have, pursuant to NRS 176.357, requested to be informed of the time, date and place scheduled for the execution.

(e) Invite a competent physician, the county coroner, a psychiatrist and not less than six reputable citizens over the age of 21 years to be present at the execution. The Director shall determine the maximum number of persons who may be present for the execution. The Director shall give preference to those eligible members or representatives of the immediate family of the victim who requested, pursuant to NRS 176.357, to attend the execution.

3. The execution must take place at the state prison.

4. A person who has not been invited by the Director may not witness the execution.

(Added to NRS by 1967, 1439; A 1977, 860; 1983, 1937; 1989, 390; 1995, 381; 2001 Special Session, 218)

NRS 176.357 Request for notification of execution of death penalty; request to attend.

1. If after a conviction for murder a judgment of death has been pronounced, each member of the immediate family of the victim who is 21 years of age or older may submit a written request to the Director to be informed of the time, date and place scheduled for the execution of the sentence of death. The request for notification may be accompanied by a written request to attend or nominate a representative to attend the execution.

2. As used in this section, "immediate family" means persons who are related by blood, adoption or marriage, within the second degree of consanguinity or affinity.

(Added to NRS by 1995, 381)

NRS 176.365 Director of Department of Corrections to make return on death warrant. After the execution, the Director of the Department of Corrections must make a return upon the death warrant to the court by which the judgment was rendered, showing the time, place, mode and manner in which it was executed.

(Added to NRS by 1967, 1439; A 1977, 860; 2001 Special Session, 219)

SUSPENSION OF EXECUTION OF DEATH PENALTY

General Provisions

NRS 176.415 When execution of death penalty may be stayed. The execution of a judgment of death must be stayed only:

1. By the State Board of Pardons Commissioners as authorized in Section 14 of Article 5 of the Constitution of the State of Nevada;

2. By the Governor if the Governor grants a reprieve pursuant to Section 13 of Article 5 of the Constitution of the State of Nevada;

3. When a direct appeal from the judgment of conviction and sentence is taken to the appellate court of competent jurisdiction pursuant to the rules fixed by the Supreme Court pursuant to Section 4 of Article 6 of the Nevada Constitution;

4. By a judge of the district court of the county in which the state prison is situated, for the purpose of an investigation of sanity or pregnancy as provided in NRS 176.425 to 176.485, inclusive;

5. By a judge of the district court in which a motion is filed pursuant to subsection 5 of NRS 175.554, for the purpose of determining whether the defendant is intellectually disabled; or

6. Pursuant to the provisions of NRS 176.0919 or 176.486 to 176.492, inclusive.

(Added to NRS by 1967, 1440; A 1987, 1221; 2003, 768; 2007, 25; 2013, 686, 1756)

Insanity or Pregnancy

NRS 176.425 Sanity investigation: Filing of petition; stay of execution.

1. If, after judgment of death, there is a good reason to believe that the defendant has become insane, the Director of the Department of Corrections to whom the convicted person has been delivered for execution may by a petition in writing, verified by a physician, petition a district judge of the district court of the county in which the state prison is situated, alleging the present insanity of such person, whereupon such judge shall:

(a) Fix a day for a hearing to determine whether the convicted person is insane;
(b) Appoint two psychiatrists, two psychologists, or one psychiatrist and one psychologist, to examine the convicted person; and
(c) Give immediate notice of the hearing to the Attorney General and to the district attorney of the county in which the conviction was had.

2. If the judge determines that the hearing on and the determination of the sanity of the convicted person cannot be had before the date of the execution of such person, the judge may stay the execution of the judgment of death pending the determination of the sanity of the convicted person.

(Added to NRS by 1967, 1440; A 1977, 861; 1991, 1002; 2001 Special Session, 219)

NRS 176.435 Sanity investigation: Conduct of hearing.

1. On the day fixed, the Director of the Department of Corrections shall bring the convicted person before the court, and the Attorney General or the Attorney General's deputy shall attend the hearing. The district attorney of the county in which the conviction was had, and an attorney for the convicted person, may attend the hearing.

2. The court shall receive the report of the examining physicians and may require the production of other evidence. The Attorney General or the Attorney General's deputy, the district attorney, and the attorney for the convicted person or such person if the convicted person is without counsel may introduce evidence and cross-examine any witness, including the examining physicians.

3. The court shall then make and enter its finding of sanity or insanity.

(Added to NRS by 1967, 1440; A 1977, 861; 2001 Special Session, 219)

NRS 176.445 Execution of judgment when defendant found sane. If it is found by the court that the convicted person is sane, the Director of the Department of Corrections must execute the judgment of death; but if the judgment has been stayed, as provided in NRS 176.425, the judge shall cause a certified copy of the order staying the execution of the judgment, together with a certified copy of the judge's finding that the convicted person is sane, to be immediately forwarded by the clerk of the court to the clerk of the district court of the county in which the conviction was had, who shall give notice thereof to the district attorney of such county. Proceedings shall then be instituted in the last mentioned district court for the issuance of a new warrant of execution of the judgment of death in the manner provided in NRS 176.495.

(Added to NRS by 1967, 1441; A 1977, 861; 2001 Special Session, 219)

NRS 176.455 Suspension of execution when defendant found insane; proceedings on recovery of sanity.

1. If it is found by the court that the convicted person is insane, the judge shall make and enter an order staying the execution of the judgment of death until the convicted person becomes sane, and shall therein order the Director of the Department of Corrections to confine such person in a safe place of confinement until the convicted person's reason is restored.

2. The clerk of the court shall serve or cause to be served three certified copies of the order, one on the Director, one on the Governor, for the use of the State Board of Pardons Commissioners, and one on the clerk of the district court of the county in which the conviction was had.

3. If the convicted person thereafter becomes sane, notice of this fact shall be given by the Director to a judge of the court staying the execution of the judgment, and the judge, upon being satisfied that such person is then sane, shall enter an order vacating the order staying the execution of the judgment.

4. The clerk of the court shall immediately serve or cause to be served three certified copies of such vacating order as follows: One on the Director, one on the Governor, for the use of the State Board of Pardons Commissioners, and one on the clerk of the district court of the county in which the conviction was had, who shall give notice thereof to the district attorney of such county, whereupon proceedings shall be instituted in the last mentioned district court for the issuance of a new warrant of execution of the judgment of death in the manner provided in NRS 176.495.

(Added to NRS by 1967, 1441; A 1977, 861; 2001 Special Session, 219)

NRS 176.465 Investigation of pregnancy: Procedure; hearing.

1. If there is good reason to believe that a female against whom a judgment of death has been rendered is pregnant, the Director of the Department of Corrections to whom she has been delivered for execution shall petition a judge of the district court of the county in which the state prison is situated, in writing, alleging such pregnancy, whereupon such judge shall summon a jury of three physicians to inquire into the alleged pregnancy and fix a day for the hearing thereon, and give immediate notice thereof to the Attorney General and to the district attorney of the county in which the conviction was had.

2. The provisions of NRS 176.425 and 176.435 apply to the proceedings upon the inquisition, except that three physicians shall be summoned. They shall certify in writing to the court their findings as to pregnancy.

(Added to NRS by 1967, 1441; A 1977, 862; 2001 Special Session, 220)

NRS 176.475 Proceedings after investigation: Execution of judgment; suspension of execution; issuance of warrant on termination of pregnancy.

1. If it is found by the court that the female is not pregnant, the Director of the Department of Corrections must execute the judgment of death; but if a stay of execution has been granted pursuant to NRS 176.425 the procedure provided in NRS 176.445 is applicable.

2. If the female is found to be pregnant, the judge shall enter an order staying the execution of the judgment of death, and shall therein order the Director to confine such female in a safe place of confinement commensurate with her condition until further order of the court.

3. When such female is no longer pregnant, notice of this fact shall be given by the Director to a judge of the court staying the execution of the judgment. Thereupon the judge, upon being satisfied that the pregnancy no longer exists, shall enter an order vacating the

order staying the execution of the judgment and shall direct the clerk of such court to serve or cause to be served three certified copies of such order, one on the Director, one on the Governor, for the use of the State Board of Pardons Commissioners, and one on the clerk of the district court of the county in which the conviction was had, who shall give notice thereof to the district attorney of such county, whereupon proceedings shall be instituted in the last mentioned district court for the issuance of a new warrant of execution of the judgment in the manner provided in NRS 176.495.

(Added to NRS by 1967, 1442; A 1977, 862; 2001 Special Session, 220)

NRS 176.485 Costs of investigations borne by State; manner of payment. The costs and expenses of the investigations provided in NRS 176.415 to 176.475, inclusive, must be borne by the State and paid in the following manner: The costs and expenses of an investigation must first be paid by county warrants drawn upon the order of the district judge. The county clerk shall then present a claim to the State Board of Examiners for the amount of such costs and expenses so ordered paid by the district judge. Upon approval of the claim by the State Board of Examiners, the State Controller shall draw a warrant for the payment thereof, and the State Treasurer shall pay the same from the Reserve for Statutory Contingency Account.

(Added to NRS by 1967, 1442; A 1991, 1753)

Petition for Postconviction Relief

NRS 176.486 Authority to enter stay of execution. A district court having proper jurisdiction, the Court of Appeals or the Supreme Court, if it has proper jurisdiction, may stay the execution of a sentence of death when a postconviction petition for habeas corpus has been filed only after appropriate notice has been given to the appropriate respondent in the case.

(Added to NRS by 1987, 1220; A 1991, 90; 2013, 1756)

NRS 176.487 Determination of whether to enter stay of execution. When a person under a sentence of death files a proper postconviction petition for habeas corpus, a district court, the Court of Appeals or the Supreme Court on a subsequent appeal shall enter a stay of execution if the court finds a stay necessary for a proper consideration of the claims for relief. In making this determination, the court shall consider whether:

1. The petition is the first effort by the petitioner to raise constitutional claims for relief after a direct appeal from a conviction and the petition raises claims other than those which could have been raised at trial or on direct appeal.
2. The petition is timely filed and jurisdictionally appropriate and does not set forth conclusory claims only.
3. If the petition is not the first petition for postconviction relief, it raises constitutional claims which are not procedurally barred by laches, the law of the case, the doctrines of abuse of the writ or successive petition or any other procedural default.
4. If the petition is a second or successive petition, it presents substantial grounds upon which relief might be granted and valid justification for the claims not having been presented in a prior proceeding.
5. The petition asserts claims based upon specified facts or law which, if true, would entitle the petitioner to relief.
6. The court cannot decide legal claims which are properly raised or expeditiously hold an evidentiary hearing on factual claims which are properly raised before the execution of sentence.

(Added to NRS by 1987, 1220; A 1991, 91; 2013, 1756)

NRS 176.488 Entry of stay of execution and necessary orders. A stay of execution must be entered by the court in writing and copies sent as soon as practicable to the Director of the Department of Corrections, the warden of the institution in which the offender is imprisoned and the Office of the Attorney General in Carson City. The court shall also enter an order and take all necessary actions to expedite further proceeding before that court.

(Added to NRS by 1987, 1221; A 2001 Special Session, 221)

NRS 176.489 Vacation of stay of execution. Any stay of execution previously entered by the court must be vacated if the court denies the petition for habeas corpus.

(Added to NRS by 1987, 1221; A 1991, 91)

NRS 176.491 Stay of execution following denial of appeal.

1. Upon the denial of any appeal pursuant to chapter 34 or 177 of NRS to the appellate court of competent jurisdiction pursuant to the rules fixed by the Supreme Court pursuant to Section 4 of Article 6 of the Nevada Constitution, the appellate court of competent jurisdiction shall dissolve any stay of execution previously entered. No stay of such execution may be entered or continued by the appellate court of competent jurisdiction after the denial of an appeal pending the filing of a petition with a federal court or a petition for a writ of certiorari with the Supreme Court of the United States.
2. The entry of a stay of issuance of a remittitur in the appellate court of competent jurisdiction does not prohibit the application of or the issuance of a warrant of execution by the district court in which the conviction was obtained.
3. To stay the execution of a sentence of death following the denial of any appeal to the appellate court of competent jurisdiction pursuant to chapter 34 or 177 of NRS, a person under sentence of death must:

(a) Apply for and obtain a stay in the federal court in which the person applies for a writ of certiorari or habeas corpus; or

(b) Obtain a stay of execution pursuant to NRS 176.487.

(Added to NRS by 1987, 1221; A 1989, 491; 2013, 1757)

NRS 176.492 Dissolution of stay of execution which was improperly entered. The respondent may file a petition with the appellate court of competent jurisdiction pursuant to the rules fixed by the Supreme Court pursuant to Section 4 of Article 6 of the Nevada Constitution within 10 days after the entry of a stay of execution by a district court to dissolve a stay which was improperly entered. The filing of the petition does not divest the district court of jurisdiction to hear the claims raised by the petition and the district court shall not delay consideration of the claims because of the filing of such a petition with the appellate court of competent jurisdiction.

(Added to NRS by 1987, 1221; A 2013, 1757)

NEW ORDER TO EXECUTE JUDGMENT OF DEATH

NRS 176.495 New warrant generally.

1. If for any reason a judgment of death has not been executed, and it remains in force, the court in which the conviction was had must, upon the application of the Attorney General or the district attorney of the county in which the conviction was had, cause another warrant to be drawn, signed by the judge and attested by the clerk under the seal of the court, and delivered to the Director of the Department of Corrections.

2. The warrant must state the conviction and judgment and appoint a week, the first day being Monday and the last day being Sunday, within which the judgment is to be executed. The first day of that week must be not less than 15 days nor more than 30 days after the date of the warrant. The Director shall execute a sentence of death within the week the judgment is to be executed, as designated by the district court. The Director may execute the judgment at any time during that week if a stay of execution is not entered by a court of appropriate jurisdiction.

(Added to NRS by 1967, 1442; A 1977, 863; 1989, 391; 2001 Special Session, 221; 2003, 2083)

NRS 176.505 Order following appeal.

1. When a remittitur showing the affirmation of a judgment of death has been filed with the clerk of the court from which the appeal has been taken, the court in which the conviction was obtained shall inquire into the facts, and, if no legal reasons exist prohibiting the execution of the judgment, shall make and enter an order requiring the Director of the Department of Corrections to execute the judgment at a specified time. The presence of the defendant in the court at the time the order of execution is made and entered, or the warrant is issued, is not required.

2. When an opinion, order dismissing appeal or other order upholding a sentence of death is issued by the appellate court of competent jurisdiction pursuant to chapter 34 or 177 of NRS, the court in which the sentence of death was obtained shall inquire into the facts and, if no legal reason exists prohibiting the execution of the judgment, shall make and enter an order requiring the Director of the Department of Corrections to execute the judgment during a specified week. The presence of the defendant in the court when the order of execution is made and entered, or the warrant is issued, is not required.

3. Notwithstanding the entry of a stay of issuance of a remittitur in the appellate court of competent jurisdiction following denial of appellate relief in a proceeding brought pursuant to chapter 34 or 177 of NRS, the court in which the conviction was obtained shall, upon application of the Attorney General or the district attorney of the county in which the conviction was obtained, cause another warrant to be drawn, signed by the judge and attested by the clerk under the seal of the court, and delivered to the Director of the Department of Corrections.

(Added to NRS by 1967, 1442; A 1977, 863; 1989, 491; 2001 Special Session, 221; 2013, 1758)

NEW TRIAL OR MOTION TO VACATE JUDGMENT

NRS 176.515 Court may grant new trial or motion to vacate judgment in certain circumstances.

1. The court may grant a new trial to a defendant if required as a matter of law or on the ground of newly discovered evidence.

2. If trial was by the court without a jury, the court may vacate the judgment if entered, take additional testimony and direct the entry of a new judgment.

3. Except as otherwise provided in NRS 176.09187, a motion for a new trial based on the ground of newly discovered evidence may be made only within 2 years after the verdict or finding of guilt.

4. A motion for a new trial based on any other grounds must be made within 7 days after the verdict or finding of guilt or within such further time as the court may fix during the 7-day period.

5. The court may grant a motion to vacate a judgment if:

(a) The judgment is a conviction for a violation of:

(1) NRS 201.354, for engaging in prostitution or solicitation for prostitution, provided that the defendant was not alleged to be a customer of a prostitute;

(2) NRS 207.200, for unlawful trespass;

(3) Paragraph (b) of subsection 1 of NRS 463.350, for loitering; or

(4) A county, city or town ordinance, for loitering for the purpose of solicitation or prostitution.

(b) The participation of the defendant in the offense was the result of the defendant having been a victim of:

(1) Trafficking in persons as described in the Trafficking Victims Protection Act of 2000, 22 U.S.C. §§ 7101 et seq.; or

(2) Involuntary servitude as described in NRS 200.463 or 200.4631; and

(c) The defendant makes a motion under this subsection with due diligence after the defendant has ceased being a victim of trafficking or involuntary servitude or has sought services for victims of such trafficking or involuntary servitude.

6. In deciding whether to grant a motion made pursuant to subsection 5, the court shall take into consideration any reasonable concerns for the safety of the defendant, family members of the defendant or other victims that may be jeopardized by the bringing of such a motion.

7. If the court grants a motion made pursuant to subsection 5, the court:

(a) Shall vacate the judgment and dismiss the accusatory pleading; and

(b) May take any additional action that the court deems appropriate under the circumstances.

(Added to NRS by 1967, 1443; A 1983, 1671; 2003, 1894; 2011, 280; 2013, 1856; 2015, 785)

ARREST OF JUDGMENT

NRS 176.525 Arrest of judgment: When granted and time in which motion is to be made. The court shall arrest judgment if the indictment, information or complaint does not charge an offense or if the court was without jurisdiction of the offense charged. The motion in arrest of judgment shall be made within 7 days after determination of guilt or within such further time as the court may fix during the 7-day period.

(Added to NRS by 1967, 1443)

NRS 176.535 Effect of arresting judgment. The effect of allowing a motion in arrest of judgment is to place the defendant in the same situation in which the defendant was before the indictment was found or information or complaint filed.

(Added to NRS by 1967, 1443)

NRS 176.545 Procedure after allowance of arrest of judgment.

1. If, from the evidence on the trial, there is reasonable ground to believe the defendant guilty, and a new indictment, information or complaint can be framed upon which the defendant may be convicted, the court may order the defendant to be recommitted to the officers of the proper county, or admitted to bail anew to answer the new indictment, information or complaint.
2. If the evidence shows the defendant guilty of another offense, the defendant shall be committed or held thereon, and in neither case shall the verdict be a bar to another prosecution.
3. But if no evidence appear sufficient to charge the defendant with any offense, the defendant shall, if in custody, be discharged; or, if admitted to bail, the defendant's bail shall be exonerated; or, if money has been deposited instead of bail, it shall be refunded to the defendant, and the arrest of judgment shall operate as an acquittal of the charge upon which the indictment, information or complaint was founded.

(Added to NRS by 1967, 1443)

MISCELLANEOUS PROVISIONS

NRS 176.555 Correction of illegal sentence. The court may correct an illegal sentence at any time.

(Added to NRS by 1967, 1443)

NRS 176.565 Clerical mistakes. Clerical mistakes in judgments, orders or other parts of the record and errors in the record arising from oversight or omission may be corrected by the court at any time and after such notice, if any, as the court orders.

(Added to NRS by 1967, 1443)

CHAPTER 176A - PROBATION AND SUSPENSION OF SENTENCE

GENERAL PROVISIONS

AUTHORITY OF THE COURT; LIMITATIONS

NRS 176A.110 Persons convicted of certain offenses required to be certified as not representing high risk to reoffend before court suspends sentence or grants probation; immunity.
NRS 176A.120 Persons convicted of certain offenses against elderly required to pay restitution before court suspends sentence or grants probation; exceptions.

PROCEDURE

NRS 176A.200 Investigation by Division.
NRS 176A.210 Promise to comply with conditions of probation; waiver of extradition.
NRS 176A.220 Delivery of copy of records to Chief Parole and Probation Officer.

ASSIGNMENT TO PROGRAM FOR TREATMENT OF MENTAL ILLNESS

NRS 176A.250 Establishment of program for treatment of mental illness or intellectual disabilities; assignment of defendant to program; progress reports.
NRS 176A.255 Transfer of jurisdiction from justice court or municipal court to district court for assignment of defendant to program.
NRS 176A.260 Conditions and limitations on assignment of defendant to program; effect of violation of terms and conditions; discharge of defendant upon fulfillment of terms and conditions; effect of discharge.
NRS 176A.265 Sealing of records after discharge.

ASSIGNMENT TO PROGRAM FOR TREATMENT OF VETERANS AND MILITARY

NRS 176A.280 Establishment of program for treatment of veterans and members of military; assignment of defendant to program; progress reports.
NRS 176A.285 Transfer of jurisdiction from justice court or municipal court to district court for assignment of defendant to program.
NRS 176A.290 Conditions and limitations on assignment of defendant to program; effect of violation of terms and conditions; discharge of defendant upon fulfillment of terms and conditions; effect of discharge.
NRS 176A.295 Sealing of records after discharge.

PROGRAM OF PROBATION SECURED BY SURETY BOND

NRS 176A.300 Execution and amount of surety bond.
NRS 176A.310 Conditions; duties of surety; probationer to report to and pay surety.
NRS 176A.320 Failure of surety to fulfill duties; failure of probationer to fulfill conditions of surety bond.
NRS 176A.330 Exoneration of surety and setting aside of forfeiture of surety bond.
NRS 176A.340 Procedure when surety not exonerated; enforcement of liability; remission of judgment of default.
NRS 176A.350 Discharge of surety and release of bond.
NRS 176A.360 Arrest of probationer.
NRS 176A.370 Money collected to be deposited in State General Fund.

TERMS AND CONDITIONS

NRS 176A.400 Imposition by court; alternative programs or treatment; prohibition on suspending term of imprisonment; placement under supervision of Chief Parole and Probation Officer.
NRS 176A.410 Required terms and conditions for sex offenders; powers and duties of court; exceptions.
NRS 176A.413 Restrictions relating to computers and use of Internet and other electronic means of communication; powers and duties of court; exceptions.
NRS 176A.416 Evaluations and counseling for offenses involving cruelty to animals; powers and duties of court.
NRS 176A.420 Tests to determine use of controlled substance.
NRS 176A.430 Restitution.
NRS 176A.440 Program of intensive supervision.
NRS 176A.450 Modification; procedure for modifying conditions relating to program of probation secured by surety bond; limitations.

DURATION; ARREST FOR ALLEGED VIOLATION

NRS 176A.500 Authority of court to fix duration; limitations; arrest for alleged violation; powers and duties of peace officers; deduction of days.

PROCEEDINGS AFTER ARREST

Residential Confinement Pending Inquiry or Consideration by Court

Inquiry to Determine Probable Cause

Consideration by Court of Alleged Violation; Assessment of Expenses

RESIDENTIAL CONFINEMENT AFTER VIOLATION

RESIDENTIAL CENTERS FOR SUPERVISION OF PROBATIONERS

PROGRAM OF REGIMENTAL DISCIPLINE

DISCHARGE

GENERAL PROVISIONS

NRS 176A.010 Definitions. As used in this chapter, unless the context otherwise requires, the words and terms defined in NRS 176A.020 to 176A.090, inclusive, have the meanings ascribed to them in those sections.

(Added to NRS by 1967, 1434; A 1969, 181; 1975, 83; 1987, 2229; 1989, 1854, 1886, 1983; 1991, 2043; 1995, 25, 1249; 1997, 1671, 2505; 2001 Special Session, 260; 2003, 1946; 2009, 104)

NRS 176A.020 "Board" defined. "Board" means the State Board of Parole Commissioners.

(Added to NRS by 1967, 1434; A 1969, 181; 1975, 83; 1987, 2229; 1989, 1854, 1886, 1983; 1991, 2043; 1995, 25, 1249; 1997, 1671, 2505)

NRS 176A.030 "Court" defined. "Court" means a district court of the State of Nevada.

(Added to NRS by 1967, 1434; A 1969, 181; 1975, 83; 1987, 2229; 1989, 1854, 1886, 1983; 1991, 2043; 1995, 25, 1249; 1997, 1671, 2505)

NRS 176A.040 "Division" defined. "Division" means the Division of Parole and Probation of the Department of Public Safety.
(Added to NRS by 1993, 1512; A 2001, 2570)

NRS 176A.043 "Member of the military" defined. "Member of the military" means a person who is presently serving in the Armed Forces of the United States, a reserve component thereof or the National Guard.
(Added to NRS by 2009, 103)

NRS 176A.045 "Mental illness" defined. "Mental illness" has the meaning ascribed to it in NRS 433.164.
(Added to NRS by 2001 Special Session, 258; A 2003, 1946)

NRS 176A.047 "Intellectual disability" defined. "Intellectual disability" has the meaning ascribed to it in NRS 433.099.
(Added to NRS by 2003, 1945; A 2013, 686)

NRS 176A.050 "Parole and probation officer" defined. "Parole and probation officer" means the Chief Parole and Probation Officer or an assistant parole and probation officer appointed in accordance with the provisions of chapter 213 of NRS.
(Added to NRS by 1967, 1434; A 1969, 181; 1975, 83; 1987, 2229; 1989, 1854, 1886, 1983; 1991, 2043; 1995, 25, 1249; 1997, 1671, 2505)

NRS 176A.060 "Residential confinement" defined. "Residential confinement" means the confinement of a person convicted of a crime to the person's place of residence under the terms and conditions established by the sentencing court.
(Added to NRS by 1967, 1434; A 1969, 181; 1975, 83; 1987, 2229; 1989, 1854, 1886, 1983; 1991, 2043; 1995, 25, 1249; 1997, 1671, 2505)

NRS 176A.070 "Standards" defined. "Standards" means the objective standards for granting or revoking parole or probation which are adopted by the Board or Chief Parole and Probation Officer.
(Added to NRS by 1967, 1434; A 1969, 181; 1975, 83; 1987, 2229; 1989, 1854, 1886, 1983; 1991, 2043; 1995, 25, 1249; 1997, 1671, 2505)

NRS 176A.080 "Surety bond" defined. "Surety bond" means a written undertaking, executed by a surety, that a person will, as a result of the bond, participate in a program of probation and that in the event that the person violates a condition of the program of probation, the surety will pay the court the amount of money specified for the bond.
(Added to NRS by 1967, 1434; A 1969, 181; 1975, 83; 1987, 2229; 1989, 1854, 1886, 1983; 1991, 2043; 1995, 25, 1249; 1997, 1671, 2505)

NRS 176A.090 "Veteran" defined. "Veteran" means a person who has served in the Armed Forces of the United States, a reserve component thereof or the National Guard and has been discharged or released therefrom.
(Added to NRS by 2009, 103)

AUTHORITY OF THE COURT; LIMITATIONS

NRS 176A.100 Authority and discretion of court to suspend sentence and grant probation; persons eligible; factors considered; intensive supervision; submission of report of presentence investigation.

1. Except as otherwise provided in this section and NRS 176A.110 and 176A.120, if a person is found guilty in a district court upon verdict or plea of:

(a) Murder of the first or second degree, kidnapping in the first degree, sexual assault, attempted sexual assault of a child who is less than 16 years of age, lewdness with a child pursuant to NRS 201.230, an offense for which the suspension of sentence or the granting of probation is expressly forbidden, or if the person is found to be a habitual criminal pursuant to NRS 207.010, a habitually fraudulent felon pursuant to NRS 207.014 or a habitual felon pursuant to NRS 207.012, the court shall not suspend the execution of the sentence imposed or grant probation to the person.

(b) A category E felony, except as otherwise provided in this paragraph, the court shall suspend the execution of the sentence imposed and grant probation to the person. The court may, as it deems advisable, decide not to suspend the execution of the sentence imposed and grant probation to the person if, at the time of sentencing, it is established that the person:

(1) Was serving a term of probation or was on parole at the time the crime was committed, whether in this State or elsewhere, for a felony conviction;

(2) Had previously had the person's probation or parole revoked, whether in this State or elsewhere, for a felony conviction;

(3) Had previously been assigned to a program of treatment and rehabilitation pursuant to NRS 453.580 and failed to successfully complete that program; or

(4) Had previously been two times convicted, whether in this State or elsewhere, of a crime that under the laws of the situs of the crime or of this State would amount to a felony.

□ If the person denies the existence of a previous conviction, the court shall determine the issue of the previous conviction after hearing all relevant evidence presented on the issue by the prosecution and the person. At such a hearing, the person may not challenge the validity of a previous conviction. For the purposes of this paragraph, a certified copy of a felony conviction is prima facie evidence of conviction of a prior felony.

(c) Another felony, a gross misdemeanor or a misdemeanor, the court may suspend the execution of the sentence imposed and grant probation as the court deems advisable.

2. In determining whether to grant probation to a person, the court shall not consider whether the person has the financial ability to participate in a program of probation secured by a surety bond established pursuant to NRS 176A.300 to 176A.370, inclusive.

3. The court shall consider the standards adopted pursuant to NRS 213.10988 and the recommendation of the Chief Parole and Probation Officer, if any, in determining whether to grant probation to a person.

4. If the court determines that a person is otherwise eligible for probation but requires more supervision than would normally be provided to a person granted probation, the court may, in lieu of sentencing the person to a term of imprisonment, grant probation pursuant to the Program of Intensive Supervision established pursuant to NRS 176A.440.

5. Except as otherwise provided in this subsection, if a person is convicted of a felony and the Division is required to make a presentence investigation and report to the court pursuant to NRS 176.135, the court shall not grant probation to the person until the court receives the report of the presentence investigation from the Chief Parole and Probation Officer. The Chief Parole and Probation Officer shall submit the report of the presentence investigation to the court not later than 45 days after receiving a request for a presentence investigation from the county clerk. If the report of the presentence investigation is not submitted by the Chief Parole and Probation Officer within 45 days, the court may grant probation without the report.

6. If the court determines that a person is otherwise eligible for probation, the court shall, when determining the conditions of that probation, consider the imposition of such conditions as would facilitate timely payments by the person of an obligation, if any, for the support of a child and the payment of any such obligation which is in arrears.

(Added to NRS by 1967, 1434; A 1973, 68, 1802; 1975, 84; 1977, 289, 658, 1631; 1979, 1460; 1981, 369; 1989, 1887; 1991, 71, 1002, 2044, 2045, 2046; 1993, 9; 1995, 224, 857, 1249, 1328, 2388, 2389; 1997, 519, 1187, 2505, 2509; 1999, 565, 1192; 2003, 846, 2827)

NRS 176A.110 Persons convicted of certain offenses required to be certified as not representing high risk to reoffend before court suspends sentence or grants probation; immunity.

1. The court shall not grant probation to or suspend the sentence of a person convicted of an offense listed in subsection 3 unless:

(a) If a psychosexual evaluation of the person is required pursuant to NRS 176.139, the person who conducts the psychosexual evaluation certifies in the report prepared pursuant to NRS 176.139 that the person convicted of the offense does not represent a high risk to reoffend based upon a currently accepted standard of assessment; or

(b) If a psychosexual evaluation of the person is not required pursuant to NRS 176.139, a psychologist licensed to practice in this State who is trained to conduct psychosexual evaluations or a psychiatrist licensed to practice medicine in this State who is certified by the American Board of Psychiatry and Neurology, Inc., and is trained to conduct psychosexual evaluations certifies in a written report to the court that the person convicted of the offense does not represent a high risk to reoffend based upon a currently accepted standard of assessment.

2. This section does not create a right in any person to be certified or to continue to be certified. No person may bring a cause of action against the State, its political subdivisions, or the agencies, boards, commissions, departments, officers or employees of the State or its political subdivisions for not certifying a person pursuant to this section or for refusing to consider a person for certification pursuant to this section.

3. The provisions of this section apply to a person convicted of any of the following offenses:

(a) Attempted sexual assault of a person who is 16 years of age or older pursuant to NRS 200.366.

(b) Statutory sexual seduction pursuant to NRS 200.368.

(c) Battery with intent to commit sexual assault pursuant to NRS 200.400.

(d) Abuse or neglect of a child pursuant to NRS 200.508.

(e) An offense involving pornography and a minor pursuant to NRS 200.710 to 200.730, inclusive.

(f) Incest pursuant to NRS 201.180.

(g) Open or gross lewdness pursuant to NRS 201.210.

(h) Indecent or obscene exposure pursuant to NRS 201.220.

(i) Sexual penetration of a dead human body pursuant to NRS 201.450.

(j) Sexual conduct between certain employees of a school or volunteers at a school and a pupil pursuant to NRS 201.540.

(k) Sexual conduct between certain employees of a college or university and a student pursuant to NRS 201.550.

(l) Luring a child or a person with mental illness pursuant to NRS 201.560, if punished as a felony.

(m) A violation of NRS 207.180.

(n) An attempt to commit an offense listed in paragraphs (b) to (m), inclusive.

(o) Coercion or attempted coercion that is determined to be sexually motivated pursuant to NRS 207.193.

(Added to NRS by 1997, 2504; A 2001, 1638, 2792; 2003, 67, 1382, 2828; 2013, 1162; 2015, 1439)

NRS 176A.120 Persons convicted of certain offenses against elderly required to pay restitution before court suspends sentence or grants probation; exceptions.

1. Except as otherwise provided in subsection 2, the court shall not grant probation to a person whose conduct during the commission of the crime for which the person was convicted satisfies the requirements for imposing an additional term of imprisonment pursuant to paragraph (h) or (i) of subsection 1 of NRS 193.167 or subsection 2 of NRS 193.167, until the convicted person has paid to the victim of the offense at least 80 percent of the amount of restitution set by the court pursuant to NRS 176.033.

2. The court shall not deny probation to a person as provided in subsection 1 unless the court determines that the person has willfully failed to make restitution to the victim of the crime and the person has the ability to make restitution.

(Added to NRS by 1997, 1031; A 1999, 43)

PROCEDURE

NRS 176A.200 Investigation by Division. The Division shall inquire into the circumstances of the offense, criminal record, social history and present condition of the defendant. Such an investigation may include a physical and mental examination of the defendant. The expense of any such examination must be paid by the county in which the indictment was found or the information filed.

(Added to NRS by 1967, 1435; A 1997, 130; 2005, 81)

NRS 176A.210 Promise to comply with conditions of probation; waiver of extradition. Upon entry of an order of probation by the court, a person:

1. Shall be deemed accepted for probation for all purposes; and
2. Shall submit to the Division for filing with the clerk of the court of competent jurisdiction a signed document stating that:

(a) The person will comply with the conditions which have been imposed by the court and are stated in the document; and

(b) If the person fails to comply with the conditions imposed by the court and is taken into custody outside of this State, the person waives all rights relating to extradition proceedings.

(Added to NRS by 1995, 25; A 2005, 81)

NRS 176A.220 Delivery of copy of records to Chief Parole and Probation Officer.

1. The court shall, upon the entering of an order of probation or suspension of sentence, as provided for in this chapter, direct the clerk of the court to deliver a copy of the records in the case to the Chief Parole and Probation Officer.
2. At the court's discretion, the court may direct the clerk of the court to deliver the copy of the records in the case in writing, by electronic means or by providing the Chief Parole and Probation Officer access to the electronic systems necessary to retrieve the records.

(Added to NRS by 1991, 2043; A 1995, 26, 1250; 2015, 2566)

ASSIGNMENT TO PROGRAM FOR TREATMENT OF MENTAL ILLNESS

NRS 176A.250 Establishment of program for treatment of mental illness or intellectual disabilities; assignment of defendant to program; progress reports. A court may establish an appropriate program for the treatment of mental illness or intellectual disabilities to which it may assign a defendant pursuant to NRS 176A.260. The assignment must include the terms and conditions for successful completion of the program and provide for progress reports at intervals set by the court to ensure that the defendant is making satisfactory progress towards completion of the program.

(Added to NRS by 2001 Special Session, 259; A 2003, 1946; 2013, 686)

NRS 176A.255 Transfer of jurisdiction from justice court or municipal court to district court for assignment of defendant to program.

1. A justice court or a municipal court may, upon approval of the district court, transfer original jurisdiction to the district court of a case involving an eligible defendant.
2. As used in this section, "eligible defendant" means a person who:

(a) Has not tendered a plea of guilty, guilty but mentally ill or nolo contendere to, or been found guilty or guilty but mentally ill of, an offense that is a misdemeanor;

(b) Appears to suffer from mental illness or to be intellectually disabled; and

(c) Would benefit from assignment to a program established pursuant to NRS 176A.250.

(Added to NRS by 2001 Special Session, 259; A 2003, 1467, 1946; 2007, 1422; 2013, 686)

NRS 176A.260 Conditions and limitations on assignment of defendant to program; effect of violation of terms and conditions; discharge of defendant upon fulfillment of terms and conditions; effect of discharge.

1. Except as otherwise provided in subsection 2, if a defendant who suffers from mental illness or is intellectually disabled tenders a plea of guilty, guilty but mentally ill or nolo contendere to, or is found guilty or guilty but mentally ill of, any offense for which the suspension of sentence or the granting of probation is not prohibited by statute, the court may, without entering a judgment of conviction and with the consent of the defendant, suspend further proceedings and place the defendant on probation upon terms and conditions that must include attendance and successful completion of a program established pursuant to NRS 176A.250.
2. If the offense committed by the defendant involved the use or threatened use of force or violence or if the defendant was previously convicted in this State or in any other jurisdiction of a felony that involved the use or threatened use of force or violence, the court may not assign the defendant to the program unless the prosecuting attorney stipulates to the assignment.
3. Upon violation of a term or condition:

(a) The court may enter a judgment of conviction and proceed as provided in the section pursuant to which the defendant was charged.

(b) Notwithstanding the provisions of paragraph (e) of subsection 2 of NRS 193.130, the court may order the defendant to the custody of the Department of Corrections if the offense is punishable by imprisonment in the state prison.

4. Upon fulfillment of the terms and conditions, the court shall discharge the defendant and dismiss the proceedings. Discharge and dismissal pursuant to this section is without adjudication of guilt and is not a conviction for purposes of this section or for purposes of employment, civil rights or any statute or regulation or license or questionnaire or for any other public or private purpose, but is a conviction for the purpose of additional penalties imposed for second or subsequent convictions or the setting of bail. Discharge and dismissal restores the defendant, in the contemplation of the law, to the status occupied before the arrest, indictment or information. The defendant may not be

held thereafter under any law to be guilty of perjury or otherwise giving a false statement by reason of failure to recite or acknowledge that arrest, indictment, information or trial in response to an inquiry made of the defendant for any purpose.

(Added to NRS by 2001 Special Session, 259; A 2003, 1467, 1946; 2007, 1422; 2013, 687)

NRS 176A.265 Sealing of records after discharge.

1. After a defendant is discharged from probation pursuant to NRS 176A.260, the court shall order sealed all documents, papers and exhibits in the defendant's record, minute book entries and entries on dockets, and other documents relating to the case in the custody of such other agencies and officers as are named in the court's order if the defendant fulfills the terms and conditions imposed by the court and the Division. The court shall order those records sealed without a hearing unless the Division petitions the court, for good cause shown, not to seal the records and requests a hearing thereon.

2. If the court orders sealed the record of a defendant discharged pursuant to NRS 176A.260, the court shall send a copy of the order to each agency or officer named in the order. Each such agency or officer shall notify the court in writing of its compliance with the order.

(Added to NRS by 2001 Special Session, 260; A 2009, 417)

ASSIGNMENT TO PROGRAM FOR TREATMENT OF VETERANS AND MILITARY

NRS 176A.280 Establishment of program for treatment of veterans and members of military; assignment of defendant to program; progress reports. A court may establish an appropriate program for the treatment of veterans and members of the military to which it may assign a defendant pursuant to NRS 176A.290. The assignment must include the terms and conditions for successful completion of the program and provide for progress reports at intervals set by the court to ensure that the defendant is making satisfactory progress towards completion of the program.

(Added to NRS by 2009, 103)

NRS 176A.285 Transfer of jurisdiction from justice court or municipal court to district court for assignment of defendant to program.

1. A justice court or a municipal court may, upon approval of the district court, transfer original jurisdiction to the district court of a case involving an eligible defendant.

2. As used in this section, "eligible defendant" means a veteran or a member of the military who:

(a) Has not tendered a plea of guilty, guilty but mentally ill or nolo contendere to, or been found guilty or guilty but mentally ill of, an offense that is a misdemeanor;

(b) Appears to suffer from mental illness, alcohol or drug abuse or posttraumatic stress disorder, any of which appear to be related to military service, including, without limitation, any readjustment to civilian life which is necessary after combat service; and

(c) Would benefit from assignment to a program established pursuant to NRS 176A.280.

(Added to NRS by 2009, 103)

NRS 176A.290 Conditions and limitations on assignment of defendant to program; effect of violation of terms and conditions; discharge of defendant upon fulfillment of terms and conditions; effect of discharge.

1. Except as otherwise provided in subsection 2, if a defendant who is a veteran or a member of the military and who suffers from mental illness, alcohol or drug abuse or posttraumatic stress disorder as described in NRS 176A.285 tenders a plea of guilty, guilty but mentally ill or nolo contendere to, or is found guilty or guilty but mentally ill of, any offense for which the suspension of sentence or the granting of probation is not prohibited by statute, the court may, without entering a judgment of conviction and with the consent of the defendant, suspend further proceedings and place the defendant on probation upon terms and conditions that must include attendance and successful completion of a program established pursuant to NRS 176A.280.

2. If the offense committed by the defendant involved the use or threatened use of force or violence or if the defendant was previously convicted in this State or in any other jurisdiction of a felony that involved the use or threatened use of force or violence, the court may not assign the defendant to the program unless the prosecuting attorney stipulates to the assignment. For the purposes of this subsection, in determining whether an offense involved the use or threatened use of force or violence, the court shall consider the facts and circumstances surrounding the offense, including, without limitation, whether the defendant intended to place another person in reasonable apprehension of bodily harm.

3. Upon violation of a term or condition:

(a) The court may enter a judgment of conviction and proceed as provided in the section pursuant to which the defendant was charged.

(b) Notwithstanding the provisions of paragraph (e) of subsection 2 of NRS 193.130, the court may order the defendant to the custody of the Department of Corrections if the offense is punishable by imprisonment in the state prison.

4. Upon fulfillment of the terms and conditions, the court shall discharge the defendant and dismiss the proceedings. Discharge and dismissal pursuant to this section is without adjudication of guilt and is not a conviction for purposes of this section or for purposes of employment, civil rights or any statute or regulation or license or questionnaire or for any other public or private purpose, but is a conviction for the purpose of additional penalties imposed for second or subsequent convictions or the setting of bail. Discharge and dismissal restores the defendant, in the contemplation of the law, to the status occupied before the arrest, indictment or information. The defendant may not be held thereafter under any law to be guilty of perjury or otherwise giving a false statement by reason of failure to recite or acknowledge that arrest, indictment, information or trial in response to an inquiry made of the defendant for any purpose.

(Added to NRS by 2009, 103; A 2013, 2093)

NRS 176A.295 Sealing of records after discharge.

1. After a defendant is discharged from probation pursuant to NRS 176A.290, the court shall order sealed all documents, papers and exhibits in the defendant's record, minute book entries and entries on dockets, and other documents relating to the case in the custody of such other agencies and officers as are named in the court's order if the defendant fulfills the terms and conditions imposed by the court and the Division. The court shall order those records sealed without a hearing unless the Division petitions the court, for good cause shown, not to seal the records and requests a hearing thereon.

2. If the court orders sealed the record of a defendant discharged pursuant to NRS 176A.290, the court shall send a copy of the order to each agency or officer named in the order. Each such agency or officer shall notify the court in writing of its compliance with the order.

(Added to NRS by 2009, 104)

PROGRAM OF PROBATION SECURED BY SURETY BOND

NRS 176A.300 Execution and amount of surety bond.

1. Whenever a person other than an indigent person has been found guilty of a category C, D or E felony upon verdict or plea, and the court has determined that the person is eligible for probation pursuant to NRS 176A.100, the court may order the person to participate in a program of probation secured by a surety bond if the court first determines that the person has the financial ability to post such a surety bond.

2. If the court orders the person to participate in a program of probation secured by a surety bond, the person shall execute a bond for the participation. The court shall require one or more sureties for the bond.

3. The court shall set the surety bond in an amount which, in the judgment of the court, will reasonably ensure the participation of the person in the program of probation.

4. A surety bond securing participation in a program of probation must:

(a) Be issued in favor of and payable to the State of Nevada;

(b) Extend for a period of 1 year;

(c) Be renewable annually; and

(d) Ensure the full compliance of the person in the program of probation with all the conditions of probation set by the court.

(Added to NRS by 1995, 1245)

NRS 176A.310 Conditions; duties of surety; probationer to report to and pay surety.

1. The court shall set the conditions of a program of probation secured by a surety bond. The conditions must be appended to and made part of the bond. The conditions may include, but are not limited to, any one or more of the following:

(a) Submission to periodic tests to determine whether the probationer is using any controlled substance or alcohol.

(b) Participation in a program for the treatment of the abuse of a controlled substance or alcohol or a program for the treatment of any other impairment.

(c) Participation in a program of professional counseling, including, but not limited to, counseling for the family of the probationer.

(d) Restrictions or a prohibition on contact or communication with witnesses or victims of the crime committed by the probationer.

(e) A requirement to obtain and keep employment.

(f) Submission to a Program of Intensive Supervision.

(g) Restrictions on travel by the probationer outside the jurisdiction of the court.

(h) Payment of restitution.

(i) Payment of fines and court costs.

(j) Supervised community service.

(k) Participation in educational courses.

2. A surety shall:

(a) Provide the facilities or equipment necessary to:

(1) Perform tests to determine whether the probationer is using any controlled substance or alcohol, if the court requires such tests as a condition of probation;

(2) Carry out a Program of Intensive Supervision, if the court requires such a Program as a condition of probation; and

(3) Enable the probationer to report regularly to the surety.

(b) Notify the court within 24 hours after the surety has knowledge of a violation of or a failure to fulfill a condition of the program of probation.

3. A probationer participating in a program of probation secured by a surety bond shall:

(a) Report regularly to the surety; and

(b) Pay the fee charged by the surety for the execution of the bond.

(Added to NRS by 1995, 1245; A 2001 Special Session, 133)

NRS 176A.320 Failure of surety to fulfill duties; failure of probationer to fulfill conditions of surety bond.

1. If a surety fails to:

(a) Provide the facilities or equipment required by paragraph (a) of subsection 2 of NRS 176A.310; or

(b) Notify the court pursuant to paragraph (b) of subsection 2 of NRS 176A.310 of a violation of or a failure to fulfill a condition of a program of probation by a probationer,

□ the surety shall pay a penalty of $15,000 to the court in addition to any other penalty imposed by law.

2. If the probationer violates or fails to fulfill a condition of the surety bond, the court shall:

(a) Declare a forfeiture of the surety bond;

(b) Direct that the surety be given notice by certified mail that the probationer has violated or failed to fulfill a condition of probation and shall execute an affidavit of such mailing to be kept as an official public record of the court;

(c) Revoke the program of probation; and

(d) Issue a warrant for violating or failing to fulfill a condition of probation and cause the defendant to be arrested.

(Added to NRS by 1995, 1246)

NRS 176A.330 Exoneration of surety and setting aside of forfeiture of surety bond. The court may exonerate the surety or set aside a forfeiture of the surety bond upon such terms as may be just if:

1. The probationer appears before the court and the court, upon hearing the matter, determines that the violation or failure of the probationer to fulfill the condition of probation was:

(a) Caused by circumstances beyond the probationer's control and occurred notwithstanding the exercise of ordinary care and in the absence of willful neglect; and

(b) Not in any way caused or aided by the surety; or

2. The surety submits an application for exoneration or an application to set the forfeiture aside on the ground that the probationer is unable to appear because the probationer:

(a) Is dead;

(b) Is ill;

(c) Is insane; or

(d) Is being detained by civil or military authorities,

□ and the court, upon hearing the matter, determines that the requirements of paragraphs (a) and (b) of subsection 1 have been met and that the surety did not in any way cause or aid the absence of the probationer from the hearing.

(Added to NRS by 1995, 1247)

NRS 176A.340 Procedure when surety not exonerated; enforcement of liability; remission of judgment of default.

1. If the surety is not exonerated and the forfeiture of the surety bond is not set aside:

(a) The court shall enter a judgment of default and execution may issue thereon; and

(b) The surety shall pay a penalty for the revocation of the program of probation to the court in an amount equal to one-half of the annual fee for the bond that the surety charged the probationer.

2. By entering into a bond the surety submits to the jurisdiction of the court and irrevocably appoints the clerk of the court as its agent upon whom any papers affecting its liability may be served. The liability may be enforced on motion and such notice of the motion as the court prescribes may be served on the clerk of the court, who shall mail copies to the surety to its last known address.

3. After entry of a judgment of default, the court shall not remit it in whole or in part unless the conditions applying to exonerating the surety and setting aside the forfeiture of the surety bond set forth in NRS 176A.330 are met.

(Added to NRS by 1995, 1247)

NRS 176A.350 Discharge of surety and release of bond. When the conditions of a surety bond securing participation in a program of probation have been satisfied or a forfeiture of a bond has been set aside or remitted, the court shall discharge the surety and release the bond.

(Added to NRS by 1995, 1247)

NRS 176A.360 Arrest of probationer. For the purpose of surrendering a probationer, a surety, at any time before it is finally discharged, and at any place within the State, may, by a written authority endorsed on a certified copy of the undertaking, cause the probationer to be arrested by a bail agent or bail enforcement agent who is licensed pursuant to chapter 697 of NRS.

(Added to NRS by 1995, 1247; A 1997, 3393)

NRS 176A.370 Money collected to be deposited in State General Fund. Money collected pursuant to NRS 176A.300 to 176A.370, inclusive, must be paid to the State Treasurer for deposit in the State General Fund.

(Added to NRS by 1995, 1247)

TERMS AND CONDITIONS

NRS 176A.400 Imposition by court; alternative programs or treatment; prohibition on suspending term of imprisonment; placement under supervision of Chief Parole and Probation Officer.

1. In issuing an order granting probation, the court may fix the terms and conditions thereof, including, without limitation:

(a) A requirement for restitution;

(b) An order that the probationer dispose of all the weapons the probationer possesses; or

(c) Any reasonable conditions to protect the health, safety or welfare of the community or to ensure that the probationer will appear at all times and places ordered by the court, including, without limitation:

(1) Requiring the probationer to remain in this State or a certain county within this State;

(2) Prohibiting the probationer from contacting or attempting to contact a specific person or from causing or attempting to cause another person to contact that person on the probationer's behalf;

(3) Prohibiting the probationer from entering a certain geographic area; or

(4) Prohibiting the probationer from engaging in specific conduct that may be harmful to the probationer's own health, safety or welfare, or the health, safety or welfare of another person.

2. In issuing an order granting probation to a person who is found guilty of a category C, D or E felony, the court may require the person as a condition of probation to participate in and complete to the satisfaction of the court any alternative program, treatment or activity deemed appropriate by the court.

3. The court shall not suspend the execution of a sentence of imprisonment after the defendant has begun to serve it.

4. In placing any defendant on probation or in granting a defendant a suspended sentence, the court shall direct that the defendant be placed under the supervision of the Chief Parole and Probation Officer.

(Added to NRS by 1991, 2043; A 1995, 1250; 1997, 3357)

NRS 176A.410 Required terms and conditions for sex offenders; powers and duties of court; exceptions.

1. Except as otherwise provided in subsection 6, if a defendant is convicted of a sexual offense and the court grants probation or suspends the sentence, the court shall, in addition to any other condition ordered pursuant to NRS 176A.400, order as a condition of probation or suspension of sentence that the defendant:

(a) Submit to a search and seizure of the defendant's person, residence or vehicle or any property under the defendant's control, at any time of the day or night, without a warrant, by any parole and probation officer or any peace officer, for the purpose of determining whether the defendant has violated any condition of probation or suspension of sentence or committed any crime.

(b) Reside at a location only if:

(1) The residence has been approved by the parole and probation officer assigned to the defendant.

(2) If the residence is a facility that houses more than three persons who have been released from prison, the facility is a facility for transitional living for released offenders that is licensed pursuant to chapter 449 of NRS.

(3) The defendant keeps the parole and probation officer assigned to the defendant informed of the defendant's current address.

(c) Accept a position of employment or a position as a volunteer only if it has been approved by the parole and probation officer assigned to the defendant and keep the parole and probation officer informed of the location of the defendant's position of employment or position as a volunteer.

(d) Abide by any curfew imposed by the parole and probation officer assigned to the defendant.

(e) Participate in and complete a program of professional counseling approved by the Division.

(f) Submit to periodic tests, as requested by the parole and probation officer assigned to the defendant, to determine whether the defendant is using a controlled substance.

(g) Submit to periodic polygraph examinations, as requested by the parole and probation officer assigned to the defendant.

(h) Abstain from consuming, possessing or having under the defendant's control any alcohol.

(i) Not have contact or communicate with a victim of the sexual offense or a witness who testified against the defendant or solicit another person to engage in such contact or communication on behalf of the defendant, unless approved by the Chief Parole and Probation Officer or the Chief Parole and Probation Officer's designee and a written agreement is entered into and signed in the manner set forth in subsection 5.

(j) Not use aliases or fictitious names.

(k) Not obtain a post office box unless the defendant receives permission from the parole and probation officer assigned to the defendant.

(l) Not have contact with a person less than 18 years of age in a secluded environment unless another adult who has never been convicted of a sexual offense is present and permission has been obtained from the parole and probation officer assigned to the defendant in advance of each such contact.

(m) Unless approved by the parole and probation officer assigned to the defendant and by a psychiatrist, psychologist or counselor treating the defendant, if any, not knowingly be within 500 feet of any place, or if the place is a structure, within 500 feet of the actual structure, that is designed primarily for use by or for children, including, without limitation, a public or private school, a school bus stop, a center or facility that provides day care services, a video arcade, an amusement park, a playground, a park, an athletic field or a facility for youth sports, or a motion picture theater. The provisions of this paragraph apply only to a defendant who is a Tier III offender.

(n) Comply with any protocol concerning the use of prescription medication prescribed by a treating physician, including, without limitation, any protocol concerning the use of psychotropic medication.

(o) Not possess any sexually explicit material that is deemed inappropriate by the parole and probation officer assigned to the defendant.

(p) Not patronize a business which offers a sexually related form of entertainment and which is deemed inappropriate by the parole and probation officer assigned to the defendant.

(q) Not possess any electronic device capable of accessing the Internet and not access the Internet through any such device or any other means, unless possession of such a device or such access is approved by the parole and probation officer assigned to the defendant.

(r) Inform the parole and probation officer assigned to the defendant if the defendant expects to be or becomes enrolled as a student at an institution of higher education or changes the date of commencement or termination of the defendant's enrollment at an institution of higher education. As used in this paragraph, "institution of higher education" has the meaning ascribed to it in NRS 179D.045.

2. Except as otherwise provided in subsection 6, if a defendant is convicted of an offense listed in subsection 6 of NRS 213.1255 against a child under the age of 14 years, the defendant is a Tier III offender and the court grants probation or suspends the sentence of the defendant, the court shall, in addition to any other condition ordered pursuant to subsection 1, order as a condition of probation or suspension of sentence that the defendant:

(a) Reside at a location only if the residence is not located within 1,000 feet of any place, or if the place is a structure, within 1,000 feet of the actual structure, that is designed primarily for use by or for children, including, without limitation, a public or private school, a school bus stop, a center or facility that provides day care services, a video arcade, an amusement park, a playground, a park, an athletic field or a facility for youth sports, or a motion picture theater.

(b) As deemed appropriate by the Chief Parole and Probation Officer, be placed under a system of active electronic monitoring that is capable of identifying the defendant's location and producing, upon request, reports or records of the defendant's presence near or within a crime scene or prohibited area or the defendant's departure from a specified geographic location.

(c) Pay any costs associated with the defendant's participation under the system of active electronic monitoring, to the extent of the defendant's ability to pay.

3. A defendant placed under the system of active electronic monitoring pursuant to subsection 2 shall:

(a) Follow the instructions provided by the Division to maintain the electronic monitoring device in working order.

(b) Report any incidental damage or defacement of the electronic monitoring device to the Division within 2 hours after the occurrence of the damage or defacement.

(c) Abide by any other conditions set forth by the Division with regard to the defendant's participation under the system of active electronic monitoring.

4. Except as otherwise provided in this subsection, a person who intentionally removes or disables or attempts to remove or disable an electronic monitoring device placed on a defendant pursuant to this section is guilty of a gross misdemeanor. The provisions of this subsection do not prohibit a person authorized by the Division from performing maintenance or repairs to an electronic monitoring device.

5. A written agreement entered into pursuant to paragraph (i) of subsection 1 must state that the contact or communication is in the best interest of the victim or witness, and specify the type of contact or communication authorized. The written agreement must be signed and agreed to by:

(a) The victim or the witness;

(b) The defendant;

(c) The parole and probation officer assigned to the defendant;

(d) The psychiatrist, psychologist or counselor treating the defendant, victim or witness, if any;

(e) If the victim or witness is a child under 18 years of age, each parent, guardian or custodian of the child; and

(f) The Chief Parole and Probation Officer or the Chief Parole and Probation Officer's designee.

6. The court is not required to impose a condition of probation or suspension of sentence listed in subsections 1 and 2 if the court finds that extraordinary circumstances are present and the court enters those extraordinary circumstances in the record.

7. As used in this section, "sexual offense" has the meaning ascribed to it in NRS 179D.097.

(Added to NRS by 1997, 1667; A 2001, 2051; 2003, 566; 2005, 2862; 2007, 1916, 2749, 3246; 2009, 1293)

NRS 176A.413 Restrictions relating to computers and use of Internet and other electronic means of communication; powers and duties of court; exceptions.

1. Except as otherwise provided in subsection 2, if a defendant is convicted of stalking with the use of an Internet or network site, electronic mail, text messaging or any other similar means of communication pursuant to subsection 3 of NRS 200.575, an offense involving pornography and a minor pursuant to NRS 200.710 to 200.730, inclusive, or luring a child or a person with mental illness through the use of a computer, system or network pursuant to paragraph (a) or (b) of subsection 4 of NRS 201.560 and the court grants probation or suspends the sentence, the court shall, in addition to any other condition ordered pursuant to NRS 176A.400, order as a condition of probation or suspension that the defendant not own or use a computer, including, without limitation, use electronic mail, a chat room or the Internet.

2. The court is not required to impose a condition of probation or suspension of sentence set forth in subsection 1 if the court finds that:

(a) The use of a computer by the defendant will assist a law enforcement agency or officer in a criminal investigation;

(b) The defendant will use the computer to provide technological training concerning technology of which the defendant has a unique knowledge; or

(c) The use of the computer by the defendant will assist companies that require the use of the specific technological knowledge of the defendant that is unique and is otherwise unavailable to the company.

3. Except as otherwise provided in subsection 1, if a defendant is convicted of an offense that involved the use of a computer, system or network and the court grants probation or suspends the sentence, the court may, in addition to any other condition ordered pursuant to NRS 176A.400, order as a condition of probation or suspension that the defendant not own or use a computer, including, without limitation, use electronic mail, a chat room or the Internet.

4. As used in this section:

(a) "Computer" has the meaning ascribed to it in NRS 205.4735.

(b) "Network" has the meaning ascribed to it in NRS 205.4745.

(c) "System" has the meaning ascribed to it in NRS 205.476.

(d) "Text messaging" has the meaning ascribed to it in NRS 200.575.

(Added to NRS by 2001, 2791; A 2003, 1383; 2009, 3010)

NRS 176A.416 Evaluations and counseling for offenses involving cruelty to animals; powers and duties of court.

1. As a condition of probation, the court may order a defendant who is convicted of a violation of chapter 574 of NRS that is punishable as a felony or gross misdemeanor to:

(a) Submit to a psychiatric evaluation; and

(b) Participate in any counseling or therapy recommended in the evaluation.

2. The court shall order a defendant, to the extent of the defendant's financial ability, to pay the cost for an evaluation and any counseling or therapy pursuant to this section.

(Added to NRS by 2001, 2891)

NRS 176A.420 Tests to determine use of controlled substance.

1. Upon the granting of probation to a person convicted of a felony or gross misdemeanor, the court may, when the circumstances warrant, require as a condition of probation that the probationer submit to periodic tests to determine whether the probationer is using any controlled substance. Any such use or any failure or refusal to submit to a test is a ground for revocation of probation.

2. Any expense incurred as a result of a test must be paid from appropriations to the Division on claims as other claims against the State are paid.

(Added to NRS by 1969, 181; A 1971, 2025; 1973, 179; 1975, 895; 1977, 262, 421; 1993, 1513)

NRS 176A.430 Restitution.

1. The court shall order as a condition of probation or suspension of sentence, in appropriate circumstances, that the defendant make full or partial restitution to the person or persons named in the order, at the times and in the amounts specified in the order unless the court finds that restitution is impracticable. Such an order may require payment for medical or psychological treatment of any person whom the defendant has injured. In appropriate circumstances, the court shall include as a condition of probation or suspension of sentence that the defendant execute an assignment of wages earned while on probation or subject to the conditions of suspension of sentence to the Division for restitution.

2. All money received by the Division for restitution must be deposited with the State Treasurer for credit to the Restitution Trust Fund.

3. The Division shall make pro rata payments from the money received from the defendant to each person to whom the restitution was ordered pursuant to this section. Such a payment must be made not less than once each fiscal year. Any money received from the defendant that is remaining at the end of each fiscal year must be paid at that time in pro rata payments to each person to whom the restitution was ordered. A final pro rata payment must be made to such persons when the defendant pays the entire restitution owed.

4. All payments from the Fund must be paid as other claims against the State are paid.

5. If restitution is not required, the court shall set forth the circumstances upon which it finds restitution impracticable in its order of probation or suspension of sentence.

6. Failure to comply with the terms of an order for restitution is a violation of a condition of probation or suspension of sentence unless the defendant's failure was caused by economic hardship resulting in his or her inability to pay the amount due. The defendant is entitled to a hearing to show the existence of such a hardship.

7. If, within 3 years after the defendant has been discharged from probation, the Division has not located the person to whom the restitution was ordered, the money paid to the Division by the defendant must be deposited with the State Treasurer for credit to the Fund for the Compensation of Victims of Crime.

(Added to NRS by 1975, 83; A 1977, 399; 1981, 1341; 1983, 245, 383; 1993, 1514; 1995, 410; 2013, 194)

NRS 176A.440 Program of intensive supervision.

1. The Chief Parole and Probation Officer shall develop a program for the intensive supervision of a person granted probation pursuant to subsection 4 of NRS 176A.100.

2. The Program of Intensive Supervision must include an initial period of electronic supervision of the probationer with an electronic device approved by the Division. The device may be capable of using the Global Positioning System, but must be minimally intrusive and limited in capability to recording or transmitting information concerning the probationer's location, including, but not limited to, the transmission of still visual images which do not concern the probationer's activities, and producing, upon request, reports or records of the probationer's presence near or within a crime scene or prohibited area or his or her departure from a specified geographic location. A device which is capable of recording or transmitting:

(a) Oral or wire communications or any auditory sound; or

(b) Information concerning the probationer's activities,

□ must not be used.

(Added to NRS by 1991, 2043; A 1993, 1514; 1995, 1251; 2015, 349)

NRS 176A.450 Modification; procedure for modifying conditions relating to program of probation secured by surety bond; limitations.

1. Except as otherwise provided in this section, by order duly entered, the court may impose, and may at any time modify, any conditions of probation or suspension of sentence. The court shall cause a copy of any such order to be delivered to the parole and probation officer and the probationer. A copy of the order must also be sent to the Director of the Department of Corrections if the probationer is under the supervision of the Director pursuant to NRS 176A.780.

2. If the probationer is participating in a program of probation secured by a surety bond, the court shall not impose or modify the conditions of probation unless the court notifies the surety and:

(a) Causes the original bond to be revoked and requires a new bond to which the original and the new conditions are appended and made part; or

(b) Requires an additional bond to which the new conditions are appended and made part.

3. The court shall not modify a condition of probation or suspension of sentence that was imposed pursuant to NRS 176A.410, unless the court finds that extraordinary circumstances are present and the court enters those extraordinary circumstances in the record.

(Added to NRS by 1967, 1435; A 1989, 1855; 1995, 1251; 1997, 1672; 2001 Special Session, 222)

DURATION; ARREST FOR ALLEGED VIOLATION

NRS 176A.500 Authority of court to fix duration; limitations; arrest for alleged violation; powers and duties of peace officers; deduction of days.

1. The period of probation or suspension of sentence may be indeterminate or may be fixed by the court and may at any time be extended or terminated by the court, but the period, including any extensions thereof, must not be more than:

(a) Three years for a:

(1) Gross misdemeanor; or

(2) Suspension of sentence pursuant to NRS 176A.260, 176A.290 or 453.3363; or

(b) Five years for a felony.

2. At any time during probation or suspension of sentence, the court may issue a warrant for violating any of the conditions of probation or suspension of sentence and cause the defendant to be arrested. Except for the purpose of giving a dishonorable discharge from probation, and except as otherwise provided in this subsection, the time during which a warrant for violating any of the conditions of probation is in effect is not part of the period of probation. If the warrant is cancelled or probation is reinstated, the court may include any amount of that time as part of the period of probation.

3. Any parole and probation officer or any peace officer with power to arrest may arrest a probationer without a warrant, or may deputize any other officer with power to arrest to do so by giving the probationer a written statement setting forth that the probationer has, in the judgment of the parole and probation officer, violated the conditions of probation. Except as otherwise provided in subsection 4, the parole and probation officer or the peace officer, after making an arrest, shall present to the detaining authorities, if any, a statement of the charges against the probationer. The parole and probation officer shall at once notify the court which granted probation of the arrest and detention or residential confinement of the probationer and shall submit a report in writing showing in what manner the probationer has violated the conditions of probation.

4. A parole and probation officer or a peace officer may immediately release from custody without any further proceedings any person the officer arrests without a warrant for violating a condition of probation if the parole and probation officer or peace officer determines that there is no probable cause to believe that the person violated the condition of probation.

5. A person who is sentenced to serve a period of probation for a felony or a gross misdemeanor must be allowed for the period of the probation a deduction as set forth in subsection 6 if the offender is in compliance with the terms and conditions of the probation as determined by the Division and is:

(a) Current with any fee to defray the cost of the supervision charged pursuant to NRS 213.1076 and with any fines, fees and restitution ordered by the court, including, without limitation, any payment of restitution required pursuant to NRS 176A.430; and

(b) Actively involved in employment or enrolled in a program of education, rehabilitation or any other program approved by the Division.

6. A person described in subsection 5 must be allowed for the period of the probation a deduction of:

(a) Ten days from that period for each month the person serves and is current on any fees to defray the cost of the supervision owed and on any fines, fees and restitution ordered by the court; and

(b) Except as otherwise provided in subsection 7, an additional 10 days from that period for each month the person serves and is actively involved in employment or enrolled in a program of education, rehabilitation or any other program approved by the Division.

7. A person who is sentenced to serve a period of probation for a felony or a gross misdemeanor and who is a participant in a specialty court program must be allowed a deduction from the period of probation for being actively involved in employment or enrolled in a program of education, rehabilitation or any other program approved by the Division only if the person successfully completes the specialty court program. Such a deduction must not exceed the length of time remaining on the person's period of probation.

8. As used in this section, "specialty court program" means a program established by a court to facilitate testing, treatment and oversight of certain persons over whom the court has jurisdiction and who the court has determined suffer from mental illnesses or abuse alcohol or drugs. Such a program includes, without limitation, a program established pursuant to NRS 176A.250or 453.580.

(Added to NRS by 1967, 1435; A 1969, 639; 1973, 169, 249; 1977, 814; 1979, 324; 1981, 370; 1983, 284; 1987, 761; 1989, 1110; 1991, 315, 1664; 1999, 1207; 2001 Special Session, 260; 2007, 3184; 2009, 105, 2513)

PROCEEDINGS AFTER ARREST

Residential Confinement Pending Inquiry or Consideration by Court

NRS 176A.530 Authority of Chief Parole and Probation Officer to order. The Chief Parole and Probation Officer may, in accordance with the provisions of NRS 176A.530 to 176A.560, inclusive, order any probationer who is arrested pursuant to NRS 176A.500 to be placed in residential confinement in lieu of detention in a county jail pending an inquiry to determine whether there is probable cause to believe that the probationer has committed any act which would constitute a violation of a condition of the probation.

(Added to NRS by 1991, 314)

NRS 176A.540 Requirements; intensive supervision; use of electronic device; limitations.

1. The Chief Parole and Probation Officer may order the residential confinement of a probationer if the Chief Parole and Probation Officer believes that the probationer poses no danger to the community and will appear at a scheduled inquiry or court hearing.

2. In ordering the residential confinement of a probationer, the Chief Parole and Probation Officer shall:

(a) Require the probationer to be confined to the probationer's residence during the time the probationer is away from any employment, community service or other activity authorized by the Division; and

(b) Require intensive supervision of the probationer, including, without limitation, unannounced visits to the probationer's residence or other locations where the probationer is expected to be to determine whether the probationer is complying with the terms of confinement.

3. An electronic device approved by the Division may be used to supervise a probationer who is ordered to be placed in residential confinement. The device may be capable of using the Global Positioning System, but must be minimally intrusive and limited in capability to recording or transmitting information concerning the probationer's location, including, but not limited to, the transmission of still visual images which do not concern the probationer's activities, and producing, upon request, reports or records of the probationer's presence near or

within a crime scene or prohibited area or his or her departure from a specified geographic location. A device which is capable of recording or transmitting:

(a) Oral or wire communications or any auditory sound; or

(b) Information concerning the probationer's activities,

□ must not be used.

4. The Chief Parole and Probation Officer shall not order a probationer to be placed in residential confinement unless the probationer agrees to the order.

5. Any residential confinement must not extend beyond the unexpired maximum term of the original sentence.

(Added to NRS by 1991, 314; 1993, 1514; 1995, 1251; 2001 Special Session, 134; 2015, 349)

NRS 176A.550 Terms and conditions; modification; notice to probationer.

1. In ordering a probationer to be placed in residential confinement, the Chief Parole and Probation Officer may establish the terms and conditions of that confinement.

2. The Chief Parole and Probation Officer may, at any time, modify the terms and conditions of the residential confinement.

3. The Chief Parole and Probation Officer shall cause a copy of the order to be delivered to the probationer.

(Added to NRS by 1991, 314)

NRS 176A.560 Termination; detention of probationer in jail.

1. The Chief Parole and Probation Officer may terminate the residential confinement of a probationer and order the detention of the probationer in a county jail pending an inquiry or court hearing if:

(a) The probationer violates the terms or conditions of the residential confinement; or

(b) The Chief Parole and Probation Officer, in his or her discretion, determines that the probationer poses a danger to the community or that there is a reasonable doubt that the probationer will appear at the inquiry or hearing.

2. A probationer has no right to dispute a decision to terminate the residential confinement.

(Added to NRS by 1991, 315)

Inquiry to Determine Probable Cause

NRS 176A.580 Inquiry required before alleged violation considered by court; qualifications of inquiring officer; time and place of inquiry; exceptions; subpoenas.

1. Before a probationer in custody for a violation of a condition of probation may be returned to the court for that violation, an inquiry must be conducted to determine whether there is probable cause to believe that the probationer has committed any act that would constitute such a violation.

2. The inquiry must be conducted before an inquiring officer who:

(a) Is not directly involved in the case;

(b) Has not made the report of violation of the probation; and

(c) Has not recommended revocation of the probation,

□ but the inquiring officer need not be a judicial officer.

3. Except in a case where the probationer is a fugitive or is under supervision in another state, the inquiry must be held at or reasonably near the place of the alleged violation or the arrest and must be held:

(a) If the probationer is on probation from another state and under supervision in this State, not later than 30 days after arrest.

(b) If the probationer is on probation from a Nevada court, promptly and not later than 15 days after arrest and confinement on the charge that the probationer has violated a condition of probation or after an order has been filed to hold the probationer on that charge if the probationer is already confined on another charge. The time for the inquiry may be extended if, within the 15-day period, the probationer is released from confinement or the order that the probationer be held is withdrawn.

4. Any conviction for violating a federal, state or local law, except a minor traffic offense, which is committed while the probationer is on probation constitutes probable cause for the purposes of this section and an inquiry need not be held.

5. For the purposes of this section, the inquiring officer may administer oaths and issue subpoenas to compel the attendance of witnesses and the production of books and papers.

(Added to NRS by 1977, 815; A 1979, 168; 1981, 479; 1983, 270)

NRS 176A.590 Enforcement of subpoena issued by inquiring officer; contempt.

1. If any witness refuses to attend or testify or produce any books and papers as required by the subpoena, the inquiring officer may report to the district court by petition, setting forth that:

(a) Due notice has been given of the time and place of attendance of the witness or the production of the books and papers;

(b) The witness has been subpoenaed by the inquiring officer pursuant to NRS 176A.580; and

(c) The witness has failed or refused to attend or produce the books and papers required by the subpoena at the inquiry which is named in the subpoena, or has refused to answer questions propounded,

□ and asking for an order of the court compelling the witness to attend and testify or produce the books and papers.

2. Upon such petition, the court shall enter an order directing the witness to appear before the court at a time and place to be fixed by the court in its order, the time to be not more than 10 days from the date of the order, and then and there show cause why the witness has not attended or testified or produced the books or papers at the inquiry. A certified copy of the order shall be served upon the witness.

3. If it appears to the court that the subpoena was regularly issued by the inquiring officer, the court shall enter an order that the witness appear at the inquiry at the time and place fixed in the order and testify or produce the required books or papers, and upon failure to obey the order the witness shall be dealt with as for contempt of court.

(Added to NRS by 1979, 168)

NRS 176A.600 Notice to probationer; rights of probationer at inquiry.

1. The parole and probation officer or detaining authority shall give the arrested probationer advance notice of:

(a) The place and time of the inquiry.

(b) The purpose of the inquiry.

(c) What violations of probation have been alleged.

2. The inquiring officer shall allow the probationer to:

(a) Appear and speak on the probationer's own behalf.

(b) Obtain counsel.

(c) Present any relevant letters or other documents and any person who can give relevant information.

(d) Confront and question any person who appears against the probationer, unless in the opinion of the inquiring officer the person would be subjected to a risk of harm by disclosure of the person's identity.

(Added to NRS by 1977, 815; A 1983, 271)

NRS 176A.610 Duties of inquiring officer; determination; detention or residential confinement of probationer upon finding probable cause.

1. Upon completion of the inquiry, the inquiring officer shall:

(a) Make a written summary of what occurred at the inquiry, noting the substance of the evidence given to support a revocation of the probation and the probationer's position and responses.

(b) Determine whether there is probable cause to hold the probationer for a court hearing on revocation.

2. If the inquiring officer determines that there is probable cause:

(a) The inquiring officer's determination is sufficient to warrant the continued detention of the probationer pending the court's hearing; or

(b) The Chief Parole and Probation Officer may order the probationer to be placed in residential confinement in accordance with the provisions of NRS 176A.530 to 176A.560, inclusive.

(Added to NRS by 1977, 816; A 1991, 316)

Consideration by Court of Alleged Violation; Assessment of Expenses

NRS 176A.630 Assignment of case; consideration of alleged violation; revocation permitted upon finding violation; alternative actions; restitution for governmental expenses. If the probationer is arrested, by or without warrant, in another judicial district of this state, the court which granted the probation may assign the case to the district court of that district, with the consent of that court. The court retaining or thus acquiring jurisdiction shall cause the defendant to be brought before it, consider the standards adopted pursuant to NRS 213.10988 and the recommendation, if any, of the Chief Parole and Probation Officer. Upon determining that the probationer has violated a condition of probation, the court shall, if practicable, order the probationer to make restitution for any necessary expenses incurred by a governmental entity in returning the probationer to the court for violation of the probation. The court may:

1. Continue or revoke the probation or suspension of sentence;
2. Order the probationer to a term of residential confinement pursuant to NRS 176A.660;
3. Order the probationer to undergo a program of regimental discipline pursuant to NRS 176A.780;
4. Cause the sentence imposed to be executed; or
5. Modify the original sentence imposed by reducing the term of imprisonment and cause the modified sentence to be executed. The court shall not make the term of imprisonment less than the minimum term of imprisonment prescribed by the applicable penal statute. If the Chief Parole and Probation Officer recommends that the sentence of a probationer be modified and the modified sentence be executed, the Chief Parole and Probation Officer shall provide notice of the recommendation to any victim of the crime for which the probationer was convicted who has requested in writing to be notified and who has provided a current address to the Division. The notice must inform the victim that he or she has the right to submit documents to the court and to be present and heard at the hearing to determine whether the sentence of a probationer who has violated a condition of probation should be modified. The court shall not modify the sentence of a probationer and cause the sentence to be executed until it has confirmed that the Chief Parole and Probation Officer has complied with the provisions of this subsection. The Chief Parole and Probation Officer must not be held responsible when such notification is not received by the victim if the victim has not provided a current address. All personal information, including, but not limited to, a current or former address, which pertains to a victim and which is received by the Division pursuant to this subsection is confidential.

(Added to NRS by 1977, 816; A 1987, 2229; 1989, 1855, 1887; 1993, 935; 1995, 1356; 1997, 3237)

NRS 176A.635 Effect of violation of condition of probation, forfeiture and restoration of credits for good behavior.

1. If a court before which a probationer is brought pursuant to NRS 176A.630 determines that the probationer has violated a condition of probation, the probationer forfeits all or part of the credits for good behavior earned pursuant to NRS 176A.500 during probation, in the discretion of the court.
2. A forfeiture may be made only by the court after proof of the violation and notice to the probationer.
3. The court may restore credits forfeited for such reasons as it considers proper.

4. If the court provides for the forfeiture or restoration of credits for good behavior of a probationer pursuant to this section, the clerk of the court shall notify the Chief Parole and Probation Officer of the forfeiture or restoration of credits.
(Added to NRS by 2009, 2512)

NRS 176A.640 Expenses of returning arrested probationer to court are charge against State; payment. The necessary expenses of returning to the court a person arrested for violation of probation are a charge against the State and must be paid from money appropriated to the Division. After the appropriation for this purpose is exhausted, money must be allocated to the Division out of the Reserve for Statutory Contingency Account, upon approval by the State Board of Examiners, for the payment of these expenses.
(Added to NRS by 1977, 816; A 1983, 237; 1991, 1753; 1993, 1515)

RESIDENTIAL CONFINEMENT AFTER VIOLATION

NRS 176A.660 Authority of court to order; requirements; intensive supervision; use of electronic device; limitations.
1. If a person who has been placed on probation violates a condition of probation, the court may order the person to a term of residential confinement in lieu of causing the sentence imposed to be executed. In making this determination, the court shall consider the criminal record of the person and the seriousness of the crime committed.
2. In ordering the person to a term of residential confinement, the court shall:
(a) Direct that the person be placed under the supervision of the Division and require:
(1) The person to be confined to the person's residence during the time the person is away from any employment, community service or other activity authorized by the Division; and
(2) Intensive supervision of the person, including, without limitation, unannounced visits to the person's residence or other locations where the person is expected to be in order to determine whether the person is complying with the terms of confinement; or
(b) If the person was placed on probation for a felony conviction, direct that the person be placed under the supervision of the Department of Corrections and require the person to be confined to a facility or institution of the Department for a period not to exceed 6 months. The Department may select the facility or institution in which to place the person.
3. An electronic device approved by the Division may be used to supervise a person ordered to a term of residential confinement. The device may be capable of using the Global Positioning System, but must be minimally intrusive and limited in capability to recording or transmitting information concerning the person's location, including, but not limited to, the transmission of still visual images which do not concern the person's activities, and producing, upon request, reports or records of the person's presence near or within a crime scene or prohibited area or his or her departure from a specified geographic location. A device which is capable of recording or transmitting:
(a) Oral or wire communications or any auditory sound; or
(b) Information concerning the person's activities,
□ must not be used.
4. The court shall not order a person to a term of residential confinement unless the person agrees to the order.
5. A term of residential confinement may not be longer than the unexpired maximum term of a sentence imposed by the court.
6. As used in this section:
(a) "Facility" has the meaning ascribed to it in NRS 209.065.
(b) "Institution" has the meaning ascribed to it in NRS 209.071.
(Added to NRS by 1987, 2228; A 1991, 57; 1993, 1515; 1995, 1252; 2001 Special Session, 135; 2007, 3185; 2009, 2514; 2015, 350)

NRS 176A.670 Terms and conditions; modification; notice.
1. In ordering a person to a term of residential confinement, a court may establish the terms and conditions of that confinement.
2. The court may, at any time, modify the terms and conditions of the residential confinement.
3. The court shall cause a copy of its order to be delivered to the person and the Division.
(Added to NRS by 1987, 2229; A 1993, 1516)

NRS 176A.680 Authority of court to modify or rescind for subsequent violation; imposition of other punishment. If it is determined that the person violated any term or condition of residential confinement, the sentence may be rescinded, modified or continued. If it is rescinded, another punishment authorized by law must be imposed.
(Added to NRS by 1987, 2229)

NRS 176A.690 Establishment of procedures by Division for supervision of persons in residential confinement. The Division shall establish procedures to administer a program of supervision for persons who are ordered to a term of residential confinement.
(Added to NRS by 1987, 2229; A 1993, 1516)

RESIDENTIAL CENTERS FOR SUPERVISION OF PROBATIONERS

NRS 176A.720 Establishment. The Division may:
1. Establish centers for the housing and supervision of probationers assigned to the centers under NRS 176A.730.
2. Contract for any services necessary to operate these centers.
(Added to NRS by 1983, 321; A 1993, 1516)

NRS 176A.730 Assignment of probationers; limitations.

1. Except as otherwise provided in subsection 2, when a district court grants probation to a person convicted of a felony or continues probation after the person's return to the court for violation of a condition of probation, the court may require as a condition of granting or continuing probation that the convicted person live for a period of time specified by the court under the supervision of the Division in a residential center established pursuant to NRS 176A.720.

2. The court may not assign a convicted person to a residential center under subsection 1:

(a) If the convicted person has served a prior prison term in any state or federal penal institution.

(b) Unless, in cases where probation is being granted rather than continued, the assignment is recommended by the Division.

(Added to NRS by 1983, 321; A 1993, 1516)

NRS 176A.740 Duties and powers of Division; management of earnings and assets of probationer; regulations.

1. The Division shall:

(a) Determine a fixed amount to be deducted from the wages of each probationer assigned to a residential center to partially offset the cost of providing the probationer with housing and meals at the center.

(b) Arrange for all earnings of a probationer assigned to a residential center to be paid directly from the employer to the probationer who shall immediately give the probationer's earnings to the Division.

(c) Deduct the amount for housing, meals and medical and dental services determined under paragraph (a), and distribute the remainder according to a court order for restitution, if any, or to a plan for the management of the probationer's assets established by the Division.

2. The Division may adopt regulations necessary to carry out the provisions of this section and NRS 176A.720 and 176A.730.

(Added to NRS by 1983, 321; A 1993, 1516)

PROGRAM OF REGIMENTAL DISCIPLINE

NRS 176A.770 Legislative declaration. The Legislature hereby determines and declares that a program of regimental discipline is not to be used as an alternative to probation, but as an alternative to incarceration.

(Added to NRS by 1989, 1852)

NRS 176A.780 Eligibility; procedure; completion; deduction of time from sentence.

1. If a defendant:

(a) Is male;

(b) Has been convicted of a felony that:

(1) Does not involve an act of violence; or

(2) Involves an act of violence, but the district attorney stipulates to the defendant's eligibility to participate in a program of regimental discipline;

(c) Is at least 18 years of age;

(d) Has not been incarcerated in jail during his lifetime for a cumulative total of more than 365 days;

(e) Has never been incarcerated in prison; and

(f) Is otherwise eligible for probation,

□ the court may order the defendant satisfactorily to complete a program of regimental discipline for 150 days before sentencing the defendant or in lieu of causing the sentence imposed to be executed upon violation of a condition of probation or suspension of sentence.

2. If the court orders the defendant to undergo a program of regimental discipline, it:

(a) Shall place the defendant under the supervision of the Director of the Department of Corrections for not more than 190 days, not more than the first 30 days of which must be used to determine the defendant's eligibility to participate in the program. In determining the defendant's eligibility to participate in the program, the Director shall:

(1) Make all reasonable efforts to accommodate the defendant in the program; and

(2) Consider the facts and circumstances of the defendant's offense based on the police report, the report of the presentence investigation and any other information available to the Director.

(b) Shall, if appropriate, direct the Chief Parole and Probation Officer to provide a copy of the defendant's records to the Director of the Department of Corrections.

(c) Shall require the defendant to be returned to the court not later than 30 days after the defendant is placed under the supervision of the Director, if the defendant is determined to be ineligible for the program.

(d) May require such reports concerning the defendant's participation in the program as it deems desirable.

3. If the defendant is ordered to complete the program before sentencing, the Director of the Department of Corrections shall return the defendant to the court not later than 150 days after the defendant began the program. The Director shall certify either that the defendant satisfactorily completed the program or that the defendant did not, and shall report the results of the Director's evaluation, including any recommendations which will be helpful in determining the proper sentence. Upon receiving the report, the court shall sentence the defendant.

4. If the defendant is ordered to complete the program in lieu of causing the sentence imposed to be executed upon the violation of a condition of probation and the defendant satisfactorily completes the program, the Director of the Department of Corrections shall, not later than 150 days after the defendant began the program, return the defendant to the court with certification that the defendant satisfactorily completed the program. The court shall direct that:

(a) The defendant be placed under the supervision of the Chief Parole and Probation Officer; and

(b) The Director of the Department of Corrections cause a copy of the records concerning the defendant's participation in the program to be provided to the Chief Parole and Probation Officer.

5. If a defendant is ordered to complete the program of regimental discipline in lieu of causing the sentence imposed to be executed upon the violation of a condition of probation, a failure by the defendant satisfactorily to complete the program constitutes a violation of that condition of probation and the Director of the Department of Corrections shall return the defendant to the court.

6. Time spent in the program must be deducted from any sentence which may thereafter be imposed.

(Added to NRS by 1989, 1852; A 1993, 1942; 2001 Special Session, 222; 2013, 1846)

DISCHARGE

NRS 176A.850 Honorable discharge from probation: When granted; restoration of civil rights; effect; documentation.

1. A person who:

(a) Has fulfilled the conditions of probation for the entire period thereof;

(b) Is recommended for earlier discharge by the Division; or

(c) Has demonstrated fitness for honorable discharge but because of economic hardship, verified by the Division, has been unable to make restitution as ordered by the court,

□ may be granted an honorable discharge from probation by order of the court.

2. Any amount of restitution remaining unpaid constitutes a civil liability arising upon the date of discharge and is enforceable pursuant to NRS 176.275.

3. Except as otherwise provided in subsection 4, a person who has been honorably discharged from probation:

(a) Is free from the terms and conditions of probation.

(b) Is immediately restored to the following civil rights:

(1) The right to vote; and

(2) The right to serve as a juror in a civil action.

(c) Four years after the date of honorable discharge from probation, is restored to the right to hold office.

(d) Six years after the date of honorable discharge from probation, is restored to the right to serve as a juror in a criminal action.

(e) If the person meets the requirements of NRS 179.245, may apply to the court for the sealing of records relating to the conviction.

(f) Must be informed of the provisions of this section and NRS 179.245 in the person's probation papers.

(g) Is exempt from the requirements of chapter 179C of NRS, but is not exempt from the requirements of chapter 179D of NRS.

(h) Shall disclose the conviction to a gaming establishment and to the State and its agencies, departments, boards, commissions and political subdivisions, if required in an application for employment, license or other permit. As used in this paragraph, "establishment" has the meaning ascribed to it in NRS 463.0148.

(i) Except as otherwise provided in paragraph (h), need not disclose the conviction to an employer or prospective employer.

4. Except as otherwise provided in this subsection, the civil rights set forth in subsection 3 are not restored to a person honorably discharged from probation if the person has previously been convicted in this State:

(a) Of a category A felony.

(b) Of an offense that would constitute a category A felony if committed as of the date of the honorable discharge from probation.

(c) Of a category B felony involving the use of force or violence that resulted in substantial bodily harm to the victim.

(d) Of an offense involving the use of force or violence that resulted in substantial bodily harm to the victim and that would constitute a category B felony if committed as of the date of honorable discharge from probation.

(e) Two or more times of a felony, unless a felony for which the person has been convicted arose out of the same act, transaction or occurrence as another felony, in which case the convictions for those felonies shall be deemed to constitute a single conviction for the purposes of this paragraph.

□ A person described in this subsection may petition a court of competent jurisdiction for an order granting the restoration of civil rights as set forth in subsection 3.

5. The prior conviction of a person who has been honorably discharged from probation may be used for purposes of impeachment. In any subsequent prosecution of the person, the prior conviction may be pleaded and proved if otherwise admissible.

6. Except for a person subject to the limitations set forth in subsection 4, upon honorable discharge from probation, the person so discharged must be given an official document which provides:

(a) That the person has received an honorable discharge from probation;

(b) That the person has been restored to his or her civil rights to vote and to serve as a juror in a civil action as of the date of honorable discharge from probation;

(c) The date on which the person's civil right to hold office will be restored pursuant to paragraph (c) of subsection 3; and

(d) The date on which the person's civil right to serve as a juror in a criminal action will be restored pursuant to paragraph (d) of subsection 3.

7. Subject to the limitations set forth in subsection 4, a person who has been honorably discharged from probation in this State or elsewhere and whose official documentation of honorable discharge from probation is lost, damaged or destroyed may file a written request with a court of competent jurisdiction to restore the person's civil rights pursuant to this section. Upon verification that the person has been honorably discharged from probation and is eligible to be restored to the civil rights set forth in subsection 3, the court shall issue an order restoring the person to the civil rights set forth in subsection 3. A person must not be required to pay a fee to receive such an order.

8. A person who has been honorably discharged from probation in this State or elsewhere may present:

(a) Official documentation of honorable discharge from probation, if it contains the provisions set forth in subsection 6; or

(b) A court order restoring the person's civil rights,

□ as proof that the person has been restored to the civil rights set forth in subsection 3.

(Added to NRS by 1967, 1436; A 1989, 1983; 1993, 1517; 1997, 1672; 2001, 1639, 1690; 2003, 67, 2685; 2005, 81, 2354; 2015, 2574)

NRS 176A.870 Dishonorable discharge. A defendant whose term of probation has expired and:

1. Whose whereabouts are unknown;
2. Who has failed to make restitution in full as ordered by the court, without a verified showing of economic hardship; or
3. Who has otherwise failed to qualify for an honorable discharge as provided in NRS 176A.850,

□ is not eligible for an honorable discharge and must be given a dishonorable discharge. A dishonorable discharge releases the probationer from any further obligation, except a civil liability arising on the date of discharge for any unpaid restitution which is enforceable pursuant to NRS 176.275, but does not entitle the probationer to any privilege conferred by NRS 176A.850.

(Added to NRS by 1967, 1437; A 1977, 274, 815; 1981, 361; 1989, 1984; 1997, 945; 2015, 2575)

CHAPTER 177 - APPEALS AND REMEDIES AFTER CONVICTION

APPEALS: WHEN ALLOWED, HOW TAKEN AND EFFECT THEREOF

NRS 177.015 Appeals to district court, court of appeals and Supreme Court. The party aggrieved in a criminal action may appeal only as follows:

1. Whether that party is the State or the defendant:

(a) To the district court of the county from a final judgment of the justice court.

(b) To the appellate court of competent jurisdiction pursuant to the rules fixed by the Supreme Court pursuant to Section 4 of Article 6 of the Nevada Constitution from an order of the district court granting a motion to dismiss, a motion for acquittal or a motion in arrest of judgment, or granting or refusing a new trial.

(c) To the appellate court of competent jurisdiction pursuant to the rules fixed by the Supreme Court pursuant to Section 4 of Article 6 of the Nevada Constitution from a determination of the district court about whether a defendant is intellectually disabled that is made as a result of a hearing held pursuant to NRS 174.098. If the appellate court of competent jurisdiction entertains the appeal, it shall enter an order staying the criminal proceedings against the defendant for such time as may be required.

2. The State may, upon good cause shown, appeal to the appellate court of competent jurisdiction pursuant to the rules fixed by the Supreme Court pursuant to Section 4 of Article 6 of the Nevada Constitution from a pretrial order of the district court granting or denying a motion to suppress evidence made pursuant to NRS 174.125. Notice of the appeal must be filed with the clerk of the district court within 2 judicial days and with the Clerk of the Supreme Court within 5 judicial days after the ruling by the district court. The clerk of the district court shall notify counsel for the defendant or, in the case of a defendant without counsel, the defendant within 2 judicial days after the filing of the notice of appeal. The appellate court of competent jurisdiction may establish such procedures as it determines proper in requiring the appellant to make a preliminary showing of the propriety of the appeal and whether there may be a miscarriage of justice if the appeal is not entertained. If the appellate court of competent jurisdiction entertains the appeal, or if it otherwise appears necessary, it may enter an order staying the trial for such time as may be required.

3. The defendant only may appeal from a final judgment or verdict in a criminal case.

4. Except as otherwise provided in subsection 3 of NRS 174.035, the defendant in a criminal case shall not appeal a final judgment or verdict resulting from a plea of guilty, guilty but mentally ill or nolo contendere that the defendant entered into voluntarily and with a full understanding of the nature of the charge and the consequences of the plea, unless the appeal is based upon reasonable constitutional, jurisdictional or other grounds that challenge the legality of the proceedings. The appellate court of competent jurisdiction may establish procedures to require the defendant to make a preliminary showing of the propriety of the appeal.

(Added to NRS by 1967, 1443; A 1971, 1450; 1973, 1489; 1981, 1705; 1991, 652; 1995, 1535; 1997, 645; 2003, 769, 1468; 2007, 1422; 2013, 687, 1758)

NRS 177.025 Appeal to court of appeals or Supreme Court taken on questions of law alone. The appeal to the appellate court of competent jurisdiction pursuant to the rules fixed by the Supreme Court pursuant to Section 4 of Article 6 of the Nevada Constitution from the district court can be taken on questions of law alone.

(Added to NRS by 1967, 1444; A 2013, 1759)

NRS 177.035 Designation of parties on appeal. The party appealing shall be known as the appellant, and the adverse party as the respondent, but the title of the action is not changed by reason of the appeal.

(Added to NRS by 1967, 1444)

NRS 177.045 Intermediate order or proceeding may be reviewed on appeal. Upon the appeal, any decision of the court in an intermediate order or proceeding, forming a part of the record, may be reviewed.

(Added to NRS by 1967, 1444)

NRS 177.055 Automatic appeal in certain cases; mandatory review of death sentence by court of appeals or Supreme Court.

1. When upon a plea of not guilty or not guilty by reason of insanity a judgment of death is entered, an appeal is deemed automatically taken by the defendant without any action by the defendant or the defendant's counsel, unless the defendant or the defendant's counsel affirmatively waives the appeal within 30 days after the rendition of the judgment.

2. Whether or not the defendant or the defendant's counsel affirmatively waives the appeal, the sentence must be reviewed on the record by the appellate court of competent jurisdiction pursuant to the rules fixed by the Supreme Court pursuant to Section 4 of Article 6 of the Nevada Constitution, which shall consider, in a single proceeding, if an appeal is taken:

(a) Any errors enumerated by way of appeal;

(b) If a court determined that the defendant is not intellectually disabled during a hearing held pursuant to NRS 174.098, whether that determination was correct;

(c) Whether the evidence supports the finding of an aggravating circumstance or circumstances;

(d) Whether the sentence of death was imposed under the influence of passion, prejudice or any arbitrary factor; and

(e) Whether the sentence of death is excessive, considering both the crime and the defendant.

3. The appellate court of competent jurisdiction pursuant to the rules fixed by the Supreme Court pursuant to Section 4 of Article 6 of the Nevada Constitution, when reviewing a death sentence, may:

(a) Affirm the sentence of death;

(b) Set the sentence aside and remand the case for a new penalty hearing before a newly impaneled jury; or

(c) Set aside the sentence of death and impose the sentence of imprisonment for life without possibility of parole.

(Added to NRS by 1967, 1444; A 1977, 1545; 1985, 1597; 1995, 2456; 2003, 770, 1468, 2084; 2013, 688, 1759)

NRS 177.075 Appeal to court of appeals or Supreme Court: Notice.

1. Except where appeal is automatic, an appeal from a district court to the appellate court of competent jurisdiction pursuant to the rules fixed by the Supreme Court pursuant to Section 4 of Article 6 of the Nevada Constitution is taken by filing a notice of appeal with the clerk of the district court. Bills of exception and assignments of error in cases governed by this chapter are abolished.

2. When a court imposes sentence upon a defendant who has not pleaded guilty or guilty but mentally ill and who is without counsel, the court shall advise the defendant of the right to appeal, and if the defendant so requests, the clerk shall prepare and file forthwith a notice of appeal on the defendant's behalf.

3. A notice of appeal must be signed:

(a) By the appellant or appellant's attorney; or

(b) By the clerk if prepared by the clerk.

(Added to NRS by 1967, 1444; A 1971, 149; 1985, 62; 1995, 2457; 2003, 1469; 2007, 1423; 2013, 1760)

NRS 177.085 Effect of appeal by State.

1. An appeal taken by the State shall in no case stay or affect the operation of a judgment in favor of the defendant; but if the appeal by the State is from an order granting a motion to set aside an indictment or information, and upon such appeal the order is reversed, the defendant shall thereupon be liable to arrest and trial upon the indictment or information. In all such cases any statute of limitations on the offense from which the appeal is taken is tolled from the time the notice of appeal is filed by the State until such appeal is heard and a ruling made thereon.

2. If the appeal by the State is from an order allowing a motion in arrest of judgment, or granting a motion for a new trial, and upon appeal the order is reversed, the trial court shall enter judgment against the defendant.

(Added to NRS by 1967, 1444; A 1969, 106)

NRS 177.095 Stay of execution upon sentence of death. A sentence of death shall be stayed if an appeal is taken.

(Added to NRS by 1967, 1445)

NRS 177.105 Stay of execution upon sentence of imprisonment. A sentence of imprisonment shall be stayed if an appeal is taken and the defendant is admitted to bail.

(Added to NRS by 1967, 1445)

NRS 177.115 Stay of execution upon fine. A sentence to pay a fine or a fine and costs, if an appeal is taken, may be stayed by a Justice Court, district court, the Court of Appeals or by the Supreme Court upon such terms as the court deems proper. The court may require the defendant pending appeal to deposit the whole or any part of the fine and costs in the registry of the court appealed from, or to give bond for the payment thereof, or to submit to an examination of assets, and it may make any appropriate order to restrain the defendant from dissipating the defendant's assets.

(Added to NRS by 1967, 1445; A 2013, 1760)

NRS 177.125 Stay of probation. An order placing the defendant on probation may be stayed if an appeal is taken.

(Added to NRS by 1967, 1445)

NRS 177.135 Admission to bail upon appeal. Admission to bail upon appeal shall be as provided in this title.

(Added to NRS by 1967, 1445)

NRS 177.145 Application for relief pending review. If application is made to a district court, the Court of Appeals or a justice of the Supreme Court for bail pending appeal or for an extension of time for filing the record on appeal or for any other relief which might have been granted by the trial court, the application shall be upon notice and shall show that:

1. Application to the court below or a judge thereof is not practicable;
2. Application has been made and denied, with the reasons given for the denial; or
3. The action on the application did not afford the relief to which the applicant considers himself or herself to be entitled.

(Added to NRS by 1967, 1445; A 2013, 1760)

NRS 177.155 Supervision of appeal. The supervision and control of the proceedings on appeal shall be in the appellate court from the time the notice of appeal is filed with its clerk, except as otherwise provided in this title. The appellate court may at any time entertain a motion to dismiss the appeal, or for directions to the trial court, or to modify or vacate any order made by the trial court or by any judge or justice of the peace in relation to the prosecution of the appeal, including any order fixing or denying bail.

(Added to NRS by 1967, 1445)

NRS 177.165 Preparation of record and papers on appeal. All appeals from a district court to the appellate court of competent jurisdiction pursuant to the rules fixed by the Supreme Court pursuant to Section 4 of Article 6 of the Nevada Constitution shall be heard on the original papers and the reporter's transcript of evidence or proceedings. The form and manner of preparation of the record and of other papers filed may be prescribed by the appellate court of competent jurisdiction, and to the extent not otherwise so prescribed shall conform to the practice in civil cases.

(Added to NRS by 1967, 1445; A 2013, 1760)

DISMISSAL OR ARGUMENT OF APPEAL

NRS 177.205 Dismissal by court of appeals or Supreme Court. The appellate court of competent jurisdiction pursuant to the rules fixed by the Supreme Court pursuant to Section 4 of Article 6 of the Nevada Constitution may, on its own motion or on motion of the respondent, dismiss an appeal:

1. If the appeal is irregular in any substantial particular.

2. If the appellant has failed to comply with the requirements for docketing of the record on appeal or filing briefs, unless for good cause shown an extension is granted.

(Added to NRS by 1967, 1446; A 1985, 63; 2013, 1761)

NRS 177.215 Date for argument. Unless good cause is shown for an earlier hearing, the appellate court of competent jurisdiction pursuant to the rules fixed by the Supreme Court pursuant to Section 4 of Article 6 of the Nevada Constitution shall set the appeal for argument on a date not less than 30 days after the expiration of the time limited for filing briefs and as soon thereafter as the state of the calendar will permit. Preference shall be given to appeals in criminal cases over appeals in civil cases.

(Added to NRS by 1967, 1446; A 2013, 1761)

JUDGMENT UPON APPEAL

NRS 177.225 Judgment may be affirmed but cannot be reversed without argument. Judgment of affirmance may be granted without argument, if the appellant fail to appear. But judgment of reversal can only be given upon argument, orally or upon written brief, though the respondent fail to appear.

(Added to NRS by 1967, 1446)

NRS 177.235 Number of counsel in argument on appeal. Upon the argument of the appeal, if the offense is punishable with death, two counsel shall be heard on each side, if they require it. In any other case the Court may, in its discretion, restrict the argument to one counsel on each side.

(Added to NRS by 1967, 1446)

NRS 177.245 Defendant need not be present. The defendant need not personally appear in the appellate court of competent jurisdiction.

(Added to NRS by 1967, 1446; A 2013, 1761)

NRS 177.255 Court to give judgment without regard to technical errors. After hearing the appeal, the Court shall give judgment without regard to technical error or defect which does not affect the substantial rights of the parties.

(Added to NRS by 1967, 1446)

NRS 177.265 Determination of appeal. The appellate court of competent jurisdiction pursuant to the rules fixed by the Supreme Court pursuant to Section 4 of Article 6 of the Nevada Constitution may reverse, affirm, or modify the judgment appealed from, and may, if necessary or proper, order a new trial.

(Added to NRS by 1967, 1447; A 2013, 1761)

NRS 177.267 Time within which court of appeals or Supreme Court shall render opinion on appeal from judgment of death. Repealed. (See chapter 442, Statutes of Nevada 2015, at page 2569.)

NRS 177.275 Defendant to be discharged on reversal without ordering new trial. If a judgment against the defendant is reversed, without ordering a new trial, the appellate court of competent jurisdiction shall direct, if the defendant is in custody, that the defendant be discharged therefrom, or if admitted to bail, that the defendant's bail be exonerated, or if money be deposited instead of bail, that it be refunded to the defendant.

(Added to NRS by 1967, 1447; A 2013, 1761)

NRS 177.285 Judgment to be executed on affirmance. On a judgment of affirmance against the defendant, the original judgment shall be carried into execution, as the appellate court of competent jurisdiction shall direct.

(Added to NRS by 1967, 1447; A 2013, 1761)

NRS 177.305 Jurisdiction of court of appeals or Supreme Court to cease after certificate of judgment remitted. After the certificate of judgment has been remitted, the appellate court of competent jurisdiction shall have no further jurisdiction of the appeal or of the proceedings thereon, and all orders which may be necessary to carry the judgment into effect shall be made by the court to which the certificate is remitted.

(Added to NRS by 1967, 1447; A 2013, 1761)

CHAPTER 178 - GENERAL PROVISIONS RIGHTS OF DEFENDANT

NRS 178.3971 Appointment of defense team for defendant accused of murder of first degree.

RECOUPMENT OF EXPENSES OF DEFENSE OF INDIGENTS

NRS 178.3975 Order for payment by defendant; remission of payment; disposition of amounts recovered; community service.
NRS 178.398 Execution against defendant's property.
NRS 178.39801 Collection of fee by certain entities.
NRS 178.39802 Additional costs and fees for collection.

INQUIRY INTO COMPETENCE OF DEFENDANT AND PROCEDURE FOLLOWING FINDING OF INCOMPETENCE

NRS 178.3981 Definitions.
NRS 178.3982 "Administrator" defined.
NRS 178.3983 "Division" defined.
NRS 178.3984 "Division facility" defined.
NRS 178.39845 "Forensic facility" defined.
NRS 178.3985 "Mental disorder" defined.
NRS 178.3986 "Person with mental illness" defined.
NRS 178.399 "Treatment to competency" defined.
NRS 178.400 Incompetent person cannot be tried or adjudged to punishment for public offense.
NRS 178.405 Suspension of trial or pronouncement of judgment when doubt arises as to competence of defendant; notice of suspension to be provided to other departments.
NRS 178.415 Appointment of person or persons to examine defendant; hearing; finding.
NRS 178.417 Certification of person who evaluates competency of defendant required.
NRS 178.420 Procedure on finding defendant competent.
NRS 178.425 Procedure on finding defendant incompetent.
NRS 178.430 Commitment of defendant exonerates bail.
NRS 178.435 Expenses of examination and transportation are charge against county or city; recovery from estate or relative.
NRS 178.440 Clerk to certify costs to county or city.
NRS 178.450 Duties of Administrator or Administrator's designee following finding of incompetence; observation and evaluation of defendant; report to court.
NRS 178.453 Access by Administrator to certain records of defendant within possession of Department of Corrections authorized for purpose of evaluating and treating defendant.
NRS 178.455 Procedure for evaluating certain defendants following finding of incompetence; report to court; procedure concerning misdemeanants.
NRS 178.460 Powers and duties of court following finding of incompetence; limitation on length of commitment.
NRS 178.461 Motion for hearing to determine whether to commit incompetent defendant to custody of Administrator; risk assessment; dismissal of motion in certain circumstances; length of commitment; review of eligibility for conditional release.
NRS 178.463 Conditional release of incompetent defendant committed to custody of Administrator: When eligible; annual review of eligibility for discharge from conditional release; maximum duration.
NRS 178.464 Procedure when defendant violates conditions of release; hearing to determine whether to continue, modify or terminate conditional release.
NRS 178.467 Person committed to custody of Administrator: Eligibility for discharge or conditional release; recommitment for failure to comply with conditions.
NRS 178.468 Hearing to determine eligibility of person committed to custody of Administrator for discharge or conditional release; report by Administrator.
NRS 178.469 Petition for discharge or conditional release by person committed to custody of Administrator.
NRS 178.471 Effect of conditional release of person committed to custody of Administrator; authority of court over person conditionally released.
NRS 178.4715 Notification of victims upon discharge, conditional release or escape.

TIME

NRS 178.472 Computation.
NRS 178.476 Enlargement.
NRS 178.478 Motions; affidavits.
NRS 178.482 Additional time after service by mail.

BAIL

NRS 178.484 Right to bail before conviction; exceptions; imposition of conditions; arrest for violation of condition.
NRS 178.4851 Release without bail; imposition of conditions; arrest for violation of condition.

NRS 178.4853 Factors considered before release without bail.
NRS 178.4855 Limitations on release without bail of certain defendants who are taken into custody while admitted to bail on other charges; notice to bail agent required.
NRS 178.486 When bail is matter of discretion, notice of application must be given to district attorney.
NRS 178.487 Bail after arrest for felony offense committed while on bail.
NRS 178.4871 Postconviction petitioner for habeas corpus: Limitations on release.
NRS 178.4873 Postconviction petitioner for habeas corpus: Release pending appeal.
NRS 178.4875 Proceeding for forfeiture of bail pending review or appeal; proceeding for recommitment of defendant.
NRS 178.488 Right to bail upon review; notice of application to be given district attorney.
NRS 178.494 Bail for witnesses; judicial review of detention or amount of bail.
NRS 178.498 Amount.
NRS 178.499 Increase in amount.
NRS 178.502 Form of bail; extension of bond or undertaking to proceedings in other courts; exoneration; place of deposit.
NRS 178.504 Justification of sureties.
NRS 178.506 Declaration of forfeiture.
NRS 178.508 Duties of court when defendant fails to appear; procedure for issuing order of forfeiture; when forfeiture becomes effective; grounds for extending date of forfeiture.
NRS 178.509 Exoneration of surety before date of forfeiture: Conditions; grounds.
NRS 178.512 Setting aside forfeiture: Conditions; grounds; when written finding is required.
NRS 178.514 Enforcement of forfeiture.
NRS 178.516 Remission of forfeited money.
NRS 178.518 Payment of forfeited deposits to county treasurer or State Controller.
NRS 178.522 Exoneration of bail.
NRS 178.524 Deposit required in certain cases.
NRS 178.526 Arrest of defendant.
NRS 178.528 Disposition of money deposited as bail.
NRS 178.532 Recommitment of defendant after having given bail or deposited money.
NRS 178.534 Contents of order for recommitment.
NRS 178.536 Arrest on order of recommitment.
NRS 178.538 Commitment of defendant on order when defendant fails to appear for judgment; if order issued for other cause, defendant may be admitted to bail.
NRS 178.542 Records: District court.
NRS 178.544 Records: Justice Court.
NRS 178.546 Records: Court of Appeals and Supreme Court.
NRS 178.548 Notification of district attorney when bail bond is forfeited.

MOTIONS

NRS 178.552 Form; contents.

DISMISSAL OF ACTIONS

NRS 178.554 Dismissal by district attorney or Attorney General by leave of court.
NRS 178.556 Dismissal by court for unnecessary delay.
NRS 178.562 Dismissal or discharge as bar to another prosecution.
NRS 178.563 Notice to defendant of provisions concerning sealing of records of proceedings leading to dismissal.

COMPROMISING CERTAIN PUBLIC OFFENSES BY LEAVE OF COURT

NRS 178.564 Certain offenses for which party injured has civil action may be compromised.
NRS 178.566 Compromise to be by permission of court; order to bar another prosecution.
NRS 178.568 No public offense to be compromised except as provided in this title.

PROTECTION OF VICTIMS AND WITNESSES

NRS 178.569 Definitions.
NRS 178.5691 Confidentiality of personal information.
NRS 178.5692 Investigation by sheriff of threats of harm; protection.
NRS 178.5694 Harassment of victim or witness by employer; notification by prosecuting attorney of continuance of proceeding.
NRS 178.5696 Separate waiting area; disposition of personal property; fees for testifying.

NRS 178.5698 Information concerning release of defendant and disposition of case provided upon request; court to inform and provide documentation to certain persons of their right to be informed of release of offender from prison in certain cases; when and whom warden must inform of release of offender from prison.

DESIGNATION OF ATTENDANT TO PROVIDE SUPPORT FOR WITNESS DURING TESTIMONY

NRS 178.571 Applicability to certain cases; persons permitted to be attendant; permissible conduct by attendant; exclusion for good cause.

IMMUNITY OF MATERIAL WITNESSES FROM PROSECUTION

NRS 178.572 Order of immunity releasing material witness from prosecution or punishment on motion of State.
NRS 178.574 Order of immunity bar to prosecution; exception.
NRS 178.576 Failure of witness granted immunity to testify is contempt.
NRS 178.578 Denial of motion.

SERVICE AND FILING OF PAPERS

NRS 178.582 Service: When required.
NRS 178.584 Service: How made.
NRS 178.586 Notice of orders.
NRS 178.588 Filing of papers.
NRS 178.589 Use of facsimile machine.

CALENDARS

NRS 178.592 Calendar of criminal actions: Preparation by clerk.
NRS 178.594 Order of disposing of issues on calendar.

EXCEPTIONS

NRS 178.596 Exceptions unnecessary.

ERROR

NRS 178.598 Harmless error.
NRS 178.602 Plain error.

RECORDS

NRS 178.606 Docket kept by deputy clerk of justice court; contents.

RULES OF COURT

NRS 178.608 Rules of justice courts and district courts not to be inconsistent with this title.
NRS 178.610 Where no procedure specifically prescribed court may proceed in lawful manner.

THE AGREEMENT ON DETAINERS

NRS 178.620 Enactment; text.
NRS 178.630 Duties of Director of Department of Corrections.
NRS 178.640 Duty of Governor.

REQUEST FOR DETAINER

MISCELLANEOUS PROVISIONS

RIGHTS OF DEFENDANT

NRS 178.388 Presence of defendant.

1. Except as otherwise provided in this title, the defendant must be present at the arraignment, at every stage of the trial including the impaneling of the jury and the return of the verdict, and at the imposition of sentence. A corporation may appear by counsel for all purposes.

2. In prosecutions for offenses not punishable by death:

(a) The defendant's voluntary absence after the trial has been commenced in the defendant's presence must not prevent continuing the trial to and including the return of the verdict.

(b) If the defendant was present at the trial through the time the defendant pleads guilty or guilty but mentally ill or is found guilty or guilty but mentally ill but at the time of sentencing is incarcerated in another jurisdiction, the defendant may waive the right to be present at the sentencing proceedings and agree to be sentenced in this State in his or her absence. The defendant's waiver is valid only if it is:

(1) Made knowingly, intelligently and voluntarily after consulting with an attorney licensed to practice in this State;

(2) Signed and dated by the defendant and notarized by a notary public or judicial officer;

(3) Signed and dated by the defendant's attorney after it has been signed by the defendant and notarized; and

(4) Accompanied by a waiver of the issuance and service of a warrant of arrest and all other procedures incidental to extradition proceedings.

3. In prosecutions for offenses punishable by fine or by imprisonment for not more than 1 year, or both, the court, with the written consent of the defendant, may permit arraignment, plea, trial and imposition of sentence in the defendant's absence, if the court determines that the defendant was fully aware of the applicable constitutional rights when the defendant gave consent.

4. The presence of the defendant is not required at the arraignment or any preceding stage if the court has provided for the use of a closed-circuit television to facilitate communication between the court and the defendant during the proceeding. If closed-circuit television is provided for, members of the news media may observe and record the proceeding from both locations unless the court specifically provides otherwise.

5. The defendant's presence is not required at the settling of jury instructions.

(Added to NRS by 1967, 1450; A 1969, 9; 1987, 2025; 1993, 933; 1995, 2457; 2003, 1470; 2007, 1426; 2015, 307)

NRS 178.391 Second prosecution for same offense prohibited. No person can be subject to a second prosecution for a public offense for which the person has once been prosecuted and duly convicted or acquitted.

(Added to NRS by 1967, 1451)

NRS 178.394 No person to be compelled to be witness against himself or herself in criminal action, or to be unnecessarily restrained. No person can be compelled, in a criminal action, to be a witness against himself or herself, nor shall a person charged with a public offense be subjected, before conviction, to any more restraint than is necessary for the person's detention to answer the charge.

(Added to NRS by 1967, 1451)

NRS 178.397 Assignment of counsel. Every defendant accused of a gross misdemeanor or felony who is financially unable to obtain counsel is entitled to have counsel assigned to represent the defendant at every stage of the proceedings from the defendant's initial appearance before a magistrate or the court through appeal, unless the defendant waives such appointment.

(Added to NRS by 1967, 1451)

NRS 178.3971 Appointment of defense team for defendant accused of murder of first degree. If a magistrate or district court appoints an attorney, other than a public defender, to represent a defendant accused of murder of the first degree in a case in which the death penalty is sought, the magistrate or court must appoint a team to defend the accused person that includes:

1. Two attorneys; and

2. Any other person as deemed necessary by the court, upon motion of an attorney representing the defendant.

(Added to NRS by 2003, 443)

RECOUPMENT OF EXPENSES OF DEFENSE OF INDIGENTS

NRS 178.3975 Order for payment by defendant; remission of payment; disposition of amounts recovered; community service.

1. The court may order a defendant to pay all or any part of the expenses incurred by the county, city or state in providing the defendant with an attorney which are not recovered pursuant to NRS 178.398. The order may be made at the time of or after the appointment of an attorney and may direct the defendant to pay the expenses in installments.

2. The court shall not order a defendant to make such a payment unless the defendant is or will be able to do so. In determining the amount and method of payment, the court shall take account of the financial resources of the defendant and the nature of the burden that payment will impose.

3. A defendant who has been ordered to pay expenses of the defendant's defense and who is not willfully or without good cause in default in the payment thereof may at any time petition the court which ordered the payment for remission of the payment or of any unpaid portion thereof. If it appears to the satisfaction of the court that payment of the amount due will impose manifest hardship on the defendant or the defendant's immediate family, the court may remit all or part of the amount due or modify the method of payment.

4. The money recovered must in each case be paid over to the city, county or public defender's office which bore the expense and was not reimbursed by another governmental agency.

5. Upon the request of a defendant, if the court finds that the defendant is suitable to perform supervised community service, the court may allow the defendant to pay all or part of any expenses incurred by the county, city or state in providing the defendant with an attorney by performing supervised community service for a reasonable number of hours, the value of which would be commensurate with such expenses incurred. The community service must be performed for and under the supervising authority of a county, city, town or other political subdivision or agency of the State of Nevada or a charitable organization that renders service to the community or its residents. The court may require a defendant who requests to perform community service to deposit with the court a reasonable sum of money to pay for the cost of policies of insurance against liability for personal injury and damage to property or for industrial insurance, or both, during those periods in which the defendant performs the community service, unless, in the case of industrial insurance, it is provided by the authority for which the defendant performs the community service.

(Added to NRS by 1975, 217; A 1977, 377; 1985, 49; 1995, 500; 2001 Special Session, 135)

NRS 178.398 Execution against defendant's property. If a defendant for whom an attorney is appointed at public expense on account of indigency has property subject to execution or acquires such property within 6 years after the termination of the attorney's representation, the court shall determine the value of the legal services provided and shall render judgment for that amount in favor of the state, county or city which furnished the public defender or otherwise paid for the defense.

(Added to NRS by 1977, 338)

NRS 178.39801 Collection of fee by certain entities.

1. If a district court orders a defendant to pay for expenses incurred by the county or State in providing the defendant with an attorney pursuant to NRS 178.3975 or makes an execution on the property of the defendant pursuant to NRS 178.398, the district court entering the judgment shall forward to the county treasurer or other office assigned by the county to make collections the information necessary to collect the fee. The county treasurer or other office assigned by the county to make collections is responsible for such collection efforts and has the authority to collect the fee.

2. If the county treasurer or other office assigned by the county to make collections is unable to collect the fee after 60 days, the county treasurer may assign to the Office of the State Controller the responsibility for collection of the fee through a cooperative agreement pursuant to NRS 353.650, so long as the Office of the State Controller is willing and able to make such collection efforts.

3. If the county treasurer and the Office of the State Controller enter into a cooperative agreement pursuant to NRS 353.650, the county treasurer or other county office assigned by the county to make collections shall forward to the Office of the State Controller the necessary information. For purposes of this section, the information necessary to collect the fee shall be considered and limited to:

(a) The name of the defendant;

(b) The date of birth of the defendant;

(c) The social security number of the defendant;

(d) The last known address of the defendant; and

(e) The nature and the amount of money owed by the defendant.

4. If the Office of the State Controller is successful in collecting the fee, the money collected must be returned to the originating county, minus the costs and fees actually incurred in collecting the fee.

5. Any money collected must be paid to the county or state public defender's office which bore the expense and which was not reimbursed by another governmental agency, pursuant to NRS 178.3975.

6. Any record created pursuant to subsection 3 that contains personal identifying information shall not be considered a public record pursuant to NRS 239.010 and must be treated pursuant to NRS 239.0105.

7. Unless otherwise prohibited by law, the entity responsible for collecting the fee pursuant to this section, has the authority to compromise the amount to be collected for the purpose of satisfying the judgment.

(Added to NRS by 2011, 910)

NRS 178.39802 Additional costs and fees for collection.

1. A defendant who owes a fee pursuant to NRS 178.39801, must be assessed by and pay to the county treasurer or other office assigned by the county to make collections, the following costs and fees if the county treasurer or other office assigned by the county to make collections is successful in collecting the fee:

(a) The costs and fees actually incurred in collecting the fee; and

(b) A fee payable to the county treasurer in the amount of 2 percent of the amount of the fee assigned to the county treasurer or other office assigned by the county to make collections.

2. The total amount of the costs and fees required to be collected pursuant to subsection 1 must not exceed 35 percent of the amount of the fee or $50,000, whichever is less.

(Added to NRS by 2011, 911)

INQUIRY INTO COMPETENCE OF DEFENDANT AND PROCEDURE FOLLOWING FINDING OF INCOMPETENCE

NRS 178.3981 Definitions. As used in NRS 178.3981 to 178.4715, inclusive, unless the context otherwise requires, the words and terms defined in NRS 178.3982 to 178.399, inclusive, have the meanings ascribed to them in those sections.
(Added to NRS by 2007, 1424, 1777; A 2009, 72, 115)

NRS 178.3982 "Administrator" defined. "Administrator" means the Administrator of the Division.
(Added to NRS by 2007, 1424)

NRS 178.3983 "Division" defined. "Division" means the Division of Public and Behavioral Health of the Department of Health and Human Services.
(Added to NRS by 2007, 1424, 1777; A 2013, 2995)

NRS 178.3984 "Division facility" defined. "Division facility" means a division facility as defined in NRS 433.094 and 435.007.
(Added to NRS by 2007, 1424; A 2013, 2995)

NRS 178.39845 "Forensic facility" defined. "Forensic facility" has the meaning ascribed to it in NRS 175.539.
(Added to NRS by 2009, 114)

NRS 178.3985 "Mental disorder" defined. "Mental disorder" means a mental illness that results from a psychiatric or neurological disorder that so substantially impairs the mental or emotional functioning of the person as to make care or treatment necessary or advisable for the welfare of the person or for the safety of the person or property of another and includes, without limitation, intellectual disabilities and related conditions.
(Added to NRS by 2007, 1424, 1777; A 2013, 689)

NRS 178.3986 "Person with mental illness" defined. "Person with mental illness" means a person who has a mental disorder.
(Added to NRS by 2007, 1424)

NRS 178.399 "Treatment to competency" defined. "Treatment to competency" means treatment provided to a defendant to attempt to cause the defendant to attain competency to stand trial or receive pronouncement of judgment.
(Added to NRS by 2003, 1947; A 2007, 1427, 1778)

NRS 178.400 Incompetent person cannot be tried or adjudged to punishment for public offense.
1. A person may not be tried or adjudged to punishment for a public offense while incompetent.
2. For the purposes of this section, "incompetent" means that the person does not have the present ability to:
(a) Understand the nature of the criminal charges against the person;
(b) Understand the nature and purpose of the court proceedings; or
(c) Aid and assist the person's counsel in the defense at any time during the proceedings with a reasonable degree of rational understanding.
[1911 Cr. Prac. § 535; RL § 7385; NCL § 11183] — (NRS A 1981, 1656; 1995, 2458; 2007, 185)

NRS 178.405 Suspension of trial or pronouncement of judgment when doubt arises as to competence of defendant; notice of suspension to be provided to other departments.
1. Any time after the arrest of a defendant, including, without limitation, proceedings before trial, during trial, when upon conviction the defendant is brought up for judgment or when a defendant who has been placed on probation or whose sentence has been suspended is brought before the court, if doubt arises as to the competence of the defendant, the court shall suspend the proceedings, the trial or the pronouncing of the judgment, as the case may be, until the question of competence is determined.
2. If the proceedings, the trial or the pronouncing of the judgment are suspended, the court must notify any other departments of the court of the suspension in writing. Upon receiving such notice, the other departments of the court shall suspend any other proceedings relating to the defendant until the defendant is determined to be competent.
[1911 Cr. Prac. § 536; A 1919, 416; 1919 RL § 7386; NCL § 11184] — (NRS A 1967, 1449; 1981, 1656; 1991, 1003; 2003, 1018; 2007, 186)

NRS 178.415 Appointment of person or persons to examine defendant; hearing; finding.
1. Except as otherwise provided in this subsection, the court shall appoint two psychiatrists, two psychologists, or one psychiatrist and one psychologist, to examine the defendant. If the defendant is accused of a misdemeanor, the court of jurisdiction shall appoint a psychiatric social worker, or other person who is especially qualified by the Division, to examine the defendant.
2. Except as otherwise provided in this subsection, at a hearing in open court, the court that orders the examination must receive the report of the examination. If a justice court orders the examination of a defendant who is charged with a gross misdemeanor or felony, the district court must receive the report of the examination.
3. The court that receives the report of the examination shall permit counsel for both sides to examine the person or persons appointed to examine the defendant. The prosecuting attorney and the defendant may:
(a) Introduce other evidence including, without limitation, evidence related to treatment to competency and the possibility of ordering the involuntary administration of medication; and

(b) Cross-examine one another's witnesses.

4. The court that receives the report of the examination shall then make and enter its finding of competence or incompetence.

5. The court shall not appoint a person to provide a report or an evaluation pursuant to this section, unless the person is certified by the Division pursuant to NRS 178.417.

[1911 Cr. Prac. § 538; A 1919, 416; 1919 RL § 7388; NCL § 11186] — (NRS A 1967, 1449; 1968, 52; 1981, 1656; 1991, 1003; 1999, 104; 2003, 1018, 1470, 1947)

NRS 178.417 Certification of person who evaluates competency of defendant required.

1. A person may not provide a report or an evaluation concerning the competency of a defendant to stand trial or receive pronouncement of judgment pursuant to this section and NRS 178.400 to 178.460, inclusive, unless the person is certified by the Division for that purpose.

2. The Division shall adopt regulations to establish:

(a) Requirements for certification of a person who provides reports and evaluations concerning the competency of a defendant pursuant to this section and NRS 178.400 to 178.460, inclusive;

(b) Reasonable fees for issuing and renewing such certificates; and

(c) Requirements for continuing education for the renewal of a certificate.

3. The fees so collected must be used only to:

(a) Defray the cost of issuing and renewing certificates; and

(b) Pay any other expenses incurred by the Division in carrying out its duties pursuant to this section.

4. The Division shall establish and administer examinations to determine the eligibility of any person who applies for certification. An applicant is entitled to certification upon satisfaction of the requirements of the Division. The Division may enter into a contract with another person, organization or agency to carry out or assist in carrying out the provisions of this subsection.

(Added to NRS by 2003, 1469)

NRS 178.420 Procedure on finding defendant competent. If the court finds that the defendant is competent, the trial must proceed, or judgment may be pronounced, as the case may be.

[1911 Cr. Prac. § 539; A 1919, 416; 1919 RL § 7389; NCL § 11187] — (NRS A 1967, 1450; 1981, 1656; 1991, 1003)

NRS 178.425 Procedure on finding defendant incompetent.

1. If the court finds the defendant incompetent, and dangerous to himself or herself or to society and that commitment is required for a determination of the defendant's ability to receive treatment to competency and to attain competence, the judge shall order the sheriff to convey the defendant forthwith, together with a copy of the complaint, the commitment and the physicians' certificate, if any, into the custody of the Administrator or the Administrator's designee for detention and treatment at a division facility that is secure. The order may include the involuntary administration of medication if appropriate for treatment to competency.

2. The defendant must be held in such custody until a court orders the defendant's release or until the defendant is returned for trial or judgment as provided in NRS 178.450, 178.455 and 178.460.

3. If the court finds the defendant incompetent but not dangerous to himself or herself or to society, and finds that commitment is not required for a determination of the defendant's ability to receive treatment to competency and to attain competence, the judge shall order the defendant to report to the Administrator or the Administrator's designee as an outpatient for treatment, if it might be beneficial, and for a determination of the defendant's ability to receive treatment to competency and to attain competence. The court may require the defendant to give bail for any periodic appearances before the Administrator or the Administrator's designee.

4. Except as otherwise provided in subsection 5, proceedings against the defendant must be suspended until the Administrator or the Administrator's designee or, if the defendant is charged with a misdemeanor, the judge finds the defendant capable of standing trial or opposing pronouncement of judgment as provided in NRS 178.400.

5. Whenever the defendant has been found incompetent, with no substantial probability of attaining competency in the foreseeable future, and released from custody or from obligations as an outpatient pursuant to paragraph (d) of subsection 4 of NRS 178.460, the proceedings against the defendant which were suspended must be dismissed. No new charge arising out of the same circumstances may be brought after a period, equal to the maximum time allowed by law for commencing a criminal action for the crime with which the defendant was charged, has lapsed since the date of the alleged offense.

6. If a defendant is found incompetent pursuant to this section, the court shall cause, within 5 business days after the finding, on a form prescribed by the Department of Public Safety, a record of that finding to be transmitted to the Central Repository for Nevada Records of Criminal History, along with a statement indicating that the record is being transmitted for inclusion in each appropriate database of the National Instant Criminal Background Check System.

7. As used in this section, "National Instant Criminal Background Check System" has the meaning ascribed to it in NRS 179A.062.

[1911 Cr. Prac. § 540; RL § 7390; NCL § 11188] — (NRS A 1967, 1450; 1968, 52; 1971, 313; 1973, 93, 252, 1406; 1981, 1656; 1991, 1003; 1999, 104; 2001, 1084; 2003, 1947; 2009, 2487;2015, 1798)

NRS 178.430 Commitment of defendant exonerates bail. The commitment of the defendant, as mentioned in NRS 178.425, shall exonerate any bail the defendant may have given, or shall entitle any person authorized to receive the property of the defendant to a return of any money the defendant may have deposited instead of bail.

[1911 Cr. Prac. § 541; RL § 7391; NCL § 11189]

NRS 178.435 Expenses of examination and transportation are charge against county or city; recovery from estate or relative. The expenses of the examination and of the transportation of the defendant to and from the custody of the Administrator or the Administrator's designee are in the first instance chargeable to the county or city from which the defendant has been sent. But the county or city may recover the money from the estate of the defendant, from a relative legally bound to care for the defendant or from the county or city of which the defendant is a resident.

[1911 Cr. Prac. § 543; RL § 7393; NCL § 11191] — (NRS A 1963, 1111; 1968, 52; 1973, 93, 252; 1981, 1657; 1991, 1004; 1999, 105; 2001, 1085)

NRS 178.440 Clerk to certify costs to county or city. The clerk of the court before which an examination has been conducted shall certify the costs to the board of county commissioners or governing body of the city, as appropriate.

[1911 Cr. Prac. § 544; RL § 7394; NCL § 11192] — (NRS A 1969, 10; 1991, 1004)

NRS 178.450 Duties of Administrator or Administrator's designee following finding of incompetence; observation and evaluation of defendant; report to court.

1. The Administrator or the Administrator's designee shall keep each defendant committed to custody under NRS 178.425 or 178.460 under observation and shall have each defendant who has been ordered to report to the Administrator as an outpatient under those sections evaluated periodically.

2. The Administrator or the Administrator's designee shall report in writing to a judge of the court which committed the person and the prosecuting attorney of the county or city to which the person may be returned for further court action whether, in his or her opinion, upon medical consultation, the defendant is of sufficient mentality to be able to understand the nature of the criminal charge against the defendant and, by reason thereof, is able to aid and assist counsel in the defense interposed upon the trial or against the pronouncement of the judgment thereafter. The Administrator or the Administrator's designee shall submit such a report, in the case of a person charged or convicted of a misdemeanor, within 3 months after the order for commitment or treatment and evaluation as an outpatient or for recommitment pursuant to paragraph (b) of subsection 4 of NRS 178.460, and at monthly intervals thereafter. In all other cases, the initial report must be submitted within 6 months after the order and at 6-month intervals thereafter. If the opinion of the Administrator or the Administrator's designee is that the defendant is not of sufficient mentality to understand the nature of the charge against the defendant and assist in the defendant's own defense, the Administrator or the Administrator's designee shall also include in the report his or her opinion whether:

(a) There is a substantial probability that the defendant can receive treatment to competency and will attain competency to stand trial or receive pronouncement of judgment in the foreseeable future; and

(b) The defendant is at that time a danger to himself or herself or to society.

3. The report must contain:

(a) The name of the defendant and the county or city to which the defendant may be returned for further court action.

(b) The circumstances under which the defendant was committed to the custody of the Administrator or the Administrator's designee and the duration of the defendant's hospitalization, or the circumstances under which the defendant was ordered to report to the Administrator or the Administrator's designee as an outpatient.

[2:292:1955] — (NRS A 1961, 476; 1968, 53; 1973, 93, 252; 1981, 1657; 1991, 1004; 1999, 105; 2001, 1085; 2003, 1948)

NRS 178.453 Access by Administrator to certain records of defendant within possession of Department of Corrections authorized for purpose of evaluating and treating defendant.

1. The Administrator or the Administrator's designee may request from the Department of Corrections access to any records in its possession which contain information that may assist in evaluating and treating a defendant who previously has served a term of imprisonment under the supervision of the Department of Corrections and who is committed to the custody of or ordered to report to the Administrator or the Administrator's designee pursuant to NRS 178.425, 178.460, 178.461 or 178.464.

2. Unless otherwise ordered by a court, upon request of the Administrator or the Administrator's designee for access to records of a defendant pursuant to subsection 1, the Department of Corrections, through the designated medical director, shall provide access to any such records, including, without limitation, relevant medical and mental health records, for the limited purpose of allowing the Administrator or the Administrator's designee to evaluate and treat the defendant.

3. No oral or written consent of the defendant is required for the Administrator or the Administrator's designee to obtain access to records from the Department of Corrections pursuant to this section.

4. As used in this section, "designated medical director" means the designated administrative officer of the Department of Corrections who is responsible for the medical treatment of offenders.

(Added to NRS by 2003, 1255; A 2007, 1778)

NRS 178.455 Procedure for evaluating certain defendants following finding of incompetence; report to court; procedure concerning misdemeanants.

1. Except as otherwise provided for persons charged with or convicted of a misdemeanor, the Administrator or the Administrator's designee shall appoint a licensed psychiatrist and a licensed psychologist from the treatment team who is certified pursuant to NRS 178.417 to evaluate the defendant. The Administrator or the Administrator's designee shall also appoint a third evaluator who must be a licensed psychiatrist or psychologist, must be certified pursuant to NRS 178.417 and must not be a member of the treatment team. Upon the completion of the evaluation and treatment of the defendant, the Administrator or the Administrator's designee shall report to the court in writing his or her specific findings and opinion upon whether the person has the present ability to:

(a) Understand the nature of the offense charged;

(b) Understand the nature and purpose of the court proceedings; and

(c) Aid and assist the person's counsel in the defense at any time during the proceedings with a reasonable degree of rational understanding.

2. If the Administrator or the Administrator's designee finds that the person does not have the present ability pursuant to paragraph (a), (b) or (c) of subsection 1 to understand or to aid and assist counsel during the court proceedings, the Administrator or the Administrator's designee shall include in the written report the reasons for the finding and whether there is a substantial probability that the person can receive treatment to competency and will attain competency in the foreseeable future.

3. A copy of the report must be:

(a) Maintained by the Administrator or the Administrator's designee and incorporated in the medical record of the person; and

(b) Sent to the office of the district attorney and to the counsel for the outpatient or person committed.

4. In the case of a person charged with or convicted of a misdemeanor, the judge shall, upon receipt of the report set forth in NRS 178.450 from the Administrator or the Administrator's designee:

(a) Send a copy of the report by the Administrator or the Administrator's designee to the prosecuting attorney and to the defendant's counsel;

(b) Hold a hearing, if one is requested within 10 days after the report is sent pursuant to paragraph (a), at which the attorneys may examine the Administrator or the Administrator's designee or the members of the defendant's treatment team on the determination of the report; and

(c) Within 10 days after the hearing, if any, or 10 days after the report is sent if no hearing is requested, enter a finding of competence or incompetence in the manner set forth in subsection 4 of NRS 178.460.

[Part 3:292:1955] — (NRS A 1961, 476; 1968, 53; 1971, 252; 1973, 93, 252; 1981, 1658; 1991, 1005; 1993, 554, 2773; 1999, 106; 2001, 1086; 2003, 1471, 1949; 2007, 186)

NRS 178.460 Powers and duties of court following finding of incompetence; limitation on length of commitment.

1. If requested by the district attorney or counsel for the defendant within 10 days after the report by the Administrator or the Administrator's designee is sent to them, the judge shall hold a hearing within 10 days after the request at which the district attorney and the defense counsel may examine the members of the treatment team on their report.

2. If the judge orders the appointment of a licensed psychiatrist or psychologist who is not employed by the Division to perform an additional evaluation and report concerning the defendant, the cost of the additional evaluation and report is a charge against the county.

3. Within 10 days after the hearing or 10 days after the report is sent, if no hearing is requested, the judge shall make and enter a finding of competence or incompetence, and if the judge finds the defendant to be incompetent:

(a) Whether there is substantial probability that the defendant can receive treatment to competency and will attain competency to stand trial or receive pronouncement of judgment in the foreseeable future; and

(b) Whether the defendant is at that time a danger to himself or herself or to society.

4. If the judge finds the defendant:

(a) Competent, the judge shall, within 10 days, forward the finding to the prosecuting attorney and counsel for the defendant. Upon receipt thereof, the prosecuting attorney shall notify the sheriff of the county or chief of police of the city that the defendant has been found competent and prearrange with the facility for the return of the defendant to that county or city for trial upon the offense there charged or the pronouncement of judgment, as the case may be.

(b) Incompetent, but there is a substantial probability that the defendant can receive treatment to competency and will attain competency to stand trial or receive pronouncement of judgment in the foreseeable future and finds that the defendant is dangerous to himself or herself or to society, the judge shall recommit the defendant and may order the involuntary administration of medication for the purpose of treatment to competency.

(c) Incompetent, but there is a substantial probability that the defendant can receive treatment to competency and will attain competency to stand trial or receive pronouncement of judgment in the foreseeable future and finds that the defendant is not dangerous to himself or herself or to society, the judge shall order that the defendant remain an outpatient or be transferred to the status of an outpatient under the provisions of NRS 178.425.

(d) Incompetent, with no substantial probability of attaining competency in the foreseeable future, the judge shall order the defendant released from custody or, if the defendant is an outpatient, released from any obligations as an outpatient if, within 10 judicial days, the prosecuting attorney has not filed a motion pursuant to NRS 178.461 or if, within 10 judicial days, a petition is not filed to commit the person pursuant to NRS 433A.200. After the initial 10 judicial days, the person may remain an outpatient or in custody under the provisions of this chapter only as long as the motion or petition is pending unless the person is committed to the custody of the Administrator pursuant to NRS 178.461 or involuntarily committed pursuant to chapter 433A of NRS.

5. Except as otherwise provided in subsection 4 of NRS 178.461, no person who is committed under the provisions of this chapter may be held in the custody of the Administrator or the Administrator's designee longer than the longest period of incarceration provided for the crime or crimes with which the person is charged or 10 years, whichever period is shorter. Upon expiration of the applicable period provided in this section, subsection 4 of NRS 178.461 or subsection 4 of NRS 178.463, the person must be returned to the committing court for a determination as to whether or not involuntary commitment pursuant to chapter 433A of NRS is required.

[Part 3:292:1955] — (NRS A 1961, 477; 1968, 54; 1973, 94, 253; 1981, 1659; 1991, 1006; 1995, 2458; 1999, 107; 2001, 1087; 2003, 1472, 1950; 2007, 187, 1779; 2009, 115)

NRS 178.461 Motion for hearing to determine whether to commit incompetent defendant to custody of Administrator; risk assessment; dismissal of motion in certain circumstances; length of commitment; review of eligibility for conditional release.

1. If the proceedings against a defendant who is charged with any category A felony or a category B felony listed in subsection 6 are dismissed pursuant to subsection 5 of NRS 178.425, the prosecuting attorney may, within 10 judicial days after the dismissal, file a motion with the court for a hearing to determine whether to commit the person to the custody of the Administrator pursuant to subsection 3. Except as otherwise provided in subsection 2, the court shall hold the hearing within 10 judicial days after the motion is filed with the court.

2. If the prosecuting attorney files a motion pursuant to subsection 1, the prosecuting attorney shall, not later than the date on which the prosecuting attorney files the motion, request from the Division a comprehensive risk assessment which indicates whether the person requires the level of security provided by a forensic facility. The Division shall provide the requested comprehensive risk assessment to the court, the prosecuting attorney and counsel for the person not later than three judicial days before the hearing. If the person was charged with any category A felony other than murder or sexual assault or a category B felony listed in subsection 6 and the comprehensive risk assessment indicates that the person does not require the level of security provided by a forensic facility, the court shall dismiss the motion.

3. At a hearing held pursuant to subsection 1, if the court finds by clear and convincing evidence that the person has a mental disorder, that the person is a danger to himself or herself or others and that the person's dangerousness is such that the person requires placement at a forensic facility, the court may order:

(a) The sheriff to take the person into protective custody and transport the person to a forensic facility; and

(b) That the person be committed to the custody of the Administrator and kept under observation until the person is eligible for conditional release pursuant to NRS 178.463 or until the maximum length of commitment described in subsection 4 has expired.

4. The length of commitment of a person pursuant to subsection 3 must not exceed 10 years, including any time that the person has been on conditional release pursuant to NRS 178.463.

5. At least once every 12 months, the court shall review the eligibility of the defendant for conditional release.

6. The provisions of subsection 1 apply to any of the following category B felonies:

(a) Voluntary manslaughter pursuant to NRS 200.050;
(b) Mayhem pursuant to NRS 200.280;
(c) Kidnapping in the second degree pursuant to NRS 200.330;
(d) Assault with a deadly weapon pursuant to NRS 200.471;
(e) Battery with a deadly weapon pursuant to NRS 200.481;
(f) Aggravated stalking pursuant to NRS 200.575;
(g) First degree arson pursuant to NRS 205.010;
(h) Burglary with a deadly weapon pursuant to NRS 205.060;
(i) Invasion of the home with a deadly weapon pursuant to NRS 205.067;
(j) Any category B felony involving the use of a firearm; and
(k) Any attempt to commit a category A felony.

(Added to NRS by 2007, 1777; A 2009, 116; 2015, 1352)

NRS 178.463 Conditional release of incompetent defendant committed to custody of Administrator: When eligible; annual review of eligibility for discharge from conditional release; maximum duration.

1. The Division or a person who is committed to the custody of the Administrator pursuant to NRS 178.461 may petition the court which committed the person for conditional release.

2. A person who is committed to the custody of the Administrator pursuant to NRS 178.461 is eligible for conditional release only after:

(a) The Division has completed a comprehensive risk assessment concerning the person;

(b) A decision to release the person from commitment with conditions imposed by the court in consultation with the Division has been made based on input from the person's treatment team, the prosecuting attorney, the counsel for the person and the team that will supervise the person in the community; and

(c) The court which committed the person has approved the conditional release.

3. If a person is serving a period of conditional release pursuant to this section, the court must, at least once every 12 months, review the eligibility of the defendant for discharge from conditional release. If, at the conclusion of the review required by this subsection, the court finds by clear and convincing evidence that the person is not a danger to himself or herself or others, the court must discharge the person from conditional release.

4. The length of the period of conditional release must not exceed 10 years, including any time that the person has been committed to the custody of the Administrator pursuant to NRS 178.461 and 178.464.

(Added to NRS by 2007, 1777; A 2009, 117; 2015, 1353)

NRS 178.464 Procedure when defendant violates conditions of release; hearing to determine whether to continue, modify or terminate conditional release.

1. The Division shall notify the court which ordered the commitment of the person pursuant to NRS 178.461 if the person violates a condition of the release from commitment.

2. If the court is notified pursuant to subsection 1 of a violation, the court shall consult with the Division, the counsel for the person and the prosecuting attorney concerning the potential risk to the community that is posed by the noncompliance of the person with the conditions of release from commitment.

3. After consulting with the persons required by subsection 2 and considering the risks to the community, the court may issue a temporary order of detention to commit the person to custody for evaluation, pending the hearing described in subsection 4. If the court issues such an order, the court must:

(a) Order the sheriff to take the person:

(1) Into protective custody and transport the person to a forensic facility; or

(2) To a jail where the person must remain in protective custody; and

(b) Provide a copy of the order to the counsel for the person and the prosecuting attorney.

4. Within 10 days after a person has been committed to the custody of the Administrator for evaluation pursuant to subsection 3, the court shall hold a hearing to determine whether to continue, modify or terminate the conditional release of the defendant.

(Added to NRS by 2007, 1778; A 2009, 117)

NRS 178.467 Person committed to custody of Administrator: Eligibility for discharge or conditional release; recommitment for failure to comply with conditions.

1. The Administrator or the Administrator's designee shall keep each person with mental illness committed to his or her custody pursuant to NRS 175.539 under observation.

2. A person committed to the custody of the Administrator pursuant to NRS 175.539 is eligible for:

(a) Discharge from commitment if the person establishes by a preponderance of the evidence that the person would not be a danger, as a result of any mental disorder, to himself or herself or to the person or property of another if discharged; or

(b) Conditional release from commitment if the person establishes by a preponderance of the evidence that the person would not be a danger, as a result of any mental disorder, to himself or herself or to the person or property of another if released from commitment with conditions imposed by the court in consultation with the Division.

3. If a person who is conditionally released from the custody of the Administrator fails to comply with any condition imposed by the court, the court shall issue an order to have the person recommitted to the custody of the Administrator.

(Added to NRS by 2007, 1424)

NRS 178.468 Hearing to determine eligibility of person committed to custody of Administrator for discharge or conditional release; report by Administrator.

1. Except as otherwise provided in this section, a court must hold a hearing not later than 60 days after:

(a) A person is committed to the custody of the Administrator pursuant to NRS 175.539; or

(b) The Division or the person committed to the custody of the Administrator files a petition for discharge or conditional release pursuant to NRS 178.469.

2. During the hearing held pursuant to subsection 1, the court shall consider any relevant information that will enable the court to determine whether the person is eligible for discharge or conditional release pursuant to NRS 178.467. The court may postpone the hearing described in this subsection for good cause or upon agreement by the person committed to the custody of the Administrator, the court and the Division.

3. Not later than 21 days before the date of the hearing held pursuant to paragraph (a) of subsection 1 and annually thereafter, the Administrator or the Administrator's designee shall prepare a written report stating whether, in his or her opinion, upon medical consultation, the person who was committed to the custody of the Administrator has recovered from the mental disorder or has improved to such an extent that the person is no longer a person with mental illness and whether or not, in his or her opinion, the person should be discharged or conditionally released. If the Administrator or the Administrator's designee determines that the person has not recovered from the mental disorder or has not improved to such an extent that the person is no longer a person with mental illness, the Administrator or the Administrator's designee shall include in the report his or her opinion concerning whether:

(a) There is a substantial probability that the person may receive treatment and recover from the mental disorder or improve to such an extent that the person is no longer a person with mental illness in the foreseeable future; and

(b) The person is at that time a danger to himself or herself or to society.

4. If the opinion of the Administrator included in the report prepared pursuant to subsection 3 provides that:

(a) The person committed to custody should not be discharged or conditionally released, the person who is committed may overcome the opinion of the Administrator by proving the elements necessary for discharge or conditional release pursuant to subsection 2 of NRS 178.467 by a preponderance of the evidence.

(b) The person committed to custody should be discharged or conditionally released, the district attorney may overcome the opinion of the Administrator by proving by a preponderance of the evidence that the person continues to be a person with mental illness.

5. Within the period prescribed in subsection 3, the Administrator or the Administrator's designee shall provide a copy of the report to:

(a) The person committed to the custody of the Administrator and the person's attorney;

(b) The prosecuting attorney; and

(c) The court.

(Added to NRS by 2007, 1424)

NRS 178.469 Petition for discharge or conditional release by person committed to custody of Administrator.

1. A person committed to the custody of the Administrator pursuant to NRS 175.539 may petition the court for discharge or conditional release not sooner than 1 year after the person is committed to the custody of the Administrator and not more than once each year thereafter.

2. The Division may file a petition for the discharge or conditional release of a person committed to the custody of the Administrator pursuant to NRS 175.539 at any time if the petition is accompanied by an affidavit of a physician or licensed psychologist which states that the mental disorder of the person has improved since the date of the most recent hearing concerning the discharge or conditional release of the person such that the physician or licensed psychologist recommends the discharge or conditional release of the person.

3. A person who is committed to the custody of the Administrator pursuant to NRS 175.539 may apply for discharge or conditional release pursuant to subsection 1 by:

(a) Filing a petition for discharge or conditional release with the court that ordered the person committed pursuant to NRS 175.539; and

(b) Providing a copy of the petition to the Division and the prosecuting attorney.

4. The Division may file a petition for discharge or conditional release pursuant to subsection 2 by:

(a) Filing the petition with the court that ordered the person committed to the custody of the Administrator pursuant to NRS 175.539;

(b) Including with the petition an affidavit of a physician or licensed psychologist pursuant to subsection 2; and

(c) Providing a copy of the petition to the person committed to the custody of the Administrator, the person's attorney and the prosecuting attorney.

(Added to NRS by 2007, 1425)

NRS 178.471 Effect of conditional release of person committed to custody of Administrator; authority of court over person conditionally released.

1. When a person is conditionally released pursuant to NRS 178.467 to 178.471, inclusive:

(a) The State and any of its agents or employees are not liable for any debts or contractual obligations, medical or otherwise, incurred or damages caused by the actions of the person; and

(b) The court shall order the restoration of full civil and legal rights as deemed necessary to facilitate the person's rehabilitation.

2. When a person is conditionally released pursuant to NRS 178.467 to 178.471, inclusive, the court shall order the Division to conduct an evaluation of the person as often as is deemed necessary to determine whether the person:

(a) Has complied with the conditions of release; or

(b) Presents a clear and present danger of harm to himself or herself or others.

3. The court may order a person who is conditionally released pursuant to NRS 178.467 to 178.471, inclusive, returned to the custody of the Administrator if the court determines that the conditional release is no longer appropriate because that person:

(a) Has violated a condition of release; or

(b) Presents a clear and present danger of harm to himself or herself or others.

(Added to NRS by 2007, 1426)

NRS 178.4715 Notification of victims upon discharge, conditional release or escape.

1. If a person is committed to the custody of the Administrator and is subject to the provisions of NRS 178.463 to 178.471, inclusive, a victim of the person may request the Administrator or the Administrator's designee to notify the victim of the person's discharge, conditional release or escape from the custody of the Administrator by submitting to the Administrator:

(a) A written request for notification; and

(b) The current address of the victim.

2. If the Administrator or the Administrator's designee receives a request for notification pursuant to subsection 1, the Administrator or the Administrator's designee shall notify the victim if the person committed to the custody of the Administrator:

(a) Will be discharged or conditionally released pursuant to NRS 178.463 to 178.471, inclusive, at least 10 days before the discharge or release; or

(b) Has escaped from the custody of the Administrator.

3. A person described in subsection 1 must not be discharged or released from commitment, temporarily or otherwise, for any purpose unless notification of the discharge or release has been mailed to the last known address of every victim of the person who has requested notification pursuant to subsection 1.

4. The Administrator or the Administrator's designee may not be held responsible for any injury proximately caused by the failure to give any notice required pursuant to this section if no address was provided to the Administrator or the Administrator's designee or if the address provided is inaccurate or not current.

5. All personal information, including, but not limited to, a current or former address, which pertains to a victim and which is received by the Administrator or the Administrator's designee pursuant to this section is confidential.

6. As used in this section, "victim" means:

(a) A person, including, without limitation, a governmental entity, against whom an act has been committed for which the person committed to the custody of the Administrator has been charged;

(b) A person who has been injured or killed as a direct result of the commission of an act for which the person committed to the custody of the Administrator has been charged; or

(c) A relative of a person described in paragraph (a) or (b). For the purposes of this paragraph, a "relative" of a person includes:

(1) A spouse, parent, grandparent or stepparent;

(2) A natural born child, stepchild or adopted child;

(3) A grandchild, brother, sister, half brother or half sister; or

(4) A parent of a spouse.

(Added to NRS by 2009, 71)

TIME

NRS 178.472 Computation. In computing any period of time the day of the act or event from which the designated period of time begins to run shall not be included. The last day of the period so computed shall be included, unless it is a Saturday, a Sunday, or a nonjudicial day, in which event the period runs until the end of the next day which is not a Saturday, a Sunday, or a nonjudicial day. When a period of time prescribed or allowed is less than 7 days, intermediate Saturdays, Sundays and nonjudicial days shall be excluded in the computation.

(Added to NRS by 1967, 1451)

NRS 178.476 Enlargement. When an act is required or allowed to be done at or within a specified time, the court for cause shown may at any time in its discretion:

1. With or without motion or notice, order the period enlarged if request therefor is made before the expiration of the period originally prescribed or as extended by a previous order; or

2. Upon motion made after the expiration of the specified period permit the act to be done if the failure to act was the result of excusable neglect,
Ê but the court may not extend the time for taking any action under NRS 176.515 or 176.525 except to the extent and under the conditions stated in those sections.
(Added to NRS by 1967, 1451; A 1969, 10; 1985, 63)

NRS 178.478 Motions; affidavits.
1. A written motion, other than one which may be heard ex parte, and notice of the hearing thereof must be served not later than 5 days before the time specified for the hearing unless a different period is fixed by rule or order of the court. For cause shown such an order may be made on ex parte application.
2. When a motion is supported by affidavit, the affidavit must be served with the motion; and opposing affidavits may be served not less than 1 day before the hearing unless the court permits them to be served at a later time.
3. A certificate of service must accompany each motion filed.
(Added to NRS by 1967, 1451; A 1991, 303)

NRS 178.482 Additional time after service by mail. Whenever a party has the right or is required to do an act within a prescribed period after the service of a notice or other paper upon the party and the notice or other paper is served by mail, 3 days shall be added to the prescribed period.
(Added to NRS by 1967, 1451)

BAIL

NRS 178.484 Right to bail before conviction; exceptions; imposition of conditions; arrest for violation of condition.
1. Except as otherwise provided in this section, a person arrested for an offense other than murder of the first degree must be admitted to bail.
2. A person arrested for a felony who has been released on probation or parole for a different offense must not be admitted to bail unless:
(a) A court issues an order directing that the person be admitted to bail;
(b) The State Board of Parole Commissioners directs the detention facility to admit the person to bail; or
(c) The Division of Parole and Probation of the Department of Public Safety directs the detention facility to admit the person to bail.
3. A person arrested for a felony whose sentence has been suspended pursuant to NRS 4.373 or 5.055 for a different offense or who has been sentenced to a term of residential confinement pursuant to NRS 4.3762 or 5.076 for a different offense must not be admitted to bail unless:
(a) A court issues an order directing that the person be admitted to bail; or
(b) A department of alternative sentencing directs the detention facility to admit the person to bail.
4. A person arrested for murder of the first degree may be admitted to bail unless the proof is evident or the presumption great by any competent court or magistrate authorized by law to do so in the exercise of discretion, giving due weight to the evidence and to the nature and circumstances of the offense.
5. A person arrested for a violation of NRS 484C.110, 484C.120, 484C.130, 484C.430, 488.410, 488.420 or 488.425 who is under the influence of intoxicating liquor must not be admitted to bail or released on the person's own recognizance unless the person has a concentration of alcohol of less than 0.04 in his or her breath. A test of the person's breath pursuant to this subsection to determine the concentration of alcohol in his or her breath as a condition of admission to bail or release is not admissible as evidence against the person.
6. A person arrested for a violation of NRS 484C.110, 484C.120, 484C.130, 484C.430, 488.410, 488.420 or 488.425 who is under the influence of a controlled substance, is under the combined influence of intoxicating liquor and a controlled substance, or inhales, ingests, applies or otherwise uses any chemical, poison or organic solvent, or any compound or combination of any of these, to a degree which renders the person incapable of safely driving or exercising actual physical control of a vehicle or vessel under power or sail must not be admitted to bail or released on the person's own recognizance sooner than 12 hours after arrest.
7. A person arrested for a battery that constitutes domestic violence pursuant to NRS 33.018 must not be admitted to bail sooner than 12 hours after arrest. If the person is admitted to bail more than 12 hours after arrest, without appearing personally before a magistrate or without the amount of bail having been otherwise set by a magistrate or a court, the amount of bail must be:
(a) Three thousand dollars, if the person has no previous convictions of battery that constitute domestic violence pursuant to NRS 33.018 and there is no reason to believe that the battery for which the person has been arrested resulted in substantial bodily harm or was committed by strangulation;
(b) Five thousand dollars, if the person has:
(1) No previous convictions of battery that constitute domestic violence pursuant to NRS 33.018, but there is reason to believe that the battery for which the person has been arrested resulted in substantial bodily harm or was committed by strangulation; or
(2) One previous conviction of battery that constitutes domestic violence pursuant to NRS 33.018, but there is no reason to believe that the battery for which the person has been arrested resulted in substantial bodily harm or was committed by strangulation; or
(c) Fifteen thousand dollars, if the person has:
(1) One previous conviction of battery that constitutes domestic violence pursuant to NRS 33.018 and there is reason to believe that the battery for which the person has been arrested resulted in substantial bodily harm or was committed by strangulation; or
(2) Two or more previous convictions of battery that constitute domestic violence pursuant to NRS 33.018.
Ê The provisions of this subsection do not affect the authority of a magistrate or a court to set the amount of bail when the person personally appears before the magistrate or the court, or when a magistrate or a court has otherwise been contacted to set the amount of bail. For the

purposes of this subsection, a person shall be deemed to have a previous conviction of battery that constitutes domestic violence pursuant to NRS 33.018 if the person has been convicted of such an offense in this State or has been convicted of violating a law of any other jurisdiction that prohibits the same or similar conduct.

8. A person arrested for violating a temporary or extended order for protection against domestic violence issued pursuant to NRS 33.017 to 33.100, inclusive, or for violating a restraining order or injunction that is in the nature of a temporary or extended order for protection against domestic violence issued in an action or proceeding brought pursuant to title 11 of NRS, or for violating a temporary or extended order for protection against stalking, aggravated stalking or harassment issued pursuant to NRS 200.591, or for violating a temporary or extended order for protection against sexual assault pursuant to NRS 200.378 must not be admitted to bail sooner than 12 hours after arrest if:

(a) The arresting officer determines that such a violation is accompanied by a direct or indirect threat of harm;

(b) The person has previously violated a temporary or extended order for protection of the type for which the person has been arrested; or

(c) At the time of the violation or within 2 hours after the violation, the person has:

(1) A concentration of alcohol of 0.08 or more in the person's blood or breath; or

(2) An amount of a prohibited substance in the person's blood or urine that is equal to or greater than the amount set forth in subsection 3 of NRS 484C.110.

9. If a person is admitted to bail more than 12 hours after arrest, pursuant to subsection 8, without appearing personally before a magistrate or without the amount of bail having been otherwise set by a magistrate or a court, the amount of bail must be:

(a) Three thousand dollars, if the person has no previous convictions of violating a temporary or extended order for protection against domestic violence issued pursuant to NRS 33.017 to 33.100, inclusive, or of violating a restraining order or injunction that is in the nature of a temporary or extended order for protection against domestic violence issued in an action or proceeding brought pursuant to title 11 of NRS, or of violating a temporary or extended order for protection against stalking, aggravated stalking or harassment issued pursuant to NRS 200.591, or of violating a temporary or extended order for protection against sexual assault pursuant to NRS 200.378;

(b) Five thousand dollars, if the person has one previous conviction of violating a temporary or extended order for protection against domestic violence issued pursuant to NRS 33.017 to 33.100, inclusive, or of violating a restraining order or injunction that is in the nature of a temporary or extended order for protection against domestic violence issued in an action or proceeding brought pursuant to title 11 of NRS, or of violating a temporary or extended order for protection against stalking, aggravated stalking or harassment issued pursuant to NRS 200.591, or of violating a temporary or extended order for protection against sexual assault pursuant to NRS 200.378; or

(c) Fifteen thousand dollars, if the person has two or more previous convictions of violating a temporary or extended order for protection against domestic violence issued pursuant to NRS 33.017 to 33.100, inclusive, or of violating a restraining order or injunction that is in the nature of a temporary or extended order for protection against domestic violence issued in an action or proceeding brought pursuant to title 11 of NRS, or of violating a temporary or extended order for protection against stalking, aggravated stalking or harassment issued pursuant to NRS 200.591, or of violating a temporary or extended order for protection against sexual assault pursuant to NRS 200.378.

Ê The provisions of this subsection do not affect the authority of a magistrate or a court to set the amount of bail when the person personally appears before the magistrate or the court or when a magistrate or a court has otherwise been contacted to set the amount of bail. For the purposes of this subsection, a person shall be deemed to have a previous conviction of violating a temporary or extended order for protection against domestic violence issued pursuant to NRS 33.017 to 33.100, inclusive, or of violating a restraining order or injunction that is in the nature of a temporary or extended order for protection against domestic violence issued in an action or proceeding brought pursuant to title 11 of NRS, or of violating a temporary or extended order for protection against stalking, aggravated stalking or harassment issued pursuant to NRS 200.591, or of violating a temporary or extended order for protection against sexual assault pursuant to NRS 200.378, if the person has been convicted of such an offense in this State or has been convicted of violating a law of any other jurisdiction that prohibits the same or similar conduct.

10. The court may, before releasing a person arrested for an offense punishable as a felony, require the surrender to the court of any passport the person possesses.

11. Before releasing a person arrested for any crime, the court may impose such reasonable conditions on the person as it deems necessary to protect the health, safety and welfare of the community and to ensure that the person will appear at all times and places ordered by the court, including, without limitation:

(a) Requiring the person to remain in this State or a certain county within this State;

(b) Prohibiting the person from contacting or attempting to contact a specific person or from causing or attempting to cause another person to contact that person on the person's behalf;

(c) Prohibiting the person from entering a certain geographic area; or

(d) Prohibiting the person from engaging in specific conduct that may be harmful to the person's own health, safety or welfare, or the health, safety or welfare of another person.

Ê In determining whether a condition is reasonable, the court shall consider the factors listed in NRS 178.4853.

12. If a person fails to comply with a condition imposed pursuant to subsection 11, the court may, after providing the person with reasonable notice and an opportunity for a hearing:

(a) Deem such conduct a contempt pursuant to NRS 22.010; or

(b) Increase the amount of bail pursuant to NRS 178.499.

13. An order issued pursuant to this section that imposes a condition on a person admitted to bail must include a provision ordering any law enforcement officer to arrest the person if the officer has probable cause to believe that the person has violated a condition of bail.

14. Before a person may be admitted to bail, the person must sign a document stating that:

(a) The person will appear at all times and places as ordered by the court releasing the person and as ordered by any court before which the charge is subsequently heard;

(b) The person will comply with the other conditions which have been imposed by the court and are stated in the document; and

(c) If the person fails to appear when so ordered and is taken into custody outside of this State, the person waives all rights relating to extradition proceedings.

Ê The signed document must be filed with the clerk of the court of competent jurisdiction as soon as practicable, but in no event later than the next business day.

15. If a person admitted to bail fails to appear as ordered by a court and the jurisdiction incurs any cost in returning the person to the jurisdiction to stand trial, the person who failed to appear is responsible for paying those costs as restitution.

16. For the purposes of subsections 8 and 9, an order or injunction is in the nature of a temporary or extended order for protection against domestic violence if it grants relief that might be given in a temporary or extended order issued pursuant to NRS 33.017 to 33.100, inclusive.

17. As used in this section, "strangulation" has the meaning ascribed to it in NRS 200.481.

(Added to NRS by 1967, 1451; A 1971, 496; 1973, 1802; 1975, 1201; 1977, 1545; 1981, 1585; 1985, 2171; 1987, 554; 1995, 26, 2293; 1997, 610, 1478, 3357; 1999, 669, 2064; 2001, 1223, 2571; 2007, 50, 1017; 2009, 93, 234, 1880)

NRS 178.4851 Release without bail; imposition of conditions; arrest for violation of condition.

1. Upon a showing of good cause, a court may release without bail any person entitled to bail if it appears to the court that it can impose conditions on the person that will adequately protect the health, safety and welfare of the community and ensure that the person will appear at all times and places ordered by the court.

2. In releasing a person without bail, the court may impose such conditions as it deems necessary to protect the health, safety and welfare of the community and to ensure that the person will appear at all times and places ordered by the court, including, without limitation, any condition set forth in subsection 11 of NRS 178.484.

3. Upon a showing of good cause, a sheriff or chief of police may release without bail any person charged with a misdemeanor pursuant to standards established by a court of competent jurisdiction.

4. Before a person may be released without bail, the person must file with the clerk of the court of competent jurisdiction a signed document stating that:

(a) The person will appear at all times and places as ordered by the court releasing the person and as ordered by any court before which the charge is subsequently heard;

(b) The person will comply with the other conditions which have been imposed by the court and are stated in the document;

(c) If the person fails to appear when so ordered and is taken into custody outside of this State, the person waives all rights relating to extradition proceedings; and

(d) The person understands that any court of competent jurisdiction may revoke the order of release without bail and may order the person into custody or require the person to furnish bail or otherwise ensure the protection of the health, safety and welfare of the community or the person's appearance.

5. If a jurisdiction incurs any costs in returning a person to the jurisdiction to stand trial, the person failing to appear is responsible for paying those costs as restitution.

6. An order issued pursuant to this section that imposes a condition on a person who is released without bail must include a provision ordering a law enforcement officer to arrest the person if the law enforcement officer has probable cause to believe that the person has violated a condition of release.

(Added to NRS by 1981, 1584; A 1987, 454; 1997, 3359; 2001, 1226; 2007, 53, 1020)

NRS 178.4853 Factors considered before release without bail. In deciding whether there is good cause to release a person without bail, the court as a minimum shall consider the following factors concerning the person:

1. The length of residence in the community;
2. The status and history of employment;
3. Relationships with the person's spouse and children, parents or other family members and with close friends;
4. Reputation, character and mental condition;
5. Prior criminal record, including, without limitation, any record of appearing or failing to appear after release on bail or without bail;
6. The identity of responsible members of the community who would vouch for the reliability of the person;
7. The nature of the offense with which the person is charged, the apparent probability of conviction and the likely sentence, insofar as these factors relate to the risk of not appearing;
8. The nature and seriousness of the danger to the alleged victim, any other person or the community that would be posed by the person's release;
9. The likelihood of more criminal activity by the person after release; and
10. Any other factors concerning the person's ties to the community or bearing on the risk that the person may willfully fail to appear.

(Added to NRS by 1981, 1584; A 1985, 809; 1997, 3360)

NRS 178.4855 Limitations on release without bail of certain defendants who are taken into custody while admitted to bail on other charges; notice to bail agent required. A defendant charged with the commission of a category A or B felony who is admitted to bail on a surety bond and who:

1. While admitted to bail, is taken into custody in the same jurisdiction in which the defendant was admitted to bail and is charged with the commission of another category A or B felony; and
2. Is ordered to be released from custody without bail,

Ê must not be released from custody pursuant to NRS 178.4851 until the law enforcement agency that conducted the initial booking procedure for the defendant for the subsequent felony has notified the bail agent that issued the surety bond of the release of the defendant.

(Added to NRS by 1999, 1845)

NRS 178.486 When bail is matter of discretion, notice of application must be given to district attorney. When the admission to bail is a matter of discretion, the court, or officer by whom it may be ordered, shall require such notice of the application therefor as the court or officer may deem reasonable to be given to the district attorney of the county where the examination is had.

(Added to NRS by 1967, 1452)

NRS 178.487 Bail after arrest for felony offense committed while on bail. Every release on bail with or without security is conditioned upon the defendant's good behavior while so released, and upon a showing that the proof is evident or the presumption great that the defendant has committed a felony during the period of release, the defendant's bail may be revoked, after a hearing, by the magistrate who allowed it or by any judge of the court in which the original charge is pending. Pending such revocation, the defendant may be held without bail by order of the magistrate before whom the defendant is brought after an arrest upon the second charge.

(Added to NRS by 1971, 574; A 1973, 348)

NRS 178.4871 Postconviction petitioner for habeas corpus: Limitations on release. A person who has filed a postconviction petition for habeas corpus:

1. Must not in any case be released on the person's own recognizance.
2. Must not be admitted to bail pending a review of the petition unless:

(a) The petition is filed in the proper jurisdiction;
(b) The petition presents substantial questions of law or fact and does not appear to be barred procedurally;
(c) The petitioner has made out a clear case on the merits; and
(d) There are exceptional circumstances deserving of special treatment in the interests of justice.

(Added to NRS by 1987, 1232; A 1991, 91)

NRS 178.4873 Postconviction petitioner for habeas corpus: Release pending appeal. If a district court denies a postconviction petition for habeas corpus, the petitioner must not be released on the petitioner's own recognizance or admitted to bail pending any appeal. If the petition is granted and a stay of the order granting relief is not entered, the district court shall admit the petitioner to bail pending appeal if the respondent files a notice of appeal.

(Added to NRS by 1987, 1232; A 1991, 91)

NRS 178.4875 Proceeding for forfeiture of bail pending review or appeal; proceeding for recommitment of defendant.

1. If the court admits a petitioner to bail pending review of the petition or pending appeal, any subsequent proceeding for forfeiture of the bail must take place in the proceeding on the petition.
2. Any subsequent proceeding for the recommitment of the defendant pursuant to NRS 178.532 may be initiated on behalf of the State in the proceeding on the petition or in the district court where the original conviction was had, if it was in a different court. If the proceeding occurs in the district court where the original conviction was had, that court must notify the court conducting the proceeding on the petition of any order for recommitment entered and subsequently enforced.

(Added to NRS by 1987, 1232)

NRS 178.488 Right to bail upon review; notice of application to be given district attorney.

1. Bail may be allowed pending appeal or certiorari unless it appears that the appeal is frivolous or taken for delay.
2. Pending appeal to a district court, bail may be allowed by the trial justice, by the district court, or by any judge thereof, to run until final termination of the proceedings in all courts.
3. Pending appeal or certiorari to the appellate court of competent jurisdiction pursuant to the rules fixed by the Supreme Court pursuant to Section 4 of Article 6 of the Nevada Constitution, bail may be allowed by the district court or any judge thereof, by the Court of Appeals or any judge thereof or by the Supreme Court or a justice thereof.
4. Any court or any judge or justice authorized to grant bail may at any time revoke the order admitting the defendant to bail.
5. The court or judge by whom bail may be ordered shall require such notice of the application therefor as the court or judge may deem reasonable to be given to the district attorney of the county in which the verdict or judgment was originally rendered.

(Added to NRS by 1967, 1452; A 1969, 10; 2013, 1762)

NRS 178.494 Bail for witnesses; judicial review of detention or amount of bail.

1. If it appears by affidavit that the testimony of a person is material in any criminal proceeding and if it is shown that it may become impracticable to secure the person's presence by subpoena, the magistrate may require bail for the person's appearance as a witness, in an amount fixed by the magistrate. If the person fails to give bail the magistrate may:

(a) Commit the person to the custody of a peace officer pending final disposition of the proceeding in which the testimony is needed;
(b) Order the person's release if the person has been detained for an unreasonable length of time; and
(c) Modify at any time the requirement as to bail.

2. Every person detained as a material witness must be brought before a judge or magistrate within 72 hours after the beginning of the detention. The judge or magistrate shall make a determination whether:

(a) The amount of bail required to be given by the material witness should be modified; and
(b) The detention of the material witness should continue.

Ê The judge or magistrate shall set a schedule for the periodic review of whether the amount of bail required should be modified and whether detention should continue.

(Added to NRS by 1967, 1452; A 1989, 327)

NRS 178.498 Amount. If the defendant is admitted to bail, the bail must be set at an amount which in the judgment of the magistrate will reasonably ensure the appearance of the defendant and the safety of other persons and of the community, having regard to:

1. The nature and circumstances of the offense charged;
2. The financial ability of the defendant to give bail;
3. The character of the defendant; and
4. The factors listed in NRS 178.4853.

(Added to NRS by 1967, 1452; A 1985, 809)

NRS 178.499 Increase in amount.

1. At any time after a district or Justice Court has ordered bail to be set at a specific amount, and before acquittal or conviction, the court may upon its own motion or upon motion of the district attorney and after notice to the defendant's attorney of record or, if none, to the defendant, increase the amount of bail for good cause shown.

2. If the defendant has been released on bail before the time when the motion to increase bail is granted, the defendant shall either return to custody or give the additional amount of bail.

(Added to NRS by 1969, 385; A 1991, 303)

NRS 178.502 Form of bail; extension of bond or undertaking to proceedings in other courts; exoneration; place of deposit.

1. A person required or permitted to give bail shall execute a bond for the person's appearance. The magistrate or court or judge or justice, having regard to the considerations set forth in NRS 178.498, may require one or more sureties or may authorize the acceptance of cash or bonds or notes of the United States in an amount equal to or less than the face amount of the bond.

2. Any bond or undertaking for bail must provide that the bond or undertaking:

(a) Extends to any action or proceeding in a Justice Court, municipal court or district court:

(1) Arising from the charge on which bail was first given in any of these courts; and

(2) Arising from a later charge, filed before the expiration of the periods provided in subsection 4, which is substantially similar to the charge upon which bail was first given and is based upon the same act or omission as that charge; and

(b) Remains in effect until exonerated by the court.

Ê This subsection does not require that any bond or undertaking extend to proceedings on appeal.

3. If an action or proceeding against a defendant who has been admitted to bail is transferred to another trial court, the bond or undertaking must be transferred to the clerk of the court to which the action or proceeding has been transferred.

4. If the action or proceeding against a defendant who has been admitted to bail is dismissed, the bail must not be exonerated until a period of 30 days has elapsed from the entry of the order of dismissal unless the defendant requests that bail be exonerated before the expiration of the 30-day period. If no formal action or proceeding is instituted against a defendant who has been admitted to bail, the bail must not be exonerated until a period of 30 days has elapsed from the day the bond or undertaking is posted unless the defendant requests that bail be exonerated before the expiration of the 30-day period.

5. If, within the periods provided in subsection 4, the defendant is charged with a public offense arising out of the same act or omission supporting the charge upon which bail was first given, the prosecuting attorney shall forthwith notify the clerk of the court where the bond was posted, the bail must be applied to the public offense later charged, and the bond or undertaking must be transferred to the clerk of the appropriate court. Within 10 days after its receipt, the clerk of the court to whom the bail is transferred shall mail notice of the transfer to the surety on the bond and the bail agent who executed the bond.

6. Bail given originally on appeal must be deposited with the magistrate or the clerk of the court from which the appeal is taken.

(Added to NRS by 1967, 1452; A 1979, 1021; 1981, 1585; 2003, 2103)

NRS 178.504 Justification of sureties.

1. Every surety, except a corporate surety which is approved as provided by law, shall justify by affidavit and may be required to describe in the affidavit:

(a) The property by which the surety proposes to justify and the encumbrances thereon;

(b) The number and amount of other bonds and undertakings for bail entered into by the surety and remaining undischarged; and

(c) All other liabilities.

2. No bond shall be approved unless the surety thereon appears to be qualified.

3. A corporate surety that is authorized to transact insurance in this State pursuant to chapter 680A of NRS is a sufficient surety for all courts and shall be deemed to be qualified for purposes of this section.

(Added to NRS by 1967, 1453; A 2009, 240)

NRS 178.506 Declaration of forfeiture. If there is a breach of condition of a bond, the court shall declare a forfeiture of the bail, subject to the provisions of NRS 178.508 and 178.509.

(Added to NRS by 1967, 1453; A 1971, 598)

NRS 178.508 Duties of court when defendant fails to appear; procedure for issuing order of forfeiture; when forfeiture becomes effective; grounds for extending date of forfeiture.

1. If the defendant fails to appear when the defendant's presence in court is lawfully required for the commission of a misdemeanor and the failure to appear is not excused or is lawfully required for the commission of a gross misdemeanor or felony, the court shall:

(a) Enter upon its minutes that the defendant failed to appear;

(b) Not later than 45 days after the date on which the defendant failed to appear, order the issuance of a warrant for the arrest of the defendant; and

(c) If the undertaking exceeds $50 or money deposited instead of bail bond exceeds $500, direct that each surety and the local agent of each surety, or the depositor if the depositor is not the defendant, be given notice that the defendant has failed to appear, by certified mail within 20 days after the date on which the defendant failed to appear. The court shall execute an affidavit of such mailing to be kept as an official public record of the court and shall direct that a copy of the notice be transmitted to the prosecuting attorney at the same time that notice is given to each surety or the depositor.

2. Except as otherwise provided in subsection 3 and NRS 178.509, an order of forfeiture of any undertaking or money deposited instead of bail bond must be prepared by the clerk of the court and signed by the court. An order of forfeiture must include the date on which the forfeiture becomes effective. The undertaking or money deposited instead of bail bond is forfeited 180 days after the date on which the notice is mailed pursuant to subsection 1.

3. The court may extend the date of the forfeiture for any reasonable period set by the court if the surety or depositor submits to the court:

(a) An application for an extension and the court determines that the surety or the depositor is making reasonable and ongoing efforts to bring the defendant before the court.

(b) An application for an extension on the ground that the defendant is temporarily prevented from appearing before the court because the defendant:

(1) Is ill;

(2) Is insane; or

(3) Is being detained by civil or military authorities,

Ê and the court, upon hearing the matter, determines that one or more of the grounds described in this paragraph exist and that the surety or depositor did not in any way cause or aid the absence of the defendant.

(Added to NRS by 1967, 1453; A 1969, 625; 1971, 598; 1979, 1400; 1983, 210; 1987, 1025; 1991, 1015; 1999, 1845; 2003, 2103; 2015, 2567)

NRS 178.509 Exoneration of surety before date of forfeiture: Conditions; grounds.

1. If the defendant fails to appear when the defendant's presence in court is lawfully required, the court shall not exonerate the surety before the date of forfeiture prescribed in NRS 178.508unless:

(a) The defendant appears before the court and the court, upon hearing the matter, determines that the defendant has presented a satisfactory excuse or that the surety did not in any way cause or aid the absence of the defendant; or

(b) The surety submits an application for exoneration on the ground that the defendant is unable to appear because the defendant:

(1) Is dead;

(2) Is ill;

(3) Is insane;

(4) Is being detained by civil or military authorities; or

(5) Has been deported,

Ê and the court, upon hearing the matter, determines that one or more of the grounds described in this paragraph exist and that the surety did not in any way cause or aid the absence of the defendant.

2. If the requirements of subsection 1 are met, the court may exonerate the surety upon such terms as may be just.

(Added to NRS by 1971, 597; A 1979, 1400; 1991, 1015; 1999, 1846; 2007, 420; 2015, 2567)

NRS 178.512 Setting aside forfeiture: Conditions; grounds; when written finding is required.

1. The court shall not set aside a forfeiture unless:

(a) The surety submits an application to set it aside on the ground that the defendant:

(1) Has appeared before the court since the date of the forfeiture and has presented a satisfactory excuse for the defendant's absence;

(2) Was dead before the date of the forfeiture but the surety did not know and could not reasonably have known of the defendant's death before that date;

(3) Was unable to appear before the court before the date of the forfeiture because of the defendant's illness or insanity, but the surety did not know and could not reasonably have known of the illness or insanity before that date;

(4) Was unable to appear before the court before the date of the forfeiture because the defendant was being detained by civil or military authorities, but the surety did not know and could not reasonably have known of the defendant's detention before that date; or

(5) Was unable to appear before the court before the date of the forfeiture because the defendant was deported, but the surety did not know and could not reasonably have known of the defendant's deportation before that date,

Ê and the court, upon hearing the matter, determines that one or more of the grounds described in this subsection exist and that the surety did not in any way cause or aid the absence of the defendant; and

(b) The court determines that justice does not require the enforcement of the forfeiture.

2. If the court sets aside a forfeiture pursuant to subsection 1 and the forfeiture includes any undertaking or money deposited instead of bail bond where the defendant has been charged with a gross misdemeanor or felony, the court shall make a written finding in support of setting aside the forfeiture.

(Added to NRS by 1967, 1453; A 1979, 1401; 1999, 1847; 2003, 2104, 3338; 2005, 108; 2015, 2568)

NRS 178.514 Enforcement of forfeiture.

1. When a forfeiture has not been set aside, the court shall on motion enter a judgment of default and execution may issue thereon.

2. If an order setting aside a forfeiture has not been entered within 180 days after the issuance of the order of forfeiture, the court shall enter judgment by default and commence execution proceedings therein.

3. By entering into a bond the obligors submit to the jurisdiction of the court and irrevocably appoint the clerk of the court as their agent upon whom any papers affecting their liability may be served. Their liability may be enforced on motion and such notice of the motion as the court prescribes may be served on the clerk of the court, who shall forthwith mail copies to the obligors to their last known addresses.

(Added to NRS by 1967, 1453; A 2003, 2105; 2015, 2568)

NRS 178.516 Remission of forfeited money. After entry of such judgment, the court shall not remit it in whole or in part unless the conditions applying to the setting aside of forfeiture in NRS 178.512 are met.

(Added to NRS by 1967, 1453; A 1979, 1402)

NRS 178.518 Payment of forfeited deposits to county treasurer or State Controller. Money collected pursuant to NRS 178.506 to 178.516, inclusive, which was collected:

1. From a person who was charged with a misdemeanor must be paid over to the county treasurer.

2. From a person who was charged with a gross misdemeanor or a felony must be paid over to the State Controller for deposit in the State General Fund for distribution in the following manner:

(a) Ninety percent for credit to the Fund for the Compensation of Victims of Crime; and

(b) Ten percent for credit to the special account established pursuant to NRS 176.0613 to assist with funding and establishing specialty court programs.

(Added to NRS by 1967, 1453; A 1981, 1672; 2001, 2922; 2003, 2105)

NRS 178.522 Exoneration of bail.

1. When the condition of the bond has been satisfied or the forfeiture thereof has been set aside or remitted, the court shall exonerate the obligors and release any bail. The court shall exonerate the obligors and release any bail at the time of sentencing the defendant, if the court has not previously done so unless the money deposited by the defendant as bail must be applied to satisfy a judgment pursuant to NRS 178.528.

2. A surety may be exonerated by a deposit of cash in the amount of the bond or by a timely surrender of the defendant into custody.

(Added to NRS by 1967, 1453; A 1969, 10; 1991, 1016; 1993, 827)

NRS 178.524 Deposit required in certain cases. If the defendant surrenders himself or herself to, is apprehended by or is in the custody of a peace officer in the State of Nevada or the Director of the Department of Corrections other than the officer to whose custody the defendant was committed at the time of giving bail, the bail may make application to the court for the discharge of the bail bond, and shall then give to the court an amount in cash or a surety bond sufficient in amount to guarantee reimbursement of any costs that may be expended in returning the defendant to the officer to whose custody the defendant was committed at the time of giving bail.

(Added to NRS by 1967, 1453; A 1977, 863; 2001 Special Session, 223)

NRS 178.526 Arrest of defendant.

1. For the purpose of surrendering a defendant, a surety, at any time before the surety is finally discharged, and at any place within this State, may, by:

(a) Written authorization for the arrest of the defendant attached to a copy of the undertaking; or

(b) A written authority endorsed on a certified copy of the undertaking,

Ê cause the defendant to be arrested by a bail agent or bail enforcement agent who is licensed pursuant to chapter 697 of NRS.

2. A bail agent or bail enforcement agent who arrests a defendant in this State or any other jurisdiction is not acting for or on behalf of this State or any of its political subdivisions.

(Added to NRS by 1967, 1454; A 1997, 3393; 1999, 1847)

NRS 178.528 Disposition of money deposited as bail. When money has been deposited, if it remains on deposit at the time of a judgment for the payment of a fine, the court, or the clerk under the direction of the court, shall apply the money in satisfaction thereof, and after satisfying the fine and costs shall refund the surplus, if any, to the person who deposited the bail, unless that person has directed, in writing, that any surplus be refunded to another.

(Added to NRS by 1967, 1454; A 1991, 303)

NRS 178.532 Recommitment of defendant after having given bail or deposited money. The court to which the committing magistrate shall return the depositions and statement, or in which an indictment or information or an appeal is pending, or to which a judgment on appeal is remitted to be carried into effect, may, by an order to be entered on its minutes, direct the arrest of the defendant and commitment to the officer to whose custody the defendant was committed at the time of giving bail, and the defendant's detention until legally discharged, in the following cases:

1. When, by reason of the defendant's failure to appear, the defendant has incurred a forfeiture of bail, or of money deposited instead thereof, as provided in NRS 178.506.

2. When it satisfactorily appears to the court that the defendant's bail, or either of them, are dead, or insufficient, or have removed from the State.

3. Upon an indictment being found or information filed in the cases provided in NRS 173.175.

(Added to NRS by 1967, 1454)

NRS 178.534 Contents of order for recommitment. The order for the recommitment of the defendant shall:

1. Recite generally the facts upon which it is founded.

2. Direct that the defendant be arrested by any sheriff, constable, marshal, police officer or other peace officer within the State, and committed to the custody of the sheriff of the county where the depositions and statement were returned, or the indictment was found, or the information was filed, or the conviction was had, as the case may be, to be detained until legally discharged.

(Added to NRS by 1967, 1454)

NRS 178.536 Arrest on order of recommitment. The defendant may be arrested pursuant to the order, upon a certified copy thereof, in any county, in the same manner as upon a warrant of arrest, except that when arrested in another county the order need not be endorsed by a magistrate of that county.

(Added to NRS by 1967, 1454)

NRS 178.538 Commitment of defendant on order when defendant fails to appear for judgment; if order issued for other cause, defendant may be admitted to bail.

1. If the order recites, as the grounds upon which it is made, the failure of the defendant to appear for judgment upon conviction, the defendant must be committed according to the requirement of the order.

2. If the order be made for any other cause, and the offense is bailable, the court may fix the amount of bail, and may cause a direction to be inserted in the order that the defendant be admitted to bail in the sum fixed, which shall be specified in the order.

(Added to NRS by 1967, 1454)

NRS 178.542 Records: District court. Each county clerk shall maintain a record containing the following information for each bail bond accepted by a district court within the county:

1. The name of the defendant;
2. The name of the surety;
3. The amount of the bond;
4. The name of the court admitting the defendant to bail and the case number;
5. The date of exoneration or forfeiture of the bond;
6. The book and page of the minute order declaring the exoneration or forfeiture; and
7. The date of notice to the district attorney of any forfeiture of the bond.

(Added to NRS by 1967, 1454; A 1983, 264)

NRS 178.544 Records: Justice Court.

1. Whenever a person is admitted to bail in a Justice Court and the bail is put in by a written undertaking, the deputy clerk of the Justice Court shall record:

(a) The name of the defendant;
(b) The names of the sureties;
(c) The amount of the bond;
(d) The name of the court;
(e) The number of the case; and
(f) Such other information as is reasonably necessary to complete the record.

2. When the bond is exonerated or forfeited, the deputy clerk of the Justice Court shall record:

(a) The date of the exoneration or forfeiture;
(b) The book and page of the minute order declaring the exoneration or forfeiture; and
(c) The date of notice to the district attorney of any forfeiture of the bond.

(Added to NRS by 1967, 1455; A 1983, 264; 1985, 53)

NRS 178.546 Records: Court of Appeals and Supreme Court.

1. Whenever a person is admitted to bail by the Court of Appeals, the Supreme Court, a judge of the Court of Appeals or a justice of the Supreme Court, the Clerk of the Supreme Court shall record:

(a) The name of the defendant;
(b) The names of the sureties;
(c) The amount of the bond; and
(d) The case number.

2. When the bond is exonerated or forfeited, the Clerk of the Supreme Court shall record:

(a) The date of the exoneration or forfeiture;
(b) The file number of the order declaring the forfeiture or exoneration;
(c) The name of the county where the defendant was convicted or if no conviction has been had, of the county where the defendant was incarcerated; and
(d) The date of the notice to the district attorney of the appropriate county of any forfeiture of the bond.

(Added to NRS by 1967, 1455; A 1983, 265; 2013, 1762)

NRS 178.548 Notification of district attorney when bail bond is forfeited. The county clerk, the deputy clerk of the justice court, or the Clerk of the Supreme Court shall notify the district attorney of the appropriate county, in writing, promptly upon the receipt of information indicating that a bail bond has been forfeited.

(Added to NRS by 1967, 1456; A 1983, 266; 1985, 53)

MOTIONS

NRS 178.552 Form; contents. An application to the court for an order shall be by motion. A motion other than one made during a trial or hearing shall be in writing unless the court permits it to be made orally. It shall state the grounds upon which it is made and shall set forth the relief or order sought. It may be supported by affidavit.

(Added to NRS by 1967, 1456)

DISMISSAL OF ACTIONS

NRS 178.554 Dismissal by district attorney or Attorney General by leave of court. The district attorney, or the Attorney General in those cases which have been initiated by the Attorney General, may by leave of court file a dismissal of an indictment, information or complaint and the prosecution shall thereupon terminate. Such a dismissal may not be filed during the trial without the consent of the defendant.

(Added to NRS by 1967, 1456)

NRS 178.556 Dismissal by court for unnecessary delay.

1. If no indictment is found or information filed against a person within 15 days after the person has been held to answer for a public offense which must be prosecuted by indictment or information, the court may dismiss the complaint. If a defendant whose trial has not been postponed upon the defendant's application is not brought to trial within 60 days after the arraignment on the indictment or information, the district court may dismiss the indictment or information.
2. If a defendant whose trial has not been postponed upon the defendant's application is not brought to trial within 60 days after the arraignment on the complaint for an offense triable in a Justice or municipal Court, the court may dismiss the complaint.

(Added to NRS by 1967, 1456; A 1985, 65; 1991, 70)

NRS 178.562 Dismissal or discharge as bar to another prosecution.

1. Except as otherwise provided in NRS 174.085, an order for the dismissal of the action, as provided in NRS 178.554 and 178.556, is a bar to another prosecution for the same offense.
2. The discharge of a person accused upon preliminary examination is a bar to another complaint against the person for the same offense, but does not bar the finding of an indictment or filing of an information.

(Added to NRS by 1967, 1456; A 1997, 2393)

NRS 178.563 Notice to defendant of provisions concerning sealing of records of proceedings leading to dismissal. Upon the entry of an order dismissing a criminal action or proceeding, the court shall provide the defendant with a written notice of the provisions of NRS 179.255 which concern the sealing of records of the proceedings leading to the dismissal.

(Added to NRS by 2001, 1692)

COMPROMISING CERTAIN PUBLIC OFFENSES BY LEAVE OF COURT

NRS 178.564 Certain offenses for which party injured has civil action may be compromised. If a defendant is held to answer on a charge of a misdemeanor for which the person injured by the act constituting the offense has a remedy by a civil action, the offense may be compromised as provided in NRS 178.566 unless the offense:

1. Was committed by or upon an officer of justice while in the execution of the duties of office;
2. Was committed riotously;
3. Was committed with the intent to commit a felony;
4. Is a battery that constitutes domestic violence pursuant to NRS 33.018; or
5. Violates a temporary or extended order for protection against domestic violence.

(Added to NRS by 1967, 1456; A 2005, 103)

NRS 178.566 Compromise to be by permission of court; order to bar another prosecution.

1. If the party injured appears before the court to which the depositions are required to be returned, at any time before trial, and acknowledges in writing that the party has received satisfaction for the injury, the court may, in its discretion, on payment of the costs incurred, order all proceedings to be stayed upon the prosecution, and the defendant to be discharged therefrom; but in such case the reasons for the order must be set forth therein, and entered on the minutes.
2. The order shall be a bar to another prosecution for the same offense.

(Added to NRS by 1967, 1457)

NRS 178.568 No public offense to be compromised except as provided in this title. No public offense shall be compromised, nor shall any proceeding for the prosecution or punishment thereof, upon a compromise, be stayed, except as provided in this title.

(Added to NRS by 1967, 1457)

PROTECTION OF VICTIMS AND WITNESSES

NRS 178.569 Definitions. As used in NRS 178.569 to 178.5698, inclusive, unless the context otherwise requires:

1. "Relative" has the meaning ascribed to it in NRS 217.060.
2. "Victim of a crime" or "victim" includes a relative of a person:

(a) Against whom a crime has been committed; or
(b) Who has been injured or killed as a direct result of the commission of a crime.
(Added to NRS by 1983, 889; A 1997, 3238)

NRS 178.5691 Confidentiality of personal information. All personal information, including, but not limited to, a current or former address, which pertains to a victim, relative, witness or other person and which is received pursuant to the provisions of NRS 178.569 to 178.5698, inclusive, is confidential.
(Added to NRS by 1997, 3238)

NRS 178.5692 Investigation by sheriff of threats of harm; protection. If a victim of a crime or a witness is cooperating with the prosecuting attorney in a criminal case and reasonably apprehends that he or she may suffer threats of harm or harm arising out of that cooperation, the sheriff of the county or the chief of police of the city shall, upon the written request of the victim or witness, investigate the circumstances, take adequate measures to protect the victim or witness where appropriate, and inform the victim or witness of the level of protection being provided.
(Added to NRS by 1983, 889)

NRS 178.5694 Harassment of victim or witness by employer; notification by prosecuting attorney of continuance of proceeding.
1. If it is difficult for such a victim or witness to assist in an investigation or cooperate with the prosecuting attorney because the victim or witness is being harassed, intimidated or subjected to conflicting requirements by his or her employer, the prosecuting attorney, sheriff or chief of police shall, upon the written request of the victim or witness, intercede on his or her behalf to minimize any loss of pay or other benefits which would result from his or her assistance or appearances in court.
2. If a proceeding in court to which such a victim or witness has been subpoenaed will not go on as scheduled, the prosecuting attorney shall:
(a) Make a reasonable effort to notify the victim or witness of that fact; or
(b) Provide a system of notification which allows the victim or witness to call by telephone and receive such information.
Ê In any case, the prosecuting attorney shall, if the victim or witness so requests in writing and provides a current address, ensure that written notice is mailed to that address. If written notice would not be timely, the prosecuting attorney shall make a reasonable effort to notify the victim or witness by some other means.
(Added to NRS by 1983, 889)

NRS 178.5696 Separate waiting area; disposition of personal property; fees for testifying.
1. A court trying a criminal case shall provide victims and witnesses a secure waiting area which is not used by the members of the jury or the defendant and the defendant's family and friends.
2. A court or law enforcement agency which has custody of any stolen or other personal property belonging to such a victim or witness shall:
(a) Upon the written request of the victim or witness, make available to the victim or witness a list describing the property held in custody, unless it is shown that the disclosure of the identity or nature of the property would seriously impede the investigation of the crime; or
(b) Return the property to the victim or witness expeditiously when it is no longer needed as evidence.
3. The prosecuting attorney shall inform each such witness of the fee to which the witness is entitled for testifying and how to obtain the fee.
(Added to NRS by 1983, 890)

NRS 178.5698 Information concerning release of defendant and disposition of case provided upon request; court to inform and provide documentation to certain persons of their right to be informed of release of offender from prison in certain cases; when and whom warden must inform of release of offender from prison.
1. The prosecuting attorney, sheriff or chief of police shall, upon the request of a victim or witness, inform the victim or witness:
(a) When the defendant is released from custody at any time before or during the trial, including, without limitation, when the defendant is released pending trial or subject to electronic supervision;
(b) If the defendant is so released, the amount of bail required, if any; and
(c) Of the final disposition of the criminal case in which the victim or witness was directly involved.
2. A request for information pursuant to subsection 1 must be made:
(a) In writing; or
(b) By telephone through an automated or computerized system of notification, if such a system is available.
3. If an offender is convicted of a sexual offense or an offense involving the use or threatened use of force or violence against the victim, the court shall provide:
(a) To each witness, documentation that includes:
(1) A form advising the witness of the right to be notified pursuant to subsection 5;
(2) The form that the witness must use to request notification in writing; and
(3) The form or procedure that the witness must use to provide a change of address after a request for notification has been submitted.
(b) To each person listed in subsection 4, documentation that includes:
(1) A form advising the person of the right to be notified pursuant to subsection 5 or 6 and NRS 176.015, 176A.630, 178.4715, 209.392, 209.3925, 209.521, 213.010, 213.040, 213.095 and 213.131 or NRS 213.10915;

(2) The forms that the person must use to request notification; and

(3) The forms or procedures that the person must use to provide a change of address after a request for notification has been submitted.

4. The following persons are entitled to receive documentation pursuant to paragraph (b) of subsection 3:

(a) A person against whom the offense is committed.

(b) A person who is injured as a direct result of the commission of the offense.

(c) If a person listed in paragraph (a) or (b) is under the age of 18 years, each parent or guardian who is not the offender.

(d) Each surviving spouse, parent and child of a person who is killed as a direct result of the commission of the offense.

(e) A relative of a person listed in paragraphs (a) to (d), inclusive, if the relative requests in writing to be provided with the documentation.

5. Except as otherwise provided in subsection 6, if the offense was a felony and the offender is imprisoned, the warden of the prison shall, if the victim or witness so requests in writing and provides a current address, notify the victim or witness at that address when the offender is released from the prison.

6. If the offender was convicted of a violation of subsection 3 of NRS 200.366 or a violation of subsection 1, paragraph (a) of subsection 2 or subparagraph (2) of paragraph (b) of subsection 2 of NRS 200.508, the warden of the prison shall notify:

(a) The immediate family of the victim if the immediate family provides their current address;

(b) Any member of the victim's family related within the third degree of consanguinity, if the member of the victim's family so requests in writing and provides a current address; and

(c) The victim, if the victim will be 18 years of age or older at the time of the release and has provided a current address,

Ê before the offender is released from prison.

7. The warden must not be held responsible for any injury proximately caused by the failure to give any notice required pursuant to this section if no address was provided to the warden or if the address provided is inaccurate or not current.

8. As used in this section:

(a) "Immediate family" means any adult relative of the victim living in the victim's household.

(b) "Sexual offense" means:

(1) Sexual assault pursuant to NRS 200.366;

(2) Statutory sexual seduction pursuant to NRS 200.368;

(3) Battery with intent to commit sexual assault pursuant to NRS 200.400;

(4) An offense involving pornography and a minor pursuant to NRS 200.710 to 200.730, inclusive;

(5) Incest pursuant to NRS 201.180;

(6) Open or gross lewdness pursuant to NRS 201.210;

(7) Indecent or obscene exposure pursuant to NRS 201.220;

(8) Lewdness with a child pursuant to NRS 201.230;

(9) Sexual penetration of a dead human body pursuant to NRS 201.450;

(10) Sexual conduct between certain employees of a school or volunteers at a school and a pupil pursuant to NRS 201.540;

(11) Sexual conduct between certain employees of a college or university and a student pursuant to NRS 201.550;

(12) Luring a child or a person with mental illness pursuant to NRS 201.560, if punished as a felony;

(13) An offense that, pursuant to a specific statute, is determined to be sexually motivated; or

(14) An attempt to commit an offense listed in this paragraph.

(Added to NRS by 1983, 890; A 1995, 407; 1997, 3238; 2001, 1140, 2792; 2003, 22, 860, 1384; 2009, 72; 2011, 69; 2013, 388, 1163; 2015, 1439)

DESIGNATION OF ATTENDANT TO PROVIDE SUPPORT FOR WITNESS DURING TESTIMONY

NRS 178.571 Applicability to certain cases; persons permitted to be attendant; permissible conduct by attendant; exclusion for good cause.

1. Except as otherwise provided in subsection 2, in a case involving any act of domestic violence pursuant to NRS 33.018, a violation of NRS 200.366, 200.368 or 200.373, a battery with intent to commit a sexual assault pursuant to NRS 200.400, a violation of any provision of NRS 200.5091 to 200.5099, inclusive, a violation of NRS 201.180, 201.210, 201.220 or 201.230 or an attempt or a conspiracy to commit any of these offenses, a witness may designate an attendant who must be allowed to attend the preliminary hearing and the trial during the witness's testimony to provide support.

2. In a case involving an offense in which a minor is a witness, the witness who is a minor may designate an attendant who must be allowed to attend the preliminary hearing and the trial during the witness's testimony to provide support.

3. The attendant may be designated by a party as a witness and, except as otherwise provided in this section, must not be excluded from the proceedings. If a party designates the attendant as a witness, the attendant must be examined and cross-examined before any other witness testifies.

4. Except as otherwise provided in this subsection and subsection 5, the attendant must not be a reporter or editorial employee of any newspaper, periodical or press association or an employee of any radio or television station. The provisions of this subsection do not apply to an attendant to a witness in a case involving a violation of any provision of NRS 200.5091 to 200.50995, inclusive.

5. The parent, child, brother or sister of the witness may serve as the attendant of the witness whether or not the attendant is a reporter or an editorial employee of any newspaper, periodical or press association or an employee of any radio or television station, but the attendant shall not make notes during the hearing or trial.

6. The court:

(a) Shall, if the witness requests, allow the attendant to sit next to the witness while the witness is testifying; or

(b) May, if the witness requests that the attendant be in another location in the courtroom while the witness is testifying, allow the attendant to be in that location while the witness is testifying.

7. Except as otherwise provided in this subsection, the court shall allow the attendant to have physical contact with the witness while the witness is testifying, if the court determines that such contact is reasonably appropriate or necessary to provide support to the witness. If the attendant attempts to influence or affect in any manner the testimony of the witness during the giving of testimony or at any other time, the court shall exclude that attendant and allow the witness to designate another attendant.

8. A party may move to exclude a particular attendant for good cause, and the court shall hear the motion out of the presence of the jury, if any. If the court grants the motion, the witness may designate another attendant.

(Added to NRS by 1983, 891; A 1995, 893, 2255; 1997, 73; 2003, 542)

IMMUNITY OF MATERIAL WITNESSES FROM PROSECUTION

NRS 178.572 Order of immunity releasing material witness from prosecution or punishment on motion of State.

1. In any investigation before a grand jury, or any preliminary examination or trial in any court of record, the court on motion of the State may order that any material witness be released from all liability to be prosecuted or punished on account of any testimony or other evidence the witness may be required to produce.

2. Any motion, hearing or order regarding the immunity of a grand jury witness must not be made public before an indictment or presentment is issued in the case.

(Added to NRS by 1967, 1457; A 1983, 1346; 1985, 1030)

NRS 178.574 Order of immunity bar to prosecution; exception. Such order of immunity shall forever be a bar to prosecution against the witness for any offense shown in whole or in part by such testimony or other evidence except for perjury committed in the giving of such testimony.

(Added to NRS by 1967, 1457)

NRS 178.576 Failure of witness granted immunity to testify is contempt. Any witness who having been granted immunity refuses to testify or produce other evidence is in contempt of court.

(Added to NRS by 1967, 1457)

NRS 178.578 Denial of motion. The court shall deny the motion of the State under NRS 178.572 if it reasonably appears to the court that such testimony or evidence would subject the witness to prosecution, except for perjury committed in the giving of such testimony, under the laws of another state or of the United States.

(Added to NRS by 1967, 1457)

SERVICE AND FILING OF PAPERS

NRS 178.582 Service: When required. Written motions other than those which are heard ex parte, written notices, designations of record on appeal and similar papers shall be served upon each of the parties.

(Added to NRS by 1967, 1457)

NRS 178.584 Service: How made.

1. Whenever under this Title or by an order of the court service is required or permitted to be made upon a party represented by an attorney, the service must be made upon the attorney unless service upon the party is ordered by the court.

2. Except as otherwise provided in NRS 178.589, service upon the attorney or upon a party must be made in the manner provided in civil actions.

(Added to NRS by 1967, 1457; A 1999, 52)

NRS 178.586 Notice of orders. Immediately upon the entry of an order made on a written motion subsequent to arraignment the clerk shall mail to each party a notice thereof and shall make a note in the docket of the mailing. Lack of notice of the entry by the clerk does not affect the time to appeal or relieve or authorize the court to relieve a party for failure to appeal within the time allowed.

(Added to NRS by 1967, 1457)

NRS 178.588 Filing of papers. Papers required to be served must be filed with the court. Except as otherwise provided in NRS 178.589, papers must be filed in the manner provided in civil actions.

(Added to NRS by 1967, 1457; A 1999, 52)

NRS 178.589 Use of facsimile machine.

1. Except when personal service of a person is ordered by the court or required by specific statute, a person who is represented by an attorney may be lawfully served with any motion, notice or other legal document by means of a facsimile machine if:

(a) The document is transmitted to the office of the attorney representing the person; and

(b) The facsimile machine is operational and is maintained by the attorney representing the person or the employer of that attorney.

2. In addition to any other document required by the court, a person who uses a facsimile machine pursuant to subsection 1 to serve any motion, notice or other legal document that is required to be filed with the court shall attach to or include with the original document filed with the court a copy of the confirmation report or other comparable evidence of the transmittal of the legal document.

3. Service of any motion, notice or other legal document by facsimile machine after 5 p.m. on the day that the document is transmitted shall be deemed delivered on the next judicial day. The time of transmittal set forth in this subsection is determined according to the time at the location of the recipient of the legal document.

4. Service of any motion, notice or other legal document by facsimile machine as authorized by this section is supplemental to and does not affect the validity of any other manner of service authorized by law.

5. As used in this section:

(a) "Facsimile machine" means a device that sends or receives a reproduction or facsimile of a document or photograph which is transmitted electronically or telephonically by telecommunications lines.

(b) "Person" includes, without limitation, a government, governmental agency or political subdivision of a government.

(Added to NRS by 1999, 51)

CALENDARS

NRS 178.592 Calendar of criminal actions: Preparation by clerk.

1. The clerk must prepare a calendar of all criminal actions pending in the court, enumerating them according to the date of filing of the indictment, information or complaint, specifying opposite the title of each action whether such action is for a felony or misdemeanor, and whether the defendant is in custody or on bail.

2. Preference shall be given to criminal proceedings as far as practicable.

(Added to NRS by 1967, 1457)

NRS 178.594 Order of disposing of issues on calendar. The issues on the calendar must be disposed of in the following order, unless for good cause the court directs an action to be tried in a different order:

1. Prosecutions for felony, when the defendant is in custody.
2. Prosecutions for misdemeanor, when the defendant is in custody.
3. Prosecutions in which the State, upon determining that the physical, emotional or mental condition of the victim of, or a material witness to, an alleged felony or gross misdemeanor is deteriorating because of age, an illness or an injury to himself or herself or his or her spouse, has demanded a trial within 60 days after the arraignment of the person accused of the felony or gross misdemeanor pursuant to NRS 174.511.
4. Prosecutions for felony, when the defendant is on bail.
5. Prosecutions for misdemeanor, when the defendant is on bail.

(Added to NRS by 1967, 1458; A 1983, 1671)

EXCEPTIONS

NRS 178.596 Exceptions unnecessary. Exceptions to rulings or orders of the court are unnecessary and for all purposes for which an exception has been necessary prior to January 1, 1968, it is sufficient that a party, at the time the ruling or order of the court is made or sought, makes known to the court the action which the party desires the court to take or the party's objection to the action of the court and the grounds therefor; but if a party has no opportunity to object to a ruling or order, the absence of an objection does not thereafter prejudice the party.

(Added to NRS by 1967, 1458)

ERROR

NRS 178.598 Harmless error. Any error, defect, irregularity or variance which does not affect substantial rights shall be disregarded.

(Added to NRS by 1967, 1458)

NRS 178.602 Plain error. Plain errors or defects affecting substantial rights may be noticed although they were not brought to the attention of the court.

(Added to NRS by 1967, 1458)

RECORDS

NRS 178.606 Docket kept by deputy clerk of justice court; contents. A docket must be kept by the deputy clerk of the justice court, in which the deputy clerk shall enter each action, and the minutes of the proceedings of the court therein.

(Added to NRS by 1967, 1458; A 1985, 53)

RULES OF COURT

NRS 178.608 Rules of justice courts and district courts not to be inconsistent with this title. Rules made by justice courts and district courts for the conduct of criminal proceedings shall not be inconsistent with this title.

(Added to NRS by 1967, 1458)

NRS 178.610 Where no procedure specifically prescribed court may proceed in lawful manner. If no procedure is specifically prescribed by this title, the court may proceed in any lawful manner not inconsistent with this title or with any other applicable statute.

(Added to NRS by 1967, 1458)

THE AGREEMENT ON DETAINERS

NRS 178.620 Enactment; text. The Agreement on Detainers, set forth in this section, is hereby enacted into law and entered into by this State with all other jurisdictions legally joining such agreement in the form substantially as follows:

The Agreement on Detainers

The contracting states solemnly agree that:

Article I

The party states find that charges outstanding against a prisoner, detainers based on untried indictments, informations or complaints, and difficulties in securing speedy trial of persons already incarcerated in other jurisdictions, produce uncertainties which obstruct programs of prisoner treatment and rehabilitation. Accordingly, it is the policy of the party states and the purpose of this agreement to encourage the expeditious and orderly disposition of such charges and determination of the proper status of any and all detainers based on untried indictments, information or complaints. The party states also find that proceedings with reference to such charges and detainers, when emanating from another jurisdiction, cannot properly be had in the absence of cooperative procedures. It is the further purpose of this agreement to provide such cooperative procedures.

Article II

As used in this agreement:

(a) "State" shall mean a state of the United States; the United States of America; a territory or possession of the United States; the District of Columbia; the Commonwealth of Puerto Rico.

(b) "Sending state" shall mean a state in which a prisoner is incarcerated at the time that the prisoner initiates a request for final disposition pursuant to Article III hereof or at the time that a request for custody or availability is initiated pursuant to Article IV hereof.

(c) "Receiving state" shall mean the state in which trial is to be had on an indictment, information or complaint pursuant to Article III or Article IV hereof.

Article III

(a) Whenever a person has entered upon a term of imprisonment in a penal or correctional institution of a party state, and whenever during the continuance of the term of imprisonment there is pending in any other party state any untried indictment, information or complaint on the basis of which a detainer has been lodged against the prisoner, the prisoner shall be brought to trial within one hundred eighty days after the prisoner shall have caused to be delivered to the prosecuting officer and the appropriate court of the prosecuting officer's jurisdiction written notice of the place of imprisonment and the prisoner's request for a final disposition to be made of the indictment, information or complaint: provided that for good cause shown in open court, the prisoner or the prisoner's counsel being present, the court having jurisdiction of the matter may grant any necessary or reasonable continuance. The request of the prisoner shall be accompanied by a certificate of the appropriate official having custody of the prisoner, stating the term of commitment under which the prisoner is being held, the time already served, the time remaining to be served on the sentence, the amount of good time earned, the time of parole eligibility of the prisoner, and any decisions of the state parole agency relating to the prisoner.

(b) The written notice and request for final disposition referred to in paragraph (a) hereof shall be given or sent by the prisoner to the warden, commissioner of corrections or other official having custody of the prisoner, who shall promptly forward it together with the certificate to the appropriate prosecuting official and court by registered or certified mail, return receipt requested.

(c) The warden, commissioner of corrections or other official having custody of the prisoner shall promptly inform the prisoner of the source and contents of any detainer lodged and shall also inform the prisoner of the right to make a request for final disposition of the indictment, information or complaint on which the detainer is based.

(d) Any request for final disposition made by a prisoner pursuant to paragraph (a) hereof shall operate as a request for final disposition of all untried indictments, informations or complaints on the basis of which detainers have been lodged against the prisoner from the state to whose prosecuting official the request for final disposition is specifically directed. The warden, commissioner of corrections or other official having custody of the prisoner shall forthwith notify all appropriate prosecuting officers and courts in the several jurisdictions within the state to which the prisoner's request for final disposition is being sent of the proceeding being initiated by the prisoner. Any notification sent pursuant to this paragraph shall be accompanied by copies of the prisoner's written notice, request, and the certificate. If trial is not had on any indictment, information or complaint contemplated hereby prior to the return of the prisoner to the original place of imprisonment, such indictment, information or complaint shall not be of any further force or effect, and the court shall enter an order dismissing the same with prejudice.

(e) Any request for a final disposition made by a prisoner pursuant to paragraph (a) hereof shall also be deemed to be a waiver of extradition with respect to any charge or proceeding contemplated thereby or included therein by reason of paragraph (d) hereof, and a waiver of extradition to the receiving state to serve any sentence there imposed upon the prisoner, after completion of the term of imprisonment in the sending state. The request for final disposition shall also constitute a consent by the prisoner to the production of the prisoner's body in any court where the prisoner's presence may be required in order to effectuate the purposes of this agreement and a further consent voluntarily to be returned to the original place of imprisonment in accordance with the provisions of this agreement. Nothing in this paragraph shall prevent the imposition of a concurrent sentence if otherwise permitted by law.

(f) Escape from custody by the prisoner subsequent to the prisoner's execution of the request for final disposition referred to in paragraph (a) hereof shall void the request.

Article IV

(a) The appropriate officer of the jurisdiction in which an untried indictment, information or complaint is pending shall be entitled to have a prisoner against whom the officer has lodged a detainer and who is serving a term of imprisonment in any party state made available in accordance with Article V (a) hereof upon presentation of a written request for temporary custody or availability to the appropriate authorities of the state in which the prisoner is incarcerated: provided that the court having jurisdiction of such indictment, information or complaint shall have duly approved, recorded and transmitted the request: and provided further that there shall be a period of thirty days after receipt by the appropriate authorities before the request be honored, within which period the governor of the sending state may disapprove the request for temporary custody or availability, either upon the governor's own motion or upon motion of the prisoner.

(b) Upon receipt of the officer's written request as provided in paragraph (a) hereof, the appropriate authorities having the prisoner in custody shall furnish the officer with a certificate stating the term of commitment under which the prisoner is being held, the time already served, the time remaining to be served on the sentence, the amount of good time earned, the time of parole eligibility of the prisoner, and any decisions of the state parole agency relating to the prisoner. Said authorities simultaneously shall furnish all other officers and appropriate courts in the receiving state who have lodged detainers against the prisoner with similar certificates and with notices informing them of the request for custody or availability and of the reasons therefor.

(c) In respect of any proceeding made possible by this Article, trial shall be commenced within one hundred twenty days of the arrival of the prisoner in the receiving state, but for good cause shown in open court, the prisoner or the prisoner's counsel being present, the court having jurisdiction of the matter may grant any necessary or reasonable continuance.

(d) Nothing contained in this Article shall be construed to deprive any prisoner of any right which the prisoner may have to contest the legality of the prisoner's delivery as provided in paragraph (a) hereof, but such delivery may not be opposed or denied on the ground that the executive authority of the sending state has not affirmatively consented to or ordered such delivery.

(e) If trial is not had on any indictment, information or complaint contemplated hereby prior to the prisoner's being returned to the original place of imprisonment pursuant to Article V (e) hereof, such indictment, information or complaint shall not be of any further force or effect, and the court shall enter an order dismissing the same with prejudice.

Article V

(a) In response to a request made under Article III or Article IV hereof, the appropriate authority in a sending state shall offer to deliver temporary custody of such prisoner to the appropriate authority in the state where such indictment, information or complaint is pending against such person in order that speedy and efficient prosecution may be had. If the request for final disposition is made by the prisoner, the offer of temporary custody shall accompany the written notice provided for in Article III of this agreement. In the case of a federal prisoner, the appropriate authority in the receiving state shall be entitled to temporary custody as provided by this agreement or to the prisoner's presence in federal custody at the place for trial, whichever custodial arrangement may be approved by the custodian.

(b) The officer or other representative of a state accepting an offer of temporary custody shall present the following upon demand:

(1) Proper identification and evidence of authority to act for the state into whose temporary custody the prisoner is to be given.

(2) A duly certified copy of the indictment, information or complaint on the basis of which the detainer has been lodged and on the basis of which the request for temporary custody of the prisoner has been made.

(c) If the appropriate authority shall refuse or fail to accept temporary custody of said person, or in the event that an action on the indictment, information or complaint on the basis of which the detainer has been lodged is not brought to trial within the period provided in Article III or Article IV hereof, the appropriate court of the jurisdiction where the indictment, information or complaint has been pending shall enter an order dismissing the same with prejudice, and any detainer based thereon shall cease to be of any force or effect.

(d) The temporary custody referred to in this agreement shall be only for the purpose of permitting prosecution on the charge or charges contained in one or more untried indictments, informations or complaints which form the basis of the detainer or detainers or for prosecution on any other charge or charges arising out of the same transaction. Except for attendance at court and while being transported to or from any place at which the prisoner's presence may be required, the prisoner shall be held in a suitable jail or other facility regularly used for persons awaiting prosecution.

(e) At the earliest practicable time consonant with the purposes of this agreement, the prisoner shall be returned to the sending state.

(f) During the continuance of temporary custody or while the prisoner is otherwise being made available for trial as required by this agreement, time being served on the sentence shall continue to run but good time shall be earned by the prisoner only if, and to the extent that, the law and practice of the jurisdiction which imposed the sentence may allow.

(g) For all purposes other than that for which temporary custody as provided in this agreement is exercised, the prisoner shall be deemed to remain in the custody of and subject to the jurisdiction of the sending state and any escape from temporary custody may be dealt with in the same manner as an escape from the original place of imprisonment or in any other manner permitted by law.

(h) From the time that a party state receives custody of a prisoner pursuant to this agreement until such prisoner is returned to the territory and custody of the sending state, the state in which the one or more untried indictments, informations or complaints are pending or in which trial is being had shall be responsible for the prisoner and shall also pay all costs of transporting, caring for, keeping and returning the prisoner. The provisions of this paragraph shall govern unless the states concerned shall have entered into a supplementary agreement providing for a different allocation of costs and responsibilities as between or among themselves. Nothing herein contained shall be construed to alter or affect any internal relationship among the departments, agencies and officers of and in the government of a party state, or between a party state and its subdivisions, as to the payment of costs, or responsibilities therefor.

Article VI

(a) In determining the duration and expiration dates of the time periods provided in Articles III and IV of this agreement, the running of said time periods shall be tolled whenever and for as long as the prisoner is unable to stand trial, as determined by the court having jurisdiction of the matter.

(b) No provision of this agreement, and no remedy made available by this agreement, shall apply to any person who is adjudged to be mentally ill.

Article VII

Each state party to this agreement shall designate an officer who, acting jointly with like officers of other party states, shall promulgate rules and regulations to carry out more effectively the terms and provisions of this agreement, and who shall provide, within and without the state, information necessary to the effective operation of this agreement.

Article VIII

This agreement shall enter into full force and effect as to a party state when such state has enacted the same into law. A state party to this agreement may withdraw herefrom by enacting a statute repealing the same. However, the withdrawal of any state shall not affect the status of any proceedings already initiated by inmates or by state officers at the time such withdrawal takes effect, nor shall it affect their rights in respect thereof.

Article IX

This agreement shall be liberally construed so as to effectuate its purposes. The provisions of this agreement shall be severable and if any phrase, clause, sentence or provision of this agreement is declared to be contrary to the constitution of any party state or of the United States or the applicability thereof to any government, agency, person or circumstance is held invalid, the validity of the remainder of this agreement and the applicability thereof to any government, agency, person or circumstance shall not be affected thereby. If this agreement shall be held contrary to the constitution of any state party hereto, the agreement shall remain in full force and effect as to the remaining states and in full force and effect as to the state affected as to all severable matters.

(Added to NRS by 1971, 640)

NRS 178.630 Duties of Director of Department of Corrections. The Director of the Department of Corrections shall comply with the provisions of Articles III and IV of The Agreement on Detainers whenever the Director has custody of a prisoner who has detainers lodged against the prisoner from other jurisdictions which are parties to such agreement.

(Added to NRS by 1971, 645; A 1977, 863; 2001 Special Session, 223)

NRS 178.640 Duty of Governor. The Governor shall appoint the officer provided in Article VII of The Agreement on Detainers.

(Added to NRS by 1971, 645; A 1983, 539)

REQUEST FOR DETAINER

NRS 178.700 Procedure for making request; time for responding; withdrawal of request; notice of receipt of detainer.

1. If the Attorney General, a prosecuting attorney or an agency of criminal justice in this State receives a request from the Department of Corrections, it shall respond in writing within 14 working days setting forth any charges that are pending against the offender.
2. If the Attorney General, a prosecuting attorney or an agency of criminal justice indicates in its response pursuant to subsection 1 that felony charges are pending against an offender, it shall, or if misdemeanor charges are pending against an offender, it may, request in the response that upon release of the offender from the custody of the Department of Corrections, the Department release the offender to an agency of criminal justice in this State that is authorized to detain a person pending prosecution. The Attorney General, a prosecuting attorney or an agency of criminal justice may submit such a request to the Department of Corrections at any other time, if charges are filed against an offender.
3. If an offender is convicted, acquitted or the charges are dropped after a request was submitted pursuant to this section, the Attorney General, prosecuting attorney or agency of criminal justice who submitted the request shall withdraw the request by providing a certified copy of the judgment to the Department of Corrections if the offender was convicted or acquitted, or by providing proof to the Department that the charges were dropped.
4. The Attorney General, a prosecuting attorney or an agency of criminal justice shall notify the Department of Corrections upon receipt of a detainer against an inmate from another jurisdiction who is transferred to the custody of the Department of Corrections.

(Added to NRS by 1997, 917; A 2001 Special Session, 223)

MISCELLANEOUS PROVISIONS

NRS 178.750 District attorney to submit annual report to Attorney General on cases filed that included charge for murder or involuntary manslaughter.

1. The district attorney for each county shall prepare and submit a report, on a form approved by the Attorney General, to the Attorney General not later than February 1 of each year concerning each case filed during the previous calendar year that included a charge for murder or voluntary manslaughter. The district attorney shall exclude from the report any charge for manslaughter that resulted from a death in a crash involving a motor vehicle.

2. The report required pursuant to subsection 1 must include, without limitation:

(a) The age, gender and race of the defendant;

(b) The age, gender and race of any codefendant or other person charged or suspected of having participated in the homicide and in any alleged related offense;

(c) The age, gender and race of the victim of the homicide and any alleged related offense;

(d) The date of the homicide and of any alleged related offense;

(e) The date of filing of the information or indictment;

(f) The name of each court in which the case was prosecuted;

(g) Whether or not the prosecutor filed a notice of intent to seek the death penalty and, if so, when the prosecutor filed the notice;

(h) The final disposition of the case and whether or not the case was tried before a jury;

(i) The race, ethnicity and gender of each member of the jury, if the case was tried by a jury; and

(j) The identity of:

(1) Each prosecuting attorney who participated in the decision to file the initial charges against the defendant;

(2) Each prosecuting attorney who participated in the decision to offer or accept a plea, if applicable;

(3) Each prosecuting attorney who participated in the decision to seek the death penalty, if applicable; and

(4) Each person outside the office of the district attorney who was consulted in determining whether to seek the death penalty or to accept or reject a plea, if any.

3. If all the information required pursuant to subsection 1 cannot be provided because the case is still in progress, an additional report must be filed with the Attorney General each time a subsequent report is filed until all the information, to the extent available, has been provided.

(Added to NRS by 2003, 2084; A 2007, 421; 2015, 1659)

CHAPTER 179 - SPECIAL PROCEEDINGS OF A CRIMINAL NATURE; SEALING RECORDS OF CRIMINAL PROCEEDINGS; REWARDS; FORMS

SEARCH WARRANTS

IDENTIFICATION OF FUNDS

FORFEITURES

FORFEITURE OF PROPERTY RELATING TO TECHNOLOGICAL CRIMES

DISPOSAL OF PROPERTY STOLEN OR EMBEZZLED

CRIMINAL EXTRADITION (UNIFORM ACT)

SEALING RECORDS OF CRIMINAL PROCEEDINGS

REWARDS

FORMS

INTERCEPTION OF WIRE, ELECTRONIC OR ORAL COMMUNICATION

MISCELLANEOUS PROVISIONS

SEARCH WARRANTS

NRS 179.015 "Property" defined. As used in NRS 179.015 to 179.115, inclusive, the term "property" includes documents, books, papers and any other tangible objects.

(Added to NRS by 1967, 1458)

NRS 179.025 Authority for issuance. A search warrant authorized by NRS 179.015 to 179.115, inclusive, may be issued by a magistrate of the State of Nevada.

(Added to NRS by 1967, 1458)

NRS 179.035 Grounds for issuance. A warrant may be issued under NRS 179.015 to 179.115, inclusive, to search for and seize any property:

1. Stolen or embezzled in violation of the laws of the State of Nevada, or of any other state or of the United States;
2. Designed or intended for use or which is or has been used as the means of committing a criminal offense; or
3. When the property or things to be seized consist of any item or constitute any evidence which tends to show that a criminal offense has been committed, or tends to show that a particular person has committed a criminal offense.

(Added to NRS by 1967, 1458)

NRS 179.045 Issuance and contents; sealing information upon which warrant is based; time for serving warrant.

1. A search warrant may issue only on affidavit or affidavits sworn to before the magistrate and establishing the grounds for issuing the warrant or as provided in subsection 3. If the magistrate is satisfied that grounds for the application exist or that there is probable cause to believe that they exist, the magistrate shall issue a warrant identifying the property and naming or describing the person or place to be searched.

2. Secure electronic transmission may be used for the submission of an application and affidavit required by subsection 1, and for the issuance of a search warrant by a magistrate. The Nevada Supreme Court may adopt rules not inconsistent with the laws of this State to carry out the provisions of this subsection.

3. In lieu of the affidavit required by subsection 1, the magistrate may take an oral statement given under oath, which must be recorded in the presence of the magistrate or in the magistrate's immediate vicinity by a certified court reporter or by electronic means, transcribed, certified by the reporter if the reporter recorded it, and certified by the magistrate. The statement must be filed with the clerk of the court.

4. Upon a showing of good cause, the magistrate may order an affidavit or a recording of an oral statement given pursuant to this section to be sealed. Upon a showing of good cause, a court may cause the affidavit or recording to be unsealed.

5. After a magistrate has issued a search warrant, whether it is based on an affidavit or an oral statement given under oath, the magistrate may orally authorize a peace officer to sign the name of the magistrate on a duplicate original warrant. A duplicate original search warrant shall be deemed to be a search warrant. It must be returned to the magistrate who authorized the signing of it. The magistrate shall endorse his or her name and enter the date on the warrant when it is returned. Any failure of the magistrate to make such an endorsement and entry does not in itself invalidate the warrant.

6. The warrant must be directed to a peace officer in the county where the warrant is to be executed. It must:

(a) State the grounds or probable cause for its issuance and the names of the persons whose affidavits have been taken in support thereof; or

(b) Incorporate by reference the affidavit or oral statement upon which it is based.

Ê The warrant must command the officer to search forthwith the person or place named for the property specified.

7. The warrant must direct that it be served between the hours of 7 a.m. and 7 p.m., unless the magistrate, upon a showing of good cause therefor, inserts a direction that it be served at any time.

8. The warrant must designate the magistrate to whom it is to be returned.

9. As used in this section, "secure electronic transmission" means the sending of information from one computer system to another computer system in such a manner as to ensure that:

(a) No person other than the intended recipient receives the information;

(b) The identity of the sender of the information can be authenticated; and

(c) The information which is received by the intended recipient is identical to the information that was sent.

(Added to NRS by 1967, 1459; A 1975, 39; 1981, 1652; 1993, 1412; 1997, 741; 2015, 2487)

NRS 179.055 Officer may break door to serve warrant after admittance refused; breaking of door or window to liberate officer or person acting in aid of officer; use of reasonable and necessary force.

1. The officer may break open any outer or inner door or window of a house, or any part of the house, or anything therein, to execute the warrant, if, after notice of authority and purpose, the officer is refused admittance.

2. The officer may break open any outer or inner door or window of a house for the purpose of liberating a person who, having entered to aid in the execution of the officer's warrant, is detained therein, or when necessary for the officer's own liberation.

3. All reasonable and necessary force may be used to effect an entry into any building or property or part thereof to execute a search warrant. In the execution of the warrant, the person executing it may reasonably detain and search any person in the place at the time in order to protect himself or herself from attack or to prevent destruction, disposal or concealment of any instruments, articles or things particularly described in the warrant.

(Added to NRS by 1967, 1459)

NRS 179.065 Person charged with felony may be searched. When a person charged with a felony is supposed to have on his or her person a dangerous weapon, or anything which may be used as evidence of the commission of the offense, the officer making the arrest shall cause the person to be searched, and the weapon or other thing to be retained, subject to the order of the court in which the defendant may be tried.

(Added to NRS by 1967, 1459)

NRS 179.075 Execution and return of warrant with inventory.

1. The warrant may be executed and returned only within 10 days after its date.

2. The officer taking property under the warrant shall give to the person from whom or from whose premises the property was taken a copy of the warrant and a receipt for the property taken or shall leave the copy and receipt at the place from which the property was taken.

3. The return shall be made promptly and shall be accompanied by a written inventory of any property taken. The inventory shall be made in the presence of the applicant for the warrant and the person from whose possession or premises the property was taken, if they are present, or in the presence of at least one credible person other than the applicant for the warrant or the person from whose possession or premises the property was taken, and shall be verified by the officer.

4. The magistrate shall upon request deliver a copy of the inventory to the person from whom or from whose premises the property was taken and to the applicant for the warrant.

(Added to NRS by 1967, 1459)

NRS 179.085 Motions for return of property and to suppress evidence.

1. A person aggrieved by an unlawful search and seizure or the deprivation of property may move the court having jurisdiction where the property was seized for the return of the property on the ground that:

(a) The property was illegally seized without warrant;

(b) The warrant is insufficient on its face;

(c) There was not probable cause for believing the existence of the grounds on which the warrant was issued;

(d) The warrant was illegally executed; or

(e) Retention of the property by law enforcement is not reasonable under the totality of the circumstances.

Ê The judge shall receive evidence on any issue of fact necessary to the decision of the motion.

2. If the motion is granted on a ground set forth in paragraph (a), (b), (c) or (d) of subsection 1, the property must be restored and it must not be admissible evidence at any hearing or trial.

3. If the motion is granted on the ground set forth in paragraph (e) of subsection 1, the property must be restored, but the court may impose reasonable conditions to protect access to the property and its use in later proceedings.

4. A motion to suppress evidence on any ground set forth in paragraphs (a) to (d), inclusive, of subsection 1 may also be made in the court where the trial is to be had. The motion must be made before trial or hearing unless opportunity therefor did not exist or the defendant was not aware of the grounds for the motion, but the court in its discretion may entertain the motion at the trial or hearing.

5. If a motion pursuant to this section is filed when no criminal proceeding is pending, the motion must be treated as a civil complaint seeking equitable relief.

(Added to NRS by 1967, 1460; A 2015, 405)

NRS 179.095 Return of papers to clerk. The magistrate who has issued a search warrant shall attach to the warrant the duplicate original warrant, if any, and a copy of the return, inventory and all other papers in connection therewith and shall file them with the clerk of the court having jurisdiction where the property was seized.

(Added to NRS by 1967, 1460; A 1981, 1653)

NRS 179.105 Retention of property taken on warrant by officer subject to court order; restoration of property to person from whom it was taken; technical irregularities will not quash warrant. All property or things taken on a warrant must be retained in an officer's custody, subject to the order of the court to which the officer is required to return the proceedings before the officer, or of any other court in which the offense in respect to which the property or things are taken is triable. If it appears that the property taken is not the same as that described in the warrant, or that there is no probable cause for believing the existence of the grounds on which the warrant was issued, the magistrate shall cause it to be restored to the person from whom it was taken. However, no search warrant shall be quashed by any magistrate or judge within this State nor shall any evidence based upon a search warrant be suppressed in any criminal action or proceeding because of mere technical irregularities which do not affect the substantial rights of the accused.

(Added to NRS by 1967, 1460)

NRS 179.115 Scope. NRS 179.015 to 179.115, inclusive, do not modify any other statute regulating search, seizure and the issuance and execution of search warrants in circumstances for which special provision is made.

(Added to NRS by 1967, 1460)

IDENTIFICATION OF FUNDS

NRS 179.1152 Identification of name, personal information and funds associated with prepaid or stored value card; contract to assist.

1. If a peace officer:

(a) Has detained a person pursuant to NRS 171.123, has arrested a person pursuant to any statutory provision authorizing or requiring the arrest of a person or is investigating a crime for which a suspect:

(1) Has not been identified; or

(2) Has been identified but was not reasonably believed by the peace officer to possess or control a prepaid or stored value card before the peace officer lawfully obtained possession of a prepaid or stored value card;

(b) Has lawfully obtained possession of a prepaid or stored value card; and

(c) Has probable cause to believe that the prepaid or stored value card represents the proceeds of a crime or has been used, is being used or is intended for use in the commission of a crime,

Ê the peace officer may use an electronic device, a necessary electronic communications network or any other reasonable means to determine the name, personal information and amount of funds associated with the prepaid or stored value card.

2. The Attorney General, the Attorney General's designee or any state or local law enforcement agency in this State may enter into a contract with any person to assist in carrying out the provisions of this section.

3. Before entering into a contract pursuant to subsection 2, the Attorney General, the Attorney General's designee or a state or local law enforcement agency shall consider the following factors:

(a) The functional benefits to all law enforcement agencies in this State of maintaining either a single database or a series of interlinked databases relating to possible criminal use of prepaid or stored value cards.

(b) The overall costs of establishing and maintaining such a database or databases.

(c) Any other factors that the Attorney General, the Attorney General's designee or the state or local law enforcement agency believe to be relevant.

4. Any contract entered into pursuant to this section:

(a) May be a sole source contract, not subject to the rules and requirements of open competitive bidding, if the period of the contract does not exceed 5 years; and

(b) Must indemnify and hold harmless any person who enters into a contract pursuant to this section, and any officers, employees or agents of that person, for claims for actions taken at the direction of a law enforcement agency in this State and within the scope of the contract.

5. As used in this section:

(a) "Prepaid or stored value card" means any instrument or device used to access funds or monetary value represented in digital electronic format, whether or not specially encrypted, and stored or capable of storage on electronic media in such a way as to be retrievable and transferable electronically.

(b) "Proceeds" has the meaning ascribed to it in NRS 179.1161.

(Added to NRS by 2009, 2243)

FORFEITURES

NRS 179.1156 Scope. Except as otherwise provided in NRS 179.1211 to 179.1235, inclusive, and 207.350 to 207.520, inclusive, the provisions of NRS 179.1156 to 179.121, inclusive, govern the seizure, forfeiture and disposition of all property and proceeds subject to forfeiture.

(Added to NRS by 1987, 1380; A 1989, 1789; 2007, 205; 2015, 2501)

NRS 179.1157 Definitions. As used in NRS 179.1156 to 179.1205, inclusive, unless the context otherwise requires, the words and terms defined in NRS 179.1158 to 179.11635, inclusive, have the meanings ascribed to them in those sections.

(Added to NRS by 1987, 1380; A 1989, 1789; 1991, 209; 2015, 2501)

NRS 179.1158 "Claimant" defined. "Claimant" means any person who claims to have:

1. Any right, title or interest of record in the property or proceeds subject to forfeiture;
2. Any community property interest in the property or proceeds; or
3. Had possession of the property or proceeds at the time of the seizure thereof by the plaintiff.

(Added to NRS by 1987, 1380)

NRS 179.1159 "Plaintiff" defined. "Plaintiff" means the law enforcement agency which has commenced a proceeding for forfeiture.

(Added to NRS by 1987, 1380)

NRS 179.1161 "Proceeds" defined. "Proceeds" means any property, or that part of an item of property, derived directly or indirectly from the commission or attempted commission of a crime.

(Added to NRS by 1987, 1380)

NRS 179.1162 "Property" defined. "Property" includes any:

1. Real property or interest in real property.
2. Fixture or improvement to real property.
3. Personal property, whether tangible or intangible, or interest in personal property.
4. Conveyance, including any aircraft, vehicle or vessel.
5. Money, security or negotiable instrument.
6. Proceeds.

(Added to NRS by 1987, 1380)

NRS 179.1163 "Protected interest" defined. "Protected interest" means the enforceable interest of a claimant in property, which interest is shown not to be subject to forfeiture.

(Added to NRS by 1987, 1380)

NRS 179.11635 "Willful blindness" defined. "Willful blindness" means the intentional disregard of objective facts which would lead a reasonable person to conclude that the property was derived from unlawful activity or would be used for an unlawful purpose.

(Added to NRS by 1991, 209)

NRS 179.1164 Property subject to seizure and forfeiture; exceptions.

1. Except as otherwise provided in subsection 2, the following property is subject to seizure and forfeiture in a proceeding for forfeiture:

(a) Any proceeds attributable to the commission or attempted commission of any felony.

(b) Any property or proceeds otherwise subject to forfeiture pursuant to NRS 179.121, 200.760, 202.257, 370.419, 453.301 or 501.3857.

2. Property may not, to the extent of the interest of any claimant, be declared forfeited by reason of an act or omission shown to have been committed or omitted without the knowledge, consent or willful blindness of the claimant.

3. Unless the owner of real property or a mobile home:

(a) Has given the tenant notice to surrender the premises pursuant to NRS 40.254 within 90 days after the owner receives notice of a conviction pursuant to subsection 2 of NRS 453.305; or

(b) Shows the court that the owner had good cause not to evict the tenant summarily pursuant to NRS 40.254,

Ê the owner of real property or a mobile home used or intended for use by a tenant to facilitate any violation of the provisions of NRS 453.011 to 453.552, inclusive, except NRS 453.336, is disputably presumed to have known of and consented to that use if the notices required by NRS 453.305 have been given in connection with another such violation relating to the property or mobile home. The holder of a lien or encumbrance on the property or mobile home is disputably presumed to have acquired an interest in the property for fair value and without knowledge or consent to such use, regardless of when the act giving rise to the forfeiture occurred.

(Added to NRS by 1987, 1380; A 1989, 1235; 1991, 209, 2286, 2288; 1995, 2534; 2001, 1066; 2003, 562; 2005, 1198)

NRS 179.1165 Seizure of property: Requirement of process.

1. Except as provided in subsection 2, property that is subject to forfeiture may only be seized by a law enforcement agency upon process issued by a magistrate having jurisdiction over the property.

2. A seizure of property may be made by a law enforcement agency without process if:

(a) The seizure is incident to:

(1) An arrest;

(2) A search pursuant to a search warrant; or

(3) An inspection pursuant to a warrant for an administrative inspection;

(b) The property is the subject of a final judgment in a proceeding for forfeiture;

(c) The law enforcement agency has probable cause to believe that the property is directly or indirectly dangerous to health or safety; or

(d) The law enforcement agency has probable cause to believe that the property is subject to forfeiture.

(Added to NRS by 1985, 1466; A 1987, 1382)

NRS 179.1169 Title in property; transfer.

1. All right, title and interest in property subject to forfeiture vests in the plaintiff:

(a) In the case of property used or intended for use to facilitate the commission or attempted commission of any felony, when the property is so used or intended for such use.

(b) In the case of property otherwise subject to forfeiture, when the event giving rise to the forfeiture occurs.

(c) In the case of proceeds, when they become proceeds.

2. Any transfer of property which occurs after title to the property has become vested in the plaintiff, and before the termination of the proceeding for forfeiture, is void as against the plaintiff, unless the person to whom the transfer is made is a good faith purchaser for value. If such a transfer is made, the purchaser must, in the proceeding for forfeiture, establish by a preponderance of the evidence that the purchaser has:

(a) An interest of record in the property;

(b) Given fair value for the interest; and

(c) Acquired the interest without notice of the proceeding or the facts giving rise to the proceeding.

Ê If the purchaser acquires the interest after the seizure of the property by the plaintiff, it is conclusively presumed that the interest has been acquired with notice of the proceeding.

(Added to NRS by 1987, 1381)

NRS 179.1171 Proceedings for forfeiture: Rules of practice; complaint; service of summons and complaint; answer; parties.

1. Except as otherwise provided in NRS 179.1156 to 179.1205, inclusive, the Nevada Rules of Civil Procedure are applicable to and constitute the rules of practice in a proceeding for forfeiture pursuant to those sections.

2. A proceeding for forfeiture is commenced by filing a complaint for forfeiture. If the property has been seized without process, the plaintiff shall file the complaint for forfeiture within 120 days after the property is seized. The property is subject to an action to claim its delivery only if the plaintiff does not file the complaint for forfeiture within 60 days after the property is seized. If the complaint for forfeiture is filed following the commencement of an action claiming delivery, the complaint must be treated as a counterclaim.

3. If a law enforcement agency seizes property, the property must not be forfeited unless:

(a) The agency files a complaint for forfeiture in the district court for the county in which the property is located; or

(b) A stipulated agreement between the parties regarding the property is reached.

4. A proceeding for forfeiture is in rem. The complaint for forfeiture must be filed in the district court for the county in which the property which is the subject of the proceeding is located.

5. The plaintiff shall cause service of the summons and complaint to be made upon each claimant whose identity is known to the plaintiff or who can be identified through the exercise of reasonable diligence. If real property or any interest in real property is affected by the proceeding, the plaintiff shall file notice of the proceeding in the manner provided in NRS 14.010.

6. Each claimant served with the summons and complaint who desires to contest the forfeiture shall, within 20 days after the service, serve and file a verified answer to the complaint. The claimant shall admit or deny the averments of the complaint and shall, in short and plain terms, describe the interest which the claimant asserts in the property. Concurrently with the answer, the claimant shall serve answers or objections to any written interrogatories served with the summons and complaint.

7. No person, other than the plaintiff and any claimant, is a proper party in the proceeding.

(Added to NRS by 1987, 1381; A 2015, 2501)

NRS 179.1173 Proceedings for forfeiture: Priority over other civil matters; order to stay; standard of proof; conviction of claimant not required; confidentiality of informants; return of property to claimant; forfeiture as part of plea or stipulated agreement.

1. Except as otherwise provided in subsection 2, the district court shall proceed as soon as practicable to a trial and determination of the matter. A proceeding for forfeiture is entitled to priority over other civil actions which are not otherwise entitled to priority.

2. At a proceeding for forfeiture, the court shall issue an order staying the proceeding that remains in effect while the criminal action which is the basis of the proceeding is pending trial. The court shall lift the stay after the trial is completed. If the claimant is acquitted during the trial, the property of the claimant must be returned to the claimant within 7 business days after the acquittal.

3. If property has been seized and the criminal charges against the owner of such property are denied or dismissed, all such property must be returned to the owner within 7 business days after the criminal charges are denied or dismissed.

4. The plaintiff in a proceeding for forfeiture must establish proof by clear and convincing evidence that the property is subject to forfeiture.

5. In a proceeding for forfeiture, the rule of law that forfeitures are not favored does not apply.

6. The plaintiff is not required to plead or prove that a claimant has been charged with or convicted of any criminal offense. If proof of such a conviction is made, and it is shown that the judgment of conviction has become final, the proof is, as against any claimant, conclusive evidence of all facts necessary to sustain the conviction.

7. The plaintiff has an absolute privilege to refuse to disclose the identity of any person, other than a witness, who has furnished to a law enforcement officer information purporting to reveal the commission of a crime. The privilege may be claimed by an appropriate representative of the plaintiff.

8. If the court determines that the property is not subject to forfeiture, the court shall order the property and any interest accrued pursuant to subsection 2 of NRS 179.1175 returned to the claimant found to be entitled to the property within 7 business days after the order is issued. If the court determines that the property is subject to forfeiture, the court shall so decree. The property, including any interest accrued pursuant to subsection 2 of NRS 179.1175, must be forfeited to the plaintiff, subject to the right of any claimant who establishes a protected interest. Any such claimant must, upon the sale or retention of the property, be compensated for the claimant's interest in the manner provided in NRS 179.118.

9. A claimant who agrees to enter a plea of guilty, guilty but mentally ill or nolo contendere to criminal charges relating to the seized property or reaches a stipulated agreement with the plaintiff may agree to the forfeiture of any property as part of the plea or agreement.

10. If the court accepts a plea or stipulated agreement pursuant to subsection 9, the court shall order forfeiture of the property that the claimant agreed to forfeit pursuant to the plea or agreement.

(Added to NRS by 1987, 1382; A 2001, 874; 2015, 2502)

NRS 179.1175 Disposition of property after seizure and forfeiture.

1. Except as otherwise provided in subsection 2, after property has been seized the agency which seized the property may:

(a) Place the property under seal;

(b) Remove the property to a place designated by the agency for the storage of that type of property; or

(c) Remove the property to an appropriate place for disposition in a manner authorized by the court.

2. If an agency seizes currency, unless otherwise ordered by the court, the agency shall deposit the currency in an interest-bearing account maintained for the purpose of holding currency seized by the agency.

3. When a court declares property to be forfeited, the plaintiff may:

(a) Retain it for official use;

(b) Sell any of it which is neither required by law to be destroyed nor harmful to the public; or

(c) Remove it for disposition in accordance with the applicable provisions of NRS.

(Added to NRS by 1985, 1467; A 1987, 1383; 2001, 875)

NRS 179.118 Distribution of proceeds from forfeited property.

1. The proceeds from any sale or retention of property declared to be forfeited and any interest accrued pursuant to subsection 2 of NRS 179.1175 must be applied, first, to the satisfaction of any protected interest established by a claimant in the proceeding, then to the proper expenses of the proceeding for forfeiture and resulting sale, including the expense of effecting the seizure, the expense of maintaining custody, the expense of advertising and the costs of the suit.

2. Any balance remaining after the distribution required by subsection 1 must be deposited as follows:

(a) Except as otherwise provided in this subsection, if the plaintiff seized the property, in the special account established pursuant to NRS 179.1187 by the governing body that controls the plaintiff.

(b) Except as otherwise provided in this subsection, if the plaintiff is a metropolitan police department, in the special account established by the Metropolitan Police Committee on Fiscal Affairs pursuant to NRS 179.1187.

(c) Except as otherwise provided in this subsection, if more than one agency was substantially involved in the seizure, in an equitable manner to be directed by the court hearing the proceeding for forfeiture.

(d) If the property was seized pursuant to NRS 200.760, in the State Treasury for credit to the Fund for the Compensation of Victims of Crime to be used for the counseling and the medical treatment of victims of crimes committed in violation of NRS 200.366, 200.710 to 200.730, inclusive, or 201.230.

(e) If the property was seized as the result of a violation of NRS 202.300, in the general fund of the county in which the complaint for forfeiture was filed, to be used to support programs of counseling of persons ordered by the court to attend counseling pursuant to NRS 62E.290.

(f) If the property was forfeited pursuant to NRS 201.351, with the county treasurer to be distributed in accordance with the provisions of subsection 4 of NRS 201.351.

(Added to NRS by 1985, 1467; A 1987, 1383; 1989, 1789; 1995, 1150; 1997, 1599; 2001, 875; 2003, 1120; 2009, 575)

NRS 179.1185 Issuance of certificate of title for forfeited vehicle or other conveyance. If a vehicle or other conveyance is forfeited of a kind which is subject to the provisions of title 43 of NRS governing certificates of title, the agency charged by law with responsibility for issuing certificates of title for conveyances of the kind shall issue a certificate of title to:

1. The governing body or the agency to whom the title was awarded by the court if the conveyance is retained for official use; or

2. The purchaser if the conveyance is sold by the governing body or the plaintiff.

(Added to NRS by 1985, 1467; A 1987, 1384; 2003, 478)

NRS 179.1187 Establishment of account for proceeds from forfeited property; restrictions on use of money in account; distribution of certain amount to school district; duties of school district and chief administrative officer of law enforcement agency.

1. The governing body controlling each law enforcement agency that receives proceeds from the sale of forfeited property shall establish with the State Treasurer, county treasurer, city treasurer or town treasurer, as custodian, a special account, known as the "................ Forfeiture Account." The account is a separate and continuing account and no money in it reverts to the State General Fund or the general fund of the county, city or town at any time. For the purposes of this section, the governing body controlling a metropolitan police department is the Metropolitan Police Committee on Fiscal Affairs.

2. The money in the account may be used for any lawful purpose deemed appropriate by the chief administrative officer of the law enforcement agency, except that:

(a) The money must not be used to pay the ordinary operating expenses of the agency.

(b) Money derived from the forfeiture of any property described in NRS 453.301 must be used to enforce the provisions of chapter 453 of NRS.

(c) Money derived from the forfeiture of any property described in NRS 501.3857 must be used to enforce the provisions of title 45 of NRS.

(d) Seventy percent of the amount of money in excess of $100,000 remaining in the account at the end of each fiscal year, as determined based upon the accounting standards of the governing body controlling the law enforcement agency that are in place on March 1, 2001, must be distributed to the school district in the judicial district. If the judicial district serves more than one county, the money must be distributed to the school district in the county from which the property was seized.

3. Notwithstanding the provisions of paragraphs (a) and (b) of subsection 2, money in the account derived from the forfeiture of any property described in NRS 453.301 may be used to pay for the operating expenses of a joint task force on narcotics otherwise funded by a federal, state or private grant or donation. As used in this subsection, "joint task force on narcotics" means a task force on narcotics operated by the Department of Public Safety in conjunction with other local or federal law enforcement agencies.

4. A school district that receives money pursuant to paragraph (d) of subsection 2 shall deposit such money into a separate account. The interest and income earned on the money in the account, after deducting any applicable charges, must be credited to the account. The money in the account must be used to purchase books and computer hardware and software for the use of the students in that school district.

5. The chief administrative officer of a law enforcement agency that distributes money to a school district pursuant to paragraph (d) of subsection 2 shall submit a report to the Director of the Legislative Counsel Bureau before January 1 of each odd-numbered year. The report must contain the amount of money distributed to each school district pursuant to paragraph (d) of subsection 2 in the preceding biennium.

(Added to NRS by 1989, 1789; A 1991, 2287; 2001, 876; 2003, 2528)

NRS 179.119 Quarterly reports by law enforcement agencies that receive forfeited property or related proceeds; inclusion of such anticipated revenue in budget prohibited.

1. Any law enforcement agency that receives forfeited property or the proceeds of a sale of such property pursuant to the provisions contained in NRS 179.1156 to 179.1205, inclusive, shall:

(a) File a quarterly report of the approximate value of the property and the amount of the proceeds with the entity that controls the budget of the agency; and

(b) Provide the entity that controls the budget of the agency with a quarterly accounting of the receipt and use of the proceeds.

2. Revenue from forfeitures must not be considered in the preparation of the budget of a law enforcement agency except as money to match money from the Federal Government.

(Added to NRS by 1985, 1468; A 1987, 1384; 1989, 1790; 2003, 2529)

NRS 179.1205 Annual reports by law enforcement agencies.

1. On an annual basis, each law enforcement agency shall report the following information about each individual seizure and forfeiture completed by the law enforcement agency under state forfeiture law:

(a) Data on seizures and forfeitures, including, without limitation, the:

(1) Date that currency, vehicles, houses or other types of property were seized;

(2) Type of property seized, including, the year, make and model, as applicable;

(3) Type of crime associated with the seizure of the property;

(4) Market value of the property seized;

(5) Disposition of the property following the seizure; and

(6) Date of the disposition of the property.

(b) Data on the use of proceeds, including, without limitation, the:

(1) Payment of all outstanding liens on the forfeited property;

(2) Payment of reasonable expenses, except personnel costs, of the seizure, storage and maintenance of custody of any forfeited property; and

(3) Distribution of proceeds pursuant to NRS 179.118, 179.1187, 179.1233 and 207.500.

(c) Any other information required by the Office of the Attorney General.

2. The Office of the Attorney General shall develop standard forms, processes and deadlines for the entry of electronic data for the annual submission of the report required by subsection 1.

3. Each law enforcement agency shall file with the Office of the Attorney General the report required by subsection 1. A null report must be filed by a law enforcement agency that did not engage in a seizure or forfeiture during the reporting period. The Office of the Attorney General shall compile the submissions and issue an aggregate report of all forfeitures in this State.

4. On or before April 1 of each year, the Office of the Attorney General shall make available:

(a) On its Internet website, the reports submitted by law enforcement agencies and the aggregate report.

(b) Upon request, printed copies of the reports submitted by law enforcement agencies and the aggregate report.

5. The Office of the Attorney General shall include in the aggregate report information on any law enforcement agencies not in compliance with this section.

(Added to NRS by 2015, 2500)

NRS 179.121 Forfeiture of personal property and conveyances used in commission of crime.

1. All personal property, including, without limitation, any tool, substance, weapon, machine, computer, money or security, which is used as an instrumentality in any of the following crimes is subject to forfeiture:

(a) The commission of or attempted commission of the crime of murder, robbery, kidnapping, burglary, invasion of the home, grand larceny or theft if it is punishable as a felony;

(b) The commission of or attempted commission of any felony with the intent to commit, cause, aid, further or conceal an act of terrorism;

(c) A violation of NRS 202.445 or 202.446;

(d) The commission of any crime by a criminal gang, as defined in NRS 213.1263; or

(e) A violation of NRS 200.463 to 200.468, inclusive, 201.300, 201.320, 202.265, 202.287, 205.473 to 205.513, inclusive, 205.610 to 205.810, inclusive, 370.380, 370.382, 370.395, 370.405, 465.070 to 465.086, inclusive, 630.400, 630A.600, 631.400, 632.285, 632.291, 632.315, 633.741, 634.227, 634A.230, 635.167, 636.145, 637.090, 637B.290, 639.100, 639.2813, 640.169, 640A.230, 644.190 or 654.200.

2. Except as otherwise provided for conveyances forfeitable pursuant to NRS 453.301 or 501.3857, all conveyances, including aircraft, vehicles or vessels, which are used or intended for use during the commission of a felony or a violation of NRS 202.287, 202.300 or 465.070 to 465.086, inclusive, are subject to forfeiture except that:

(a) A conveyance used by any person as a common carrier in the transaction of business as a common carrier is not subject to forfeiture under this section unless it appears that the owner or other person in charge of the conveyance is a consenting party or privy to the felony or violation;

(b) A conveyance is not subject to forfeiture under this section by reason of any act or omission established by the owner thereof to have been committed or omitted without the owner's knowledge, consent or willful blindness;

(c) A conveyance is not subject to forfeiture for a violation of NRS 202.300 if the firearm used in the violation of that section was not loaded at the time of the violation; and

(d) A forfeiture of a conveyance encumbered by a bona fide security interest is subject to the interest of the secured party if the secured party neither had knowledge of nor consented to the felony. If a conveyance is forfeited, the appropriate law enforcement agency may pay the existing balance and retain the conveyance for official use.

3. For the purposes of this section, a firearm is loaded if:

(a) There is a cartridge in the chamber of the firearm;

(b) There is a cartridge in the cylinder of the firearm, if the firearm is a revolver; or

(c) There is a cartridge in the magazine and the magazine is in the firearm or there is a cartridge in the chamber, if the firearm is a semiautomatic firearm.

4. As used in this section, "act of terrorism" has the meaning ascribed to it in NRS 202.4415.

(Added to NRS by 1983, 1135; A 1985, 638, 1239; 1989, 656, 1187, 1188, 1241, 1242, 1453; 1991, 210, 2287, 2288; 1995, 1150, 1424; 1997, 639; 1999, 2711; 2003, 2952; 2005, 90, 1199; 2007, 1269; 2009, 575; 2013, 1857, 2248, 2420; 2015, 2311)

FORFEITURE OF PROPERTY RELATING TO TECHNOLOGICAL CRIMES

NRS 179.1211 Definitions. As used in NRS 179.1211 to 179.1235, inclusive, unless the context otherwise requires, the words and terms defined in NRS 179.1213, 179.1215 and 179.1217 have the meanings ascribed to them in those sections.

(Added to NRS by 2007, 201)

NRS 179.1213 "Proceeds" defined. "Proceeds" means any property, or that part of an item of property, derived directly or indirectly from a technological crime.

(Added to NRS by 2007, 201)

NRS 179.1215 "Property" defined. "Property" includes, without limitation, any:

1. Real property or interest in real property.
2. Fixture or improvement to real property.
3. Personal property, whether tangible or intangible, or interest in personal property.
4. Conveyance, including, without limitation, any aircraft, vehicle or vessel.
5. Money, security or negotiable instrument.
6. Proceeds.

(Added to NRS by 2007, 201)

NRS 179.1217 "Technological crime" defined. "Technological crime" has the meaning ascribed to it in NRS 205A.030.

(Added to NRS by 2007, 201)

NRS 179.1219 Property subject to forfeiture; substitution for unreachable property.

1. Except as otherwise provided in NRS 179.1221, if an indictment or information filed in a criminal proceeding alleges that property was derived from, realized through, or used or intended for use in the course of a technological crime which is punishable as a felony and the extent of that property:

(a) The jury; or
(b) If the trial is without a jury, the court,

Ê shall, upon a conviction, determine at a separate hearing the extent of the property to be forfeited. If the indictment or information does not include such an allegation, the property is not subject to criminal forfeiture pursuant to this section.

2. If, at a hearing to determine the extent of the property to be forfeited pursuant to subsection 1, the jury or, if the hearing is without a jury, the court determines by a preponderance of the evidence that the property:

(a) Was used or intended to be used in, or was used or intended to be used to facilitate, a technological crime; or
(b) Was acquired during a technological crime or within a reasonable time after the technological crime and there was no likely source of such property other than the technological crime,

Ê the court shall order the forfeiture of the property.

3. The following property is subject to criminal forfeiture pursuant to subsection 1:

(a) Any proceeds attributable to a technological crime;
(b) Any property acquired directly or indirectly from a technological crime; and
(c) Any property used or intended to be used in, or used or intended to be used to facilitate, a technological crime.

4. If property which is ordered to be criminally forfeited pursuant to subsection 1:

(a) Cannot be located;
(b) Has been sold to a purchaser in good faith for value;
(c) Has been placed beyond the jurisdiction of the court;
(d) Has been substantially diminished in value by the conduct of the defendant;
(e) Has been commingled with other property which cannot be divided without difficulty or undue injury to innocent persons; or
(f) Is otherwise unreachable without undue injury to innocent persons,

Ê the court shall order the forfeiture of other property of the defendant up to the value of the property that is unreachable.

(Added to NRS by 2007, 201)

NRS 179.1221 Forfeiture as part of plea agreement.

1. A defendant who agrees to enter a plea of guilty to a technological crime may agree to the forfeiture of any property as part of the agreement.

2. If the court accepts the plea of guilty, the court shall order the forfeiture of the property that the defendant agreed to forfeit pursuant to subsection 1.

(Added to NRS by 2007, 202)

NRS 179.1223 Temporary restraining order to preserve property.

1. The prosecuting attorney may apply for, and a court may issue without notice or hearing, a temporary restraining order to preserve property which would be subject to criminal forfeiture pursuant to NRS 179.1219 if:

(a) An indictment or information alleging a technological crime has been filed in a criminal proceeding and the extent of criminally forfeitable property is included therein or the court believes there is probable cause for such an inclusion;
(b) The property is in the possession or control of the party against whom the order will be entered; and
(c) The court determines that the nature of the property is such that it can be concealed, disposed of or placed beyond the jurisdiction of the court before a hearing on the matter.

2. A temporary restraining order which is issued without notice may be issued for not more than 10 days and may be extended only for good cause or by consent. The court shall provide notice and hold a hearing on the matter before the order expires.

(Added to NRS by 2007, 202)

NRS 179.1225 Orders to secure property.

1. After an information or indictment alleging a technological crime is filed in a criminal proceeding, the prosecuting attorney may request the court to:

(a) Enter a restraining order or injunction;
(b) Require the execution of a satisfactory bond;
(c) Appoint a receiver; or
(d) Take any other necessary action,

Ê to secure property which is subject to criminal forfeiture.

2. The court shall, after a hearing for which notice was given to any person whose rights in the property proposed for forfeiture would be affected, order such an action if the prosecuting attorney shows by a preponderance of the evidence that the action is necessary to preserve the defendant's property which is subject to criminal forfeiture.

3. If no indictment or information alleging a technological crime has been filed, the court may, after such a hearing and upon a showing of the prosecuting attorney that:

(a) There is probable cause to believe that the property for which the order is sought would be subject to criminal forfeiture; and
(b) The requested order would not result in substantial and irreparable harm or injury to the party against whom the order is to be entered that outweighs the need to secure the property for the potential criminal forfeiture,

Ê order an action to secure the property. Such an order may not be effective for more than 90 days unless it is extended for good cause or an indictment or information alleging a technological crime is filed and the extent of the criminally forfeitable property is listed therein.

(Added to NRS by 2007, 202)

NRS 179.1227 Order of forfeiture; order to protect interests of State.

1. Upon a verdict of guilty or a plea of guilty to a technological crime, the court may order the forfeiture of the appropriate property.

2. Upon entry of such an order, the court may:

(a) Enter a restraining order or injunction;

(b) Require the execution of a satisfactory bond;

(c) Appoint a receiver; or

(d) Take any other necessary action,

Ê to protect the interests of the State.

(Added to NRS by 2007, 203)

NRS 179.1229 Property subject to civil forfeiture; required proof; where action must be instituted.

1. Except as otherwise provided in subsection 2, all property used in the course of, intended for use in the course of, derived from or gained through a technological crime is subject to civil forfeiture to the State.

2. Upon a showing by the owner of the property of the requisite facts, the following is not subject to forfeiture under this section:

(a) Except as otherwise provided in paragraph (b), property used without the knowledge or consent of its owner; and

(b) A means of transportation used by a person in the transaction of business as a common carrier unless it appears the owner or person in charge of the common carrier consented to or had knowledge of the technological crime.

3. The State is not required to plead or prove that a person has been charged with or convicted of any technological crime. If proof of such conviction is made, and it is shown that the judgment of conviction has become final, the proof against any person is conclusive evidence of all facts necessary to sustain the conviction.

4. Any civil action or proceeding under this section must be instituted in the district court of the State in the county in which the prospective defendant resides or has committed any act which subjects the prospective defendant to criminal or civil liability pursuant to the provisions of NRS 179.1211 to 179.1235, inclusive.

(Added to NRS by 2007, 203)

NRS 179.1231 Seizure of property before forfeiture and final disposition; institution of proceedings; intercession by district attorney or Attorney General; interlocutory actions by court; order of forfeiture.

1. Property subject to forfeiture under NRS 179.1219 or 179.1229 may be seized by a law enforcement agency upon process issued by a court. Before an order of civil forfeiture is issued without legal process, notice of the claim for forfeiture of real property may be given in the manner provided in NRS 14.010 and 14.015. A seizure of personal property may be made without legal process if the seizure is incident to:

(a) A lawful arrest or search; or

(b) An inspection under an administrative warrant.

2. Property seized or made the subject of notice under this section is deemed to be in the custody of the agency, subject only to orders of the court which has jurisdiction over the proceedings for forfeiture. An agency which has seized such property without process shall begin proceedings for forfeiture promptly. Such an action takes precedence over other civil proceedings. The seized property is subject to an action to claim the delivery of the property if the agency does not file the complaint for forfeiture within 60 days after the property is seized. If a complaint for forfeiture is filed after an affidavit claiming delivery, the complaint must be treated as a counterclaim.

3. When property is seized pursuant to this section, pending forfeiture and final disposition, the law enforcement agency may:

(a) Place the property under seal.

(b) Remove the property to a place designated by the court.

(c) Require another agency authorized by law to take custody of the property and remove it to an appropriate location.

4. The district attorney or the Attorney General may institute civil proceedings under this section for the forfeiture of property subject to forfeiture pursuant to NRS 179.1229. The district attorney and the Attorney General shall determine by agreement between themselves which of them will institute such a proceeding in a particular case. If a district attorney or the Attorney General has not instituted such a proceeding or has not pursued one which was instituted in accordance with the agreement, the other may intercede after giving the prosecutor designated in the agreement 30 days' written notice of the intention to do so. In any action so brought, the district court shall proceed as soon as practicable to the hearing and determination. Pending final determination in an action brought pursuant to this section, the district court may at any time enter such injunctions, prohibitions or restraining orders, or take such actions, including, without limitation, the acceptance of satisfactory performance bonds, as the court deems proper in connection with any property or interest subject to forfeiture.

5. Upon a finding of civil liability under this section, the court may order the forfeiture of the appropriate property.

(Added to NRS by 2007, 203; A 2013, 823)

NRS 179.1233 Sale of forfeited property; use of proceeds; deposit of balance of proceeds in Account for the Technological Crime Advisory Board; payment of certain encumbrances.

1. The State, county or city shall sell any property forfeited pursuant to NRS 179.1219 or 179.1229 as soon as commercially feasible. Except as otherwise provided in subsection 2, the proceeds from such a sale must be used first for payment of all proper expenses of any proceedings for the forfeiture and sale, including, without limitation, any expenses for the seizure and maintenance of the property, advertising and court costs. The balance of the proceeds, if any, must be deposited in the Account for the Technological Crime Advisory Board created pursuant to NRS 205A.090.

2. If the property forfeited is encumbered by a bona fide security interest and the secured party shows that the secured party did not consent or have knowledge of the violation causing the forfeiture, the State, county or city shall pay the existing balance or return the property to the secured party.

(Added to NRS by 2007, 204)

NRS 179.1235 Limitation of actions. A criminal action or proceeding pursuant to NRS 179.1219 may be commenced at any time within 5 years after the technological crime occurs. Except as otherwise provided in NRS 217.007, a civil action or proceeding pursuant to NRS 179.1229 may be commenced at any time within 5 years after the technological crime occurs. If a criminal prosecution, civil action or other proceeding is brought to punish, prevent or restrain a technological crime, the running of the period of limitations prescribed by this section with respect to any cause of action arising under NRS 179.1229, which is based in whole or in part upon any matter complained of in the prosecution or proceeding, is suspended during the pendency of the prosecution or proceeding and for 2 years following termination of the prosecution or proceeding.

(Added to NRS by 2007, 204)

DISPOSAL OF PROPERTY STOLEN OR EMBEZZLED

NRS 179.125 Stolen or embezzled property held by peace officer subject to magistrate's order. Except as provided in NRS 52.385, when property, alleged to have been stolen or embezzled, shall come into the custody of a peace officer, the peace officer shall hold the same subject to the order of the magistrate authorized by NRS 179.135 to direct the disposal thereof.

(Added to NRS by 1967, 1460; A 1975, 1184)

NRS 179.135 Order for delivery to owner; payment of expenses. On satisfactory proof of the title of the owner of the property, the magistrate to whom the information is laid, or who shall examine the charge against the person accused of stealing or embezzling the property, may order it to be delivered to the owner, on the owner's paying the reasonable and necessary expenses incurred in its preservation, to be certified by the magistrate. The order shall entitle the owner to demand and receive the property.

(Added to NRS by 1967, 1460)

NRS 179.145 Magistrate to deliver property to owner when it comes into magistrate's custody; proof of title and payment of expenses. If the property stolen or embezzled come into the custody of the magistrate, it shall be delivered to the owner on satisfactory proof of title, and on the owner's paying the necessary expenses incurred in its preservation, to be certified by the magistrate.

(Added to NRS by 1967, 1461)

NRS 179.155 Court may order return of property to owner. If the property stolen or embezzled has not been delivered to the owner, the court before which a conviction is had for stealing or embezzling it may, on proof of title, order it to be restored to the owner.

(Added to NRS by 1967, 1461)

NRS 179.165 Notice must be provided by law enforcement agency to owner, pawnbroker and other interested persons; contents of notice; sale or disposal of unclaimed property by county treasurer; records.

1. Except as otherwise provided in subsections 2 and 3, a law enforcement agency which has custody of property that has been stolen or embezzled shall, if the agency knows or can reasonably discover the name and address of the owner or the person entitled to possession of the property, notify the owner or the person entitled to possession of the property by letter of the location of the property and the method by which the owner or the person entitled to possession of the property may claim it.

2. If the property that has been stolen or embezzled is a firearm, the law enforcement agency shall notify only the owner of the firearm of the location of the property and the method by which the owner may claim it.

3. If the property that has been stolen or embezzled was obtained from a pawnbroker pursuant to NRS 646.047, the law enforcement agency shall, in addition to notifying the persons described in subsection 1 or 2, as appropriate, notify the pawnbroker from whom it was obtained.

4. The notice must be mailed by certified or registered mail:

(a) Upon the conviction of the person who committed the offense;

(b) Upon the decision of the police or district attorney not to pursue or prosecute the case; or

(c) When the case is otherwise terminated.

5. If the property stolen or embezzled is not claimed by the owner or the person entitled to possession of the property before the expiration of 6 months after the date the notice is mailed or, if no notice is required, after the date notice would have been sent if it were required, the magistrate or other officer having it in custody shall, except as otherwise provided in this subsection, on payment of the necessary expenses incurred for its preservation, deliver it to the county treasurer, who shall dispose of the property as provided in subsection 6. If a metropolitan police department which is organized pursuant to chapter 280 of NRS has custody of the property, the sheriff of the department may deliver it to the county treasurer and accept the net proceeds, if any, from the disposition of the property pursuant to subsection 6 in lieu of the payment of expenses incurred for the property's preservation.

6. Upon receiving stolen or embezzled property pursuant to this section, the county treasurer shall petition the district court for an order authorizing the county treasurer to:

(a) Conduct an auction for the disposal of salable property;

(b) Dispose of property not deemed salable by donations to charitable organizations or by destruction;

(c) Destroy property the possession of which is deemed illegal or dangerous; or

(d) Dispose of property not purchased at an auction by donations to charitable organizations or by destruction.

7. Records of the property disposed of by sale, destruction or donation and an accounting of the cash received by the county treasurer from the sales must be filed with the county clerk.

(Added to NRS by 1967, 1461; A 1973, 565; 1989, 382; 1999, 753)

CRIMINAL EXTRADITION (UNIFORM ACT)

NRS 179.177 Short title. NRS 179.177 to 179.235, inclusive, may be cited as the Uniform Criminal Extradition Act.
(Added to NRS by 1967, 1098)

NRS 179.179 Definitions. As used in NRS 179.177 to 179.235, inclusive, unless the context requires otherwise:
1. "Executive authority" means the governor, and any person performing the functions of governor in a state other than this state.
2. "Governor" means any person performing the functions of Governor by authority of the law of this state.
3. "State," when referring to a state other than this state, means any other state or territory, organized or unorganized, of the United States of America.
(Added to NRS by 1967, 1098)

NRS 179.181 Fugitives from justice; duty of Governor. Subject to the provisions of NRS 179.177 to 179.235, inclusive, the provisions of the Constitution of the United States controlling, and any and all Acts of Congress enacted in pursuance thereof, it is the duty of the Governor of this state to have arrested and delivered up to the executive authority of any other state of the United States any person charged in that state with treason, felony or other crime, who has fled from justice and is found in this state.
(Added to NRS by 1967, 1098)

NRS 179.183 Form of demand. No demand for the extradition of a person charged with crime in another state shall be recognized by the Governor unless it is:
1. In writing alleging, except in cases arising under NRS 179.189, that the accused was present in the demanding state at the time of the commission of the alleged crime, and that thereafter the accused fled from the state; and
2. Accompanied by a copy of an indictment found or by information supported by affidavit in the state having jurisdiction of the crime, or by a copy of an affidavit made before a magistrate there, together with a copy of any warrant which was issued thereupon; or
3. Accompanied by a copy of a judgment of conviction or of a sentence imposed in execution thereof, together with a statement by the executive authority of the demanding state that the person claimed has escaped from confinement or has broken the terms of the person's bail, probation or parole.
Ê The indictment, information or affidavit made before the magistrate must substantially charge the person demanded with having committed a crime under the law of that state; and the copy of indictment, information, affidavit, judgment of conviction or sentence must be authenticated by the executive authority making the demand.
(Added to NRS by 1967, 1098)

NRS 179.185 Governor may investigate case. When a demand is made upon the Governor of this state by the executive authority of another state for the surrender of a person so charged with crime, the Governor may call upon the Attorney General or any prosecuting officer in this state to investigate or assist in investigating the demand, and to report to the Governor the situation and circumstances of the person so demanded, and whether the person ought to be surrendered.
(Added to NRS by 1967, 1099)

NRS 179.187 Extradition of persons imprisoned or awaiting trial in another state or who have left demanding state under compulsion.
1. When it is desired to have returned to this state a person charged in this state with a crime, and such person is imprisoned or is held under criminal proceedings then pending against the person in another state, the Governor of this state may agree with the executive authority of such other state for the extradition of such person before the conclusion of such proceedings or the person's term of sentence in such other state, upon condition that such person be returned to such other state at the expense of this state as soon as the prosecution in this state is terminated.
2. The Governor of this state may also surrender on demand of the executive authority of any other state any person in this state who is charged in the manner provided in NRS 179.223 with having violated the laws of the state whose executive authority is making the demand, even though such person left the demanding state involuntarily.
(Added to NRS by 1967, 1099)

NRS 179.189 Extradition of persons not present in demanding state at time of commission of crime. The Governor of this state may also surrender, on demand of the executive authority of any other state, any person in this state charged in such other state in the manner provided in NRS 179.183 with committing an act in this state, or in a third state, intentionally resulting in a crime in the state whose executive authority is making the demand, and the provisions of NRS 179.177 to 179.235, inclusive, not otherwise inconsistent shall apply to such cases, even though the accused was not in that state at the time of the commission of the crime, and has not fled therefrom.
(Added to NRS by 1967, 1099)

NRS 179.191 Governor's warrant of arrest.
1. If the Governor decides that the demand should be complied with, the Governor shall sign a warrant of arrest, which must be sealed with the state seal, and be directed to any peace officer or other person whom the Governor may think fit to entrust with the execution thereof. The warrant must substantially recite the facts necessary to the validity of its issuance.
2. A telegraphic copy or an abstract of the Governor's warrant may be sent by telegraph, teletype or any other electronic device to the person entrusted with the execution of the warrant. The copy or abstract is as effectual as the original warrant issued by the Governor.
3. The person who causes a telegraphic copy or abstract of the Governor's warrant to be sent must certify as correct, and file in the telegraphic office from which the copy or abstract is sent, a copy of the warrant, and must return the original with a statement of the person's actions under the warrant.
(Added to NRS by 1967, 1099; A 1987, 91)

NRS 179.193 Manner and place of execution. Such warrant shall authorize the peace officer or other person to whom directed to:

1. Arrest the accused at any time and any place where the accused may be found within the State;
2. Command the aid of all peace officers or other persons in the execution of the warrant; and
3. Deliver the accused, subject to the provisions of NRS 179.177 to 179.235, inclusive, to the duly authorized agent of the demanding state.

(Added to NRS by 1967, 1099)

NRS 179.195 Authority of arresting officer. Every such peace officer or other person empowered to make the arrest shall have the same authority, in arresting the accused, to command assistance therein as peace officers have by law in the execution of any criminal process directed to them, with like penalties against those who refuse their assistance.

(Added to NRS by 1967, 1100)

NRS 179.197 Rights of accused person; application for writ of habeas corpus.

1. No person arrested upon such warrant shall be delivered over to the agent whom the executive authority demanding the person has appointed to receive the person unless the person is first taken forthwith before a judge of a court of record in this state, who shall inform the person of the demand made for surrender and of the crime with which the person is charged, and that the person has the right to demand and procure legal counsel.
2. If the prisoner or the prisoner's counsel state that the prisoner or they desire to test the legality of the arrest, the judge of such court of record shall fix a reasonable time to be allowed within which to apply to the district court for a writ of habeas corpus.
3. When such writ is applied for, notice thereof, and of the time and place of hearing thereon, shall be given to the prosecuting officer of the county in which the arrest is made and in which the accused is in custody, and to the agent of the demanding state.

(Added to NRS by 1967, 1100; A 1983, 539)

NRS 179.199 Penalty for noncompliance with NRS 179.197. Any officer who delivers to the agent for extradition of the demanding state a person in the officer's custody under the Governor's warrant, in willful disobedience to NRS 179.197, shall be guilty of a misdemeanor.

(Added to NRS by 1967, 1100)

NRS 179.201 Confinement in jail or detention facility when necessary.

1. The officer or persons executing the Governor's warrant of arrest, or the agent of the demanding state to whom the prisoner may have been delivered may, when necessary, confine the prisoner in the jail or detention facility of any county or city through which he or she may pass, and the keeper of the jail or detention facility shall receive and safely keep the prisoner until the officer or person having charge of the prisoner is ready to proceed on his or her route, such officer or person being chargeable with the expense of keeping.
2. The officer or agent of a demanding state to whom a prisoner may have been delivered following extradition proceedings in another state, or to whom a prisoner may have been delivered after waiving extradition in another state, and who is passing through this state with a prisoner for the purpose of immediately returning the prisoner to the demanding state may, when necessary, confine the prisoner in the jail or detention facility of any county or city through which he or she may pass, and the keeper of the jail or detention facility shall receive and safely keep the prisoner until the officer or agent having charge of the prisoner is ready to proceed on his or her route, such officer or agent being chargeable with the expense of keeping. The officer or agent shall produce and show to the keeper of the jail or detention facility satisfactory written evidence of the fact that the officer or agent is actually transporting a prisoner to the demanding state after a requisition by the executive authority of the demanding state. The prisoner is not entitled to demand a new requisition while in this state.

(Added to NRS by 1967, 1100; A 1989, 1178)

NRS 179.203 Arrest before requisition.

1. Whenever any person within this state is charged on the oath of any credible person before any judge or magistrate of this state with the commission of any crime in any other state and, except in cases arising under NRS 179.189, with having fled from justice, or with having been convicted of a crime in that state and having escaped from confinement, or having broken the terms of the person's bail, probation or parole; or
2. Whenever complaint has been made before any judge or magistrate in this state setting forth on the affidavit of any credible person in another state that a crime has been committed in such other state and that the accused has been charged in such state with the commission of the crime, and, except in cases arising under NRS 179.189, has fled from justice, or with having been convicted of a crime in that state and having escaped from confinement, or having broken the terms of the person's bail, probation or parole and is believed to be in this state,

Ê the judge or magistrate shall issue a warrant directed to any peace officer commanding the peace officer to apprehend the person named therein, wherever the person may be found in this state, and to bring the person before the same or any other judge, magistrate or court who or which may be available in or convenient of access to the place where the arrest may be made, to answer the charge or complaint and affidavit. A certified copy of the sworn charge or complaint and affidavit upon which the warrant is issued shall be attached to the warrant.

(Added to NRS by 1967, 1100)

NRS 179.205 Arrest without warrant. The arrest of a person may be lawfully made also by any peace officer or a private person, without a warrant upon reasonable information that the accused stands charged in the courts of a state with a crime punishable by death or imprisonment for a term exceeding 1 year; but when so arrested the accused must be taken before a judge or magistrate with all practicable speed and complaint must be made against the person under oath setting forth the ground for the arrest as in NRS 179.203. Thereafter the answer shall be heard as if the person had been arrested on a warrant.

(Added to NRS by 1967, 1101)

NRS 179.207 Commitment to await requisition; bail. If from the examination before the judge or magistrate it appears that the person held is the person charged with having committed the crime alleged and, except in cases arising under NRS 179.189, that the person has fled from justice, the judge or magistrate must, by a warrant reciting the accusation, commit the person to the county jail for such a time, not exceeding 30 days and specified in the warrant, as will enable the arrest of the accused to be made under a warrant of the Governor on a requisition of the executive authority of the state having jurisdiction of the offense, unless the accused gives bail as provided in NRS 179.209, or until the accused is legally discharged.

(Added to NRS by 1967, 1101; A 1967, 1389)

NRS 179.209 Bail: In what cases; conditions of bond. Unless the offense with which the prisoner is charged is shown to be an offense punishable by death or life imprisonment under the laws of the state in which it was committed, or unless the prisoner is charged as a parole violator or escaped convict, a judge or magistrate in this state may admit the person arrested to bail by bond, with sufficient sureties, and in such sum as the judge or magistrate deems proper, conditioned for the prisoner's appearance at a time specified in such bond, and for the person's surrender, to be arrested upon the warrant of the Governor of this state. No prisoner may be admitted to bail after having been arrested upon the warrant of the Governor of this state.

(Added to NRS by 1967, 1101; A 1973, 800)

NRS 179.211 Extension of time of commitment; adjournment. If the accused is not arrested under warrant of the Governor by the expiration of the time specified in the warrant or bond, a judge or magistrate may discharge or may recommit the accused for a further period not to exceed 60 days, or a judge or magistrate judge may again take bail for the accused's appearance and surrender, as provided in NRS 179.209, but within a period not to exceed 60 days after the date of such new bond.

(Added to NRS by 1967, 1101)

NRS 179.213 Forfeiture of bail. If the prisoner is admitted to bail, and fails to appear and surrender according to the conditions of the prisoner's bond, the judge, or magistrate by proper order, shall declare the bond forfeited and order the prisoner's immediate arrest without warrant if the prisoner is within this state. Recovery may be had on such bond in the name of the State as in the case of other bonds given by the accused in criminal proceedings within this state.

(Added to NRS by 1967, 1102)

NRS 179.215 Persons under criminal prosecution in this State at time of requisition. If a criminal prosecution has been instituted against such person under the laws of this State and is still pending, the Governor, in the Governor's discretion, either may surrender the person on demand of the executive authority of another state or hold the person until the person has been tried and discharged or convicted and punished in this State.

(Added to NRS by 1967, 1102)

NRS 179.217 Guilt or innocence of accused: When inquired into. The guilt or innocence of the accused as to the crime of which the accused is charged may not be inquired into by the Governor or in any proceeding after the demand for extradition accompanied by a charge of crime in legal form as above provided has been presented to the Governor, except as it may be involved in identifying the person held as the person charged with the crime.

(Added to NRS by 1967, 1102)

NRS 179.219 Governor may recall warrant or issue alias. The Governor may recall a warrant of arrest or may issue another warrant whenever the Governor deems proper.

(Added to NRS by 1967, 1102)

NRS 179.221 Fugitives from this State; duty of Governor. Whenever the Governor of this State demands a person charged with crime or with escaping from confinement or breaking the terms of bail, probation or parole in this State, from the executive authority of any other state, or from the Chief Justice or an associate justice of the Supreme Court of the District of Columbia authorized to receive such demand under the laws of the United States, the Governor shall issue a warrant under the seal of this State, to some agent, commanding the agent to receive the person so charged if delivered and convey the person to the proper officer of the county in this State in which the offense was committed.

(Added to NRS by 1967, 1102)

NRS 179.223 Application for issuance of requisition: By whom made; contents.

1. When the return to this state of a person charged with crime in this state is required, the district attorney shall present to the Governor a written application for a requisition for the return of the person charged in which application must be stated:

(a) The name of the person so charged;

(b) The crime charged against the person;

(c) The approximate time, place and circumstances of its commission;

(d) The state in which the person is believed to be, including the location of the accused therein at the time the application is made; and

(e) A certification that, in the opinion of the district attorney, the ends of justice require the arrest and return of the accused to this state for trial and that the proceeding is not instituted to enforce a private claim.

2. When the return to this state is required of a person who has been convicted of a crime in this state and has escaped from confinement or broken the terms of the person's bail, probation or parole, the district attorney of the county in which the offense was

committed, the State Board of Parole Commissioners, the Chief Parole and Probation Officer, the Director of the Department of Corrections or the sheriff of the county from which escape was made shall present to the Governor a written application for a requisition for the return of the person, in which application must be stated:

(a) The name of the person;

(b) The crime of which the person was convicted;

(c) The circumstances of the person's escape from confinement or of the breach of the terms of bail, probation or parole; and

(d) The state in which the person is believed to be, including the location of the person therein at the time application is made.

3. The application must be verified by affidavit, executed in duplicate and accompanied by two certified copies of the indictment returned, or information and affidavit filed, or of the complaint made to the judge or magistrate, stating the offense with which the accused is charged, or of the judgment of conviction or of the sentence. The district attorney, State Board of Parole Commissioners, Chief Parole and Probation Officer, Director of the Department of Corrections or sheriff may also attach such further affidavits and other documents in duplicate as deemed proper to be submitted with the application. One copy of the application, with the action of the Governor indicated by endorsement thereon, and one of the certified copies of the indictment, complaint, information and affidavits, or of the judgment of conviction or of the sentence must be filed in the Office of the Secretary of State of the State of Nevada to remain of record in that office. The other copies of all papers must be forwarded with the Governor's requisition.

(Added to NRS by 1967, 1102; A 1969, 15; 1977, 864; 1985, 149; 2001 Special Session, 224)

NRS 179.225 Costs and expenses.

1. If the punishment of the crime is the confinement of the criminal in prison, the expenses must be paid from money appropriated to the Office of the Attorney General for that purpose, upon approval by the State Board of Examiners. After the appropriation is exhausted, the expenses must be paid from the Reserve for Statutory Contingency Account upon approval by the State Board of Examiners. In all other cases, they must be paid out of the county treasury in the county wherein the crime is alleged to have been committed. The expenses are:

(a) If the prisoner is returned to this State from another state, the fees paid to the officers of the state on whose governor the requisition is made;

(b) If the prisoner is returned to this State from a foreign country or jurisdiction, the fees paid to the officers and agents of this State or the United States; or

(c) If the prisoner is temporarily returned for prosecution to this State from another state pursuant to this chapter or chapter 178 of NRS and is then returned to the sending state upon completion of the prosecution, the fees paid to the officers and agents of this State,

Ê and the per diem allowance and travel expenses provided for state officers and employees generally incurred in returning the prisoner.

2. If a person is returned to this State pursuant to this chapter or chapter 178 of NRS and is convicted of, or pleads guilty, guilty but mentally ill or nolo contendere to, the criminal charge for which the person was returned or a lesser criminal charge, the court shall conduct an investigation of the financial status of the person to determine the ability to make restitution. In conducting the investigation, the court shall determine if the person is able to pay any existing obligations for:

(a) Child support;

(b) Restitution to victims of crimes; and

(c) Any administrative assessment required to be paid pursuant to NRS 62E.270, 176.059, 176.0611, 176.0613, 176.062 and 176.0623.

3. If the court determines that the person is financially able to pay the obligations described in subsection 2, it shall, in addition to any other sentence it may impose, order the person to make restitution for the expenses incurred by the Office of the Attorney General or other governmental entity in returning the person to this State. The court shall not order the person to make restitution if payment of restitution will prevent the person from paying any existing obligations described in subsection 2. Any amount of restitution remaining unpaid constitutes a civil liability arising upon the date of the completion of the sentence.

4. If the court orders a person to make restitution for the expenses incurred by the Office of the Attorney General in returning the person to this State pursuant to this section, the Office of the Attorney General shall assign the collection of such restitution to the State Controller in accordance with the provisions of NRS 353C.195.

5. The Attorney General may adopt regulations to carry out the provisions of this section.

(Added to NRS by 1967, 1103; A 1968, 22; 1969, 640; 1973, 170; 1983, 727; 1991, 1754; 1993, 305, 935; 1995, 2459; 1997, 150, 1599; 2003, 1121, 1473, 2105; 2007, 598, 1427; 2013, 820, 1072)

NRS 179.227 Immunity from service of process in certain civil actions. A person brought into this State by, or after waiver of, extradition based on a criminal charge shall not be subject to service of personal process in civil actions arising out of the same facts as the criminal proceeding to answer which the person is being or has been returned, until the person has been convicted in the criminal proceeding, or, if acquitted, until the person has had reasonable opportunity to return to the state from which the person was extradited.

(Added to NRS by 1967, 1103)

NRS 179.229 Written waiver of extradition proceedings.

1. Except as otherwise provided in subsection 3, a person arrested in this State who is charged with having committed a crime in another state or who is alleged to have escaped from confinement, or broken the terms of the person's bail, probation or parole may waive the issuance and service of the warrant provided for in NRS 179.191 and 179.193 and all other procedure incidental to extradition proceedings, by executing or subscribing in the presence of a judge of a court of record within this State a writing which states that the person consents to return to the demanding state. Before the waiver is executed or subscribed, the judge shall inform the person of the rights to the issuance and service of a warrant of extradition and to obtain a writ of habeas corpus as provided for in NRS 179.197.

2. An executed waiver must be forwarded immediately to the Office of the Attorney General of this State and filed therein. The judge shall remand the person to custody without bail, unless otherwise stipulated by the district attorney with the concurrence of the other state,

and shall direct the officer having the person in custody to deliver the person immediately to an accredited agent of the demanding state, and shall deliver or cause to be delivered to the agent a copy of the waiver.

3. A law enforcement agency which has custody of a person in this State who is alleged to have broken the terms of the person's probation, parole, bail or other release shall, after the resolution of all criminal charges filed in this State against that person, immediately deliver that person to the accredited agent of the demanding state without a warrant issued pursuant to NRS 179.191 and 179.193 if:

(a) The person has signed a waiver of extradition as a condition of probation, parole, bail or other release in the demanding state; and

(b) The law enforcement agency has received:

(1) An authenticated copy of the waiver of extradition signed by the person; and

(2) A photograph and copy of the fingerprints of the person that identify him or her as the person who signed the waiver.

4. This section does not limit:

(a) The right of the accused person to return voluntarily and without formality to the demanding state;

(b) The powers, rights or duties of the officers of the demanding state or of this State; or

(c) Other procedures concerning the waiver of extradition.

(Added to NRS by 1967, 1103; A 1991, 153; 1993, 249; 1997, 151)

NRS 179.231 Nonwaiver by this State. Nothing contained in NRS 179.177 to 179.235, inclusive, shall be deemed to constitute a waiver by this State of its right, power or privilege to try such demanded person for crime committed within this State, or of its right, power or privilege to regain custody of such person by extradition proceedings or otherwise for the purpose of trial, sentence or punishment for any crime committed within this State, nor shall any proceedings had under NRS 179.177 to 179.235, inclusive, which result in, or fail to result in, extradition be deemed a waiver by this State of any of its rights, privileges or jurisdiction in any way whatsoever.

(Added to NRS by 1967, 1104)

NRS 179.233 No right of asylum; no immunity from other criminal prosecutions while in this State. After a person has been brought back to this State by or after waiver of extradition proceedings, the person may be tried in this State for other crimes which the person may be charged with having committed here as well as that specified in the requisition for extradition.

(Added to NRS by 1967, 1104)

NRS 179.235 Interpretation. The provisions of NRS 179.177 to 179.235, inclusive, shall be so interpreted and construed as to effectuate their general purposes to make uniform the law of those states which enact them.

(Added to NRS by 1967, 1104)

SEALING RECORDS OF CRIMINAL PROCEEDINGS

NRS 179.241 Definitions. As used in NRS 179.241 to 179.301, inclusive, unless the context otherwise requires, the words and terms defined in NRS 179.242, 179.243 and 179.244 have the meanings ascribed to them in those sections.

(Added to NRS by 2013, 107)

NRS 179.242 "Agency of criminal justice" defined. "Agency of criminal justice" has the meaning ascribed to it in NRS 179A.030.

(Added to NRS by 2013, 107)

NRS 179.243 "Disposition" defined. "Disposition" has the meaning ascribed to it in NRS 179A.050.

(Added to NRS by 2013, 107)

NRS 179.244 "Record" defined. "Record" has the meaning ascribed to "record of criminal history" in NRS 179A.070.

(Added to NRS by 2013, 107)

NRS 179.245 Sealing records after conviction: Persons eligible; petition; notice; hearing; order.

1. Except as otherwise provided in subsection 5 and NRS 176A.265, 176A.295, 179.259, 453.3365 and 458.330, a person may petition the court in which the person was convicted for the sealing of all records relating to a conviction of:

(a) A category A or B felony after 15 years from the date of release from actual custody or discharge from parole or probation, whichever occurs later;

(b) A category C or D felony after 12 years from the date of release from actual custody or discharge from parole or probation, whichever occurs later;

(c) A category E felony after 7 years from the date of release from actual custody or discharge from parole or probation, whichever occurs later;

(d) Except as otherwise provided in paragraph (e), any gross misdemeanor after 5 years from the date of release from actual custody or discharge from probation, whichever occurs later;

(e) A violation of NRS 422.540 to 422.570, inclusive, other than a felony, a violation of NRS 484C.110 or 484C.120 other than a felony, or a battery which constitutes domestic violence pursuant to NRS 33.018 other than a felony, after 7 years from the date of release from actual custody or from the date when the person is no longer under a suspended sentence, whichever occurs later; or

(f) Any other misdemeanor after 2 years from the date of release from actual custody or from the date when the person is no longer under a suspended sentence, whichever occurs later.

2. A petition filed pursuant to subsection 1 must:

(a) Be accompanied by the petitioner's current, verified records received from:

(1) The Central Repository for Nevada Records of Criminal History; and

(2) All agencies of criminal justice which maintain such records within the city or county in which the conviction was entered;

(b) If the petition references NRS 453.3365 or 458.330, include a certificate of acknowledgment or the disposition of the proceedings for the records to be sealed from all agencies of criminal justice which maintain such records;

(c) Include a list of any other public or private agency, company, official or other custodian of records that is reasonably known to the petitioner to have possession of records of the conviction and to whom the order to seal records, if issued, will be directed; and

(d) Include information that, to the best knowledge and belief of the petitioner, accurately and completely identifies the records to be sealed, including, without limitation, the:

(1) Date of birth of the petitioner;

(2) Specific conviction to which the records to be sealed pertain; and

(3) Date of arrest relating to the specific conviction to which the records to be sealed pertain.

3. Upon receiving a petition pursuant to this section, the court shall notify the law enforcement agency that arrested the petitioner for the crime and the prosecuting attorney, including, without limitation, the Attorney General, who prosecuted the petitioner for the crime. The prosecuting attorney and any person having relevant evidence may testify and present evidence at the hearing on the petition.

4. If, after the hearing, the court finds that, in the period prescribed in subsection 1, the petitioner has not been charged with any offense for which the charges are pending or convicted of any offense, except for minor moving or standing traffic violations, the court may order sealed all records of the conviction which are in the custody of any agency of criminal justice or any public or private agency, company, official or other custodian of records in the State of Nevada, and may also order all such records of the petitioner returned to the file of the court where the proceeding was commenced from, including, without limitation, the Federal Bureau of Investigation, the California Bureau of Criminal Identification and Information and all other agencies of criminal justice which maintain such records and which are reasonably known by either the petitioner or the court to have possession of such records.

5. A person may not petition the court to seal records relating to a conviction of:

(a) A crime against a child;

(b) A sexual offense;

(c) A violation of NRS 484C.110 or 484C.120 that is punishable as a felony pursuant to paragraph (c) of subsection 1 of NRS 484C.400;

(d) A violation of NRS 484C.430;

(e) A homicide resulting from driving or being in actual physical control of a vehicle while under the influence of intoxicating liquor or a controlled substance or resulting from any other conduct prohibited by NRS 484C.110, 484C.130 or 484C.430;

(f) A violation of NRS 488.410 that is punishable as a felony pursuant to NRS 488.427; or

(g) A violation of NRS 488.420 or 488.425.

6. If the court grants a petition for the sealing of records pursuant to this section, upon the request of the person whose records are sealed, the court may order sealed all records of the civil proceeding in which the records were sealed.

7. As used in this section:

(a) "Crime against a child" has the meaning ascribed to it in NRS 179D.0357.

(b) "Sexual offense" means:

(1) Murder of the first degree committed in the perpetration or attempted perpetration of sexual assault or of sexual abuse or sexual molestation of a child less than 14 years of age pursuant to paragraph (b) of subsection 1 of NRS 200.030.

(2) Sexual assault pursuant to NRS 200.366.

(3) Statutory sexual seduction pursuant to NRS 200.368, if punishable as a felony.

(4) Battery with intent to commit sexual assault pursuant to NRS 200.400.

(5) An offense involving the administration of a drug to another person with the intent to enable or assist the commission of a felony pursuant to NRS 200.405, if the felony is an offense listed in this paragraph.

(6) An offense involving the administration of a controlled substance to another person with the intent to enable or assist the commission of a crime of violence pursuant to NRS 200.408, if the crime of violence is an offense listed in this paragraph.

(7) Abuse of a child pursuant to NRS 200.508, if the abuse involved sexual abuse or sexual exploitation.

(8) An offense involving pornography and a minor pursuant to NRS 200.710 to 200.730, inclusive.

(9) Incest pursuant to NRS 201.180.

(10) Open or gross lewdness pursuant to NRS 201.210, if punishable as a felony.

(11) Indecent or obscene exposure pursuant to NRS 201.220, if punishable as a felony.

(12) Lewdness with a child pursuant to NRS 201.230.

(13) Sexual penetration of a dead human body pursuant to NRS 201.450.

(14) Sexual conduct between certain employees of a school or volunteers at a school and a pupil pursuant to NRS 201.540.

(15) Sexual conduct between certain employees of a college or university and a student pursuant to NRS 201.550.

(16) Luring a child or a person with mental illness pursuant to NRS 201.560, if punishable as a felony.

(17) An attempt to commit an offense listed in this paragraph.

(Added to NRS by 1971, 955; A 1983, 1088; 1991, 303; 1993, 38; 1997, 1673, 1803, 3159; 1999, 647, 648, 649; 2001, 1167, 1692; 2001 Special Session, 261; 2003, 312, 316, 319, 1385; 2005, 2355; 2007, 2751; 2009, 105, 418, 1884; 2013, 107, 980, 1165, 1382; 2015, 909, 1441)

NRS 179.255 Sealing of records after dismissal, decline of prosecution or acquittal: Petition; notice; hearing; order; inspection of records.

1. If a person has been arrested for alleged criminal conduct and the charges are dismissed, the prosecuting attorney having jurisdiction declined prosecution of the charges or such person is acquitted of the charges, the person may petition:

(a) The court in which the charges were dismissed, at any time after the date the charges were dismissed;

(b) The court having jurisdiction in which the charges were declined for prosecution:
(1) Any time after the applicable statute of limitations has run;
(2) Any time 10 years after the arrest; or
(3) Pursuant to a stipulation between the parties; or
(c) The court in which the acquittal was entered, at any time after the date of the acquittal,
Ê for the sealing of all records relating to the arrest and the proceedings leading to the dismissal, declination or acquittal.

2. If the conviction of a person is set aside pursuant to NRS 458A.240, the person may petition the court that set aside the conviction, at any time after the conviction has been set aside, for the sealing of all records relating to the setting aside of the conviction.

3. A petition filed pursuant to subsection 1 or 2 must:
(a) Be accompanied by the petitioner's current, verified records received from:
(1) The Central Repository for Nevada Records of Criminal History; and
(2) All agencies of criminal justice which maintain such records within the city or county in which the petitioner appeared in court;
(b) Except as otherwise provided in paragraph (c), include the disposition of the proceedings for the records to be sealed;
(c) If the petition references NRS 453.3365 or 458.330, include a certificate of acknowledgment or the disposition of the proceedings for the records to be sealed from all agencies of criminal justice which maintain such records;
(d) Include a list of any other public or private agency, company, official and other custodian of records that is reasonably known to the petitioner to have possession of records of the arrest and of the proceedings leading to the dismissal, declination or acquittal and to whom the order to seal records, if issued, will be directed; and
(e) Include information that, to the best knowledge and belief of the petitioner, accurately and completely identifies the records to be sealed, including, without limitation, the:
(1) Date of birth of the petitioner;
(2) Specific charges that were dismissed or of which the petitioner was acquitted; and
(3) Date of arrest relating to the specific charges that were dismissed or of which the petitioner was acquitted.

4. Upon receiving a petition pursuant to subsection 1, the court shall notify the law enforcement agency that arrested the petitioner for the crime and:
(a) If the charges were dismissed, declined for prosecution or the acquittal was entered in a district court or justice court, the prosecuting attorney for the county; or
(b) If the charges were dismissed, declined for prosecution or the acquittal was entered in a municipal court, the prosecuting attorney for the city.
Ê The prosecuting attorney and any person having relevant evidence may testify and present evidence at the hearing on the petition.

5. Upon receiving a petition pursuant to subsection 2, the court shall notify:
(a) If the conviction was set aside in a district court or justice court, the prosecuting attorney for the county; or
(b) If the conviction was set aside in a municipal court, the prosecuting attorney for the city.
Ê The prosecuting attorney and any person having relevant evidence may testify and present evidence at the hearing on the petition.

6. If, after the hearing on a petition submitted pursuant to subsection 1, the court finds that there has been an acquittal, that the prosecution was declined or that the charges were dismissed and there is no evidence that further action will be brought against the person, the court may order sealed all records of the arrest and of the proceedings leading to the acquittal, declination or dismissal which are in the custody of any agency of criminal justice or any public or private company, agency, official or other custodian of records in the State of Nevada.

7. If, after the hearing on a petition submitted pursuant to subsection 2, the court finds that the conviction of the petitioner was set aside pursuant to NRS 458A.240, the court may order sealed all records relating to the setting aside of the conviction which are in the custody of any agency of criminal justice or any public or private company, agency, official or other custodian of records in the State of Nevada.

8. If the prosecuting attorney having jurisdiction previously declined prosecution of the charges and the records of the arrest have been sealed pursuant to subsection 6, the prosecuting attorney may subsequently file the charges at any time before the running of the statute of limitations for those charges. If such charges are filed with the court, the court shall order the inspection of the records without the prosecuting attorney having to petition the court pursuant to NRS 179.295.

(Added to NRS by 1971, 955; A 1997, 3160; 2001, 1693; 2009, 1439; 2013, 110, 1385)

NRS 179.259 Sealing records after completion of program for reentry: Persons eligible; procedure; order; inspection of sealed records by certain entities.

1. Except as otherwise provided in subsections 3, 4 and 5, 5 years after an eligible person completes a program for reentry, the court may order sealed all documents, papers and exhibits in the eligible person's record, minute book entries and entries on dockets, and other documents relating to the case in the custody of such other agencies and officers as are named in the court's order. The court may order those records sealed without a hearing unless the Division of Parole and Probation of the Department of Public Safety petitions the court, for good cause shown, not to seal the records and requests a hearing thereon.

2. If the court orders sealed the record of an eligible person, the court shall send a copy of the order to each agency or officer named in the order. Each such agency or officer shall notify the court in writing of its compliance with the order.

3. A professional licensing board is entitled, for the purpose of determining suitability for a license or liability to discipline for misconduct, to inspect and to copy from a record sealed pursuant to this section.

4. The Division of Insurance of the Department of Business and Industry is entitled, for the purpose of determining suitability for a license or liability to discipline for misconduct, to inspect and to copy from a record sealed pursuant to this section.

5. A person may not petition the court to seal records relating to a conviction of a crime against a child or a sexual offense.

6. As used in this section:
(a) "Crime against a child" has the meaning ascribed to it in NRS 179D.0357.
(b) "Eligible person" means a person who has:

(1) Successfully completed a program for reentry, which the person participated in pursuant to NRS 209.4886, 209.4888, 213.625 or 213.632; and

(2) Been convicted of a single offense which was punishable as a felony and which did not involve the use or threatened use of force or violence against the victim. For the purposes of this subparagraph, multiple convictions for an offense punishable as a felony shall be deemed to constitute a single offense if those offenses arose out of the same transaction or occurrence.

(c) "Program for reentry" means:

(1) A correctional program for reentry of offenders and parolees into the community that is established by the Director of the Department of Corrections pursuant to NRS 209.4887; or

(2) A judicial program for reentry of offenders and parolees into the community that is established in a judicial district pursuant to NRS 209.4883.

(d) "Sexual offense" has the meaning ascribed to it in paragraph (b) of subsection 7 of NRS 179.245.

(Added to NRS by 2001, 1166; A 2003, 26, 2586; 2007, 2753; 2015, 3509)

NRS 179.265 Rehearings after denial of petition: Time for; number.

1. A person whose petition is denied under NRS 179.245 or 179.255 may petition for a rehearing not sooner than 2 years after the denial of the previous petition.

2. No person may petition for more than two rehearings.

(Added to NRS by 1971, 956)

NRS 179.275 Order sealing records: Distribution to Central Repository and persons named in order; compliance. Where the court orders the sealing of a record pursuant to NRS 176A.265, 176A.295, 179.245, 179.255, 179.259, 453.3365 or 458.330, a copy of the order must be sent to:

1. The Central Repository for Nevada Records of Criminal History; and

2. Each agency of criminal justice and each public or private company, agency, official or other custodian of records named in the order, and that person shall seal the records in his or her custody which relate to the matters contained in the order, shall advise the court of compliance and shall then seal the order.

(Added to NRS by 1971, 956; A 1991, 304; 1999, 2089; 2001, 1168; 2001 Special Session, 261; 2003, 312; 2009, 107, 420; 2013, 111)

NRS 179.285 Order sealing records: Effect; proceedings deemed never to have occurred; restoration of civil rights. Except as otherwise provided in NRS 179.301:

1. If the court orders a record sealed pursuant to NRS 176A.265, 176A.295, 179.245, 179.255, 179.259, 453.3365 or 458.330:

(a) All proceedings recounted in the record are deemed never to have occurred, and the person to whom the order pertains may properly answer accordingly to any inquiry, including, without limitation, an inquiry relating to an application for employment, concerning the arrest, conviction, dismissal or acquittal and the events and proceedings relating to the arrest, conviction, dismissal or acquittal.

(b) The person is immediately restored to the following civil rights if the person's civil rights previously have not been restored:

(1) The right to vote;

(2) The right to hold office; and

(3) The right to serve on a jury.

2. Upon the sealing of the person's records, a person who is restored to his or her civil rights pursuant to subsection 1 must be given:

(a) An official document which demonstrates that the person has been restored to the civil rights set forth in paragraph (b) of subsection 1; and

(b) A written notice informing the person that he or she has not been restored to the right to bear arms, unless the person has received a pardon and the pardon does not restrict his or her right to bear arms.

3. A person who has had his or her records sealed in this State or any other state and whose official documentation of the restoration of civil rights is lost, damaged or destroyed may file a written request with a court of competent jurisdiction to restore his or her civil rights pursuant to this section. Upon verification that the person has had his or her records sealed, the court shall issue an order restoring the person to the civil rights to vote, to hold office and to serve on a jury. A person must not be required to pay a fee to receive such an order.

4. A person who has had his or her records sealed in this State or any other state may present official documentation that the person has been restored to his or her civil rights or a court order restoring civil rights as proof that the person has been restored to the right to vote, to hold office and to serve as a juror.

(Added to NRS by 1971, 956; A 1981, 1105; 1991, 304; 2001, 1169, 1694; 2001 Special Session, 262; 2003, 312, 316, 319, 2687; 2009, 108, 420; 2011, 22)

NRS 179.295 Reopening of sealed records.

1. The person who is the subject of the records that are sealed pursuant to NRS 176A.265, 176A.295, 179.245, 179.255, 179.259, 453.3365 or 458.330 may petition the court that ordered the records sealed to permit inspection of the records by a person named in the petition, and the court may order such inspection. Except as otherwise provided in this section, subsection 8 of NRS 179.255 and NRS 179.259 and 179.301, the court may not order the inspection of the records under any other circumstances.

2. If a person has been arrested, the charges have been dismissed and the records of the arrest have been sealed, the court may order the inspection of the records by a prosecuting attorney upon a showing that as a result of newly discovered evidence, the person has been arrested for the same or a similar offense and that there is sufficient evidence reasonably to conclude that the person will stand trial for the offense.

3. The court may, upon the application of a prosecuting attorney or an attorney representing a defendant in a criminal action, order an inspection of such records for the purpose of obtaining information relating to persons who were involved in the incident recorded.

4. This section does not prohibit a court from considering a conviction for which records have been sealed pursuant to NRS 176A.265, 176A.295, 179.245, 179.255, 179.259, 453.3365 or 458.330 in determining whether to grant a petition pursuant to NRS 176A.265, 176A.295, 179.245, 179.255, 179.259, 453.3365 or 458.330 for a conviction of another offense.

(Added to NRS by 1971, 956; A 1981, 1105; 1991, 304; 1997, 3160; 2001, 1169, 1694; 2001 Special Session, 262; 2003, 312, 316, 319; 2009, 108, 420; 2013, 1386)

NRS 179.301 Inspection of certain sealed records by certain persons and agencies.

1. The Nevada Gaming Control Board and the Nevada Gaming Commission and their employees, agents and representatives may inquire into and inspect any records sealed pursuant to NRS 179.245 or 179.255, if the event or conviction was related to gaming, to determine the suitability or qualifications of any person to hold a state gaming license, manufacturer's, seller's or distributor's license or registration as a gaming employee pursuant to chapter 463 of NRS. Events and convictions, if any, which are the subject of an order sealing records:

(a) May form the basis for recommendation, denial or revocation of those licenses.

(b) Must not form the basis for denial or rejection of a gaming work permit unless the event or conviction relates to the applicant's suitability or qualifications to hold the work permit.

2. The Division of Insurance of the Department of Business and Industry and its employees may inquire into and inspect any records sealed pursuant to NRS 179.245 or 179.255, if the event or conviction was related to insurance, to determine the suitability or qualifications of any person to hold a license, certification or authorization issued in accordance with title 57 of NRS. Events and convictions, if any, which are the subject of an order sealing records may form the basis for recommendation, denial or revocation of those licenses, certifications and authorizations.

3. A prosecuting attorney may inquire into and inspect any records sealed pursuant to NRS 179.245 or 179.255 if:

(a) The records relate to a violation or alleged violation of NRS 202.575; and

(b) The person who is the subject of the records has been arrested or issued a citation for violating NRS 202.575.

4. The Central Repository for Nevada Records of Criminal History and its employees may inquire into and inspect any records sealed pursuant to NRS 179.245 or 179.255 that constitute information relating to sexual offenses, and may notify employers of the information in accordance with NRS 179A.180 to 179A.240, inclusive.

5. Records which have been sealed pursuant to NRS 179.245 or 179.255 and which are retained in the statewide registry established pursuant to NRS 179B.200 may be inspected pursuant to chapter 179B of NRS by an officer or employee of the Central Repository for Nevada Records of Criminal History or a law enforcement officer in the regular course of his or her duties.

6. The State Board of Pardons Commissioners and its agents and representatives may inquire into and inspect any records sealed pursuant to NRS 179.245 or 179.255 if the person who is the subject of the records has applied for a pardon from the Board.

7. As used in this section:

(a) "Information relating to sexual offenses" means information contained in or concerning a record relating in any way to a sexual offense.

(b) "Sexual offense" has the meaning ascribed to it in NRS 179A.073.

(Added to NRS by 1981, 1105; A 1987, 1759; 1997, 1674; 2003, 2688, 2833; 2003, 20th Special Session, 16; 2005, 973; 2011, 23; 2013, 111; 2015, 3510)

REWARDS

NRS 179.310 Reward for apprehension of robber.

1. The Governor shall offer a standing reward of $250 for the arrest of:

(a) Each person engaged in the robbery of, or in the attempt to rob, any person upon, or having in charge in whole or in part, any railroad train or other conveyance engaged at the time in conveying passengers, or any private conveyance within this State.

(b) Each person engaged in the robbery of, or in the attempt to rob, any person upon any highway in this State.

2. The reward must be paid to the person or persons making the arrest immediately upon the conviction of the person so arrested, but no reward may be paid except after such a conviction.

3. The reward must be paid from the Reserve for Statutory Contingency Account upon approval by the State Board of Examiners.

4. The provisions of this section do not apply to any sheriff, constable, marshal or police officer who makes an arrest in the performance of the duties of his or her office in the county where the officer resides or in which the official duties are required to be performed.

[1:53:1877; A 1885, 35; BH § 1918; C § 1927; RL § 3905; NCL § 6720] — (NRS A 1963, 1111; 1991, 1754)

FORMS

NRS 179.315 Use of authorized forms.

1. Unless otherwise expressly required by this title, no particular form of words is required to be used in any pleading, warrant, order, motion or other paper incident to a criminal proceeding. Substantial compliance with any statutory requirement as to content, or in the absence of any such requirement, language which reasonably informs the defendant or other person to whom such paper is directed of its nature, is sufficient.

2. The use of one of the forms set out in NRS 179.320 to 179.400, inclusive, modified as may be necessary to fit the case, is prima facie sufficient for their respective purposes.

(Added to NRS by 1967, 1461)

NRS 179.320 Warrant of arrest. A warrant of arrest may be in substantially the following form:

Warrant of Arrest

County of .... The State of Nevada, to any sheriff, constable, marshal, police officer, or peace officer in this State: A complaint, upon oath, has been this day laid before me by A. B. that the crime of (designate it) has been committed, and accusing C. D. thereof; you are therefore commanded forthwith to arrest the above-named C. D. and bring him or her before me at (naming the place), or, in case of my absence or inability to act, before the nearest or most accessible magistrate in this county.

Dated at ...., this .... day of the month of .... of the year ....

....
(Signature and official title of magistrate)

(Added to NRS by 1967, 1461; A 2001, 39)

NRS 179.325 Summons. A summons may be in substantially the following form:

Summons

State of Nevada }
}ss.
County of..................................... }

The State of Nevada to the (naming defendant or corporation):

You are hereby summoned to appear before me at (naming the place) on (specifying the day and hour), to answer a charge made against you upon the complaint of A. B. for (designating the offense generally).

Dated at ...., this .... day of the month of .... of the year ....

....
(Signature and official title of magistrate)

(Added to NRS by 1967, 1462; A 2001, 39)

NRS 179.330 Search warrant. A search warrant may be in substantially the following form:

Search Warrant

State of Nevada }
}ss.
County of..................................... }

The State of Nevada, to any peace officer in the County of .... Proof by affidavit having been made before me by (naming every person whose affidavit has been taken) that (stating the grounds or probable cause for issuance).

You are hereby commanded to search (naming the person or describing with reasonable particularity the place to be searched) for the following property (describing it with reasonable particularity), making the search (in the daytime or at any time, as determined by the magistrate) and if any such property is found there to seize it, prepare a written inventory of the property seized and bring the property before me (or another designated magistrate).

Dated at ...., this .... day of the month of .... of the year ....

....
(Signature and official title of magistrate)

(Added to NRS by 1967, 1462; A 2001, 40)

NRS 179.335 Motion for return of seized property and suppression of evidence. A motion for the return of seized property and the suppression of evidence may be in substantially the following form:

Motion for the Return of Seized Property
and the Suppression of Evidence

Defendant (naming defendant) hereby moves this court to direct that certain property of which the defendant is the owner, a schedule of which is annexed hereto, and which on (stating date and time), at (describing the place), was unlawfully seized and taken from the defendant by a peace officer of the State of Nevada (name and designation of peace officer, or, if so, state "whose true name is unknown to the petitioner"), be returned and that it be suppressed as evidence against the defendant in any criminal proceeding.

The petitioner further states that the property was seized against his or her will and without a search warrant (or other reason why the warrant is defective or illegal).

....
(Attorney for Petitioner)

(Added to NRS by 1967, 1462)

NRS 179.340 Bail: After arrest and before preliminary examination. An undertaking for bail after arrest and before preliminary examination may be in substantially the following form:

Undertaking

A warrant having been issued on the .... day of the month of .... of the year ...., by ...., a justice of the peace of .... County, for the arrest of .... (stating name of the accused), upon a charge of .... (stating briefly the nature of the offense), upon which the accused has been arrested and duly ordered admitted to bail in the sum of .... dollars and ordered to appear before the magistrate who issued the warrant, we, ..., of ...., and .... (stating their names and place of residence), hereby undertake that the above-named .... shall appear and answer the charge above mentioned, at .... o'clock ...m., on the .... day of the month of .... of the year ...., before ...., the magistrate issuing the warrant, at the magistrate's office in ...., ... County, State of Nevada, and that the above-named (insert name of accused) shall appear and answer the charge above mentioned in whatever court and before whatever magistrate it may be prosecuted, or before which the accused may be required to appear by law, and shall at all times render himself or herself amenable to the orders and process of the court and the requirements of the law, and if convicted shall appear for judgment and render himself or herself in execution thereof; or if the accused fails to perform any of these conditions, that we will pay to the State of Nevada the sum of .... dollars (inserting the sum in which the defendant is admitted to bail).

....

....
(Signatures of Sureties)

(Added to NRS by 1967, 1463; A 2001, 40)

NRS 179.345 Endorsement on warrant of arrest for commitment for preliminary examination. An endorsement on a warrant of arrest for commitment for preliminary examination may be in substantially the following form:

Endorsement

The within-named A. B., having been brought before me under this warrant, is committed for examination to the sheriff (or other appropriate peace officer) of the County of ....

....
(Signature and official title of magistrate)

(Added to NRS by 1967, 1463)

NRS 179.350 Discharge after preliminary examination. A discharge after preliminary examination may be in substantially the following form:

Discharge

There being no sufficient cause to believe the within-named A. B. guilty of the offense within named, I order A.B. to be discharged.

....
(Signature and official title of magistrate)

(Added to NRS by 1967, 1463)

NRS 179.355 Commitment and bail after preliminary examination. Commitment and bail may be in substantially the following form:

Commitment and Bail

It appearing to me by the within depositions and statement (if any) that the offense therein named (or any other offense according to the fact, stating generally the nature thereof) has been committed, and that there is sufficient cause to believe the within-named A. B. guilty thereof, I order that A. B. be held to answer the same (and A. B. is hereby committed to the sheriff of the County of ....) or (and I have admitted A. B. to bail to answer by the undertaking hereto annexed) or (and that A. B. be admitted to bail in the sum of .... dollars, and is committed to the sheriff of the County of .... until A. B. give such bail).

....
(Signature and official title of magistrate)

(Added to NRS by 1967, 1463)

NRS 179.360 Commitment where defendant held to answer after preliminary examination. A commitment where defendant is held to answer after a preliminary examination may be in substantially the following form:

Commitment

County of .... (as the case may be).

The State of Nevada to the sheriff of the County of ....: An order having been this day made by me that A. B. be held to answer upon a charge of (stating briefly the nature of the offense, and giving as near as may be the time when and the place where the same was committed), you are commanded to receive A. B. into your custody and detain A. B. until A. B. is legally discharged.

Dated this .... day of the month of .... of the year ....

....
(Signatures and official title of magistrate)

(Added to NRS by 1967, 1464; A 2001, 41)

NRS 179.365 Bail after preliminary examination and before arraignment. An undertaking for bail after preliminary examination and before arraignment may be in substantially the following form:

Undertaking

An order having been made on the .... day of the month of .... of the year .... by A. B., a justice of the peace of .... County (or as the case may be), that C. D. be held to answer upon a charge of (stating briefly the nature of the offense), upon which C. D. has been duly admitted to bail in the sum of .... dollars, we, E. F. and G. H. (stating their place of residence), hereby undertake that the above-named C. D. shall appear and answer the charge above mentioned, in whatever court it may be prosecuted, and shall at all times render himself or herself amenable to the orders and process of the court, and, if convicted, shall appear for judgment and render himself or herself in execution thereof, or, if C. D. fail to perform any of these conditions, that we will pay to the State of Nevada the sum of .... dollars (inserting the sum in which the defendant is admitted to bail).

....

....
(Signature of Sureties)

(Added to NRS by 1967, 1464; A 2001, 41)

NRS 179.370 Indictment. An indictment may be substantially in the following form:

Indictment

State of Nevada }
}ss.
County of....................................... }

The State of Nevada, plaintiff, against A. B., defendant (or John Doe, whose real name is unknown). Defendant A. B., above named, is accused by the grand jury of the County of ...., of a felony (or of the crime of murder or other name of crime), committed as follows: The said A. B., on the .... day of the month of .... of the year ...., or thereabouts, at the County of ...., State of Nevada, without authority of law and with malice aforethought, killed Richard Roe, by shooting with a pistol (or with a gun or other weapon, according to the facts).

....
District Attorney
or District Attorney, by Deputy.

(Added to NRS by 1967, 1464; A 2001, 42)

NRS 179.375 Information. An information may be in substantially the following form:

Information

State of Nevada }
}ss.
County of..................................... }

In the .... court. The State of Nevada against A. B., C. D. district attorney within and for the County of .... in the State aforesaid, in the name and by the authority of the State of Nevada, informs the court that A. B. on the .... day of the month of .... of the year ...., at the County of ...., did (here state offense) against the peace and dignity of the State of Nevada.

....
C. D., District Attorney
or C. D., District Attorney, by H. M., Deputy.

(Added to NRS by 1967, 1465; A 2001, 42)

NRS 179.380 Warrant upon finding of presentment, indictment or information. A warrant upon the finding of a presentment, indictment or information may be in substantially the following form:

Warrant

County of .... The State of Nevada, to any sheriff, constable, marshal, police officer, or peace officer in this State: A presentment having been made or an indictment having been found (or information filed) on the .... day of the month of .... of the year ...., in the district court of the ...., County of ...., charging C. D. with the crime of (designating it generally), you are therefore commanded forthwith to arrest the above-named C. D. and bring C. D. before that court to answer the presentment, indictment or information; or if the court is not in session that you deliver C. D. into the custody of the sheriff of the County of .... By order of the court. Given under my hand with the seal of the court affixed this .... day of the month of .... of the year ....

....
(Seal) E. F., Clerk.

(Added to NRS by 1967, 1465; A 2001, 43)

NRS 179.385 Bail after arrest on warrant following finding of presentment, indictment or information. An undertaking for bail after arrest on a warrant following the finding of a presentment, indictment or information may be in substantially the following form:

Undertaking

A presentment having been made (or an indictment having been found or an information having been filed), on the .... day of the month of .... of the year ...., in the District Court of the .... Judicial District of the State of Nevada, in and for the County of .... (as the case may be), charging A. B. with the crime of (indicating it generally), and A. B. having been duly admitted to bail in the sum of .... dollars, we, C. D. and E. F. (stating their place of residence), hereby undertake that the above-named A. B. shall appear and answer the indictment or information above mentioned in whatever court it may be prosecuted, and shall at all times render himself or herself amenable to the orders and processes of the court, and, if convicted, shall appear for judgment and render himself or herself in execution thereof; or, if A. B. fails to perform either of these conditions, that we will pay to the State of Nevada the sum of .... dollars (inserting the sum in which the defendant is admitted to bail).

....

....
(Signature of Sureties)

(Added to NRS by 1967, 1465; A 2001, 43)

NRS 179.390 Subpoena; subpoena duces tecum. A subpoena or subpoena duces tecum may be in substantially the following form:

Subpoena

The State of Nevada to A. B.: You are commanded to appear before C. D., a justice of the peace of .... township, in .... County (or, the court of ...., as the case may be), at (naming the place), on (stating the day and hour), as a witness in a criminal action, prosecuted by the State of Nevada against E. F. Given under my hand this .... day of the month of .... of the year .... G. H., Justice of the Peace (seal) (or "By order of the court, L. M., Clerk (seal)" as the case may be). (If books, papers or documents are required, a direction to the following effect must be contained in the subpoena: "And you are required also to bring with you the following (describing intelligibly the books, papers or documents required).")

(Added to NRS by 1967, 1466; A 1987, 124; 2001, 44)

NRS 179.395 Bench warrant after conviction. A bench warrant may be in substantially the following form:

Bench Warrant

State of Nevada }
}ss.
County of..................................... }

The State of Nevada, to any sheriff, constable, marshal, police officer or other peace officer in this state: A. B. having been on the .... day of the month of .... of the year .... duly convicted in the .... Judicial District Court of the State of Nevada and in and for the County of ...., of the crime of (designating it generally); you are therefore commanded forthwith to arrest the above-named A. B. and bring A. B. before that court for judgment, or if the court has adjourned, that you deliver A. B. into the custody of the sheriff of the County of .... Given, by order of the court, under my hand with the seal of the court affixed, this the .... day of the month of .... of the year ....

....
(Seal) E. F., Clerk.

(Added to NRS by 1967, 1466; A 2001, 44)

NRS 179.400 Undertaking on recommitment. When bail is taken upon the recommitment of the defendant, the undertaking shall be in substantially the following form:

Undertaking

An order having been made on the .... day of the month of .... of the year ...., by the court (naming it), that A. B. be admitted to bail in the sum of $.........., in an action pending in that court against A. B., in behalf of the State of Nevada, upon a (presentment, indictment, information, or appeal, as the case may be), we, C. D. and E. F., of (stating their place of residence), hereby undertake that the above-named A. B. shall appear in that or any other court in which A. B.'s appearance may be lawfully required, upon that (presentment, indictment, information, or appeal, as the case may be), and shall at all times render himself or herself amenable to its orders and processes, and appear for judgment, and surrender himself or herself in execution thereof; or, if A. B. fail to perform any of these conditions, that we will pay to the State of Nevada the sum of $.......... (inserting the sum in which the defendant is admitted to bail).

....

....
(Signature of Sureties)

(Added to NRS by 1967, 1466; A 2001, 44)

INTERCEPTION OF WIRE, ELECTRONIC OR ORAL COMMUNICATION

NRS 179.410 Definitions. As used in NRS 179.410 to 179.515, inclusive, except where the context otherwise requires, the words and terms defined in NRS 179.415 to 179.455, inclusive, have the meanings ascribed to them in those sections.

(Added to NRS by 1973, 1742; A 1989, 658; 2015, 2488)

NRS 179.415 "Aggrieved person" defined. "Aggrieved person" means a person who was a party to any intercepted wire, electronic or oral communication or a person against whom the interception was directed.

(Added to NRS by 1973, 1742; A 2015, 2488)

NRS 179.420 "Contents" defined. "Contents" when used with respect to any wire, electronic or oral communication includes any information concerning the identity of the parties to such communication or the existence, substance, purport or meaning of that communication.

(Added to NRS by 1973, 1742; A 2015, 2488)

NRS 179.421 "Electronic communication" defined. "Electronic communication" means a transfer of signs, signals, writings, images, sounds, data or intelligence of any nature transferred in whole or in part by a wire, radio, electromagnetic, photoelectric or photo-optical system. The term does not include:

1. A wire or oral communication.
2. A communication made through a tone-only paging device.
3. A communication from a tracking device.
4. Electronic funds transfer information stored by a financial institution in a communication system used for the electronic storage and transfer of funds.
5. The incoming or outgoing electronic or other impulses that identify the originating number of an instrument or device from which or to which a wire or electronic communication was transmitted.

(Added to NRS by 2015, 2485)

NRS 179.423 "Electronic communication service" defined. "Electronic communication service" means a service that provides to users of the service the ability to send or receive a wire or electronic communication.

(Added to NRS by 2015, 2486)

NRS 179.425 "Electronic, mechanical or other device" defined. "Electronic, mechanical or other device" means any device or apparatus which can be used to intercept a wire, electronic or oral communication other than:

1. Any telephone instrument, equipment or facility, or any component thereof:

(a) Furnished to the subscriber or user by a provider of electronic communication service in the ordinary course of its business and being used by the subscriber or user in the ordinary course of its business;

(b) Furnished by the subscriber or user for connection to the facilities of an electronic communication service and being used by the subscriber or user in the ordinary course of its business; or

(c) Being used by a provider of electronic communication service in the ordinary course of its business, or by an investigative or law enforcement officer in the ordinary course of his or her duties.

2. A hearing aid or similar device being used to correct subnormal hearing to not better than normal.
3. A portable event recording device, as defined in NRS 289.830 or 480.365.

(Added to NRS by 1973, 1742; A 2013, 1959; 2015, 573, 2488, 3665)

NRS 179.430 "Intercept" defined. "Intercept" means the aural acquisition of the contents of any wire, electronic or oral communication through the use of any electronic, mechanical or other device or of any sending or receiving equipment.

(Added to NRS by 1973, 1743; A 2015, 2488)

NRS 179.435 "Investigative or law enforcement officer" defined. "Investigative or law enforcement officer" means any officer of the United States or this State or a political subdivision thereof who is empowered by the law of this state to conduct investigations of or to make arrests for felonies, and any attorney authorized by law to prosecute or participate in the prosecution of such offenses.

(Added to NRS by 1973, 1743; A 2015, 2488)

NRS 179.440 "Oral communication" defined. "Oral communication" means any verbal message uttered by a person exhibiting an expectation that such communication is not subject to interception, under circumstances justifying such expectation. The term does not include an electronic communication.

(Added to NRS by 1973, 1743; A 2015, 2488)

NRS 179.443 "Peace officer" defined. "Peace officer" means a category I peace officer, as defined in NRS 289.460.

(Added to NRS by 2015, 2486)

NRS 179.445 "Person" defined. "Person" means any official, employee or agent of the United States or any state or political subdivision thereof, and any individual, partnership, association, joint-stock company, trust or corporation.

(Added to NRS by 1973, 1743)

NRS 179.450 "State" defined. "State" means any state of the United States, the District of Columbia, the Commonwealth of Puerto Rico and any territory or possession of the United States.

(Added to NRS by 1973, 1743)

NRS 179.451 "Tracking device" defined. "Tracking device" means an electronic or mechanical device that permits the tracking of the movement of a person or an object.

(Added to NRS by 2015, 2486)

NRS 179.453 "User" defined. "User" means a person or entity who:

1. Uses an electronic communication service; and
2. Is authorized by the provider of the electronic communication service to engage in such use.

(Added to NRS by 2015, 2486)

NRS 179.455 "Wire communication" defined. "Wire communication" means any aural transfer made in whole or in part through the use of facilities for the transmission of communications by the aid of wire, cable or other like connection between the point of origin and the point of reception, including the use of such connection in a switching station, furnished or operated by any person engaged in providing or operating such facilities for the transmission of intrastate, interstate or foreign communications.

(Added to NRS by 1973, 1743; A 2015, 2489)

NRS 179.458 Provisions inapplicable to recording of certain telephone calls by public utility. The provisions of NRS 179.410 to 179.515, inclusive, do not prohibit the recording of any telephone call by a public utility pursuant to NRS 704.195.

(Added to NRS by 1989, 658)

NRS 179.460 Circumstances in which interception of communications may be authorized; immunity.

1. The Attorney General or the district attorney of any county may apply to a Supreme Court justice or to a district judge in the county where the interception is to take place for an order authorizing the interception of wire, electronic or oral communications, and the judge may, in accordance with NRS 179.470 to 179.515, inclusive, grant an order authorizing the interception of wire, electronic or oral communications by investigative or law enforcement officers having responsibility for the investigation of the offense as to which the application is made, when the interception may provide evidence of the commission of murder, kidnapping, robbery, extortion, bribery, escape of an offender in the custody of the Department of Corrections, destruction of public property by explosives, a sexual offense against a child, sex trafficking, a violation of NRS 200.463, 200.464 or 200.465, trafficking in persons in violation of NRS 200.467 or 200.468 or the commission of any offense which is made a felony by the provisions of chapter 453 or 454 of NRS.

2. A provider of electronic communication service or a public utility, an officer, employee or agent thereof or another person associated with the provider of electronic communication service or public utility who, pursuant to an order issued pursuant to subsection 1, provides information or otherwise assists an investigative or law enforcement officer in the interception of a wire, electronic or oral communication is immune from any liability relating to any interception made pursuant to the order.

3. As used in this section, "sexual offense against a child" includes any act upon a child constituting:

(a) Incest pursuant to NRS 201.180;
(b) Lewdness with a child pursuant to NRS 201.230;
(c) Sado-masochistic abuse pursuant to NRS 201.262;
(d) Sexual assault pursuant to NRS 200.366;
(e) Statutory sexual seduction pursuant to NRS 200.368;
(f) Open or gross lewdness pursuant to NRS 201.210; or
(g) Luring a child or a person with mental illness pursuant to NRS 201.560, if punished as a felony.

(Added to NRS by 1973, 1743; A 1975, 1520; 1993, 99; 2001, 2794; 2003, 1387; 2011, 20; 2013, 2421; 2015, 2489)

NRS 179.463 Circumstances in which interception, listening or recording of communications by peace officer or certain other persons not unlawful.

1. The interception, listening or recording of a wire, electronic or oral communication by a peace officer specifically designated by the Attorney General or the district attorney of any county, or a person acting under the direction or request of a peace officer, is not unlawful if the peace officer or person is intercepting the communication of a person who has:

(a) Barricaded himself or herself and is not exiting or surrendering at the lawful request of a peace officer, in circumstances in which there is imminent risk of harm to the life of another person as a result of the barricaded person's actions or the actions of law enforcement in resolving the barricade situation;

(b) Created a hostage situation; or

(c) Threatened the imminent illegal use of an explosive.

2. For the purposes of subsection 1:

(a) A barricade occurs when a person:

(1) Refuses to come out from a covered or enclosed position after being provided an order to exit by a peace officer; or

(2) Is contained in an open area and the presence or approach of a peace officer precipitates an imminent risk of harm to the life of another person.

(b) A hostage situation occurs when a person holds another person against the other person's will, regardless of whether the person holding the other person has made a demand.

(Added to NRS by 2015, 2486)

NRS 179.465 Disclosure or use of intercepted communications.

1. Any investigative or law enforcement officer who, by any means authorized by NRS 179.410 to 179.515, inclusive, or 704.195 or 18 U.S.C. §§ 2510 to 2522, inclusive, has obtained knowledge of the contents of any wire, electronic or oral communication, or evidence

derived therefrom, may disclose the contents to another investigative or law enforcement officer or use the contents to the extent that the disclosure or use is appropriate to the proper performance of the official duties of the officer making or receiving the disclosure.

2. Any person who has received, by any means authorized by NRS 179.410 to 179.515, inclusive, or 704.195 or 18 U.S.C. §§ 2510 to 2522, inclusive, or by a statute of another state, any information concerning a wire, electronic or oral communication, or evidence derived therefrom intercepted in accordance with the provisions of NRS 179.410 to 179.515, inclusive, may disclose the contents of that communication or the derivative evidence while giving testimony under oath or affirmation in any criminal proceeding in any court or before any grand jury in this state, or in any court of the United States or of any state, or in any federal or state grand jury proceeding.

3. An otherwise privileged wire, electronic or oral communication intercepted in accordance with, or in violation of, the provisions of NRS 179.410 to 179.515, inclusive, or 18 U.S.C. §§ 2510 to 2522, inclusive, does not lose its privileged character.

4. When an investigative or law enforcement officer engaged in intercepting wire, electronic or oral communications as authorized by NRS 179.410 to 179.515, inclusive, intercepts wire, electronic or oral communications relating to offenses other than those specified in the order provided for in NRS 179.460, the contents of the communications and the evidence derived therefrom may be disclosed or used as provided in subsection 1. The direct evidence derived from the communications is inadmissible in a criminal proceeding, but any other evidence obtained as a result of knowledge obtained from the communications may be disclosed or used as provided in subsection 2 when authorized or approved by a justice of the Supreme Court or district judge who finds upon application made as soon as practicable that the contents of the communications were intercepted in accordance with the provisions of NRS 179.410 to 179.515, inclusive, or 18 U.S.C. §§ 2510 to 2522, inclusive.

(Added to NRS by 1973, 1743; A 1983, 117; 1989, 658; 2015, 2489)

NRS 179.467 Order requiring provider of electronic communication service to disclose contents of electronic or wire communication or records pertaining to customers; immunity.

1. The Nevada Supreme Court and the district courts of this State may issue orders requiring a provider of electronic communication service to disclose the contents of a wire or electronic communication or a record or other information pertaining to a subscriber to, or customer of, such service upon the application of a district attorney or the Attorney General, or their deputies, supported by an affidavit of a peace officer under the circumstances and upon the conditions prescribed by 18 U.S.C. § 2703.

2. A provider of electronic communication service, an officer, employee or agent thereof or another person associated with the provider of electronic communication service who, pursuant to an order issued by a district court pursuant to subsection 1, discloses the contents of a wire or electronic communication or a record or other information pertaining to a subscriber to, or customer of, the electronic communication service is immune from any liability relating to any disclosure made pursuant to the order.

(Added to NRS by 2015, 2486)

NRS 179.470 Application for order authorizing interception of communications; prerequisites to issuance of order.

1. Each application for an order authorizing the interception of a wire, electronic or oral communication must be made in writing upon oath or affirmation to a justice of the Supreme Court or district judge and must state the applicant's authority to make such application. Each application must include the following information:

(a) The identity of the investigative or law enforcement officer making the application, and the officer authorizing the application.

(b) A full and complete statement of the facts and circumstances relied upon by the applicant to justify the applicant's belief that an order should be issued, including:

(1) Details as to the particular offense that is being, has been or is about to be committed.

(2) A particular description of the nature and location of the facilities from which or the place where the communication is to be intercepted, the facilities to be used and the means by which such interception is to be made.

(3) A particular description of the type of communications sought to be intercepted.

(4) The identity of the person, if known, who is committing, has committed or is about to commit an offense and whose communications are to be intercepted.

(c) A full and complete statement as to whether or not other investigative procedures have been tried and failed or why they reasonably appear to be unlikely to succeed if tried or to be too dangerous.

(d) A statement of the period of time for which the interception is required to be maintained. If the nature of the investigation is such that the authorization for interception should not automatically terminate when the described type of communication has been obtained, a particular description of facts establishing probable cause to believe that additional communications of the same type will occur thereafter.

(e) A full and complete statement of the facts concerning all previous applications known to the person authorizing and making the application made to any judge for authorization to intercept wire, electronic or oral communications involving any of the same persons, facilities or places specified in the application, and the action taken by the judge on each such application.

(f) Where the application is for the extension of an order, a statement setting forth the results thus far obtained from the interception, or a reasonable explanation of the failure to obtain such results.

2. The judge may require the applicant to furnish additional testimony or documentary evidence under oath or affirmation in support of the application. Oral testimony must be reduced to writing.

3. Upon such application the judge may enter an ex parte order, as requested or as modified, authorizing interception of wire, electronic or oral communications within the territorial jurisdiction of the court in which the judge is sitting, if the judge determines on the basis of the facts submitted by the applicant that:

(a) There is probable cause for belief that a person is committing, has committed or is about to commit an offense for which interception is authorized by NRS 179.460.

(b) There is probable cause for belief that particular communications concerning that offense will be obtained through such interception.

(c) Normal investigative procedures have been tried and have failed or reasonably appear to be unlikely to succeed if tried or appear to be too dangerous.

(d) There is probable cause for belief that the facilities from which, or the place where, the wire, electronic or oral communications are to be intercepted are being used or are about to be used by such person in connection with the commission of such offense or are leased to, listed in the name of, or commonly used by such person.

4. The judge may accept a facsimile or electronic copy of the signature of any person required to give an oath or affirmation as part of an application submitted pursuant to this section as an original signature to the application.

(Added to NRS by 1973, 1744; A 1983, 118; 2015, 2490)

NRS 179.475 Order authorizing interception of communications: Contents; duration; extension.

1. Each order authorizing the interception of any wire, electronic or oral communication must specify:

(a) The identity of the person, if known, whose communications are to be intercepted.

(b) The nature and location of the place where or communication facilities to which authority to intercept is granted, the facilities to be used and the means by which such interceptions will be made.

(c) A particular description of the type of communication sought to be intercepted, and a statement of the particular offense to which it relates.

(d) The identity of the agency authorized to intercept the communications, and of the person authorizing the application.

(e) The period of time during which such interception is authorized, including a statement as to whether or not the interception will automatically terminate when the described communication has been first obtained.

2. An order authorizing the interception of a wire, electronic or oral communication shall, upon request of the applicant, direct that a provider of electronic communication service, landlord, custodian or other person shall furnish the applicant forthwith all information, facilities, and technical assistance necessary to accomplish the interception unobtrusively and with a minimum of interference with the services that such provider of electronic communication service, landlord, custodian, or person is according the person whose communications are to be intercepted. Any provider of electronic communication service, landlord, custodian or other person furnishing such facilities or technical assistance must be compensated therefor by the applicant at the prevailing rates.

3. No order entered under this section may authorize the interception of any wire, electronic or oral communication for any period longer than is necessary to achieve the objective of the authorization, and in no event longer than 30 days. Extensions of an order may be granted, but only upon application for an extension made in accordance with the procedures provided in NRS 179.470. The period of extension must be no longer than the authorizing judge deems necessary to achieve the purposes for which it was granted and in no event for longer than 30 days. Every order and extension thereof must contain a provision that the authorization to intercept must be executed as soon as practicable, must be conducted in such a way as to minimize the interception of communications not otherwise subject to interception under this statute, and will terminate upon attainment of the authorized objective, or in any event in 30 days.

(Added to NRS by 1973, 1745; A 2015, 2491)

NRS 179.480 Progress reports to judge. Whenever an order authorizing interception is entered pursuant to NRS 179.410 to 179.515, inclusive, the order may require reports to be made to the judge who issued the order showing what progress has been made toward achievement of the authorized objective and the need for continued interception. Such reports shall be made at such intervals as the judge may require.

(Added to NRS by 1973, 1746)

NRS 179.485 Recording. The contents of any wire, electronic or oral communication intercepted by any means authorized by NRS 179.410 to 179.515, inclusive, must, if possible, be recorded on tape or wire or other comparable device. The recording of the contents of any wire, electronic or oral communication under this section must be done in such a way as will protect the recording from editing or other alterations. Immediately upon the expiration of the period of the order, or extensions thereof, such recordings must be made available to the judge issuing such order and sealed under the judge's directions. Custody of the recordings must be placed with whomever the judge directs. They must not be destroyed except upon an order of the judge issuing such order and in any event must be kept for 10 years. Duplicate recordings may be made for use or disclosure pursuant to the provisions of subsection 1 of NRS 179.465 for investigations. The presence of the seal provided for by this section, or a satisfactory explanation for the absence thereof, is a prerequisite for the use or disclosure of the contents of any wire, electronic or oral communication or evidence derived therefrom under subsection 2 of NRS 179.465.

(Added to NRS by 1973, 1746; A 2015, 2492)

NRS 179.490 Sealing of applications and orders; disclosure.

1. Applications made and orders granted under this statute shall be sealed by the judge. Custody of the applications and orders shall be placed with whomever the judge orders. Such applications and orders shall be disclosed only upon a showing of good cause before a judge of a court of competent jurisdiction and shall not be destroyed except on order of the judge who issued or denied the order, and in any event shall be kept for 10 years.

2. Any violation of the provisions of this section may be punished as contempt of court.

(Added to NRS by 1973, 1747)

NRS 179.495 Notice to parties to intercepted communications.

1. Within a reasonable time but not later than 90 days after the termination of the period of an order or any extension thereof, the judge who issued the order shall cause to be served on the chief of the Investigation Division of the Department of Public Safety, persons named in the order and any other parties to intercepted communications, an inventory which must include notice of:

(a) The fact of the entry and a copy of the order.

(b) The fact that during the period wire, electronic or oral communications were or were not intercepted.

Ê Except as otherwise provided in NRS 239.0115, the inventory filed pursuant to this section is confidential and must not be released for inspection unless subpoenaed by a court of competent jurisdiction.

2. The judge, upon receipt of a written request from any person who was a party to an intercepted communication or from the person's attorney, shall make available to the person or the person's counsel those portions of the intercepted communications which contain the person's conversation. On an ex parte showing of good cause to a district judge, the serving of the inventory required by this section may be postponed for such time as the judge may provide.

(Added to NRS by 1973, 1747; A 1975, 1520; 1983, 119; 1985, 1976; 2001, 2572; 2007, 2077; 2015, 2493)

NRS 179.500 Contents of intercepted communications inadmissible in evidence unless transcript provided to parties before trial. The contents of any intercepted wire, electronic or oral communication or evidence derived therefrom must not be received in evidence or otherwise disclosed in any trial, hearing or other proceeding in any court of this state unless each party, not less than 10 days before the trial, hearing or proceeding, has been furnished with a copy of the court order and accompanying application under which the interception was authorized and a transcript of any communications intercepted. Such 10-day period may be waived by the judge if the judge finds that it was not possible to furnish the party with such information 10 days before the trial, hearing or proceeding and that the party will not be prejudiced by the delay in receiving such information.

(Added to NRS by 1973, 1747; A 2015, 2493)

NRS 179.505 Motion to suppress.

1. Any aggrieved person in any trial, hearing or proceeding in or before any court, department, officer, agency or other authority of this State, or a political subdivision thereof, may move to suppress the contents of any intercepted wire, electronic or oral communication, or evidence derived therefrom, on the grounds that:

(a) The communication was unlawfully intercepted.

(b) The order of authorization under which it was intercepted is insufficient on its face.

(c) The interception was not made in conformity with the order of authorization.

(d) The period of the order and any extension had expired.

2. Such a motion must be made before the trial, hearing or proceeding unless there was no opportunity to make such a motion or the person was not aware of the grounds of the motion. If the motion is granted, the contents of the intercepted wire, electronic or oral communication, or evidence derived therefrom, must be treated as having been obtained in violation of NRS 179.410 to 179.515, inclusive. The judge, upon the filing of such motion by the aggrieved person, may in the judge's discretion make available to the aggrieved person or the aggrieved person's counsel for inspection such portions of the intercepted communication or evidence derived therefrom as the judge determines to be in the interest of justice.

(Added to NRS by 1973, 1747; A 2015, 2493)

NRS 179.510 Appeal by State from order granting motion to suppress. In addition to any other right to appeal the State may appeal from an order granting a motion to suppress made under NRS 179.505 if the Attorney General or district attorney certifies to the judge or other official granting such motion that the appeal is not taken for purposes of delay. Such appeal shall be taken within 30 days after the date the order of suppression was entered and shall be diligently prosecuted as in the case of other interlocutory appeals or under such rules as the Supreme Court may adopt.

(Added to NRS by 1973, 1748)

NRS 179.515 Reports by justices of Supreme Court, district judges, Attorney General and district attorneys.

1. In January of each year, the Attorney General and the district attorney of each county shall report to the Administrative Office of the United States Courts the information required to be reported pursuant to 18 U.S.C. § 2519. A copy of the report must be filed with the Investigation Division of the Department of Public Safety. In the case of a joint application by the Attorney General and a district attorney both shall make the report.

2. Every justice of the Supreme Court or district judge who signs an order authorizing or denying an interception shall, within 30 days after the termination of the order or any extension thereof, file with the Investigation Division of the Department of Public Safety on forms approved by the Division a report containing the same information required to be reported pursuant to 18 U.S.C. § 2519. The report must also indicate whether a party to an intercepted wire, electronic or oral communication had consented to the interception.

3. The willful failure of any officer to report any information known to the officer which is required to be reported pursuant to subsection 1 or 2 constitutes malfeasance in office and, in such cases, the Secretary of State shall, when the wrong becomes known to the Secretary of State, institute legal proceedings for the removal of that officer.

4. The Investigation Division of the Department of Public Safety shall, on or before April 30 of each year, compile a report consisting of a summary and analysis of all reports submitted to the Division pursuant to this section during the previous calendar year. The report is a public record and may be inspected by any person during the regular office hours of the Division.

(Added to NRS by 1973, 1748; A 1975, 1520; 1981, 2009; 1983, 120; 1985, 1977; 2001, 2573; 2015, 2494)

MISCELLANEOUS PROVISIONS

NRS 179.525 Temporary changes in telephone service permitted where hostages are being held or suspects are barricaded.

1. A supervising peace officer who, with other officers, or any peace officer who, alone, is attempting to gain control of a situation in which a person:

(a) Is holding another as a hostage, whether or not the life of the hostage has been threatened; or

(b) Has committed or is believed to have committed a crime, is barricaded in an area or structure and is resisting arrest through the use or threatened use of force,
Ê may direct the public utility which provides telephone service to the area or structure in which the hostages are being held or persons are barricaded, or to an area which is close to that area or structure, to interrupt the service on, divert, reroute or otherwise make temporary changes in telephone lines to enable the peace officer making the request to establish communication with the person holding the hostage, or among peace officers, or to deny communication to the person holding the hostage.

2. Each public utility which provides telephone service in this State shall designate an employee and an alternate to supervise in performing the orders of a peace officer who is carrying out the purposes of this section.

3. A reliance in good faith by a public utility on the order of a peace officer pursuant to this section constitutes a complete defense to any civil or criminal action brought against the public utility on account of any interruption, diversion, rerouting or change in telephone service made in response to the order.

(Added to NRS by 1981, 1561)

NRS 179.530 Order authorizing use of pen register or trap and trace device.

1. District courts of this state may issue orders authorizing the use of a pen register or trap and trace device upon the application of a district attorney, the Attorney General or their deputies, supported by an affidavit of a peace officer under the circumstances and upon the conditions prescribed by 18 U.S.C. §§ 3121-3127 as those provisions existed on July 1, 1989.

2. As used in this section, "peace officer" means:

(a) Sheriffs of counties and metropolitan police departments and their deputies;

(b) Personnel of the Department of Public Safety who have the powers of peace officers pursuant to NRS 289.270;

(c) Police officers of cities and towns;

(d) Agents of the Nevada Gaming Control Board who are investigating any violation of subsection 2 or 3 of NRS 463.360 or chapter 465 of NRS;

(e) Special investigators employed by the Attorney General who have the powers of peace officers pursuant to NRS 289.170;

(f) Investigators employed by a district attorney who have the powers of peace officers pursuant to NRS 289.170; and

(g) The Inspector General of the Department of Corrections and the criminal investigators employed by the Department who have the powers of peace officers pursuant to NRS 289.220.

3. A public utility that relies, in good faith, upon an order of a district court authorizing the use of a pen register or trap and trace device is not liable in any civil or criminal action brought against the public utility for the use of the pen register or trap and trace device in accordance with the order of the court.

(Added to NRS by 1989, 1134; A 1991, 969; 1993, 83, 2528; 2001, 2573; 2011, 21, 726)

NRS 179.535 Receipt for property taken from person arrested for public offense. When money or other property is taken from a defendant arrested upon a charge of a public offense, the officer taking it shall at the time give duplicate receipts therefor, specifying particularly the amount of money and the kind of property taken, one of which receipts the officer shall deliver to the defendant, and the other of which the officer shall forthwith file with the clerk of the court to which the deposition and statements must be sent.

(Added to NRS by 1967, 1461)

CHAPTER 179A - RECORDS OF CRIMINAL HISTORY AND INFORMATION RELATING TO PUBLIC SAFETY

GENERAL PROVISIONS

CENTRAL REPOSITORY FOR NEVADA RECORDS OF CRIMINAL HISTORY

TRANSMITTAL OF MENTAL HEALTH INFORMATION TO NATIONAL INSTANT CRIMINAL BACKGROUND CHECK SYSTEM AND NATIONAL CRIME INFORMATION CENTER

PROGRAM FOR REPORTING CRIMES RELATED TO PREJUDICE

DISSEMINATION OF INFORMATION RELATING TO CERTAIN OFFENSES

ACCOUNT TO INVESTIGATE BACKGROUND OF VOLUNTEERS WHO WORK WITH CHILDREN

REPOSITORY FOR INFORMATION CONCERNING ORDERS FOR PROTECTION AGAINST DOMESTIC VIOLENCE

REPOSITORY FOR INFORMATION CONCERNING CRIMES AGAINST OLDER PERSONS

NATIONAL CRIME PREVENTION AND PRIVACY COMPACT

PENALTIES

GENERAL PROVISIONS

NRS 179A.010 Definitions. As used in this chapter, unless the context otherwise requires, the words and terms defined in NRS 179A.020 to 179A.073, inclusive, have the meanings ascribed to them in those sections.
(Added to NRS by 1979, 1850; A 1987, 1764; 2005, 2864; 2009, 1834, 2490; 2015, 1799)

NRS 179A.020 "Administration of criminal justice" defined. "Administration of criminal justice" means detection, apprehension, detention, release pending trial or after trial, prosecution, adjudication, correctional supervision or rehabilitation of accused persons or criminal offenders, and includes criminal identification activities and the collection, storage and dissemination of records of criminal history.
(Added to NRS by 1979, 1850)

NRS 179A.030 "Agency of criminal justice" defined. "Agency of criminal justice" means:
1. Any court; and
2. Any governmental agency or subunit of any governmental agency which performs a function in the administration of criminal justice pursuant to a statute or executive order, and which allocates a substantial part of its budget to a function in the administration of criminal justice.
(Added to NRS by 1979, 1850; A 2013, 112)

NRS 179A.045 "Central Repository" defined. "Central Repository" means the Central Repository for Nevada Records of Criminal History.
(Added to NRS by 1985, 912)

NRS 179A.047 "Child" defined. "Child" means a person under the age of 16 years.
(Added to NRS by 1987, 1760)

NRS 179A.049 "Department" defined. "Department" means the Department of Public Safety.
(Added to NRS by 1987, 1760; A 2001, 2574)

NRS 179A.050 "Disposition" defined. "Disposition" means the formal conclusion of a criminal proceeding at any point in the administration of criminal justice which shows the nature of the conclusion.
(Added to NRS by 1979, 1850)

NRS 179A.060 "Dissemination" defined. "Dissemination" means disclosing records of criminal history or the absence of records of criminal history to a person or agency outside the organization which has control of the information.
(Added to NRS by 1979, 1850; A 1985, 912)

NRS 179A.061 "National Crime Information Center" defined. "National Crime Information Center" means the computerized information system created and maintained by the Federal Bureau of Investigation pursuant to 28 U.S.C. § 534.
(Added to NRS by 2015, 1799)

NRS 179A.062 "National Instant Criminal Background Check System" defined. "National Instant Criminal Background Check System" means the national system created by the federal Brady Handgun Violence Prevention Act, Public Law 103-159.
(Added to NRS by 2009, 2488)

NRS 179A.066 "Offender convicted of a crime against a child" defined. "Offender convicted of a crime against a child" has the meaning ascribed to it in NRS 179D.0559.
(Added to NRS by 2005, 2864; A 2007, 2753)

NRS 179A.070 "Record of criminal history" defined.
1. "Record of criminal history" means information contained in records collected and maintained by agencies of criminal justice, the subject of which is a natural person, consisting of descriptions which identify the subject and notations of summons in a criminal action, warrants, arrests, citations for misdemeanors issued pursuant to NRS 171.1773, citations issued for violations of NRS

484C.110, 484C.120, 484C.130 and 484C.430, detentions, decisions of a district attorney or the Attorney General not to prosecute the subject, indictments, informations or other formal criminal charges and dispositions of charges, including, without limitation, dismissals, acquittals, convictions, sentences, information set forth in NRS 209.353 concerning an offender in prison, any postconviction relief, correctional supervision occurring in Nevada, information concerning the status of an offender on parole or probation, and information concerning a convicted person who has registered as such pursuant to chapter 179C of NRS. The term includes only information contained in a record, maintained in written or electronic form, of a formal transaction between a person and an agency of criminal justice in this State, including, without limitation, the fingerprints of a person who is arrested and taken into custody and of a person who is placed on parole or probation and supervised by the Division of Parole and Probation of the Department.

2. "Record of criminal history" does not include:

(a) Investigative or intelligence information, reports of crime or other information concerning specific persons collected in the course of the enforcement of criminal laws;

(b) Information concerning juveniles;

(c) Posters, announcements or lists intended to identify fugitives or wanted persons and aid in their apprehension;

(d) Original records of entry maintained by agencies of criminal justice if the records are chronological and not cross-indexed;

(e) Records of application for and issuance, suspension, revocation or renewal of occupational licenses, including, without limitation, permits to work in the gaming industry;

(f) Except as otherwise provided in subsection 1, court indexes and records of public judicial proceedings, court decisions and opinions, and information disclosed during public judicial proceedings;

(g) Except as otherwise provided in subsection 1, records of traffic violations constituting misdemeanors;

(h) Records of traffic offenses maintained by the Department to regulate the issuance, suspension, revocation or renewal of drivers' or other operators' licenses;

(i) Announcements of actions by the State Board of Pardons Commissioners and the State Board of Parole Commissioners, except information concerning the status of an offender on parole or probation; or

(j) Records which originated in an agency other than an agency of criminal justice in this State.

(Added to NRS by 1979, 1850; A 1985, 1977; 1987, 1764; 1995, 2069; 1997, 1327; 1999, 2089; 2005, 164; 2007, 2810)

NRS 179A.071 "Record of registration" defined. "Record of registration" has the meaning ascribed to it in NRS 179D.070.

(Added to NRS by 2005, 2864; A 2011, 220)

NRS 179A.0715 "Records of criminal history of the United States or another state" defined. "Records of criminal history of the United States or another state" means records which originated in an agency of criminal justice of the Federal Government or an agency of criminal justice of another state.

(Added to NRS by 2009, 1834)

NRS 179A.072 "Sex offender" defined. "Sex offender" has the meaning ascribed to it in NRS 179D.095.

(Added to NRS by 2005, 2864)

NRS 179A.073 "Sexual offense" defined.

1. "Sexual offense" includes acts upon a child constituting:

(a) Sexual assault under NRS 200.366;

(b) Statutory sexual seduction under NRS 200.368;

(c) Use of a minor in producing pornography under NRS 200.710;

(d) Promotion of a sexual performance of a minor under NRS 200.720;

(e) Possession of a visual presentation depicting the sexual conduct of a child under NRS 200.730;

(f) Incest under NRS 201.180;

(g) Lewdness with a child under NRS 201.230; or

(h) Luring a child or a person with mental illness pursuant to NRS 201.560, if punished as a felony.

2. "Sexual offense" also includes acts committed outside the State that would constitute any of the offenses in subsection 1 if committed in the State, and the aiding, abetting, attempting or conspiring to engage in any of the offenses in subsection 1.

(Added to NRS by 1987, 1760; A 2001, 2794; 2003, 1388; 2013, 1167)

CENTRAL REPOSITORY FOR NEVADA RECORDS OF CRIMINAL HISTORY

NRS 179A.075 Creation; duties of agencies of criminal justice and certain other agencies; duties and powers of General Services Division of Department and Central Repository.

1. The Central Repository for Nevada Records of Criminal History is hereby created within the General Services Division of the Department.

2. Each agency of criminal justice and any other agency dealing with crime or delinquency of children shall:

(a) Collect and maintain records, reports and compilations of statistical data required by the Department; and

(b) Submit the information collected to the Central Repository in the manner approved by the Director of the Department.

3. Each agency of criminal justice shall submit the information relating to records of criminal history that it creates, issues or collects, and any information in its possession relating to the DNA profile of a person from whom a biological specimen is obtained pursuant to NRS 176.09123 or 176.0913, to the Division. The information must be submitted to the Division:

(a) Through an electronic network;

(b) On a medium of magnetic storage; or

(c) In the manner prescribed by the Director of the Department,

Ê within 60 days after the date of the disposition of the case. If an agency has submitted a record regarding the arrest of a person who is later determined by the agency not to be the person who committed the particular crime, the agency shall, immediately upon making that determination, so notify the Division. The Division shall delete all references in the Central Repository relating to that particular arrest.

4. The Division shall, in the manner prescribed by the Director of the Department:

(a) Collect, maintain and arrange all information submitted to it relating to:

(1) Records of criminal history; and

(2) The DNA profile of a person from whom a biological specimen is obtained pursuant to NRS 176.09123 or 176.0913.

(b) When practicable, use a record of the personal identifying information of a subject as the basis for any records maintained regarding him or her.

(c) Upon request, provide the information that is contained in the Central Repository to the State Disaster Identification Team of the Division of Emergency Management of the Department.

(d) Upon request, provide, in paper or electronic form, the information that is contained in the Central Repository to a multidisciplinary team to review the death of the victim of a crime that constitutes domestic violence organized or sponsored by the Attorney General pursuant to NRS 228.495.

5. The Division may:

(a) Disseminate any information which is contained in the Central Repository to any other agency of criminal justice;

(b) Enter into cooperative agreements with repositories of the United States and other states to facilitate exchanges of information that may be disseminated pursuant to paragraph (a); and

(c) Request of and receive from the Federal Bureau of Investigation information on the background and personal history of any person whose record of fingerprints or other biometric identifier the Central Repository submits to the Federal Bureau of Investigation and:

(1) Who has applied to any agency of the State of Nevada or any political subdivision thereof for a license which it has the power to grant or deny;

(2) With whom any agency of the State of Nevada or any political subdivision thereof intends to enter into a relationship of employment or a contract for personal services;

(3) Who has applied to any agency of the State of Nevada or any political subdivision thereof to attend an academy for training peace officers approved by the Peace Officers' Standards and Training Commission;

(4) For whom such information is required or authorized to be obtained pursuant to NRS 62B.270, 62G.223, 62G.353, 424.031, 432A.170, 432B.198, 433B.183, 449.123 and 449.4329; or

(5) About whom any agency of the State of Nevada or any political subdivision thereof is authorized by law to have accurate personal information for the protection of the agency or the persons within its jurisdiction.

6. To request and receive information from the Federal Bureau of Investigation concerning a person pursuant to subsection 5, the Central Repository must receive:

(a) The person's complete set of fingerprints for the purposes of:

(1) Booking the person into a city or county jail or detention facility;

(2) Employment;

(3) Contractual services; or

(4) Services related to occupational licensing;

(b) One or more of the person's fingerprints for the purposes of mobile identification by an agency of criminal justice; or

(c) Any other biometric identifier of the person as it may require for the purposes of:

(1) Arrest; or

(2) Criminal investigation,

Ê from the agency of criminal justice or agency of the State of Nevada or any political subdivision thereof and submit the received data to the Federal Bureau of Investigation for its report.

7. The Central Repository shall:

(a) Collect and maintain records, reports and compilations of statistical data submitted by any agency pursuant to subsection 2.

(b) Tabulate and analyze all records, reports and compilations of statistical data received pursuant to this section.

(c) Disseminate to federal agencies engaged in the collection of statistical data relating to crime information which is contained in the Central Repository.

(d) Investigate the criminal history of any person who:

(1) Has applied to the Superintendent of Public Instruction for the issuance or renewal of a license;

(2) Has applied to a county school district, charter school or private school for employment; or

(3) Is employed by a county school district, charter school or private school,

Ê and notify the superintendent of each county school district, the governing body of each charter school and the Superintendent of Public Instruction, or the administrator of each private school, as appropriate, if the investigation of the Central Repository indicates that the person has been convicted of a violation of NRS 200.508, 201.230, 453.3385, 453.339 or 453.3395, or convicted of a felony or any offense involving moral turpitude.

(e) Upon discovery, notify the superintendent of each county school district, the governing body of each charter school or the administrator of each private school, as appropriate, by providing the superintendent, governing body or administrator with a list of all persons:

(1) Investigated pursuant to paragraph (d); or

(2) Employed by a county school district, charter school or private school whose fingerprints were sent previously to the Central Repository for investigation,

Ê who the Central Repository's records indicate have been convicted of a violation of NRS 200.508, 201.230, 453.3385, 453.339 or 453.3395, or convicted of a felony or any offense involving moral turpitude since the Central Repository's initial investigation. The superintendent of each county school district, the governing body of a charter school or the administrator of each private school, as applicable, shall determine whether further investigation or action by the district, charter school or private school, as applicable, is appropriate.

(f) Investigate the criminal history of each person who submits one or more fingerprints or other biometric identifier or has such data submitted pursuant to NRS 62B.270, 62G.223, 62G.353, 424.031, 432A.170, 432B.198, 433B.183, 449.122, 449.123 or 449.4329.

(g) On or before July 1 of each year, prepare and post on the Central Repository's Internet website an annual report containing the statistical data relating to crime received during the preceding calendar year. Additional reports may be posted to the Central Repository's Internet website throughout the year regarding specific areas of crime if they are approved by the Director of the Department.

(h) On or before July 1 of each year, prepare and post on the Central Repository's Internet website a report containing statistical data about domestic violence in this State.

(i) Identify and review the collection and processing of statistical data relating to criminal justice and the delinquency of children by any agency identified in subsection 2 and make recommendations for any necessary changes in the manner of collecting and processing statistical data by any such agency.

(j) Adopt regulations governing biometric identifiers and the information and data derived from biometric identifiers, including, without limitation:

(1) Their collection, use, safeguarding, handling, retention, storage, dissemination and destruction; and

(2) The methods by which a person may request the removal of his or her biometric identifiers from the Central Repository and any other agency where his or her biometric identifiers have been stored.

8. The Central Repository may:

(a) In the manner prescribed by the Director of the Department, disseminate compilations of statistical data and publish statistical reports relating to crime or the delinquency of children.

(b) Charge a reasonable fee for any publication or special report it distributes relating to data collected pursuant to this section. The Central Repository may not collect such a fee from an agency of criminal justice, any other agency dealing with crime or the delinquency of children which is required to submit information pursuant to subsection 2 or the State Disaster Identification Team of the Division of Emergency Management of the Department. All money collected pursuant to this paragraph must be used to pay for the cost of operating the Central Repository.

(c) In the manner prescribed by the Director of the Department, use electronic means to receive and disseminate information contained in the Central Repository that it is authorized to disseminate pursuant to the provisions of this chapter.

9. As used in this section:

(a) "Biometric identifier" means a fingerprint, palm print, scar, bodily mark, tattoo, voiceprint, facial image, retina image or iris image of a person.

(b) "Mobile identification" means the collection, storage, transmission, reception, search, access or processing of a biometric identifier using a handheld device.

(c) "Personal identifying information" means any information designed, commonly used or capable of being used, alone or in conjunction with any other information, to identify a person, including, without limitation:

(1) The name, driver's license number, social security number, date of birth and photograph or computer-generated image of a person; and

(2) A biometric identifier of a person.

(d) "Private school" has the meaning ascribed to it in NRS 394.103.

(Added to NRS by 1985, 912; A 1987, 666, 1765; 1989, 376, 559, 564; 1991, 825; 1995, 1910; 1997, 415, 1535, 3259, 3266; 1999, 459, 463, 1251, 2090, 2097, 3123, 3135; 2001, 146, 1853, 3034, 3038; 2003, 2834; 2005, 17, 900, 2421; 2007, 1221, 2928; 2009, 1834, 2369; 2011, 994, 3551; 2013, 138, 179, 462, 1073, 2100; 2015, 544, 841, 1799, 2762)

NRS 179A.078 Uniform Program for Reporting Crimes: Establishment; purpose. The Director of the Department shall establish within the Central Repository a Uniform Program for Reporting Crimes that is designed to collect statistical data relating to crime or delinquency of children and to facilitate the collection and analysis of statistical data relating to crime at a central location.

(Added to NRS by 1991, 824; A 1993, 362; 1997, 454; 2005, 903)

NRS 179A.079 Advisory Committee on Nevada Criminal Justice Information Sharing: Creation; members; duties; terms of office; meetings.

1. The Director of the Department shall establish within the Department the Advisory Committee on Nevada Criminal Justice Information Sharing.

2. The Advisory Committee consists of:

(a) The Director of the Department or the Director's designee;

(b) The Attorney General or the Attorney General's designee;

(c) The Director of the Department of Corrections or the Director's designee;

(d) One member who is a representative of the Judicial Branch of State Government, appointed by the Chief Justice of the Supreme Court;

(e) One member appointed by the Nevada Sheriffs' and Chiefs' Association, or a successor organization;

(f) One member appointed by the Nevada District Attorneys Association, or a successor organization;

(g) One member appointed by the Director of the Department who uses the Central Repository to obtain information relating to records of criminal history for purposes other than criminal justice, which may include, without limitation, for purposes of determining eligibility of persons for employment or licensure;

(h) One member of the Senate appointed by the Majority Leader of the Senate; and

(i) One member of the Assembly appointed by the Speaker of the Assembly.

3. The Advisory Committee shall:

(a) Recommend policies and procedures that apply the best management practices to the activities at the Central Repository;

(b) Advise on technological support for the Central Repository; and

(c) Advise on the integrated information sharing of statistical data relating to crime or the delinquency of children.

4. Each member that is appointed to the Advisory Committee pursuant to subsection 2, other than a member of the Senate or the Assembly, shall serve a term of 3 years. A member of the Senate and the Assembly appointed to the Advisory Committee shall serve until a replacement is appointed. Any vacancy occurring in the membership of the Advisory Committee must be filled in the same manner as the original appointment.

5. The Advisory Committee shall meet twice annually.

6. The Director may assign such other employees of the Department as the Director deems necessary to assist the Advisory Committee in its duties.

7. Members of the Advisory Committee serve without compensation. If sufficient money is available, members are entitled to travel allowances provided for state officers and employees generally while attending meetings of the Advisory Committee.

(Added to NRS by 2005, 900)

NRS 179A.080 Duties of Director of Department. The Director of the Department is responsible for administering this chapter and may adopt regulations for that purpose. The Director shall:

1. Adopt regulations for the security of the Central Repository so that it is adequately protected from fire, theft, loss, destruction, other hazards and unauthorized access.

2. Adopt regulations and standards for personnel employed by agencies of criminal justice in positions of responsibility for maintenance and dissemination of information relating to records of criminal history and information disseminated pursuant to NRS 179A.180 to 179A.240, inclusive.

3. Provide for audits of informational systems by qualified public or private agencies, organizations or persons.

(Added to NRS by 1979, 1854; A 1981, 2010; 1985, 913, 1978; 1987, 1765; 2003, 2837)

NRS 179A.090 Prerequisite to dissemination of records; exceptions. No agency of criminal justice in Nevada may disseminate any record of criminal history which includes information about a felony or a gross misdemeanor without first making inquiry of the Central Repository, to obtain the most current and complete information available, unless:

1. The information is needed for a purpose in the administration of criminal justice for which time is essential, and the Central Repository is not able to respond within the required time;

2. The full information requested and to be disseminated relates to specific facts or incidents which are within the direct knowledge of an officer, agent or employee of the agency which disseminates the information;

3. The full information requested and to be disseminated was received as part of a summary of records of criminal history from the Central Repository within 30 days before the information is disseminated;

4. The statute, executive order, court rule or court order under which the information is to be disseminated refers only to information which is in the files of the agency which makes the dissemination;

5. The information requested and to be disseminated is for the express purpose of research, evaluation or statistical activities to be based upon information maintained in the files of the agency or agencies from which the information is sought; or

6. The information is requested by a compensation officer of the State Board of Examiners pursuant to NRS 217.090.

(Added to NRS by 1979, 1851; A 1981, 1673; 1985, 913)

NRS 179A.100 Records that may be disseminated without restriction; records that must be disseminated upon request; information that must be disseminated regardless of written consent; information that must be disseminated only with written consent.

1. The following records of criminal history may be disseminated by an agency of criminal justice without any restriction pursuant to this chapter:

(a) Any which reflect records of conviction only; and

(b) Any which pertain to an incident for which a person is currently within the system of criminal justice, including parole or probation.

2. Without any restriction pursuant to this chapter, a record of criminal history or the absence of such a record may be:

(a) Disclosed among agencies which maintain a system for the mutual exchange of criminal records.

(b) Furnished by one agency to another to administer the system of criminal justice, including the furnishing of information by a police department to a district attorney.

(c) Reported to the Central Repository.

3. An agency of criminal justice shall disseminate to a prospective employer, upon request, records of criminal history concerning a prospective employee or volunteer which are the result of a name-based inquiry and which:

(a) Reflect convictions only; or

(b) Pertain to an incident for which the prospective employee or volunteer is currently within the system of criminal justice, including parole or probation.

4. In addition to any other information to which an employer is entitled or authorized to receive from a name-based inquiry, the Central Repository shall disseminate to a prospective or current employer, or a person or entity designated to receive the information on behalf of

such an employer, the information contained in a record of registration concerning an employee, prospective employee, volunteer or prospective volunteer who is a sex offender or an offender convicted of a crime against a child, regardless of whether the employee, prospective employee, volunteer or prospective volunteer gives written consent to the release of that information. The Central Repository shall disseminate such information in a manner that does not reveal the name of an individual victim of an offense or the information described in subsection 7 of NRS 179B.250. A request for information pursuant to this subsection must conform to the requirements of the Central Repository and must include:

(a) The name and address of the employer, and the name and signature of the person or entity requesting the information on behalf of the employer;

(b) The name and address of the employer's facility in which the employee, prospective employee, volunteer or prospective volunteer is employed or volunteers or is seeking to become employed or volunteer; and

(c) The name and other identifying information of the employee, prospective employee, volunteer or prospective volunteer.

5. In addition to any other information to which an employer is entitled or authorized to receive, the Central Repository shall disseminate to a prospective or current employer, or a person or entity designated to receive the information on behalf of such an employer, the information described in subsection 4 of NRS 179A.190 concerning an employee, prospective employee, volunteer or prospective volunteer who gives written consent to the release of that information if the employer submits a request in the manner set forth in NRS 179A.200 for obtaining a notice of information. The Central Repository shall search for and disseminate such information in the manner set forth in NRS 179A.210 for the dissemination of a notice of information.

6. Except as otherwise provided in subsection 5, the provisions of NRS 179A.180 to 179A.240, inclusive, do not apply to an employer who requests information and to whom such information is disseminated pursuant to subsections 4 and 5.

7. Records of criminal history must be disseminated by an agency of criminal justice, upon request, to the following persons or governmental entities:

(a) The person who is the subject of the record of criminal history for the purposes of NRS 179A.150.

(b) The person who is the subject of the record of criminal history when the subject is a party in a judicial, administrative, licensing, disciplinary or other proceeding to which the information is relevant.

(c) The Nevada Gaming Control Board.

(d) The State Board of Nursing.

(e) The Private Investigator's Licensing Board to investigate an applicant for a license.

(f) A public administrator to carry out the duties as prescribed in chapter 253 of NRS.

(g) A public guardian to investigate a ward or proposed ward or persons who may have knowledge of assets belonging to a ward or proposed ward.

(h) Any agency of criminal justice of the United States or of another state or the District of Columbia.

(i) Any public utility subject to the jurisdiction of the Public Utilities Commission of Nevada when the information is necessary to conduct a security investigation of an employee or prospective employee or to protect the public health, safety or welfare.

(j) Persons and agencies authorized by statute, ordinance, executive order, court rule, court decision or court order as construed by appropriate state or local officers or agencies.

(k) Any person or governmental entity which has entered into a contract to provide services to an agency of criminal justice relating to the administration of criminal justice, if authorized by the contract, and if the contract also specifies that the information will be used only for stated purposes and that it will be otherwise confidential in accordance with state and federal law and regulation.

(l) Any reporter for the electronic or printed media in a professional capacity for communication to the public.

(m) Prospective employers if the person who is the subject of the information has given written consent to the release of that information by the agency which maintains it.

(n) For the express purpose of research, evaluative or statistical programs pursuant to an agreement with an agency of criminal justice.

(o) An agency which provides child welfare services, as defined in NRS 432B.030.

(p) The Division of Welfare and Supportive Services of the Department of Health and Human Services or its designated representative, as needed to ensure the safety of investigators and caseworkers.

(q) The Aging and Disability Services Division of the Department of Health and Human Services or its designated representative, as needed to ensure the safety of investigators and caseworkers.

(r) An agency of this or any other state or the Federal Government that is conducting activities pursuant to Part D of Subchapter IV of Chapter 7 of Title 42 of the Social Security Act, 42 U.S.C. §§ 651 et seq.

(s) The State Disaster Identification Team of the Division of Emergency Management of the Department.

(t) The Commissioner of Insurance.

(u) The Board of Medical Examiners.

(v) The State Board of Osteopathic Medicine.

(w) The Board of Massage Therapists and its Executive Director.

(x) The Board of Examiners for Social Workers.

(y) A multidisciplinary team to review the death of the victim of a crime that constitutes domestic violence organized or sponsored by the Attorney General pursuant to NRS 228.495.

8. Agencies of criminal justice in this State which receive information from sources outside this State concerning transactions involving criminal justice which occur outside Nevada shall treat the information as confidentially as is required by the provisions of this chapter.

(Added to NRS by 1979, 1852; A 1985, 913; 1987, 1765; 1989, 5, 560, 562, 991; 1991, 130; 1995, 374, 1656; 1997, 1965, 2333, 3261; 1999, 492, 1253, 3126; 2001, 2254, 2577; 2001 Special Session, 16; 2003, 236, 2837; 2005, 2528, 2864; 2007, 274, 2931; 2009, 1837, 2583; 2013, 182, 969; 2015, 3861)

NRS 179A.103 Service to conduct name-based search of records of employee, prospective employee, volunteer or prospective volunteer.

1. There is hereby established within the Central Repository a service to conduct a name-based search of records of criminal history of an employee, prospective employee, volunteer or prospective volunteer.

2. An eligible person that wishes to participate in the service must enter into a contract with the Central Repository.

3. The Central Repository may charge a reasonable fee for participation in the service.

4. A participant of the service may inquire about the records of criminal history of an employee, prospective employee, volunteer or prospective volunteer to determine the suitability of the employee or prospective employee for employment or the suitability of the volunteer or prospective volunteer for volunteering.

5. The Central Repository shall disseminate to a participant of the service information which:

(a) Reflects convictions only; or

(b) Pertains to an incident for which an employee, prospective employee, volunteer or prospective volunteer is currently within the system of criminal justice, including parole or probation.

6. An employee, prospective employee, volunteer or prospective volunteer who is proposed to be the subject of a name-based search must provide his or her written consent for the Central Repository to perform the search and to release the information to a participant. The written consent form may be:

(a) A form designated by the Central Repository; or

(b) If the participant is an employment screening service, a form that complies with the provisions of 15 U.S.C. § 1681b(b)2 for the procurement of a consumer report.

7. An employment screening service that is designated to receive records of criminal history on behalf of an employer or volunteer organization may provide such records of criminal history to the employer or volunteer organization upon request of the employer or volunteer organization.

8. The Central Repository may audit a participant, at such times as the Central Repository deems necessary, to ensure that records of criminal history are securely maintained.

9. The Central Repository may terminate participation in the service if a participant fails:

(a) To pay the fees required to participate in the service; or

(b) To address, within a reasonable period, deficiencies identified in an audit conducted pursuant to subsection 8.

10. As used in this section:

(a) "Consumer report" has the meaning ascribed to it in 15 U.S.C. § 1681a(d).

(b) "Eligible person" includes:

(1) An employer.

(2) A volunteer organization.

(3) An employment screening service.

(c) "Employer" means a person in this State that:

(1) Employs an employee; or

(2) Enters into a contract with an independent contractor.

(d) "Employment" includes performing services for an employer as an independent contractor.

(e) "Employment screening service" means a person or entity designated by an employer or volunteer organization to provide employment or volunteer screening services to the employer or volunteer organization.

(Added to NRS by 2015, 704)

NRS 179A.105 Immunity of employer who fails to request certain information concerning volunteer. An employer who fails to request:

1. The information contained in a record of registration concerning a volunteer or prospective volunteer who is a sex offender or an offender convicted of a crime against a child, as authorized pursuant to subsection 4 of NRS 179A.100; or

2. The information described in subsection 4 of NRS 179A.190 concerning a volunteer or prospective volunteer, as authorized pursuant to subsection 5 of NRS 179A.100,

Ê is not liable to a child served by the employer for civil damages suffered by the child as a result of an offense listed in subsection 4 of NRS 179A.190 committed against the child by such a volunteer or prospective volunteer.

(Added to NRS by 2003, 2834; A 2005, 2866)

NRS 179A.110 Records to be used solely for purpose requested; further dissemination of information or records. A record of criminal history or any records of criminal history of the United States or another state obtained pursuant to this chapter must be used solely for the purpose for which the record was requested. No person who receives information relating to records of criminal history pursuant to this chapter or who receives information pursuant to NRS 179A.180 to 179A.240, inclusive, may disseminate the information further without express authority of law or in accordance with a court order. This section does not prohibit the dissemination of material by an employee of the electronic or printed media in a professional capacity for communication to the public.

(Added to NRS by 1979, 1853; A 1987, 1767; 2003, 2839; 2009, 1839)

NRS 179A.120 Disclosures to victims of crime.

1. Agencies of criminal justice may disclose to victims of a crime, members of their families or their guardians the identity of persons suspected of being responsible for the crime, including juveniles who have been certified to stand trial as adults, together with information, including dispositions, which may be of assistance to the victim in obtaining redress for an injury or loss in a civil action. This disclosure may

be made regardless of whether charges have been filed, and even if a prosecuting attorney has declined to file charges or the charge has been dismissed.

2. Disclosure of investigative information pursuant to this section does not establish a duty to disclose any additional information concerning the same incident or make any disclosure of information obtained by an investigation, except as compelled by legal process.

(Added to NRS by 1979, 1853; A 1981, 2025)

NRS 179A.130 Log to be maintained of dissemination of information relating to records of criminal history. Each agency of criminal justice which maintains and disseminates information relating to records of criminal history must maintain a log of each dissemination of that information other than a dissemination of the fact that the agency has no record relating to a certain person. The log must be maintained for at least 1 year after the information is disseminated, and must contain:

1. An entry showing to what agency or person the information relating to records of criminal history were provided;
2. The date on which the information was provided;
3. The person who is the subject of the information; and
4. A brief description of the information provided.

(Added to NRS by 1979, 1853; A 1987, 1767; 2003, 2839)

NRS 179A.140 Fee for furnishing information relating to records of criminal history; use of money collected.

1. Except as otherwise provided in this section, an agency of criminal justice may charge a reasonable fee for information relating to records of criminal history provided to any person or governmental entity.

2. An agency of criminal justice shall not charge a fee for providing such information to another agency of criminal justice if the information is provided for purposes of the administration of criminal justice, or for providing such information to the State Disaster Identification Team of the Division of Emergency Management of the Department.

3. The Central Repository shall not charge such a fee:

(a) For information relating to a person regarding whom the Central Repository provided a similar report within the immediately preceding 6 months in conjunction with the application by that person for professional licensure; or

(b) For information provided to any organization that meets the criteria established by regulation pursuant to paragraph (b) of subsection 5 of NRS 179A.310.

4. The Director may request an allocation from the Contingency Account pursuant to NRS 353.266, 353.268 and 353.269 to cover the costs incurred by the Department to carry out the provisions of paragraph (b) of subsection 3.

5. All money received or collected by the Department pursuant to this section must be used to defray the cost of operating the Central Repository.

(Added to NRS by 1979, 1855; A 1985, 915; 1987, 1767; 1995, 1912; 1997, 1305, 3263; 2001, 2578; 2003, 2839; 2005, 2867; 2007, 542)

NRS 179A.150 Inspection and correction of information contained in record of criminal history.

1. The Central Repository and each state, municipal, county or metropolitan police agency shall permit a person, who is or believes he or she may be the subject of information relating to records of criminal history maintained by that agency, to appear in person during normal business hours of the agency and inspect any recorded information held by that agency pertaining to that person. This right of access does not extend to data contained in intelligence, investigative or other related files, and does not include any information other than information contained in a record of criminal history.

2. Each such agency shall adopt regulations and make available necessary forms to permit inspection and review of information relating to other records of criminal history by those persons who are the subjects thereof. The regulations must specify:

(a) The reasonable periods during which the records are available for inspection;

(b) The requirements for proper identification of the persons seeking access to the records; and

(c) The reasonable charges or fees, if any, for inspecting records.

3. Each such agency shall procure for and furnish to any person who requests it and pays a reasonable fee therefor, all of the information contained in the Central Repository which pertains to the person making the request.

4. The Director of the Department shall adopt regulations governing:

(a) All challenges to the accuracy or sufficiency of information relating to records of criminal history by the person who is the subject of the allegedly inaccurate or insufficient record;

(b) The correction of any information relating to records of criminal history found by the Director to be inaccurate, insufficient or incomplete in any material respect;

(c) The dissemination of corrected information to those persons or agencies which have previously received inaccurate or incomplete information; and

(d) A time limit of not more than 90 days within which inaccurate or insufficient information relating to records of criminal history must be corrected and the corrected information disseminated. The corrected information must be sent to each person who requested the information in the 12 months preceding the date on which the correction was made, and notice of the correction must be sent to each person entitled thereto pursuant to NRS 179A.210, to the address given by each person who requested the information when the request was made.

(Added to NRS by 1979, 1854; A 1981, 2010; 1985, 915, 1978; 1987, 1767; 2003, 2839)

NRS 179A.160 Removal of certain records where disposition of case favorable to accused.

1. If a person has been arrested or issued a citation, or has been the subject of a warrant for alleged criminal conduct and the person is acquitted of the charge or the disposition of the charge is favorable to the person, at any time after the charge is dismissed, acquittal is entered or disposition of the charge in favor of the person is final, the person who is the subject of a record of criminal history relating to the

arrest, citation or warrant may apply in writing to the Central Repository and the agency which maintains the record to have it removed from the files which are available and generally searched for the purpose of responding to inquiries concerning the criminal history of a person.

2. The Central Repository and the agency shall remove the record unless:

(a) The defendant is a fugitive;

(b) The case is under active prosecution according to a current certificate of a prosecuting attorney;

(c) The disposition of the case was a deferred prosecution, plea bargain or other similar disposition;

(d) The person who is the subject of the record has a prior conviction for a felony or gross misdemeanor in any jurisdiction in the United States; or

(e) The person who is the subject of the record has been arrested for or charged with another crime, other than a minor traffic violation, since the arrest, citation or warrant which the person seeks to have removed from the record.

3. This section does not restrict the authority of a court to order the deletion or modification of a record in a particular cause or concerning a particular person or event.

(Added to NRS by 1979, 1853; A 1985, 916; 2001, 1694)

TRANSMITTAL OF MENTAL HEALTH INFORMATION TO NATIONAL INSTANT CRIMINAL BACKGROUND CHECK SYSTEM AND NATIONAL CRIME INFORMATION CENTER

NRS 179A.163 Transmittal of mental health information to National Instant Criminal Background Check System and National Crime Information Center; person who is subject of record may petition; removal of information; action to compel.

1. Upon receiving a record transmitted pursuant to NRS 159.0593, 174.035, 175.533, 175.539, 178.425 or 433A.310, the Central Repository:

(a) Shall take reasonable steps to ensure that the information reported in the record is included in each appropriate database of the National Instant Criminal Background Check System; and

(b) May take reasonable steps to ensure that the information reported in the record is included in each appropriate database of the National Crime Information Center.

2. Except as otherwise provided in subsection 3, if the Central Repository receives a record described in subsection 1, the person who is the subject of the record may petition the court for an order declaring that:

(a) The basis for the adjudication reported in the record no longer exists;

(b) The adjudication reported in the record is deemed not to have occurred for purposes of 18 U.S.C. § 922(d)(4) and (g)(4) and NRS 202.360; and

(c) The information reported in the record must be removed from the National Instant Criminal Background Check System and the National Crime Information Center.

3. To the extent authorized by federal law, if the record concerning the petitioner was transmitted to the Central Repository pursuant to NRS 159.0593, 174.035, 175.533, 175.539, 178.425 or 433A.310, the petitioner may not file a petition pursuant to subsection 2 until 3 years after the date of the order transmitting the record to the Central Repository.

4. A petition filed pursuant to subsection 2 must be:

(a) Filed in the court which made the adjudication or finding pursuant to NRS 159.0593, 174.035, 175.533, 175.539, 178.425 or 433A.310; and

(b) Served upon the district attorney for the county in which the court described in paragraph (a) is located.

5. The Nevada Rules of Civil Procedure govern all proceedings concerning a petition filed pursuant to subsection 2.

6. The court shall grant the petition and issue the order described in subsection 2 if the court finds that the petitioner has established that:

(a) The basis for the adjudication or finding made pursuant to NRS 159.0593, 174.035, 175.533, 175.539, 178.425 or 433A.310 concerning the petitioner no longer exists;

(b) The petitioner's record and reputation indicate that the petitioner is not likely to act in a manner dangerous to public safety; and

(c) Granting the relief requested by the petitioner pursuant to subsection 2 is not contrary to the public interest.

7. Except as otherwise provided in this subsection, the petitioner must establish the provisions of subsection 6 by a preponderance of the evidence. If the adjudication or finding concerning the petitioner was made pursuant to NRS 159.0593 or 433A.310, the petitioner must establish the provisions of subsection 6 by clear and convincing evidence.

8. The court, upon entering an order pursuant to this section, shall cause, on a form prescribed by the Department of Public Safety, a record of the order to be transmitted to the Central Repository.

9. Within 5 business days after receiving a record of an order transmitted pursuant to subsection 8, the Central Repository shall take reasonable steps to ensure that information concerning the adjudication or finding made pursuant to NRS 159.0593, 174.035, 175.533, 175.539, 178.425 or 433A.310 is removed from the National Instant Criminal Background Check System and the National Crime Information Center, if applicable.

10. If the Central Repository fails to remove a record as provided in subsection 9, the petitioner may bring an action to compel the removal of the record. If the petitioner prevails in the action, the court may award the petitioner reasonable attorney's fees and costs incurred in bringing the action.

11. If a petition brought pursuant to subsection 2 is denied, the person who is the subject of the record may petition for a rehearing not sooner than 2 years after the date of the denial of the petition.

(Added to NRS by 2009, 2488; A 2015, 1802)

NRS 179A.165 Confidentiality of records; immunity for performing or failing to perform certain acts.

1. Any record described in NRS 179A.163 is confidential and is not a public book or record within the meaning of NRS 239.010. A person may not use the record for any purpose other than for a purpose related to criminal justice, including, without limitation, inclusion in the appropriate database of the National Instant Criminal Background Check System and the National Crime Information Center, if applicable. The Central Repository may disclose the record to any agency of criminal justice.

2. If a person or governmental entity is required to transmit, report or take any other action concerning a record pursuant to NRS 159.0593, 174.035, 175.533, 175.539, 178.425, 179A.163 or 433A.310, no action for damages may be brought against the person or governmental entity for:

(a) Transmitting or reporting the record or taking any other required action concerning the record;

(b) Failing to transmit or report the record or failing to take any other required action concerning the record;

(c) Delaying the transmission or reporting of the record or delaying in taking any other required action concerning the record; or

(d) Transmitting or reporting an inaccurate or incomplete version of the record or taking any other required action concerning an inaccurate or incomplete version of the record.

(Added to NRS by 2009, 2489; A 2015, 1803)

NRS 179A.167 Inspection and correction of information relating to records of mental health; regulations.

1. The Central Repository shall permit a person who is or believes he or she may be the subject of information relating to records of mental health held by the Central Repository to inspect and correct any information contained in such records.

2. The Central Repository shall adopt regulations and make available necessary forms to permit inspection, review and correction of information relating to records of mental health by those persons who are the subjects thereof. The regulations must specify:

(a) The requirements for proper identification of the persons seeking access to the records; and

(b) The reasonable charges or fees, if any, for inspecting records.

3. The Director of the Department shall adopt regulations governing:

(a) All challenges to the accuracy or sufficiency of information or records of mental health by the person who is the subject of the allegedly inaccurate or insufficient record;

(b) The correction of any information relating to records of mental health found by the Director to be inaccurate, insufficient or incomplete in any material respect;

(c) The dissemination of corrected information to those persons or agencies which have previously received inaccurate or incomplete information; and

(d) A reasonable time limit within which inaccurate or insufficient information relating to records of mental health must be corrected and the corrected information disseminated.

4. As used in this section, "information relating to records of mental health" means information contained in a record:

(a) Transmitted to the Central Repository pursuant to NRS 159.0593, 174.035, 175.533, 175.539, 178.425 or 433A.310; or

(b) Transmitted to the National Instant Criminal Background Check System or the National Crime Information Center pursuant to NRS 179A.163.

(Added to NRS by 2009, 2489; A 2015, 1803)

PROGRAM FOR REPORTING CRIMES RELATED TO PREJUDICE

NRS 179A.175 Establishing program; adoption of guidelines for collection of statistical data; report; data to be used only for research or statistical purposes.

1. The Director of the Department shall establish within the Central Repository a program for reporting crimes that manifest evidence of prejudice based on race, color, religion, national origin, physical or mental disability, sexual orientation or gender identity or expression.

2. The program must be designed to collect, compile and analyze statistical data about crimes that manifest evidence of prejudice based on race, color, religion, national origin, physical or mental disability, sexual orientation or gender identity or expression. The Director shall adopt guidelines for the collection of the statistical data, including, but not limited to, the criteria to establish the presence of prejudice.

3. The Central Repository shall include in any appropriate report an independent section relating solely to the analysis of crimes that manifest evidence of prejudice based on race, color, religion, national origin, physical or mental disability, sexual orientation or gender identity or expression.

4. Data acquired pursuant to this section must be used only for research or statistical purposes and must not contain any information that may reveal the identity of an individual victim of a crime.

5. As used in this section, "gender identity or expression" has the meaning ascribed to it in NRS 193.0148.

(Added to NRS by 1995, 2706; A 2013, 65; 2015, 845, 2765)

DISSEMINATION OF INFORMATION RELATING TO CERTAIN OFFENSES

NRS 179A.180 Definitions. As used in NRS 179A.180 to 179A.240, inclusive, unless the context otherwise requires:

1. "Employee" means a person who renders time and services to an employer, and whose regular course of duties places that person in a position to:

(a) Exercise supervisory or disciplinary control over children;

(b) Have direct access to or contact with children served by the employer; or

(c) Have access to information or records maintained by the employer relating to identifiable children served by the employer,

Ê and includes a prospective employee, but does not include a volunteer or prospective volunteer.

2. "Employer" means a person, or a governmental agency or political subdivision of this State that is not an agency of criminal justice, whose employees regularly render services to children, including without limitation care, treatment, transportation, instruction, companionship, entertainment and custody.

(Added to NRS by 1987, 1760; A 1989, 993)

NRS 179A.190 Notice of information may be disseminated to employers; use by employer; employer not liable for discrimination; other dissemination or release; offenses for which notice may be disseminated.

1. Notice of information relating to the offenses listed in subsection 4 may be disseminated to employers pursuant to NRS 179A.180 to 179A.240, inclusive.

2. An employer may consider such a notice of information concerning an employee when making a decision to hire, retain, suspend or discharge the employee, and is not liable in an action alleging discrimination based upon consideration of information obtained pursuant to NRS 179A.180 to 179A.240, inclusive.

3. The provisions of NRS 179A.180 to 179A.240, inclusive, do not limit or restrict any other statute specifically permitting the dissemination or release of information relating to the offenses listed in subsection 4.

4. The offenses for which a notice of information may be disseminated pursuant to subsection 1 includes information contained in or concerning a record of criminal history, or the records of criminal history of the United States or another state, relating in any way to:

(a) A sexual offense;

(b) A conviction for a felony within the immediately preceding 7 years;

(c) An act committed outside this State that would constitute a sexual offense if committed in this State or a conviction for an act committed outside this State that would constitute a felony if committed in this State; and

(d) The aiding, abetting, attempting or conspiring to engage in any such act in this State or another state.

(Added to NRS by 1987, 1761; A 2003, 2840)

NRS 179A.200 Employer may request notice of information; requirements for making request.

1. In addition to any other information which an employer is authorized to request pursuant to this chapter, an employer may request from the Central Repository notice of information relating to the offenses listed in subsection 4 of NRS 179A.190 concerning an employee.

2. A request for notice of information relating to the offenses listed in subsection 4 of NRS 179A.190 from an employer must conform to the requirements of the Central Repository. The request must include:

(a) The name and address of the employer, and the name and signature of the person requesting the notice on behalf of the employer;

(b) The name and address of the employer's facility in which the employee is employed or seeking to become employed;

(c) The name, a complete set of fingerprints and other identifying information of the employee;

(d) Signed consent by the employee authorizing:

(1) The employer to forward the fingerprints of the employee to the Central Repository for submission to the Federal Bureau of Investigation for its report;

(2) A search of information relating to the offenses listed in subsection 4 of NRS 179A.190 concerning the employee; and

(3) The release of a notice concerning that information;

(e) The mailing address of the employee or a signed waiver of the right of the employee to be sent a copy of the information disseminated to the employer as a result of the search of the records of criminal history; and

(f) The signature of the employee indicating that the employee has been notified of:

(1) The types of information for which notice is subject to dissemination pursuant to NRS 179A.210, or a description of the information;

(2) The employer's right to require a check of the records of criminal history as a condition of employment; and

(3) The employee's right, pursuant to NRS 179A.150, to challenge the accuracy or sufficiency of any information disseminated to the employer.

(Added to NRS by 1987, 1761; A 2003, 2841)

NRS 179A.210 Request by employer for notice of information; search by Central Repository; dissemination of notice; written report required; correction of information; receipt of new information.

1. Upon receipt of a request from an employer for notice of information relating to the offenses listed in subsection 4 of NRS 179A.190, the Central Repository shall undertake a search for the information, unless the request does not conform to the requirements of the Repository. The search must be based on the fingerprints of the employee, or on a number furnished to the employee for identification pursuant to a previous search, as provided by the employer, and must include:

(a) Identifying any information relating to the offenses listed in subsection 4 of NRS 179A.190 concerning the employee in the Central Repository;

(b) Requesting information relating to the offenses listed in subsection 4 of NRS 179A.190 concerning the employee from repositories of the United States or other states, if authorized by federal law or an agreement entered into pursuant to NRS 179A.075;

(c) If the information pertains to an arrest for which no disposition has been reported, contacting appropriate officers in the local jurisdiction where the arrest or prosecution occurred to verify and update the information; and

(d) Determining whether the information relating to the offenses listed in subsection 4 of NRS 179A.190 is the type of information for which notice is subject to dissemination pursuant to this section.

2. Notice of information relating to the offenses listed in subsection 4 of NRS 179A.190 may be disseminated to an employer who has requested it only if a check of the pertinent records indicates:

(a) A conviction for any such offense, or a conviction based on an arrest or on an initial charge for any such offense;

(b) An arrest or an initial charge for a sexual offense that is pending at the time of the request; or

(c) Two or more incidents resulting in arrest or initial charge for a sexual offense that have not resulted in a conviction.

3. If a search of the records of the Central Repository reveals no information for which notice is subject to release, the Central Repository shall submit the fingerprints of the employee to the Federal Bureau of Investigation for a search of its records of criminal history. The Central Repository shall review all information received from the Federal Bureau of Investigation. Notice of any information received from the Federal Bureau of Investigation may be disseminated only if the information is of a kind for which notice is subject to release pursuant to this section.

4. Within 30 days after receipt of a request by an employer for notice of information relating to the offenses listed in subsection 4 of NRS 179A.190, the Central Repository shall send a written report of the results of the search to the employer and to the employee, except that if the employee has waived the right to receive the results of the search, the report must be sent only to the employer. If the search revealed:

(a) No information for which notice is subject to release, the report must include a statement to that effect; or

(b) Information about the employee for which notice is subject to release, the report must include a notice of the type of information, limited to the descriptions set forth in subsection 2, revealed by the search. The notice must not include any further facts or details concerning the information. A statement of the purpose for which the notice is being disseminated, and the procedures by which the employee might challenge the accuracy and sufficiency of the information, must also be included with the report.

5. Upon receipt of corrected information relating to the offenses listed in subsection 4 of NRS 179A.190 for which notice was disseminated under this section, the Central Repository shall send written notice of the correction to:

(a) The employee who was the subject of the search, unless the employee has waived the right to receive such a notice;

(b) All employers to whom notice of the results of the search were disseminated within 3 months before the correction; and

(c) Upon request of the employee, any other employers who previously received the information.

6. Upon receipt of new information relating to the offenses listed in subsection 4 of NRS 179A.190 concerning an employee who was the subject of a search within the previous 3 months, for which notice is subject to dissemination under this section, the Central Repository shall send written notice of the information to:

(a) The employee who was the subject of the search, unless the employee has waived the right to receive such a notice;

(b) All employers to whom a report of the results of the search were disseminated within 3 months before the correction; and

(c) Upon request of the employee, any other employers who previously received a report of the results of the search.

(Added to NRS by 1987, 1761; A 1989, 561; 2003, 2841; 2009, 1839)

NRS 179A.220 Hearings. All hearings arising under NRS 179A.180 to 179A.240, inclusive, must be held as provided in NRS 233B.121 to 233B.150, inclusive.

(Added to NRS by 1987, 1763)

NRS 179A.230 When person who is subject of notice of information may bring action for damages; when child who is victim of offense committed by employee may bring action for damages against employer; statute of limitations.

1. A person who is the subject of a request for notice of information pursuant to NRS 179A.180 to 179A.240, inclusive, may recover actual damages in a civil action against:

(a) The Central Repository for an intentional or grossly negligent:

(1) Dissemination of information relating to the offenses listed in subsection 4 of NRS 179A.190 not authorized for dissemination; or

(2) Release of information relating to the offenses listed in subsection 4 of NRS 179A.190 to a person not authorized to receive the information;

(b) The Central Repository for an intentional or grossly negligent failure to correct any notice of information relating to the offenses listed in subsection 4 of NRS 179A.190 which was disseminated pursuant to NRS 179A.180 to 179A.240, inclusive; or

(c) An employer, representative of an employer or employee for an intentional or grossly negligent violation of NRS 179A.110. Punitive damages may be awarded against an employer, representative of an employer or employee whose violation of NRS 179A.110 is malicious.

2. An employer is liable to a child served by the employer for damages suffered by the child as a result of an offense listed in subsection 4 of NRS 179A.190 committed against the child by an employee if, at the time the employer hired the employee, the employee was the subject of information relating to the offenses for which notice was available for dissemination to the employer and the employer:

(a) Failed, without good cause, to request notice of the information pursuant to NRS 179A.180 to 179A.240, inclusive; or

(b) Was unable to obtain the information because the employee refused to consent to the search and release of the information, and the employer hired or retained the employee despite this refusal.

Ê The amount of damages for which an employer is liable pursuant to this subsection must be reduced by the amount of damages recovered by the child in an action against the employee for damages sustained as a result of an offense listed in subsection 4 of NRS 179A.190.

3. An action pursuant to this section must be brought within 3 years after:

(a) The occurrence upon which the action is based; or

(b) The date upon which the party bringing the action became aware or reasonably should have become aware of the occurrence, whichever was earlier, if the party was not aware of the occurrence at the time of the occurrence.

4. This section does not limit or affect any other rights, claims or causes of action arising by statute or common law.

(Added to NRS by 1987, 1763; A 1989, 993; 2003, 2843)

NRS 179A.240 Unlawful acts. A person who knowingly and willfully:

1. Uses NRS 179A.180 to 179A.240, inclusive, to obtain or seek to obtain information relating to the offenses listed in subsection 4 of NRS 179A.190 under false pretenses;

2. Disseminates or attempts to disseminate information relating to the offenses listed in subsection 4 of NRS 179A.190 that the person knows was not received in accordance with the provisions of this chapter; or

3. Disseminates or attempts to disseminate information relating to the offenses listed in subsection 4 of NRS 179A.190 that the person knows is false, inaccurate or incomplete,

Ê is guilty of a misdemeanor.

(Added to NRS by 1987, 1764; A 2003, 2844)

ACCOUNT TO INVESTIGATE BACKGROUND OF VOLUNTEERS WHO WORK WITH CHILDREN

NRS 179A.310 Creation; administration; purpose; regulations; failure to apply for grant or request background investigation is not evidence of negligence or causation.

1. The Revolving Account to Investigate the Background of Volunteers Who Work With Children is hereby created in the State General Fund.

2. The Director of the Department shall administer the Account to Investigate the Background of Volunteers Who Work With Children. The money in the Account must be expended only to pay the costs of the Central Repository to process requests from nonprofit agencies to determine whether a volunteer of a nonprofit agency who works directly with children or a prospective volunteer of the nonprofit agency who will work directly with children has committed an offense listed in subsection 4 of NRS 179A.190. The existence of the Account to Investigate the Background of Volunteers Who Work With Children does not create a right in any person to receive money from the Account.

3. The Director of the Department may apply for and accept any gift, donation, bequest, grant or other source of money. Any money so received must be deposited in the Account to Investigate the Background of Volunteers Who Work With Children.

4. The interest and income earned on money in the Account from any gift, donation or bequest, after deducting any applicable charges, must be credited to the Account. Money from any gift, donation or bequest that remains in the Account at the end of the fiscal year does not revert to the State General Fund, and the balance in the Account must be carried forward to the next fiscal year.

5. The Director of the Department shall adopt regulations to carry out the provisions of this section. The regulations must include, without limitation:

(a) The procedure by which a person may apply for a grant of money from the Account to Investigate the Background of Volunteers Who Work With Children;

(b) The criteria that the Department will consider in determining whether to award such a grant of money from the Account; and

(c) Procedures to distribute the money in the Account in a fair and equitable manner.

6. The following facts must not be considered as evidence of negligence or causation in any civil action brought against a nonprofit agency:

(a) The fact that the nonprofit agency did not apply for a grant of money from the Account.

(b) The fact that the nonprofit agency did not request that the Central Repository, through the use of the Account, determine whether a volunteer or prospective volunteer of the nonprofit agency has committed an offense listed in subsection 4 of NRS 179A.190.

(Added to NRS by 1999, 2054; A 2003, 2844)

NRS 179A.315 Donations to Account: Forms and procedures; deposit with State Treasurer. A state or local governmental agency:

1. May establish forms and procedures for a person to donate money to the Account to Investigate the Background of Volunteers Who Work With Children while the person is transacting business with the State or local governmental agency; and

2. Shall deposit any money received for the Account to Investigate the Background of Volunteers Who Work With Children with the State Treasurer for credit to the Account.

(Added to NRS by 1999, 2055)

REPOSITORY FOR INFORMATION CONCERNING ORDERS FOR PROTECTION AGAINST DOMESTIC VIOLENCE

NRS 179A.350 Creation; contents; prompt entry of information; accessibility; submission of report to Legislature.

1. The Repository for Information Concerning Orders for Protection Against Domestic Violence is hereby created within the Central Repository.

2. Except as otherwise provided in subsection 6, the Repository for Information Concerning Orders for Protection Against Domestic Violence must contain a complete and systematic record of all temporary and extended orders for protection against domestic violence issued or registered in the State of Nevada, in accordance with regulations adopted by the Director of the Department, including, without limitation, any information received pursuant to NRS 33.095. Information received by the Central Repository pursuant to NRS 33.095 must be entered in the Repository for Information Concerning Orders for Protection Against Domestic Violence not later than 8 hours after it is received by the Central Repository.

3. The information in the Repository for Information Concerning Orders for Protection Against Domestic Violence must be accessible by computer at all times to each agency of criminal justice.

4. On or before July 1 of each year, the Director of the Department shall submit to the Director of the Legislative Counsel Bureau a written report concerning all temporary and extended orders for protection against domestic violence issued pursuant to NRS 33.020 during the previous calendar year that were transmitted to the Repository for Information Concerning Orders for Protection Against Domestic Violence. The report must include, without limitation, information for each court that issues temporary or extended orders for protection against domestic violence concerning:

(a) The total number of temporary and extended orders that were granted by the court pursuant to NRS 33.020 during the calendar year to which the report pertains;

(b) The number of temporary and extended orders that were granted to women;

(c) The number of temporary and extended orders that were granted to men;
(d) The number of temporary and extended orders that were vacated or expired;
(e) The number of temporary orders that included a grant of temporary custody of a minor child; and
(f) The number of temporary and extended orders that were served on the adverse party.

5. The information provided pursuant to subsection 4 must include only aggregate information for statistical purposes and must exclude any identifying information relating to a particular person.

6. The Repository for Information Concerning Orders for Protection Against Domestic Violence must not contain any information concerning an event that occurred before October 1, 1998.

(Added to NRS by 1997, 1803; A 2007, 2483; 2015, 2765)

REPOSITORY FOR INFORMATION CONCERNING CRIMES AGAINST OLDER PERSONS

NRS 179A.450 Creation; contents; submission of report to Legislature; confidentiality of data.

1. The Repository for Information Concerning Crimes Against Older Persons is hereby created within the Central Repository.

2. The Repository for Information Concerning Crimes Against Older Persons must contain a complete and systematic record of all reports of the abuse, neglect, exploitation, isolation or abandonment of older persons in this State. The record must be prepared in a manner approved by the Director of the Department and must include, without limitation, the following information:

(a) All incidents that are reported to any entity.
(b) All cases that are currently under investigation and the type of such cases.
(c) All cases that are referred for prosecution and the type of such cases.
(d) All cases in which prosecution is declined or dismissed and any reason for such action.
(e) All cases that are prosecuted and the final disposition of such cases.
(f) All cases that are resolved by agencies which provide protective services and the type of such cases.

3. The Director of the Department shall compile and analyze the data collected pursuant to this section to assess the incidence of the abuse, neglect, exploitation, isolation or abandonment of older persons.

4. On or before July 1 of each year, the Director of the Department shall prepare and submit a report to the Director of the Legislative Counsel Bureau for transmittal to the Legislature that sets forth statistical data on the abuse, neglect, exploitation, isolation or abandonment of older persons.

5. The data acquired pursuant to this section is confidential and must be used only for the purpose of research. The data and findings generated pursuant to this section must not contain information that may reveal the identity of an individual victim or a person accused of the abuse, neglect, exploitation, isolation or abandonment of older persons.

6. As used in this section:

(a) "Abandonment" has the meaning ascribed to it in NRS 200.5092.
(b) "Abuse" has the meaning ascribed to it in NRS 200.5092.
(c) "Exploitation" has the meaning ascribed to it in NRS 200.5092.
(d) "Isolation" has the meaning ascribed to it in NRS 200.5092.
(e) "Neglect" has the meaning ascribed to it in NRS 200.5092.
(f) "Older person" means a person who is 60 years of age or older.

(Added to NRS by 2007, 746; A 2009, 2447; 2011, 82; 2015, 826)

NATIONAL CRIME PREVENTION AND PRIVACY COMPACT

NRS 179A.800 Enactment; text. The National Crime Prevention and Privacy Compact is hereby ratified, enacted into law and entered into with all jurisdictions legally joining in the Compact, in substantially the form set forth in this section:

Article I. Definitions

As used in this Compact, the following definitions apply:

(1) "Attorney General" means the Attorney General of the United States.

(2) "Compact officer" means:

(a) With respect to the Federal Government, an official so designated by the Director of the FBI; and

(b) With respect to a party state, the chief administrator of the state's criminal history record repository or a designee of the chief administrator who is a regular full-time employee of the repository.

(3) "Council" means the Compact Council established under Article VI.

(4) "Criminal history record repository" means the state agency designated by the governor or other appropriate executive official or the legislature of a state to perform centralized recordkeeping functions for criminal history records and services in the state.

(5) (a) "Criminal history records" means information collected by criminal justice agencies on individuals consisting of identifiable descriptions and notations of arrests, detentions, indictments, or other formal criminal charges and any disposition arising therefrom, including acquittal, sentencing, correctional supervision, or release.

(b) The term does not include identification information such as fingerprint records if the information does not indicate involvement of the individual with the criminal justice system.

(6) "Criminal justice" includes activities relating to the detection, apprehension, detention, pretrial release, posttrial release, prosecution, adjudication, correctional supervision, or rehabilitation of accused persons or criminal offenders. The administration of criminal justice includes criminal identification activities and the collection, storage, and dissemination of criminal history records.

(7) (a) "Criminal justice agency" means:
(i) Courts; and
(ii) A governmental agency or any subunit of an agency that performs the administration of criminal justice pursuant to a statute or executive order and allocates a substantial part of its annual budget to the administration of criminal justice.
(b) The term includes federal and state inspector general offices.
(8) "Criminal justice services" means services provided by the FBI to criminal justice agencies in response to a request for information about a particular individual or as an update to information previously provided for criminal justice purposes.
(9) "Direct access" means access to the national identification index by computer terminal or other automated means not requiring the assistance of or intervention by any other party or agency.
(10) "Executive order" means an order of the President of the United States or the chief executive officer of a state that has the force of law and that is promulgated in accordance with applicable law.
(11) "FBI" means the Federal Bureau of Investigation.
(12) (a) "III System" means the Interstate Identification Index System, which is the cooperative federal-state system for the exchange of criminal history records.
(b) The term includes the national identification index, the national fingerprint file, and to the extent of their participation in the system, the criminal history record repositories of the states and the FBI.
(13) "National fingerprint file" means a database of fingerprints or of other uniquely personal identifying information that relates to an arrested or charged individual and that is maintained by the FBI to provide positive identification of record subjects indexed in the III System.
(14) "National identification index" means an index maintained by the FBI consisting of names, identifying numbers, and other descriptive information relating to record subjects about whom there are criminal history records in the III System.
(15) "National indexes" means the national identification index and the national fingerprint file.
(16) "Noncriminal justice purposes" means uses of criminal history records for purposes authorized by federal or state law other than purposes relating to criminal justice activities, including employment suitability, licensing determinations, immigration and naturalization matters, and national security clearances.
(17) "Nonparty state" means a state that has not ratified this Compact.
(18) "Party state" means a state that has ratified this Compact.
(19) "Positive identification" means a determination, based upon a comparison of fingerprints or other equally reliable biometric identification techniques, that the subject of a record search is the same person as the subject of a criminal history record or records indexed in the III System. Identifications based solely upon a comparison of subjects' names or other nonunique identification characteristics or numbers, or combinations thereof, does not constitute positive identification.
(20) "Sealed record information" means:
(a) With respect to adults, that portion of a record that is:
(i) Not available for criminal justice uses;
(ii) Not supported by fingerprints or other accepted means of positive identification; or
(iii) Subject to restrictions on dissemination for noncriminal justice purposes pursuant to a court order related to a particular subject or pursuant to a federal or state statute that requires action on a sealing petition filed by a particular record subject; and
(b) With respect to juveniles, whatever each state determines is a sealed record under its own law and procedure.
(21) "State" means any state, territory, or possession of the United States, the District of Columbia, and the Commonwealth of Puerto Rico.

Article II. Purposes

The purposes of this Compact are to:
(1) Provide a legal framework for the establishment of a cooperative federal-state system for the interstate and federal-state exchange of criminal history records for noncriminal justice uses;
(2) Require the FBI to permit use of the national identification index and the national fingerprint file by each party state and to provide, in a timely fashion, federal and state criminal history records to requesting states, in accordance with the terms of this Compact and with rules, procedures, and standards established by the Council under Article VI;
(3) Require party states to provide information and records for the national identification index and the national fingerprint file and to provide criminal history records, in a timely fashion, to criminal history record repositories of other states and the Federal Government for noncriminal justice purposes, in accordance with the terms of this Compact and with rules, procedures, and standards established by the Council under Article VI;
(4) Provide for the establishment of a Council to monitor III System operations and to prescribe system rules and procedures for the effective and proper operation of the III System for noncriminal justice purposes; and
(5) Require the FBI and each party state to adhere to III System standards concerning record dissemination and use, response times, system security, data quality, and other duly established standards, including those that enhance the accuracy and privacy of such records.

Article III. Responsibilities of Compact Parties

(1) The Director of the FBI shall:
(a) Appoint an FBI Compact officer who shall:
(i) Administer this Compact within the Department of Justice and among federal agencies and other agencies and organizations that submit search requests to the FBI pursuant to Article V(3);

(ii) Ensure that Compact provisions and rules, procedures, and standards prescribed by the Council under Article VI are complied with by the Department of Justice and the federal agencies and other agencies and organizations referred to in subsection (1)(a)(i) of this Article III; and

(iii) Regulate the use of records received by means of the III System from party states when such records are supplied by the FBI directly to other federal agencies;

(b) Provide to federal agencies and to state criminal history record repositories criminal history records maintained in its database for the noncriminal justice purposes described in Article IV, including:

(i) Information from nonparty states; and

(ii) Information from party states that is available from the FBI through the III System, but is not available from the party state through the III System;

(c) Provide a telecommunications network and maintain centralized facilities for the exchange of criminal history records for both criminal justice purposes and the noncriminal justice purposes described in Article IV and ensure that the exchange of the records for criminal justice purposes has priority over exchange for noncriminal justice purposes; and

(d) Modify or enter into user agreements with nonparty state criminal history record repositories to require them to establish record request procedures conforming to those prescribed in Article V.

(2) Each party state shall:

(a) Appoint a Compact officer who shall:

(i) Administer this Compact within that state;

(ii) Ensure that Compact provisions and rules, procedures, and standards established by the Council under Article VI are complied with in the state; and

(iii) Regulate the in-state use of records received by means of the III System from the FBI or from other party states;

(b) Establish and maintain a criminal history record repository, which shall provide:

(i) Information and records for the national identification index and the national fingerprint file; and

(ii) The state's III System-indexed criminal history records for noncriminal justice purposes described in Article IV;

(c) Participate in the national fingerprint file; and

(d) Provide and maintain telecommunications links and related equipment necessary to support the criminal justice services set forth in this Compact.

(3) In carrying out their responsibilities under this Compact, the FBI and each party state shall comply with III System rules, procedures, and standards duly established by the Council concerning record dissemination and use, response times, data quality, system security, accuracy, privacy protection, and other aspects of III System operation.

(4) (a) Use of the III System for noncriminal justice purposes authorized in this Compact must be managed so as not to diminish the level of services provided in support of criminal justice purposes.

(b) Administration of Compact provisions may not reduce the level of service available to authorized noncriminal justice users on the effective date of this Compact.

Article IV. Authorized Record Disclosures

(1) To the extent authorized by section 552a of Title 5, United States Code (commonly known as the Privacy Act of 1974), the FBI shall provide on request criminal history records, excluding sealed record information, to state criminal history record repositories for noncriminal justice purposes allowed by federal statute, federal executive order, or a state statute which has been approved by the Attorney General and which authorizes national indexes checks.

(2) The FBI, to the extent authorized by section 552a of Title 5, United States Code (commonly known as the Privacy Act of 1974), and state criminal history record repositories shall provide criminal history records, excluding sealed record information, to criminal justice agencies and other governmental or nongovernmental agencies for noncriminal justice purposes allowed by federal statute, federal executive order, or a state statute that has been approved by the Attorney General, that explicitly authorizes national indexes checks.

(3) Any record obtained under this Compact may be used only for the official purposes for which the record was requested. Each Compact officer shall establish procedures, consistent with this Compact and with rules, procedures, and standards established by the Council under Article VI, which procedures shall protect the accuracy and privacy of the records and shall:

(a) Ensure that records obtained under this Compact are used only by authorized officials for authorized purposes;

(b) Require that subsequent record checks are requested to obtain current information whenever a new need arises; and

(c) Ensure that record entries that may not legally be used for a particular noncriminal justice purpose are deleted from the response and, if no information authorized for release remains, an appropriate "no record" response is communicated to the requesting official.

Article V. Record Request Procedures

(1) Subject fingerprints or other approved forms of positive identification must be submitted with all requests for criminal history record checks for noncriminal justice purposes.

(2) Each request for a criminal history record check utilizing the national indexes made under any approved state statute must be submitted through that state's criminal history record repository. A state criminal history record repository shall process an interstate request for noncriminal justice purposes through the national indexes only if the request is transmitted through another state criminal history record repository or the FBI.

(3) Each request for criminal history record checks utilizing the national indexes made under federal authority must be submitted through the FBI or, if the state criminal history record repository consents to process fingerprint submissions, through the criminal history

record repository in the state in which the request originated. Direct access to the national identification index by entities other than the FBI and state criminal history records repositories may not be permitted for noncriminal justice purposes.

(4) A state criminal history record repository or the FBI:

(a) May charge a fee, in accordance with applicable law, for handling a request involving fingerprint processing for noncriminal justice purposes; and

(b) May not charge a fee for providing criminal history records in response to an electronic request for a record that does not involve a request to process fingerprints.

(5) (a) If a state criminal history record repository cannot positively identify the subject of a record request made for noncriminal justice purposes, the request, together with fingerprints or other approved identifying information, must be forwarded to the FBI for a search of the national indexes.

(b) If, with respect to a request forwarded by a state criminal history record repository under subsection (5)(a), the FBI positively identifies the subject as having a III System-indexed record or records:

(i) The FBI shall so advise the state criminal history record repository; and

(ii) The state criminal history record repository is entitled to obtain the additional criminal history record information from the FBI or other state criminal history record repositories.

Article VI. Establishment of Compact Council

(1) (a) There is established a Council to be known as the Compact Council, which has the authority to promulgate rules and procedures governing the use of the III System for noncriminal justice purposes, not to conflict with FBI administration of the III System for criminal justice purposes.

(b) The Council shall:

(i) Continue in existence as long as this Compact remains in effect;

(ii) Be located, for administrative purposes, within the FBI; and

(iii) Be organized and hold its first meeting as soon as practicable after the effective date of this Compact.

(2) The Council must be composed of 15 members, each of whom must be appointed by the Attorney General, as follows:

(a) Nine members, each of whom shall serve a 2-year term, who must be selected from among the Compact officers of party states based on the recommendation of the Compact officers of all party states, except that in the absence of the requisite number of Compact officers available to serve, the chief administrators of the criminal history record repositories of nonparty states must be eligible to serve on an interim basis;

(b) Two at-large members, nominated by the Director of the FBI, each of whom shall serve a 3-year term, of whom:

(i) One must be a representative of the criminal justice agencies of the Federal Government and may not be an employee of the FBI; and

(ii) One must be a representative of the noncriminal justice agencies of the Federal Government;

(c) Two at-large members, nominated by the Chair of the Council once the Chair is elected pursuant to subsection (3) of this Article VI, each of whom shall serve a 3-year term, of whom:

(i) One must be a representative of state or local criminal justice agencies; and

(ii) One must be a representative of state or local noncriminal justice agencies;

(d) One member who shall serve a 3-year term and who shall simultaneously be a member of the FBI's Advisory Policy Board on Criminal Justice Information Services, nominated by the membership of that Policy Board; and

(e) One member, nominated by the Director of the FBI, who shall serve a 3-year term and who must be an employee of the FBI.

(3) (a) From its membership, the Council shall elect a Chair and a Vice Chair of the Council. Both the Chair and Vice Chair of the Council:

(i) Must be a Compact officer, unless there is no Compact officer on the Council who is willing to serve, in which case the Chair may be an at-large member; and

(ii) Shall serve 2-year terms and may be reelected to only one additional 2-year term.

(b) The Vice Chair of the Council shall serve as the Chair of the Council in the absence of the Chair.

(4) (a) The Council shall meet at least once each year at the call of the Chair. Each meeting of the Council must be open to the public. The Council shall provide prior public notice in the Federal Register of each meeting of the Council, including the matters to be addressed at the meeting.

(b) A majority of the Council or any committee of the Council shall constitute a quorum of the Council or of a committee, respectively, for the conduct of business. A lesser number may meet to hold hearings, take testimony, or conduct any business not requiring a vote.

(5) The Council shall make available for public inspection and copying at the Council office within the FBI and shall publish in the Federal Register any rules, procedures, or standards established by the Council.

(6) The Council may request from the FBI reports, studies, statistics, or other information or materials that the Council determines to be necessary to enable the Council to perform its duties under this Compact. The FBI, to the extent authorized by law, may provide assistance or information upon a request.

(7) The Chair may establish committees as necessary to carry out this Compact and may prescribe their membership, responsibilities, and duration.

Article VII. Ratification of Compact

This Compact takes effect upon being entered into by two or more states as between those states and the Federal Government. When additional states subsequently enter into this Compact, it becomes effective among those states and the Federal Government and each party state that has previously ratified it. When ratified, this Compact has the full force and effect of law within the ratifying jurisdictions. The form of ratification must be in accordance with the laws of the executing state.

Article VIII. Miscellaneous Provisions

(1) Administration of this Compact may not interfere with the management and control of the Director of the FBI over the FBI's collection and dissemination of criminal history records and the advisory function of the FBI's Advisory Policy Board chartered under the Federal Advisory Committee Act (5 U.S.C. App.) for all purposes other than noncriminal justice.

(2) Nothing in this Compact requires the FBI to obligate or expend funds beyond those appropriated to the FBI.

(3) Nothing in this Compact diminishes or lessens the obligations, responsibilities, and authorities of any state, whether a party state or a nonparty state, or of any criminal history record repository or other subdivision or component thereof, under the Departments of State, Justice, and Commerce, the Judiciary, and Related Agencies Appropriation Act, 1973 (Public Law 92-544), or regulations and guidelines promulgated thereunder, including the rules and procedures promulgated by the Council under Article VI(1), regarding the use and dissemination of criminal history records and information.

Article IX. Renunciation

(1) This Compact shall bind each party state until renounced by the party state.

(2) Any renunciation of this Compact by a party state must:

(a) Be effected in the same manner by which the party state ratified this Compact; and

(b) Become effective 180 days after written notice of renunciation is provided by the party state to each other party state and to the Federal Government.

Article X. Severability

The provisions of this Compact are severable. If any phrase, clause, sentence, or provision of this Compact is declared to be contrary to the constitution of any participating state or to the Constitution of the United States or if the applicability of any phrase, clause, sentence, or provision of this Compact to any government, agency, person, or circumstance is held invalid, the validity of the remainder of this Compact and the applicability of the remainder of the Compact to any government, agency, person, or circumstance is not affected by the severability. If a portion of this Compact is held contrary to the constitution of any party state, all other portions of this Compact remain in full force and effect as to the remaining party states and in full force and effect as to the party state affected, as to all other provisions.

Article XI. Adjudication of Disputes

(1) The Council:

(a) Has initial authority to make determinations with respect to any dispute regarding:

(i) Interpretation of this Compact;

(ii) Any rule or standard established by the Council pursuant to Article VI; and

(iii) Any dispute or controversy between any parties to this Compact; and

(b) Shall hold a hearing concerning any dispute described in subsection (1)(a) at a regularly scheduled meeting of the Council and only render a decision based upon a majority vote of the members of the Council. The decision must be published pursuant to the requirements of Article VI(5).

(2) The FBI shall exercise immediate and necessary action to preserve the integrity of the III System, to maintain system policy and standards, to protect the accuracy and privacy of records, and to prevent abuses until the Council holds a hearing on the matters.

(3) The FBI or a party state may appeal any decision of the Council to the Attorney General and after that appeal may file suit in the appropriate District Court of the United States that has original jurisdiction of all cases or controversies arising under this Compact. Any suit arising under this Compact and initiated in a state court must be removed to the appropriate District Court of the United States in the manner provided by section 1446 of Title 28, United States Code, or other statutory authority.

(Added to NRS by 1999, 771)

PENALTIES

NRS 179A.900 Unlawful acts. Any person who:

1. Willfully requests, obtains or seeks to obtain records of criminal history under false pretenses;
2. Willfully communicates or seeks to communicate records of criminal history to any agency or person except pursuant to this chapter; or
3. Willfully falsifies any record of criminal history or any record relating to records of criminal history,

Ê is guilty of a misdemeanor.

(Added to NRS by 1979, 1855)

CHAPTER 179B - STATEWIDE REGISTRY OF SEX OFFENDERS AND OFFENDERS CONVICTED OF A CRIME AGAINST A CHILD

GENERAL PROVISIONS

ESTABLISHMENT AND CONTENTS

COMMUNITY NOTIFICATION WEBSITE

LIMITATIONS ON LIABILITY AND THE DISCLOSURE OF INFORMATION

GENERAL PROVISIONS

NRS 179B.010 Definitions. As used in this chapter, unless the context otherwise requires, the words and terms defined in NRS 179B.020 to 179B.140, inclusive, have the meanings ascribed to them in those sections.
(Added to NRS by 1997, 1644; A 1999, 1288; 2003, 2829; 2005, 2868)

NRS 179B.020 "Central Repository" defined. "Central Repository" means the Central Repository for Nevada Records of Criminal History.
(Added to NRS by 1997, 1644)

NRS 179B.023 "Community notification website" defined. "Community notification website" means the website on the Internet established and maintained by the Department pursuant to NRS 179B.250.
(Added to NRS by 2005, 2867)

NRS 179B.025 "Convicted" defined. "Convicted" has the meaning ascribed to it in NRS 179D.035.
(Added to NRS by 1999, 1288)

NRS 179B.030 "Crime against a child" defined. "Crime against a child" has the meaning ascribed to it in NRS 179D.0357.

(Added to NRS by 1997, 1644; A 2007, 2754)

NRS 179B.040 "Department" defined. "Department" means the Department of Public Safety.
(Added to NRS by 1997, 1644; A 2001, 2578)

NRS 179B.050 "Director" defined. "Director" means the Director of the Department.
(Added to NRS by 1997, 1644)

NRS 179B.060 "Division" defined. "Division" means the Division of Parole and Probation of the Department.
(Added to NRS by 1997, 1644)

NRS 179B.070 "Law enforcement officer" defined. "Law enforcement officer" includes, but is not limited to:

1. A prosecuting attorney or an attorney from the Office of the Attorney General;
2. A sheriff of a county or a sheriff's deputy;
3. An officer of a metropolitan police department or a police department of an incorporated city;
4. An officer of the Division;
5. An officer of the Department of Corrections;
6. An officer of a law enforcement agency from another jurisdiction; or
7. Any other person upon whom some or all of the powers of a peace officer are conferred pursuant to NRS 289.150 to 289.360, inclusive, if the person is seeking information as part of a criminal investigation.

(Added to NRS by 1997, 1644; A 2001 Special Session, 225)

NRS 179B.073 "Offender" defined. "Offender" means a sex offender or an offender convicted of a crime against a child.
(Added to NRS by 2003, 2829)

NRS 179B.075 "Offender convicted of a crime against a child" defined. "Offender convicted of a crime against a child" has the meaning ascribed to it in NRS 179D.0559.
(Added to NRS by 1999, 1288; A 2007, 2754)

NRS 179B.090 "Record of registration" defined. "Record of registration" has the meaning ascribed to it in NRS 179D.070.
(Added to NRS by 1997, 1645; A 2011, 220)

NRS 179B.100 "Requester" defined. "Requester" means a person who requests information from the community notification website.
(Added to NRS by 1997, 1645; A 2005, 2868)

NRS 179B.110 "Sex offender" defined. "Sex offender" has the meaning ascribed to it in NRS 179D.095.
(Added to NRS by 1997, 1645)

NRS 179B.130 "Statewide registry" defined. "Statewide registry" means the statewide registry of sex offenders and offenders convicted of a crime against a child established within the central repository pursuant to NRS 179B.200.
(Added to NRS by 1997, 1645)

NRS 179B.140 "Subject of the search" defined. "Subject of the search" means the person about whom a requester seeks information.
(Added to NRS by 1997, 1645)

ESTABLISHMENT AND CONTENTS

NRS 179B.200 Establishment of registry; contents; search of registry by law enforcement officer; access by other persons; contents deemed record of criminal history for limited purposes.

1. The Director shall establish within the Central Repository a statewide registry of sex offenders and offenders convicted of a crime against a child that consists of the record of registration for each such offender and all other information concerning each such offender that is obtained pursuant to law.
2. The statewide registry must be organized so that a law enforcement officer may search the records of registration in the registry by entering certain search information, including, but not limited to:
   (a) A name, alias, physical description or address of an offender.
   (b) A geographic location where an offense was committed.
   (c) The age, gender, race or general physical description of a victim.
   (d) The method of operation used by an offender, including, but not limited to:
      (1) The specific sexual acts committed against a victim;
      (2) The method of obtaining access to a victim, such as the use of enticements, threats, forced entry or violence against a victim;
      (3) The type of injuries inflicted on a victim;
      (4) The types of instruments, weapons or objects used;

(5) The type of property taken; and
(6) Any other distinctive characteristic of the behavior or personality of an offender.

3. Except as otherwise provided in this subsection or by specific statute, information in the statewide registry may be accessed only by a law enforcement officer in the regular course of the law enforcement officer's duties and officers and employees of the Central Repository. The Director may permit the following persons to have access to information in the statewide registry:

(a) Except as otherwise provided in chapter 179A of NRS or by specific statute, an officer or employee of a governmental agency that is investigating the background of a person for the purposes of employment.

(b) Any other person for the limited purposes of research or statistical analysis.

4. Information contained in the statewide registry, including, but not limited to, the record of registration of an offender, shall be deemed a record of criminal history only for the purposes of those provisions of chapter 179A of NRS that are consistent with the provisions of this chapter.

(Added to NRS by 1997, 1645; A 1999, 1288)

COMMUNITY NOTIFICATION WEBSITE

NRS 179B.250 Establishment, maintenance and content of website; information to be included with each inquiry; duties, authorizations and prohibitions of Central Repository.

1. The Department shall establish and maintain within the Central Repository a community notification website to provide the public with access to certain information contained in the statewide registry in accordance with the procedures set forth in this section.

2. The community notification website is the source of record for information available to the public concerning offenders listed in the statewide registry, and must:

(a) Be maintained in a manner that will allow the public to obtain relevant information for each offender by a single query for any given zip code or geographical radius set by the user;

(b) Include in its design all the search field capabilities needed for full participation in the Dru Sjodin National Sex Offender Public Website maintained by the Attorney General of the United States pursuant to 42 U.S.C. § 16920;

(c) Include, to the extent practicable, links to sex offender safety and education resources;

(d) Include instructions on how to seek correction of information that a person contends is erroneous; and

(e) Include a warning that the information on the website should not be used to unlawfully injure, harass or commit a crime against any person named in the registry or residing or working at any reported address and a notice that any such action could result in civil or criminal penalties.

3. For each inquiry to the community notification website, the requester may provide:

(a) The name of the subject of the search;

(b) Any alias of the subject of the search;

(c) The zip code of the residence, place of work or school of the subject of the search; or

(d) Any other information concerning the identity or location of the subject of the search that is deemed sufficient in the discretion of the Department.

4. For each inquiry to the community notification website made by the requester, the Central Repository shall:

(a) Explain the levels of registration and community notification that are assigned to sex offenders pursuant to NRS 179D.010 to 179D.550, inclusive; and

(b) Explain that the Central Repository is prohibited by law from disclosing certain information concerning certain offenders, even if those offenders are listed in the statewide registry.

5. If an offender listed in the statewide registry matches the information provided by the requester concerning the identity or location of the subject of the search, the Central Repository shall disclose to the requester information in the statewide registry concerning the offender as provided pursuant to subsection 6.

6. After each inquiry to the community notification website made by the requester, the Central Repository shall inform the requester that:

(a) No offender listed in the statewide registry matches the information provided by the requester concerning the identity or location of the subject of the search;

(b) The search of the statewide registry has not produced information that is available to the public through the statewide registry; or

(c) An offender listed in the statewide registry matches the information provided by the requester concerning the identity or location of the subject of the search. Except as otherwise provided in subsection 7, if a search of the statewide registry results in a match pursuant to this paragraph, the Central Repository shall provide the requester with the following information:

(1) The name of the offender and all aliases that the offender has used or under which the offender has been known.
(2) A complete physical description of the offender.
(3) A current photograph of the offender.
(4) The year of birth of the offender.
(5) The complete address of any residence at which the offender resides or will reside.
(6) The address of any location where the offender is or will be:
(I) A student, as defined in NRS 179D.110; or
(II) A worker, as defined in NRS 179D.120.
(7) The license plate number and a description of any motor vehicle owned or operated by the offender.
(8) The following information for each offense for which the offender has been convicted:
(I) The offense that was committed, including a citation to and the text of the specific statute that the offender violated.
(II) The court in which the offender was convicted.

(III) The name under which the offender was convicted.

(IV) The name and location of each penal institution, school, hospital, mental facility or other institution to which the offender was committed for the offense.

(V) The city, township or county where the offense was committed.

(9) The tier level of registration and community notification assigned to the offender pursuant to NRS 179D.010 to 179D.550, inclusive.

(10) Any other information required by federal law.

7. If a search of the statewide registry results in a match pursuant to paragraph (c) of subsection 6, the Central Repository shall not provide the requester with:

(a) The identity of any victim of a sexual offense or crime against a child;

(b) Any information relating to a Tier I offender unless the offender has been convicted of a sexual offense against a child or a crime against a child;

(c) The social security number of the offender;

(d) The name of any location where the offender is or will be:

(1) A student, as defined in NRS 179D.110; or

(2) A worker, as defined in NRS 179D.120;

(e) Any reference to arrests of the offender that did not result in conviction;

(f) Any other information that is included in the record of registration for the offender other than the information required pursuant to paragraph (c) of subsection 6; or

(g) Any other information exempted from disclosure by the Attorney General of the United States pursuant to federal law.

8. A person may not use information obtained through the community notification website as a substitute for information relating to the offenses listed in subsection 4 of NRS 179A.190 that must be provided by the Central Repository pursuant to NRS 179A.180 to 179A.240, inclusive, or another provision of law.

9. The provisions of this section do not prevent law enforcement officers, the Central Repository and its officers and employees, or any other person from:

(a) Accessing information in the statewide registry pursuant to NRS 179B.200;

(b) Carrying out any duty pursuant to chapter 179D of NRS; or

(c) Carrying out any duty pursuant to another provision of law.

10. As used in this section, "Tier I offender" has the meaning ascribed to it in NRS 179D.113.

(Added to NRS by 1997, 1646; A 1999, 1289; 2003, 2829, 2845; 2005, 2868; 2007, 2754; 2013, 372)

NRS 179B.270 Restrictions on use of information. Except as otherwise authorized pursuant to specific statute, a person shall not use information obtained from the community notification website for any purpose related to any of the following:

1. Insurance, including health insurance.
2. Loans.
3. Credit.
4. Employment.
5. Education, scholarships or fellowships.
6. Housing or accommodations.
7. Benefits, privileges or services provided by any business establishment.

(Added to NRS by 2005, 2867)

NRS 179B.280 Misuse of information: Civil liabilities. Any person who uses information obtained from the community notification website in violation of the provisions of NRS 179B.250 or 179B.270 is liable:

1. In a civil action brought by or on behalf of a person injured by the violation, for damages, attorney's fees and costs incurred as the result of the violation; and

2. In a civil action brought in the name of the State of Nevada by the Attorney General, for a civil penalty not to exceed $25,000 and for the costs of the action, including investigative costs and attorney's fees.

(Added to NRS by 2005, 2868)

NRS 179B.285 Criminal penalties for using information to commit crime. In addition to any civil liability provided pursuant to NRS 179B.280, if any person uses information obtained from the community notification website to commit a crime punishable as:

1. A misdemeanor, the person is guilty of a gross misdemeanor.

2. A gross misdemeanor, the person is guilty of a category E felony and shall be punished as provided in NRS 193.130.

(Added to NRS by 2007, 2754)

NRS 179B.290 Misuse of information: Attorney General may file action for injunctive relief.

1. If there is reasonable cause to believe that a person or group of persons has engaged in or is about to engage in any act or practice, or any pattern of acts or practices, which involves the use of information obtained from the community notification website and which violates any provision of this section, NRS 179B.250, 179B.270 or 179B.280, the Attorney General may file an action for injunctive relief in the appropriate district court to prevent the occurrence or continuance of that act or practice or pattern of acts or practices.

2. An injunction pursuant to this section:

(a) May be issued without proof of actual damage sustained by any person; and

(b) Does not preclude or affect the availability of any other remedy including, without limitation, the criminal prosecution of a violator or the filing or maintenance of a civil action for damages or a civil penalty pursuant to NRS 179B.280.

(Added to NRS by 2005, 2868)

LIMITATIONS ON LIABILITY AND THE DISCLOSURE OF INFORMATION

NRS 179B.300 Prohibition on disclosing name of victim; immunity for Central Repository and law enforcement agencies.

1. Information in the statewide registry, including information in the community notification website, that is accessed or disclosed pursuant to the provisions of this chapter must not reveal the name of an individual victim of an offense.

2. The Central Repository and its officers and employees are immune from criminal or civil liability for an act or omission relating to information obtained, maintained or disclosed pursuant to the provisions of this chapter, including, but not limited to, an act or omission relating to:

(a) The accuracy of information in the statewide registry; or

(b) The disclosure of or the failure to disclose information in the statewide registry.

3. A law enforcement agency and its officers and employees are immune from criminal or civil liability for an act or omission relating to information obtained pursuant to the provisions of this chapter, including, but not limited to, an act or omission relating to:

(a) The accuracy of information obtained from the statewide registry; or

(b) The disclosure of or the failure to disclose information obtained from the statewide registry.

(Added to NRS by 1997, 1647; A 2005, 2870)

CHAPTER 179C - REGISTRATION OF CONVICTED PERSONS

GENERAL PROVISIONS

REQUIREMENTS AND PROCEDURE

DISSEMINATION OF INFORMATION

PROHIBITED ACTS AND PENALTIES

GENERAL PROVISIONS

NRS 179C.010 "Convicted person" defined.

1. Except as otherwise provided in subsection 2, as used in this chapter, unless the context otherwise requires, "convicted person" means:

(a) A person convicted in the State of Nevada or convicted in any place other than the State of Nevada of two or more offenses punishable as felonies.

(b) A person convicted in the State of Nevada of an offense punishable as a category A felony.

(c) A person convicted in the State of Nevada or convicted in any place other than the State of Nevada of a crime that would constitute a category A felony if committed in this State on or after July 1, 2003.

2. For the purposes of this chapter, "convicted person" does not include:

(a) A person who has been convicted of a crime against a child, as defined in NRS 179D.0357, or a sexual offense, as defined in NRS 179D.097; or

(b) Except as otherwise provided in this chapter, a person whose conviction is or has been set aside in the manner provided by law.

[1:123:1955]—(NRS A 1959, 216; 1963, 89; 1967, 519; 1971, 932; 1973, 1061; 1975, 1633; 1979, 322, 1019; 1981, 362, 1295, 1296; 1987, 703; 1991, 789, 2268; 1997, 1325, 1682; 1999, 435; 2003, 2688; 2007, 2756)

REQUIREMENTS AND PROCEDURE

NRS 179C.100 Registration with local law enforcement officer within 48 hours; duties and procedures; registration card may not be required; effect of restoration of civil rights.

1. It is unlawful for a convicted person to be or remain in the State of Nevada for a period of more than 48 hours without, during such 48-hour period, registering with the sheriff of a county or the chief of police of a city in the manner prescribed in this section.

2. A convicted person who does not reside in the State of Nevada but who has a temporary or permanent place of abode outside the State of Nevada, and who comes into the State on five occasions or more during any 30-day period, is subject to the provisions of this chapter.

3. A person who has registered as a convicted person with the sheriff of a county or the chief of police of a city shall register again as provided in this section if the person subsequently commits another offense described or referred to in this chapter.

4. A person required by this section to register shall do so by filing with the sheriff or chief of police a statement in writing, upon a form prescribed and furnished by the sheriff or chief of police, which is signed by the person and which provides the following information:

(a) The person's true name and each alias that the person has used or under which the person may have been known;

(b) A full and complete description of his or her person;

(c) The kind, character and nature of each crime of which the person has been convicted;

(d) The place in which the person was convicted of each crime;

(e) The name under which the person was convicted in each instance and the date thereof;

(f) The name, if any, and the location of each prison, reformatory, jail or other penal institution in which the person was confined or to which the person was sentenced;

(g) The location and address of the person's residence, stopping place, living quarters or place of abode, and if more than one residence, stopping place or place of abode, that fact must be stated and the location and address of each given;

(h) The kind of residence, stopping place, or place of abode in which the person resides, including whether it is a private residence, hotel, apartment house or other building or structure;

(i) The length of time the person has occupied each place of residence, stopping place or place of abode, and the length of time the person expects or intends to remain in the State of Nevada; and

(j) Any further information that may be required by the sheriff or chief of police for the purpose of aiding and assisting in carrying into effect the provisions and intent of this chapter.

5. The sheriff of a county or the chief of police of a city shall not require a convicted person to carry a registration card, and no convicted person who is required to register pursuant to this section may be punished for the failure to carry a registration card.

6. When so ordered in the individual case by the district court in which the conviction was obtained, by the State Board of Parole Commissioners or by the State Board of Pardons Commissioners, whichever is appropriate, the provisions of this section do not apply to a convicted person who has had his or her civil rights restored.

[2:123:1955]—(NRS A 1969, 406; 1973, 1843; 1979, 1461; 1997, 1326; 2003, 2689)

NRS 179C.110 Convicted person to notify local law enforcement officer of change of address; procedure. A convicted person, except a nonresident, who is required to register under the provisions of this chapter and who changes his or her place of residence, stopping place or place of abode, shall, within 48 hours after the change, and a nonresident mentioned in subsection 2 of NRS 179C.100 who has registered and who changes his or her place of residence, stopping place or place of abode, shall, upon the next entry into the State after the change, notify the sheriff or chief of police of the change and furnish to the sheriff or chief of police the address of his or her new residence, stopping place or place of abode by filing with the sheriff or chief of police a written statement, upon a form prescribed and furnished by the sheriff or chief of police, which is signed by the person and which provides the following information:

1. The person's true name and each alias that the person has used or under which the person may have been known;
2. The kind, character and nature of each crime of which the person has been convicted;
3. The place in which the person was convicted of each crime;
4. The name under which the person was convicted in each instance and the date thereof; and
5. The location and address of the person's residence, stopping place, living quarters or place of abode, and, if there is more than one, the location and address of each residence, stopping place, living quarters or place of abode.

[3:123:1955]—(NRS A 1997, 1327)

NRS 179C.120 Fingerprinting of convicted persons. Each convicted person, at the time of registering and furnishing the information required by this chapter, shall be fingerprinted by the sheriff or chief of police, who shall cause such fingerprints to be made a part of the record required by this chapter.

[4:123:1955]

DISSEMINATION OF INFORMATION

NRS 179C.160 Registration information forwarded to Central Repository. Upon registering a convicted person pursuant to the provisions of this chapter, a sheriff or a chief of police shall forward all information concerning such registration to the Central Repository for Nevada Records of Criminal History in the manner prescribed by the Director of the Department of Public Safety.

(Added to NRS by 1997, 1325; A 2001, 2579)

NRS 179C.170 Registration information placed in separate file; inspection of information; information may be transmitted to certain agencies and persons.

1. The statements and fingerprints provided for in this chapter must at all times be kept by the sheriff or chief of police in a file separate and apart from other files and records maintained and kept by the sheriff or chief of police, and must not be open to inspection by the public, or by any person other than a regular law enforcement officer.

2. Copies of those statements and fingerprints may be transmitted to:

(a) The sheriff of any county in this State;

(b) The head of any organized police department of any municipality in this State;

(c) The head of any department of the State of Nevada engaged in the enforcement of any criminal law of this State;

(d) The Nevada Gaming Commission and Nevada Gaming Control Board or any successor thereto;

(e) The head of any federal law enforcement agency;

(f) Any sheriff or chief of police of a municipality; or

(g) The head of any other law enforcement agency in any state or territory outside of this State, if a request is made in writing by such sheriff or other head of a law enforcement agency asking for the record of a certain person named therein, or for the record of a person whose fingerprints reasonably correspond with fingerprints submitted with the request, and stating that the record is deemed necessary for the use of that law enforcement officer or agency in or concerning the investigation of any crime, or any person who is accused of committing a crime, or any crime which is reported to have been committed, and further stating that the record will be used only for that purpose.

3. A sheriff or chief of police shall, upon the written request of a county clerk or registrar of voters, furnish the county clerk or registrar of voters with a list containing the name and current address of the residence of each person required to register pursuant to this chapter.

[5:123:1955]—(NRS A 1965, 1031; 1989, 2173)

PROHIBITED ACTS AND PENALTIES

NRS 179C.200 Misleading information prohibited. No person required by any provision of this chapter to furnish a statement shall in such statement give any false or fictitious address or any address other than a true address or intended address, or furnish in the making of any such report any false, untrue or misleading information or statement, relating to any information required by any of the provisions thereof to be made or furnished.

[6:123:1955]

NRS 179C.210 Continuing duty to furnish statement; separate offenses. The duty to furnish statements when and in the manner provided by this chapter is hereby declared to be a continuing one, and for each day that any person required under the provisions of this chapter to furnish a statement fails to do so, such failure shall constitute a separate offense; provided:

1. That no person may be convicted more than once on account of violations occurring by reason of failure, on a series of days, to furnish such statements; and

2. That nothing contained herein shall be deemed a bar to subsequent prosecutions for violations of the provisions of this chapter occurring subsequent to a prior conviction or acquittal of a violation thereof.

[7:123:1955]

NRS 179C.220 Penalty. Any person violating the provisions of this chapter is guilty of a misdemeanor.

[8:123:1955]—(NRS A 1967, 520)

CHAPTER 179D - REGISTRATION OF SEX OFFENDERS AND OFFENDERS CONVICTED OF A CRIME AGAINST A CHILD

GENERAL PROVISIONS

NRS 179D.045 "Institution of higher education" defined.
NRS 179D.050 "Local law enforcement agency" defined.
NRS 179D.0557 "Nonresident offender or sex offender who is a student or worker within this State" and "nonresident offender or sex offender" defined.
NRS 179D.0559 "Offender convicted of a crime against a child" and "offender" defined.
NRS 179D.065 "Primary address" defined.
NRS 179D.070 "Record of registration" defined.
NRS 179D.075 "Registration" defined.
NRS 179D.080 "Release" defined.
NRS 179D.090 "Resides" defined.
NRS 179D.095 "Sex offender" defined.
NRS 179D.097 "Sexual offense" defined.
NRS 179D.100 "Sexual penetration" defined.
NRS 179D.110 "Student" defined.
NRS 179D.113 "Tier I offender" defined.
NRS 179D.115 "Tier II offender" defined.
NRS 179D.117 "Tier III offender" defined.
NRS 179D.120 "Worker" defined.

ADVISORY COMMITTEE TO STUDY LAWS CONCERNING SEX OFFENDER REGISTRATION

NRS 179D.130 "Committee" defined.
NRS 179D.132 Creation; members and appointing authorities; Chair; terms; vacancies; meetings; quorum; salaries and per diem; staff.
NRS 179D.134 Organization authority to appoint member.
NRS 179D.136 Duties of Committee.
NRS 179D.138 Grants, bequests, devises, donations and gifts; Special Account for the Support of the Committee.

RECORD OF REGISTRATION

NRS 179D.151 Contents.
NRS 179D.160 Inspection.
NRS 179D.170 Record and information concerning offender or sex offender provided to Federal Bureau of Investigation.

REGISTRATION

NRS 179D.441 Duty to register and to keep registration current.
NRS 179D.443 Information required for registration; provision of biological specimen; duties of local law enforcement agency.
NRS 179D.445 Initial registration with local law enforcement agency of jurisdiction in which convicted.
NRS 179D.447 Duty to update information after change of name, residence, employment or student status; duty of local law enforcement agency.
NRS 179D.450 Registration after conviction; duties and procedure; offender or sex offender informed of duty to register; effect of failure to inform; duties and procedure upon receipt of notification from another jurisdiction or Federal Bureau of Investigation.
NRS 179D.460 Registration with local law enforcement agency within 48 hours; duties of offender or sex offender and procedure; local law enforcement agency to inform offender or sex offender of duties after registration; duties of local law enforcement agency when notified of certain information about offender or sex offender who enrolls in or works at institution of higher education.
NRS 179D.470 Sex offender to notify appropriate agencies of change of address and provide updated information; duties and procedure.
NRS 179D.475 Community notification.
NRS 179D.480 When offender or sex offender is required to appear in person and provide certain information to local law enforcement agency; duties of Central Repository if offender or sex offender fails to comply.
NRS 179D.490 Duration of duty to register; termination of duty; procedure; exceptions.
NRS 179D.495 Duty of Central Repository to determine whether person is required to register as a Tier I, Tier II or Tier III offender.
NRS 179D.550 Prohibited acts; penalties; duties of local law enforcement agency.

CENTRAL REPOSITORY

NRS 179D.570 Duty to share information with certain agencies; requirements of information; regulations.

LIMITATIONS ON LIABILITY AND THE DISCLOSURE OF INFORMATION

NRS 179D.850 Name of victim not to be disclosed; immunity from liability for certain entities and their officers and employees for act or omission relating to information obtained, maintained or disclosed.

GENERAL PROVISIONS

NRS 179D.010 Definitions. As used in this chapter, unless the context otherwise requires, the words and terms defined in NRS 179D.015 to 179D.120, inclusive, have the meanings ascribed to them in those sections.
(Added to NRS by 1997, 1647; A 1999, 1291; 2003, 568; 2007, 2762)

NRS 179D.015 "Campus police department" defined. "Campus police department" means any campus police department or campus security department at an institution of higher education.
(Added to NRS by 2003, 567)

NRS 179D.020 "Central Repository" defined. "Central Repository" means the Central Repository for Nevada Records of Criminal History.
(Added to NRS by 1997, 1647)

NRS 179D.030 "Community notification" defined. "Community notification" means notification of a community pursuant to the provisions of NRS 179D.475.
(Added to NRS by 1997, 1647; A 2007, 2763)

NRS 179D.035 "Convicted" defined. "Convicted" includes, but is not limited to, an adjudication of delinquency by a court having jurisdiction over juveniles if:
1. The adjudication of delinquency is for the commission of a sexual offense that is listed in NRS 62F.200; and
2. The offender was 14 years of age or older at the time of the offense.
(Added to NRS by 1999, 1290; A 2001, 1311, 2795; 2003, 45, 1122, 1389; 2007, 2763)

NRS 179D.0357 "Crime against a child" defined. "Crime against a child" means any of the following offenses if the victim of the offense was less than 18 years of age when the offense was committed:
1. Kidnapping pursuant to NRS 200.310 to 200.340, inclusive, unless the offender is the parent or guardian of the victim.
2. False imprisonment pursuant to NRS 200.460, unless the offender is the parent or guardian of the victim.
3. Involuntary servitude of a child pursuant to NRS 200.4631, unless the offender is the parent or guardian of the victim.
4. An offense involving sex trafficking pursuant to subsection 2 of NRS 201.300 or prostitution pursuant to NRS 201.320.
5. An attempt to commit an offense listed in this section.
6. An offense committed in another jurisdiction that, if committed in this State, would be an offense listed in this section. This subsection includes, without limitation, an offense prosecuted in:
(a) A tribal court.
(b) A court of the United States or the Armed Forces of the United States.
7. An offense against a child committed in another jurisdiction, whether or not the offense would be an offense listed in this section, if the person who committed the offense resides or has resided or is or has been a student or worker in any jurisdiction in which the person is or has been required by the laws of that jurisdiction to register as an offender who has committed a crime against a child because of the offense. This subsection includes, without limitation, an offense prosecuted in:
(a) A tribal court.
(b) A court of the United States or the Armed Forces of the United States.
(c) A court having jurisdiction over juveniles.
(Added to NRS by 2007, 2757; A 2013, 1858, 2422)

NRS 179D.040 "Division" defined. "Division" means the Division of Parole and Probation of the Department of Public Safety.
(Added to NRS by 1997, 1647; A 2001, 2579)

NRS 179D.045 "Institution of higher education" defined. "Institution of higher education" means:
1. A university, college or community college which is privately owned or which is part of the Nevada System of Higher Education; and
2. A postsecondary educational institution, as defined in NRS 394.099, or any other institution of higher education.
(Added to NRS by 2003, 567)

NRS 179D.050 "Local law enforcement agency" defined. "Local law enforcement agency" means:
1. The sheriff's office of a county;
2. A metropolitan police department; or
3. A police department of an incorporated city.
(Added to NRS by 1997, 1648)

NRS 179D.0557 "Nonresident offender or sex offender who is a student or worker within this State" and "nonresident offender or sex offender" defined. "Nonresident offender or sex offender who is a student or worker within this State" or "nonresident offender or sex offender" means an offender or sex offender who is a student or worker within this State but who is not otherwise deemed a resident offender or sex offender pursuant to subsection 2 or 3 of NRS 179D.460.

(Added to NRS by 2007, 2757)

NRS 179D.0559 "Offender convicted of a crime against a child" and "offender" defined.

1. "Offender convicted of a crime against a child" or "offender" means a person who, after July 1, 1956, is or has been:

(a) Convicted of a crime against a child that is listed in NRS 179D.0357; or

(b) Adjudicated delinquent by a court having jurisdiction over juveniles of a crime against a child that is listed in NRS 62F.200 if the offender was 14 years of age or older at the time of the crime.

2. The term includes, without limitation, an offender who is a student or worker within this State but who is not otherwise deemed a resident offender pursuant to subsection 2 or 3 of NRS 179D.460.

(Added to NRS by 2007, 2757)

NRS 179D.065 "Primary address" defined. "Primary address" means the address at which:

1. A student primarily attends any course of academic or vocational instruction within this state.
2. A worker primarily engages in any type of occupation, employment, work or volunteer service within this state.

(Added to NRS by 1999, 1290)

NRS 179D.070 "Record of registration" defined. "Record of registration" means a record of registration that contains the information required by NRS 179D.151.

(Added to NRS by 1997, 1647; A 2011, 222)

NRS 179D.075 "Registration" defined. "Registration" means registration as an offender or sex offender pursuant to NRS 179D.010 to 179D.550, inclusive.

(Added to NRS by 2007, 2758)

NRS 179D.080 "Release" defined. "Release" means release from incarceration or confinement. The term includes, but is not limited to:

1. Release on probation, parole or any other type of supervised release.
2. Release after a term of incarceration expires.
3. Release from confinement in a school, hospital, mental facility or other institution.

(Added to NRS by 1997, 1648)

NRS 179D.090 "Resides" defined. "Resides" means the place where an offender resides or, if the offender is incarcerated or confined, the place where the offender will reside upon release.

(Added to NRS by 1997, 1648)

NRS 179D.095 "Sex offender" defined.

1. "Sex offender" means a person who, after July 1, 1956, is or has been:

(a) Convicted of a sexual offense listed in NRS 179D.097; or

(b) Adjudicated delinquent by a court having jurisdiction over juveniles of a sexual offense listed in NRS 62F.200 if the offender was 14 years of age or older at the time of the offense.

2. The term includes, without limitation, a sex offender who is a student or worker within this State but who is not otherwise deemed a resident offender pursuant to subsection 2 or 3 of NRS 179D.460.

(Added to NRS by 2007, 2758)

NRS 179D.097 "Sexual offense" defined.

1. "Sexual offense" means any of the following offenses:

(a) Murder of the first degree committed in the perpetration or attempted perpetration of sexual assault or of sexual abuse or sexual molestation of a child less than 14 years of age pursuant to paragraph (b) of subsection 1 of NRS 200.030.

(b) Sexual assault pursuant to NRS 200.366.

(c) Statutory sexual seduction pursuant to NRS 200.368.

(d) Battery with intent to commit sexual assault pursuant to subsection 4 of NRS 200.400.

(e) An offense involving the administration of a drug to another person with the intent to enable or assist the commission of a felony pursuant to NRS 200.405, if the felony is an offense listed in this subsection.

(f) An offense involving the administration of a controlled substance to another person with the intent to enable or assist the commission of a crime of violence pursuant to NRS 200.408, if the crime of violence is an offense listed in this section.

(g) Abuse of a child pursuant to NRS 200.508, if the abuse involved sexual abuse or sexual exploitation.

(h) An offense involving pornography and a minor pursuant to NRS 200.710 to 200.730, inclusive.

(i) Incest pursuant to NRS 201.180.

(j) Open or gross lewdness pursuant to NRS 201.210.

(k) Indecent or obscene exposure pursuant to NRS 201.220.

(l) Lewdness with a child pursuant to NRS 201.230.

(m) Sexual penetration of a dead human body pursuant to NRS 201.450.

(n) Sexual conduct between certain employees of a school or volunteers at a school and a pupil pursuant to NRS 201.540.

(o) Sexual conduct between certain employees of a college or university and a student pursuant to NRS 201.550.

(p) Luring a child or a person with mental illness pursuant to NRS 201.560, if punished as a felony.
(q) Sex trafficking pursuant to NRS 201.300.
(r) Any other offense that has an element involving a sexual act or sexual conduct with another.
(s) An attempt or conspiracy to commit an offense listed in paragraphs (a) to (r), inclusive.
(t) An offense that is determined to be sexually motivated pursuant to NRS 175.547 or 207.193.
(u) An offense committed in another jurisdiction that, if committed in this State, would be an offense listed in this subsection. This paragraph includes, without limitation, an offense prosecuted in:
(1) A tribal court.
(2) A court of the United States or the Armed Forces of the United States.
(v) An offense of a sexual nature committed in another jurisdiction, whether or not the offense would be an offense listed in this section, if the person who committed the offense resides or has resided or is or has been a student or worker in any jurisdiction in which the person is or has been required by the laws of that jurisdiction to register as a sex offender because of the offense. This paragraph includes, without limitation, an offense prosecuted in:
(1) A tribal court.
(2) A court of the United States or the Armed Forces of the United States.
(3) A court having jurisdiction over juveniles.
2. Except for the offenses described in paragraphs (n) and (o) of subsection 1, the term does not include an offense involving consensual sexual conduct if the victim was:
(a) An adult, unless the adult was under the custodial authority of the offender at the time of the offense; or
(b) At least 13 years of age and the offender was not more than 4 years older than the victim at the time of the commission of the offense.
(Added to NRS by 2007, 2758; A 2013, 1167, 2423; 2015, 1444)

NRS 179D.100 "Sexual penetration" defined. "Sexual penetration" means cunnilingus, fellatio or any intrusion, however slight, of any part of the victim's body or any object manipulated or inserted by a person into the genital or anal openings of the body of the victim. The term includes, but is not limited to, anal intercourse and sexual intercourse in what would be its ordinary meaning.
(Added to NRS by 1999, 1290)

NRS 179D.110 "Student" defined. "Student" means a person who is enrolled in and attends, on a full-time or part-time basis within this State, any course of academic or vocational instruction conducted by a public or private educational institution or school, including, but not limited to, any of the following institutions or schools:
1. An institution of higher education.
2. A trade school or vocational school.
3. A secondary school.
(Added to NRS by 1999, 1290; A 2003, 568; 2007, 2763)

NRS 179D.113 "Tier I offender" defined. "Tier I offender" means an offender convicted of a crime against a child or a sex offender other than a Tier II offender or Tier III offender.
(Added to NRS by 2007, 2759)

NRS 179D.115 "Tier II offender" defined. "Tier II offender" means an offender convicted of a crime against a child or a sex offender, other than a Tier III offender, whose crime against a child is punishable by imprisonment for more than 1 year or whose sexual offense:
1. If committed against a child, constitutes:
(a) Luring a child pursuant to NRS 201.560, if punishable as a felony;
(b) Abuse of a child pursuant to NRS 200.508, if the abuse involved sexual abuse or sexual exploitation;
(c) An offense involving sex trafficking pursuant to NRS 201.300 or prostitution pursuant to NRS 201.320;
(d) An offense involving pornography and a minor pursuant to NRS 200.710 to 200.730, inclusive; or
(e) Any other offense that is comparable to or more severe than the offenses described in 42 U.S.C. § 16911(3);
2. Involves an attempt or conspiracy to commit any offense described in subsection 1;
3. If committed in another jurisdiction, is an offense that, if committed in this State, would be an offense listed in this section. This subsection includes, without limitation, an offense prosecuted in:
(a) A tribal court; or
(b) A court of the United States or the Armed Forces of the United States; or
4. Is committed after the person becomes a Tier I offender if any of the person's sexual offenses constitute an offense punishable by imprisonment for more than 1 year.
(Added to NRS by 2007, 2759; A 2013, 2424)

NRS 179D.117 "Tier III offender" defined. "Tier III offender" means an offender convicted of a crime against a child or a sex offender who has been convicted of:
1. Murder of the first degree committed in the perpetration or attempted perpetration of sexual assault or of sexual abuse or sexual molestation of a child less than 14 years of age pursuant to paragraph (b) of subsection 1 of NRS 200.030;
2. Sexual assault pursuant to NRS 200.366;
3. Battery with intent to commit sexual assault pursuant to subsection 4 of NRS 200.400;

4. Abuse of a child pursuant to NRS 200.508, if the abuse involved sexual abuse or sexual exploitation and if the victim of the offense was less than 13 years of age when the offense was committed;

5. Kidnapping pursuant to NRS 200.310 to 200.340, inclusive, if the victim of the offense was less than 18 years of age when the offense was committed, unless the offender is the parent or guardian of the victim;

6. Any sexual offense or crime against a child after the person becomes a Tier II offender;

7. Any other offense that is comparable to or more severe than the offenses described in 42 U.S.C. § 16911(4);

8. An attempt or conspiracy to commit an offense described in subsections 1 to 7, inclusive; or

9. An offense committed in another jurisdiction that, if committed in this State, would be an offense listed in this section. This subsection includes, without limitation, an offense prosecuted in:

(a) A tribal court; or

(b) A court of the United States or the Armed Forces of the United States.

(Added to NRS by 2007, 2759)

NRS 179D.120 "Worker" defined. "Worker" means a person who is self-employed or who engages in or who knows or reasonably should know that he or she will engage in any type of occupation, employment, work or volunteer service, whether or not the person engages in or will engage in the occupation, employment, work or volunteer service for compensation.

(Added to NRS by 1999, 1291; A 2007, 2763)

ADVISORY COMMITTEE TO STUDY LAWS CONCERNING SEX OFFENDER REGISTRATION

NRS 179D.130 "Committee" defined. As used in NRS 179D.130 to 179D.138, inclusive, "Committee" means the Advisory Committee to Study Laws Concerning Sex Offender Registration.

(Added to NRS by 2009, 427)

NRS 179D.132 Creation; members and appointing authorities; Chair; terms; vacancies; meetings; quorum; salaries and per diem; staff.

1. The Advisory Committee to Study Laws Concerning Sex Offender Registration is hereby created.

2. The Committee consists of the following members:

(a) The Attorney General or the Attorney General's designee;

(b) One member of the Assembly appointed by the Speaker of the Assembly;

(c) One member of the Senate appointed by the Majority Leader of the Senate;

(d) One member appointed by the Nevada Sheriffs' and Chiefs' Association, or a successor organization;

(e) One member appointed by the Nevada District Attorneys Association, or a successor organization;

(f) One member who is a public defender, appointed by the governing body of the State Bar of Nevada;

(g) One member appointed by the American Civil Liberties Union, or a successor organization;

(h) One member who is a mental health professional, appointed by the Attorney General; and

(i) Any member appointed by an organization that has been authorized by the Attorney General to appoint a member of the Committee pursuant to NRS 179D.134.

3. The Attorney General or the Attorney General's designee is the Chair of the Committee.

4. Each member who is appointed to the Committee serves a term of 2 years. Except as otherwise provided in subsection 3 of NRS 179D.134:

(a) Members may be reappointed for additional terms of 2 years in the same manner as the original appointments; and

(b) Any vacancy occurring in the membership of the Committee must be filled in the same manner as the original appointment not later than 30 days after the vacancy occurs.

5. The Committee shall meet at least twice each year and may meet at such further times as deemed necessary by the Chair.

6. A majority of the members of the Committee constitutes a quorum for the transaction of business, and a majority of those members present at any meeting is sufficient for any official action taken by the Committee.

7. The Committee shall comply with the provisions of chapter 241 of NRS, and all meetings of the Committee must be conducted in accordance with that chapter.

8. For each day or portion of a day during which a member of the Committee who is a Legislator attends a meeting of the Committee or is otherwise engaged in the business of the Committee, except during a regular or special session of the Legislature, the Legislator is entitled to receive the:

(a) Compensation provided for a majority of the members of the Legislature during the first 60 days of the preceding regular session;

(b) Per diem allowance provided for state officers generally; and

(c) Travel expenses provided pursuant to NRS 218A.655.

Ê The compensation, per diem allowances and travel expenses of the members of the Committee who are Legislators must be paid from the Legislative Fund.

9. While engaged in the business of the Committee, to the extent of legislative appropriation, the members of the Committee who are not Legislators are entitled to receive the per diem allowance and travel expenses provided for state officers and employees generally.

10. A member of the Committee who is an officer or employee of this State or a political subdivision of this State must be relieved from his or her duties without loss of regular compensation so that he or she may prepare for and attend meetings of the Committee and perform any work necessary to carry out the duties of the Committee in the most timely manner practicable. A state agency or political subdivision of this State shall not require an officer or employee who is a member of the Committee to:

(a) Make up the time the member is absent from work to carry out his or her duties as a member of the Committee; or

(b) Take annual leave or compensatory time for the absence.

11. The Attorney General shall provide the Committee with such staff as is necessary to carry out the duties of the Committee.
(Added to NRS by 2009, 427; A 2011, 222)

NRS 179D.134 Organization authority to appoint member.
1. An organization which is concerned with state and federal laws concerning the registration of sex offenders and which wishes to appoint a member to the Committee pursuant to paragraph (i) of subsection 2 of NRS 179D.132 may apply to the Attorney General, or the Attorney General's designee, for authorization to appoint a member to the Committee. At the Attorney General's discretion, the Attorney General may authorize the organization to appoint a member to the Committee.
2. At any time after the Attorney General has authorized an organization to appoint a member to the Committee, the Attorney General may revoke the organization's authorization to appoint a member to the Committee.
3. If, after receiving authorization to appoint a member to the Committee, an organization ceases to exist or has its authorization to appoint a member to the Committee revoked by the Attorney General, any member of the Committee appointed by the organization may complete the term to which the member was appointed, and upon the completion of that term, the organization, or a successor organization, may not appoint a member to the Committee.
(Added to NRS by 2009, 428; A 2011, 224)

NRS 179D.136 Duties of Committee. The Committee shall:
1. Identify and study issues relating to state and federal law concerning the registration of sex offenders and any litigation concerning those laws.
2. Prepare a report of the activities and findings of the Committee and any recommendations for proposed legislation concerning the registration of sex offenders developed by the Committee.
3. On or before September 1 of each even-numbered year, submit the report prepared pursuant to subsection 2 to the Director of the Legislative Counsel Bureau for submission to the Legislative Commission.
(Added to NRS by 2009, 429)

NRS 179D.138 Grants, bequests, devises, donations and gifts; Special Account for the Support of the Committee.
1. The Attorney General may apply for and accept any available grants and may accept any bequests, devises, donations or gifts from any public or private source to carry out the provisions of NRS 179D.130 to 179D.138, inclusive.
2. Any money received pursuant to this section must be deposited in the Special Account for the Support of the Committee, which is hereby created in the State General Fund. Interest and income earned on money in the Account must be credited to the Account. Money in the Account may only be used for the support of the Committee and its activities pursuant to NRS 179D.130 to 179D.138, inclusive.
(Added to NRS by 2009, 429)

RECORD OF REGISTRATION

NRS 179D.151 Contents.
1. A record of registration must include, if the information is available:
(a) Information identifying the offender or sex offender, including, but not limited to:
(1) The name of the offender or sex offender and all aliases that the offender or sex offender has used or under which he or she has been known;
(2) A complete physical description of the offender or sex offender, a current photograph of the offender or sex offender and the fingerprints and palm prints of the offender or sex offender;
(3) The date of birth and the social security number of the offender or sex offender;
(4) The identification number from a driver's license or an identification card issued to the offender or sex offender by this State or any other jurisdiction and a photocopy of such driver's license or identification card;
(5) Information indicating whether the DNA profile and DNA record of the offender or sex offender has been entered in CODIS; and
(6) Any other information that identifies the offender or sex offender.
(b) Except as otherwise provided in paragraph (c), information concerning the residence of the offender or sex offender, including, but not limited to:
(1) The address at which the offender or sex offender resides;
(2) The length of time the offender or sex offender has resided at that address and the length of time the offender or sex offender expects to reside at that address;
(3) The address or location of any other place where the offender or sex offender expects to reside in the future and the length of time the offender or sex offender expects to reside there; and
(4) The length of time the offender or sex offender expects to remain in the county where the offender or sex offender resides and in this State.
(c) If the offender or sex offender has no fixed residence, the address of any dwelling that is providing the offender or sex offender temporary shelter, or any other location where the offender or sex offender habitually sleeps, including, but not limited to, the cross streets, intersection, direction and identifiable landmarks of the city, county, state and zip code of that location.
(d) Information concerning the offender's or sex offender's occupations, employment or work or expected occupations, employment or work, including, but not limited to, the name, address and type of business of all current and expected future employers of the offender or sex offender.
(e) Information concerning the offender's or sex offender's volunteer service or expected volunteer service in connection with any activity or organization within this State, including, but not limited to, the name, address and type of each such activity or organization.

(f) Information concerning the offender's or sex offender's enrollment or expected enrollment as a student in any public or private educational institution or school within this State, including, but not limited to, the name, address and type of each such educational institution or school.

(g) Information concerning whether:

(1) The offender or sex offender is, expects to be or becomes enrolled as a student at an institution of higher education or changes the date of commencement or termination of the offender's or sex offender's enrollment at an institution of higher education; or

(2) The offender or sex offender is, expects to be or becomes a worker at an institution of higher education or changes the date of commencement or termination of the offender's or sex offender's work at an institution of higher education,

Ê including, but not limited to, the name, address and type of each such institution of higher education.

(h) The license plate number and a description of all motor vehicles registered to or frequently driven by the offender or sex offender.

(i) The level of registration and community notification of the offender or sex offender.

(j) The criminal history of the offender or sex offender, including, without limitation:

(1) The dates of all arrests and convictions of the offender or sex offender;

(2) The status of parole, probation or supervised release of the offender or sex offender;

(3) The status of the registration of the offender or sex offender; and

(4) The existence of any outstanding arrest warrants for the offender or sex offender.

(k) The following information for each offense for which the offender or sex offender has been convicted:

(1) The court in which the offender or sex offender was convicted;

(2) The text of the provision of law defining each offense;

(3) The name under which the offender or sex offender was convicted;

(4) The name and location of each penal institution, school, hospital, mental facility or other institution to which the offender or sex offender was committed;

(5) The specific location where the offense was committed;

(6) The age, the gender, the race and a general physical description of the victim; and

(7) The method of operation that was used to commit the offense, including, but not limited to:

(I) Specific sexual acts committed against the victim;

(II) The method of obtaining access to the victim, such as the use of enticements, threats, forced entry or violence against the victim;

(III) The type of injuries inflicted on the victim;

(IV) The types of instruments, weapons or objects used;

(V) The type of property taken; and

(VI) Any other distinctive characteristic of the behavior or personality of the offender or sex offender.

(l) Any other information required by federal law.

2. As used in this section:

(a) "CODIS" has the meaning ascribed to it in NRS 176.09113.

(b) "DNA profile" has the meaning ascribed to it in NRS 176.09115.

(c) "DNA record" has the meaning ascribed to it in NRS 176.09116.

(Added to NRS by 2011, 220; A 2013, 1075)

NRS 179D.160 Inspection.

1. Except as otherwise provided by specific statute, the contents of a record of registration:

(a) Are confidential and not subject to inspection by the general public.

(b) May be inspected only by a law enforcement officer in the regular course of the law enforcement officer's duties or by the offender named in the record of registration.

2. As used in this section, "law enforcement officer" includes, but is not limited to:

(a) A prosecuting attorney or an attorney from the Office of the Attorney General;

(b) A sheriff of a county or a sheriff's deputy;

(c) An officer of a metropolitan police department or a police department of an incorporated city;

(d) An officer of the Division;

(e) An officer of the Department of Corrections;

(f) An officer of a law enforcement agency from another jurisdiction; or

(g) Any other person upon whom some or all of the powers of a peace officer are conferred pursuant to NRS 289.150 to 289.360, inclusive, if the person is seeking information as part of a criminal investigation.

(Added to NRS by 1997, 1649; A 2001 Special Session, 225; 2013, 375)

NRS 179D.170 Record and information concerning offender or sex offender provided to Federal Bureau of Investigation. Upon receiving from a local law enforcement agency, pursuant to NRS 179D.010 to 179D.550, inclusive:

1. A record of registration;
2. Fingerprints, palm prints or a photograph of an offender or sex offender;
3. A new address of an offender or sex offender; or
4. Any other updated information,

Ê the Central Repository shall immediately provide the record of registration, fingerprints, palm prints, photograph, new address or updated information to the Federal Bureau of Investigation.

(Added to NRS by 1997, 1650; A 2003, 569; 2007, 2765)

REGISTRATION

NRS 179D.441 Duty to register and to keep registration current. Each offender convicted of a crime against a child and each sex offender shall:

1. Register initially with the local law enforcement agency of the jurisdiction in which the offender or sex offender was convicted as required pursuant to NRS 179D.445;
2. Register with the appropriate law enforcement agency as required pursuant to NRS 179D.460 and 179D.480; and
3. Keep the registration current as required pursuant to NRS 179D.447.

(Added to NRS by 2007, 2760)

NRS 179D.443 Information required for registration; provision of biological specimen; duties of local law enforcement agency.

1. When an offender convicted of a crime against a child or a sex offender registers with a local law enforcement agency as required pursuant to NRS 179D.445, 179D.460 or 179D.480, or updates the registration as required pursuant to NRS 179D.447:

(a) The offender or sex offender shall provide the local law enforcement agency with the following:

(1) The name of the offender or sex offender and all aliases that the offender or sex offender has used or under which the offender or sex offender has been known;

(2) The social security number of the offender or sex offender;

(3) The address of any residence or location at which the offender or sex offender resides or will reside;

(4) The name and address of any place where the offender or sex offender is a worker or will be a worker;

(5) The name and address of any place where the offender or sex offender is a student or will be a student;

(6) The license plate number and a description of all motor vehicles registered to or frequently driven by the offender or sex offender; and

(7) Any other information required by federal law.

(b) If the offender or sex offender has not previously provided a biological specimen pursuant to NRS 176.09123, 176.0913 or 176.0916, the offender or sex offender shall provide a biological specimen to the local law enforcement agency. The local law enforcement agency shall provide the specimen to the forensic laboratory that has been designated by the county in which the offender or sex offender resides, is present or is a worker or student to conduct or oversee genetic marker analysis for the county pursuant to NRS 176.0917.

(c) The local law enforcement agency shall ensure that the record of registration of the offender or sex offender includes, without limitation:

(1) A complete physical description of the offender or sex offender, a current photograph of the offender or sex offender and the fingerprints and palm prints of the offender or sex offender;

(2) The text of the provision of law defining each offense for which the offender or sex offender is required to register;

(3) The criminal history of the offender or sex offender, including, without limitation:

(I) The dates of all arrests and convictions of the offender or sex offender;

(II) The status of parole, probation or supervised release of the offender or sex offender;

(III) The status of the registration of the offender or sex offender; and

(IV) The existence of any outstanding arrest warrants for the offender or sex offender;

(4) Information indicating whether the DNA profile and DNA record of the offender or sex offender has been entered in CODIS;

(5) The identification number from a driver's license or an identification card issued to the offender or sex offender by this State or any other jurisdiction and a photocopy of such driver's license or identification card; and

(6) Any other information required by federal law.

2. As used in this section:

(a) "CODIS" has the meaning ascribed to it in NRS 176.09113.

(b) "DNA profile" has the meaning ascribed to it in NRS 176.09115.

(c) "DNA record" has the meaning ascribed to it in NRS 176.09116.

(Added to NRS by 2007, 2760; A 2007, 3262; 2013, 1078)

NRS 179D.445 Initial registration with local law enforcement agency of jurisdiction in which convicted.

1. In addition to any other registration that is required pursuant to NRS 179D.010 to 179D.550, inclusive, each offender or sex offender who, on or after October 1, 2007, is or has been convicted of a crime against a child or a sexual offense shall register initially with the appropriate local law enforcement agency of the jurisdiction in which the offender or sex offender was convicted pursuant to the provisions of this section.

2. An offender or sex offender shall initially register with a local law enforcement agency as required pursuant to subsection 1:

(a) If the offender or sex offender is sentenced to a term of imprisonment for the crime, before being released from incarceration or confinement for the crime; and

(b) If the offender or sex offender is not sentenced to a term of imprisonment for the crime, not later than 3 business days after the date on which the offender or sex offender was sentenced for the crime.

(Added to NRS by 2007, 2761; A 2007, 3263)

NRS 179D.447 Duty to update information after change of name, residence, employment or student status; duty of local law enforcement agency.

1. An offender convicted of a crime against a child or a sex offender convicted of a sexual offense who changes his or her name, residence, employment or student status shall, not later than 3 business days after such change of name, residence, employment or student status:

(a) Appear in person in at least one of the jurisdictions in which the offender or sex offender resides, is a student or worker; and

(b) Provide all information concerning such change to the appropriate local law enforcement agency.

2. The local law enforcement agency shall immediately provide the updated information provided by an offender or sex offender pursuant to subsection 1 to the Central Repository and to all other jurisdictions in which the offender or sex offender is required to register.

(Added to NRS by 2007, 2761)

NRS 179D.450 Registration after conviction; duties and procedure; offender or sex offender informed of duty to register; effect of failure to inform; duties and procedure upon receipt of notification from another jurisdiction or Federal Bureau of Investigation.

1. If the Central Repository receives notice from a court pursuant to NRS 176.0926 that an offender has been convicted of a crime against a child, pursuant to NRS 176.0927 that a sex offender has been convicted of a sexual offense or pursuant to NRS 62F.220 that a juvenile has been adjudicated delinquent for an offense for which the juvenile is subject to registration and community notification pursuant to NRS 179D.010 to 179D.550, inclusive, the Central Repository shall:

(a) If a record of registration has not previously been established for the offender or sex offender, notify the local law enforcement agency so that a record of registration may be established; or

(b) If a record of registration has previously been established for the offender or sex offender, update the record of registration for the offender or sex offender and notify the appropriate local law enforcement agencies.

2. If the offender or sex offender named in the notice is granted probation or otherwise will not be incarcerated or confined, the Central Repository shall:

(a) Immediately provide notification concerning the offender or sex offender to the appropriate local law enforcement agencies and, if the offender or sex offender resides in a jurisdiction which is outside of this State, to the appropriate law enforcement agency in that jurisdiction; and

(b) Immediately provide community notification concerning the offender or sex offender pursuant to the provisions of NRS 179D.475.

3. If an offender or sex offender is incarcerated or confined and has previously been convicted of a crime against a child as described in NRS 179D.0357 or a sexual offense as described in NRS 179D.097, before the offender or sex offender is released:

(a) The Department of Corrections or a local law enforcement agency in whose facility the offender or sex offender is incarcerated or confined shall:

(1) Inform the offender or sex offender of the requirements for registration, including, but not limited to:

(I) The duty to register initially with the appropriate law enforcement agency in the jurisdiction in which the offender or sex offender was convicted if the offender or sex offender is not a resident of that jurisdiction pursuant to NRS 179D.445;

(II) The duty to register in this State during any period in which the offender or sex offender is a resident of this State or a nonresident who is a student or worker within this State and the time within which the offender or sex offender is required to register pursuant to NRS 179D.460;

(III) The duty to register in any other jurisdiction during any period in which the offender or sex offender is a resident of the other jurisdiction or a nonresident who is a student or worker within the other jurisdiction;

(IV) If the offender or sex offender moves from this State to another jurisdiction, the duty to register with the appropriate law enforcement agency in the other jurisdiction;

(V) The duty to notify the local law enforcement agency for the jurisdiction in which the offender or sex offender now resides, in person, and the jurisdiction in which the offender or sex offender formerly resided, in person or in writing, if the offender or sex offender changes the address at which the offender or sex offender resides, including if the offender or sex offender moves from this State to another jurisdiction, or changes the primary address at which the offender or sex offender is a student or worker; and

(VI) The duty to notify immediately the appropriate local law enforcement agency if the offender or sex offender is, expects to be or becomes enrolled as a student at an institution of higher education or changes the date of commencement or termination of the offender or sex offender's enrollment at an institution of higher education or if the offender or sex offender is, expects to be or becomes a worker at an institution of higher education or changes the date of commencement or termination of the offender or sex offender's work at an institution of higher education; and

(2) Require the offender or sex offender to read and sign a form stating that the requirements for registration have been explained and that the offender or sex offender understands the requirements for registration, and to forward the form to the Central Repository.

(b) The Central Repository shall:

(1) Update the record of registration for the offender or sex offender;

(2) Provide community notification concerning the offender or sex offender pursuant to the provisions of NRS 179D.475; and

(3) Provide notification concerning the offender or sex offender to the appropriate local law enforcement agencies and, if the offender or sex offender will reside upon release in a jurisdiction which is outside of this State, to the appropriate law enforcement agency in that jurisdiction.

4. The failure to provide an offender or sex offender with the information or confirmation form required by paragraph (a) of subsection 3 does not affect the duty of the offender or sex offender to register and to comply with all other provisions for registration.

5. If the Central Repository receives notice from another jurisdiction or the Federal Bureau of Investigation that an offender or sex offender is now residing or is a student or worker within this State, the Central Repository shall:

(a) Immediately provide notification concerning the offender or sex offender to the appropriate local law enforcement agencies;

(b) Establish a record of registration for the offender or sex offender; and

(c) Immediately provide community notification concerning the offender or sex offender pursuant to the provisions of NRS 179D.475.

(Added to NRS by 1997, 1655; A 1999, 1300; 2001, 2058; 2001 Special Session, 227; 2003, 289, 573, 1122; 2007, 2765, 3252)

NRS 179D.460 Registration with local law enforcement agency within 48 hours; duties of offender or sex offender and procedure; local law enforcement agency to inform offender or sex offender of duties after registration; duties of local law enforcement agency when notified of certain information about offender or sex offender who enrolls in or works at institution of higher education.

1. In addition to any other registration that is required pursuant to NRS 179D.450, each offender or sex offender who, after July 1, 1956, is or has been convicted of a crime against a child or a sexual offense shall register with a local law enforcement agency pursuant to the provisions of this section.

2. Except as otherwise provided in subsection 3, if the offender or sex offender resides or is present for 48 hours or more within:

(a) A county; or

(b) An incorporated city that does not have a city police department,

Ê the offender or sex offender shall be deemed a resident offender or sex offender and shall register with the sheriff's office of the county or, if the county or the city is within the jurisdiction of a metropolitan police department, the metropolitan police department, not later than 48 hours after arriving or establishing a residence within the county or the city.

3. If the offender or sex offender resides or is present for 48 hours or more within an incorporated city that has a city police department, the offender or sex offender shall be deemed a resident offender or sex offender and shall register with the city police department not later than 48 hours after arriving or establishing a residence within the city.

4. If the offender or sex offender is a nonresident offender or sex offender who is a student or worker within this State, the offender or sex offender shall register with the appropriate sheriff's office, metropolitan police department or city police department in whose jurisdiction the offender or sex offender is a student or worker not later than 48 hours after becoming a student or worker within this State.

5. A resident or nonresident offender or sex offender shall immediately notify the appropriate local law enforcement agency if:

(a) The offender or sex offender is, expects to be or becomes enrolled as a student at an institution of higher education or changes the date of commencement or termination of the offender or sex offender's enrollment at an institution of higher education; or

(b) The offender or sex offender is, expects to be or becomes a worker at an institution of higher education or changes the date of commencement or termination of the offender or sex offender's work at an institution of higher education.

Ê The offender or sex offender shall provide the name, address and type of each such institution of higher education.

6. To register with a local law enforcement agency pursuant to this section, the offender or sex offender shall:

(a) Appear personally at the office of the appropriate local law enforcement agency;

(b) Provide all information that is requested by the local law enforcement agency, including, but not limited to, fingerprints and a photograph; and

(c) Sign and date the record of registration or some other proof of registration of the local law enforcement agency in the presence of an officer of the local law enforcement agency.

7. When an offender or sex offender registers, the local law enforcement agency shall:

(a) Inform the offender or sex offender of the duty to notify the local law enforcement agency if the offender or sex offender changes the address at which the offender or sex offender resides, including if the offender or sex offender moves from this State to another jurisdiction, or changes the primary address at which the offender or sex offender is a student or worker; and

(b) Inform the offender or sex offender of the duty to register with the local law enforcement agency in whose jurisdiction the sex offender relocates.

8. After the offender or sex offender registers with the local law enforcement agency, the local law enforcement agency shall forward to the Central Repository the information collected, including the fingerprints and a photograph of the offender or sex offender.

9. If the Central Repository has not previously established a record of registration for an offender or sex offender described in subsection 8, the Central Repository shall:

(a) Establish a record of registration for the offender or sex offender;

(b) Provide notification concerning the offender or sex offender to the appropriate local law enforcement agencies; and

(c) Provide community notification concerning the offender or sex offender pursuant to the provisions of NRS 179D.475.

10. When an offender or sex offender notifies a local law enforcement agency that:

(a) The offender or sex offender is, expects to be or becomes enrolled as a student at an institution of higher education or changes the date of commencement or termination of the offender or sex offender's enrollment at an institution of higher education; or

(b) The offender or sex offender is, expects to be or becomes a worker at an institution of higher education or changes the date of commencement or termination of the offender or sex offender's work at an institution of higher education,

Ê and provides the name, address and type of each such institution of higher education, the local law enforcement agency shall immediately provide that information to the Central Repository and to the appropriate campus police department.

(Added to NRS by 1997, 1657; A 1999, 1302; 2001, 2059; 2003, 575; 2007, 2767, 3253)

NRS 179D.470 Sex offender to notify appropriate agencies of change of address and provide updated information; duties and procedure.

1. If a sex offender changes the address at which he or she resides, including moving from this State to another jurisdiction, changes the primary address at which he or she is a student or worker or remains in a jurisdiction longer than 30 days after initially reporting a stay of less than 30 days, the sex offender shall, not later than 48 hours after such a change in status, provide notice of the change in status, including, without limitation, the new address, in person, to the local law enforcement agency in whose jurisdiction the sex offender now resides and, in person or in writing, to the local law enforcement agency in whose jurisdiction the sex offender formerly resided and shall provide all other information that is relevant to updating the record of registration, including, but not limited to, any change in the sex offender's name, occupation, employment, work, volunteer service or driver's license and any change in the license number or description of a motor vehicle registered to or frequently driven by the sex offender.

2. Upon receiving a change of address from a sex offender, the local law enforcement agency shall immediately forward the new address and any updated information to the Central Repository and:

(a) If the sex offender has changed an address within this State, the Central Repository shall immediately provide notification concerning the sex offender to the local law enforcement agency in whose jurisdiction the sex offender is now residing or is a student or worker and shall notify the local law enforcement agency in whose jurisdiction the sex offender last resided or was a student or worker; or

(b) If the sex offender has changed an address from this State to another jurisdiction, the Central Repository shall immediately provide notification concerning the sex offender to the appropriate law enforcement agency in the other jurisdiction and shall notify the local law enforcement agency in whose jurisdiction the sex offender last resided or was a student or worker.

3. In addition to any other requirement pursuant to this section and upon notification of the requirements of this subsection, any sex offender who has no fixed residence shall at least every 30 days notify the local law enforcement agency in whose jurisdiction the sex offender resides if there are any changes in the address of any dwelling that is providing the sex offender temporary shelter or any changes in location where the sex offender habitually sleeps. The court may dismiss any criminal charges filed for failure to comply with this subsection if the sex offender immediately updates his or her record of registration.

(Added to NRS by 1997, 1658; A 1999, 1304; 2001, 2061; 2011, 224)

NRS 179D.475 Community notification.

1. Except as otherwise provided in subsection 3, the Central Repository shall immediately provide all updated information obtained pursuant to NRS 179D.445, 179D.447, 179D.460 or 179D.480 to:

(a) The Attorney General of the United States;

(b) The appropriate local law enforcement agencies for each jurisdiction in which the offender or sex offender resides or is a student or worker;

(c) Each jurisdiction in which the offender or sex offender now resides or is a student or worker and the jurisdiction in which the offender or sex offender most recently resided or was a student or worker, if the offender or sex offender changes the address at which he or she resides or is a student or worker;

(d) Any agency responsible for conducting employment-related background checks pursuant to 42 U.S.C. § 5119a; and

(e) Any organization, company or person who requests such notification.

2. Except as otherwise provided in subsection 3, a local law enforcement agency:

(a) Shall immediately provide all updated information obtained from the Central Repository pursuant to subsection 1 to:

(1) Each school, religious organization, youth organization and public housing authority in which the offender or sex offender resides or is a student or worker;

(2) Each agency which provides child welfare services as defined in NRS 432B.030;

(3) Volunteer organizations in which contact with children or other vulnerable persons might occur; and

(4) If the offender or sex offender is a Tier III offender, members of the public who are likely to encounter the offender or sex offender; and

(b) May provide any updated information obtained from the Central Repository pursuant to subsection 1 to any other person or entity whom the law enforcement agency determines warrants such notification.

3. An entity or person described in paragraph (e) of subsection 1 or subparagraph (1) of paragraph (a) of subsection 2 may request to receive the updated information obtained pursuant to subsection 1 not less frequently than once every 5 business days.

(Added to NRS by 2007, 2762)

NRS 179D.480 When offender or sex offender is required to appear in person and provide certain information to local law enforcement agency; duties of Central Repository if offender or sex offender fails to comply.

1. Except as otherwise provided in subsection 3, an offender convicted of a crime against a child or a sex offender shall appear in person in at least one jurisdiction in which the offender or sex offender resides or is a student or worker:

(a) Not less frequently than annually, if the offender or sex offender is a Tier I offender;

(b) Not less frequently than every 180 days, if the offender or sex offender is a Tier II offender; or

(c) Not less frequently than every 90 days, if the offender or sex offender is a Tier III offender,

Ê and shall allow the appropriate local law enforcement agency to collect a current set of fingerprints and palm prints, a current photograph and all other information that is relevant to updating the offender or sex offender's record of registration, including, but not limited to, any change in the offender or sex offender's name, occupation, employment, work, volunteer service or driver's license and any change in the license number or description of a motor vehicle registered to or frequently driven by the offender or sex offender.

2. If an offender or sex offender does not comply with the provisions of subsection 1, the Central Repository shall:

(a) Immediately notify the appropriate local law enforcement agencies and the Attorney General of the United States; and

(b) Update the record of registration for the sex offender to reflect the failure to comply with the provisions of subsection 1.

3. An offender or sex offender is not required to comply with the provisions of subsection 1 during any period in which the offender or sex offender is incarcerated or confined.

(Added to NRS by 1997, 1658; A 1999, 1304; 2001, 2061; 2007, 2769)

NRS 179D.490 Duration of duty to register; termination of duty; procedure; exceptions.

1. An offender convicted of a crime against a child or a sex offender shall comply with the provisions for registration for as long as the offender or sex offender resides or is present within this State or is a nonresident offender or sex offender who is a student or worker within this State, unless the period of time during which the offender or sex offender has the duty to register is reduced pursuant to the provisions of this section.

2. Except as otherwise provided in subsection 3, the full period of registration is:

(a) Fifteen years, if the offender or sex offender is a Tier I offender;

(b) Twenty-five years, if the offender or sex offender is a Tier II offender; and

(c) The life of the offender or sex offender, if the offender or sex offender is a Tier III offender,
Ê exclusive of any time during which the offender or sex offender is incarcerated or confined.

3. If an offender or sex offender complies with the provisions for registration:

(a) For an interval of at least 10 consecutive years, if the offender or sex offender is a Tier I offender; or

(b) For an interval of at least 25 consecutive years, if the offender or sex offender is a Tier III offender adjudicated delinquent for the offense which required registration as an offender or sex offender,

Ê during which the offender or sex offender is not convicted of an offense for which imprisonment for more than 1 year may be imposed, is not convicted of a sexual offense, successfully completes any periods of supervised release, probation or parole, and successfully completes a sex offender treatment program certified by the State or by the Attorney General of the United States, the offender or sex offender may file a petition to reduce the period of time during which the offender or sex offender has a duty to register with the district court in whose jurisdiction the offender or sex offender resides or, if he or she is a nonresident offender or sex offender, in whose jurisdiction the offender or sex offender is a student or worker. For the purposes of this subsection, registration begins on the date that the Central Repository or appropriate agency of another jurisdiction establishes a record of registration for the offender or sex offender or the date that the offender or sex offender is released, whichever occurs later.

4. If the offender or sex offender satisfies the requirements of subsection 3, the court shall hold a hearing on the petition at which the offender or sex offender and any other interested person may present witnesses and other evidence. If the court determines from the evidence presented at the hearing that the offender or sex offender satisfies the requirements of subsection 3, the court shall:

(a) If the offender or sex offender is a Tier I offender, reduce the period of time during which the offender or sex offender is required to register by 5 years; and

(b) If the offender or sex offender is a Tier III offender adjudicated delinquent for the offense which required registration as an offender or sex offender, reduce the period of time during which the offender or sex offender is required to register from the life of the offender or sex offender to that period of time for which the offender or sex offender meets the requirements of subsection 3.

(Added to NRS by 1997, 1659; A 1999, 1305; 2001, 2062; 2007, 2770)

NRS 179D.495 Duty of Central Repository to determine whether person is required to register as a Tier I, Tier II or Tier III offender. If a person who is required to register pursuant to NRS 179D.010 to 179D.550, inclusive, has been convicted of an offense described in paragraph (r) of subsection 1 of NRS 179D.097, paragraph (e) of subsection 1 or subsection 3 of NRS 179D.115 or subsection 7 or 9 of NRS 179D.117, the Central Repository shall determine whether the person is required to register as a Tier I offender, Tier II offender or Tier III offender.

(Added to NRS by 2007, 2762; A 2013, 1168, 2424; 2015, 1445)

NRS 179D.550 Prohibited acts; penalties; duties of local law enforcement agency.

1. Except as otherwise provided in subsection 2, an offender or sex offender who:

(a) Fails to register with a local law enforcement agency;

(b) Fails to notify the local law enforcement agency of a change of name, residence, employment or student status as required pursuant to NRS 179D.447;

(c) Provides false or misleading information to the Central Repository or a local law enforcement agency; or

(d) Otherwise violates the provisions of NRS 179D.010 to 179D.550, inclusive,

Ê is guilty of a category D felony and shall be punished as provided in NRS 193.130.

2. An offender or sex offender who commits a second or subsequent violation of subsection 1 within 7 years after the first violation is guilty of a category C felony and shall be punished as provided in NRS 193.130. A court shall not grant probation to or suspend the sentence of a person convicted pursuant to this subsection.

3. If a local law enforcement agency is aware that an offender or sex offender in its jurisdiction has failed to comply with a provision of NRS 179D.010 to 179D.550, inclusive, the local law enforcement agency must take any appropriate action to ensure compliance.

(Added to NRS by 1997, 1661; A 1999, 1306; 2001, 2063; 2005, 2872; 2007, 100, 2771)

CENTRAL REPOSITORY

NRS 179D.570 Duty to share information with certain agencies; requirements of information; regulations.

1. The Central Repository shall, in accordance with the requirements of this section, share information concerning sex offenders and offenders convicted of a crime against a child with:

(a) The Nevada Gaming Control Board to carry out the provisions of NRS 463.335 pertaining to the registration of a gaming employee who is a sex offender or an offender convicted of a crime against a child. The Central Repository shall, at least once each calendar month, provide the Nevada Gaming Control Board with the name and other identifying information of each offender who is not in compliance with the provisions of this chapter, in the manner and form agreed upon by the Central Repository and the Nevada Gaming Control Board.

(b) The Department of Motor Vehicles to carry out the provisions of NRS 483.283, 483.861 and 483.929.

2. The information shared by the Central Repository pursuant to this section must indicate whether a sex offender or an offender convicted of a crime against a child is in compliance with the provisions of this chapter.

3. The Central Repository shall share information pursuant to this section as expeditiously as possible under the circumstances.

4. The Central Repository may adopt regulations to carry out the provisions of this section.

(Added to NRS by 2005, 2871; A 2007, 2772)

LIMITATIONS ON LIABILITY AND THE DISCLOSURE OF INFORMATION

NRS 179D.850 Name of victim not to be disclosed; immunity from liability for certain entities and their officers and employees for act or omission relating to information obtained, maintained or disclosed.

1. Information that is disclosed pursuant to the provisions of this chapter must not reveal the name of an individual victim of an offense.

2. A law enforcement agency and its officers and employees, the Central Repository and its officers and employees, and a campus police department and its officers and employees are immune from criminal or civil liability for an act or omission relating to information obtained, maintained or disclosed pursuant to the provisions of this chapter, including, but not limited to, an act or omission relating to:

(a) The accuracy of information in a record of registration; or

(b) The disclosure of or the failure to disclose information pursuant to the provisions of this chapter.

(Added to NRS by 1997, 1665; A 2003, 578)

CHAPTER 180 - STATE PUBLIC DEFENDER

NRS 180.010 Office created; term; qualifications; private practice of law prohibited; supervision; assignment of additional duties.

1. The Office of State Public Defender is hereby created within the Department of Health and Human Services.

2. The Governor shall appoint the State Public Defender for a term of 4 years, and until a successor is appointed and qualified.

3. The State Public Defender:

(a) Must be an attorney licensed to practice law in the State of Nevada.

(b) Is in the unclassified service of the State.

(c) Except as otherwise provided in NRS 7.065, shall not engage in the private practice of law.

4. No officer or agency of the State, other than the Governor and the Director of the Department of Health and Human Services, may supervise the State Public Defender. No officer or agency of the State, other than the Governor, may assign the State Public Defender duties in addition to those prescribed by this chapter.

(Added to NRS by 1971, 1410; A 1973, 707; 1977, 1176; 1989, 202; 1993, 1518)

NRS 180.030 Employment of deputies and other employees; qualifications of deputies.

1. The State Public Defender may employ:

(a) Deputy state public defenders in the unclassified service of the State.

(b) Clerical, investigative and other necessary staff in the classified service of the State.

2. Each deputy state public defender must be an attorney licensed to practice law in the State of Nevada, and shall not engage in the practice of law, except in performing the duties of office and as otherwise provided in NRS 7.065.

(Added to NRS by 1971, 1411; A 1977, 159; 1981, 1270; 1985, 394; 1989, 202)

NRS 180.040 Office; branch offices.

1. The Office of the State Public Defender shall be in Carson City, Nevada, and the Buildings and Grounds Section of the State Public Works Division of the Department of Administration shall provide necessary office space.

2. The State Public Defender may establish branch offices necessary to perform the State Public Defender's duties. The State Public Defender shall designate a deputy state public defender to supervise each such office.

(Added to NRS by 1971, 1411)

NRS 180.050 Contracts for legal services.

1. The State Public Defender may contract with attorneys licensed to practice law in the State of Nevada and with county public defenders to provide services required by this chapter if it is impracticable for the State Public Defender or the State Public Defender's deputies to provide such services for any reason.

2. All such contract services shall be performed under the supervision and control of the State Public Defender.

(Added to NRS by 1971, 1411; A 1973, 706)

NRS 180.060 Duties: Representation of indigent persons; contracts to render services.

1. The State Public Defender may, before being designated as counsel for that person pursuant to NRS 171.188, interview an indigent person when the indigent person has been arrested and confined for a public offense or for questioning on suspicion of having committed a public offense.

2. The State Public Defender shall, when designated pursuant to NRS 62D.030, 62D.100, 171.188 or 432B.420, and within the limits of available money, represent without charge each indigent person for whom the State Public Defender is appointed.

3. When representing an indigent person, the State Public Defender shall:

(a) Counsel and defend the indigent person at every stage of the proceedings, including revocation of probation or parole; and

(b) Prosecute any appeals or other remedies before or after conviction that the State Public Defender considers to be in the interests of justice.

4. In cases of postconviction proceedings and appeals arising in counties in which the office of public defender has been created pursuant to the provisions of chapter 260 of NRS, where the matter is to be presented to the appellate court of competent jurisdiction pursuant to the rules fixed by the Supreme Court pursuant to Section 4 of Article 6 of the Nevada Constitution, the State Public Defender shall prepare and present the case and the public defender of the county shall assist and cooperate with the State Public Defender.

5. The State Public Defender may contract with any county in which the office of public defender has been created to provide representation for indigent persons when the court, for cause, disqualifies the county public defender or when the county public defender is otherwise unable to provide representation.

(Added to NRS by 1971, 1411; A 1973, 358; 1975, 41; 1977, 338; 1985, 1398; 2003, 1124; 2013, 1762)

NRS 180.080 Duties: Reports to Governor, participating counties and Legislative Commission.

1. The State Public Defender shall submit:

(a) A report on or before December 1 of each year to the Governor and to each participating county containing a statement of:

(1) The number of cases that are pending in each participating county;

(2) The number of cases in each participating county that were closed in the previous fiscal year;

(3) The total number of criminal defendants represented in each participating county with separate categories specifying the crimes charged and whether the defendant was less than 18 years of age or an adult;

(4) The total number of working hours spent by the State Public Defender and the State Public Defender's staff on work for each participating county; and

(5) The amount and categories of the expenditures made by the State Public Defender's office.

(b) To each participating county, on or before December 1 of each even-numbered year, the total proposed budget of the State Public Defender for that county, including the projected number of cases and the projected cost of services attributed to the county for the next biennium.

(c) Such reports to the Legislative Commission as the regulations of the Commission require.

2. As used in this section, "participating county" means each county in which the office of public defender has not been created pursuant to NRS 260.010.

(Added to NRS by 1971, 1412; A 1977, 331; 1995, 498)

NRS 180.090 Application. Except as provided in subsections 4 and 5 of NRS 180.060, the provisions of this chapter apply only to counties in which the office of public defender has not been created pursuant to the provisions of chapter 260 of NRS.

(Added to NRS by 1971, 1412; A 1975, 42; 1977, 338)

NRS 180.100 Other protections and sanctions not excluded. The provisions of this chapter do not exclude any protection or sanction that the law otherwise provides.

(Added to NRS by 1971, 1412)

NRS 180.110 Collection of charges to counties for services.

1. Each fiscal year the State Public Defender may collect from the counties amounts which do not exceed those authorized by the Legislature for use of the State Public Defender's services during that year.

2. The State Public Defender shall submit to the county an estimate on or before the first day of May and that estimate becomes the final bill unless the county is notified of a change within 2 weeks after the date on which the county contribution is approved by the Legislature. The county shall pay the bill:

(a) In full within 30 days after the estimate becomes the final bill or the county receives the revised estimate; or

(b) In equal quarterly installments on or before the 1st day of July, October, January and April, respectively.

Ê The counties shall pay their respective amounts to the State Public Defender who shall deposit the amounts with the Treasurer of the State of Nevada and shall expend the money in accordance with the State Public Defender's approved budget.

(Added to NRS by 1973, 719; A 1975, 714; 1977, 309; 1983, 528; 1991, 995)

CHAPTER 189 - JUSTICE COURTS

PROCEDURE IN JUSTICE COURTS

APPEALS TO DISTRICT COURT

Appeal by Defendant

Appeal by State

PROCEDURE IN JUSTICE COURTS

NRS 189.005 Applicability of other provisions of title. Except as otherwise expressly provided in this chapter, criminal proceedings in justice courts are governed by the provisions of this title.

(Added to NRS by 1967, 1467)

NRS 189.007 Grounds for dismissal of complaint. Any complaint, upon motion of the defendant, may be dismissed by the justice of the peace upon any of the following grounds:

1. That the justice of the peace does not have jurisdiction of the offense.
2. That more than one offense is charged in any one count of the complaint.
3. That the facts stated do not constitute a public offense.

(Added to NRS by 1979, 36)

APPEALS TO DISTRICT COURT

Appeal by Defendant

NRS 189.010 Appeal must be taken within 10 days. Except as otherwise provided in NRS 177.015, a defendant in a criminal action tried before a justice of the peace may appeal from the final judgment therein to the district court of the county where the court of the justice of the peace is held, at any time within 10 days from the time of the rendition of the judgment.

[1911 Cr. Prac. § 662; RL § 7512; NCL § 11309] — (NRS A 1995, 1536)

NRS 189.020 Notice of intention to appeal: Filing and service; stay of judgment pending appeal.

1. The party intending to appeal must file with the justice and serve upon the district attorney a notice entitled in the action, setting forth the character of the judgment, and the intention of the party to appeal therefrom to the district court.
2. Stay of judgment pending appeal is governed by NRS 177.105 and 177.115.

[1911 Cr. Prac. § 663; RL § 7513; NCL § 11310] — (NRS A 1967, 1467)

NRS 189.030 Transmission of transcript, other papers, sound recording and copy of docket to district court.

1. The justice shall, within 10 days after the notice of appeal is filed, transmit to the clerk of the district court the transcript of the case, all other papers relating to the case and a certified copy of the docket.
2. The justice shall give notice to the appellant or the appellant's attorney that the transcript and all other papers relating to the case have been filed with the clerk of the district court.
3. If the district judge so requests, before or after receiving the record, the justice of the peace shall transmit to the district judge the sound recording of the case.

[1911 Cr. Prac. § 664; RL § 7514; NCL § 11311] — (NRS A 1973, 631; 1979, 1512)

NRS 189.035 Procedure where transcript defective.

1. Except as provided in subsection 2, if the district court finds that the transcript of a case which was recorded by sound recording equipment is materially or extensively defective, the case must be returned for retrial in the justice court from which it came.
2. If all parties to the appeal stipulate to being bound by a particular transcript of the proceedings in the justice court, or stipulate to a particular change in the transcript, an appeal based on that transcript as accepted or changed may be heard by the district court without regard to any defects in the transcript.

(Added to NRS by 1979, 1512)

NRS 189.050 Action to be judged on record. An appeal duly perfected transfers the action to the district court to be judged on the record.

[Part 1911 Cr. Prac. § 666; RL § 7516; NCL § 11313] — (NRS A 1979, 1512)

NRS 189.060 Grounds for dismissal of appeal; enforcement of judgment.

1. The appeal may be dismissed on either of the following grounds:

(a) For failure to take the same in time.

(b) For failure to appear in the district court when required.

2. If the appeal is dismissed, a copy of the order of dismissal must be remitted to the justice, who may proceed to enforce the judgment.

[Part 1911 Cr. Prac. § 666; RL § 7516; NCL § 11313]

NRS 189.065 Dismissal for failure to set or reset appeal for hearing.

1. An appeal must be dismissed by the district court unless perfected by application of the defendant, within 60 days after the appeal is filed in the justice court, by having it set for hearing.

2. If an appeal has been set for hearing and the hearing is vacated at the request of the appellant, the appeal must be dismissed unless application is made by the appellant to reset the hearing within 60 days after the date on which the hearing was vacated.

(Added to NRS by 1965, 376; A 1985, 57, 972)

NRS 189.070 Grounds for dismissal of complaint on appeal. Any complaint, upon motion of the defendant, may be dismissed upon any of the following grounds:

1. That the justice of the peace did not have jurisdiction of the offense.

2. That more than one offense is charged in any one count of the complaint.

3. That the facts stated do not constitute a public offense.

[1911 Cr. Prac. § 667; RL § 7517; NCL § 11314] — (NRS A 1979, 36)

Appeal by State

NRS 189.120 Appeal by State from order granting defendant's motion to suppress evidence.

1. The State may appeal to the district court from an order of a justice court granting the motion of a defendant to suppress evidence.

2. Such an appeal shall be taken:

(a) Within 2 days after the rendition of such an order during a trial or preliminary examination.

(b) Within 5 days after the rendition of such an order before a trial or preliminary examination.

3. Upon perfecting such an appeal:

(a) After the commencement of a trial or preliminary examination, further proceedings in the trial shall be stayed pending the final determination of the appeal.

(b) Before trial or preliminary examination, the time limitation within which a defendant shall be brought to trial shall be extended for the period necessary for the final determination of the appeal.

(Added to NRS by 1969, 1079)

Made in the USA
Middletown, DE
18 April 2022

64459170R00133